Fundamentals of
MANAGEMENT
ACCOUNTING

THE
WILLARD J. GRAHAM SERIES
IN ACCOUNTING

CONSULTING EDITOR

ROBERT N. ANTHONY *Harvard University*

Fundamentals of
MANAGEMENT
ACCOUNTING

ROBERT N. ANTHONY
Graduate School of Business Administration
Harvard University

and

GLENN A. WELSCH
College of Business Administration
University of Texas at Austin

 1974

RICHARD D. IRWIN, INC. *Homewood, Illinois 60430*
Irwin-Dorsey International, London, England   WC2H 9NJ
Irwin-Dorsey Limited, Georgetown, Ontario   L7G 4B3

First Printing, April 1974
Second Printing, September 1974
Third Printing, October 1974
Fourth Printing, November 1975

Case material of the Harvard Graduate School of
Business Administration is made possible by the
cooperation of business firms who may wish to remain
anonymous by having names, quantities, and other
identifying details disguised while basic relationships
are maintained. Cases are prepared as the basis for
class discussion rather than to illustrate either effective
or ineffective handling of administrative situations.

ISBN 0-256-01541-4
Library of Congress Catalog Card No. 73–91788

Printed in the United States of America

LEARNING SYSTEMS COMPANY—
a division of Richard D. Irwin, Inc.—has developed a
PROGRAMMED LEARNING AID
to accompany texts in this subject area.
Copies can be purchased through your bookstore
or by writing PLAIDS,
1818 Ridge Road, Homewood, Illinois   60430.

To our wives,
Katherine and Irma

Preface

Many accounting instructors believe that it is sound pedagogy to divide the first course in accounting into two parts, the first semester or quarter focusing on financial accounting and the second on management accounting. Most texts, however, are not arranged so that such an approach is feasible with a single text. Consequently, instructors tend to select one text for financial accounting and a different text for management accounting, which causes a certain amount of confusion because of differences in terminology, point of view, and coverage. Moreover, the second text usually contains considerable review material on financial accounting because its author could not assume that students would have a common body of knowledge.

This volume and its companion, *Fundamentals of Financial Accounting,* are designed to overcome these problems. They provide material for a fully coordinated first course. As their titles indicate, this volume deals with the fundamentals of management accounting, and its companion with the fundamentals of financial accounting. Each volume can be used either for a one-semester or a one-quarter course. Both are designed to provide maximum flexibility for the instructor in the selection and order of materials for the classroom. They emphasize those aspects of accounting we believe essential for interpretation and use of accounting information. Mechanical and procedural details are minimized, while the conceptual, measurement, and communication aspects are emphasized.

Partly because the treatment of management accounting as a separate subject is relatively new, a satisfactory pedagogical framework for it—one that provides a way of organizing and unifying the several

viii

separate topics—has been difficult to devise. In financial accounting, the accounting equation, Assets = Liabilities + Owners' Equity, provides a unifying theme.

No such unified structure exists for management accounting. On the contrary, instructors spend much time emphasizing the point that "different figures are used for different purposes." This is a fundamental point, and it is valid, but it does tend to create confusion on the part of the student. In one chapter of the usual text he is told that in figuring cost he is supposed to include an allocated share of overhead costs; in another chapter he is told that the allocated costs are irrelevant and should be disregarded. In still another chapter he is told that costs must be related to personal responsibility, whereas in most other places no mention is made of personal responsibility.

The vagueness of the notion that there are *several* purposes adds to the student's problem of comprehending what the course is all about. How many purposes are there? Does each type of alternative choice problem (for example, make-or-buy, dropping a product, equipment replacement, buy-or-lease) constitute a separate purpose, with its own peculiar requirements for accounting information? Do the purposes mentioned in the book constitute *all* the purposes, or are there others? Are there topics not mentioned in the elementary course that he must learn about in advanced courses?

After a good many years of wrestling with the problem, the authors have concluded that it is possible to devise a framework for management accounting that overcomes these pedagogical difficulties. This volume is constructed around such a framework. We arrived at the framework by shifting the focus from the notion of "purpose" to the notion of "types of accounting information." It seems to us that there are three, and only three, different ways of constructing accounting information for use by management. One is conventional cost accounting, with its emphasis on full cost and its close ties to generally accepted financial accounting principles and to the financial accounting system. A second is the notion variously labelled as the "differential," "marginal," or "incremental" approach. The third is what has come to be called "responsibility accounting"; it focuses on the costs, revenues, and assets of responsibility centers.

It is not possible to relate each of these constructions to a single purpose. Planning, for example, uses all three types. For some pricing problems, full costs are relevant; whereas for others, differential costs are relevant. Nevertheless, if the three topics are arranged in the order given above, it is possible to describe, under the first topic, uses that require the use of full cost data; under the second topic, uses that require differential costs and revenue; and under the third topic, uses that require responsibility accounting data.

Another advantage of this approach is that it encourages the student to make a clear distinction among these three different types of information. Failure to appreciate this distinction is a basic cause of the difficulty that some students have in understanding what management accounting is all about.

We chose labels that are descriptive of the type of cost that is appropriate for each of the three purposes. These are: (1) full cost accounting, (2) differential accounting, and (3) responsibility accounting. Each of the three main parts of the book focuses on one of these topics. Together, they constitute the field of management accounting. The following brief descriptions will suggest their general nature:

Full cost accounting measures the total amount of resources used for a cost objective. These resources are the direct costs plus a fair share of the indirect costs associated with the cost objective.

Differential accounting focuses on the costs and revenues that are expected to be different if one alternative course of action, rather than another alternative, is adopted.

Responsibility accounting focuses on costs, revenues, and assets that are associated with the work of a responsibility center. It measures the inputs and outputs of responsibility centers.

In stressing the differences among the three types of management accounting information, we run the risk that the student will not appreciate that the three categories use many common elements, that they overlap, and that they constitute a single management accounting system, rather than three separate systems. We have taken steps to minimize these risks.

It can of course be argued that there are more than three types of management accounting information. Our three categories do not suggest such distinctions as long run v. short run, historical v. future, opportunity v. incurred, regulatory v. nonregulatory, direct v. indirect, or strategic planning v. management control. It would be possible to construct frameworks based on any or all of these distinctions. Instead of doing this, we have chosen to discuss these topics at the appropriate place in each of our main categories. We have found it feasible, without straining, to fit all these concepts under our three main topics, and this fact increases our confidence in the conclusion that the three categories are inclusive. If the student comes away from the course with the clear recognition that three types of management accounting information exist, and if he understands how to use them for appropriate purposes, he will be ahead of a great many people (including Congressmen and others in public life, and even some businessmen who imply in their speeches and actions that there is such a thing as "the" cost of something).

PLAN OF THE BOOK

Within each of the three categories, our objective is to discuss both the characteristics of the accounting information that is useful in that category, and also the way in which such information should be used. In general, the early chapters in each section focus on the background characteristics, and the later chapters focus on the use.

The discussion of full cost accounting comes first because this topic is closely related to the subject matter of this text's companion volume, *Fundamentals of Financial Accounting*. Full costs are used to measure inventory amounts in financial accounting, and their construction is essentially governed by generally accepted financial accounting principles. Thus, this topic provides a good way of making the transition from financial accounting to management accounting. In discussing the uses of full cost information, more attention is given to its use as a basis for pricing than is the case with many accounting books. Whatever the theoretical merits of marginal-cost pricing may be, the fact is that in the real world the great majority of selling prices are based on full costs, and the student should therefore learn how costs are constructed and used for this purpose. (Marginal cost pricing is discussed in Part Two.)

Part Two deals with differential costs, differential revenues, and differential investments. These constructions are used in alternative choice decisions of various types, and the use of accounting information for these purposes is discussed in Chapters 7, 8, and 9. As background for this discussion, Chapter 6 contains a description of the behavior of costs, particularly the relationship among costs, volume, and profit. Part Three focuses on responsibility accounting, that is, on costs, revenues, and investments that are associated with the activities of responsibility centers. As background, Chapters 10 and 13 discuss the management control structure and process respectively. Chapters 11, 14, and 15 discuss the use of accounting information in budgeting, in the analysis of variances, and in reports on performance.

Part Three also contains a chapter on standard costs. Logically, this chapter could just as well have been located in Part One since standard costs are a part of many cost accounting systems. Students find standard costs quite difficult and complicated, however, and this is the reason for deferring this topic until a later chapter. (The chapter can be assigned following Chapter 4 if an instructor wants to treat standard costs along with other cost accounting topics.)

Chapter 16, on information processing, is more isolated from the main framework of the book than is ideal. We treat it separately because the subject is relevant for all three categories of accounting information, and therefore it is not appropriately included in any single one of them, to the exclusion of the other two.

Most books on management accounting do not contain a summary chapter. This one does, in Chapter 17. The essential rationale for a summary is that the emphasis on the three types of cost construction in the body of the book may have created the impression that management accounting consists of three separate, and largely unrelated, systems.

The summary attempts to correct any such misconception by showing the interrelationships that in fact exist.

The list of students and faculty members to whom the authors feel a sense of gratitude for ideas and suggestions is too long to enumerate here. With respect to this volume, we are particularly grateful to the following individuals who devoted considerable time in discussions, reviewing manuscript, and testing materials: Professors Gale E. Newell, Western Michigan University; Michael J. Barrett, University of Minnesota; Richmond O. Bennett, Lamar University; Henry A. Genery, Colby College; Vern Odmark, San Diego State College; and Jack Helmkamp, Purdue University. Yvonne Knight, Colby College, prepared many of the questions and problems. Jean McElroy, Carolyn Torgerson, and Christy Boyer did much of the typing.

The Liquid Chemical Company Case is copyrighted by David Solomons, University of Pennsylvania. Other cases in the problems are copyrighted by the President and Fellows of Harvard College. Permission to use these cases is appreciated.

March 1974   ROBERT N. ANTHONY
                                                GLENN A. WELSCH

Contents

xiii

The capital expenditure budget. Appendix: *The mechanics of budget preparation.*

Purpose of the chapter. Nature and uses of standard costs: *Nature of standard costs. Variances. Uses of standard costs.* Setting the cost standards: *Separation of quantity and price. Types of standards. Standard direct material cost. Standard direct labor costs. Standard overhead costs. Adjustments in standards. Mechanics of the system. Variations in the standard cost idea.*

Purpose of the chapter. Responsibility centers: *Reality versus information. Expense centers. Profit centers. Transfer prices. Investment centers.* Additional control concepts. Effectiveness and efficiency. Controllable costs: *Degree of influence. Contrast with direct costs. Contrast with variable costs. Converting noncontrollable costs to controllable costs. Reporting noncontrollable costs.* Engineered, discretionary, and committed costs: *Engineered costs. Discretionary costs. Committed costs.*

Purpose of the chapter. Overview of the analytical process: *Structure of the analysis.* Revenue variances: *Joint variance. Gross margin analysis.* Direct labor and direct material variances: *Direct labor. Direct material.* Overhead variances: *Production volume variance. Spending variance. Calculation of overhead variances.* Relation of variances to the accounts. Use and limitations of variance analysis: *Validity of the standard. Noncomparable data. Significance of variances.*

Purpose of the chapter. General nature of control reports: *Information reports versus control reports. Purpose of comparisons. Ingredients of control reports. Criteria for control reports.* Focus on personal responsibility. Selection of a standard. Highlighting significant information: *Rounding. Management by exception.* Timing of reports: *The control period. Report timing.* Clarity of communication. Integrated reports. Cost of reporting. Format of control reports. Use of control reports: *Feedback. Identification. Investigation. Action.* Economic appraisal.

Purpose of the chapter. Nature of information processing: *Criteria for information processing. Historical development of systems. Manual systems. Punched card machines.* Automated data processing: *Input. Storage. Processing. Output. Processing modes. Time sharing. Minicalculators.* Implications for accounting: *General impact. The input problem. Operating data. Financial accounting. Full cost accounting. Differential accounting. Responsibility accounting. Integrated data processing.*

1 The nature of management accounting

Purpose of the chapter

The companion volume of this book, *Fundamentals of Financial Accounting,** focuses on financial accounting, where the principal objective is to furnish information that is useful to investors and other persons who are *outside* the organization. In this volume, the focus is on management accounting, where the principal objective is to furnish information that is useful to managers, that is, to persons who are *inside* the organization.

This chapter gives a general description of the work that managers do and the information that they use in doing this work. Accounting information is one type of information that managers use. The nature of management accounting and the similarities and differences between management accounting and financial accounting are discussed. The three types of management accounting information and the purposes for which they are used are introduced.

Characteristics of an organization

An organization is a group of people who work together for some purpose. Let us look at a specific organization, the Morgan Ford Company. This company sells and services Ford automobiles in the city of Morgan. Such an organization is customarily called a "dealership."

OBJECTIVES

The purposes for which an organization exists are called its objectives. The Morgan Ford Company is a corporation. Its owners, that is,

---

* Glenn A. Welsch and Robert N. Anthony, *Fundamentals of Financial Accounting* (Homewood, Ill.: Richard D. Irwin, Inc., 1974).

1

its shareholders, have voluntarily invested money in the corporation. They did so in the expectation of earning a return, or profit, on that investment. A central objective of the Morgan Ford Company, therefore, is to earn profits. The shareholders hold Mr. Carroll, the president of Morgan Ford Company, responsible for managing the activities of the company in such a way that a satisfactory return is earned on the funds they have invested in it.

As we discuss in *Fundamentals of Financial Accounting,* earning a satisfactory profit is an important objective of most private businesses; and for this reason such businesses are called "profit-oriented" companies to distinguish them from government organizations, hospitals, colleges, and other organizations that have quite different objectives.

Although earning profits is one objective, it is not the only objective of the Morgan Ford Company. Its owners want to be well regarded in the community, they want to create jobs, they want to encourage the growth of the city of Morgan. The profit objective is tempered by the existence of these other objectives.

STRATEGY

There are many ways in which an automobile dealership can earn a satisfactory profit. The management of Morgan Ford Company has selected from the various possible alternatives certain courses of action that seem best to it. These are its **strategies.** They are often called its **policies.**

Mr. Carroll, with the assent of the owners, has decided that the best strategies for the Morgan Ford Company are to sell new Ford automobiles, to sell used cars of any make, and to service automobiles. He has ruled out several other possible strategies. For example, he has decided not to sell trucks, not to operate a gasoline service station, not to lease automobiles, and not to operate a taxi service, because he doubts that the income that might be earned from these activities would provide an adequate return on the investment that the company would have to make in them. Other automobile dealers do engage in some or all of these activities; that is, they follow different strategies.

Within his staked-out domain of selling and servicing automobiles, Mr. Carroll also has a choice of strategies. Some automobile dealers are "volume" dealers; that is, they sell at low unit prices[1] and/or they spend much money on advertising, in the expectation that the lower profit per unit will be more than made up by the relatively large number of units sold. Others are "quality" dealers; that is, they maintain a relatively high selling price but attract customers by providing excellent

---

[1] Automobile dealers customarily quote the manufacturers' suggested retail price, which is the same for everyone, but they vary the actual selling price by making allowances and discounts from it. Buyers therefore do not necessarily pay the suggested retail price.

service and by creating an aura of trustworthiness. Again, the selection of one of these or similar strategies is a matter of management judgment. Some dealers make money one way, some another. (And, of course, some dealers lose money if the strategy they select does not work out satisfactorily.)

Every business has a set of strategies, although often they are not written down. Essentially they state (1) the products the business has decided to manufacture, and/or the services it has decided to offer; and (2) which of the available alternatives for manufacturing and marketing these products and services it has decided on.

Incidentally, the fact that investors make their own decisions as to where to invest their money and the fact that individual companies can select their own strategies are two of the great strengths of the free enterprise system. They result in a constant search for new opportunities, and this helps to keep the economy dynamic. Governments in Soviet countries have discovered that the socialist system, as originally conceived, did not permit adequate flexibility in channeling investment funds or in selecting strategies, and they are now experimenting with various capitalistic devices that will provide more flexibility.

ORGANIZATION STRUCTURE

Mr. Carroll does not execute his strategies by himself; the Morgan Ford Company has 52 employees. Since he cannot personally supervise the work of so many people, Mr. Carroll has organized Morgan Ford employees into groups, called departments. Each department has an assigned job to do, and each is headed by a manager. Mr. Carroll has four line departments and one staff department.

The **line departments** are responsible for activities that are directly associated with the objectives of the organization. They are (1) new car sales department, which is responsible for selling new automobiles; (2) used car sales department, which is responsible for selling used automobiles; (3) service department, which services and repairs automobiles for customers and also reconditions used cars taken in trade; and (4) parts and accessories department, which furnishes parts and accessories to the service department and sells them to customers and other dealers. The managers of the two car sales departments report to a vice president in charge of car sales.

A **staff department** provides services to other departments. The controller department, which is the one staff department of Morgan Ford Company, collects, reports, and analyzes accounting information and other information, and prepares reports for both internal and external use.

Exhibit 1–1 is an *organization chart* depicting this arrangement of people. The boxes represent the various organization units, and the lines connecting the boxes represent the relationships of the units to one an-

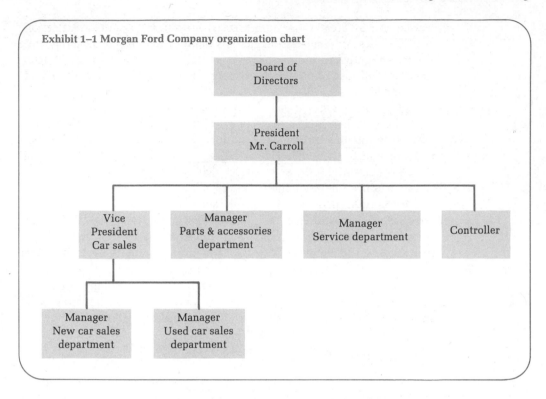

Exhibit 1–1 Morgan Ford Company organization chart

other. They show that the manager of the new car sales department and
the manager of the used car sales department are responsible to the vice
president for all car sales. All other managers are responsible to the
president, Mr. Carroll. Mr. Carroll in turn is responsible to the board
of directors, who represent the shareholders. **An organization chart
shows the responsibility relationships among managers in an organization.**

The lines connecting the boxes on the organization chart show the
formal responsibility relationships; for example, the line between "Manager, used car department" and "Vice president, car sales" means that
the manager of the used car department reports to, is responsible to,
the vice president for car sales. The chart does not depict *informal* relationships. These exist and are important in any organization. For example, even though there is no line that connects "Manager, used car sales
department" with "Manager, service department," these two people
must work closely together for the overall good of Morgan Ford
Company.

In its essentials, this organization chart is similar to that in many
medium-size companies. There are a number of line departments and
one or more staff departments. In many companies there would be several staff units that do not exist in the Morgan Ford Company, including
any or all of the following: finance, purchasing, research and develop-

ment, personnel, labor relations, advertising, public relations, and legal.

In larger or more complex companies, the organization is naturally more complicated. There may be a number of layers in the organization, that is, subdepartments reporting to departments, subsubdepartments reporting to subdepartments, and so on. The complete organization chart for the Ford Motor Company, which has over 400,000 employees, requires many hundreds of 8½-by-11-inch pages. It is so large and complicated that it is doubtful that any one person is familiar with all its details; each manager knows the part that affects his responsibility relationships within the company.

There is no standard designation of the names of organization units. The terms "divisions," "departments," "units," and "sections" stand for different things in different companies. In this book, the word "division" is used for a relatively large and relatively self-contained organization, such as the Chicago division of a company that operates a number of separate automobile dealerships, and the word "department" is used for a unit that performs a single line or staff function. In other words, as used here, departments are part of divisions, not vice versa.

RESPONSIBILITY CENTERS

Each box on Exhibit 1–1 represents a group of people (or, as in the case of "President, Mr. Carroll" and "Vice president, car sales," a single person). The group has a job to do, that is, it has a defined responsibility. Each person in the group reports to someone, whom we shall designate the manager. We shall use the term **responsibility center** for any such group, that is, for **an organization unit with a defined responsibility and headed by a manager.** Moreover, we shall use the term responsibility center to include aggregations of individual boxes on the organization chart. Thus, each department is a responsibility center; the company as a whole is also a responsibility center consisting of the aggregate of the lower level responsibility centers, with the president as its manager. If there were divisions, each of them would be responsibility centers. The responsibility center is a key concept in our discussion of management accounting.

THE CONTROLLER

In the Morgan Ford Company the manager who is responsible for collecting and reporting accounting information is called the **controller**, and the responsibility center which he heads is called the **controller department.** The controller department is a staff department; it provides service—that is, information—to the other departments and to top management. With our focus on accounting, we are in this book particularly interested in the work of the controller department and in the use by other departments of the information it prepares.

Although the word "controller" is widely used, the title "financial vice president" is used in some companies and (but less commonly) "chief accountant" is used in others. The word "comptroller" is an obsolete spelling of "controller" but continues to be used in some organizations; "comptroller" is *pronounced* the same as "controller."

THE FUNCTIONS OF MANAGEMENT

Although a manager may personally sell automobiles or do other work directly related to the objectives of the organization, his principal responsibility is *not* to do the work himself. Rather, the principal responsibility of a manager is to see to it that the work gets done by the persons who report to him. The principal responsibility of the service manager is not personally to repair cars; it is to see to it that his mechanics do a good job of repairing cars. The manager of the new car sales department does not personally deal with each customer; there simply is not time for him to meet the dozens of customers who visit the Morgan Ford Company every day. Rather, his primary responsibility is to see to it that the eight salesmen in the new car sales department do an effective sales job with these customers. The manager may, of course, spend some of his time dealing with customers, and he often participates in the closing of deals, but this is not his *primary* responsibility, and when he does these things he is *not* acting as a manager.

This is not the place for a detailed discussion of the functions that a manager performs in carrying out his responsibilities; textbooks on management discuss these at length. Various authors classify these functions in different ways, but there is general agreement that they include at least the following:

1. Planning.
2. Directing.
3. Controlling.

Each manager performs these functions for his own responsibility center, and he participates in the corresponding processes for the company as a whole.

In **planning, the manager decides what actions should be taken to help the organization achieve its objectives.** A customer who walks into the Morgan Ford Company sees employees who are engaged in a variety of activities; he sees machines ready to service his automobile, and he sees bins full of parts. If he stops to think about this (and there is no particular reason why he should do so), he realizes that much thought and action has been involved in creating the organization and the physical resources that are ready to serve him. This is planning. An important planning activity, especially at higher levels in the organization, is that of **coordination,** which means **melding the plans of individ-**

ual responsibility centers into an integrated, balanced plan for the whole company.

In **directing, the manager oversees the conduct of day-to-day operations.** The service manager assigns mechanics to jobs, he helps a mechanic who can't locate the source of trouble in an automobile, he settles disputes that arise between mechanics, he goes to bat for his mechanics in disputes that they have with the parts and accessories departments. These are the activities that the customer observes, and outsiders may therefore believe that these activities are the only function of the manager; this is by no means the case. Directing is the process involved with the here and now.

In **controlling, the manager takes steps to insure that his responsibility center is operating in the best possible way.** In order to do this, he studies reports on past operations, and from these he tries to find ways of making operations better in the future. In other words, he uses the lessons learned from past experience to make better plans for the future. The process of using past experience to modify future plans is also called **feedback.** His evaluations of the past are made in two general areas. First, there is an appraisal of **activities or functions** which may lead to improvements in ways of doing things or even to a change in strategy. Second, there is an appraisal of the **performance of individuals** which leads to praise, promotion, criticism, constructive suggestions, or other actions with respect to these individuals. As we shall see, the information that is needed for one of these types of appraisals is significantly different from that needed for the other.

SIMILARITIES AMONG ORGANIZATIONS

Although each of the millions of organizations in the United States in some sense is unique, nearly all of them have the general characteristics described above; that is, they have one or more objectives, they have a strategy for achieving these objectives, their personnel are arranged in an organization structure, there are one or more managers in this structure, and these managers plan, direct, and control the activities of the organization.

In this book we shall describe the nature and uses of management accounting in all types of organizations. Because of the basic similarities among organizations, many statements can be made that apply to organizations generally. Because of the differences among organizations of various types, however, some statements will apply only to certain types of organizations. For example, there are important differences between a profit-oriented organization, such as the Morgan Ford Company, and a nonprofit organization, such as a government entity, a hospital, a college, or a church. A nonprofit organization, by definition, does not have profit as one of its objectives. It does have objectives, however; and the management accounting information in these organizations is intended to help management attain these objectives, whatever they may be.

Information

The purpose of this section is to distinguish management accounting information from other types of information. First, let us define **information as a fact, datum, observation, perception, or any other thing that adds to knowledge.** The number 1,000 taken by itself is not information; it doesn't tell anyone anything. The statement that 1,000 students are enrolled in a certain school *is* information. Management accounting is one type of information. Its place in the whole picture is shown in Exhibit 1–2.

Information can be either quantitative or nonquantitative. Impressions from the senses (hearing, vision, etc.), conversations, television programs, and newspaper stories are examples of nonquantitative information. Management accounting is not, strictly speaking, concerned with nonquantitative information.

There are many types of quantitative information, of which accounting is one. Accounting information is distinguished from the other types in that it usually is expressed in monetary terms. Data on the age, experience level, and other characteristics of an employee are quantitative, but they are not usually designated as accounting information. The

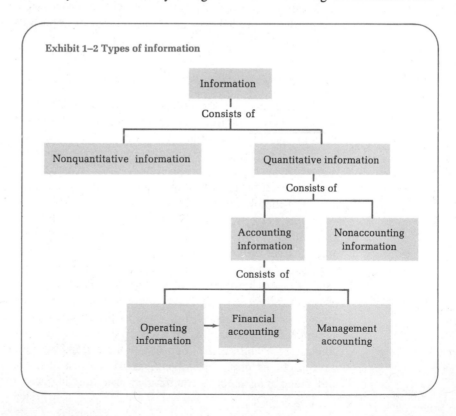

Exhibit 1–2 Types of information

line here is not sharply drawn, however; much nonmonetary information is included in accounting reports when it assists the reader in understanding what the report is intended to convey. For example, reports on sales for the Morgan Ford Company would show, in addition to the monetary amount of sales revenue, the number of automobiles sold, which is nonmonetary information. There is no point in debating the question of whether this is or is not accounting. The important point is that the focus of accounting information is monetary, but that nonmonetary information is reported when it is helpful to do so.

OPERATING INFORMATION

The bottom section of Exhibit 1–2 indicates the general nature of accounting information. By far the largest quantity of such information consists of **operating information.** Operation information provides the raw material for (1) management accounting and (2) financial accounting.

In the course of its daily operations, a company like the Morgan Ford Company generates a vast amount of accounting information. Viewed close up and in detail, the mass of this information is bewildering; but if one steps back a bit from the detail, one can see that most of it can be classified into a relatively few main streams. The principal such streams are:

1. *Production.* These are records showing the detail on orders received from customers, instructions for manufacturing the goods to meet these orders, instructions for manufacturing goods that are to be held in inventory until orders are received, and corresponding detail on services rendered. In the Morgan Ford Company, this stream is not as large as it would be in a manufacturing company, but it does exist in the form of work orders for cars to be serviced.

The nature of the production stream varies widely in different industries, but it tends to be similar for companies within a given industry. In some industries, such as banks and insurance companies, the majority of employees are engaged in processing production records; these employees process "paper" in essentially the same way that employees in a factory process material.

2. *Purchasing and materials.* These are records having to do with material and services ordered, with their receipt, with keeping track of material while it is in inventory, and with its issue to the production departments.

3. *Payroll.* These are records which show how much each employee has earned, the nature of the work that he did, and how much he has been paid. Every company is required by law to furnish to its employees and to the government specified information on earnings, and because of this requirement there is a great deal of similarity in the payroll records of most companies.

4. *Plant and equipment.* These are records of the cost, location, and condition of each significant item of building, equipment, or other noncurrent asset used by the company, together with the related depreciation data.

5. *Sales and accounts receivable.* For every cash sale, there is a cash register record of some sort. For every credit sale there is an invoice giving detail of what was sold and to whom. For every customer there is a record of the amount he owes and the amount he has paid.

6. *Finance.* These are the checkbook and bank deposits that are familiar to everyone, and the less familiar but equally important records required to keep track of investments, the incurrence and payment of liabilities, and dividends and other transactions with stockholders.

7. *Cost.* These are records of costs incurred in manufacturing goods or rendering services. In the Morgan Ford Company, these are records of the labor costs, material costs, and other costs incurred for each automobile repair job in the service department.

8. *Responsibility accounting.* This is a record of the revenues, expenses, and investment of each responsibility center.

These eight streams of data constitute the bulk of the information that exists in most companies. There are a wide variety of minor streams and variations on these main streams that need not concern us. The relative importance and complexity of these streams varies greatly in different types of businesses.

In a department store, the stream of data on sales and accounts receivable is relatively large because of the paperwork connected with charge purchases, while the payroll stream is relatively small because the number of employees per dollar of revenue is relatively small, and because the method of compensating employees is usually straightforward. In an automobile manufacturing company, the reverse would be the case. Its customers, who are automobile dealers, are no more numerous than those in a retail store that has sales a 10th of 1 percent as great, yet it has tens of thousands of employees, and must keep records on what each of them earn and what work they do.

The eight streams of data, although separately identifiable, are interrelated. Thus, the accounts receivable stream is connected to the financial stream when cash payments are received from customers; and the purchases stream is connected to the financial stream when vendors are paid and to the production stream when material is used in the production process.

Management accounting

In *Fundamentals of Financial Accounting,* we focus on the financial statements, namely, the balance sheet, the income statement, and the statement of changes in financial position. Most of the information used in the preparation of these financial statements is obtained from summaries of the streams of operating information that were listed above.

In *Fundamentals of Management Accounting,* our focus is on accounting information that is useful to management. The financial statements obviously are useful to management. Exhibit 1–3 is an income statement of Morgan Ford Company. It is useful in thinking about plans for the company (e.g., it suggest questions about the relative profitability of the various departments), and it is also useful as a basis for control (e.g., it can be used as a basis for discussion with the several department managers about their performance). In this sense, therefore, both the volumes, *Fundamentals of Financial Accounting* and *Fundamentals of Management Accounting,* are concerned with management accounting.

Exhibit 1–3

MORGAN FORD COMPANY
Income statement
For the year ended December 31, 1973

	Revenue	*Costs*	*Gross Margin*
New cars....................	$ 764,375	$ 631,281	$133,094
Used cars..................	479,138	431,455	47,683
Service.....................	189,502	151,397	38,105
Parts and accessories.........	67,316	56,862	10,454
Total................	$1,500,331	$1,270,995	$229,336
Expenses:			
Sales salaries............................		$60,786	
Other salaries............................		62,846	
Advertising..............................		9,372	
Depreciation.............................		14,275	
Maintenance.............................		12,323	
Other...................................		6,340	165,942
Income before taxes.......................			$ 63,394
Income taxes.............................			28,650
Net Income..............................			$ 34,744

There is obviously no point in repeating the material we discuss in *Fundamentals of Financial Accounting,* however; so in this volume we shall limit the scope of management accounting to the *additional* accounting information, beyond that contained in the financial statements, that is useful to management. The several streams of operating information provide much of the raw material of management accounting. Much of this information is not of direct interest to managers, however. In the normal course of events, a manager does not care about the amount of money that an individual customer owes, or the amount that an individual employee earned last week, or the amount that was deposited in the bank yesterday, or the placement of an individual purchase order for the replenishment of parts. For obvious reasons, records must be kept of all these facts, but ordinarily these records are used by operating personnel rather than by managers. The manager is interested in summaries drawn from these records rather than in the records themselves.

In general, therefore, management accounting information is *summary* information. In order to understand it, we do need to know something about the source of raw material used for these summaries, but we need only enough of the detail to be able to understand the resulting summaries.

MANAGEMENT'S NEED FOR ACCOUNTING INFORMATION

In an earlier section we pointed out that among the manager's functions are: (1) planning, (2) directing day-to-day operations, and (3) controlling. Management needs accounting information for each of these functions, as discussed in a preliminary way below.

Planning. There are two somewhat different types of planning activities: (1) planning what action to take about specific problems, often called alternative choice decisions; and (2) making overall plans for the whole enterprise.

Alternative choice decisions. Many management decisions involve making a choice between two or more alternatives. These decisions relate to all sorts of problems, but accounting information is especially useful in connection with one broad category of problem, that having to do with the allocation of resources. Although resources are usually measured in terms of money, it is best to think of them in terms of the more fundamental physical realities that the money amounts stand for—materials of various types, machines, services of employees, and services furnished by others. In any company, resources are limited, and they have a cost. They must be used in the best way to accomplish the company's objectives. To give just a few examples from the long list of alternative choice problems that arise in the Morgan Ford Company: the used car sales manager decides whether or not to place newspaper advertisements for his cars; the service manager decides whether or not to buy a new machine that will help the mechanics do a better job of servicing cars; the parts and accessories manager decides whether or not to add a new item to his inventory, and if so, how many to order and from whom it should be purchased.

Overall planning. A good manager does not wait for a problem to arise and then decide what to do about it. Rather, to the extent that he can, he anticipates the problems and decides what should be done before they press for immediate attention. This is the process of overall planning. It can take many forms, but we are especially interested in the formal planning technique called **budgeting.** A budget is a plan, usually annual, and usually expressed in financial terms.

Accounting information that is used for planning can be classified in various ways. Simon[2] draws a useful distinction between **attention-**

---

[2] Herbert A. Simon, *Administrative Behavior* (2d ed.; New York: The MacMillan Co., 1957), p. 20.

directing information and **problem-solving** information. The former alerts management to the existence of a problem or of an opportunity; the latter helps management decide on the best way of solving the problem or taking advantage of the opportunity.

Directing day-to-day operations. Accounting information is useful for many purposes in the conduct of day-to-day operations. For example, when a customer has his car repaired, he expects that his bill will be based on the costs incurred in doing the repair job. Thus, the price charged for repair work is normally based on the cost of doing that work. In order to determine what the price should be, there must be a record of what costs were incurred.

In the Morgan Ford Company, all the repair work takes place in a single room, and the measurement of costs incurred is a relatively simple task. In a manufacturing company, such as the Ford Motor Company, where the thousands of parts in an automobile are fabricated in dozens of different departments, and where the complete manufacturing process for these parts and for assembling the automobile extends over a period of weeks, the job of measuring costs is much more complicated, but the purpose is essentially the same as in the Morgan Ford Company: to help decide what price should be charged for the finished product. Although selling prices are related to costs in a great many situations, there are numerous other situations in which they are not so related; we shall discuss both types of situations.

Controlling. As noted in the description of the Morgan Ford Company, the manager must make judgments both about activities and about persons. With respect to the former, he must decide how well things are going; in particular, whether they are going as planned. If he decides that they are not going well, he needs to find out why and take corrective action. Even though things are going reasonably well, he may spot opportunities for making them even better. Accounting information helps in this process of evaluation. Since the evaluation leads to new decisions, the process is one of feedback, in the same sense that a thermostat senses the temperature of a room and feeds back information to the furnace if the temperature is not satisfactory. The manager must also make judgments about how well his subordinates are doing. Accounting information helps in these judgments.

TYPES OF MANAGEMENT ACCOUNTING INFORMATION

The several purposes described above require somewhat different types of accounting information. Financial accounting is essentially a single process, governed by a single set of generally accepted accounting principles, and unified by the basic equation Assets = Liabilities + Owners' equity. By contrast, in management accounting there are *several* processes; there are *several* sets of principles that govern the compilation of the data; and there is no single unifying equation. Three different types of management accounting data exist, each of which is useful for certain purposes but invalid if applied to other purposes. It is essential that the differences among these types be appreciated. To emphasize this point, each of the three main parts of this book focuses on one of these three types. It would be premature to attempt an explanation of each type now, but at least they should be listed:

1. *Full cost accounting.* This type of accounting measures the full cost of goods and services. It is useful in the course of ordinary operations, particularly in arriving at selling prices. The determination of the price for an automobile repair job, mentioned above, is an example. Full cost accounting is also used, in some situations, in measuring and analyzing performance, which is a part of the control process.

2. *Differential accounting.* This type of accounting measures, or estimates, how costs and revenues would be different if one course of action were adopted as compared with an alternative course of action. It is therefore helpful in the analysis of alternative choice problems, which is part of the planning process.

3. *Responsibility accounting.* This type of accounting measures the costs, revenues, and investment in responsibility centers. It is the principal type of accounting information used in the control process, and it also is used in budgeting, which is an important part of planning.

It should be emphasized that *there is not a one-to-one correspondence between the three types of management accounting information and the three management functions.* The task of understanding management accounting would be much simpler if such a correspondence existed, but it does not. Overall planning uses primarily responsibility accounting, but to a certain extent it also uses full cost accounting and differential accounting. Some operating decisions use full cost information, while others use differential accounting information.

Thus, the central scheme of this book is to discuss each of the three types of management accounting separately, first explaining what it is, and then discussing its use for various management purposes. At this point the reader is not expected to remember, or even to understand, the classifications given above. The fact to be emphasized here is the fact of diversity.

PLACE OF MANAGEMENT ACCOUNTING

Since our interest is focused here on management accounting, we may have a tendency to overemphasize its importance. In order to counteract this tendency, two points are stated here, and will be repeated in other contexts later on.

Nonaccounting information. The first point is that accounting information is only part of the information that a manager uses. A manager uses whatever information is available, whether it be accounting or nonaccounting, quantitative or nonquantitative. A telephoned message, or even a rumor, that an important customer is so dissatisfied with a company's product that he is about to take his business elsewhere, is not accounting and not even quantitative, but it is certainly an imporant piece of information.

Necessity for judgment. The second point is that accounting information, and indeed any information, rarely provides the complete answer to a management problem. The most that accounting information can do is to help the manager. The actual decision requires, in all except the most trivial situations, that judgment be exercised. Accounting information can help the manager make sound decisions; it assists the manager's judgment, but it is not a substitute for judgment.

Management accounting and financial accounting   We have mentioned some differences between management accounting and financial accounting. In order to facilitate the transition from the study of financial accounting in *Fundamentals of Financial Accounting* to the study of management accounting in this volume, it seems desirable to recapitulate these differences, add others, and also point out similarities.

DIFFERENCES BETWEEN MANAGEMENT ACCOUNTING AND FINANCIAL ACCOUNTING

In contrast with financial accounting, management accounting—

1. Has no single unifying concept.
2. Is not necessarily governed by generally accepted principles.
3. Is optional rather than mandatory.
4. Includes more nonmonetary information.
5. Has more emphasis on the future.
6. Focuses on segments as well as on the whole of business.
7. Has less emphasis on precision.
8. Is part of other processes rather than an end in itself.

1. *Lack of a unifying concept.* As already noted, financial accounting is built around the fundamental equation: Assets = Liabilities + Owners' equities, whereas in management accounting there are three types of accounting, each with its own conceptual framework.

2. *Not governed by generally accepted principles.* Financial accounting information must be prepared in accordance with generally accepted accounting principles. Outsiders, who usually have no choice but to accept information just as the company provides it, need assurance that the financial statements are prepared in accordance with a mutually understood set of ground rules. Otherwise, they could not make sense out of the figures. Generally accepted accounting principles provide these common ground rules. The management of a company, by contrast, can make and enforce whatever rules it finds most useful for its own purposes, without worrying about whether these conform to some outside standard. Thus, in management accounting there may well be information on sales orders received (i.e., the order "backlog"), even though these are not financial accounting transactions; fixed assets may be stated at appraisal values, overhead costs may be omitted from inventories, or revenue may be recorded before it is realized, even though each of these concepts is inconsistent with generally accepted accounting principles. The basic question in management accounting is the pragmatic one: "Is the information useful?" rather than, "Does it conform to generally accepted principles?"

3. *Optional.* Financial accounting *must* be done. Enough effort must be expended to collect data in acceptable form and with an acceptable degree of accuracy to meet the requirements of outside parties, whether or not the accountant regards this information as useful. For most sizable corporations, these requirements are specified by the Securities and Exchange Commission (SEC). Even those companies that are not covered by SEC regulations have their financial statements examined by professional outside accountants, in most cases, and these accountants insist that certain requirements be met. And all companies must keep records for income tax purposes, according to regulations of the taxing authorities. Management accounting, by contrast, is entirely optional. No outside agencies specify what must be done, or indeed that anything need be done. Being optional, there is no point in collecting a piece of information for management purposes unless its value, as an aid to management, is believed to exceed the cost of collecting it.

4. *Nonmonetary information.* The financial statements, which are the end product of financial accounting, include primarily monetary information. Management accounting deals with nonmonetary as well as monetary information. Although the accounts themselves contain only money amounts, much of the information on management accounting reports is nonmonetary. They contain quantities of material, as well as the monetary cost of material; number of employees, as well as labor costs; units of products sold, as well as dollar amounts of sales revenue; and so on.

5. *Future information.* Financial accounting records the financial history of an enterprise. Entries are made in the accounts only after transactions have occurred. Financial accounting information is indeed used as a basis for making future plans, but the information itself is historical. Management accounting includes, in its formal structure, numbers that represent estimates and plans for the future, as well as information about the past. (Some financial accounting entries, such as those for depreciation, require that estimates of future conditions be made; the basic thrust of financial accounting is nevertheless historical.)

6. *Focus on segments.* The financial statements relate to the business as a whole. Some companies do subdivide total revenue according to the main lines of business in which they engage, and other companies subdivide certain costs in a similar fashion. The main focus, however,

is on the entire business entity. In management accounting, by contrast, the main focus is on segments, that is, on products; or on individual activities; or on divisions, departments, and other responsibility centers. As we shall see, the necessity for dividing the total costs of the business among these individual segments creates important problems in management accounting that do not exist in financial accounting.

7. *Less emphasis on precision.*   Management needs information rapidly, and is often willing to sacrifice some precision in order to gain speed in reporting. Thus, in management accounting, approximations are often as useful as, or even more useful than, numbers that are worked out to the last penny. Financial accounting cannot be absolutely precise either, so the difference is one of degree. The approximations used in management accounting are greater than those in financial accounting.

8. *A means rather than an end.*   The purpose of financial accounting is to produce financial statements. When the statements have been produced, the purpose has been accomplished. (The accountant can, to be sure, play an important role in helping users to analyze and understand the statements, but this activity takes place after the completion of the financial accounting process.) Management accounting information is only a means to an end, the end being the planning, directing, and controlling activities described above. The management accountant assists management in using accounting data. He should not adopt the attitude that the accounting numbers are an end in themselves.

SIMILARITIES BETWEEN MANAGEMENT ACCOUNTING AND FINANCIAL ACCOUNTING

Although differences do exist, most elements of financial accounting are also found in management accounting. There are two reasons for this. First, the same considerations that make generally accepted accounting principles sensible for the purposes of financial accounting are likely to be present for purposes of management accounting. For example, management cannot base its reporting system on unverifiable, subjective estimates of profits submitted by lower echelons, which is the same reason that financial accounting adheres to the cost and realization concepts. Second, the operating accounting system must furnish the information used in preparing the financial statements. There is a presumption therefore, that the basic data will be collected in accordance with generally accepted financial accounting principles, for to do otherwise would require duplication of data collecting activities.

SOURCE DISCIPLINES

Accounting is an applied science (or "art," as some prefer). All applied subjects are developed from foundations and concepts developed in a basic science or discipline. Management accounting has two such source disciplines. Part of management accounting is related to **economics,** which deals with the principles governing decisions on the use of scarce resources. Another part is related to **social psychology,**[3] which deals with the principles governing the behavior of people in organizations. These two sets of principles are quite different from one another, and this fact causes problems both in understanding the principles of management accounting and in applying these principles in the real world. For example, for the purpose of deciding whether to purchase a new machine, we shall use accounting information developed according to principles that the economist specifies, but for the purpose of preparing a budget for the responsibility center in which that same machine is used we shall take account of the principles of social psychology; the latter may lead to quite different accounting constructions.

Some economists and some behavioral scientists criticize management accounting. Much of this criticism arises because each has the mistaken belief that management accounting relates solely to his discipline. One of the significant problems in the real world is to give the appropriate weight to each of these disciplines.

Summary

Any organization has objectives. In a business company, an important objective is to earn a satisfactory profit. A company selects a set of strategies for attaining its objectives, and the people in the company are organized in a way that presumably is best for carrying out these strategies. The various units in this organization are called responsibility centers. Each is headed by a manager. Management accounting exists to provide useful information to these managers. Among other functions, managers perform the following for which accounting information is useful: planning and coordinating the future activities of the responsibility center, directing day-to-day operations, and control, which involves evaluating results and taking appropriate action.

Accounting is one type of information. The total amount of information available to a manager includes nonquantitative as well as quantitative elements. The quantitative elements include both monetary and nonmonetary amounts. Accounting is essentially monetary, but includes related nonmonetary data.

Accounting information can be divided into three categories. The largest, in terms of quantity of data, is operating information. The mass of operating data flowing through a company consists of these streams: production, purchasing and materials, payroll, sales and accounts receivable, plant and equipment, financial, cost, and responsibility accounting. Data in these streams provide the raw material for both

---

[3] The boundaries of social psychology are not entirely clear. We mean to include those principles of psychology and of sociology that are intended to explain how individuals behave in situations ranging from two-person interactions to large groups.

financial accounting and management accounting; that is, accounting reports are essentially summaries of these data, constructed in various ways to meet the needs of investors and other outside parties and of managers inside the business, respectively.

There is no single, unified management accounting system. Rather, there are three different types of information, each used for different purposes. These are labeled: (1) full cost accounting, (2) differential accounting, and (3) responsibility accounting. Each of the three main parts of this book is devoted to one of these types.

As contrasted with financial accounting, management accounting has several concepts rather than one; is not necessarily governed by generally accepted principles; includes more nonmonetary information; has more emphasis on the future; is optional rather than mandatory; focuses on segments of a business rather than on the whole; has less emphasis on precision; and is a means to an end rather than an end in itself. Nevertheless, the two subjects have much in common.

Management accounting is built on concepts from two source disciplines: economics and social psychology. This fact causes problems in deciding on the relative importance to be given to concepts from each discipline in various situations.

Important terms

At the end of each chapter, a list of the important terms introduced in that chapter is given. You should understand the meaning of these terms. The list for Chapter 1, arranged in the order in which they appear in the text, is:

Organization	**Planning**
Strategy or policy	**Directing**
Line department	**Controlling**
Staff department	**Feedback**
Organization chart	**Information**
Responsibility center	**Operating information**
Manager	**Management accounting**
Controller	

Questions for discussion

1. A football team is an organization. Can you describe this organization in the terms used in the text, that is, its objectives, its strategies, its organization structure, and the functions of its managers?

2. Name some of the strategies that are available to a company in the retail grocery business.

3. An important planning activity is *coordination*. Give examples of the coordination that must take place in the Morgan Ford Company.

4. Some of the items on the income statement in Exhibit 1–3 are especially important to each manager in the Morgan Ford Company.

Which items would each manager shown on the organization chart be especially interested in?

5. A college or university is a nonprofit organization. Discuss the similarities and differences, in terms of the characteristics given in the text, between a college or university and the Morgan Ford Company.

6. What is the difference between information and data?

7. Is the material in this book information? Is it management information?

8. Does a newspaper contain management information?

9. Refer to Exhibit 1–3. Does it contain both financial accounting and management accounting information? Describe similar management accounting reports for the Morgan Ford Company that (*a*) emphasized the future rather than the past, (*b*) focused on segments rather than the whole, and (*c*) had nonmonetary as well as monetary information.

10. How does information needed for planning differ from information needed for control?

11. Why is precision less important in management accounting than in financial accounting?

12. Give some examples of situations in which estimates of the future affect financial accounting information.

13. Why do generally accepted accounting principles affect management accounting even though there is no requirement that management accounting adhere to such principles?

14. Explain the differences between management accounting and financial accounting.

15. Control, or the analysis of performance, is related both to (*a*) activities or functions and (*b*) persons. What source discipline probably governs the control of activities or functions? the control of persons?

16. The controller department is generally responsible for all record-keeping. Why don't the managers of line departments keep their own records?

17. The controller department is a staff or service organization. If the department consists of several sections such as accounts receivable, payroll, cost accounting, etc., does the controller have line responsibility for these sections?

Problems   1–1.   Suburbia Department Store sells four different lines:
a. Men's and boys' wear.
b. Ladies' wear.
c. Home furnishings.
d. Notions.

Each of these departments is headed by a manager (called the "buyer") who directs the activities of sales, inventory control, and clerical personnel in his department. There is a merchandising division manager who is directly responsible to the president. The buyers are responsible to the division manager. The store has three others also responsible to the president—an advertising manager, the controller of the accounting division, and the store personnel manager.

Required:

Devise an organization chart which clearly distinguishes between the line and staff functions described.

1–2. Below is a list of selected management positions in Baker Corporation and a list of various ledger accounts.

Required:

Choose the accounts which reflect the area for which each member of management would be responsible.

Management Position	*Accounts*
Treasurer	Cash
Controller	Salaries and Wages—Accounting
Credit manager	Salaries and Wages—Salesman
Marketing manager	Equipment—Delivery
Purchasing manager	Equipment—Bookkeeping Machines
Production manager	Depreciation—Receiving Department Equipment
	Inventory—Finished Goods
	Inventory—Raw Materials
	Machinery and Equipment—Factory
	Salaries and Wages—Factory
	Accounts Receivable

1–3. Following is a management accounting report for the Morgan Ford Company. You are asked to contrast this report with a financial accounting report (as, for example, Exhibit 1–3), according to the list of differences given in the text.

MORGAN FORD COMPANY
Service Department Report
September 1974

	Planned	*Actual*	*Difference**
Number of jobs completed.....	200	183	(17)
Number of employee days.....	370	368	2
Expenses:			
Employees wages..........	$11,000	$11,386	$ (386)
Parts used...............	8,000	6,287	1,713
Supplies used............	2,500	2,412	88
Other expenses...........	3,000	3,312	(312)
Total Expenses........	$24,500	$23,397	$ 1,103
Revenue...................	30,000	27,234	(2,766)
Profit.................	$ 5,500	$ 3,837	$(1,663)

* ( ) means unfavorable.

1–4. The purpose of some management accounting is "attention directing." What questions can be raised about the performance of the service department from the information given in the report in Problem 1–3?

part one Full cost accounting

In Chapter 1, we described briefly three different types of management accounting information. These are:

1. Full cost accounting.
2. Differential accounting.
3. Responsibility accounting.

Part One focuses on the first of these types of cost, that is, on full cost accounting. This topic is described first because financial accounting, the subject of the companion volume of this book, uses full cost information; and full costs therefore provide, in a sense, a bridge between this volume and its companion. Moreover, the earliest management accounting systems were systems for collecting full costs. We shall describe these systems in Chapters 2, 3, and 4. Chapter 5 describes management uses of full cost information.

It follows from the above that there are two somewhat different reasons for studying systems for collecting full cost information. First, these systems provide data that are used in financial accounting, and an understanding of them is essential to a thorough understanding of the meaning of certain items on the balance sheet and income statement. Second, and quite apart from their financial accounting uses, full cost data are useful for certain management purposes. By far the most important of these purposes is pricing, in the broad meaning of this term. The selling prices of many goods and services are related to the full costs of these goods and services. Many contracts provide that the buyer pay the seller an amount that equals the sum of full cost plus a specified profit. We hasten to add that in many other situations selling

23

prices are based on differential costs rather than on full costs; these situations are discussed in Part Two.

Because the uses of full cost information for pricing and for other purposes cannot be discussed in detail until the necessary groundwork has been laid, a discussion of uses is necessarily deferred to Chapter 5. Nevertheless, in studying the cost accumulation systems described in Chapters 2, 3, and 4, the reader should keep in mind that cost information is being collected for certain purposes, and that these purposes are essentially those described above.

2 Cost accounting systems

This is the first of three chapters that describe the concepts and practices of cost accounting. Although the term "cost accounting" would appear to refer to accounting for costs of any type, cost accounting systems usually are designed to collect primarily one type of cost, which is called full cost. In this chapter, we discuss the meaning of "full cost," describe the main elements of cost accounting systems, and describe the two main types of systems used for accumulating full costs, namely, job order costing and process costing.

"Cost" is one of the most slippery words used in accounting. It is used for a number of quite different notions. If someone says, without elaboration, "The cost of a widget is $1.80," it is practically impossible to understand exactly what is meant. The word "cost" becomes more meaningful when it is preceded by a modifier, making phrases such as "direct cost," "full cost," "opportunity cost," "differential cost," and so on; but even these phrases do not convey a clear meaning unless the context in which they are used is clearly understood. We shall be discussing the various contexts throughout this book.

GENERAL DEFINITION

In *Fundamentals of Financial Accounting*, there were numerous references to the word "cost," and from these it is possible to derive a generic definition:

> **Cost is a measurement, in monetary terms, of the amount of resources used for some purpose.**

25

Three important ideas are included in this definition. First, and most basic, is the notion that cost measures the use of resources. The elements that constitute the cost of making something are physical quantities of material, hours of labor service, and quantities of other services. Cost measures how much of these resources was used. The second idea is that cost measurements are expressed in monetary terms. Money provides a common denominator that permits the amounts of individual resources, each measured according to its own scale, to be combined so that the total amount of all resources used can be determined. Third, cost measurement always relates to a stated purpose. Much confusion can arise if this purpose is not clearly spelled out.

> *EXAMPLE:* Consider the building of a house. The purpose here is the house. The resources used in building the house are lumber; hardware of various types; roofing material; hours of effort by carpenters, plumbers, electricians, and other tradesmen; hours of effort by supervisors; permit fees; trucks, power saws, and other items of equipment; and so on.
>
> For some purposes, the amount of resources used need not be expressed in monetary terms. In ordering the lumber, the construction supervisor can say: "Deliver 1,000 board feet of 2 by 4's." In assigning the tradesmen, he can say: "Mr. X, you are to work all next week on the house."
>
> For other purposes, however, it is necessary to find the sum of all the resources used to build the house. In order to do this, the separate resources must be expressed in terms of some common denominator so that they can be added together. Since cost is expressed as a monetary amount, it provides such a common denominator. We cannot add together 1,000 board feet of lumber and 1,000 hours of labor, but if the price of the lumber is 50 cents a board foot and if the price of labor is $8 per hour, we can express the lumber as $500, the labor as $8,000, and add these to the monetary measures of other resources to obtain the total amount of resources used for the house. Each of these amounts is an element of cost, and the total is the cost of the house.

COST OBJECTIVE

Cost objective is the technical name for the purpose for which costs are measured.

In each instance, the cost objective must be carefully stated and clearly understood. In a certain shoe factory, for example, the manufacture of one case (i.e., 12 or 24 pair) of Style 607 shoes may be one cost objective, the manufacture of one case of Style 608 shoes may be another cost objective, and the manufacture *and sale* of a case of Style 607 shoes may be still another cost objective.

In this and the next chapter, we shall focus on cost objectives that are tangible goods, such as shoes, but it should be kept in mind that a cost objective is *any* purpose for which costs are measured. A cost objective can be a service, such as repairing a television set; it can be a fixed asset, such as a new building constructed by a company's own work force; it can be a current asset, such as material purchased for inventory.

A specific cost objective can be defined as broadly or as narrowly as one wishes. At one extreme, all the shoes manufactured in a shoe factory could be considered as a single cost objective, but if such a broad definition were used, differences in the resources used for the various styles of shoes would not be measured. At the other extreme, each pair of shoes could be considered as a single cost objective, but if such a narrow definition were used, the amount of recordkeeping involved would be great. As it happens, many shoe factories use a "case" of shoes, which consists of 12 pair or 24 pair of a single style, as the unit of costing. The shoes in a single case may consist of several sizes, and each size requires slightly different amounts of leather, but these differences are not considered important enough to warrant the effort of measuring the cost of each size.

FULL COST

The type of cost that we shall be discussing in these three chapters is called **full cost.** It means total cost, that is, **all the resources used for a cost objective.** In some circumstances, full cost is easily measured. If Mr. X pays $20 for a pair of shoes at a shoe store, the full cost of the pair of shoes to Mr. X is $20; that is, he used $20 of his resources—in this case, money—to acquire the pair of shoes.

But suppose we ask: What was the full cost of manufacturing the pair of shoes? This is a much more difficult question. A shoe factory may make thousands of pairs of shoes a month. Some are plain while others have intricate patterns, some are made of leather while others are made of synthetic material, and some are large while some are small. Clearly, different amounts of resources are used for these different styles of shoes; that is, they have different costs. One task of cost accounting is to assign amounts in such a way that significant differences in the amount of resources used are measured.

In a factory, the costs of cost objectives are measured in what is essentially a two-step process. First, all the costs applicable to the manufacturing operations of a given accounting period are collected, and, secondly, these costs are divided on a rational basis among all the cost objectives that were worked on in the factory during that accounting period.

The first step, the collection of the costs that are applicable to operations in a given accounting period, is a problem in financial accounting. The underlying accounting concept is known as the accrual concept, which, as explained in *Fundamentals of Financial Accounting,* is to be distinguished from the cash basis of measurement. According to the accrual concept, labor costs for an accounting period represent the labor services *performed* in the period rather than the wages actually *paid* in cash in the period; material costs represent the amount of material *consumed* in the period rather than the amount of materials *purchased* or paid for in the period; fixed asset costs are represented by depreciation for the period rather than by the cost of fixed assets purchased in the period; and so on. In general, the accrual concept focuses on the *use* of resources rather than on *outlays* for resources, and thus is consistent with the basic idea that cost measures the use of resources. Since these distinctions are discussed at length in *Fundamentals of Financial Accounting,* they will not be repeated here.

The second step, the division of total costs among cost objectives, is the province of cost accounting. In order to explain this step, we first introduce the distinction between direct and indirect costs.

Direct costs are items of costs that are specifically traceable to or directly caused by a cost objective. Leather used in manufacturing a case of shoes is a direct cost of that case of shoes, and so are the wages earned by the employees who worked directly in making that case of shoes.

Indirect costs are elements of costs that are associated with or caused by two or more cost objectives jointly, but are not directly traceable to each of them individually. The nature of an indirect cost is such that it is not possible or feasible to measure directly how much of the cost is attributable to a single cost objective. Some part of the factory superintendent's salary and some part of the cost of heat and light are elements of the cost of making each case of shoes, but there is no direct, observable way of measuring how much of these cost elements belong to each case.

Governing principle. **A governing principle of cost accounting is that the full cost of a cost objective is the sum of (1) its direct costs, plus (2) a fair share of its indirect costs.** This principle requires an explanation, for although it is intuitively obvious that the cost elements directly traceable to a cost objective are a part of the cost of that cost objective, it is by no means obvious that some fraction of the elements of indirect cost are part of the cost. One can actually see the leather in a pair of shoes, and it is obvious that certain labor services were involved in fashioning this leather into shoes, so there is no doubt of the appropriateness of counting such material and labor as part of the cost of the shoes. But what is the connection between the salary of the factory superintendent and the cost of the shoes made in the factory? The superintendent did not work on the shoes; for most of the time he probably was not even in the same room where the shoes were being manufactured.

The basic rationale is that the indirect costs in the factory are incurred for the several cost objectives in the factory; to argue otherwise would be to assert that indirect costs are sheer waste. Consistent with this rationale, some fraction of the indirect costs must be part of the costs of each cost objective. The fact that indirect costs cannot be traced directly to *individual* cost objectives does not alter this conclusion. We shall defer until later the question of how the fraction, or fair share, of indirect costs applicable to each cost objective can be measured.

> *EXAMPLE:* Consider the salary of the superintendent of a shoe factory. The superintendent has responsibilities for all the work done in the factory; his monthly salary is part of the total cost of operating the factory. If 1,000 cases of shoes are manufactured in a certain month, then some fraction of the superintendent's salary for that month is part of the full cost of each of these cases of shoes. This is so, even though there is no traceable relationship between the superintendent's salary and any one case of shoes.

Elements of cost

Elements of cost are either material, labor, or services. In a full cost accounting system, these elements are customarily recorded in certain categories. These categories are shown in Exhibit 2–1 and are defined and described below.

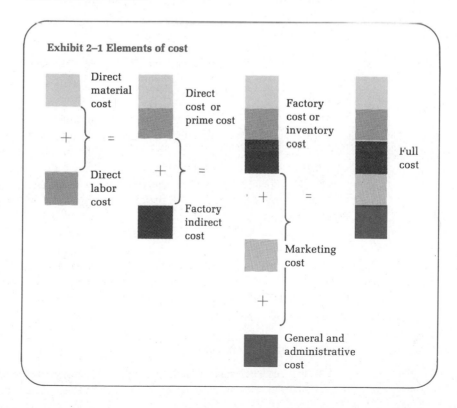

Exhibit 2–1 Elements of cost

Direct material cost
+ } =
Direct labor cost

Direct cost or prime cost
+ } =
Factory indirect cost

Factory cost or inventory cost
+ } =

Marketing cost
+

General and administrative cost

Full cost

DIRECT MATERIAL COST

Direct materials (sometimes called "stores" or "raw materials") **are those materials which actually enter into and become part of the specified finished product.** They are to be distinguished from *supplies,* which are materials used in the operation of the business but not directly in the product itself, such as lubricating oil used in machinery. Direct material costs include, in addition to the purchase price, the cost of inward freight on the materials, and many companies also include storage and handling costs associated with the direct material. Purchase discounts are often deducted from the invoice price of goods purchased. (See Chapter 6 of *Fundamentals of Financial Accounting* for further details.)

DIRECT LABOR COST

Direct labor is labor used to convert raw material into the finished product. **The direct labor costs of a product are those which can be specifically traced to or identified with the product or which vary so closely with the number of units produced that a direct relationship can be presumed to be present.** The wages and related costs of workers who assemble parts into a finished product, or who operate machines in the process of production, or who work on the product with tools, would be direct labor cost of the product.

PRIME COST

Prime cost is the sum of direct labor cost and direct material cost.

SERVICES

Services are distinguished from material in that they are intangible; they have no physical substance. Electricity, heat, and insurance protection are examples. Services are distinguished from labor in that they are performed by persons who are not employees of the responsibility center. If a product is tested for quality by company personnel, the cost is a labor cost; but if the product is tested by an outside testing laboratory, the cost is a service cost.

Although, conceptually, services can be either direct or indirect, the amount of *direct* services in most manufacturing companies is relatively small. Thus, in most cost accounting systems for manufacturing operations, all services are classified as indirect cost. It follows that total direct cost is the sum of direct material and direct labor cost, that is, the prime cost.

FACTORY INDIRECT COST

Factory indirect cost, sometimes called "factory overhead" or "burden," **includes all manufacturing costs other than direct material and**

direct labor. One element of factory indirect cost is indirect labor, which represents wages and salaries earned by employees who do not work directly on a single product or other cost objective but whose services are related to the overall process of production; for example, janitors, forklift operators, toolroom personnel, inspectors, timekeepers, and foremen. Another element of factory indirect cost is indirect material cost, which is the cost of material used in the factory but not traced directly to individual products or other cost objectives; for example, lubricants for machines, supplies, and material items which, although a part of the final product, are too insignificant to be included in direct material cost (such as the glue, thread, and eyelets used in manufacturing shoes). Factory indirect cost also includes such elements of cost as heat, light, power, maintenance, depreciation, taxes, and insurance on assets used in the manufacturing process.

FACTORY COST OR INVENTORY COST

Factory cost is the sum of direct and indirect factory costs. Under generally accepted accounting principles (i.e., the cost principle), **this is the cost at which completed manufactured goods are carried as inventory, and the amount that is shown as cost of sales when the goods are sold.**[1]

Note that the cost at which goods are carried in inventory does not include marketing costs, or those general and administrative costs that are unrelated to manufacturing operations. It includes only the costs that are incurred "up to the factory exit door."

MARKETING COST

Marketing cost, also called "distribution costs" or "selling costs," can be classified as either *order-getting costs* or *logistics cost*. **Order-getting costs,** such as marketing management, advertising, sales promotion, and salesperson's compensation and expenses, **are those incurred in the efforts to make sales. Logistics costs are those costs incurred "beyond the factory exit door" in storing the completed product, in transferring it to the customer, and in doing the associated record-keeping.** They include warehousing costs, billing costs, and transportation costs. Logistics costs are also called *order-filling costs.*

GENERAL AND ADMINISTRATIVE COST

General and administrative is a catchall classification to cover items not included in the above categories. Examples of such items are: costs incurred in the general and executive offices; research, development, and

---

[1] As noted in *Fundamentals of Financial Accounting,* Chapter 7, inventory is carried at cost unless (as is unusual) its market value is less than its cost.

engineering costs (which some companies include in factory indirect cost); public relations costs (which some companies include in marketing cost); donations; and miscellaneous items. General and administrative costs may include the cost of interest on borrowed capital, but in many companies interest is not counted as a cost at all for the purpose of measuring the full cost of cost objectives; instead, it is counted as an overall financial cost of the company.

The foregoing is only a brief, preliminary description of the elements of cost. We shall discuss them in greater depth in Chapters 3 and 4.

Systems for cost accumulation

A cost accounting system is a particular method of collecting costs and assigning them to cost objectives. There are many types of such systems. At this point we shall describe the essentials of a common type of system that is used to assign factory costs to products in a manufacturing company. The measurement of factory costs is necessary in order to obtain the proper amounts for the inventory items on the balance sheet and for the cost of goods sold item on the income statement.

INVENTORY ACCOUNTS

As of any moment of time, such as the date of a balance sheet, the current assets of a manufacturing company include three types of inventory accounts: raw materials, goods in process, and finished goods. **Raw Materials Inventory** reflects the acquisition cost of the raw materials on hand. These materials will be used subsequently in the manufacturing process. **Goods in Process** (or **Work in Process**) **Inventory** reflects the costs accumulated to date for those products on which production has been started but not yet completed as of the end of the accounting period. This cost includes the direct material, direct labor, and factory indirect costs assigned to such products. **Finished Goods Inventory** reflects the total manufacturing costs of products that have been manufactured but not yet sold. Finished Goods Inventory is comparable to the Merchandise Inventory account in a merchandising company, such as a retail store or a wholesaler. A merchandising company has no raw materials or goods in process inventory. (Refer to Chapters 6 and 7 of *Fundamentals of Financial Accounting* for a more complete discussion.)

THE ACCOUNT FLOWCHART

The flow of costs through the inventory accounts, ending with their appearance on the income statement as cost of goods sold, is described in the next section. As an aid in understanding this flow, the concept of the account flowchart is introduced here. Such a flowchart depicts the accounts used in a system, shown in T-account form, with lines indicating the flow of amounts from one account to another.

Most of the accounts on a cost accounting flowchart are either asset accounts or expense accounts. A characteristic of both asset and expense accounts is that increases are shown on the debit side and decreases are shown on the credit side. Since a line on a flowchart indicates a transfer "from" one account "to" another account, signifying that the first account is being decreased and the second account is being increased, it follows that the typical line on a cost accounting flowchart leads from the credit side of one account to the debit side of another. These flows represent events that happen during the manufacturing process. In addition to the lines designating "flow," other lines indicate entries for certain external transactions that are associated with the manufacturing process; an example is the entry for the acquisition of raw material from an outside vendor, which is a debit to Raw Materials Inventory and a credit to Accounts Payable or Cash.

FLOW OF COSTS

Exhibit 2–2 illustrates the flowchart concept and shows the essential cost flows in a manufacturing company. This flowchart contains a hypothetical set of figures for a month's operation in a small company that manufactures smoking pipes.

The flowchart is divided into three sections: (1) *acquisition,* containing the accounts related to the acquisition of resources, which are asset and liability accounts; (2) *manufacture,* containing the accounts related to the manufacturing process; and (3) *sale,* the accounts related to the sale of products.

The cycle of operations depicted on the flowchart may be explained as follows:

1. During the month, $6,000 of raw material was purchased on open account, $8,400 of various other assets were purchased for cash, and $7,000 of accounts payable were paid. The journal entries recording these transactions are as follows:

```
(a)  Raw Materials Inventory............. 6,000
         Accounts Payable................           6,000
(b)  (Various asset accounts)........... 8,400
         Cash..........................           8,400
(c)  Accounts Payable................... 7,000
         Cash..........................           7,000
```

2. During the month, raw materials costing $8,000 (principally briar wood, hard rubber blanks for stems, and filters) were withdrawn

Exhibit 4–2

Accounting flow chart of a pipe company

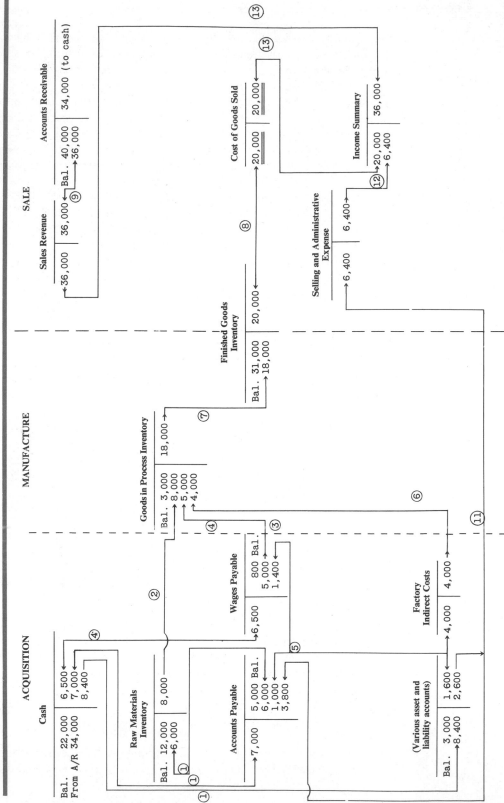

from inventory and sent to the factory to be worked on. This decrease in Raw Materials Inventory and increase in Goods in Process Inventory is recorded in the following journal entry:

```
Goods in Process Inventory.............. 8,000
    Raw Materials Inventory.............         8,000
```

3. During the month, employees worked on this material and fashioned it into pipes. The amount which they earned, $5,000, adds to the amount of Goods in Process Inventory, and the resulting liability increases Wages Payable, as recorded in the following journal entry:

```
Goods in Process Inventory.............. 5,000
    Wages Payable.......................         5,000
```

4. Employees were paid $6,500 cash. This decreases the liability account, Wages Payable, and also decreases Cash. (The payment of wages also involves social security taxes, withholding taxes, and certain other complications; these matters have been omitted from this introductory diagram.) The journal entry follows:

```
Wages Payable........................... 6,500
    Cash................................         6,500
```

5. Factory indirect costs were incurred during the month amounting to $4,000. Of the total, $1,000 was ascertained from current invoices for such things as electricity and telephone bills, so the offsetting credits were to Accounts Payable. Indirect labor costs were $1,400, with the offsetting credit to Wages Payable. The remaining $1,600 represented depreciation, the charge-off of prepaid expenses, and other credits to asset accounts. All of these items are here summed up in the general account, Factory Indirect Costs, but in practice they are usually recorded in separate indirect cost accounts, one for each type of cost. The journal entry follows:

```
Factory Indirect Costs.................. 4,000
    Accounts Payable....................  .        1,000
    Wages Payable.......................           1,400
    (Various assets and liability accounts)        1,600
```

6. Since the factory indirect cost is a part of the cost of the pipes that were worked on during the month, the total cost incurred is

transferred to Goods in Process Inventory, as in the following journal entry:

```
Goods in Process Inventory............... 4,000
        Factory Indirect Costs...............          4,000
```

7. Pipes whose total cost was $18,000 were completed during the month and were transferred to Finished Goods Inventory. This resulted in a decrease in Goods in Process Inventory and an increase in Finished Goods Inventory, as recorded in the following journal entry:

```
Finished Goods Inventory............... 18,000
        Goods in Process Inventory.........          18,000
```

8. Pipes with a cost of $20,000 were sold during the month. Physically, these pipes were removed from inventory and shipped to the customer. On the accounting records, this is reflected by a credit to Finished Goods Inventory and a debit to Cost of Goods Sold, as in the following journal entry:

```
Cost of Goods Sold.................... 20,000
        Finished Goods Inventory...........          20,000
```

9. For the same pipes, sales revenue of $36,000 was earned, and this is recorded in the accounts as a credit to Sales and a debit to Accounts Receivable. Note that the Sales Revenue credit described here and the Cost of Goods Sold debit described in Entry No. 8 related to *the same physical products,* the same pipes. The difference between the balances in the Sales Revenue and Cost of Goods Sold accounts, which is $16,000, therefore represents the gross margin earned on pipes sold during the month. The journal entry for the sales transaction is as follows:

```
Accounts Receivable.................... 36,000
        Sales Revenue......................          36,000
```

10. Accounts receivable collected during the month amounted to $34,000. Some of these accounts were for sales made in the current month, but most were for sales made in previous months. The journal entry follows:

```
Cash..................................... 34,000
        Accounts Receivable................          34,000
```

11. During the month $6,400 of selling and administrative expenses were incurred, $3,800 of which represented credits to Accounts Payable and $2,600 credits to various asset and liability accounts. These are recorded in the following journal entry:

```
Selling and Administrative Expense....... 6,400
    Accounts Payable.....................        3,800
    (Various asset and liability
        accounts)........................        2,600
```

12. Since these expenses were applicable to the current period, the Selling and Administrative Expense account is closed to the Income Summary account, as in the following journal entry:

```
Income Summary........................... 6,400
    Selling and Administrative Expense...        6,400
```

13. The balances in the Sales and Cost of Goods Sold accounts are also closed to Income Summary. The balance in Income Summary then reflects the pretax income for the period. (To simplify the example, income taxes and certain nonoperating and financial items normally appearing on income statements have been excluded.) These closing journal entries follow:

```
Sales Revenue............................ 36,000
    Income Summary.......................        36,000
Income Summary........................... 20,000
    Cost of Goods Sold...................        20,000
```

Strictly speaking, the cost accounting system as such ends with Entry No. 8. The other entries are given in order to show the complete set of events for the company.

The income statement for the pipe factory is shown in Exhibit 2–3.

Exhibit 2–3

PIPE COMPANY
Income statement
For the month of ——

Sales......................................	$36,000
Cost of goods sold.........................	20,000
Gross margin...............................	$16,000
Selling and administrative expense.........	6,400
Income (before income taxes)...............	$ 9,600

SOME IMPLICATIONS OF COST ACCOUNTING

Before going more deeply into the mechanics of cost accounting, let us pause to consider some of the important points that are implicit in the brief description given above.

First, observe that **cost accounting in a manufacturing company is not a separate accounting system.** It is an integral part of the financial accounting system, with accounts, journal entries, and the same rules for debit and credit that were described and illustrated in *Fundamentals of Financial Accounting.* Since there are books and manuals that have "cost accounting" in their title, some may get the impression that cost accounting is a separate accounting system, off by itself; this is not so.

Second, note what happens in the Goods in Process Inventory account. This account can be visualized as an accounting representation of the factory itself. As labor, material, and services flow into the factory, the monetary representation of these resources flow to Goods in Process Inventory as debits. The physical movement of products out of the factory and into the finished goods warehouse is represented by a credit to Goods in Process Inventory and a debit to Finished Goods Inventory. The balance in the Goods in Process Inventory account represents the costs that have been accumulated on partially completed products that are still in the factory at the end of the period. This balance corresponds to physical quantities of products still in the factory.

Third, observe the difference in the timing of the impact of costs on net income between a merchandising or service company and a manufacturing company. If a clerk in a retail store earns $600 in September, that $600 is an expense in September, and net income in September is reduced correspondingly. But if a factory employee in our pipe factory earns $600 in September, that $600 becomes a part of the cost of the pipes on which he works. In September, it appears in Goods in Process Inventory; then it moves to Finished Goods Inventory in the month in which the pipes are completed, where it remains until the pipes are sold. Thus, a factory employee's wages affect cost of goods sold, and hence net income, only when the pipes are sold, which may be in October or some later month. During the interval between the date of cost incurrence and the date of sale, the $600 of direct labor costs, together with all the other elements of manufacturing costs, appear in either Goods in Process or Finished Goods Inventory accounts; that is, they are part of the current assets.

In a merchandising or service company, costs of labor, supplies used, depreciation, and other elements affect net income *in the accounting period in which these costs are incurred,* that is, wage expense for September, the supplies used in September, and depreciation expense for September, all have an impact on the net income for September. In a manufacturing company, by contrast, those labor and other costs that are associated with the manufacturing process affect, initially, the value of inventory; **they affect net income only in the accounting period in** which the products containing these costs are sold. This may be a later accounting period than that in which the product was manufactured. The larger the inventory in relation to sales and the longer the production process, then the longer is the time interval that elapses between the incurrence of a manufacturing cost and its impact on net income.

Finally, note the difference between "manufacturing cost" and "costs of goods manufactured." **Manufacturing cost** (or factory cost) **refers to all the resources put into the manufacturing process during an accounting period.** In other words, it is the sum of the debits to the Goods in Process Inventory account. **Cost of goods manufactured refers to the cost of the products completed during the accounting period;** it is the credit to Goods in Process Inventory. These two terms sound almost identical, but they stand for quite different concepts. Manufacturing cost would equal cost of goods manufactured in a given period only if the balance in the Goods in Process Inventory account were the same at the end of the period as at the beginning.

Job costing and process costing

Consider the entries that transfer the cost of completed pipes from Goods in Process Inventory to Finished Goods Inventory, and from Finished Goods Inventory to Cost of Goods Sold. (These were Entries No. 7 and No. 8 in Exhibit 2–2 in the amount of $18,000 and $20,000 respectively.) The number and types of physical units (i.e., pipes) involved in these transfers can be ascertained readily by counting the pipes, but in order to assign dollar amounts that correspond to these physical units, a *cost per unit* must be established.

If the company manufactured only one style of pipe during a certain period and had no partially completed pipes at the end of the period, it would be possible to divide the total amount of debits to Goods in Process Inventory by the total number of units worked on during the period to obtain the cost per unit; this unit cost could then be used to calculate the amount that is recorded for the transfer of completed pipes from Goods in Process Inventory to Finished Goods Inventory, and when pipes of this type were sold, the same unit cost could be used to calculate the amount that is debited to Cost of Goods Sold and credited to Finished Goods Inventory. If the factory made more than one kind of product, however, such a simple calculation would not give results that fitted the facts, since one product probably required more material, more labor, or more overhead—that is, it cost more—than another. If the entries transferring completed goods from Goods in Process Inventory to Finished Goods Inventory and subsequently to Cost of Goods Sold are to reflect the facts of the situation, there must be some means of taking these differences into account.

> *EXAMPLE:* Assume the pipe factory made two grades of pipe, one with a factory cost of $2 per unit and the other with a factory cost

of $4 per unit. The transfers from Goods in Process Inventory to Finished Goods Inventory and from Finished Goods Inventory to Cost of Goods Sold should recognize these differences in cost. If, in one month, 8,000 of the $2 pipes and 2,000 of the $4 pipes were sold, the debit to Cost of Goods Sold should be $24,000, whereas in another month if 2,000 of the $2 pipes and 8,000 of the $4 pipes were sold the cost should be $36,000, even though the same *number* of pipes, 10,000, were sold in each month.

There are two principal systems for accumulating the costs of individual products. They are called, respectively, job order costing and process costing. Each is discussed below.

These cost accounting systems correspond to the two principal types of manufacturing operations. In one type of manufacturing, which is often called the **job shop** type, the factory works on a series of discrete jobs, each one of which has different specifications. The different styles of shoes in a shoe factory have already been mentioned. Other examples are the various types of furniture made in a furniture factory and the products made in a machine tool factory. In the other type of manufacturing, often called the **process** type, a single product, or an unvarying mix of products, is produced continuously. Petroleum refineries and many other chemical processing plants are of this type.

> **Essentially, a job order cost system collects cost for each physically identifiable job or batch of work as it moves through the factory, regardless of the accounting period in which the work is done; while a process cost system collects costs for all the products worked on during an accounting period, and determines unit costs by dividing the total costs by the total number of units worked on.**

JOB ORDER COSTING

The "job" in a job order cost system may consist of a single unit (e.g., a turbine or a house), or it may consist of all units of identical or similar products covered by a single job or production order (e.g., 1,000 printed books or 10 dozen Style 652 girdles). Usually each job is given an identification number, and its costs are collected on a separate record that is set up for that number. Anyone who has had an automobile repaired at a garage has seen such a record, except that the amounts that the customer sees have been converted from costs to retail prices. Exhibit 2–4 shows such a **job cost record.** It contains spaces to record the individual elements of cost that are charged to that job. These costs are recorded as the job moves through the various departments in the factory. When the job is completed, these cost elements are totaled to find the total cost of that job. The sum of all the costs charged to all the jobs worked on in the factory during an accounting period is the basis for the entries debiting Goods in Process Inventory

Exhibit 2–4

Job cost record

Product: Item 607					Job No.: 227
Date Started: 3/6 Date Completed: 3/18					
Units Started: 100 Units Completed: 100					

			Costs		
Week Ending	Dept. No.	Direct Material	Direct Labor	Factory Indirect	Total
March 6	12	$642.00	$108.00	$108.00	
13	12	. . .	422.00	422.00	
20	14		270.00	216.00	
Total		642.00	800.00	746.00	$2,188.00
Unit cost		6.42	8.00	7.46	21.88

and crediting Raw Materials Inventory, Wages Payable, and Factory Indirect Costs accounts (i.e., Entries No. 2, 3, and 6 in Exhibit 2–2). When each job is completed, the total cost recorded on the job cost record is the basis for the entry transferring the product from Goods in Process Inventory to Finished Goods Inventory (i.e., Entry No. 7), and this same cost is the basis for the entry transferring the product from Finished Goods Inventory to Cost of Goods Sold when the product is sold (Entry No. 8). The total cost recorded on all job cost records for products that are still in the factory as of the end of an accounting period equals the total of the Goods in Process Inventory account at that time.

In summary, in a job order cost system:

1. A separate job cost record is established for each job.
2. Costs chargeable to the job are entered on this record and are also debited to Goods in Process Inventory.
3. When the job is completed and transferred out of the factory, the total cost accumulated on the job cost record is the amount used to debit Finished Goods Inventory and to credit Goods in Process Inventory.
4. The balance in Goods in Process Inventory at the end of the accounting period is therefore the sum of the costs accumulated on all jobs still in the factory as reflected on the job cost records for uncompleted jobs.

PROCESS COSTING

In a **process cost system,** all manufacturing costs for an accounting period, such as a month, are collected in Goods in Process Inventory. These costs are *not* identified with specific units of product. A record of the number of units worked on is also maintained. By dividing total costs by total units, one derives a cost per unit; and this cost per unit is used as the basis for calculating the dollar amount of the entries which records the transfer from Goods in Process Inventory to Finished Goods Inventory, and the subsequent transfer from Finished Goods Inventory to Cost of Goods Sold.

> *EXAMPLE:* In a factory using a process cost system, the total factory cost in October was $200,000 and the number of units manufactured was 100,000. The cost per unit was therefore $2, and this unit cost was used to make the transfers from Goods in Process Inventory to Finished Goods Inventory.

Equivalent production. One special problem that arises in a process cost system is that of taking into account the products that are only partially completed at the end of an accounting period. The units that were *worked on* in September include the following: (1) units that were both started and completed during September; plus (2) units that were worked on but not completed by the end of September; plus (3) units that were started in August (or earlier) and completed in September.

Since 100 percent of the costs of the first type were incurred in September but only a portion of the costs of the second and third types, production   activity for September cannot be determined simply by adding up the number of units worked on during September. The three types of units must be converted to a common base, called **equivalent production,** that is, the equivalent of one completed unit. In order to convert the number of uncompleted products into their equivalence in terms of completed units, the assumption is often made that units still in process at the end of the period are 50 percent complete, and similarly that units in process at the beginning of the period were 50 percent complete at that time. Thus, in order to calculate the costs per unit worked on, each unit completed would be given a weight of one, each unit in process at the end of the period would be given a weight of one half, and each unit in process at the beginning of the period also would be given a weight of one half.[2]

> *EXAMPLE:* In a certain factory, costs incurred in September amounted to $22,000. During September, units were worked on as shown in Exhibit 2–5, that is, 2,000 units were started and completed, another 300 units were started but not completed, and 100 units that had been started in August were completed. Thus, some work was done during September on a total of 2,400 units. The unit cost is *not*

---

[2] A more precise procedure would be to estimate the actual stage of completion, but this involves more effort. At the other extreme, some companies disregard the units in process and show no Goods in Process Inventory account. If the goods in process inventory is small, or if it remains relatively constant in size, no serious error is introduced. Another variation is to apply the 50 percent assumption separately to each department through which the product passes rather than to the factory as a whole.

Exhibit 2–5

Calculation of equivalent production

Period in Which Costs Were Incurred

Units	*August*	*September*	*October*
A. 2,000 all in current month		2,000	
B. 300 completed next month		½ of 300	½ of 300
C. 100 started in prior month	½ of 100	½ of 100	

Calculation of Equivalent Production

	Gross Units	*Equivalent Production*
A.	2,000	2,000
B.	300 (×½)	150
C.	100 (×½)	50
Total	2,400	2,200

Unit cost: $22,000 ÷ 2,200 units = $10

Goods in Process Inventory

```
Beginning balance              To Finished Goods
   (100 units)        500         Inventory
                                  (2,100 units)    21,000
Costs incurred     22,000      Ending balance
                                  (300 units)       1,500
                   _____                          _____
                   22,500                          22,500
```

calculated by dividing $22,000 by the 2,400 units worked on, however, for to do so would be to neglect the costs incurred in the prior months for some units and the costs that will be incurred in the next month for still other units. Instead, it is assumed that in September one half of the work was done on partially completed units, so that each of them is equivalent to one half a unit that was begun and completed within the month. The number of equivalent units was therefore $2,000 + ½(300) + ½(100) = 2,200$ units. Since total factory costs for September were $22,000, the unit cost was $10.

The 2,100 units transferred to Finished Goods Inventory would be costed at $10 per unit, a total of $21,000. The 300 partially completed units remaining in Goods in Process Inventory at the end of September would be costed at *one half* the unit cost, or $5 per unit since it is assumed that they are only half completed.

The foregoing applies to direct labor costs and to factory indirect costs. Direct material costs may be treated differently, however, depending on when direct material enters the production process. If material is added evenly throughout the production process, it could reasonably be costed by use of the 50 percent assumption described above. If, as is perhaps more common, all the raw material for a unit is issued at the beginning of the process, the direct material cost per unit would be obtained by dividing the total cost of material used by the number of units *started* during the period.

In any event, some reasonable assumption has to be made. In a process cost system, there is no precise way of determining the amount of costs attributable to partially completed units.

> *EXAMPLE:* Assume that the $22,000 of cost in the above example excludes direct material cost. All the direct material is issued at the beginning of the production process. In September, the total cost of direct material put into production was $6,900. During the month, 2,300 units were started into production (items A and B on Exhibit 2–5). The unit raw material cost was therefore $3.
>
> The inclusion of direct material costs would modify the amounts given in Exhibit 2–5. If we now take the $10 per unit cost computed there and add to it the $3 per unit direct material cost, the total unit cost becomes $13. The 2,100 units transferred to Finished Goods Inventory would be costed at $13 × 2,100 = $27,300. The 300 units in Goods in Process Inventory at the end of September would be costed at material cost of $3 per unit plus other costs of ½ ($10) = $5 per unit (because, it will be recalled, it is assumed that only one half the other costs have been incurred). The total unit cost for these items is therefore $8, and the total inventory amount for the 300 units is $2,400.

Summary.   In summary, a process cost system works like this:

1.   The costs of resources used in the manufacturing process during the accounting period are accumulated as debits to the Goods in Process Inventory account.
2.   For cost elements, such as direct labor and factory indirect cost, that are incurred *throughout* the manufacturing process:
     a.   Production is measured in terms of the number of equivalent units of production.
     b.   A cost per unit is found by dividing total cost by the number of equivalent units.
3.   For cost elements, such as direct material, that are incurred at the *beginning* of the manufacturing process, the cost per unit is found by dividing total cost by the number of units that started the production process.
4.   Finished Goods Inventory is debited, and Goods in Process Inventory is credited, by an amount that is equal to the number of units completed in the period multiplied by these costs per unit.
5.   Assuming that all direct material is issued at the beginning of the production process, the balance in Goods in Process Inventory at the end of an accounting period is the direct material cost of the

units still in the factory plus an appropriate share (say, 50 percent) of the total direct labor and factory indirect cost of these units.

CHOICE OF A SYSTEM

Since a process cost system requires less recordkeeping than a job order system, there is a tendency to use it even though the products manufactured are not entirely alike. Thus, a manufacturer of children's shoes may use a process cost system, even though there are some differences in cost among the various sizes, styles, and colors of shoes manufactured.

In a process cost system, the unit costs are averages derived from the total cost of the period. Differences in the costs of individual products are not revealed. Thus, if there are important reasons for keeping track of the differences between one product and another, or between one production lot of the same type of product and another, then a job cost system is more appropriate. For example, a job cost system would invariably be used if the customer paid for the specific item or production order on the basis of its cost (as is often the case in machine shops, print shops, and other "job shop" companies). Also, use of a job cost system makes it possible to examine actual costs on specific jobs, and this may help one to locate trouble spots; in a process cost system, costs cannot be traced to specific jobs.

For our purposes, there is no need to study differences in the detailed records required for the two types of systems. Both systems are essentially devices for collecting full cost information. Either furnishes the information required for the accounting entries illustrated in Exhibit 2–2. In practice, there are many cost accounting systems that use job costing in some departments and process costing in other departments.

VARIATIONS IN PRACTICE

The accounting system outlined in Exhibit 2–2 will probably never be precisely duplicated in actual practice since it is a schematic representation of underlying structures. Companies build on the basic structure by adding accounts that collect the data in more detail so as to meet their particular needs for information. A company may, for example, set up several raw material inventory accounts, each one covering a different type of material, instead of a single account as shown in Exhibit 2–2. Alternatively, the Raw Material Inventory account may be a controlling account, controlling thousands of individual subsidiary accounts.[3] Another common variation is to have several goods in process accounts, one for each main department or "cost

---

[3] See *Fundamentals of Financial Accounting,* Chapter 6, Appendix A, for the operation of such accounts.

Exhibit 2-6

Cost system with departmental accounts

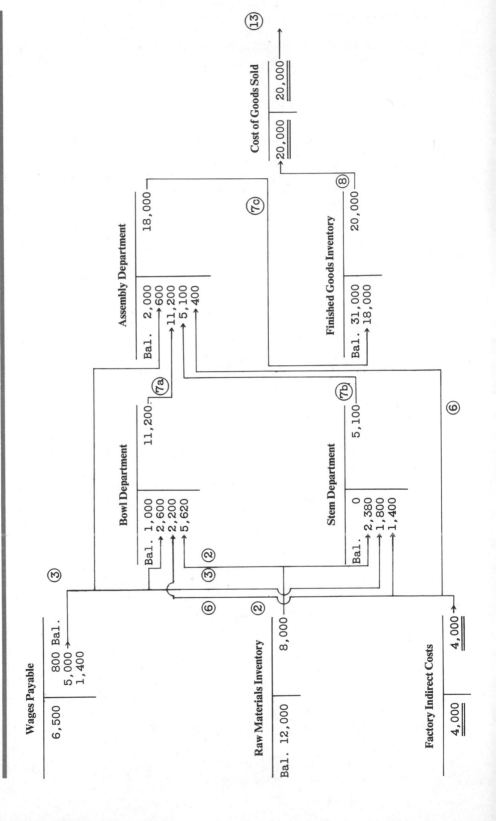

center" in the factory. A system using several goods in process accounts is shown in Exhibit 2–6. It will be noted that such a system is essentially like that shown in Exhibit 2–2 except that work is transferred from one department to another. The finished goods of one department become, in effect, the raw material of the next department.

Demonstra-
tion case

PART A

This demonstration case has two parts, A and B.

Refer to Exhibit 2–6. You are asked to describe the nature of each of the entries depicted on the flow diagram. Although this requires careful attention to detail, it will aid your understanding of the flow of costs through a cost accounting system.

After you have traced the entries, you can check your understanding by referring to Exhibit 2–7. This exhibit shows how much of the three

Exhibit 2–7

Assignment of cost elements

Entry	Total	Bowl	Stem	Assembly
Beginning balance..................	$3,000	$ 1,000	0	$ 2,000
2. Direct material......................	8,000	5,620	$2,380	0
3. Direct labor........................	5,000	2,600	1,800	600
6. Factory indirect....................	4,000	2,200	1,400	400
7a. From Bowl.........................				11,200
7b. From Stem.........................				5,100
Total debits to Goods in Process..		$11,420	$5,580	$19,300
Credits to Goods in Process..........		11,200	5,100	18,000
Ending balance in Goods in Process....	$2,000	$ 220	$ 480	$ 1,300

elements of cost—direct material, direct labor, and factory indirect—were debited to each of the three departments. Observe that the total for each element agrees with the amount debited to Goods in Process Inventory for that item, as shown on Exhibit 2–2. This correspondence arises because the accounts for Bowl Department, Stem Department, and Assembly Department are in fact goods in process inventory accounts.

Observe also the transfers between departments, that is, the $11,200 credited to Bowl Department and debited to Assembly Department, and the transfer of $5,100 from Stem Department to Assembly Department. The $11,200 represents the costs of the bowls completed during the month, and the $5,100 represents the cost of the pipe stems completed.

The other transactions on Exhibit 2–6 are the same as those on Exhibit 2–2. If you had difficulty with any of them, refer back to the explanations given for that Exhibit.

PART B

Unit costs. To review your understanding of equivalent production units, assume that the pipe factory used a process cost system in the stem department, that raw material entered at the beginning of the process, and that the number of units in the stem department was as follows:

	Units
On hand, beginning of month.............	0
Completed during the month............	30,000
On hand, end of month................	4,000

You are asked to calculate the cost per stem for the month, and to explain how the ending balance of $480 in the Stem Department and the transfer from Stem Department to Assembly Department of $5,100 were calculated.

After you have made this calculation, you can check your work, as follows:

For direct material, the total amount used was $2,380. Since material is used at the beginning of the process, this amount applies to all units started, which was 30,000 + 4,000 = 34,000. Direct material cost per unit was therefore $2,380 ÷ 34,000 = $0.07.

For direct labor and factory indirect costs, we must calculate the equivalent production. Since no stems were on hand at the beginning of the month, equivalent production is the number of units completed plus one half the number of units on hand at the end of the month, that is, 30,000 + ½ (4,000) = 32,000. Total direct labor and factory indirect costs were $3,200. The equivalent unit cost was therefore $3,200 ÷ 32,000 = $0.10.

The unit cost applicable to the transfer to Assembly Department was:

Material................	$0.07
Labor and overhead.......	0.10
Unit cost............	$0.17

The total cost of the stems transferred to Assembly was therefore 30,000 × $0.17 = $5,100.

The cost applicable to the stems on hand at the end of the month was:

	Units	Unit Cost	Cost
Material.....................	4,000	$0.07	$280
Labor and indirect...........	2,000	0.10	200
Total, Goods in Process Inventory..............			$480

Summary   Cost is a word of many meanings. In this chapter we have discussed cost in the sense of the full cost of a cost objective; cost in this sense measures all the resources used for a cost objective. The measurement of full costs is a two-step process: First, all the costs applicable to an accounting period are collected, and, secondly, these costs are assigned to all the cost objectives that were worked on during that accounting period.

The second of these steps is the province of cost accounting. It is accomplished by assigning to cost objectives (1) their direct costs, that is, the costs that are directly traceable to each cost objective; and (2) a fair share of the indirect costs, that is, those costs incurred for several cost objectives.

A cost accounting system collects costs and assigns them to cost objectives. In a factory, costs are accumulated in a Goods in Process Inventory account as resources are used in the manufacturing process and these costs are then transferred to a Finished Goods Inventory account when the products have been completed. In order to make the transfer from Goods in Process to Finished Goods, there must be some procedure for measuring the cost of individual completed units. There are two such procedures: (1) job order costing, in which costs are accumulated separately for each individual item or for a lot of similar items; and (2) process costing, in which costs are accumulated for all units together, and then are divided between completed units and partially completed units according to some reasonable assumption as to the stage of completion at the end of the period.

Important terms	Cost	Direct labor cost
	Cost objective	Prime cost
	Full cost	Factory indirect cost
	Direct cost	Job order costing
	Indirect cost	Process costing
	Direct material cost	Equivalent production

Questions for discussion

1. Explain, with an example, why not all items of cost can be classified as direct costs.

2. Distinguish between direct labor cost and indirect labor cost, giving an example of each.

3. Distinguish between direct material cost and indirect material cost, giving an example of each.

4. Distinguish among raw material inventory, goods in process inventory, and finished goods inventory.

5. Distinguish between factory cost and full cost. What elements of cost make up the difference between them?

6. The cost objectives in a certain motel are (*a*) room rentals and (*b*) meals. List some of the elements of cost you would expect to find in a motel, distinguishing between those that are direct costs of each of these cost objectives and those that are indirect costs.

7. Would you expect to find Raw Materials, Goods in Process, and Finished Goods Inventory accounts in the accounting system of a motel? Why?

8. Which of the following are part of the full cost of building a certain house? Explain why.
    (a) Depreciation expense on the builders' trucks that haul material to the house.
    (b) Lumber originally delivered to the site but later removed because it was in excess of that needed.
    (c) Cost of the architect's plans which were used to build this and five other identical houses.
    (d) Fees paid to the municipality on account of inspections required to see that the house conformed to building codes.
    (e) Advertising expenses incurred to sell the house.

9. Distinguish between the factory costs of a month and the cost of goods manufactured in that month.

10. Under what circumstances is job order costing rather than process costing appropriate?

11. In the example given for process costing (page 44), it was assumed that direct materials were used at the beginning of the production process. Suppose that direct materials were added evenly throughout the production process. What amount would be transferred to Finished Goods Inventory? What would be the amount of Goods in Process Inventory at the end of the period?

12. Consider that the course you are now taking is one cost objective. List as specifically as you can the items of direct costs *to the school* (not to you as an individual) of that cost objective and give examples of indirect costs of that cost objective.

13. Marketing costs are not included as part of the inventory cost of a product. Why?

14. In an account flow chart for a cost accounting system, the flow is usually from the credit side of one account to the debit side of another account. Why is the flow in this direction, rather than the reverse?

Problems   2–1. Refer to the situation illustrated in Exhibits 2–2 and 2–3. Assume that each of the following events occurred instead of those actually depicted:
    (a) No raw material was purchased for the month.
    (b) Costs were incurred as indicated, but no pipes were completed during the month. Sales were as indicated.
    (c) The factory was shut down during the month. Factory overhead costs continued at $4,000 and were charged as an ex-

pense on the income statement. No direct material or direct labor costs were incurred.

(d)   No sales were made during the month.

Required:

Considering each of these four events separately:

(1)   What changes would be required in Exhibit 2–2 and the related journal entries?

(2)   What would be the effect on the income statement, Exhibit 2–3?

2–2.   The Apex Assembly Company began business on January 1. Its employees earn $3 per hour. It incurred materials costs as indicated below. It purchased and received $10,000 of raw material on January 1. It had no other costs. During January it worked on three jobs, as follows:

	Job No. 1	Job No. 2	Job No. 3
Materials...............	$1,600	$3,000	$2,000
Labor.................	100 hours	200 hours	50 hours
Status, January 31......	Complete	Complete	Incomplete
	Sold for	Not sold	
	$3,000		
	cash		

Required:

(1)   What are the balances in the inventory accounts as of January 31?

(2)   Prepare an income statement for January.

2–3.   Following are partial data for the Carol Company for February:

Direct material used....................	$ 70,000
Direct labor cost......................	80,000
Total manufacturing cost...............	200,000
Beginning goods in process inventory.....	60,000
Ending goods in process inventory........	90,000

Required:

(1)   What was the factory indirect cost for February?

(2)   What was the cost of goods manufactured (i.e., transferred to Finished Goods Inventory)?

2–4.   A partial summary of the Carol Company's operations for March are given below:

Materials purchased....................	$25,000
Beginning balance—raw material..........	10,000
Ending balance—raw material............	2,000
Direct labor cost......................	14,000
Beginning balance—goods in process.......	3,000
Ending balance—goods in process........	25,000
Beginning balance—finished goods........	20,000
Ending balance—finished goods..........	10,000
Cost of goods sold.....................	50,000
Revenue.............................	80,000

Required:

(1) Give the journal entry for the transfer from Raw Material Inventory to Goods in Process Inventory.

(2) Give the journal entry for the transfer from Goods in Process Inventory to Finished Goods Inventory. (Hint: This amount can be determined by analysis of the Finished Goods Inventory transactions; use a T-account.)

(3) What was the amount of factory indirect cost for March? (Hint: Use a T-account for Goods in Process Inventory.)

(4) Prepare an income statement.

2–5. The Daley Company manufactures Gedol. Five units of raw material are required to manufacture one unit of Gedol. During April 20,000 units of raw material were purchased. Inventory balances for April were as follows, in units:

	Beginning	Ending
Raw material...............	5,000	2,000
Finished goods............	1,000	3,000
Goods in process..........	0	0

Required:

How many units of Gedol were sold in April?

2–6. A plant food is produced in two departments, Mixing and Bottling. During December, Mixing produced 7,000 gallons costing $7,000. The bottling process, which adds 5,000 gallons of water, incurred a total cost of $4,200. The plant food is bottled in 8-ounce bottles and packed in cases of 12 bottles each.

Required:

(1) Assuming no loss or breakage, what is the cost per case of plant food for December?

(2) If the plant food sells for $0.29 per bottle, compute the gross profit on the sale of one case.

2–7. The Camden Carburetor Company has received an order from the Sno-Go Snowmobile Corporation for 500 custom-made, racing-type carburetors. Below is the job cost record for this order:

Job No. 6—SG Corporation

Date	Materials	Labor	Factory Indirect	Credits	Balance
Jan. 1					0
18	4,000				4,000
30		3,000	1,500		8,500
Feb. 2	3,000				11,500
15		2,000	500		14,000
17				14,000	0

Required:

Journalize the entries necessary to reflect the above data in the Goods in Process Inventory and Finished Goods Inventory accounts.

2–8. The Handy Tool Company manufactures various tools and parts for small gasoline engines, some for special order and some for stock. At the end of April a summary of job cost sheets reflects the following data:

Job No.	Customer or Stock No.	Total Cost
1,002.................	Part No. 32	$4,500
1,100.................	Customer No. 45	7,800
1,205.................	Customer No. 69	7,200

During May two new jobs were started: 1,206 for stock Part No. 18, and 1,207 for Customer No. 70. Job Nos. 1,002, 1,100, and 1,206 were completed during May. Customer No. 45 paid $20,000 in full for his order. None of the stock parts were sold. Total costs incurred in May are shown below by job number:

Job No.	Amount
1,002.................	$4,900
1,100.................	8,000
1,205.................	600
1,206.................	5,000
1,207.................	3,100

Required:

(1) Produce a summary job cost sheet to show the jobs still in process May 31.

(2) Compute the cost of goods completed (manufactured) for May.

(3) Compute the gross margin for May.

2–9. Complete a job order cost record to show the accumulation of costs for Job No. 786, for a special-order refrigeration unit. Data pertinent to the costs of the job are as follows:

January

1 100 pounds of raw material C costing $10 per pound were requisitioned from the storeroom and used on the job.

7 Direct labor incurred on the job amounted to 100 hours at $3 per hour.

10 Raw material D was purchased at a cost of $1,500 for 150 pounds. This material will be used on Job No. 786 and on other future jobs requiring the same material.

11 Five pounds of raw material D were requisitioned from the storeroom and used on the job.

14 Direct labor cost incurred on the job amounted to 200 hours at $3 per hour and 10 hours at $5 per hour.

15 Factory indirect cost is assigned to the job on the basis of 150 percent of direct labor.

16 The job is completed.

2–10. Purity Enterprises manufactures a single product, maple sundae topping. Syrup, flavoring, and preservatives are mixed, cooked for several hours in vats, cooled, and put into gallon cans to await shipment. On March 1, the vats were empty. During March 24,000 gallons of topping were completed. On March 31, there were 4,000 gallons left in the vats, all completed as to raw materials and 50 percent complete as to labor and factory indirect cost. Actual costs incurred in March manufacturing were $56,000 for materials, $10,400 for labor, and $13,000 for factory indirect cost.

Required:

(1) Compute the average cost of manufacturing a gallon of topping during March.
(2) Journalize the entry to transfer the March production to finished goods inventory.

2–11. During the first month of operations, June, the Lotos Detergent Company incurred the following costs:

Direct material..........	$ 30,000
Direct labor..............	50,000
Factory indirect..........	50,000
	$130,000

Three hundred thousand pounds of detergent were produced and transferred to the warehouse in June, and another 300,000 pounds remained one-third completed as to direct labor and materials and factory indirect costs.

Required:

On separate sheet of paper complete the blanks in the flowchart below to illustrate June production activity. Show the computation of the June cost per pound.

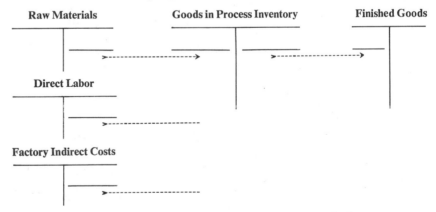

2–12. Diversified Products, Inc., manufactures a product in four processes. Below are data relating to the final process, Process 4, for the month of March:

Goods in Process 4 on March 1 were 600 units shown at a cost of $1,200. Of this amount, $600 was the cost as transferred from Process 3, and $600 was direct labor and overhead of Process 4. These units were assumed to be 50 percent complete as to labor and overhead.

During March $6,000 of direct labor cost and $6,600 of overhead cost were incurred in Process 4.

During March 4,400 units, at $1 each, were transferred from Process 3, and 4,000 units were completed and transferred to finished goods inventory.

Units in process at the end of March were assumed to be 50 percent complete as to direct labor and overhead. (No direct material was added in Process 4.)

Required:

1. What was the goods in process inventory in units on March 31?
2. What were the equivalent units of production in March?
3. What was the direct labor and overhead cost per equivalent unit in March?
4. What was the dollar amount transferred to finished goods inventory?
5. What was the balance in goods in process inventory as of April 1?

2–13. Complete the postings to a flowchart like the model below and use arrows to reflect the flow of costs from raw material through the cost of goods sold. Other data pertinent to operations for the month of April for Simplex Manufacturing Corp. follow (000's omitted):

Raw material purchases	230	Factory rent		50
Freight–in on purchases	10	Rental of retail store		20
Factory supplies used	15	Office heat, light, power		8
Indirect labor	80	Raw material used in pro-		
Direct labor	400	duction		200
Depreciation of factory		Cost of goods completed		
machinery	75	during April		700
Factory heat, light, power	12	Finished goods ending		
Repairs to factory	10	inventory		150

Raw Material Inventory

3/31/
Inventory 50

Direct Labor

Manufacturing Overhead

Goods in Process Inventory

3/31/
Inventory 60

Finished Goods Inventory

3/31/
Inventory 200

Cost of Goods Sold

2–14.   Journalize the entries for the transactions reflected in the T-accounts below for the Connecticut Barrel Company for the month of December:

Cash

Bal. 11/30	10,000	60,000
	70,000	

Accounts Receivable

Bal. 11/30	15,000	70,000
	80,000	

Sales

80,000	80,000

Cost of Sales

50,000	50,000

Raw Material Inventory

Bal. 11/30	14,000	25,000
	27,000	

Goods in Process Inventory

Bal. 11/30	12,000	65,000
	23,000	
	25,000	
	18,000	

Finished Goods Inventory

Bal. 11/30 25,000	50,000
65,000	

Accounts Payable

60,000	Bal. 11/30 11,000
	76,000

Direct Labor

23,000	23,000

Factory Indirect Costs

18,000	18,000

Selling and Administrative Expense

8,000	8,000

Income Summary

50,000	80,000
8,000	

2–15.   Following is a summary of the transactions of Trial Run Corporation for the month of February:

1.   Materials and supplies purchased on account:
     Raw material........................ $ 220,000
     Factory supplies used................   10,000

2. Labor costs paid in cash:
Factory direct labor....................	$ 300,000
Factory indirect labor...................	60,000
Selling and administrative wages........	30,000

3. Depreciation for the month:
Manufacturing assets..................	$ 30,000
Selling and administrative assets........	10,000

4. Other cash payments during February:
Freight–in on raw material.............	$ 9,000
Miscellaneous factory indirect costs.......	120,000
Miscellaneous selling and administrative expense......................	700,000
Payments on accounts payable for inventory purchases.................	190,000

5. Sales on account for February............... $2,000,000
6. Collections on accounts receivable for February......................... $1,600,000
7. Inventory data follows:

	January 31	February 28
Raw material.............	65,000	70,000
Goods in process...........	23,000	20,000
Finished goods...........	90,000	110,000

Required:

Journalize the following entries to record February operations:
1. To compute the net raw material purchases.
2. To close net purchases to raw material used.
3. To adjust the raw materials used for raw material inventories.
4. To transfer raw material used to the cost of goods manufactured.
5. To add direct labor to the cost of goods manufactured.
6. To add all factory indirect costs to the cost of goods manufactured.
7. To adjust the cost of goods manufactured for the goods in process inventories.
8. To transfer the cost of goods manufactured to the cost of goods sold.
9. To adjust the cost of goods sold for the finished goods inventories.

2–16. Using the data in Problem 2–15 above, prepare an income statement for the Trial Run Corporation for the month ended February 28. Show the details of the computations of the cost of goods manufactured and sold. You may ignore income taxes.

Suggestions for further study

(These books relate to the material in Chapters 2–5.)

Fremgen, James M. *Accounting for Managerial Analysis*. Rev. ed. Homewood, Ill.: Richard D. Irwin, Inc., 1972.

Horngren, Charles T. *Cost Accounting: A Managerial Emphasis*. 3d ed. Englewood Cliffs, N.J.: Prentice-Hall, Inc., 1972.

Matz, Adolph, and Curry, Othel J. *Cost Accounting Planning and Control.* 5th ed. Cincinnati: Southwestern Publishing Co., 1972.

Neuner, John J. W. *Cost Accounting: Principles and Practice.* 8th ed. Homewood, Ill.: Richard D. Irwin, Inc., 1973.

Shillinglaw, Gordon. *Cost Accounting: Analysis and Control.* 3d ed. Homewood, Ill.: Richard D. Irwin, Inc., 1972.

3 Measurement of manufacturing costs

Purpose of
the chapter In Chapter 2, we gave an overview of cost accounting. The essence of that description was that cost accounting measures the resources used for cost objectives and that the full cost of a cost objective is the sum of (1) its direct costs and (2) a fair share of its indirect costs. In Chapter 3 we shall describe in more detail how the manufacturing costs of products are measured, and in Chapter 4 we shall describe the measurement of nonmanufacturing cost.

The measurement of direct costs is relatively straightforward. The measurement of indirect costs of products is somewhat more complicated, however; and we shall describe each step in this measurement process in some detail.

Knowledge of the cost accounting process is essential to an understanding of the meaning of the costs that are the end product of the process. The purpose of the chapter is to facilitate such an understanding.

SOURCE OF COST PRINCIPLES

As emphasized in *Fundamentals of Financial Accounting,* financial accounting is governed by "generally accepted accounting principles." These are man-made rather than being derived from laws of nature. They are established principally by the Financial Accounting Standards Board and by the Securities and Exchange Commission.

There is no similar authoritative body of principles applicable to full cost accounting. Until 1971, no official source of authority even existed. In that year, Congress created the Cost Accounting Standards Board

59

(CASB), and some cost accounting standards (which is a term synonymous with "principles") have now been published by that Board. Although the CASB's authority explicitly includes only the measurement of full costs on *government contracts,* its pronouncements have a considerable influence on other types of full cost measurement because in most respects problems involved in measuring the full cost of government contracts are the same as problems involved in measuring full costs in other situations. To the extent that CASB has published principles, they are therefore incorporated in the following description.

Direct costs

There are two general criteria for deciding whether or not a cost item is direct with respect to a specified cost objective. An item of cost is *direct:*

(1) if the specified cost objective was intended to *benefit* from that item of costs; or
(2) if the specified cost objective *caused* incurrence of the cost.[1]

If the benefit or the causal relationship for a single item of cost applies to two or more cost objectives, the item is indirect.

In this chapter, the cost objectives we are interested in are the manufacture of physical products, such as shoes. For these cost objectives, direct costs are those that directly benefit or are caused by the manufacture of products. For other types of cost objectives, the word "direct" could refer to quite different items of cost. Thus the salary of a department foreman is a direct cost of the department that he supervises, but it is an indirect cost of the products made in that department because no beneficial or causal relationship exists between any single product and the foreman's salary. If the department made only a single product, however, the foreman's salary could be classified as a direct cost of that product. Even in this situation, many companies classify the foreman's salary as an indirect cost; they limit direct labor costs to the costs of employees who work physically on the product.

> *EXAMPLE:* In a factory that manufactures shirts, the employees who operate the machines which are used to cut the cloth, sew the pieces together, make buttonholes, sew on buttons, attach the label, press the completed shirt, and inspect it, are direct workers. The employees who carry the material from one work station to another and those who do production planning, timekeeping, and supervision are indirect workers.

We shall now discuss in more detail the two principal types of direct product costs: direct labor costs and direct material cost.

---

[1] Cost Accounting Standards Board, *Statement of Operating Policies, Procedures, and Objectives,* March 1973, p. 17.

DIRECT LABOR

There are essentially two problems in the measurement of direct labor cost: (1) measuring the *quantity* of labor time expended on the product, and (2) ascertaining the *price* per unit of labor time.

Measuring the **quantity** of labor time is relatively easy. A daily time-card, or comparable record, is usually kept for each direct worker; and on it a record is made of the time he spends *on each job*. Or, if direct workers are paid a piece rate, the record shows the number of pieces completed. These timecards are used both to measure labor costs and also as a basis for payroll computations. Problems do arise concerning the treatment of idle time, personal time, overtime, and so on, but these problems are beyond the scope of this introductory treatment.

Deciding on the best way to **price** these labor times is conceptually more difficult than measuring the quantity of time. The great majority of companies have a simple solution to this problem; they price direct labor at the amounts actually earned by the employees concerned (so much an hour if employees are paid on a day-rate or hourly rate basis; so much a piece if they are paid on a piece-rate basis). There may be either a separate labor rate for each employee or an average labor rate for all the direct labor employees in a department.

> *EXAMPLE:* Assume that a certain job is worked on in four departments and that the time worked in each department (as shown by the timecards) and the labor rates are as indicated below. The direct labor cost of the job would be computed as follows:

Department	Direct Labor Hours on Job	Departmental Hourly Rate	Total Amount
A.	20	$5.00	$100.00
B.	3	4.50	13.50
C.	6	3.80	22.80
D.	40	3.00	120.00
Total direct labor cost of job.			$256.30

Some companies add **labor-related costs** to the basic wage rate. They reason that each hour of labor effort costs the company not only the wages paid to the employee but also the social security taxes, pension contributions, and other fringe benefits paid by the employer.[2] The company must pay these labor-related benefits; they are caused by the fact that the employee works, and they are therefore part of the real cost of using the employee's services. Other companies even include a share

---

[2] But *not* the *employee's* social security contribution. This is a deduction from the employee's earnings; it is therefore not a cost to the company. (*See Fundamentals of Financial Accounting*, Chapter 10, Appendix A.)

of the costs of the personnel department and employee welfare programs in a part of direct labor cost. Using such a higher labor cost
gives a more accurate picture of direct labor costs. It also involves
additional recordkeeping, however, and many companies do not believe
the gain in accuracy is worthwhile.

DIRECT MATERIAL

The measurement of direct material cost (or "raw materials cost")
also has the two aspects of the *quantity* of material used and the *price*
per unit of quantity. The quantity is usually determined from requisitions or similar documents that order material out of the storeroom and
into production. The problem of pricing this material is similar to that
for pricing direct labor. Material may be priced at solely its purchase
or invoice cost, or there may be added some or all of the following
material-related costs: inward freight, inspection costs, moving costs,
purchasing department costs, and interest and space charges associated
with holding material in inventory.

As was the case with labor costs, it is conceptually desirable to count
these material-related items as part of material cost, but to do so may
involve more recordkeeping than a company believes worthwhile.

The measurement of direct material costs is also affected by the assumption made about the flow of inventory costs, that is, Lifo, Fifo, or
average cost. The effect of these alternative flow assumptions is discussed in Chapter 7 of *Fundamentals of Financial Accounting*.

Indirect costs

DISTINCTION BETWEEN DIRECT AND INDIRECT COSTS

It is conceptually desirable that a given item of cost be classified as
a direct cost rather than as an indirect cost. This is because an item of
direct cost is assigned directly to a single cost objective, whereas, as will
be discussed in a later section, the assignment of indirect costs to cost
objectives is a more roundabout and usually less accurate process.
Nevertheless, the category of indirect costs does, and must, exist.

Costs are not traced directly to a product, for one of three reasons:
(1) It is *impossible* to do so, as in the case of the factory superintendent's salary already mentioned. (2) It is *not feasible* to do so; that is,
the recordkeeping required for such a direct tracing would cost too
much. (For example, the nails, the sewing thread, the eyelets, and the
glue that are used on a pair of shoes cost only a few pennies, and it is
not worthwhile to trace them to each case of shoes; they are therefore
classified as indirect materials.) (3) Management *chooses* not to do so;
that is, many companies classify certain items of costs as indirect simply
because it has become customary in the industry to do so, or because
they are not aware of appropriate procedures for assigning them directly.

Problems of drawing distinctions. Problems arise in attempting to

define the precise line between items of cost that are caused by or benefit a product and other costs. For example, a cost may not be caused
by a product even though it is incurred at the same time as the product
is being manufactured.

> *EXAMPLE:* In a certain factory, Products A, B, and C were manu-
> factured during regular working hours, and Product D was manu-
> factured after regular hours. Overtime wages were paid to the em-
> ployees who worked on Product D. These overtime wages might, or
> might not, be a direct cost of Product D. If the factory worked over-
> time because the general volume of orders was high, then the over-
> time is attributable to all the products worked on, and was an in-
> direct cost. If, on the other hand, the overtime work on Product D
> was occasioned by a special request of the customer for Product D,
> then the overtime is a direct cost of Product D. It could also happen
> that the overtime was occasioned by a special need to make Product
> C quickly, and in order to meet this need, Product D was re-
> scheduled from the regular work period to the overtime period; in
> this case, the overtime is truly a direct cost of Product C, even
> though overtime was not in fact paid during the hours in which
> Product C was being manufactured.

Moreover, there are differences of opinion as to how close the causal
or beneficial relationship between the cost and cost objective must be
in order to classify a cost item as direct. In many production operations,
such as assembly lines of all types, refineries, and similar continuous
process operations, a basic work force is required no matter what products are manufactured. Some would argue that the labor cost of this
work force constitutes a cost that is required to operate the plant in
general, much like depreciation on the machinery, and that it is therefore an indirect cost. Nevertheless, most companies consider such costs
as direct labor.

DISTINCTION BETWEEN FACTORY COSTS AND GENERAL AND ADMINISTRATIVE COSTS

In thinking about the items that should be included in factory costs,
one may be misled if he pictures the "factory" as a physical building or
group of buildings and concludes that only the costs that are incurred
inside these premises are factory costs. Conceptually at least, part of
the *general and administrative* costs of the company are also indirect
factory costs. General and administrative costs are costs incurred by
corporate staff departments—personnel, finance, research and development, controller, marketing, and the like; costs of the president's office
and related general management activities; and general corporate costs,
such as donations to charitable organizations and memberships in associations.

Although general and administrative costs are not incurred physically
inside the factory, some of them are incurred, at least in part, *for the*

benefit of the manufacturing process. The personnel department, for example, may be responsible for hiring and training employees some of whom are factory employees; the controller maintains accounting records, some of which are factory records. Despite the conceptual justification for assigning a part of the general and administrative costs as factory costs, many companies do not do so. They have decided that the extra paperwork that would be required would not be worthwhile.

Allocating indirect costs

In Chapter 2, we stated the guiding principle that the cost of a cost objective includes, in addition to its direct costs, a *fair share* of the indirect costs that were incurred for several cost objectives, of which the cost objective in question is one. Thus, the factory cost of a case of shoes includes a fair share of all the indirect costs in the shoe factory. The idea of "fair share" sounds vague, and it is vague, but it is the only way of approaching the problem of measuring the indirect costs of a cost objective.

What is a fair share? Perhaps the best way to think about this question is from the viewpoint of the customer. Under ordinary circumstances, a customer should be willing to pay the cost of the product he buys plus a reasonable profit. Consider, for example, the customer of a job shop that offers printing services. A customer whose job requires the use of an expensive four-color printing press should expect to pay his share of the costs of operating that press, and he should expect to pay more per hour of press time than the customer whose job required only a small, inexpensive press. The customer whose job required a long time should expect to pay a relatively large share of the cost of plant facilities. Collectively, moreover, all the customers should expect to pay all the costs.

From the above line of reasoning, it follows that (1) all items of factory cost should be assigned to cost objectives, and (2) the amount assigned to an individual cost objective should depend on the benefits received or a causal incurrence, to the extent that a beneficial or causal relationship exists.

The process of assigning indirect costs to individual cost objectives is called allocation. The verb "to allocate" means "to assign indirect costs to individual cost objectives." Unfortunately, there is not general agreement on this terminology. In this book, we use "assign" or "charge" as general terms applying to both direct and indirect costs, and we restrict "allocate" to indirect costs only.[3] In some of its pronouncements, however, the Cost Accounting Standards Board has defined "allocate" as being synonymous with "assign." This terminology is, to say the least, confusing; and it would leave us with no good label for the process of assigning indirect costs to cost objectives.

Exhibit 3–1 is a diagram of the procedure for assigning indirect

---

[3] In Great Britain the word "apportion" is used instead of "allocate."

factory costs to products. Before describing this diagram, we need to explain the idea of *cost center,* which is a new term appearing thereon.

COST CENTERS

A cost center is an accounting device for accumulating items of cost that have common characteristics. After costs have been accumulated in a cost center, the next step is to charge them to another cost center or to a final cost objective, and the characteristics that the items of cost have in common relate to this next step; that is, all the costs assigned to a cost center should be sufficiently similar so that they rationally can be charged out of the cost center in some common fashion. Thus, the costs assigned to a cost center are said to be relatively **homogeneous.**

> *EXAMPLE:* A department that manufactures bowls in a pipe factory may be a cost center. All the items of indirect cost assigned to that cost center have in common the characteristic that they are associated with the manufacture of bowls. They therefore can be allocated to the product cost of pipes in accordance with the type of bowl that the pipe has.

Although a cost center may be a responsibility center, such as the department that makes bowls in a pipe factory, there is no necessary correspondence between cost centers and responsibility centers.

Recall from Chapter 1 that a responsibility center is an organization unit, such as a department, headed by a responsible manager. Some cost centers are responsibility centers; others are not. Many departments are both a responsibility center and a cost center; however, as will be illustrated below, there can be several cost centers within a single responsibility center. Also, some cost centers do not correspond to any responsibility center. An "occupancy" cost center, in which depreciation, light, heat, and other costs of a factory are accumulated, is an example.

There are two types of cost centers: production cost centers and service cost centers.

A production cost center is a cost center through which a product, or a product component, passes. Often a production cost center corresponds to a production department, but a group of similar machines (such as a bank of screw machines) may be a production cost center, and so may a single machine (such as each printing press in a printing job shop).

A service cost center is a responsibility center or other unit that does not work directly on products or components. The maintenance department, the power plant, and general factory offices are examples. The term "service cost center" calls to mind an observable physical entity, such as a department. Our procedure must provide, however, for the accumulation of indirect costs which are not readily identified with specific organizational units. The periodic depreciation on the factory building, for example, is clearly an indirect cost. This cost, together with the costs of heating, lighting, and maintaining the factory premises are often grouped together in a service cost center. Service cost centers are often called **indirect cost pools;** the term "pool" conveys the notion of a container into which indirect costs flow.

GENERAL PROCEDURE

We now return to the procedure for allocating indirect factory costs to products, as diagrammed in Exhibit 3–1. The exhibit and illustrations

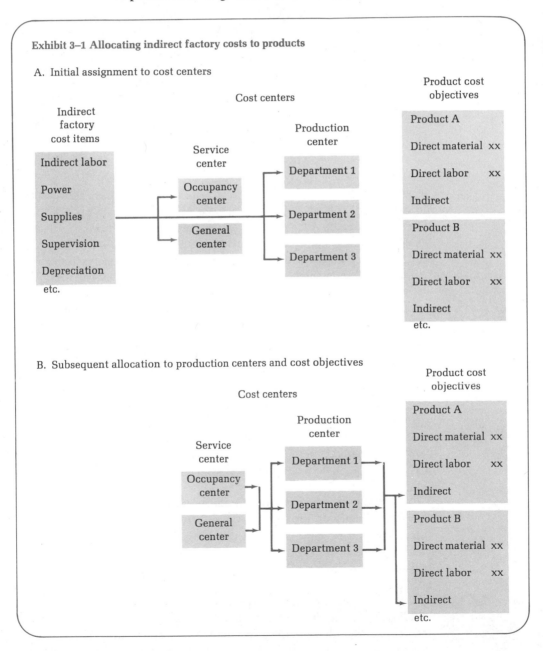

Exhibit 3–1 Allocating indirect factory costs to products

A. Initial assignment to cost centers

B. Subsequent allocation to production centers and cost objectives

to be given subsequently refer to a simple factory, that of manufacturing smoking pipes. In this factory are three production departments, Department 1, Department 2, and Department 3. Each of these production departments is a production cost center. In addition, the factory has two service cost centers, Occupancy and General. The Occupancy cost center is used to accumulate all costs associated with the factory building, such as building depreciation, building maintenance, heat, light, and property insurance. The General cost center is used to accumulate the cost of factory supervision and other general costs that are not directly traceable to the other cost centers.

There are three steps in the process of allocating indirect factory costs:

1. **All indirect factory costs for an accounting period are charged to some service or production cost center.** This flow is illustrated in Section A of Exhibit 3–1.

2. **The total cost accumulated in each service cost center is reassigned to production cost centers.** This flow is illustrated in Section B of Exhibit 3–1.

3. **The total of the indirect costs accumulated in each production cost center, including the reassigned service center costs, is allocated to the products that pass through the production cost center.** This flow is illustrated in Section B of Exhibit 3–1.

We shall describe these three steps in more detail. First, as a pedagogical device for explaining the concept, we shall describe them in the order listed above. We shall then show that by changing this order, we can arrive at the desired end result—the factory cost of products—by a simpler technique and one that produces more useful information for management.

INDIRECT COST ACCUMULATION BY COST CENTERS

The first step in the allocation of indirect costs is to assign all items of indirect factory costs for the period to some cost center (see A of Exhibit 3–1). Indirect labor costs are assigned to the cost centers in which the employees work. The costs of supplies and other indirect materials are assigned to the cost centers in which the materials are used. Depreciation on machinery and power costs associated with the machine are assigned to cost centers in which the machines are located. In this step, each item of indirect cost is assigned to one, and only one, cost center, so that the sum of the costs for all the cost centers exactly equals the total indirect costs for the whole factory.

> *EXAMPLE:* The first line of Exhibit 3–2 shows that $3,100 of indirect labor cost was assigned to Department 1, $2,700 to Department 2, and so on. These amounts were the actual indirect labor costs

Exhibit 3–2

Allocating indirect factory costs to products

| | | Production Centers | | | Service Centers | |
Cost Item	Total	Dept. 1	Dept. 2	Dept. 3	Occu-pancy	General
A. Initial Assignment to Cost Centers						
Indirect labor..............................	$ 9,700	$ 3,100	$2,700	$ 0	$ 0	$ 3,900
Indirect supplies...........................	4,000	900	600	500	400	1,600
Other......................................	12,000	3,900	1,200	700	4,300	1,900
Subtotals...........................	$25,700	$ 7,900	$4,500	$1,200	$4,700	$ 7,400
B. Assignment of Service Center Costs						
Occupancy.................................		1,900	1,400	900	(4,700)	500
General....................................		3,600	2,600	1,700		$(7,900)
Total indirect cost...................	$25,700	$13,400	$8,500	$3,800		
C. Allocation to Products						
Direct labor hours..........................		2,200	4,000	2,000		
Overhead rate per direct labor hour...........		$6.10	$2.12	$1.90		

incurred in these cost centers. (Department 3 had no indirect labor, nor did the occupancy cost center.)

ASSIGNMENT OF SERVICE CENTER COSTS

The second step in the allocation of indirect costs is to assign the total cost accumulated in each service cost center so that eventually all indirect costs are assigned to some production cost center (see Section B of Exhibit 3–1). Some service center costs are assigned directly to the cost centers that receive the service. Maintenance department costs may be charged to operating departments on the basis of the maintenance service actually performed, for example. The costs of a power-generating plant may be assigned according to the metered usage of electricity in each cost center, just as if the electricity had been purchased from an outside company.

Note, incidentally, the use of the word "directly" in the above paragraph. With respect to the final cost objective, that is, the product, all the items of cost that we are now discussing are indirect. With respect to individual cost centers, however, some of the items of cost are direct. We referred to this distinction earlier, and it is important that it not be overlooked.

The costs of some service cost centers cannot be directly assigned to other cost centers, these costs must be allocated; that is, the costs must be assigned to other cost centers on some reasonable basis. The basis of allocation should correspond, as closely as is feasible, to one of the two criteria listed above; that is, it should have some connection with either benefits received or a causal relationship. The dozens of alternative bases of allocations that are used in practice can be grouped into the following principal categories.

1. *Payroll related.* Social security taxes paid by the employer, accident insurance, fringe benefits, and other costs associated with amounts earned by employees may be allocated on the basis of the total labor costs. Alternatively, as mentioned above, some or all of these costs may enter into the calculation of direct labor costs; if so they will not appear as indirect costs at all. If certain indirect costs are ultimately charged to products by means of a direct labor rate (as will be described below), the ultimate effect of treating these costs as indirect is approximately the same as if they were charged as part of direct labor costs.

2. *Personnel related.* Personnel department costs, and other costs that are associated with the number of employees rather than with the amount that they are paid, may be allocated on the basis of number of employees. (The distinction between "payroll related" and "personnel related" is a subtle one. Many companies do not attempt to make such a distinction; instead they allocate both types of costs together, usually on the basis of direct labor costs.)

3. *Material related.* This category of cost may be allocated on the basis of either the quantity or the cost of direct material used in production cost centers, or, alternatively, it may be excluded from indirect costs and charged to products as part of direct material cost, as already mentioned. The latter practice is conceptually preferable but it usually involves more recordkeeping.

4. *Space related.* Some items of cost are associated with the space that the cost center occupies, and they are allocated to cost centers on the basis of their relative area or cubic content. Occupancy cost in Exhibit 3–2 is an example.

5. *Activity related.* Some costs are roughly related to the overall volume of activity in the cost center, or at least there is a presumption that the more work that a cost center does, the more costs are properly allocated to it. Electrical power costs and steam costs, if not directly assigned, fall into this category; and so do the costs of a variety of other service cost centers which, although not demonstrably a function of activity, are more realistically allocated in this way than in any other. The measure of activity may be an overall indication of the amount of work done by the cost center, such as its total labor cost, its total direct costs, or the total cost of its output. Alternatively, the measure of activity may be more closely related to the function of the service cost center whose costs are being allocated; for example, electric costs may be allocated on the basis of the total horsepower of motors installed in each cost center.

> EXAMPLE: The middle section of Exhibit 3–2 illustrates the assignment of service center costs to production cost centers. Occupancy

costs are allocated on the basis of the relative floor space in each cost center; the total cost of $4,700 is divided among the three production cost centers and the General service cost center using the percentages 40, 30, 19, and 11 because these represent each cost center's percentage of the total floor space.

The costs of the General cost center are then allocated on the basis of the total direct costs (i.e., direct material + direct labor) charged to the three production cost centers. The total General cost is, after the addition of the allocated share of Occupancy cost, $7,900. Of this amount 46 percent is allocated to Department 1, 33 percent to Department 2, and 21 percent of Department 3 because these are the percentages that each department's direct cost are to total direct cost.

Step-down order. Note that in Exhibit 3–2, part of the cost of the Occupancy service cost center is charged to the General service cost center. It may well be that part of the cost of the General cost center should be charged to the Occupancy cost center, and this creates a problem. Whenever there are a number of service cost centers, the interrelationships among them could theoretically lead to a long series of distributions, redistributions, and re-redistributions. In practice, however, these redistributions are avoided by allocating the service center costs in a prescribed order, which is called the **step-down order.** In general, the least significant service centers are allocated first. In the illustration, the prescribed order is Occupancy first, and General second. No additional cost is allocated to a service cost center after its costs have been allocated. Since the step-down order is adhered to in all calculations, the results are always consistent.

ALLOCATION OF INDIRECT COSTS TO PRODUCTS

Overhead rates. Having assembled all the indirect costs in production cost centers, we now seek some equitable means of loading a portion of these costs onto each product as it passes through the cost center; this is the third step in the process of allocating indirect costs (see Section B of Exhibit 3–1). Factory indirect costs accumulated in production cost centers are allocated to products by a device called an **overhead rate.** [4]

The function of the overhead rate is to assign an equitable amount of indirect cost to each product. In thinking about how this rate should be constructed, therefore, we need to address the question: Why, in all fairness, should one product have a higher indirect, or overhead, cost than another product? Depending on the circumstances, the following are among the plausible answers to this question:

---

[4] Since we have here referred to these costs as "indirect costs," it would be consistent to use the term "indirect cost rate." In practice, the term "overhead rate" is more widely used. "Burden rate" is also used.

1. Because more labor effort was expended on one product than on another, and indirect costs are presumed to vary with the amount of labor effort.
2. Because one product used more machine time than another, and indirect costs are presumed to vary with the amount of machine time.
3. Because one product had higher direct costs than another and was therefore able to "afford" a higher amount of indirect costs.

Each of these answers suggests a quantitative basis of activity that can be used to allocate indirect costs to products, viz:

1. The number of labor hours or labor dollars required for the product.
2. The number of machine-hours.
3. The total direct costs (i.e., direct material plus direct labor).

The machine-hours basis is common for production cost centers that consist primarily of one machine (such as a papermaking machine) or a group of related machines. The direct labor cost basis is frequently used in other situations, since the direct labor cost is readily available on the job cost card. Direct labor hours are often used if a record of the number of hours worked on each job is readily available. In general, a monetary basis, such as direct labor dollars, is less preferable than a nonmonetary basis, such as direct labor hours, since the monetary basis is affected by changes in prices (e.g., wage rates) as well as by changes in physical amounts of activity.

The decision as to the best measure of activity is judgmental. It is guided by the criteria of benefits received and causal relationships; but, by definition, there is no objective way of measuring how much indirect cost actually should attach to each product.

Having selected what appears to be the most appropriate measure, the overhead rate for a production cost center is calculated by dividing the total indirect cost of the production cost center by the total amount of activity for the period.

> EXAMPLE: Continuing with the example in Exhibit 3–2, let us assume that the number of direct labor hours is the appropriate activity measure for the allocation of indirect costs to products. In Department 1, the direct labor hours for the period totaled 2,200. This, divided into the total indirect cost of $13,400, gives an overhead rate per direct labor hour of $6.10.

Allocation to products. The indirect cost for each product that passes through the production cost center is calculated by multiplying the cost center overhead rate by the number of activity units accumulated for that product.

> EXAMPLE: Referring to the situation in Exhibit 3–2, if in this factory a certain job, Job No. 307, required 30 direct labor hours

in Department 1, 20 direct labor hours in Department 2, and 5 direct labor hours in Department 3, its total indirect cost would be calculated as follows:

Production Cost Center	Direct Labor Hours	Overhead Rate	Indirect Cost
Department 1................... 30		$6.10	$183.00
Department 2................... 20		2.12	42.40
Department 3................... 5		1.90	9.50
Total indirect cost of Job No. 307.........			$234.90

PREDETERMINED OVERHEAD RATES

The preceding description of the accumulation of indirect costs and their allocation to products followed the same chronological order as that used for the description of accounting for direct material and direct costs; that is, the amount of cost was first ascertained, and subsequently the amount was allocated to products. This approach was taken for pedagogical reasons. Although it would be possible to account for indirect costs in this fashion, and although a few companies in fact do this, **a better way of allocating overhead costs in most situations is to establish an overhead rate for each production cost center in advance, usually once a year, and then to use these predetermined overhead rates throughout the year.**

There are three reasons why the calculation of an annual overhead rate in advance is preferable to calculating a rate at the end of each month based on the actual indirect costs incurred in that month.

1. The most important reason is that if overhead rates were calculated monthly, they would be unduly affected by conditions peculiar to that month. Heating costs in the winter, for example, are higher than heating costs in the summer, but no useful purpose would be served by reporting that shoes manufactured in the winter cost more than shoes manufactured in the summer. As will be explained below, fluctuations in the volume of activity can cause gyrations in overhead rates; and misleading information on indirect costs would be presented if the indirect costs assigned to products were affected by month-to-month variations in the volume of activity.

2. The use of a predetermined overhead rate permits product costs to be calculated more promptly. Direct material and direct labor costs can be assigned to products as soon as the time records and material requisitions are available; but if overhead rates were calculated only at the end of each month, after all the information on indirect costs for the month had been assembled, indirect costs could not be assigned to

products until after this calculation had been completed. With the use of a predetermined overhead rate, indirect costs can be allocated to products at the same time that direct costs are assigned to them.

3. The calculations of an overhead rate once a year requires less effort than going through the same calculations every month.

Procedure for establishing predetermined overhead rates. In order to establish overhead rates that will be used during a forthcoming year, a calculation is made that follows exactly the same steps described above; that is, indirect costs are accumulated in cost centers, costs of service cost centers are reassigned to production cost centers, an activity basis for each production cost center is selected, and the amount of indirect cost in each cost center is divided by the amount of activity to arrive at an overhead rate. The only difference is that instead of using the *actual* indirect costs and activity rates for the period, the procedure uses *estimates* of what the costs and activity levels will be for the forthcoming year. These estimates do not, in fact, involve additional work, for they are made in the normal course of events as a part of the *budgeting* process, which will be described in Chapter 11. Because the calculation of predetermined overhead rates is otherwise exactly the same as the calculation of overhead rates which has already been described and illustrated in Exhibit 3–2, the mechanics are not repeated here.

Estimating volume. The most uncertain part of the process of establishing predetermined overhead rates is estimating what the volume of activity will be in the forthcoming year. This estimate of volume has a significant effect on overhead rates. This amount is called the **standard volume.** In most companies, important items of indirect cost do not vary with changes in volume; they are called *fixed costs.* To take the extreme case, if *all* indirect costs were fixed, the overhead rate would vary directly with the level of volume estimated for the forthcoming year. To the extent that not all costs are fixed, changes in overhead rates associated with changes in the estimate of volume are not as severe, but they are nevertheless important in most situations. It is therefore important that careful attention be given to making the best possible estimate of volume as part of the procedure of calculating predetermined overhead rates.

> *EXAMPLE:* A papermaking machine is a large, expensive machine that either runs at capacity or doesn't run at all. Its depreciation, the costs associated with the building in which it is housed, and most other items of indirect cost are unaffected by how many hours a year the machine operates. Assume that these indirect costs are estimated to be $1,000,000 a year, and that they are entirely fixed, that is, they are estimated to be $1,000,000 regardless of how many hours the machine operates during the year. If the measure of activity used in establishing the overhead rate is machine-hours, overhead rates will vary as shown below for various estimates of machine-hours to be operated during the year:

Indirect Cost	No. of Machine-Hours	Overhead Rate (per Machine-Hour)
$1,000,000	8,000	$125
1,000,000	6,000	167
1,000,000	4,000	250

The effect of the volume estimate on the amount of overhead cost assigned to products during the year is therefore great. Indeed, in a situation like this, in which indirect fixed costs are large relative to total costs, including direct labor and direct material, the accounted cost of the product may be affected more by the estimate of annual volume than by any other single factor.

The important point to remember is that the predetermined overhead rate will be relatively low if the estimated volume of activity is relatively high because the same amount of fixed cost will be spread over a larger number of units. This point will be discussed in more depth in Chapter 6.

UNABSORBED AND OVERABSORBED OVERHEAD

If a predetermined overhead rate is used, the amount of indirect costs allocated to products in a given month are likely to differ from the amount of indirect costs actually incurred in that month. This is because the actual indirect costs assigned to the cost center in the month, and/or the actual activity level for the month, are likely to be different from the estimates that were used when the predetermined overhead rate was calculated. If the amount of indirect cost allocated to products exceeds the amount actually assigned to the cost center, overhead is said to be **overabsorbed;** and if the amount is less, indirect costs are **underabsorbed** (or more commonly, **unabsorbed**). For management purposes, the amount of unabsorbed or overabsorbed overhead is useful information, as will be discussed in Chapter 14.

EXAMPLE: Assume in a certain production cost center, the predetermined overhead rate was calculated as follows:

	Annual	Average Month
Estimated indirect costs	$1,200,000	$100,000
Estimated direct labor hours	300,000	25,000
Overhead rate, per direct labor hour	$4	$4

In January, actual indirect costs were $110,000 and actual direct labor hours were 25,000. The amount of overhead allocated to products would be 25,000 × $4 = $100,000. The amount of unabsorbed cost would be $110,000 − $100,000 = $10,000.

In February, actual indirect costs were $150,000 and actual direct labor hours were 40,000. The amount of overhead allocated to products would be 40,000 × $4 = $160,000. The amount of overabsorbed cost would be $160,000 − $150,000 = $10,000.

The January numbers in the above example are typical of the situation that exists when costs get "out of control"; that is, costs were $10,000 higher than they should have been. The February example typifies the situation when actual volume exceeds estimated volume.

For financial accounting purposes, the amount of unabsorbed or overabsorbed overhead in a given month is usually held in suspense as a temporary item on the balance sheet in the expectation that unabsorbed overhead in one month will be offset by overabsorbed overhead in another month. Any balance that exists at the end of the year is divided among Goods in Process Inventory, Finished Goods Inventory, and Cost of Goods Sold in proportion to the relative size of these accounts.

In the interests of simplicity, no account for overabsorbed or unabsorbed overhead was shown in the cost accounting flowchart given in Chapter 2, Exhibit 2–2. Such an account is often labeled an **Overhead Variance account.** The journal entry debits Goods in Process Inventory for the amount of costs absorbed, credits indirect cost accounts for the amount of indirect costs incurred, and debits or credits Overhead Variance for the difference.

> *EXAMPLE:* Exhibit 2–2 is constructed on the assumption that all indirect costs are allocated to products. If a predetermined overhead were used, and if its use gave rise to unabsorbed overhead, the accounts would be as depicted in Exhibit 3–3. The situation illustrated there is that in which actual factory indirect costs incurred exceeded the amount absorbed in a given month, that is, the costs were unabsorbed. The journal entry is:

```
Goods in Process Inventory..............4,000
Overhead Variance.......................  500
        Factory Indirect Costs..............       4,500
```

Exhibit 3–3

Overhead Variance account

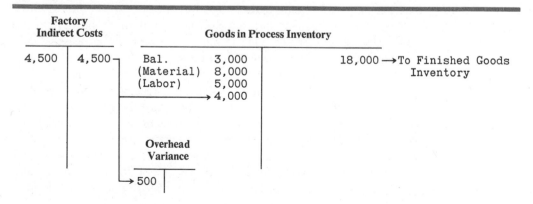

Factory Indirect Costs		Goods in Process Inventory		
4,500	4,500	Bal.	3,000	18,000 →To Finished Goods Inventory
		(Material)	8,000	
		(Labor)	5,000	
		→	4,000	
		Overhead Variance		
		→ 500		

STANDARD COSTS

The predetermined overhead rate has the effect of incorporating into the cost accounting system numbers that represent what indirect costs are *estimated to be,* as contrasted with what they *actually were.* This device provides information about the difference between estimated and actual costs that is useful to management. We can extend this same concept to direct material costs and direct labor costs; that is, we can incorporate in the system *estimates* of these costs, prepared in advance of actual operations. A system that does this is called a **standard cost system.** Since its principal use is in connection with the management control process, a detailed description is deferred until Chapter 12. The general idea of a standard cost system can be inferred from the discussion of overhead rates above.

Joint products and by-products

Joint products are two or more dissimilar end products that may be produced from a single batch of raw material or from a single production process. The classic example is the variety of end products that are made from a steer. The end products include hides, many different cuts of meat, frozen meat dishes, pet food, fertilizers, and a variety of chemicals. Up to a certain point in the production process, the raw material is treated as a single unit. Beyond that point, which is called the **split-off point,** separate end products are identified, and costs are accumulated for each of these end products during subsequent stages of the manufacturing process. For example, up to the point at which the steer is slaughtered and dressed, feed, grazing, transportation, and other costs are accumulated for the steer as a whole; beyond that point, these costs must be divided among the many end products that are made from the steer. The problem of joint costing is to find some reasonable basis for allocating to each of the joint products the direct and indirect costs that were incurred up to the split-off point.

This problem is essentially the same as that of allocating indirect costs to cost centers. In both cases, the objective is to assign a fair share of the joint or common costs to the separate end products, and in neither case can the results be an entirely accurate measure of the actual costs.

One common basis of allocating joint costs is in proportion to the *sales value* of the end products, minus the separate processing and marketing costs that are estimated to be incurred for each end product beyond the split-off point. If the selling price depends on cost, this method involves a certain amount of circular reasoning, but there may be no better alternative. If gasoline sells for twice the price of kerosene, it is reasonable that gasoline should bear twice as much of the crude oil and joint refining costs. Another basis of apportionment is *weight,* that is, the joint costs are divided in proportion to the weight of the joint material in the several end products. In the case of the steer, this method implicitly assumes that the stew meat is as valuable as the tenderloin, which is unrealistic; but in other situations, the assumption that costs are related to weight might be reasonable. In any event, the amount of cost charged to each end product must be recognized as resulting from a judgmental decision, and hence not entirely accurate.

By-products. By-products are a special kind of joint product. If management wishes to manufacture Products A and B in some predetermined proportion, or if it wishes to make as much of each end product as possible from a given quantity of raw material, then these products are ordinary joint products. On the other hand, **if management's objective is to make Product A, but in so doing some quantity of Product B inevitably emerges from the production process, then Product A is a main product and Product B is a by-product.** The intention is to make from a given amount of raw material as much of the main product and as little of the by-product as is possible. As management's intention changes, the classification changes. In the early part of the 20th century kerosene was the main product made from crude oil; subsequently, with the growth in consumption of gasoline, kerosene became a by-product; currently, kerosene has become a main product again because it is an important component of jet engine fuel.

A number of alternative procedures are used in measuring the cost of by-products. At one extreme, a by-product may be assigned zero cost, with all the costs being assigned to the main products. In such a case, the profit on the by-product is equal to its sales revenue. At the other extreme, by-products may be assigned a cost that is equal to their sales value, with the result that no profit or loss is attributed to the by-product and the entire profit of the process is attributed to the main product. The latter method sounds sloppy because there is no logical reason for asserting that the cost of a by-product actually is equal to its sales value. Since the by-product is, by its nature, of minor importance, no significant distortion usually arises from this assumption. Peculiar results sometimes occur, however. For example, animal feed is a by-product of the process of milling flour; at certain times the sales value of feed fluctuates widely, and these changes can have a significant effect on the cost assigned to the flour.

Validity of product costs   From the above description, it should be apparent that the factory cost of a product cannot be measured with complete accuracy if some items of cost are indirect, as is usually the case; and it should also be apparent that differences in cost accounting practice among companies result in different cost measures for the same physical item.

ACCURACY OF DIRECT COSTS

Since companies differ in where they draw the line between direct and indirect costs, a comparison of the direct costs of two different companies may be misleading. If Company A classifies only the wages of direct workers as direct labor, its direct labor costs will be less than those in Company B if Company B includes labor-related costs. Since labor-related costs (social security taxes, vacation pay, pensions, and the like) may amount to 20 percent or more of wages, this difference can be substantial. Corresponding differences usually do not exist within a single company, for all its responsibility centers presumably use similar definitions (although such similarity may not exist if the company consists of subsidiaries or divisions with a considerable degree of autonomy).

ACCURACY OF INDIRECT COSTS

The indirect costs allocated to a product cannot measure the "actual" amount of resources used in making the product—that is, the "actual" cost incurred—in any literal sense of the word "actual." By means of the collection and allocation mechanism described above, we have indeed succeeded in adding a portion of building depreciation, for example, onto the cost of each unit of product, but judgments as to what is fair and reasonable were involved in each step of this process: (1) in deciding on the amount of costs applicable to the *accounting period* (what really is the depreciation expense of this period?), (2) in deciding how much of this item of cost is applicable to each *cost center,* and (3) in deciding how much of the cost center's cost is applicable to each product. Two equally capable accountants can arrive at quite different amounts of indirect cost for a given product; and there is no way of proving that one is right and the other wrong, that is, that one indirect figure is accurate and the other is inaccurate. This difference is inherent in the definition of indirect costs; that is, it is impossible to measure how much of the resources they represent should actually be assigned to each product.

DEFINITION OF COST CENTER

The amount of indirect cost allocated to a product can be significantly influenced by judgment as to how a cost center is defined. In some companies, each important machine is a cost center. At the other extreme, the entire plant may be a single cost center (giving rise to a **plantwide overhead rate**). There are a number of choices between these two extremes. In general, the more narrow the definition of a cost center, the more equitable is the resulting indirect cost allocated to the product.

> *EXAMPLE:* Assume a plant with two production cost centers, Departments A and B. In Department A, machining work is done with expensive machine tools requiring much floor space, power, and supplies; and in Department B bench work and assembly are done with inexpensive hand tools. Overhead rates are determined as follows:

Cost Center	Estimated Annual Direct Labor Hours	Estimated Annual Indirect Cost	Overhead Rate per Direct Labor Hour
A..................	20,000	$200,000	$10.00
B..................	40,000	100,000	2.50
Total plant.........	60,000	$300,000	5.00

Assume a certain job required 20 direct labor hours in Department A and 100 direct labor hours in Department B. If the company used separate overhead rates for each department, the indirect cost allocated to this job would be:

Cost Center	Indirect Cost Allocated
A................................	20 hours × $10.00 = $200
B................................	100 hours × 2.50 = 250
Total overhead cost.................	$450

By contrast, if the company used a plantwide overhead rate, the indirect cost allocated to the same job would be:

$$120 \text{ direct labor hours} \times \$5 = \$600$$

The amount of $600 is a less equitable allocation than the $450 derived from the use of separate departmental overhead rates because the plantwide rate costed $5 of indirect cost for each direct labor hour, despite the fact that almost all the direct labor hours on this job were incurred in Department B, where the overhead rate was only $2.50 per hour.

On the other hand, it is also true that the more narrow the definition of the cost centers, the more cost centers there will be, and therefore more clerical work will be required to compute and apply separate overhead rates. The choice of cost centers in a particular situation depends on the balance between the increase in the validity of the overhead rates as cost centers are more narrowly defined, on the one hand, and the increased clerical work involved on the other hand. If all products require approximately the same proportion of time in each department, the differences in indirect costs assigned by means of a series of rates for each department and the indirect costs assigned by a plantwide rate will be small. In such a situation, little increase in validity is gained by using a large number of overhead rates.

Demonstra-
tion case

As a means of solidifying your understanding of how overhead rates are established and used, you are asked to calculate overhead rates for 1975 for the company whose indirect costs are given in Exhibit 3–2. The data in Exhibit 3–2 are for a month. Assume that data for the *average* month in 1975 will be changed in the following respects:

1. Indirect labor costs are estimated to be 130 percent of the amounts shown.
2. Other items of cost are estimated to be 120 percent of the amounts shown.
3. Direct labor hours are estimated to be 125 percent of the amounts shown.

The basis of assignment of service centers costs is as given in the text.

Required:

1. Calculate the overhead rates for 1975.
2. Calculate the factory indirect cost allocated to a product that required 30 direct labor hours in Department 1, 20 hours in Department 2, and 5 hours in Department 3.

After you have made the calculation of the overhead rate, check your answer with Exhibit 3–4.

Exhibit 3–4

Calculation of overhead rate, 1975

		Production Centers			Service Centers	
Cost Item	Total	Dept. 1	Dept. 2	Dept. 3	Occu-pancy	General
A. Initial Assignment to Cost Centers						
Indirect labor..........................	$12,610	$ 4,030	$ 3,510	$ 0	$ 0	$ 5,070
Indirect supplies.......................	4,800	1,080	720	600	480	1,920
Other..................................	14,400	4,680	1,440	840	5,160	2,280
Subtotals.........................	$31,810	$ 9,790	$ 5,670	$1,440	$5,640	$ 9,270
B. Assignment of Service Center Costs						
Occupancy.............................		2,256	1,692	1,072	(5,640)	620
General................................		4,549	3,264	2,077		$(9,890)
Total indirect cost.................	$31,810	$16,595	$10,626	$4,589		
C. Allocation to Products						
Direct labor hours......................		2,750	5,000	2,500		
Overhead rate per direct labor hour.........		$6.03	$2.13	$1.84		

Solution: The calculation of the factory indirect cost of the product is:

Department	Hours	Overhead Rate	Factory Indirect Cost
1................................	30	$6.03	$180.90
2................................	20	2.13	42.60
3................................	5	1.84	9.20
Total factory indirect cost.........			$232.70

Summary   Direct costs of a cost objective are those that are specifically traceable
to that cost objective. In addition to its direct costs, the factory cost of a
product includes a fair share of the indirect costs incurred in or for the
factory. The distinction between direct costs and indirect costs varies
among companies. Items of cost are indirect because it is not possible to
assign them directly, because it is not worthwhile to do so, or because
the management chooses not to do so.

Factory indirect costs are allocated to products by means of an overhead rate. This rate is calculated prior to the beginning of the period,
usually once a year. The procedure is as follows:

1.   The amount of indirect costs for each cost center is estimated.
2.   The estimated costs of service cost centers are assigned to pro-
     duction cost centers on some basis that reflects benefits received or
     a causal relationship. After this step has been completed, all indirect
     costs end up in production cost centers.
3.   A measure of activity for each production cost center is selected,
     and the level of activity, according to that measure, is estimated.
     This is usually the most uncertain number in the estimate.
4.   The activity level is divided into the total indirect cost to arrive at
     the overhead rate.

The overhead rate is used to allocate indirect costs to the products
that pass through the production cost center. The number of units of
activity required for each product multiplied by the overhead rate gives
the total amount of indirect cost allocated to that product.

Appendix   CONCEPTS OF STANDARD VOLUME

The level of activity selected for use in calculating the overhead rate
is called the *standard volume*. The text suggests that standard volume is
the volume anticipated for the next year. Some companies use instead
the *average volume* expected over a *number of years* in the future. The
overhead rate is lower if the estimated volume is high because the same
amount of fixed cost is spread over a larger number of units. Therefore,
the overhead rates resulting from the use of one of these concepts of
standard volume can differ substantially from those calculated on the
other concept.

When the standard volume is taken as the volume expected next year,
the resulting overhead rate is such that total overhead costs incurred in
the year will be approximately absorbed onto products if the estimates
are made with reasonable accuracy; that is, the amount of unabsorbed or
overabsorbed overhead will be small. This method therefore meets the
objective of financial accounting because it attaches all overhead costs
to products. It may, however, cause difficulty if the costs are being used
as a basis for pricing, for unit costs will tend to be high in a year of low
volume and low in a year of high volume. If the low volume implies a
business recession, the high unit cost may lead to an increase in selling

prices at the very time when it is probably most unwise to attempt such an increase. Conversely, in a year of high volume, the low rate may lead to a decrease in selling prices when such a decrease is unnecessary.

A standard volume based on an average of several years is used by automobile manufacturers and by a number of other leading companies. It avoids the pricing paradox mentioned above, but it does result in a large amount of overabsorbed overhead in a year of abnormally high volume, and a large amount of unabsorbed overhead in a year of abnormally low volumes.

> EXAMPLE: In a hypothetical company, the number of units manu-
> factured is as low as 30,000 in some years and as high as 60,000
> in other years, but is 40,000 units in an average year. Fixed costs
> are $120,000 a year, whatever the volume in that year may be. (The
> impact of inflation is ignored in the interest of simplicity.) Variable
> costs are $5 per unit. Exhibit 3–5 shows how the product costs would
> be calculated under the alternative ways of measuring volume.

Exhibit 3–5

Effect of volume measure on costs

	High Volume Year	Average Year	Low Volume Year
Units manufactured.............	60,000	40,000	30,000
Total fixed costs................	$120,000	$120,000	$120,000
Unit costs:			
A. *Overhead rate based on annual volume:*			
Variable cost...........	$5.00	$5.00	$5.00
Fixed cost.............	2.00	3.00	4.00
Total cost per unit..	$7.00	$8.00	$9.00
B. *Overhead rate based on average volume:*			
Variable cost...........	$5.00	$5.00	$5.00
Fixed cost.............	3.00	3.00	3.00
Total cost per unit..	$8.00	$8.00	$8.00

If the overhead rate is based on the volume level in each year, then it will be $2 per unit (= $120,000 ÷ 60,000) in a year when volume is 60,000 units and $4 per unit (= $120,000 ÷ 30,000) in a year when volume is 30,000 units. The total cost per unit is $7 in the year of high volume and $9 in the year of low volume. If prices are based on cost, there will be a tendency to charge low prices in a year in which volume is high, which is the very time when the heavy demand indicates that high prices can be obtained. Correspondingly, there will be a tendency to charge high prices in a year in which volume is low, which is the very time when customers are reluctant to buy the product.

If the overhead rate is based on the average volume of 40,000 units, the fixed costs will be $3 per unit (= $120,000 ÷ 30,000) regardless of what the volume is in a given year. Correspondingly, the total unit cost will not fluctuate with changes in volume.

Important terms		
	Allocation	**Standard volume**
	Cost center	**Overabsorbed overhead**
	Production cost center	**Unabsorbed (or underabsorbed) overhead**
	Service cost center	**Overhead variance account**
	Indirect cost pool	**Standard cost system**
	Step-down order	**Joint products**
	Overhead rate	**By-products**
	Predetermined over-	**Plantwide overhead rate**
	head rate	

Questions for discussion

1. Explain what is meant by "benefits received" and "causal relationship" as bases for assigning costs to cost objectives.

2. Consider a factory that manufactures several types of wooden desks. List items of cost that probably would be treated as direct costs and other items that would be treated as factory indirect costs for these desks.

3. Below are listed certain service cost centers and the five bases for allocation that are used in a certain factory. Which basis of allocation is most appropriate for each cost center? Explain your answer.

	Service Cost Center		*Basis for Allocation*
a.	Medical department	1.	Direct labor cost
b.	Employee pensions	2.	Number of employees
c.	Purchasing department	3.	Direct material cost
d.	Building maintenance	4.	Square feet of space
e.	Machine maintenance	5.	Direct material plus direct
f.	Employee cafeteria		labor cost
g.	Telephone department		
h.	Factory superintendent		

4. Distinguish between "assign," "assign directly," and "allocate" as used in this text.

5. Why are predetermined overhead rates better than overhead rates determined after the fact?

6. Exhibit 3–4 shows that average monthly indirect supplies cost for 1975 is estimated to be $4,800. Describe in your own words each step in the procedure that results in some fraction of this $4,800 being allocated to products (i.e., pipes) manufactured in 1975.

7. Give several reasons why factory overhead costs would be overabsorbed in a given month.

8. The text gives the journal entry for unabsorbed overhead costs. Give the corresponding entry for overabsorbed overhead, assuming any numbers that you wish.

9. Is it true that unabsorbed overhead is always reflected by a debit to the Overhead Variance account and overabsorbed overhead is always reflected as a credit?

10. Suppose that before closing, the Overhead Variance account for a year has a credit balance. Does this fact indicate that the Finished Goods Inventory balance is overstated? Explain.

11. "Since all factory indirect costs are allocated to some product, they all wind up in inventory or in cost of goods sold. It therefore makes no difference how they are allocated." Comment.

12. "The Delia Company set selling prices on each job that are equal to cost plus 10 percent. Its total profit will therefore be 10 percent of cost, no matter how the costs are allocated to each job. It therefore makes no difference how the costs are allocated." Comment.

13. "It is absolutely impossible to measure the true cost of any cost objective if indirect costs are present." Comment.

14. The overhead rates for Department 1 and Department 3 are higher on Exhibit 3–2 than on Exhibit 3–4, whereas the overhead rate for Department 2 is the same on each exhibit. Explain how this happened.

15. The factory indirect cost of a job calculated in connection with Exhibit 3–4 was $232.25, whereas for the same job calculated in connection with Exhibit 3–2, it was $234.90. Why did the factory indirect cost decrease?

16. Distinguish between joint products and by-products.

17. The text states that fluctuations in the sales value of a by-product, such as animal feed, can influence the cost of the main product, flour. Explain, using illustrative numbers, how this can happen.

18. Following is a diagram of the flow of costs into and out of inventory accounts in a certain period. Describe what amounts each of the letters represent.

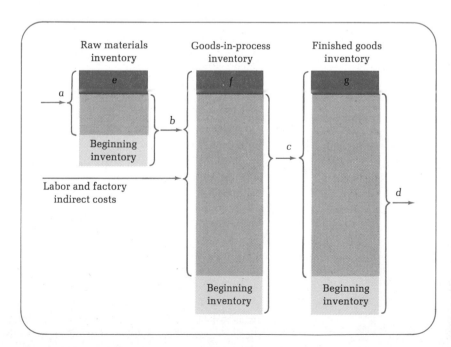

Problems 3–1. The Carter Company allocates factory indirect costs to jobs on the basis of direct labor dollars. Its estimated average monthly costs for 1975 are as follows:

	Average Monthly Costs
Direct material.................................	$30,000
Direct labor (other than overtime).................	40,000
Overtime payments to direct workers	10,000
Factory indirect costs (other than overtime)	50,000

Among the jobs worked on in November 1975 were two jobs, E and F, for which the following information was collected:

	Job E	Job F
Direct material cost......................	$3,000	$3,000
Direct labor cost (other than overtime).....	4,000	4,000
Overtime cost*.........................		1,000

* This cost was caused strictly by Job F.

Required:
1. Compute the overhead rate and the total factory costs of Jobs E and F on *each* of the following assumptions:
   a. Overtime is classified as direct labor cost.
   b. Overtime is classified as factory indirect cost.
2. Discuss which of the above methods is preferable.

3–2. The Drake Company allocates factory indirect costs to jobs on the basis of direct labor hours. Its estimated average monthly factory costs for 1974 are as follows:

	Average Monthly Costs
Direct material....	$ 50,000
Direct labor (other than items below).............	80,000
Overtime payments to direct workers.............	10,000
Fringe benefits on direct labor (including payroll taxes) (20% of direct labor)..................	16,000
Other factory indirect costs.....................	100,000

Its estimated average monthly direct labor hours is 20,000.

Among the jobs worked on in November 1974 were two jobs, G and H, for which the following information was collected:

	Job G	Job H
Direct material cost.....................	$5,000	$ 5,000
Direct labor cost (other than overtime and fringe benefits)....................	8,000	10,000
Overtime cost.........................	1,000	0
Direct labor hours......................	2,000	2,000

Assume that no fringe benefits were paid on overtime work.

Required:

1. Compute the overhead rate and the total factory costs of Jobs G and H on each of the following assumptions:
    a. Overtime and fringe benefits are classified as factory indirect costs.
    b. Fringe benefits are classified as factory indirect cost and overtime as direct labor.
    c. Overtime and fringe benefits are classified as direct labor cost.
2. Discuss which of the above methods is preferable.

3–3. The Smith Company estimated that costs of production for the following year would be:

Raw materials.............	$50,000
Direct labor...............	60,000
Factory indirect............	90,000

Required:

1. Calculate the overhead rate for the next year, assuming that it is based on direct labor dollars.
2. Journalize the entry necessary to show the total cost of production for the month of April if the raw materials put into production totaled $4,000 and direct labor was $5,100.
3. If actual factory indirect costs incurred in April were $7,500, calculate the overabsorbed or unabsorbed overhead for the month.

3–4. Following is a summary of transactions for 1974 for the Teetor Company:

Transactions

1. Raw materials purchased on account, $17,000.
2. Sales made on account were billed at $30,000 and cost of goods sold was $19,000.
3. Paid bills in cash, as follows:

Machine repairs....................	$ 2,000
Direct labor........................	7,600
Indirect labor......................	1,500
Administrative costs................	500
Salespersons' salaries................	1,500
Miscellaneous indirect factory costs...	500
Accounts payable..................	18,000

4. Received $32,000 from customers on account.
5. Raw material withdrawn from warehouse and put into production, $15,000.
6. Direct labor applied to production, $7,600.

7. Overhead rate, 60 percent of direct labor cost.
8. Cost of units of production completed during year, $31,000.
9. Any overabsorbed or unabsorbed overhead is allocated to the units sold.

Required:

1. Journalize these transactions, and any necessary adjusting entries. Post to T-accounts.
2. Prepare an income statement.

3–5. The Cable Company estimates that production costs for the operations of the coming year will be $400,000 for materials, $600,000 for labor, and $840,000 for factory overhead (i.e., factory indirect cost). Overhead is charged to cost objectives on the basis of percentage of direct labor cost.

Required:

1. Calculate the overhead rate for the estimated production for the coming year.
2. Compute the *debits* to goods in process for the month of January, assuming actual costs were $25,000 for direct materials, $35,000 for direct labor, and $75,000 for overhead.
3. Calculate the overabsorbed and unabsorbed overhead for January.
4. Assume that no changes are made in estimated production for the whole year. What disposition should be made of the overabsorbed or unabsorbed overhead?

3–6. At the end of the accounting period a partial list of the accounts of Samson, Inc., show the following balances:

	Debit	Credit
Raw material ending inventory	$10,000	
Goods in process ending inventory	12,000	
Finished goods ending inventory	8,000	
Cost of goods sold	40,000	
Selling and administrative expenses	6,000	
Overhead variance		$ 3,000
Sales revenue		55,000

Required:

1. Show the allocation of the overabsorbed or unabsorbed overhead to the proper accounts.
2. Compute the gross margin for the period.

3–7. The Smith Machine Company manufactures shoe-making machinery to customer specifications. On April 30, certain accounts appeared as follows prior to closing the books for the month:

Raw Materials Inventory			Goods in Process Inventory			Finished Goods Inventory	
Bal. 3/31			Bal. 3/31			Bal. 3/31	
18,000	1,600	(#436)	8,000	11,300		10,000	10,000
11,000	11,000	(#437)	12,600			11,300	
			10,000				
			7,000				

Cost of Goods Sold		Direct Labor			Factory Indirect Cost		Sales Revenue
10,000		10,000	1,000	(#436)	3,000	7,000	15,200
			9,000	(#437)	2,500		
					500		
					1,000		

The March 31 inventory of goods in process consisted of partly finished Job No. 436, which contains charges for raw materials, $3,800, direct labor, $3,000, and factory indirect cost, $1,200. The finished goods consisted of Job No. 435 which was sold during April. Job No. 436 was finished during the month and placed in the finished goods warehouse, and Job No. 437 was started. Factory indirect cost is allocated to individual jobs at $0.70 per dollar of direct labor cost.

Required:

1. Journalize the entries from which the April ledger postings were made in the inventory accounts.
2. Show the manufacturing costs allocated to Jobs No. 436 and No. 437 as of April 30.
3. Prepare a partial income statement through the gross margin, showing the details of the calculation of the cost of goods sold.

3–8. The adjusted trial balance of Troy Corporation includes the following costs which are to be distributed before the books are closed to its three cost centers, A, B, and C.

	Total	Building	Furniture—Fixtures	Machinery—Equipment
Heat, light, power........	$40,000			
Depreciation............	23,800	$3,000	$800	$20,000
Insurance:				
Inventories............	200			
Other................	2,210	1,300	60	850
Repairs................	5,900	4,000		1,900
Telephone expense.......	1,800			
	$73,910			

Data used for cost distribution follow:

	Cost Center		
	A	B	C
Cubic feet.............................	700,000	200,000	100,000
Square feet of floor space...............	48,000	9,000	3,000
Number of telephone extensions.........	6	30	9

Three fourths of the furniture and fixtures are in Cost Center B and one fourth are in Cost Center C. Half of the inventory is in Cost Center A and half is in Cost Center B. Assume that all building costs except utilities are allocated on the basis of floor space. All machinery is in Cost Center A.

Required:

Calculate the amount of cost to be allocated to each cost center.

3–9.   The Northwest Company calculated expected indirect costs for the coming year as shown in Exhibit 3–6.

Exhibit 3–6

Departmental expected cost distribution

		Production Centers			Service Centers		
	Basis for						*Gen'l*
Expense	*Distribution*	*Stamping*	*Grinding*	*Assembly*	*Stores*	*Personnel*	*Factory*
Indirect wages.......	Payroll dollars	$ 50,000	$ 95,000	$10,000	$4,000	$29,000	$15,000
Rent...............	Square feet	1,200	1,200	600	1,200	240	360
Depreciation—							
Buildings..........	Square feet	2,400	2,400	1,200	2,400	480	720
Machinery........	Value	89,750	8,650	1,785	10	15	820
Insurance..........	Value	300	280	150	15	15	60
Taxes—building.....	Square feet	600	600	300	600	120	180
Heat...............	Radiators	400	400	200	250	50	70
Power.............	Direct meter	450	450	175	25	80	40
Total.........		$145,100	$108,980	$14,410	8,500	$30,000	$17,250

Additional data pertaining to the departments above:

Area in square feet..................	10,000	10,000	5,000	10,000	2,000	3,000
Number of employees................	10	15	2	1	5	2
Expected raw materials issued........	$11,000	$ 3,000	$ 1,000			
Expected direct labor................	114,400	110,400	14,400			
Actual direct labor—January..........	15,000	16,000	4,000			
Raw material—January...............	40,000					
Actual indirect costs—January........	23,000	19,000	6,000			

Required:

1.   Allocate the indirect costs of the service centers to the product centers utilizing the step-down procedure as follows:
Personnel—on basis of employees.
General factory—on basis of square feet of area.
Stores—on basis of requisitions.

2.   Compute the overhead rate per direct labor dollar for each product center.

3.   Calculate the overabsorbed or unabsorbed overhead for each product center for January.

3–10.   The Northwest Company (referred to in the previous problem) has been using an overhead rate based on direct labor dollars for each product center. A review of operations reveals the following facts:

1. Work starts in the stamping department where the use of costly stamping machinery is the prime reason for cost incurrence.
2. Stamped goods are then sent to the grinding department where the major cost is for the time spent grinding.
3. In assembly, a great deal of skill is required in some jobs, very little skill in others, causing varying hourly wages.

Required:

Use the following data to calculate the overhead rate for each product center, using the most appropriate allocation basis.

	Stamping	Grinding	Assembly
Expected indirect costs.....	$172,800	$152,000	$24,000
Total direct labor hours....	48,000	60,000	12,000
Total direct labor dollars....	$180,000	$192,000	$48,000
Machine-hours.............	9,600	240	120

3–11. The Middy Company uses a job order cost system. The following relate to the month of March:

Order No.	Raw Materials Issued	Direct Labor Hours	Direct Labor Dollars
11..............	$ 2,000	1,000	$ 4,000
12..............	6,100	2,000	8,000
13..............	7,000	5,000	19,000
14..............	5,300	2,000	9,000
15..............	6,200	3,000	12,000
Total...........	$26,600	13,000	$52,000

Factory indirect cost is applied to production on the basis of $4 per direct labor hour.

Factory indirect cost for the month was $55,000.

Production orders 11, 13, 14, and 15 were completed during the month.

Production orders 11 and 14 were shipped and invoiced to customers during the month at a price double the total factory cost.

Required:

1. Prepare the following journal entries:
   a. Transferring raw material to goods in process.
   b. Transferring direct labor to goods in process.
   c. Transferring factory indirect cost to goods in process.
   d. Transferring from goods in process to finished goods inventory.
   e. Recording sales revenue and cost of goods sold.
2. Prepare a job cost record for Order No. 12.
3. What was the gross margin for the month?

3–12. The Tempo Company has three production departments, A, B, and C, for which expected average monthly factory indirect cost and direct labor hours are as follows:

	Total	A	B	C
Factory indirect cost.......	$300,000	$210,000	$50,000	$40,000
Direct labor hours.........	60,000	30,000	10,000	20,000

Among the jobs worked on in January were the following, together with the direct labor hours of each:

		Direct Labor Hours		
Job	*Total*	*Dept. A*	*Dept. B*	*Dept. C*
150...............	600	200	100	300
151...............	600	300	100	200
152...............	600	100	100	400

The company considered the whole plant as one cost center (i.e., it used a plantwide overhead rate). The rate was based on direct labor hours.

Required:

1. Compute the factory indirect cost allocated to each job in January.
2. Suppose that, instead of having a single cost center, each department was treated as a separate cost center. What would the factory indirect costs of the three departments have been?
3. Discuss whether the single cost center is preferable to having three cost centers.

3–13. The Wendell Canning Company has a busy season lasting six months from September through February and a slack season lasting from March through August. Typical data for these seasons are as follows:

	Busy Season	Slack Season
Average monthly direct labor hours............	12,000	4,000
Average monthly factory indirect costs........	$24,000	$12,000

Factory indirect cost is allocated to cases of canned goods on the basis of direct labor hours. The typical case requires one direct labor hour. The same type of products is packed in all months. On December 31, it has 20,000 cases in finished goods inventory.

Required:

1. If the company allocated each month's factory indirect costs to the products made in that month, what would be the factory

indirect cost per case in the busy season and in the slack season, respectively? What would be the factory indirect cost component of finished goods inventory?

2. If, instead, the company used a predetermined annual overhead rate, what would be its cost per case? What would be the factory indirect cost component of finished goods inventory?

3. Discuss which method of overhead allocation is preferable.

3–14. The Nutrient Company manufactures soybean oil and soybean meal. The company pays $64 per ton (2,000 pounds) for soybeans and incurs processing costs of $36 per ton. The average output from a ton of soybeans is 800 pounds of soybean oil and 1,200 pounds of soybean meal. Soybean oil is sold for $12 per cwt. (100 pounds), and soybean meal is sold for $3 per cwt.

Required:

1. Calculate the cost per cwt. of each product if:
    a. Costs are allocated on the basis of weight.
    b. Costs are allocated on the basis of market value.
    c. Soybean meal is treated as a by-product.
2. Which method of costing is preferable?
3. If output were 800 pounds of soybean oil, 1,100 pounds of soybean meal, and 100 pounds of chaff which had no market value, how, if at all, would your answer to Question 1 be different? (You are *not* required to make new calculations.)

3–15. The production processes involved in making maple syrup can also produce maple sugar. Vermont Sugar Enterprises wishes to produce only syrup, but on occasion some sugaring takes place. Production for March produced the following results:

	Syrup	*Sugar*	*Total*
Units produced..............	10,000	500	10,500
Unit selling price.............	$7.50	$1.00	
Total process costs:			
After split-off..............	$ 6,000	$155	$ 6,155
Joint costs.................			55,000

Required:

1. Calculate the cost of the syrup if the sugar is considered a by-product and the gross profit from its sale is considered to be a reduction of syrup cost.
2. Calculate product costs assuming this company decided to make and sell as much maple sugar as possible after filling all syrup orders.

3–16. The Haley Manufacturing Company makes a main product called Main-Pro in two processes, and makes a by-product which emerges at the end of Process 1, and is called By-Pro. Debit balances in certain accounts were:

```
Raw materials................... $50,000
Direct labor....................   15,000
Factory indirect costs...........   14,000
Goods in process—I.............        0
Goods in process—II............    8,000
Finished goods—By-Pro..........      300
Finished goods—Main-Pro.......   12,000
Costs of goods sold.............        0
```

Transactions

(1) Requisitioned $20,000 of raw material for Process I and $13,000 for Process II.

(2) Assigned direct labor—$9,000 to Process I and $6,000 to Process II.

(3) Allocation of actual factory indirect costs to processes on basis of direct labor dollars.

(4) Completion of all work started in Process I and transferred to Process II in amount of $37,000 and balance in this account was transferred to By-Pro finished goods.

(5) Completed $50,000 of work in Process II.

(6) Sold By-Pro costing $200 and Main-Pro costing $47,000.

Required:

Set up T-accounts for the items listed. Prepare journal entries for the transactions, and post them to the T-accounts.

4 Measurement of nonmanufacturing costs

Purpose of
the chapter In Chapter 3 we focused on the measurement of costs for one type of cost objective, that is, the manufacture of tangible goods. In the present chapter, the description of cost measurement is expanded to include (1) costs incurred by manufacturing companies outside their manufacturing facilities, and (2) the costs of services. Included in the first category are marketing costs, research and development costs, other general and administrative costs, and financial costs. Services are distinguished from goods simply by the fact that goods are tangible—they have physical properties such that they can be seen, felt, weighed, and measured—whereas services are intangible.

The general principles of cost measurement are the same for non-manufacturing costs as for manufacturing costs, and the same for services as for goods. In this chapter, we are simply extending these principles to additional types of cost and to additional types of cost objectives.

Types of
nonmanufac-
turing costs Until the last two or three decades, most cost accounting systems dealt exclusively with the measurement of the manufacturing costs of tangible goods. This was probably because these were the only items of cost that needed to be assigned to goods in order to prepare the financial statements. Manufacturing costs of goods must be measured in order to obtain the amounts for Goods in Process Inventory and Finished Goods Inventory accounts on the balance sheet and the amount for cost of goods sold on the income statement. Other costs were reported as expenses on the income statement in aggregate amounts. In more recent

94

years, cost accounting systems have been expanded to include the collection of information on other types of cost, that is, on costs not related to the manufacture of goods.

A list of the types of nonmanufacturing costs, as they are found in many industrial companies, is given in Exhibit 4–1. Although there is

Exhibit 4–1

Types of nonmanufacturing costs

1. *Marketing costs*
   A. *Order-getting costs*
      Advertising and other sales promotion
      Field selling:
         Selection and training of personnel
         Solicitation of orders
      Sales office expenses
      Market research
      General marketing management, policy, and planning
   B. *Logistics costs*
      Warehousing
      Packing and shipping
      Delivery (including transportation-out)
      Installation and service
      Order and invoice handling

2. *General and administrative costs*
   A. *Research and development costs*
   B. *Other general and administrative costs*
      (1) Staff and service units
            Control staff
            Personnel staff
            Finance staff
            Secretary and his staff
            Public relations staff
            Legal staff

      (2) General corporate costs
            General management
            Donations
            Litigation costs
            Public responsibility activities

3. *Financial costs*

considerable diversity in the way companies classify nonmanufacturing activities, this list is sufficiently representative to serve as a basis for the description that follows. We shall discuss items in the first two main categories in some detail. The third category, financial costs, will not be discussed. **Financial costs** include interest cost on borrowed funds (not dividends on stock; dividends are a distribution of earnings rather than a cost). Most companies do not include financial costs in their cost accounting system. In effect, they separate their operating activities from their financing activities. Interest is therefore an item of expense that appears below operating income on the income statement, and this is why we shall not discuss financial costs further.

GUIDING PRINCIPLES

For nonmanufacturing costs, the guiding principles of cost measurement are the same as those already discussed in connection with manufacturing costs; namely, (1) that the full cost of a cost objective is the sum of its direct costs plus an equitable share of indirect costs, (2) that as many items of cost as are feasible should be treated as direct costs, and (3) that indirect costs should be allocated to individual cost objectives on the basis of intended benefits or a causal relationship.

Marketing costs

Marketing costs comprise the costs of performing two quite dissimilar activities: (1) order getting, and (2) logistics (or order filling). The rationale for treating these costs under the single heading of marketing is primarily that these two activities are usually the responsibility of a single organization in the company, which is often called the marketing organization.

ORDER-GETTING COSTS

Order-getting costs are costs that are incurred in efforts to get orders. They include advertising and other sales promotion costs; the costs of field salespersons and sales offices, including the salaries, travel, and entertainment expense, costs of training salespersons and holding sales meetings, commissions of salespersons, and the costs associated with operating sales offices; market research costs; and the costs of general marketing management activities.

Order-getting costs are as necessary to the profitable operation of a business as are manufacturing costs. It is, however, much more difficult to measure the order-getting costs of an individual product than to measure its manufacturing cost. Order-getting activities are often carried on at field sales offices which may be widely dispersed geographically, whereas manufacturing is usually carried on within the four walls of one plant. Usually, salespersons and others in the marketing organization sell several products, so most of the order-getting costs applicable to a single product are indirect costs. Manufacturing activities tend to be standardized and repetitive, whereas each call that is made by a salesperson must be tailored to fit the needs and whims of the particular customer. Most importantly, although many order-getting activities do not in fact result in orders, the cost of the *entire* order-getting effort is properly associated with the sales revenue that results from those orders that are obtained. For example, if a salesperson's cost averages $10 per call, and if one order is received, on the average, for every three calls that the salesperson makes, the cost per order is not the $10 cost of the call which resulted in the order but rather the $30 cost of the three calls.

For these and other reasons, few companies attempt to measure the order-getting cost of each product separately in a manner similar to the method they use to measure manufacturing costs. Instead of establishing either a job order or process cost accounting system to collect the order-getting costs of each product, most companies measure the cost of each order-getting function, that is, advertising, direct selling, etc. If, however, a company is organized so that different organization units are each responsible for all order-getting functions for individual products or groups of related products (i.e., *product lines*), then it is feasible and worthwhile to measure order-getting costs by products or product lines.

Whether order-getting costs are measured by function or by product, the total cost includes some elements that are direct and other elements that are indirect. Amounts paid to media are direct costs of advertising, for example. A salesperson's compensation is a direct cost of the products that he or she sells if paid on a *commission* basis, that is, if the compensation is a percentage of the dollar value of the orders obtained, the compensation is clearly a direct cost. If the salesperson is paid a salary and sells many products, the compensation may not be traceable to individual products and therefore is an indirect cost of the products.

Classification of costs.   Information on order-getting costs, together with information on the sales that are generated by order-getting efforts, is used in reports to management that are designed to show what is happening in this area and where the problems are. Sales and cost information may be classified in any number of ways, including:

1.   Sales territories or sales offices.
2.   Individual salespersons.
3.   Customers, classified by—
    a.   Industry, or line of business.
    b.   Size of order.
    c.   Geographical territory.
    d.   Frequency of salesperson's call.
4.   Types of selling effort, such as media advertising, point-of-sale advertising, sales promotion, coupons, etc.

The desirability of reporting on order-getting costs and the associated revenues in several different ways means that these costs and revenues must be accumulated in the cost accounting system by several categories simultaneously; that is, if all the information listed above is deemed to be useful in a given company, that company must classify each transaction by each of the categories listed. Although it might seem that much recordkeeping would be required to make such cross classifications, they are in fact easily accomplished by devising an appropriate coding system, and then coding each cost and revenue transaction accordingly. If a computer is available, the work involved in accumulating information by numerous classifications may be relatively small.

LOGISTICS COSTS

Logistics (or order-filling) costs are those costs incurred between the time a product enters finished goods inventory and the time it is delivered to the customer, together with the recordkeeping costs associated with processing the customer's order and accounts receivable. These costs include: costs of warehousing, that is, holding the completed product in inventory until it is shipped to the customer; costs of packing and otherwise preparing the product for shipment; costs of shipping the product to the customer, including transportation costs if the customer does not pay for these separately; costs of installation and servicing, if the customer does not pay for these separately; costs of preparing the invoice and the related costs of recording the transaction in the company's accounts; the costs of processing the payment when it is received from the customer, collection cost and bad debt expense. In the terminology of economics, logistics costs provide **place utility,** in contrast with manufacturing costs which provide **form utility.**

As is the case with order-getting costs, logistics costs are part of the full costs of products in the sense that a product cannot be said to be profitable unless its sales revenue exceeds all its costs, including logistics costs. Thus, in estimating full costs as a basis for setting selling prices, logistics costs must be taken into account.

Exhibit 4–2

Analysis of profitability by customer class (thousands omitted)

	Customer Class*			
	Small	*Medium*	*Large*	*Total*
Sales revenue..................	$800	$1,800	$1,400	$4,000
Cost of goods sold............	390	760	650	1,800
Gross margin.............	$410	$1,040	$ 750	$2,200
Logistics costs:				
Transportation.............	$ 64	$ 174	$ 93	$ 331
Handling..................	58	78	85	221
Other.....................	80	155	41	276
Subtotal...............	$202	$ 407	$ 219	$ 828
Profit after logistics costs......	$208	$ 633	$ 531	$1,372
Logistics costs as % of gross margin....................	49	39	29	38
Order-getting costs:				
Direct selling...............	$148	$ 262	$ 142	$ 552
Advertising................	92	207	161	460
Subtotal...............	$240	$ 469	$ 303	$1,012
Profit or (loss)...............	$(32)	$ 164	$ 228	$ 360
Percent of sales revenue.......	...	9.1	16.3	9.0

* Small = Customers who purchase less than $1,000 annually.
  Medium = Customers who purchase $1,000–$25,000 annually.
  Large = Customers who purchase over $25,000 annually.

Also, like order-getting costs, logistics costs are classified in various ways in order to facilitate reporting them in ways that facilitate management planning and control. An example of an analysis of both logistics and order-getting costs is given in Exhibit 4–2, which shows revenues and costs classified by size of customer. The analysis indicates that the customers who place small quantities of orders are not, as a class, profitable, and that this is in large part because the logistics costs of these small orders are a relatively large percentage of gross margin. On the basis of this information, managerial attention should be focused on this class of customers in an effort to reduce costs, or possibly to place a restriction on the minimum size of customer that salespersons should solicit.

DISTINCTION BETWEEN LOGISTICS AND ORDER-GETTING COSTS

From a management standpoint, a fundamental distinction should be made between logistics costs and order-getting costs. Logistics costs are *caused by* the sales transaction in the sense that once an order has been accepted, a chain of events begins that culminates in the delivery of the product to the customer and the collection of cash from him. These events involve costs, and the costs are a more-or-less inevitable consequence of accepting the order. Order-getting costs have an opposite cause-and-effect relationship. They *cause* the sales order, rather than being *caused by* the sales order. They are in the nature of "bread cast upon the waters." We shall return to the significance of this distinction in later chapters.

General and administrative costs Exhibit 4–1 lists two categories of general and administrative costs. **General and administrative** is a catchall category. **It includes general costs and also the costs of various administrative activities applicable to the company as a whole,** but the distinction between "general" and "administrative" is not important enough to warrant separate treatment of these two categories. Research and development is so different from the other general and administrative activities that there are good reasons for making it a separate main classification. Indeed, this is done in some companies, particularly those in which research and development expenditures are sizable.

RESEARCH AND DEVELOPMENT COSTS

Research and development costs are the costs associated with efforts to find and perfect new or improved products or processes. Although there is a technical distinction between "research" and "development," it is unimportant for our purposes since both types of effort are usually carried on by the same organization unit.

Research and development is a gamble. Only a relatively few research projects—in many companies, fewer than 5 percent—produce successful results. In a narrow sense, the money spent on the unsuccessful projects is lost, but it is an unavoidable loss since no one knows at the beginning of a research effort whether the effort will succeed. Thus, it is realistic to view the whole research and development effort as an overall cost of the company. In this view, all the research and development costs would be allocated to all the products.

Various refinements on this broad view are possible. Some product lines may inherently require more research and development effort than others because they are technologically based and thus threatened by early obsolescence unless extensive research and development effort is devoted to improving existing products or developing new products. Management may decide to allocate all, or greater than a proportional share of, research and development costs to these product lines. Also some research and development projects may be specifically identifiable with a particular product, such as research that is undertaken to correct a defect that has been discovered on that product; if so, these projects are a direct cost of that product.

Project costing. Within the research and development organization, the unit of costing—that is, the cost objective—is generally each individual research and development project. If management decides that the therapeutic possibilities of some new chemical formulation should be investigated, it sets up a **project** for this specific purpose and assigns one or more researchers to it. The resources used for this project are measured in a way that is similar to the job order cost system in the factory; that is, each project is a job to which is assigned its direct costs and an allocated portion of the indirect costs of the research and development organization. In order to allocate overhead costs, a research and development overhead rate is calculated, using a procedure similar to that described in Chapter 3.

In addition to working on projects, researchers typically spend some of their time on nonproject investigations, trying out their own ideas. The costs of such work are collected in a "catchall" or miscellaneous project that is set up for this purpose.

OTHER GENERAL AND ADMINISTRATIVE COSTS

Examples of the functions included in the category of "other general and administrative costs" are listed on Exhibit 4–1. Costs of these functions are sometimes referred to as *corporate* costs or as *home office* costs. For the purpose of measuring and analyzing costs, these functions can be classified as either (1) staff and service units or (2) general corporate costs.

Staff and service units. All companies except the smallest have central staff units that provide assistance to the line units and to top management. These include the control staff, headed by the controller, whose functions were described in Chapter 1; the personnel staff, which is usually responsible for hiring and training personnel and for establishing wage and salary scales and other personnel policies; the finance staff, which is responsible for negotiating loans, arranging for issues of stock, and managing cash and short-term securities; the corporate secretary's staff, which is responsible for general corporate affairs and relationships with stockholders; the public relations staff, which is responsible for maintaining a favorable public attitude toward the company; the legal staff, which prepares or checks contracts and other legal documents and represents the company in litigation, and a number of others.

To the extent that these staff units provide services that can be traced directly to individual line departments, the cost of these services is a direct cost of the departments receiving them; if these line departments are production cost centers, the costs of the staff units become part of the costs of the products that these departments work on. Other staff and service costs are indirect and are allocated to cost objectives.

General corporate costs. Corporate costs include the costs of general management, that is, the chief executive, other top executives who have general management (as distinguished from functional management) responsibilities, and their personal staffs. Corporate costs also include donations to charitable organizations, dues and other costs associated with trade association membership, settlement of lawsuits and other litigation costs that are in addition to the costs of the legal staff, expenditures to meet the company's public responsibility, and similar activities. Since the activities of general management are spread across the whole business and since these and other general corporate costs can rarely be traced directly to a specific cost center, almost all general corporate costs are indirect costs.

ASSIGNMENT OF GENERAL AND ADMINISTRATIVE COSTS

As pointed out in Chapter 3, since general and administrative costs are intended to benefit the whole company, and since the manufacturing organization is one part of the company, it follows that conceptually some fraction of total general and administrative costs should be assigned to production cost centers and thereby become a part of the factory cost of products passing through these centers. Some companies do not follow this practice, however.

The Cost Accounting Standards Board (CASB) has prescribed bases of allocation in some detail. Although its standard is specifically related to the problem of allocating "home office" (i.e., corporate headquarters) costs to segments (i.e., divisions, plants, or other major subdivisions of a company), the same general principles apply to the allocation of general and administrative costs to other types of cost objectives. The CASB criteria are as follows.[1]

(1) *Centralized service functions.* Expenses of centralized service functions performed by a home office for its segments shall be allocated to segments on the basis of the services received by each segment. Centralized service functions performed by a home office for its segments are considered to consist of specific functions, which but for the existence of a home office would be performed or acquired by some or all of the segments individually, or would not be available to a segment. Examples include centrally performed personnel administration and centralized data processing.

(2) *Staff management of certain specific activities of segments.* The expenses incurred by a home office for staff management, supervisory, or policy functions related to specific activities of segments shall be allocated to appropriate segments over a base, or bases, representative of the total specific activity being managed or supervised. Staff management, supervision, or policy guidance to segments is commonly provided in the performance of specific segment activities such as manufacturing, accounting, and engineering.

(3) *Staff management not identifiable with any certain specific activities of segments.* The expenses incurred by a home office for staff management, supervisory, or policy functions which, for reasons of management policy, are not related to specific activities of segments shall be allocated . . . as residual expenses.

(4) *Line management of particular segments or groups of segments.* The expense of line management shall be allocated only to the particular segment or group of segments which are being managed or supervised. If more than one segment is managed or supervised, the expenses shall be allocated over a base or bases representative of the total activity of such segments. Line management is considered to consist of management or supervision of a segment as a whole.

Exhibit 4–3 gives examples of allocation bases that are suggested by CASB for various general and administrative expenses and functions.

Residual expenses. Those items of general and administrative costs that cannot realistically be related to activities by one of the bases described above are called **residual expenses.** They include the general corporate costs and in some companies a portion of staff and service costs. The Cost Accounting Standards Board requires[2] that residual costs be allocated to cost objectives by what is called the **Massachusetts Formula.** This formula provides that the percentage of residual expenses allocated to any cost center (i.e., department, division, or other segment) is the *arithmetical average* of the following three percentages:

---

[1] Cost Accounting Standard 403.40.

[2] Cost Accounting Standard 403.40 (7).

Exhibit 4–3

Bases for allocating general and administrative costs

Home Office Expense or Function	*Alternative Allocation Bases*
Centralized service functions:	
1. Personnel administration........ 1.	Number of personnel, labor hours, payroll, number of hires.
2. Data processing services........ 2.	Machine time, number of reports.
3. Centralized purchasing and sub- 3. contracting.	Number of purchase orders, value of purchases, number of items.
4. Centralized warehousing........ 4.	Square footage, value of material, volume.
5. Company aircraft service....... 5.	Actual or standard rate per hour, mile, passenger mile, or similar unit.
6. Central telephone service........ 6.	Usage costs, number of instruments.
Staff management of specific activities:	
1. Personnel management.......... 1.	Number of personnel, labor hours, payroll, number of hires.
2. Manufacturing policies (quality 2. control, industrial engineering, production scheduling, tooling, inspection, and testing, etc.).	Manufacturing cost input, manufacturing direct labor.
3. Engineering policies............ 3.	Total engineering costs, engineering direct labor, number of drawings.
4. Material/purchasing policies..... 4.	Number of purchase orders, value of purchases.
5. Marketing policies............. 5.	Sales, segment marketing costs.

Source: Cost Accounting Standards 403.60.

a. The percentage of the cost center's payroll to the total payroll of all cost centers;

b. The percentage of the cost center's revenue to the total operating revenue of all cost centers; and

c. The percentage of the net book value of the cost center's tangible assets to the total net book value of the tangible assets of all cost centers.

The Massachusetts Formula is complicated, and it is therefore not now widely used except for measuring the costs applicable to those government contracts that are within the jurisdiction of the Cost Accounting Standards Board. Because of the increasing use of CASB standards for other purposes, its use seems likely to grow, however.

Converting allocated costs to direct costs. Some costs which are allocated could, with some effort, be assigned directly to cost objectives. For example, if the controller department operates a computer, the costs of this computer may be allocated to other cost centers. Alternatively, computer costs could be assigned directly to users by setting up an hourly rate for computer time and charging each user for computer time at this rate. It is worthwhile to go to some effort to develop procedures for assigning costs directly, for at least two reasons: (1) direct assignment is a more accurate way of assigning costs than an allocation; and

(2) as will be discussed in Chapter 10, direct assignment of costs assists in the control of these costs.

Implications
for users of
cost
information

We have now completed our description of the methods used by companies to measure full costs of goods. Before turning to another topic, it is appropriate to think about the description in this and the two preceding chapters from the viewpoint of the user of cost information, for the user needs to understand the effect of cost accounting practices in order to understand the nature and significance of the cost information that is generated by these practices.

EFFECT OF ALTERNATIVE PRACTICES ON INCOME MEASUREMENT

Cost measures the use of resources. The total costs of a period can be classified into one of these categories depending on the purpose for which resources were used: (1) capital costs, (2) product costs, or (3) expenses.

Capital costs are the costs associated with the acquisition, construction, and installation of newly acquired fixed assets. These costs are reported in the fixed assets section of the balance sheet. At the moment of acquisition, capitalized costs have no effect on net income. They are amortized (i.e., depreciated) and become expenses in the future years during which the assets provide benefits to the company. In *Fundamentals of Financial Accounting,* we discuss how the line between capital expenditures and other costs should be drawn.

Product costs (also called **inventoriable costs or factory costs**) consist of the direct costs plus a fair share of the factory indirect costs that are involved in manufacturing products. These costs "attach" to the product; that is, as the product physically moves through the factory, the accounting system accumulates elements of cost for it in each of the production cost centers through which it moves. Initially, these costs appear as part of Goods in Process Inventory. As soon as the manufacturing process has been completed, the product physically moves to finished goods inventory, and its cost enters the Finished Goods Inventory account. When the product is sold, its cost is reported on the income statement as cost of goods sold. Thus, product costs affect net income only in the period in which the product is sold.

Note that the product cost is the cost of *manufacturing* the product; it does not include costs incurred "beyond the factory door." Product costs are therefore less than the full cost of a product; full cost includes marketing and general and administrative costs as well as factory cost.

Expenses are those costs that are matched against revenue in a given accounting period. They are also called **period costs.** As discussed earlier, it is important to understand that although the terms "costs" and "expenses" are sometimes used interchangeably, they are in fact different concepts. **All expenses are costs, but not all costs are expenses.** The acquisition of a building involves a cost but not an expense in the period in which the building was acquired; the acquisition cost becomes an expense in future periods via the depreciation mechanism. The manufacture of a product involves a cost in the period of manufacture; the corresponding expense is reported in the period in which the product is sold.

Importance of the distinction. The decisions on how a given item of cost is classified can have an important effect on the amount of income reported for a given accounting period. The effect is shown in the diagram in Exhibit 4–4. Consider any resource, such as labor services,

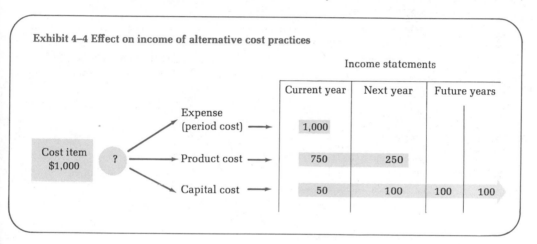

Exhibit 4–4 Effect on income of alternative cost practices

Income statements

	Current year	Next year	Future years
Expense (period cost)	1,000		
Product cost	750	250	
Capital cost	50	100	100 100

Cost item $1,000   ?

material, supplies, or whatever. The cost of this resource, assumed to be $1,000, can be recorded in one of three ways. If it is classified as an expense, the whole $1,000 affects net income of the current year. If it is classified as a product cost and three fourths of the products containing this cost are sold in the current year, then $750 of the cost affects net income in the current year. The remaining $250 winds up in inventory, which is an asset on the balance sheet as of the end of the current year. It has no effect on the current year's income; rather, it affects income in the next year, the year in which the product is sold. Finally, if the $1,000 is capitalized, it affects net income in a succession of future years. In the diagram, it is assumed that the asset is depreciated over a period of 10 years, with one half a year's depreciation occurring in the first year.

IMPORTANCE OF RECOGNIZING DIFFERENCES IN PRACTICE

In addition to differences in the way in which companies distinguish between product costs and expenses, other differences in practice have been described in these chapters. In order to understand the full meaning of an item of cost information, therefore, one must understand the system from which it comes. Does it or does it not include an allocation of marketing costs, or of some or all of general administrative costs? If so, what basis of allocation is used? What items of cost are counted as direct costs? How are indirect manufacturing costs allocated? The way that a particular company answers these questions has an effect on the way it measures costs. Despite these differences, there are forces which result in a basic similarity in the cost accounting systems of many companies. The set of generally accepted accounting principles is one such force. Moreover, in certain industries, companies have similar cost accounting systems because a trade association has fostered a common accounting system for use by the industry (as is the case with hospitals, most of which use a system developed by the American Hospital Association), or because companies in the industry have adopted the system of a leading company (as in the automobile manufacturing industry, in which all systems are similar to that developed by General Motors Corporation).

Measuring the full cost of services

In Chapters 2 and 3 and so far in Chapter 4, we have focused on methods of measuring the full cost of goods.[3] We now extend the discussion to include the measurement of the full cost of **services,** that is **intangible outputs of an organization.** The principles of measurement and the general approach already described for goods are applicable for services, but there are some additional complications involved in measuring the cost of services.

In the United States many more persons are employed in service organizations than in organizations that manufacture tangible goods, and, as is characteristic of highly developed economies, the proportion of the total work force that is employed in service industries is steadily increasing. Exhibit 4–5 gives an indication of the magnitude of the various types of organizations that are generally included in the service category. Note that government organizations constitute the largest segment of this category, that transportation, communication, and energy companies (also called *public utilities*) is the second largest, real estate operations is third, and health care is fourth.

Companies that engage in retail or wholesale selling are called **trading, merchandising,** or **commercial** companies (thus the distinction between "industry" and "commerce"). These companies usually are not

---

[3] Terminology can be confusing. Ideally, it would be preferable if everyone adopted this general practice: *products* are all outputs of an organization; products are either tangible *goods* or intangible *services.* However, many people use "products" to refer only to tangible goods; they therefore do not count services as products. The context usually makes the meaning unambiguous. We have attempted to follow general practice.

Exhibit 4–5

Size of service industries, 1968

	Value Added ($ Billion)
Government and government enterprises	105.0
Transportation, communication, energy	45.1
Real estate	52.5
Health care	23.6
Legal and other professional	14.0
Banking	12.7
Business services	11.5
Insurance	9.8
Personal services (e.g., laundries, cleaners, beauty shops, barber shops, funeral services)	7.3
Nonprofit membership organizations (i.e., business, professional, labor, civic, political, religious, and charitable organizations)	7.0
Educational	5.9
Amusements and recreation	4.2
Hotels and lodging	3.7
Repair services	3.1

Source: U.S. Department of Commerce.

included in the category of service organizations; they are in a separate category, called trade. The cost accounting practices of trading companies are similar to those of service organizations. The cost accounting problems of trading firms therefore will not be discussed separately here. The costs involved are not only the costs of the merchandise that is sold but include also the costs of the various functions that are carried out by the company.

NONPROFIT ORGANIZATIONS

A nonprofit organization is an organization whose primary objective is something other than earning a profit; it is to be contrasted with a *profit-oriented* organization. Most nonprofit organizations provide services rather than manufacture tangible products, so they are included in the services category. Of the types listed in Exhibit 4–5, health care, educational, membership, and government organizations are predominantly nonprofit organizations. The cost accounting practices of nonprofit organizations are in many respects similar to those of profit-oriented organizations. Both nonprofit and profit-oriented organizations use resources; and in both cases, the problem of cost measurement is to identify the amount of resources that are used for each of the various cost objectives that the organization has.

Two important differences exist, however: (1) nonprofit organizations tend to make less use of the accrual concept, and (2) some of them do not measure depreciation. Each is discussed below.

Less use of accrual accounting. Since cost measures the use of resources, valid information on costs cannot be collected unless the underlying accounting data are structured in such a way that monetary information on the use of resources is available. In a profit-oriented organization, adherence to the accrual and matching concepts assures that cost measures the *use* of resources. Some, but not all, service organizations have accounting systems that adhere to these concepts. A great many government organizations—local, state, and federal—do not have accrual accounting systems; that is, their systems measure the cost of resources *acquired* in a given period but not the cost of resources *used* in that period.

The reason for this discrepancy is primarily historical. Accrual accounting started in manufacturing companies because of the need to measure the costs of products in inventory. It developed further in manufacturing companies as those companies perceived ways in which management could make additional uses of accounting data. The trend toward accrual accounting in profit-oriented service organizations has been a fairly recent one. In the last few years banks, other financial institutions, and insurance companies have adopted accounting principles that permitted independent accountants to certify that their financial statements were "prepared in accordance with generally accepted accounting principles." Such a statement still cannot be made for many nonprofit organizations, particularly colleges and universities, religious organizations, and government organizations. In the absence of accrual accounting, monetary information on the amount of resources used for cost objectives cannot be obtained from the accounting records. Instead, approximations must be made on the basis of information obtained outside the accounting records. Without the control that debit and credit provides, such approximations are often unreliable.

> *EXAMPLE:* In many government organizations, an accounting record is made when material is *purchased,* but no record is made when material is *used.* Material cost is deducted from revenue in the period in which the material was purchased, in clear violation of the matching principle. Thus, no accounting record shows the monetary amount of material *used* in a given period, either in individual cost centers or for the organization as a whole. Similarly, contracts (such as for painting a building) are recorded in the period in which the contract is signed rather than in the period in which the work was done (e.g., the period in which the building was painted).

Less use of depreciation. Many nonprofit organizations do not record depreciation expense. In profit-oriented companies, depreciation accounting is essential; a company cannot be said to have made a profit unless its revenue exceeds all its costs, including the cost of the fixed assets that it uses. Many nonprofit organizations do not have the same need to match depreciation expense with revenue because they derive funds for fixed assets from gifts (as in the case of private colleges and religious organizations) or from special appropriations made for that purpose (as in the case of government organizations), rather than from operating revenues. Nonprofit organizations whose operating revenues are supposed to cover all costs (e.g., government-owned electric, water, and transportation organizations) do use depreciation accounting.

SIMILARITY TO PRODUCT COST MEASUREMENT

As in the case with manufacturing companies, some service organizations use job order cost systems and others use process cost systems. Many garages that service and repair automobiles use a job cost system, that is, they accumulate on a job cost record the costs incurred for each automobile that they service. Many hospitals and medical clinics set up a job cost record for each patient. Many other service organizations use a process cost system; that is, they assign costs to cost centers, they measure in some way the number of units of service furnished by the cost center, and they find the unit cost by dividing the total cost of the center by the number of units of services rendered. Some of the terminology used in service organizations differs from that discussed earlier for product organizations. For example, instead of the term "production cost center," the term **mission cost center** is used. A mission cost center works directly on the services that the organization provides, as contrasted with a **support cost center** that provides services to other cost centers in the organization. A support cost center corresponds to a service cost center in a manufacturing company, and the only reason for the difference in terminology is to avoid the confusion that might otherwise arise if the word "service" was used both for a type of cost center and for the output of the whole organization.

Because of the basic similarity in the methods of measuring cost in both service organizations and manufacturing organizations, there is no need to repeat the description of cost measurement methods that has already been given.

DEFINING COST OBJECTIVES AND OUTPUTS

The output of a manufacturing company is tangible; it has physical properties that can be described unambiguously and that can be readily counted or measured in most cases. The output of a service organization, by contrast, is intangible: in many situations the service cannot be clearly described, let alone counted or measured. In the absence of a practical way of measuring the real output of the organization, a surrogate measure is used. A **surrogate measure is one that approximates the real output, although it is not the same as the real output.**

> *EXAMPLE:* The real output of an educational institution is education, but the amount of education that each student receives cannot be accurately measured. Therefore, the number of students who attend,

or the number of students who graduate, is used as a surrogate output measure.

The cost objectives of a service organization are related to these surrogates of output. In designing a cost accounting system, much thought needs to be given to defining cost objectives in the most useful way. Usually, two criteria are important in deciding on what the cost objectives should be: (1) they should be useful as a basis for setting selling prices, and (2) they should provide useful information for management planning and control.

EXAMPLE NO. 1: A university may designate its entire educational program as a single cost objective. Alternatively, it may establish two cost objectives, one for undergraduate and the other for graduate education. Going into still more detail, it may decide to measure the cost of individual fields of instruction, or even of individual courses in each field. Depending on the cost objectives selected, the university can arrive at a cost per student, a cost per undergraduate (as distinguished from graduate) student, a cost per student majoring in a given field, or a cost per course or per credit hour. The choice of cost objectives depends on how, if at all, the resulting cost information can be used for pricing (e.g., setting tuition charges in private universities or obtaining funds from the legislature in the case of public universities), and the usefulness of the cost detail in making management decisions.

EXAMPLE NO. 2: Long-distance trucking companies collect commodities, move them from one city to another, and deliver them. Each city in which a company operates is called a terminal. Movement of freight between two cities is called a traffic lane. Three types of cost objectives are used in the trucking industry. Some companies assign all costs and revenues to *terminals*, including a share of the costs of hauling freight from one terminal to another. Other companies assign costs and revenue to *traffic lanes*, including a share of the costs of operating facilities in each terminal. Still other companies assign costs to *classes of commodities* transported. Some companies use two of these approaches in combination. Their choice depends on their judgment as to which type of cost objective provides the most useful information to management.

SYSTEMS PRESCRIBED BY REGULATORY AGENCIES

Many service organizations are regulated by government agencies. Among these are gas companies, electric companies, water companies, trucking companies, railroads, airlines, bus companies, pipeline companies, telephone companies, broadcasting companies, banks, investment trusts, and insurance companies. Most regulatory agencies require that each regulated company submit revenue and cost reports, and the agency prescribes, usually in considerable detail, how costs are to be measured on these reports. The fact that the method of measuring costs is prescribed in detail has one important advantage, but in certain industries it has an equally important disadvantage. The advantage is that the data are comparable among companies so that valid comparisons of the costs of various cost objectives can be made. Indeed, the regulatory agency usually publishes averages and other compilations of cost in order to facilitate such comparisons. The disadvantage is that in some regulated industries, the cost objectives and the methods of assigning costs to cost objectives specified by the regulatory agency are of little use for management. Usually, such systems were instituted prior to the development of modern cost accounting principles and have not been modified in the light of recent developments. In these industries, the regulated companies are in the unfortunate position of being required to maintain two "sets of books," one to meet the requirements of the regulatory agency, but useless for other purposes, and the other to meet the needs of management. Not only does this requirement cause additional recordkeeping expense, but also it leads to misunderstanding when information from one set of books is confused with that from the other set of books.

> *EXAMPLE:* The cost accounting system prescribed by the Civil Aeronautics Board for airline companies is an example of a system that provides information that is useful both to the regulatory agency and to the managements of airline companies. By contrast, the system prescribed by the Interstate Commerce Commission for railroads is an antiquated one which requires that costs be collected in a way that is not useful to management, and probably of little use to the needs of the ICC.

ESTIMATES OF VOLUME

In Chapter 3 we emphasized both the importance of making a good estimate of volume, that is, the level of activity, as a part of the process of arriving at overhead rates and also the difficulty of arriving at a good estimate in a manufacturing company because of the uncertainties about what sales activity will be in the forthcoming year. Service organizations also must make volume estimates in order to arrive at overhead rates, but in some of them, the problem is much less difficult than that in the typical manufacturing company. A college or university knows, within reasonably close limits, what its level of activity will be for the whole academic year as soon as students have registered in the fall. The activity level of religious organizations and of many other membership organizations is determined by the amount that can be raised from dues or contributions, and this amount often can be estimated within close limits prior to the beginning of the year. Government organizations that depend on financial support from the legislature know, usually before the beginning of the year, how much money they are going to receive, and this determines the level of services that they can furnish. In these organizations, the problem of estimating the level of activity is much less serious than it is in a typical manufacturing company.

Demonstration case

The following problem has two purposes: (1) to encourage you to review your understanding of methods of allocating nonmanufacturing costs to products, and (2) to permit you to see the impact of various allocation methods on the data that are furnished to management. Exhibit 4–6 shows revenue and cost information for the Allstol Com-

Exhibit 4–6

Revenue and cost data for Allstol Company (thousands omitted)

	Total	Product A	Product B
Sales......................................	$2,400	$1,600	$800
Direct cost:			
Direct material.....................	$ 200	$ 150	$ 50
Direct labor.......................	500	400	100
Factory indirect......................	500	450	50
Total factory cost..............	$1,200	$1,000	$200
Marketing costs......................	600	280	320
General and administrative costs.......	400	220	180
Full costs....................	$2,200	$1,500	$700
Pretax operating revenue..............	$ 200	$ 100	$100
Percent of sales revenue..............	8.3	6.2	12.5

pany. This company makes two products. Product A is sold in large quantities to a relatively few buyers. Product B requires extensive advertising and sales promotion effort, and has relatively high logistics costs because the average size of each order is small. In Exhibit 4–6 costs have been allocated to products by first collecting elements of cost in a number of cost pools and then allocating the total amount in each pool according to benefits received or a causal relationship. You are asked to calculate what the costs assigned to each product would have been if instead of the basis actually used the company had used each of the following methods of handling indirect costs:

1. Marketing and general and administrative costs are allocated on the basis of the relative direct labor cost of each product.
2. Marketing and general and administrative costs are allocated on the basis of the relative amount of total factory costs.

Required:

Calculate the dollar amount of income and its percentage of revenue for each product under each of the above methods. Having made these calculations, think about the usefulness of these various approaches to management.

Solution:

The calculations for the allocation of marketing and general and administrative costs on the basis of direct labor are made after determining that the direct labor of Product A is 400 ÷ 500 = 80 percent of total direct labor, and of Product B, 20 percent. They are:

Allocated by Direct Labor	A	B
Proportion allocated..................	80%	20%
Amount allocated...................	$ 800	$200
Total cost.........................	1,800	400
Income............................	(200)	400
Percent of sales revenue.............	(12.5)	50.0

The calculations for the allocation of marketing and general and administrative costs on the basis of total factory costs are derived from the fact that the total factory costs of Product A are 1,000 ÷ 1,200 = 83 percent of total factory costs, and those of Product B are 17 percent. The calculations are:

Allocated by Total Factory Cost	A	B
Proportion allocated...............	83%	17%
Amount allocated..................	$ 830	$170
Total cost.........................	1,830	370
Income............................	(230)	430
Percent of sales revenue............	(14.4)	53.8

These three methods of calculation give quite different results. The carefully worked out allocations given in Exhibit 4–6 show that Product B has 12.5 percent profit per dollar of revenue compared with 6.2 percent for Product A; that is, each revenue dollar of Product B produces twice as much income as a revenue dollar of Product A.

By contrast, the impression conveyed by either of the other two methods is that Product A is being sold at a loss and all the company's income is being generated by Product B.

The conclusion is that unless careful methods of indirect cost allocation are used, management may be misled by the resulting cost information. The most useful information is the careful allocation shown in Exhibit 4–6, for this is the closest approximation to the amount of resources actually used for each of the two products.

Summary   This chapter concludes our description of cost accounting systems that are designed to measure the full costs of cost objectives. For a manufacturing company, costs incurred outside the factory are marketing costs and general and administrative costs. Marketing consists of two quite different activities, order-getting and logistics (or order-filling). The differences must be kept in mind in examining the costs related to each type. Marketing costs are usually recorded by functions, customers, and activities, rather than by products. Research and development costs are collected by projects using a procedure that is similar to the job order cost system in a factory. Other general and administrative costs are assigned to cost objectives, to the extent feasible, on a basis that reflects intended benefits or causal relationship. There is usually a certain class of residual costs for which no rational basis for allocation exists, and an arbitrary formula must be used to allocate such costs.

There is no uniform way of measuring costs, so cost comparisons among companies must be made cautiously. Nevertheless, the measurement procedures for companies within a given industry tend to be similar.

Service organizations include nonprofit as well as profit-oriented organizations. The cost accounting problems and practices of service organizations are similar to those of manufacturing organizations, except that some nonprofit service organizations do not use accrual accounting and some do not account for depreciation; cost objectives are more difficult to define and measure in service organizations; regulated service organizations must adhere to practices prescribed by the regulatory agency; and volume is relatively easy to estimate in some service organizations.

Important terms	
Marketing costs	**Massachusetts Formula**
Order-getting costs	**Capital cost**
Logistics costs	**Period cost (or expense)**
General and administrative costs	**Services**
Research and development costs	**Nonprofit organization**
Residual expenses	**Surrogate**

Questions for discussion

1. Distinguish between financial costs and costs of the finance function.
2. Why are order-getting costs ordinarily not collected by products? Under what circumstances is it appropriate to collect order-getting costs by products?
3. "If a salesperson obtains an order on one out of every three calls that are made, and if costs are $10 per call, the cost per order is $10, because the other two calls were unproductive." Do you agree? Why?
4. Why are production activities said to give "form utility" and logistics activities "place utility"?
5. In analyzing costs, what is the importance of the distinction between order-getting costs and logistics costs?
6. Describe the similarity between accounting for research and development cost and accounting for job orders in a factory.

7. How, if at all, do general and administrative costs become part of finished goods inventory?

8. Why is it preferable to charge users so much an hour for the computer time they use rather than to allocate computer costs along with other general and administrative costs?

9. What do you suppose is the rationale behind the Massachusetts Formula?

10. Distinguish between product costs and period costs.

11. As between capital costs, product costs, and expenses, which has the most immediate impact on net income, and which has the least immediate impact? Why?

12. The U.S. Postal Service is a large nonprofit organization. Does it need a cost accounting system? Why?

13. Many government organizations do not have an accrual accounting system. How would management benefit from such a system?

14. What would be appropriate cost objectives for a large church or synagogue?

15. Why, if at all, should the cost accounting system for a profit-oriented electric power company be different from that of a government-owned, nonprofit electric company?

Problems **4–1.** The central regional sales manager for the Toddler Toy Company is held responsible for the control of the following expenses incurred in June and July:

Expense	June	July
Supervision	$ 5,000	$ 5,500
Salesmen's salaries	8,334	8,000
Commissions	4,500	4,666
Salesmen's travel	7,000	6,600
Supplies—sales office	1,000	1,080
Salaries—sales office	2,500	2,834
Miscellaneous sales expense	1,240	1,330
Rent	2,500	3,000
Total	$ 32,074	$ 33,010
Net Sales Revenue	$151,600	$170,000

Required:

After computing the amount of expense per dollar of net sales for each expense category, answer the following:

1. What was the total cost per dollar of the added July sales?

2. What can be said about the sales manager's control of salesmen's salaries?

3. What possible relationship might exist between travel expense and sales?

4–2. The following are items relating to the marketing expenses and sales of Callo Cosmetics for a week in January and February. The sales manager is held responsible for all expense items below:

Expense	January	February
Supervisory..........................	$ 1,250	$ 1,375
Salesmen's salaries..................	2,083	2,000
Commissions.........................	1,125	1,167
Salesmen's travel....................	1,750	1,650
Supplies—sales office................	250	270
Salaries—sales office................	625	708
Miscellaneous sales expense...........	310	333
Rent................................	625	750
Total......................	$ 8,018	$ 8,253
Net Sales Revenue..................	$37,900	$42,500

Required:

After computing the amount of expenses per dollar of net sale for each expenditure, answer the following:

1. What was the total cost per dollar of added February sales?
2. What can be said about the manager's control of salesmen's salaries?
3. What is a possible relationship between travel expense and sales?

4–3. The Whitney Company incurred the following costs in manufacturing and selling its products:

Salesmen's commissions...................	$20,000
Raw materials purchased.................	80,000
Cost of salesmen's salesbooks..............	350
Cost of invoices used to bill customers......	500
Salary of finished goods warehouse janitor...	5,000
Wages of credit department clerks..........	8,000
Salesmen's travel expense.................	3,700
Rent on materials warehouse.............	800
Rent on finished goods warehouse..........	1,200
Interest on finished goods warehouse loan...	500

Required:

Compute separately the order-getting and logistics costs included above.

4–4. The New Mode Corporation incurred the following costs in the manufacturer and sale of its products:

Processing of salesmen's orders.............	$ 2,200
Processing of raw material purchase orders..	1,100
Insurance on raw material storage.........	100
Insurance on finished goods storage........	250
Salaries of salesmen.....................	18,000
Cost of customer billing..................	3,000
Accounts receivable collection costs........	700
Transportation-in—materials..............	1,500
Transportation-out—sales.................	2,000
Salaries of raw material clerk	6,000
Salary of purchasing agent................	10,000

Required:

Compute separately the order-getting and logistics costs included above.

4–5. Below is a breakdown, by product, of the 1975 sales and costs of producing and selling the four products in the line of East-West, Inc.

	For the Year Ended December 31, 1975			
	Product A	Product B	Product C	Product D
Sales.................	$60,000	$40,000	$50,000	$30,000
Cost of goods sold.....	33,000	20,800	26,000	15,300
Selling expenses.......	11,000	10,000	9,500	10,700
General expenses.......	9,000	6,000	9,500	3,000
Operating income......	7,000	3,200	5,000	1,000

Required:

1. Calculate the change in gross margin which would result if logistics costs totaling 10 percent of total selling expenses were treated as a factory cost instead of marketing cost.
2. Rate the products according to their profitability.

4–6. The results of operations for the year 1974 for the North-South Company are summarized below:

	For the Year 1974			
	Product A	Product B	Product C	Product D
Sales.................	$120,000	$80,000	$100,000	$60,000
Cost of goods sold....	66,000	41,600	52,000	30,600
Selling expenses......	22,000	20,000	19,000	21,400
General expenses.....	18,000	12,000	19,000	6,000
Net income..........	14,000	6,400	10,000	2,000

Required:

1. Logistics costs total 10 percent of selling expenses. Calculate the change in gross margin which would result if these were treated as factory costs.
2. Which product is the most profitable? The least profitable?

4–7. Consider two hypothetical companies, A and B. Their operations are identical in all respects, and their income statement data, for 1975, excluding the items listed below, are also identical, as follows:

Sales revenue.............................	$1,100,000
Cost of goods sold........................	600,000
Gross margin.............................	$ 500,000
Marketing expense........................	$ 130,000
General and administrative expense..........	200,000
Operating income.........................	$ 170,000

One half of the manufacturing costs for the year remain in Finished Goods Inventory as of December 31, and the other half are in Cost of Goods Sold.

The companies' accounting treatment of certain items differs as follows:

1. Freight on shipments to customers is $50,000. Company A classifies this as a marketing expense. Company B deducts this from sales revenue, in arriving at net sales.
2. Freight on shipments from one company warehouse to another is $40,000. Company A classifies this as a product cost. Company B classifies it as a marketing cost.
3. Certain staff costs, not included in the $200,000 listed above, amount to $20,000. Company A classifies these as a product cost. Company B classifies them as a period cost because they were incurred for the benefit of the manufacturing division.
4. Certain other administrative costs not included in the $200,000 listed above, and amounting to $30,000, are for the administration of the marketing function. Company A classifies these as marketing expenses, and Company B as general and administrative expenses.

Required:

1. Prepare an income statement for Company A and another for Company B.
2. Calculate the percentage of each item to net sales. Explain why these differ for the two companies.
3. Discuss which of the alternative treatments is preferable for each of the four items.

4-8. The controller of Canton Sales, Inc., produced the following statement of income by product line for the month of May:

	Total	Product A	Product B	Product C
Sales.........................	$14,000	$2,800	$4,200	$7,000
Cost of goods sold.............	5,400	1,080	1,620	2,700
Gross margin..................	$ 8,600	$1,720	$2,580	$4,300
Order getting.................	6,600	800	2,200	3,600
Profit before general and admin. ...	$ 2,000	$ 920	$ 380	$ 700

Order-getting costs were allocated by charging each product with its fair share according to the number of customer calls, number of miles traveled by salesmen, number of telephone calls made, number of invoices sent, number of orders received, and similar bases.

The sales manager said that these allocations of order-getting costs were so much "hocus-pocus," and that the commonsense way of allocating the $6,600 was either in proportion to sales revenue or in proportion to gross margin.

Required:

1. Calculate the profitability of the three products in accordance with each of the two methods suggested by the sales manager.
2. Which product is actually the most profitable? Explain your answer as if you were the controller discussing this matter with the sales manager.

5 Uses of full cost information

In Chapters 2, 3, and 4 we described how the full cost of a cost objective is measured. In the present chapter, we describe some of the uses that management makes of full cost information. These uses are the following: (1) in financial accounting; (2) in answering the question: "What did it cost?"; (3) in arriving at regulated prices; (4) in normal pricing; and (5) in analysis of profitability. Of these, we shall give special emphasis to normal pricing and shall describe the uses of full cost information in a variety of pricing practices.

We have already described how full cost information is used in developing financial statements. To summarize:

1. Partially completed products are reported on the balance sheet as goods in process inventory. The amounts reported represent the factory costs incurred on these goods as of the end of the accounting period.

2. Completed but unsold products are reported on the balance sheet as finished goods inventory. The amounts reported are the total factory cost of each item in the inventory.

3. When a product is sold, its total factory cost is reported on the income statement as cost of goods sold.

4. When a company constructs a building, a machine, or some other fixed asset for its own use, the amount at which this asset is recorded in the accounts and reported on the balance sheet is its full cost.

SEGMENT REPORTING

Cost accounting information is also used in certain companies to measure the income of the principal segments of the business. Some

120

companies, called **diversified companies** or **conglomerates,** do business in several different industries. The Securities and Exchange Commission (SEC) requires that these companies report to it "(i) total sales and revenues and (ii) income (or loss) before income taxes and extraordinary items, attributable to each line of business. . . ." In order to calculate income, it is of course necessary to subtract the applicable costs from revenue. Two principal problems arise in complying with this requirement: (1) the definition of "line of business" or segment, and (2) the measurement of costs applicable to each segment. (A third problem area, the measurement of revenue for each segment, is usually not a difficult matter.)

The SEC has not specified in detail what criteria are to be used in defining a **line of business.** In general, a line of business can be thought of as a separate industry, such as steel manufacturing as contrasted with electronics or with food. It is intended that the term be defined broadly enough so that no company is required to divide its total activities into more than 10 segments; few companies report more than 5 or 6.

Neither is the SEC specific as to how the costs attributable to a given segment are to be measured. The guiding principle is the same as that already stated; namely, that the full cost of a segment is the sum of its direct cost plus an equitable share of the applicable indirect costs. In this situation, indirect costs include the general and administrative costs of the company. As we have already seen, there are wide variations in practice used by companies in allocating these indirect costs. Accounting reports on the profitability of segments must be treated cautiously because the reported profitability can be affected significantly by the methods of allocation that a company selects. The principle of consistency, however, requires that a company continue to use the same method of allocation from one year to another, so comparisons of one company's report of profitability by segments over a period of years should not be affected by differences in the method of allocation.

What did it cost?

The problem of measuring the cost of something arises in a great many contexts: What did the Vietnam War cost? What did one bombing raid in that war cost? What did the last Presidential election cost? What was the cost of police protection in city X? What did it cost the U.S. Postal Service to send a letter from Chicago to San Francisco? What was the cost of operating a school cafeteria? What was the cost of a certain research project?

The question also arises when two or more companies engage in a **joint venture.** Several petroleum companies may agree to undertake a joint exploration program, or they may agree to develop a newly discovered oil field jointly, with each company paying for a specified fraction of the full cost. Company A may agree to do research that is also of interest to Company B, with Company B paying a stipulated share of the full cost.

In measuring the cost in such situations, there is a likelihood of misunderstanding and friction unless there is a clear and complete statement of exactly how "cost" is to be defined. There can be confusion as to what the cost objective is, there can be confusion as to what items of cost are to be assigned to the cost objective, and there can be confusion as to how indirect costs are to be allocated. The first two of these possible sources of confusion are discussed below; the third is the, by now, familiar problem of cost allocation.

DEFINITION OF COST OBJECTIVE

A televised public service message, whose purpose was to encourage gifts to higher education, contained the following statement: "Tuition covers only 25 percent of the cost of education in private colleges and universities." Evidently this percentage was arrived at by dividing tuition revenue by the total cost of operating these institutions. Such a calculation is incorrect, because universities engage in research, in community service programs, in providing board and room, and in many other noneducational activities; the total cost of operation includes the cost of these activities. If the cost objective is taken as being the education of students, then all these noneducational costs should be excluded. The correct percentage of tuition to total *education* cost of all private colleges and universities is probably closer to 75 percent than to 25 percent.

Even if the cost objective is properly defined as education, there is room for confusion as to exactly what constitutes educational activities. How does one distinguish between that part of the library which exists for faculty research and that part which exists for student education? Are athletic facilities a part of education? Questions like these need to be thought about carefully in order to arrive at an unambiguous answer. In many cases, the description of the objective for which costs are collected is taken as being more obvious than it really is.

> *EXAMPLE:* A salesman's boss tells him: "Please take Mr. Jones (a customer) out to dinner tonight; the company will pay what it costs." By "it," the boss may have in mind the bill for the two dinners, but the salesman may have in mind that "it" means the cost of the dinners plus the cost of drinks before dinner, the cost of his automobile trip to pick up Mr. Jones, and the cost of parking his car. Further, if it is agreed that "it" includes the cost of using the salesman's automobile, there are a number of uncertainties as to how this cost should be measured. Should it include just gasoline and oil? Or should it also include an allowance for depreciation, insurance, and/or fees?

After a few instances of misunderstanding that arose because of vagueness in the definition of "entertainment" in situations like that in the above example, a company undoubtedly would work out rules that clarified what the cost objective is to include. It must work out similar rules in a great many other situations. Does the product or service that is being priced include shipping costs to the customer? Is the company expected to furnish assistance in installation? If the product is unsatisfactory, will the company incur additional costs in remedying it? The list can be extended indefinitely.

DEFINITION OF COST

As we have seen there is much room for differences of opinion as to how full cost is to be measured. In particular, one cannot rely on the statement: "Measure costs according to generally accepted accounting principles," for accounting principles are not specific enough to resolve many of the detailed questions that arise. In some situations, one does not even know whether a cost is intended to represent full cost or some other type of cost.

EXAMPLE: Exhibit 5–1 shows some of the estimates that have been made of the "cost" of the Vietnam War in its peak year, which was fiscal year (FY) 1969. The highest estimate is four times the lowest.

Exhibit 5–1

Estimate of cost of the Vietnam War in fiscal year 1969

Source of Estimate	Cost (billions)
James Clayton	$86.4
Department of Defense, at the time	35.8
Senator Stuart Symington	32.0
Melvin Laird, as a congressman	29.0
Department of Defense, in 1970	21.5

Source: Congressional testimony.

Clayton's estimate includes the cost of pensions and other veterans' benefits that will be paid out in future years to those who served in the Armed Forces during FY 1969. The Department of Defense estimate is an attempt to measure full cost including a share of general and administrative cost, but excluding veterans' benefits. The next two estimates are also of full costs. The last estimate is of direct costs only.

In order to reduce confusion as to what is to be included in cost, it is often necessary to specify in some detail how direct costs are to be defined, what elements of indirect costs are to be included, how these elements are to be measured, and what method is to be used to allocate them to the cost objective.

COST-TYPE CONTRACTS

Agreement on the details of how cost is to be measured is especially important in situations in which one party has agreed to buy products or services from another party at a price that is based on cost. There are tens of billions of dollars of such contracts annually. Under the Medicare and Medicaid programs, the federal government reimburses hospitals and other providers of health care for the cost of providing service to eligible patients. Blue Cross, Blue Shield, and insurance companies do the same thing for their subscribers and policyholders. The federal government pays for 90 percent of the cost of certain highway construction, and either 100 percent or some lesser percentage of the cost of urban renewal programs, welfare programs, programs for assistance to small business, disaster relief programs, and a variety of others. The price of many construction projects, ranging in size from a private home to a skyscraper, is stated as cost plus an allowance for profit. When the cost of a product cannot be estimated accurately in advance, as is the case with new weapons systems and other newly developed products, the price is necessarily based on cost plus an allowance for profit.

In all these situations, the word "cost" means full cost. Again, because of differences in methods of measuring cost, it is necessary that the method to be used in the particular contract be spelled out in some detail so as to avoid misunderstanding. For example, the Armed Services Procurement Regulations contain dozens of pages of description as to the elements of cost that are appropriately counted in measuring the cost of cost-type contracts entered into by the Department of Defense. Even this lengthy description was so inadequate that in 1971 the Congress created the Cost Accounting Standards Board whose function is to develop better descriptions of how the costs of such contracts are to be measured.

Setting regulated prices

Although Americans live in what is generally regarded as being a market economy, many of the prices that they pay are set not by the forces of the marketplace but rather by regulatory agencies. These include prices for electricity; gas and water; passenger and/or freight transportation by train, airplane, truck, bus, barge, and pipeline; telephone and telegraph; insurance premiums; services in buying and selling securities; and a long list of others. In each of these cases, the regulatory agency (Federal Communications Commission, Interstate Commerce Commission, state public utility and insurance commissions, etc.) allows a price that is equal to full cost plus an allowance for profit. In most cases, the regulatory agency provides a manual, which may contain several hundred pages, spelling out in great detail how costs are to be measured. The principles underlying the rules in these manuals are those described in Chapters 2, 3, and 4, but the details differ greatly depending partly on the nature of the product or service whose price is regulated and partly on the personal preferences of the regulatory body.

In World War II, in the Korean War, and in the early 1970s, substantially all prices in the United States were made subject to regulation by a government agency. The general principle of these regulations was that prices could be increased only to the extent that full costs had increased.

Normal pricing

RATIONALE FOR PRICING

As we discuss in Chapter 16 of *Fundamentals of Financial Accounting,* a principal economic objective of a business is to earn a satisfactory return on its investment, that is, on the assets that it uses. If the return on investment is too low, investors will refuse to put additional capital into the business. If the return on investment is too high, investors who observe the lucrative profit opportunities will pour funds into competing businesses, and the additional capacity that results from this will lead to a reduction in selling prices and hence in the return on investment. Furthermore, a business with an extraordinarily high return on investment will be exposed to charges that it is gouging the public which can lead to pressure—legal, political, and public—for price reduction. Thus, powerful forces work to keep return on investment within a range which can be designated as "satisfactory."

In order to earn a satisfactory return, revenues from the sale of goods and services must be large enough both to (1) recover all costs, and (2) earn a profit that is large enough to provide a satisfactory return on investment. The total amount of revenue is governed by the quantity of products sold and the unit selling price. One can usefully think of the selling price as consisting of two components: (1) an amount to recover costs, and (2) profit.

If a business makes a single product, the measurement of the cost of that product is simple. Thus, if a contractor agrees to build a house for a customer at "cost plus 10 percent," he can easily set up a record-keeping system that will measure the full cost of building the house, and the price of the house is found simply by adding 10 percent to that cost. If, however, a business handles a number of products, either manufacturing them or selling them, or both, the problem is much more difficult. It essentially is this: The business will prosper if *for all the products combined,* total sales revenues exceed total costs by a sufficiently large amount. But selling prices must be set separately *for each product.* How can this be done for *each* product so that a satisfactory profit is earned for *all* products?

The general answer to this question is that each product should bear a *fair share* of the total costs of the business. We can expand this statement to say that **in general the selling price of a product should be high** enough (1) to recover its direct costs, (2) to recover a fair share of all applicable indirect costs, and (3) to yield a satisfactory profit. Such a price is a **normal price.** Systems for assigning costs to products are set up so that a selling price that meets this criterion can be developed.

It must be understood that the foregoing is a statement of general tendency rather than a prescription for setting the selling price for each and every product. For a number of reasons to be discussed subsequently, the selling price of a given product is not set simply by ascertaining each of the components listed above and then adding them up. Nevertheless, the measurement of the cost of a product provides a starting point in an analysis of what the actual selling price should be.

ADJUSTMENT TO HISTORICAL COST

The problems of measuring product costs have been discussed in the preceding chapters. They are not repeated here, but one new element is introduced. The discussion in earlier chapters focused on the measurement of costs that actually *were* incurred, that is, on historical costs. If the purpose is to set selling prices for products that will be manufactured at some future time, the relevant costs are the costs that *will be* incurred at that time, not the costs that *were* incurred at some earlier time. Thus, in estimating costs for the purpose of arriving at selling prices, historical costs should be adjusted if it is believed that the costs that will be incurred to fill the future orders will be significantly different from the costs that have been incurred in the past. There are four principal reasons why future costs may not be the same as historical costs: (1) inflation, (2) volume, (3) productivity, and (4) specification changes. Each is discussed below.

Inflation. Since the United States, along with most countries of the world, seems to be in a more-or-less permanent condition of inflation, an allowance for this factor often needs to be made. In many situations, this can be done by increasing the historical full cost by an appropriate percentage. If different elements of cost are expected to increase at different rates of inflation, however, it may be necessary to make more detailed calculations. For example, one rate may be applied to the direct labor element and another rate to the direct material element.

> *EXAMPLE:* For a certain product, direct material costs are expected to increase 7 percent, direct labor costs 5 percent, and other costs 6 percent. The revised estimate of unit costs is calculated as follows:

	Current Unit Cost	*Adjustment for Inflation*	*Adjusted Unit Cost*
Direct material	$10.00	107%	$10.70
Direct labor	15.00	105	15.75
Other costs	20.00	106	21.20
Total unit cost	$45.00		$47.65

Volume. The importance of changes in volume on units costs has been mentioned in Chapter 3 and will be discussed in detail in Chapter 6. For present purposes, it is sufficient to call attention to the fact that fixed costs *per unit* vary inversely with changes in the level of activity.

> EXAMPLE: In the current year, for a certain product, fixed costs are estimated to be $120,000 in total, and 10,000 units are manufactured. The unit fixed cost is therefore $12. It is estimated that in the next year the dollar amount of fixed costs will be unchanged, but that 12,000 units will be manufactured. The fixed cost per unit is therefore estimated to be $10, a decrease of $2.

Productivity. More efficient methods of production are constantly being developed, and these reduce costs. This increase in productivity averages about 3 percent a year for all American industry, but there are wide variations among companies and among products within a single company. In order to estimate the effect of productivity changes, the *quantity* of resources used for the product must be recalculated and then converted to monetary terms at the estimated prices.

> EXAMPLE: If it is estimated that productivity gains will reduce the number of labor hours required per unit of product from 3.0 to 2.7, then there is a productivity gain of 10 percent. In estimating the labor cost, the 2.7 hours must be costed at the estimated future labor rate, which usually is higher than the current labor rate because of inflation.

Specification changes. The specifications of the product may be changed with a corresponding change in its cost. The estimated cost must be calculated on the basis of the revised specifications. The specifications for a 1975 Chevrolet two-door Impala differ from those of a 1974 model in dozens of ways; each of these must be taken into account in estimating the 1975 cost.

THE PROFIT COMPONENT OF PRICE

We now discuss the other component of price, the profit element. This is often called the *profit margin.* It is the amount added to costs, however they are measured, to arrive at the selling price.

The fact that an economic objective of a business earns a satisfactory return on assets employed suggests that logically the profit component of the selling price should be related to assets employed in making the product. Nevertheless, it is common pricing practice to relate the profit component of the price to costs rather than to the amount of assets employed.

In some situations, it is easy to establish a profit margin expressed as a percentage of cost in such a way that the resulting selling price will give a satisfactory return on assets employed. In general, this is the case

when all products have approximately the same unit cost and/or when
the assets employed by products vary proportionately with their cost.

> *EXAMPLE:* A retail shoe store decides that a satisfactory profit is a
> 15 percent return (before income taxes) on its investment. If its total
> investment in inventory, accounts receivable, and other assets is es-
> timated to be $200,000 then its profit must be $200,000 × 15 percent
> = $30,000 for the year. If its total operating costs, excluding the cost
> of the shoes, are estimated to be $70,000, then its selling prices must
> be such that the profit margin above the costs of the shoes comes out
> to $70,000 + $30,000 = $100,000. If the store expects to sell shoes
> that cost in total $300,000, then total sales revenue must be $400,000
> in order to obtain this $100,000. The store can obtain the desired
> $100,000 by setting a selling price that is 33⅓ percent above the cost
> of the shoes (source: $400,000 ÷ $300,000 = 133⅓ percent). This
> pricing policy would generate revenue of $400,000 for the year if the
> expected sales volume were realized, of which $300,000 would go for
> the cost of the shoes, $70,000 for operating costs, and $30,000 for
> profit. Shoe store owners customarily describe such a set of numbers
> as demonstrating that they make a profit of 7.5 percent on sales
> (= $30,000 ÷ $400,000), but what is more important is that it is a
> return of 15 percent on assets employed (= $30,000 ÷ $200,000).

Although setting the profit margin as a percentage of costs or of
selling price works satisfactorily if the assets employed for each product
are proportionate to the costs of each product, it breaks down if this
condition does not exist. Products, or companies, with a relatively low
asset turnover require a relatively high profit margin, as a percentage of
costs or of selling price, in order to earn a satisfactory return on assets
employed. (*Asset turnover* means revenues divided by assets employed.
If sales revenues are $2,000,000 and assets employed are $1,000,000,
then asset turnover is two times. Each dollar of assets employed is
said to "generate" two dollars of sales revenue.)

> *EXAMPLE 1:* Department stores discovered the importance of recog-
> nizing assets employed when they started in the 1940s and 1950s to
> sell "big ticket" items, such as television sets. Initially, they arrived at
> prices for television sets by adding the same percentage profit margin
> to cost as they customarily used for other products. At these prices,
> not many television sets were sold. Observing this situation, some in-
> novative people started a new kind of store—the discount house; they
> arrived at the price for television sets by using a significantly lower
> profit margin percentage. The discount houses quickly gained a large
> share of the television business; consequently, their inventory turn-
> over was much more rapid than that of the department stores. In-
> ventory was the largest single component of investment of assets em-
> ployed in both department stores and discount houses. The discount
> houses further reduced the amounts of assets employed by eliminating
> accounts receivable, that is, by requiring customers to pay cash. Dis-
> count houses therefore were able to earn a satisfactory return on assets

employed, even though their profit as a percentage of sales was much smaller than that of department stores. Department stores were forced to adjust their prices accordingly.

EXAMPLE 2: A company manufactures two products, A and B, the full cost of each being $6 per unit. If the company prices each product so that the profit is 50 percent of cost, the profit margin would be $3 per unit and the selling price would be $9 (= $6 + $3). If 100,000 units of each product were sold, the total profit would be $600,000 (= 200,000 units × $3). If, on the other hand, the company used return-on-investment pricing, it would first estimate the total amount of assets employed for the two products. Assume that this works out to $3 million, or $30 per unit, for Product A and $1 million, or $10 per unit, for Product B. If the company desires a 15 percent return on its investment, the profit margin would be $4.50 for Product A (= $30 × 15 percent) and $1.50 for Product B (= $10 × 15 percent), making the selling prices $10.50 and $7.50 respectively. These selling prices produce the same total profit, $600,000, as the prices calculated at a 50 percent profit on cost. The $10.50 and $7.50 prices are more equitable than the $9 price since they reflect the fact that more assets are required to make a unit of Product A than a unit of Product B.

EXAMPLE 3: The General Accounting Office and others have recommended that profits on Defense contracts should be calculated on the basis of assets employed rather than as a percentage of cost, and experiments with such a method were begun in 1973. The rationale is suggested by the following: Assume two contractors, each with a contract that specifies that a certain product be manufactured with an estimated cost of $1,000,000. Under previous Department of Defense contracting practice, each contractor would be allowed a profit of approximately 7 percent of estimated cost, or $70,000. If Contractor A had assets employed of $500,000 (which is about average for manufactured products costing $1,000,000), his $70,000 profit would be a return of 14 percent on assets employed. If Contractor B, because he used government-owned fixed assets, or because he leased assets rather than owning them, or because he received progress payments which reduced the funds tied up in inventory, or for other reasons, had assets employed of only $200,000 (and such cases are by no means rare), his profit of $70,000 would be a return of 35 percent on his assets employed. It is difficult to justify this difference in return on equitable grounds. If different products require different amounts of assets, the profit margin should reflect this fact.

Assigning assets employed to products involves essentially the same techniques as assigning costs to products. These techniques are not described in detail here. Until fairly recently, it was widely believed that the accounting effort required to assign assets employed to products was so great and the results so unreliable that the effort was not worthwhile, but it is now recognized that practical ways of doing this are not so difficult as had been believed.

Specific
pricing
practices

GROSS MARGIN PRICING

Retailers, wholesalers, distributors, and other companies that sell but do not manufacture products tend to set selling prices at a certain percentage above the cost of individual products. This percentage is called the **mark-on percentage**.[1] Although applied to cost, there is a mathematical relationship between the mark-on percentage and the **gross margin percentage** which is the margin expressed as a percentage of sales revenue.[2] As indicated in the example of the shoe store given above, this mark-on is intended both to cover the operating costs of the business and also to provide a satisfactory return on assets employed. Operating costs and the amount of assets employed vary greatly in different types of trading companies, and there is a corresponding variation in their mark-ons. The higher the asset turnover and the lower the operating cost per dollar of sales, the smaller the mark-on needs to be in order to produce a satisfactory return on assets employed.

> *EXAMPLE 1:* A food retailer that provides delivery service and personalized service to customers, that carries a relatively large inventory, and that has charge accounts that are outstanding for a month or two, requires a relatively high mark-on. By contrast, a supermarket that has no delivery service and hence a lower operating cost per sales dollar, that has a relatively small inventory in relation to sales, and that has no assets tied up in accounts receivable, and hence a high asset turnover, requires a relatively low mark-on.

> *EXAMPLE 2:* The typical wholesaler's sales volume per salesman is much higher than that of the typical retailer so the wholesaler can make the same return on assets employed as the retailer with a much lower mark-on. The distributor, who carries no inventory, has relatively a small amount of assets per dollar of sales, and thus requires a lower mark-on than either the wholesaler or the retailer.

Differences in operating costs per sales dollar and in asset turnover are two important reasons for differences in mark-ons and in gross margin percentages in businesses of various types. There are others. Products with high risks tend to have high profit margins. For example, the margins on women's fashion apparel are relatively high because of the risk that if the merchandise cannot be sold during a given season, it will become obsolete. Moreover, individual businesses will have margins that differ from the average in their industry because of differences in management skill, in public acceptance, or in similar factors.

---

[1] The use of "mark-on" and "markup" in practice is confusing. Some people use "mark-on" and/or "markup" to mean the percentage of profit to *selling price,* rather than to cost, as defined above. In this text, *gross margin percentage* is used to refer to the percentage of profit to selling price.

[2] The gross margin percentage can be converted to a mark-on by dividing it by 100 minus the gross margin percentage. For example, if the gross margin percentage is 25, the mark-on percentage is $25 \div (100 - 25) = 33\frac{1}{3}$. The mark-on is always larger than the gross margin percentage.

Thus, at best, the factors influencing margins are tendencies; they do not give rise to formulas that permit precise calculations. Management judgment must be used in arriving at them.

DIRECT COST PRICING

Some manufacturing businesses set selling prices at **a certain percentage above the direct costs incurred in manufacturing their products;** this is called **direct cost pricing.** Such a pricing policy is similar to the use of a uniform gross margin percentage by retailers and other merchandising companies. It is a sensible policy when the same general conditions exist as those in merchandising companies that use this policy, namely, when the amount of indirect costs that equitably should be borne by each product are substantially the same percentage of direct costs, and when the assets employed in each product are also substantially similar. When these conditions do not exist, the practice of setting selling prices as a certain percentage above direct cost can have unsatisfactory results. One reason why this practice is followed is that the allocation of indirect costs to products involves judgment, and some businessmen believe that the results are not sufficiently valid to be useful in making decisions on selling prices. They prefer to base pricing decisions on direct costs because these costs can be measured with a high degree of accuracy.

EXAMPLE 1: In a certain company, the indirect costs of all products were 80 percent of direct costs. The company desired a profit equal to 10 percent of total cost. It could arrive at its selling price in either of two ways:

	A *Full Costing*	*B* *Direct Costing*
Direct costs.	$ 6.00	$ 6.00
Indirect costs.	4.80	
Total cost.	$10.80	
Mark-on.	1.08	5.88
Price.	$11.88	$11.88

Under the full cost method (A), its costs as shown by its cost accounting system would be the sum of its direct and indirect costs, $10.80. A mark-on of 10 percent added to this is $1.08, making the price $11.88. Under the direct cost method (B), the company finds what mark-on percentage is required to cover indirect costs plus the desired 10 percent profit. Since indirect costs are 80 percent of direct costs, this percentage is the same for all products. It turns out to be 98 percent.[3] It applies this to the direct cost, and arrives at the same price, $11.88, as that obtained by using the full cost method.

---

[3] The markon percentage $= 80\% + 10\% + (10\% \times 80\%) = 98\%$. The third term in this equation reflects the fact that the company wants a 10 percent profit on the 80 percent of costs that are indirect.

EXAMPLE 2: Product A is made on expensive machine tools while Product B requires only assembly labor. Unless Product A is sold at a higher mark-on above direct cost than Product B, its selling price will not recover the high costs associated with the use of these machine tools. If each product is sold at the same mark-on above direct costs, customers who buy Product B can complain, with justification, that they are required to help pay for costs that are actually attributable to Product A.

EXAMPLE 3: A television set manufacturer manufactured its own picture tubes. Its direct material and direct labor costs were $100 per television set (of which $25 was direct material and direct labor for the picture tube). The company arrived at a selling price by adding a mark-on of 150 percent to its direct costs for the television set; the selling price was therefore $100 + $150 = $250. It made a satisfactory profit at this $250 price. If the manufacturer should decide to purchase the complete picture tube for $75 (which was an increase of $50 above its direct costs of manufacturing the picture tube), its direct costs would increase to $150; and if it used the same 150 percent mark-on, its selling price for the television sets would increase to $375. Presumably, the decision to purchase the picture tube was made in the belief that purchasing would lower, not increase, the total costs of making the set. Certainly, nothing has happened that justifies a higher price for the completed set. A uniform mark-on above direct costs is *not* appropriate in these circumstances.

It can be argued that direct cost pricing gives satisfactory results, even when the cost characteristics of the products are different, because the differences in margin will offset one another and the company overall will make a satisfactory profit—"what we lose on the bananas, we make up on the oranges." There are two weaknesses in this argument. First, the differences will balance out only if the sales quantities of each product are in the same proportion as was originally contemplated when the prices were set. If a higher proportion of the high-cost products and a lower proportion of the low-cost products are sold, the company overall will earn less total profit than it estimated. Second, the differences may produce peculiar results in the marketplace. Some products will be sold for a price that is lower than reasonably can be justified, and profits on these products will be inadequate; other products will have a price that is higher than is justified by their cost, so business will be lost to competitors who price so as to earn only a satisfactory return on such products.

FULL COST PRICING

As the above examples illustrate, when the amount of indirect cost that is appropriately assignable to a product varies from one product to another, problems are likely to arise unless these differences are taken into account in arriving at selling prices. The methods of collecting indirect costs and of allocating them to products as described in the preceding chapters are intended to overcome these difficulties. They allocate to each product an equitable share of all the elements of cost incurred in the company. Because these costs are indirect, there is by definition no way of proving that the amounts so allocated are exactly the "right" amount of cost. Nevertheless, use of procedures that allocate costs to products according to the criteria discussed in Chapters 3 and 4 does assure that the recorded cost of the product is reasonable, and a selling price based on this cost should be a reasonable price.

TIME AND MATERIAL PRICING

In the preceding discussion, it was assumed that selling prices were arrived at by first calculating costs and then adding an allowance for profit. An alternative approach is called **time and material pricing. In this method one pricing rate is established for direct labor and a separate pricing rate for direct material. Each of these rates is constructed so that it includes allowances for indirect costs and for profit.** This method of pricing is used in automobile garages, in job printing shops, in television repair shops, and in similar types of service establishments. It is also used by many professional persons and professional organizations, including physicians, lawyers, engineers, ski instructors, consultants of various types, and public accounting firms.

In time and material pricing the **time** component is expressed as a labor rate per hour, which is calculated as the sum of (1) direct salary and fringe benefit costs of the employee; (2) an equitable share of all indirect costs, except those related to material; and (3) an allowance for profit. The material component includes a **material loading** which is added to the invoice cost of parts and other material used on the job. This loading consists of an allowance for material handling costs and storage costs plus an allowance for profit. The loading might well be approximately 20 percent to 40 percent of the invoice cost of the materials.

With such a pricing method, it is possible to arrive at a price for the job that is reasonably equitable because it is related to the amount of labor and the amount of material actually used on the job; moreover, the price of the job is easily calculated, and the calculation does not reveal the profit margin to the customer. Because of differences in indirect costs or in the amount of assets employed, this method may not be entirely equitable to the customer under all circumstances. The inequities can be reduced if special charges are made for those jobs that require more than an average amount of indirect costs. For example, if an expensive engine analyzer were used on a automobile repair job, a special charge might be made for this equipment, over and above the usual time and material charges.

The time component of the time and material charge may be calculated on a machine-hour basis rather than on a labor-hour basis. A machine-hour basis is generally used in printing shops, for example, because there is a substantial difference in the costs of using the various types of presses and other printing equipment. An hourly rate is built up for each type of equipment, in a manner similar to that described above for labor, and each job that uses the equipment is charged at the appropriate hourly rate.

ADJUSTING COSTS TO PRICES

Pricing, quite naturally, is usually thought of as the process of arriving at selling prices. There are some situations in which the process works in reverse; that is, the selling price that must be charged in order to meet competition is taken as a given; the problem then is to determine how much cost the company can afford to incur if it is to earn a satisfactory profit at the given price. In the apparel business, for example, it is customary to use discrete price points—$19.75, $29.75, $39.75, and so on. The manufacturer designs individual garments to "fit" one of these price points. In order to insure that the company makes a satisfactory profit on a garment, the selling price is taken as a given, and the company calculates how much it can afford to spend on cloth, on labor, and on other elements of cost and still have a satisfactory profit margin. If an acceptable product cannot be manufactured at the assumed price, then either the proposed item is dropped from the line or the calculations are redone, taking the next higher price point as the given.

When a manufacturer contemplates making a product which competitors have already introduced and which has become well established in the market, at a price that consumers are accustomed to, he knows that it is prudent to start with this market price as a given. He calculates whether his costs are such that he can make a satisfactory profit at that price. If the results of such a calculation are disappointing, he either attempts to redesign the product so that its costs are lower or he drops the project. Occasionally, he may decide to market the product at a price that is higher than that charged by competitors, but this is a risky course of action; he must persuade consumers that some difference in the product justifies the higher price.

The foregoing type of analysis is used for many products with a mass market and a customary selling price, such as television and radio sets, most types of household appliances, clothing, branded foods, household furnishings, office supplies, office equipment, and general-purpose factory equipment.

PRICE REGULATIONS

The Robinson-Patman Amendment to the Clayton Antitrust Act prohibits differentials in the prices charged competing customers unless these differentials "make due allowance for differences in the cost of manufacture, sale, or delivery resulting from the differing methods or quantities in which commodities are to such purchasers sold or delivered." The courts have interpreted these "due allowances" as related to full costs (i.e., the sum of direct costs and applicable indirect costs) rather than to direct costs alone. This is another reason why it is advisable to calculate both the direct and the indirect costs attributable to products and to base prices on such calculations. Similarly, many states prohibit the sale of certain products or services below cost, with "cost" either specified as, or interpreted as meaning, full cost. For income tax purposes, certain transactions between a company and its affiliates must be handled at prices that are based on full cost.

PRICING STRATEGY

The foregoing discussion has emphasized the role of costs in arriving at selling prices. It would be unfortunate if the reader were left with the impression that pricing consists of the mechanical task of adding up the costs and tacking on a profit margin. Actually, many companies have no pricing problem. A market price exists, customers will not pay more than this price, and there is no reason why the product should be sold at a lower price. Wheat and other products traded on commodity markets are the classic examples, but the situation also exists for companies in many other industries, such as small companies in industries where one or a few large companies exercise price leadership. Under such circumstances, a company makes no pricing calculations; it simply charges the market price.

If a company does have the problem of determining its selling prices, **cost information at best provides a first approximation to the selling price.** The price arrived at by the methods described above is often described as a **target price.** It is important information, but by no means is it the only information used in the final pricing decision. The selling price is one of the tactics used in marketing a product.

The whole marketing problem can be visualized in terms of a football game. Each team wants to win, and each has a set of offensive and defensive plays designed to achieve this objective. Each uses these plays at various times according to its perception of the strengths and weaknesses of the opposing team. The situation in business is roughly similar, but much more complicated because there are more than two teams, there are more variables in the environment, and the "plays" occur in much larger time and space dimensions than the 60 minutes and 100 yards of a football game. In its struggle to attain its profit objective, each company competes with a number of other companies. It attempts both to take business away from competitors and to expand the total amount of business in the industry. It has a number of tactics or plays to use in this struggle—advertising, other promotional activities, salesmen, the product itself, its packaging, and the selling price.[4]

The selling price, therefore, is one tactical device in the competitive game. It can be varied in either direction—lowered in an effort to take business away from competitors, or raised in the hope that additional profits will be generated without undue loss of volume. Marketing managers use all the tactical devices, not just one. The selling price is, of course, an important one; and the manager needs information about the cost components of each product as a basis for making the pricing decision.

Adjustments to the target price. What does the marketing expert do with the first approximation that is given by the cost calculations? For one thing, he realizes that the target prices are averages, and that prices on individual products might well deviate from the average. In a typical family of products, some are "big brothers," some are average, and some are "weak sisters." The big brothers earn a higher-than-average profit margin. The weak sisters earn a below-average profit margin but they are carried in the line because customers expect the company to supply them, and they might take all their business elsewhere if this were not done or for other reasons. The marketing expert has to decide on the basis of what he knows about the market, whether a product can be sold at "big brother" prices, whether the profit margin on current "weak sisters" can be increased either by raising the price or by decreasing the cost, or whether the product is really needed in the line. Thus, his analysis does not focus on a single product; rather, he considers a whole product line, and he realizes that the total profit on the product line will be satisfactory if there are enough big brothers and not too many weak sisters.

Moreover, the marketing expert is not thinking solely about the selling price. It is the *difference* between selling price and cost that is important. In many circumstances, instead of raising selling prices, this difference can best be widened by redesigning the product or by reducing costs in other ways.

In making decisions about whether or not to discontinue an existing product, similar considerations normally govern. A new product is normally added to the line only if it is expected to produce a satisfactory return on the assets employed in making it. If an existing product has a low profit margin, and if the situation cannot be corrected by increasing prices or reducing costs, then the product normally is replaced with a more profitable one. Again, marketing considerations may dictate departures from the normal procedure. Many low-margin products are retained so that the company may offer its customers a full line; equipment may be sold at a low margin in order to induce the sale of high-

---

[4] For a more complete discussion, see Joe S. Bain, *Price Theory* (New York: Holt, Rhinehart & Winston, Inc., 1963).

margin accessories and supplies;[5] no replacement product with an adequate margin may be available; and so on.

CONTRIBUTION PRICING

In the situations described above, the company makes pricing decisions with information on full costs as a first approximation. There are other situations in which individual products may be sold at a loss, that is, at a price that is below full costs. Even though these products are sold at a loss, under certain conditions they may increase the company's total profit. These are special situations, and they require special cost constructions. The approach is called contribution pricing, and it is described in Chapter 7.

Analysis of profitability

In *Fundamentals of Financial Accounting* we discuss ratios and other techniques that are useful in analyzing the profitability of an entire business. Cost accounting makes it possible to make similar analyses of individual segments of a business. Such a segment might be an individual product, a product line (which is a family of related products), a plant, a division, a sales territory, or any other subdivision of the whole business that is of interest. Using the principles of cost accounting, the direct costs and an appropriate share of the indirect costs of the segment being reviewed can be determined. If the segment does not earn a reasonable profit, that is, if the revenue generated by this segment does not exceed these costs by an amount that represents a reasonable return on assets employed, there is an indication that something is wrong.

In the short run, a product, a division, or other segment of a business generally can be tolerated if its revenues at least exceed its out-of-pocket costs, but any part of the business which does not earn a satisfactory return on assets employed is not healthy, and consideration should be given to shifting the investment to a more attractive use. Techniques for pinpointing the cause of the unsatisfactory situation are discussed in Chapter 14.

Summary

Information on the full cost of products and services is used—

1. In financial accounting, to derive certain balance sheet and income statement amounts and to derive income by "lines of business" or segments.
2. To answer the question, "What did X cost?" This question is asked in many contexts. Of particular interest is the fact that many con-

---

[5] A company cannot *compel* its customers to buy its own accessories and supplies. Such "tie-in" agreements are illegal.

tracts require that the buyer pay the seller either full cost or full cost plus a stipulated profit.

3. As a basis for setting regulated prices.
4. As a first approximation in deciding on selling prices under normal circumstances.
5. To measure the profitability of products, divisions, plants, or other segments of a business, so as to facilitate an analysis of the operations of these segments.

Of these uses, our attention was focused primarily on full cost pricing decisions. The usual practice is to compute a target price by adding a profit margin to the full costs of the product. The profit margin is figured either as a percentage of cost or, preferably, as a percentage return on the assets employed in making the product. This target price is modified to take into account the strength of competition, the necessity of fitting the price into customary price lines (such as $19.75 dresses), and many other marketing considerations. Consequently, actual prices, and hence actual profit margins on specific products, may differ widely from the cost-based first approximation. The intent is, however, that the desired profit will be obtained, on the average, with extra profits on high-margin products offsetting thin profits on low-margin products.

Adjustments to this first approximation may take the form of changing costs as well as changing profit margins. If it is thought that the computed price is too high, then the product may be redesigned to bring its cost down so that a satisfactory profit can be made at the attainable price.

Appendix   THE ECONOMISTS' APPROACH TO PRICING

Students who have had a first course in economics will probably have noticed that the description of pricing in this chapter differs substantially from what they have read in their introductory economics text. They therefore justifiably can ask for a reconciliation of these different points of view. The purpose of this appendix is to provide such an explanation.

PRICING IN ECONOMICS

The description of pricing in the standard economics text is essentially stated in terms of "the law of supply and demand." The *demand* for a product is determined by how many customers want to buy it. For most products, it is reasonable to expect that the lower the price, the more people will want to buy it. This can be expressed graphically as in Exhibit 5–2, which is called a demand curve; it is nothing more than a graphic representation of the statement made above—the lower the price, the more units will be sold.

The *supply* part of the law refers to the product's cost. A supply curve is given in Exhibit 5–3. It reflects the fact that unit costs decrease

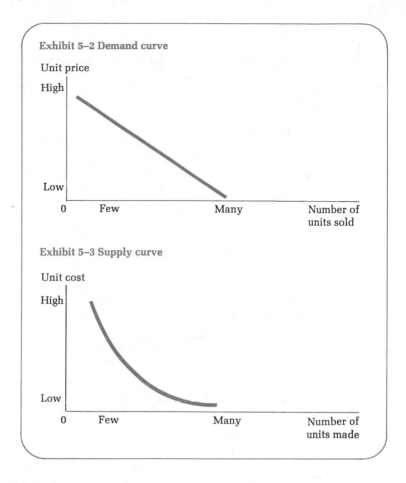

Exhibit 5–2 Demand curve

Unit price

High

Low

0   Few   Many   Number of
units sold

Exhibit 5–3 Supply curve

Unit cost

High

Low

0   Few   Many   Number of
units made

as volume increases. This is because the fixed costs of the company are spread over more and more units as volume increases. The rationale for the supply curve can be seen from the following table, which shows what happens to unit costs when fixed costs are $50,000 per month, variable costs are $100 per unit, and volume increases from 500 units to 2,000 units. Unit costs for various quantities would be as follows:

Quantity (Units)	Fixed Cost Total	Fixed Cost Per Unit	Variable Cost Total	Variable Cost Per Unit	Total Cost	Unit Cost
500	$50,000	$100	$ 50,000	$100	$100,000	$200
1,000	50,000	50	100,000	100	150,000	150
1,500	50,000	33	150,000	100	200,000	133
2,000	50,000	25	200,000	100	250,000	125

In Exhibit 5–4, these general notions of supply and demand are applied to a specific situation. It is assumed, as above, that a company

Exhibit 5–4

Pricing analysis

Unit Selling Price	*Estimated Quantity Sold*	*Total Revenue*	*Fixed Cost*	*Variable Cost (at $100 per unit)*	*Total Cost*	*Profit*
$250	500	$125,000	$50,000	$ 50,000	$100,000	$25,000
200	1,000	200,000	50,000	100,000	150,000	50,000*
150	1,500	225,000	50,000	150,000	200,000	25,000
125	2,000	250,000	50,000	200,000	250,000	0

* Preferred alternative.

has fixed costs of $50,000, regardless of volume. Column 1 shows various alternative selling prices, and Column 2 shows the estimated quantity that will be sold at each selling price. The quantity sold increases as the selling price decreases, in accordance with the law of demand. The next column shows the revenue earned at each selling price, which is the quantity sold at that price multiplied by the unit selling price. The next three columns show the costs estimated to be incurred for each quantity; they are the same as those calculated above. The final column shows the profit, which is the difference between revenue and cost. Clearly, $200 is the best selling price, for at that price profit is $50,000, which is higher than the profit at either a higher or a lower price.

This illustration suggests a general rule, namely, that the way to arrive at selling price is to estimate revenue and costs at several possible selling prices and select that price at which the difference between revenue and costs is the largest. This differs from the approach described in the text of this chapter in that the cost calculations given there were based on a single estimate of quantity sold, rather than on estimates of costs for each of several different quantities.

Another difference between the economics and the cost accounting approaches is implicit in Exhibit 5–4. Observe that the fixed costs are a constant; they are $50,000 at each level of volume. They therefore could be eliminated from the calculation without changing the result. A selling price of $200 per unit produces the highest profit, whether profit is measured as the difference between revenue and total cost or as the difference between revenue and variable cost.

MARGINAL COSTS AND MARGINAL REVENUE

The preceding analysis was stated in terms of total costs and total revenue. Economists build up a similar argument in terms of marginal cost and marginal revenue. The marginal cost is the cost of making one additional unit beyond that currently being manufactured; it is essen-

true only if perfect comp.

tially the same as the variable cost of that unit. Marginal revenue is the selling price of that additional unit. (*true only when m a A = a = price*)

The rule advocated in introductory economics texts is that a company should sell an additional unit at any price that exceeds its marginal cost. Using the preceding example, in which variable costs are $100 per unit, it is said that if the company can sell an additional unit at $101, it should do so; for it will incur additional costs of $100, will earn additional revenue of $101, and therefore will add $1 to profits.

DIFFERENCES BETWEEN ECONOMICS AND ACCOUNTING

The approach advocated in economics therefore differs from that in accounting in two respects:

1. The economist recommends that revenues and costs be estimated for a number of possible levels of volume, whereas accounting calculations of full cost are usually based on a single volume estimate.

2. The economist pays no attention to fixed costs. In the calculation of profit at various volumes, fixed costs are disregarded since they are constant and hence do not affect the final result. In the marginal cost/ marginal revenue approach, fixed costs are also excluded. In accounting the emphasis is on full costs which include an appropriate share of fixed costs. Introductory economics texts specifically reject the whole procedure of allocating indirect costs to products as described in Chapters 3 and 4 as being irrelevant and unnecessary.

If the economics analysis is appropriate for real-life pricing problems, the student has indeed wasted his time in learning the procedures for collecting and allocating indirect costs as described in preceding chapters. Obviously, we did not believe this to be the case. In the real world full costs are useful as a basis for pricing decisions, and learning how to measure full costs is therefore *not* a waste of time.

KNOWLEDGE OF SUPPLY AND DEMAND

Perhaps the best way to reconcile the economics approach and the accounting approach is to say that economics describes certain general tendencies, whereas accounting focuses on specific situations. If the law of supply and demand is to be applied in a specific situation, management must be able to make numerical estimates of the shape of the supply curve and that of the demand curve. Economics assumes that these estimates can be made, but this assumption is unrealistic in most real-world situations.

Management usually can estimate the supply curve with tolerable accuracy, that is, it knows reasonably well what costs will be incurred at various volume levels. There are, however, only a few situations in which management can estimate the *demand* curve, that is, the quantity of products that will be sold at each of the possible unit prices. Indeed, we know of no principles of economics text that gives even one real-world example of a demand curve.

To illustrate the difficulty of estimating the demand curve, consider the Chevrolet Division of General Motors Corporation. The annual pricing decision on Chevrolet automobiles involves millions of dollars of profits. If it were possible to obtain a reliable estimate on the number of Chevrolets that would be sold at various prices, General Motors management would certainly spare no expense in doing so. But General Motors does not decide on the Chevrolet price by an analysis like that recommended by the economists. Instead, it builds up full costs by methods similar to those described in the context of this book, and it adds a profit margin to these costs in order to arrive at a target price. It uses this approach because it cannot estimate what the demand schedule is for automobiles in general; and more importantly, it cannot estimate the demand schedule for Chevrolets, as one of many automobiles, because it does not know how the other automobile manufacturers will style or price their products, and these styles and prices affect the number of Chevrolets that will be sold relative to other automobiles.

If the manufacturer of Chevrolets, an established product, cannot use the approach advocated by the economists, how much less likely it is that other manufacturers can do so? Who can estimate what quantity of product will be sold at one price, let alone at a wide range of prices? Indeed, the difficulty is so great that few companies ever attempt to estimate a demand schedule, and few managers have ever even seen one. Without a demand schedule, the diagrams and equations that economists have built up cannot be used to solve real-world pricing problems.

OTHER ASSUMPTIONS

The assumption that management can estimate demand is the most important limitation on application of the law of supply and demand to real-world problems. Several other assumptions implicit in the law are also rarely found in the real world. Some are mentioned below.

The economic analysis usually assumes that the firm produces only one product; thus, if production facilities are not used for that product, they will be idle. In actual practice, most firms make a variety of products; if facilities are committed to one product, the same facilities cannot be used to manufacture other products. Indirect costs are, in a sense, a measure of the sacrifice involved in using facilities for one product rather than for another. They are therefore a genuine cost of that product and should not be disregarded.

The economic analysis assumes that the consumer's decision to buy a product is primarily influenced by its price. Actually, as we have seen, price is but one of several elements in a total marketing strategy. Advertising, sales promotion efforts, channels of distribution, salespersons' tactics, and the characteristics of the product itself (quality, style, etc.) are other elements that management can make decisions about. Price is rarely the only variable in the market equation, and often it is not the most important.

The economic analysis assumes that changes in price do not cause retaliation by competitors. In the real world, competitors often meet the new price, and the quantity sold by one firm is therefore relatively unaffected.

The economic analysis assumes that changes in cost and demand conditions occur infrequently, so that the picture will "hold still" while an analysis of supply and demand is made and the resulting pricing decision is implemented. In the real world, all elements of the problem are likely to be fluid.

In summary, the marginal cost/marginal revenue principle works only if businessmen are clairvoyant. In the real world, a businessman does not know what will happen if he sells one additional unit at a price that is only $1 above its marginal cost. Perhaps this sale will have repercussions on the price at which other units are sold so that on balance his total profit is decreased rather than increased. Perhaps he actually could sell the additional unit for much more than that marginal dollar if he tried hard enough to do so. Perhaps he could use the same manufacturing capacity for another product on which a satisfactory profit can be earned.

The marginal approach also leads to the rule: "Price as high as you can above marginal cost." Since no businessman would think of selling at a price that is less than marginal cost, this rule reduces to "price as high as you can, period." Such a rule has two defects. First, it doesn't provide much in the way of guidance to management. How high is high? Secondly, it can lead to behavior that society is increasingly unwilling to tolerate: gouging the customer and taking advantage of unusual circumstances. (Should a garage triple its towing charges on a snowy night just because the demand is high?)

Clearly, if the marginal principle of pricing were applied to normal pricing problems, the company would have no assurance that its prices were high enough to cover *all* its costs and provide a satisfactory profit as well. There are special situations in which this approach is applicable, however. These situations are discussed in Chapter 7.

RATIONALE FOR THE ECONOMISTS' APPROACH

If the economists' approach doesn't work in the real world, why do economists describe it in their introductory texts? There are two excellent reasons for doing so. First, the law of supply and demand is perfectly valid as a general tendency, and it is important that the student understand this law and its implications. Secondly, this approach permits the use of rigorous analysis which is useful in developing the intellectual capacity of students. If one accepts the idea that a demand curve can be found, then sophisticated reasoning can be applied to the pricing problem. Economists believe that students should be challenged to develop such reasoning power. (For similar reasons, physics teachers sometimes ask their students to think about a world in which gravity is 10 times the force of earth gravity, or a world in which there is no mechanical friction.) These are useful intellectual exercises, provided the student realize that the conclusions developed from them are rarely applicable in specific real-world situations.

A few economists attempt to justify the fact that their approach to pricing differs from actual business practice on other grounds, namely that businessmen are ignorant and do not price the way they should. This argument is becoming increasingly difficult to sustain. Many managers have studied economics. The reason that they do not apply the principles stated in their introductory economics text is clearly *not* that they are ignorant; it means that they have found that the approach described in the text does not work in the real world.

Most economists understand this fact, and most texts caution the student about the practical difficulty of applying the techniques of economic analysis to real-world pricing problems. In his efforts to master the techniques, the student unfortunately often overlooks, or forgets, the caution.

Important terms	Line of business	Gross margin percentage
	Normal price	**Direct cost pricing**
	Profit margin	**Time and material pricing**
	Asset turnover	**Material loading**
	Mark-on percentage	**Target price**

Questions for discussion		
	1.	If you were asked to calculate the full cost of undergraduate education in a certain college or university, what items of cost would you include?
	2.	Does the full cost of the Vietnam War include the pensions that will be paid at some future time to members of the Armed Forces who served during the war? Explain.
	3.	The federal government agrees to pay to the states 90 percent of the full cost of certain highway construction. Should the full cost include the salaries of state engineers who design the highways? Explain.
	4.	The text uses "return on assets employed" and "return on investment" interchangeably. Explain why these terms have the same meaning. (Hint: You should recall the discussion in *Fundamentals of Financial Accounting*, particularly the relationship between assets and investments on a balance sheet.)

5. The principal determinants of the total profit of a business are (1) selling price per unit, (2) cost per unit, and (3) one other factor. What is that other factor? Why is it important?

6. Consider a passenger automobile, such as a Ford Galaxy. In deciding on next year's selling prices, what types of adjustment to last year's costs should management take into account?

7. The example on page 128 describes how a retail shoe store can set selling prices so as to earn a 15 percent return on assets employed. Explain this procedure in your own words.

8. Is the normal profit margin percentage that a retailer uses for setting the selling price of fine watches higher than that used by a super-market in setting the selling price for cornflakes? List the factors that explain the difference.

9. Why is the mark-on percentage for a given item always higher than the gross margin percentage?

10. Some supermarkets vary their profit margin percentage according to the number of square feet of shelf space that a given item occupies. What is the rationale for this approach? Do you agree with this rationale?

11. Explain the difference between direct cost pricing and full cost pricing.

12. Under what circumstances will a pricing policy of charging the same mark-on above direct costs for all products lead to unsatisfactory results?

13. In time and material pricing, a profit is included both in the time component and also in the material component. Does this mean that profits are double counted? Explain.

14. A shoe manufacturer is designing a new style of shoes to sell at $17 a pair. His estimates show that costs of the contemplated design will not produce a satisfactory profit at this price. What types of action should he consider?

Problems   5–1.   Conrad owns a taxicab, which is operated 112 hours a week. He agrees to rent it to Werner for use 56 hours a week, with costs to be shared equitably. Costs for the first year were as follows:

Registration	$ 800
Depreciation	2,000
Gasoline and oil	1,500
Tires (changed every 25,000 miles)	600
Routine maintenance (every month)	1,000

During the year Conrad drove the taxicab 30,000 miles and Werner 20,000. All the above costs were paid by Conrad. In addition, Werner paid $25 for his operator's license. In addition to his share of the cost, Werner agreed to pay 10 percent of cost to Conrad.

Required:

How much does Werner owe Conrad?

5–2. Truro Company manufactures a number of products. In 1974 the selling price of Product A, whose sales are normally 10,000 units per year, was calculated as follows:

	Unit Costs Product A
Direct material................................	$ 2.00
Direct labor.....................................	4.00
Factory indirect................................	3.00
General and administrative.......................	2.00
Total unit cost............................	$11.00
Profit (10 percent).............................	1.10
Selling price....................................	$12.10

In 1975 the company estimates that direct material cost and direct labor costs will increase by 5 percent. It estimates that factory indirect costs will increase by $5,000 and that general and administrative costs will remain unchanged.

Required:

What is the target selling price for Product A in 1975?

5–3. Fred and John are brothers. Fred operates a grocery store and John operates a jewelry store. Each brother has $50,000 invested in assets. Fred maintains that John must have a higher return on his assets and therefore be more profitable because jewelry stores have a higher profit margin than his grocery store which has a 1 percent margin. John maintains that his return on sales is higher at 5 percent than Fred's, but that since John had only $100,000 of sales compared to Fred's $500,000 per year, that Fred must be more profitable.

Required:

Comment on the above arguments, and support your comments with appropriate calculations.

5–4. Mary Martin is considering investing in a business, and has narrowed the choice to two possibilities, A and B, with the following characteristics for first year's operations:

	Business A	*Business B*
Investment required..................	$ 50,000	$ 25,000
Sales revenue........................	150,000	100,000
Income before tax....................	4,000	2,500

Required:

1. Compute the asset turnover, percentage return on sales, and return on investment for each business.
2. Disregarding other considerations, which of these businesses is the better investment?

5–5. The Smith Company has introduced two new products to its line. A sales manager has been assigned to each product. The results of operations for the first year these two products were on the market were as follows:

	Product A	Product B
Assets employed.....................	$200,000	$1,200,000
Net income........................	30,000	180,000
Return on sales.....................	5%	20%

Required:

Which sales manager is doing the better job? Comment.

5–6. Hallow Manufacturing Company makes a line of brooms and brushes. The following data relate to the production and sale of floor brush No. 826:

Sales per year—500,000 units @ $0.55 each
Direct costs per brush—$0.30
Other costs, per year—$100,000
Total assets employed—$100,000

Required:

1. How much income does the sale of brush No. 826 generate for the company?
2. How many brushes must be sold to earn a 10 percent return before tax on assets?

5–7. Bright, Inc., manufactures furniture polishes and cleaners. The following data relate to the production and sale of Shine, a large seller:

Sales per year—250,000 cans @ $1.10 each
Direct costs—$0.60 per unit
Other costs—$105,000
Total assets employed—$125,000

Required:

1. Compute the income which Shine generates for the company.
2. How many cans of Shine must be sold to earn a 10 percent return on assets before taxes?

5–8. Trevor Company and Margill Company make similar snowblowers. Each sells 100,000 per year. Their unit costs are as follows:

	Unit Costs	
	Trevor	*Margill*
Direct material..........................	$16	$52
Direct labor............................	32	12
Indirect costs..........................	24	8
Total unit costs...................	$72	$72

These costs reflect the fact that Trevor manufactures most of the components of the snowblower while Margill purchases components from other manufacturers and merely assembles them.

Required:

1. If each company's pricing policy was to charge direct cost plus 80 percent, what would the target price of each snowblower be?
2. If each company's pricing policy was to charge full cost plus 20 percent, what would the target price of each snowblower be?
3. Discuss the relative merits of each pricing policy.

5–9. Kendall Company services television sets. It charges customers on a time and material basis. It has three employees, who earn $9,000 per year each and who spend 1,000 hours per year each on service calls. It sells annually parts that have a purchase cost of $20,000 per year. Other costs are $13,000 per year, of which $9,000 is allocated to labor and $4,000 to parts. The company has a target profit of $10,000 per year. It desires to make the same profit margin percentage on labor as on parts.

Required:

1. How much should the company charge for labor?
2. What mark-on percentage should it apply to the purchase cost of parts?

5–10. Kendex Company manufactures two products, A and B. It expects to sell approximately 1,000 units of each product next year. Estimated unit costs are as follows:

	Costs per Unit	
	Product A	Product B
Cost of goods sold.	$60	$40
Direct marketing costs.	10	10
Total direct costs.	$70	$50
Indirect costs.	20	10
Total costs.	$90	$60

The controller estimates that $100 of assets are employed in connection with one unit of Product A annually, and that $200 of assets are employed on one unit of Product B. Income taxes are to be disregarded. The company estimates that a reasonable and attainable rate of profit is 10 percent on assets employed.

Required:

1. How much total profit does the company need to earn for the year in order to earn 10 percent return on assets employed if sales are as estimated above?
2. If the company sets selling prices at a uniform percentage above direct costs, what should be the selling price of each product in order to earn the desired total amount of profit?

3. If the company sets selling prices at a uniform percentage above total costs, what should the selling prices be?

4. If the company sets selling prices so as to earn a 10 percent return on the assets employed on each product, what should the selling prices be?

5. If, during the year the company actually sold 800 units of Product A and 1,000 units of Product B, but unit costs and unit amounts of assets employed were as estimated above, what would be its percentage return on total assets employed under each of the sets of selling prices calculated in Questions 2 through 4 above?

6. What do these calculations indicate as to the effects of various pricing policies?

part two Differential accounting

In Part One we focused on the collection and use of information on the full costs of products or other cost objectives. We now turn to a second type of management accounting information. Various names are given to this type; we shall use the term "differential" accounting. Differential accounting has three closely related facets: differential costs, differential revenues, and differential investment (i.e., the amount of assets employed). Of these, we shall give most emphasis to differential costs because these involve the most difficult problems of understanding.

Chapter 6 introduces the concept of differential costs and describes how costs on certain items change with the level of activity and with other factors. It provides a technical background for Chapters 7, 8, and 9 which discuss the use of differential accounting information in various types of business problems.

Difficulty is sometimes experienced in understanding clearly the similarities and the differences between the differential cost construction discussed in this Part Two and the full cost construction discussed in Part One. The full cost accounting system described in Part One does provide much of the raw data that is used to construct the differential costs whose use will be described in Part Two. In Part Two, however, we shall use not the full costs but rather only those items of cost that are relevant to a particular problem. In Part Two, we shall also use some cost data that does *not* come from a cost accounting system. Cost accounting systems are generally governed by the principles of financial accounting, one of which is that assets and expenses are recorded at the monetary amounts that were exchanged at the time the company acquired the asset or incurred the expense. In Part Two we are not bound

151

by this principle; we shall use certain elements of costs that are *not* represented by identifiable monetary exchanges, and we shall disregard as being irrelevant certain other elements of costs, even though they are represented by monetary exchanges.

The essential reason for the differences in the cost constructions that are relevant to Part Two and those that were relevant in Part One is one of purpose. When the student thoroughly understands the central idea that different purposes require different cost constructions, the confusion over different types of cost constructions should at least be diminished; hopefully it will disappear.

6 The behavior of costs

Purpose of the chapter In this chapter we introduce the concept of differential costs (and also differential revenues) and contrast this concept with that of full costs which was our focus in Part One. The chapter explains in an introductory way what the differential cost concept is and how differential costs aid the decision maker in his analysis of business problems. As a background for discussing the analysis of business problems, we describe how costs behave in certain situations, and particularly the effect that a change in volume has on costs.

Concept of differential costs and revenues In Part One we focused on the measurement of full costs, which is one type of cost construction. In the present chapter we introduce a second main type of cost construction, called *differential costs.* Some people have difficulty in accepting the idea that there is more than one type of cost construction. They say, "When I pay a company $180 for a desk, the desk surely cost me $180. How could the cost be anything else?" It is appropriate therefore that we establish the points that (a) "cost" does have more than one meaning, (b) that differences in cost constructions relate to the *purpose* for which the cost information is to be used, and (c) that unless these differences are understood, serious mistakes can be made.

To explain these points, let us consider a furniture company that, among other things, manufactures and sells desks. According to its cost accounting records, maintained as described in Part One, the full cost of manufacturing a certain desk would be $200. Suppose that a customer offered to buy such a desk for $180. If the company considered

153

that the only relevant cost for this desk was the $200 full cost, it would of course refuse the order because its revenue would be only $180 and its costs would be $200; therefore the management would conclude that it would incur a loss of $20 on the order. But it might well be that the additional out-of-pocket costs of making this one desk—the lumber and other material and the wages paid to the cabinetmaker who worked on the desk—would be only $125. The other items making up the $200 of full cost as measured in the cost accounting system were items of cost which would not be affected by this one order. The management might therefore decide to accept this order at $180. If it did, the company's costs would increase by $125, its revenue would increase by $180, and its income would increase by the difference, or $55. Thus, the company would be $55 better off by accepting this order than by refusing it. Evidently in this problem, the wrong decision could be made if the company relied on the full cost information.

In this example, we used both $200 and $125 as measures of the "cost" of the desk. These numbers represent two types of cost constructions, each of which is used for a different purpose. The $200 measures the full cost of the desk, which is the cost used for the purposes described in Chapter 5. The $125 is another type of cost construction, and it is used for other purposes, one of which is to decide, under certain circumstances, whether an order for the desk should be accepted. We shall label this latter type of cost construction *differential cost*.

Differential costs are costs that are different under one set of conditions than they would be under another set of conditions.[1] The term refers both to certain elements of cost and to amounts of cost. Thus, in many situations direct labor is an item of differential cost; also, if the amount of cost that differs in a certain problem is $1,000, the $1,000 is said to be the amount of differential cost.

Differential costs always relate to a specific situation. In the example described above, the differential cost of the desk in question was $125. Under another set of circumstances—for example, if a similar problem arose several days later—the differential costs might well be something other than $125. The differential cost to the *buyer* of the desk was $180. He paid $180 for the desk, which he would not have paid if he had not purchased the desk.

DIFFERENTIAL REVENUES

The differential concept also applies to revenues; that is, *differential revenues* are those that are different under one set of conditions than they would be under another set of conditions. In the example of the desk, the differential revenue to the furniture manufacturer was $180;

---

[1] Differential costs are also called *relevant* costs.

his revenue would differ by $180 if he accepted the order for the desk from what it would be if he did not accept the order.

VARIABLE AND FIXED COSTS

In the example of the desk given above, the volume, or output, of the furniture manufacturer would be higher, by one desk, if it accepted the order compared with what it would have been if it did not accept the order. The proposal under consideration therefore had an effect on volume as well as on costs. This is the case with a great many problems involving differential costs, and we shall therefore discuss in some detail the relation of costs to volume. In order to do so, we introduce the concepts of variable costs and fixed costs.

In general usage, the word "variable" means simply "changeable," but in accounting, "variable" has a more restricted meaning. Variable refers not to changes in cost that take place over time, nor to changes associated with the seasons, but only to changes associated with the *level of activity,* that is, with the volume of output. If an item of cost goes up as volume goes up, the item is a variable cost; otherwise, it is not. There are three types of cost patterns: variable, fixed, and semivariable (partly variable).

Variable costs are items of cost that vary directly and proportionately with volume; that is, as volume increases by 10 percent, the amount of cost also increases by 10 percent. Direct labor, direct material, lubricants, power costs, and supplies often are examples of variable costs.

Fixed costs do not vary at all with volume. Building depreciation, property taxes, supervisory salaries, and occupancy costs (heat and light) often behave in this fashion. These costs are incurred because of the passage of time, rather than because of the volume within a specified period of time. Although the term "fixed cost" may imply that the amount of cost is fixed and hence cannot be changed, such an implication is incorrect. The term refers only to items of cost that do not change with changes in *volume.* Fixed costs can be changed for other reasons, for example, a deliberate management decision to change them. The term "nonvariable" is therefore more appropriate than "fixed," but since "fixed cost" is in widespread business use, we use it here.

> *EXAMPLE:* Plant protection costs, such as the wages of guards and watchmen, are ordinarily fixed costs since these costs do not vary with changes in volume. Plant protection costs will increase, however, if management decides that the current level of plant protection is inadequate. Alternatively, they will decrease if management decides that reductions in the current level are prudent.

Semivariable costs vary in the same direction as, but less than proportionately with, changes in volume; that is, if volume increases by 10 percent, the amount of cost will increase, but by less than 10 percent.

Semivariable costs are also called "semifixed" or "partly variable" costs. Examples may be indirect labor, maintenance, and clerical costs.

Relation to unit costs. The foregoing description of the three types of cost was expressed in terms of total costs for a period. In terms of unit costs, the description of these types of cost is quite different. Variable cost per unit of volume is a *constant;* that is, it does not change as volume changes. Fixed cost per unit does change with changes in volume; as volume increases, fixed cost per unit decreases. Semivariable cost per unit also changes with changes in volume, but the amount of change is smaller than that for fixed cost. These relationships have already been described briefly in Chapters 4 and 5, but an additional example is given for emphasis.

EXAMPLE: Costs at three levels of volume are given below:

	Volume (Units)		
	100	125	150
Total cost:			
Variable cost....................	$400	$500	$600
Fixed cost.....................	300	300	300
Semivariable cost...............	300	350	400
Unit cost:			
Variable cost....................	$4.00	$4.00	$4.00
Fixed cost.....................	3.00	2.40	2.00
Semivariable cost...............	3.00	2.80	2.67

Observe that as volume increases by 50 percent (i.e., from 100 to 150 units),

- Total variable cost increases by 50 percent.
- Total fixed cost remains unchanged.
- Total semivariable cost increases but by less than 50 percent.
- Variable cost per unit remains unchanged.
- Fixed cost per unit decreases.
- Semivariable cost per unit decreases, but not as rapidly as fixed cost per unit.

Variable costs versus direct costs. We need to distinguish carefully between variable cost and direct cost. A *direct* cost is an element of cost that can be traced to a single cost objective, as contrasted with an indirect cost which applies to more than one cost objective. The labor cost for the time that a worker spends making Product X is a *direct* cost of Product X. Direct labor cost is also a *variable* cost for Product X because in normal circumstances it takes twice as much labor time to make two units as it takes to make one unit.

There are, however, many circumstances in which a direct cost is not a variable cost. If a certain machine is used exclusively for Product X and for no other products, then the depreciation on that machine is a direct cost of Product X; however, it is not normally a *variable* cost because the amount of depreciation is ordinarily accounted for as a function of the passage of time rather than of the quantity of items produced. The cost of electric power required to operate such a machine would be both a variable cost and a direct cost.

As a general rule, **all items of variable cost are direct, but not all items of direct cost are variable.**

Contribu-
tion analysis
In this section we introduce a technique called *contribution analysis*. We do so both because contribution analysis is an important tool in analyzing differential costs and also because in explaining the technique we can clarify the relationships among, and differences between, variable costs, fixed costs, direct costs, indirect costs, full costs, and differential costs. Contribution analysis focuses on what is called the contribution margin.

The **contribution margin for a product, service, or other segment of a business is the difference between its revenue and its variable costs.** Exhibit 6–1 contrasts the conventional income statement for a laundry and dry cleaning company with the same data rearranged so as to measure the contribution margin for each of its two services, dry cleaning and laundry. Analysis of the underlying records shows that of the $7,000 total revenue in June, $5,400 was earned on dry cleaning work and $1,600 on laundry. The expense items[2] on the income statement were analyzed to determine which amounts were variable, and of these, how much was attributable to dry cleaning and how much to laundry. Of the total amount of $3,300 for salaries and wages, $1,300 of wages was a variable expense of dry cleaning and $700 was a variable expense of laundry; the remaining $1,300 of salaries was a fixed expense, applicable to the business as a whole. The other variable expenses were found to be supplies and power. The total amount of variable expense was $3,050 for dry cleaning and $1,050 for laundry.

The contribution margin, which is the difference between revenue and total variable expenses, was therefore $2,350 for dry cleaning and $550 for laundry.

In addition to variable expenses, dry cleaning had $600 of direct fixed expense; this was the depreciation on the dry cleaning equipment. Laundry had $200 of direct fixed expenses. Subtracting these direct, but fixed, expenses from the contribution margin shows how much each service contributed to the indirect fixed costs of the business; the amounts were $1,750 for dry cleaning and $350 for laundry, a total of

---

[2] Since this is an income statement, amounts deducted from revenue are called *expenses*. As pointed out in Chapter 3, expenses are one type of cost. Thus, although the description in this chapter uses the broader term, "costs," it applies equally well to that type of cost which is labeled "expense."

Exhibit 6–1

Contrast between conventional income statement and contribution analysis

---

A. Income Statement—Conventional Basis
Month of June

Revenue...		$7,000
Expenses:		
Salaries and wages.............................	$3,300	
Supplies.......................................	1,800	
Heat, light, and power.........................	400	
Advertising....................................	200	
Rent...	700	
Depreciation on equipment......................	800	
Other (telephone, insurance, etc.).............	300	
Total expense.............................		7,500
Net Loss..		$ (500)

B. Income Statement—Contribution Margin Basis
Month of June

	Dry Cleaning		Laundry	
Revenue.............................		$5,400		$1,600
Variable expenses:				
Wages............................	$1,300		$700	
Supplies.........................	1,500		300	
Power............................	250		50	
Total variable expenses.........		3,050		1,050
Contribution margin.................	(44%)	$2,350	(34%)	$ 550
Direct fixed expenses:				
Depreciation on equipment..........		600		200
Contribution to indirect expenses......		$1,750		$ 350

Total contribution...............		$2,100
Indirect fixed expenses:		
Salaries.........................	$1,300	
Heat and light...................	100	
Advertising......................	200	
Rent.............................	700	
Other............................	300	
Total indirect fixed expenses....		2,600
Net Loss............................		$ (500)

$2,100. Since the total of these indirect fixed costs was $2,600, this contribution was not large enough to produce net income for the month; the difference was the net loss of $500.

We shall use these numbers to illustrate the types of costs listed above:

• Variable costs (here expenses) are $3,050 for dry cleaning and $1,050 for laundry. They are variable because they vary with the volume of dry cleaning and laundry done.

- Fixed costs are the $800 of depreciation on equipment plus the $2,600 of ~~indirect~~ fixed expenses, a total of $3,400.
- Direct costs include not only the variable costs ($4,100) but also the depreciation of the dry cleaning equipment ($600) and of the laundry equipment ($200), a total of $4,900. These are direct because they are traceable directly to the separate services, but they are not all variable costs because the amount of depreciation does not change with the volume of work done.
- Indirect costs are those amounts (totaling $2,600) that are not traced directly to dry cleaning or to laundry.
- Full costs are not shown on the analysis. In order to obtain full costs, it would be necessary to allocate the $2,600 of indirect costs to dry cleaning and to laundry, on some reasonable basis.

In the above list, we omitted mention of differential costs. This is because we cannot identify differential costs in general; rather we must always relate them to a specific alternative choice problem. Three of several possible problems are discussed below. (The discussion is greatly simplified; many considerations are omitted in order to focus on the types of costs.)

Case A. Suppose the management is considering certain actions that are intended to increase the volume of dry cleaning work and asks how increased volume will affect income. In this situation, the differential costs are the variable costs (and the revenue is, of course, differential revenue). Each additional dollar of dry cleaning business is expected to add 44 cents to profit, the percentage difference between revenue and variable costs.

Case B. Suppose the management is considering getting out of the laundry business. The analysis indicates that such a move would reduce costs by $1,250 (the sum of laundry variable expenses plus depreciation on the laundry equipment that will no longer be needed). The differential costs are therefore $1,250. However, $1,600 of laundry revenue also would be lost, so the move would result in a greater decrease in revenue than the saving in cost; the net loss would be increased by $350.

Case C. Suppose management was considering shutting down the whole business. In this case, all the costs, including the indirect costs of $2,600, would be eliminated, so the differential costs would be $7,500.

Thus, in Case A, the differential costs are the variable costs; in Case B, they are the variable costs plus the direct fixed costs; and in Case C, they are the total costs. In short, differential costs cannot be identified except in terms of a specific situation that is being analyzed.

Observe also how the message conveyed by the contribution analysis differs from the message conveyed by the conventional income statement. The income statement indicates that the business operated at a loss.

Moreover, if the indirect expenses were allocated to the two services in proportion to their variable expenses, each of the two services would also show a loss, viz:

	Total	*Dry Cleaning*	*Laundry*
Contribution to indirect expenses	$2,100	$1,750	$ 350
Allocated indirect expenses	2,600	1,934	666
Net Loss	$ (500)	$ (184)	$(316)

From these numbers, someone might conclude that one or the other of these services should be discontinued in order to reduce losses. By contrast, the contribution analysis shows that each of the services made a contribution to indirect costs and that the total loss of the business would therefore not be reduced by discontinuing either of them. The loss would have been $1,750 greater if dry cleaning were eliminated and $350 greater if laundry were eliminated.

CONTRASTS BETWEEN FULL COSTS AND DIFFERENTIAL COSTS

From the description given thus far in this chapter, we can identify three important differences between full costs and differential costs. One is in the nature of the costs, a second is in the source of data, and the third is in the relevant time perspective. Each is discussed below.

The full costs of a product or other cost objective are the sum of its direct costs plus an equitable share of applicable indirect costs. Differential costs include only those elements of cost that are different under a certain set of conditions. This is the most important difference between full costs and differential costs.

Information on full costs is taken directly from a company's cost accounting system. The system is designed to measure full costs on a regular basis, and to report these costs routinely. There is no comparable system for collecting differential costs. The appropriate items that constitute differential costs are assembled to meet the requirements of a specific problem. Each problem is different. Some of the data used to construct differential costs may come from the cost accounting system, but other data comes from other sources.

Finally, the full cost accounting system collects costs on a historical basis, that is, it measures what the costs *were*. For certain purposes, such as setting selling prices, these historical costs are adjusted to reflect the estimated impact of future conditions; but for other purposes, such as financial reporting, the historical costs are used without change. **Differential costs always relate to the future;** they are intended to show what the costs **would be** if a certain course of action were adopted, rather than what the costs were. Historical costs are relevant only as a starting point for estimating what costs will be in the future. This point has not been emphasized adequately in the introductory examples given to this point. For example, in discussing differential costs in the laundry and dry cleaning situation shown in Exhibit 6–1, we used data from the company's historical records, which was an oversimplification. Actually, the differential costs in this, and in any other problem in which differential costs are relevant, are estimates of what the costs *are going to be,* not what *they were.*

Relation of
costs to
volume

Since many differential cost problems involve changes in volume, that is, the level of activity, we need to consider carefully the effect that changes in volume have on costs. This section describes such cost-volume relationships and some of the tools that are helpful in analyzing these relationships.

COST-VOLUME DIAGRAMS

The relationship between costs and volume can be displayed on a cost-volume diagram, as in Exhibit 6–2. In such diagrams, cost is always plotted on the vertical, or *y,* axis, and volume is plotted on the horizontal, or *x,* axis. This follows a conventional rule in geometry: the "dependent variable" is plotted on the *y* axis, and the "independent variable" is plotted on the *x* axis. In a cost-volume diagram, therefore, cost is implicitly assumed to be the "dependent variable" and volume the "independent variable"; that is, the amount of the cost *depends on* the volume or level of activity, rather than *vice versa.*

For the present, think of volume as meaning the number of units or products manufactured or sold in a given time period, such as a month. Alternative methods of measuring and expressing volume will be discussed in a subsequent section.

Exhibit 6–2 gives a generalized picture of the behavior of the three types of cost described earlier in this chapter. The fixed cost is $300 *for a period of time* regardless of the volume in that period. The variable cost is $0.80 *per unit of volume,* which means that the total variable cost varies proportionately with volume. The semivariable cost starts at $200 and increases at a rate of $0.20 per unit of volume. Note that the semivariable cost can be decomposed into two elements, a fixed element of $200 per period of time and a variable element of $0.20 per unit of volume.

BEHAVIOR OF TOTAL COSTS

If each separate cost element behaves according to one of the three patterns shown above, then the total cost, which is the sum of these separate elements, must vary with volume in the manner shown in

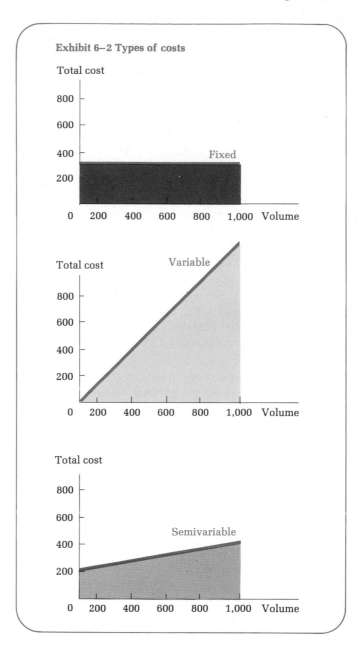

Exhibit 6–2 Types of costs

Exhibit 6–3, which was constructed simply by combining the three separate elements shown in Exhibit 6–2.

Since a semivariable cost can be split into fixed and variable components, the **behavior of total costs can be described in terms of only two components—a fixed component, which is a total amount per period, and a variable component, which is an amount per unit of volume.** In Exhibit 6–3, the fixed amount is $500 per period (=$300 +

$200) and the variable amount is $1 per unit of volume (=$0.80 + $0.20). The semivariable cost has disappeared as a separate entity, part of it being combined with the variable cost and the remainder being combined with the fixed cost. This combination can be made for any semivariable cost item that is expressed as a fixed dollar amount per period plus a rate per unit of volume. There is therefore no need to consider semivariable costs as a separate category. From this point on, we shall consider only the fixed and variable components of cost. Subsequently, we shall describe techniques for separating a semivariable cost into a variable rate per unit of volume and a fixed amount per time period.

COST ASSUMPTIONS

Exhibit 6–3 is based on several implicit assumptions as to the behavior of costs, two of which are discussed below. The first is usually a reasonable one, but the second is actually quite unrealistic.

The linear assumption. One cost behavior assumption is that all costs behave according to one of the three patterns described above, each of which is expressed by a straight line; that is, each relationship is *linear*. Actually, some items of costs may vary in steps, as in Exhibit 6–4. This happens when the cost occurs in discrete "chunks," as when one indirect worker is added for every 500 additional hours of direct

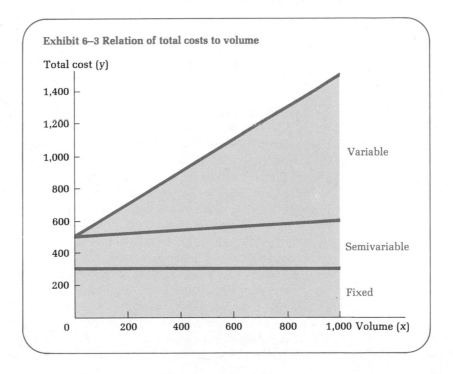

Exhibit 6–3 Relation of total costs to volume

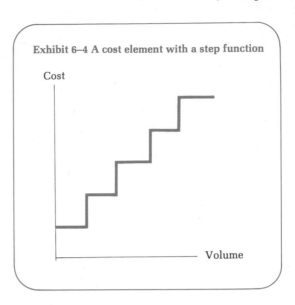

Exhibit 6–4 A cost element with a step function

Cost

Volume

labor per month. Other items of cost may vary along a curve rather than a straight line; and in rare circumstances still others, such as the maintenance cost of idle machines, may actually decrease as volume increases.

In most situations, however, the effect of these discontinuities and nonlinear cost functions on total costs is minor, and the assumption that total costs vary in a linear relationship with volume is a satisfactory working approximation. This is a most fortunate fact. Many theoretical treatises discuss cost functions with various types of complicated curves. Such complicated curves are rarely used in practice, however, for it is usually found that the simple straight-line assumption, although perhaps not a perfect representation of cost-volume relationships, is close enough for practical purposes. In this book, therefore, we describe only linear relationships. If a real-life problem does involve nonlinear relationships, the general approach is similar to that described here; the only difference is that the arithmetic is more complicated.

Full-range assumption. A second cost behavior assumption implicit in Exhibit 6–3 is that costs move along a straight line throughout *the whole range* of volume, from zero to whatever number is at the far right of the diagram. This assumption is unrealistic. For example, at zero volume (i.e., when the factory is not operating at all), management decisions may cause costs to be considerably higher or considerably lower than the $500 shown in the diagram. When production gets so high that a second shift is required, costs may behave quite differently from the way in which they behave under one-shift operations. Even within the limits of a single shift, it is to be expected that costs will behave differently when the factory is very busy, from the way they do

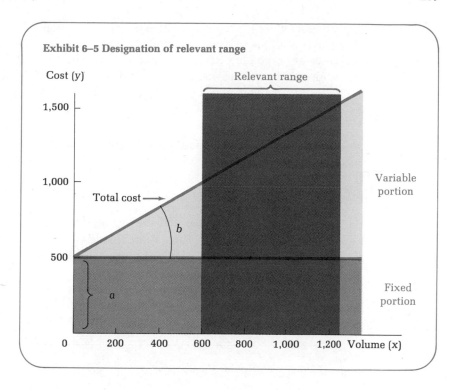

Exhibit 6–5 Designation of relevant range

when the factory is operating at a significantly lower volume. In short, the single straight line gives a good approximation of the behavior of costs *only within a certain range of volume*. This range is referred to as the **relevant range** because it is the range that is relevant for the situation being analyzed.

Exhibit 6–5 shows the same cost pattern as Exhibit 6–3, and the relevant range is indicated by the shaded area from 600 units to 1,200 units. Although the cost line extends back to zero, it does not imply that costs actually will behave in this fashion at volumes lower than 600 units; rather, it is drawn on the diagram solely as a means of identifying the fixed component of total costs. The fixed component (i.e., $500 per period) is the amount of costs indicated by the point where the cost line crosses the y axis, which is zero volume.

It is also important to note that the diagram shows the estimated relationship between costs and volume under a *certain set of conditions*. This is not an assumption; it is a fact. If any of these conditions should change—for example, if there is an increase in wage rates—the diagram is obsolete, and a new one must be drawn.

FORMULA FOR THE COST LINE

As already pointed out, total costs at any volume are the sum of the fixed component ($500 per period in Exhibit 6–5) and the variable component ($1 per unit). For example, at a volume of 1,000 units, cost is $500 + ($1 per unit times 1,000 units) = $1,500. Designating costs as y, volume as x, the fixed component as a, and the variable component as b, the cost at any volume can be found from the formula, $a + bx = y$. This is simply the general formula for a straight line.[3] Recapitulating:

Equation:	a	$+$	(b	$\cdot$	x)	$=$	y
Words:	Fixed per period	+	(Variable per unit	$\cdot$	Units)	=	Total cost
Numbers:	$500	+	($1	$\cdot$	1,000)	=	$1,500

UNIT COSTS

It should be emphasized that the line we are studying represents *total* costs at various volumes. Such a line should not be confused with a line that represents *unit* costs. If total costs have a linear relationship with volume, then unit costs will always be a curve that slopes downward to the right; it reflects the fact that unit costs decrease as volume increases. Exhibit 6–6 is a unit cost curve derived from Exhibit 6–5. Since unit cost is simply total cost divided by the number of units, Exhibit 6–6

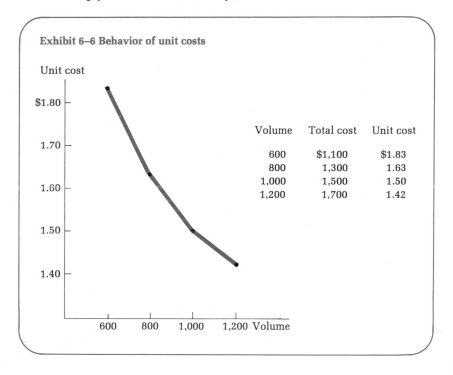

Exhibit 6–6 Behavior of unit costs

Volume	Total cost	Unit cost
600	$1,100	$1.83
800	1,300	1.63
1,000	1,500	1.50
1,200	1,700	1.42

---

[3] In some mathematics texts, the notation used is $y = mx + b$. In such a notation, m represents the *slope*, or cost per unit, and b represents the fixed cost per period. This difference in notation reflects the personal preference of mathematicians and has no other significance whatsoever.

was obtained simply by dividing total cost at various volume levels by the amount of volume at those levels, plotting the results of each such calculation, and joining the dots.

ESTIMATING COST-VOLUME RELATIONSHIP

In order to construct a cost-volume diagram, estimates must be made of what the amount of costs are expected to be. These estimates often are made as part of the *budgeting* process, which is described in Chapter 11. In this process, estimates are made of all significant items of revenue and cost; these show what revenues and costs are expected to be in some future period, usually the following year.

Any of the following methods can be used to derive the *a* and *b* terms for the cost-volume formula as a part of this process:

1. Estimate total costs at each of two volume levels; this establishes two points on the line. (This is often called the **high-low method** because one of the volumes selected is likely to be quite high and the other is likely to be quite low; the upper and lower limits of the relevant range often are selected for this purpose.) Then proceed as follows:

a. Subtract total cost at the lower volume from total cost at the higher volume, and subtract the number of units for the lower volume from the number of units for the higher volume.

b. Divide the difference in cost by the difference in volume, which gives *b*, the amount by which total cost changes with a change of one unit of volume.

c. Multiply either of the volumes by *b* and subtract the result from the total cost at that volume, thus removing the variable component and leaving the fixed component *a*.

> *EXAMPLE:* It is determined that costs are $1,200 when volume is 700 units and $1,500 when volume is 1,000 units. The calculation of the formula for the line is as follows:

	Observations		
	High	*Low*	*Difference*
Volume, units..............	1,000	700	300
Cost.....................	$1,500	$1,200	$300

$b =$ $300 difference in cost $\div$ 300 difference in units
    $=$ $1 per unit; this is the *variable* component
$a =$ $1,200 $-$ (700 $\times$ $1)
    $=$ $500; this is the *fixed* component

or

$a =$ $1,500 $-$ (1,000 $\times$ $1) $=$ $500

Therefore, the formula for the line is:

$500 $+$ $1x = y$

2. Estimate total costs at one volume, and estimate how costs will change with a given change in volume. This gives *b* directly, and *a* can be found by subtraction, as described above.

3. Build up separate estimates of the behavior of each of the items that make up total costs. From these estimates, derive the *a* and *b* components directly.

4. Make a **scatter diagram** in which actual costs recorded in past periods are plotted (on the *y* axis) against the volume levels in those periods (on the *x* axis). Data on costs and volumes for each of the preceding several months might be used for this purpose. Draw a line that best fits these observations. Such a diagram is shown in Exhibit 6–7. The line of best fit either can be drawn by visual inspection of the plotted points, or it can be fitted by a statistical technique called the **method of least squares** (see Appendix A). In many cases a line drawn by visual inspection is just as good as, and in some cases is better than, a mathematically fitted line, because judgment can be used to adjust for unusual observations.

If the line is fitted visually, the *a* and *b* values can be determined by reading the values for any two points on the line and then using the high-low method described above. If the line is fitted statistically, the procedure gives the *a* and *b* values directly.

Problems with scatter diagrams. Estimating cost-volume relationships by means of a scatter diagram or by a least-squares calculation is a common practice, but the results can be misleading. In the first place, this technique shows, at best, what the relationship between costs and volumes **was in the past,** whereas we are interested in what the relation-

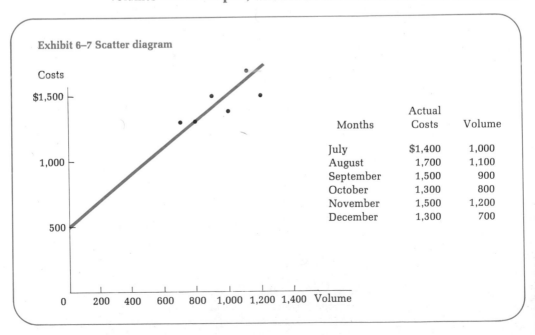

Exhibit 6–7 Scatter diagram

Months	Actual Costs	Volume
July	$1,400	1,000
August	1,700	1,100
September	1,500	900
October	1,300	800
November	1,500	1,200
December	1,300	700

ship will be in the future. The past is not necessarily a mirror of the future. Also, the relationship we seek is that obtaining under a *single set of operating conditions,* whereas each point on a scatter diagram may represent changes in factors other than the two being studied, namely, cost and volume.

Exhibit 6–8 shows a common source of difficulty. In this scatter diagram, volume is represented by sales revenue, as is often the case. Each dot is located by plotting the costs for one year on the y axis and the sales revenue for that year on the x axis. The dots lie along a well-

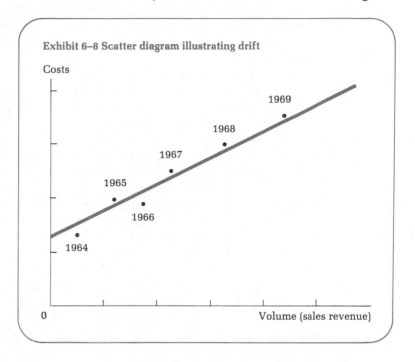

Exhibit 6–8 Scatter diagram illustrating drift

defined path, which is indicated by the straight line, but this line may *not* indicate a relationship between costs and volume. It may, instead, indicate nothing more than the tendency for both revenues and costs to increase over the past six years because of inflationary factors. If this is the case, then the line shows the trend, or **drift,** of costs **through time,** not the relationship between cost and volume **at a given time.** Any scatter diagram covering a period of years in which sales were generally increasing each year, or generally decreasing each year, is likely to have this characteristic; and the longer the period covered, the more un- reliable the diagram becomes.

MEASURES OF VOLUME

Thus far, we have used "volume" as an abstract concept, but in a real-world situation volume must be measured in some concrete fashion.

In Chapter 3 we described how indirect costs were allocated to products by means of an overhead rate. Such an overhead rate can be expressed as an amount per unit of product, per direct labor hour, per direct labor dollar, or in other ways. Each of these bases of overhead allocation is a measure of volume. Presumably, a certain measure is selected because it most closely reflects the conditions that cause costs to change. It is appropriate here to discuss the problem of selecting the best volume measure in more depth than we did in Chapter 3.

Essentially, two basic questions must be answered: (1) should the measure be based on *inputs,* or should it be based on *outputs?* and (2) should the measure be expressed in terms of *money amounts,* or should it be expressed in terms of *physical quantities?* Each of these questions is discussed below.

Input versus output measures. **Input measures** relate to the resources that are used in a cost center. Examples for a production cost center are the number of direct labor hours worked, dollars of direct labor cost, number of machine-hours operated, or pounds of raw material used. **Output measures** relate to the work done by the cost center; in a production cost center, this is the amount of products produced, expressed either in terms of the number of units worked on or their dollar value. For cost-volume diagrams that show the relationship between overhead costs and volume, an input measure, such as direct labor costs, may be a good measure of volume since many elements of overhead cost tend to vary more closely with other input factors than with output. For example, it is reasonable to expect that indirect cost items associated with direct labor, such as fringe benefits, social security taxes, and payroll accounting, vary more closely with the amount of direct labor used than with the amount of products produced. Some indirect costs, such as inspection costs and plant transportation, might vary more closely with the quantity of products produced, however.

If the diagram represents total costs for a cost center, and if volume is measured in terms of direct labor, which is itself one element of cost, it can be argued that the same numbers affect both costs and volume. This is true, but the line nevertheless reflects changes in costs other than direct labor and is therefore useful.

Monetary versus nonmonetary measures. A volume measure expressed in physical quantities, such as direct labor hours, is often better than one expressed in dollars, such as direct labor cost, because the former is unaffected by changes in prices. A wage increase would cause direct labor costs to increase, even if there were no actual increase in the volume of activity. If volume is measured in terms of direct labor dollars, such a measure could be misleading. On the other hand, if price changes are likely to affect both labor and overhead to the same degree, the use of a monetary measure of volume may be a means of allowing implicitly for the effect of these price changes.

Choice of a measure. These considerations must be tempered by practicality. Total direct labor costs are often available in the cost accounting system without extra calculation, whereas the computation of total direct labor hours, or machine-hours, may require considerable additional work. Also, since the measure of volume for analytical purposes is often (but not always) the same as that used in allocating overhead costs to products for the purpose of financial accounting, the appropriateness of the measure for the latter purpose must also be taken into account.

The profit-graph and break-even analysis

The cost-volume diagram in Exhibit 6–5 can be amplified into a useful device called the *profitgraph* (or "Profit-Volume graph," or "P/V graph") simply by the addition of a revenue line to it, for a **profitgraph is a diagram showing the expected relationship between total cost and revenue at various volumes.**[4] A profitgraph can be constructed either for the business as a whole, or for some segment of the business such as a product, a product line, or a division.

On a profitgraph, the measure of volume may be the number of units produced and sold, or it may be dollars of sales revenue. We have already stated the formula for the cost line: $a + bx = y$. Revenue is plotted on the profitgraph on the assumption of a constant selling price per unit. Assuming that volume is to be measured as units of product sold and designating the unit selling price as p, the number of units of volume as x, and the total revenue as y, the total revenue (y) equals the unit selling price (p) times the number of units of volume (x); or $px = y$. For example, if the unit selling price is $2, the total revenue from the sale of 1,000 units will be $2,000.

A profitgraph showing these relationships is shown in Exhibit 6–9. Although not shown explicitly on the diagram, it should be understood that the relationships are expected to hold only within the relevant volume range, as in Exhibit 6 5. Sometimes, several revenue lines are drawn on a profitgraph, each one showing what revenue would be at a specified unit selling price. This procedure helps to show how a change in selling price affects the profit at any given volume.

At the **break-even volume,** total costs equal total revenue. This is simply a geometric fact. The break-even point is of little practical interest in a profitable company, because attention is focused on the profit area, which should be considerably above the break-even point. At lower volumes, a loss is expected; and at higher volumes, a profit is expected. The amount of loss or profit expected at any volume is the difference between points on the total cost and revenue lines at that volume. The break-even volume is not the same as the "standard" volume used as a basis for determining overhead rates. In a profitable

---

[4] This device is also called a "break-even chart," but such a label has the unfortunate implication that the objective of a business is merely to break even.

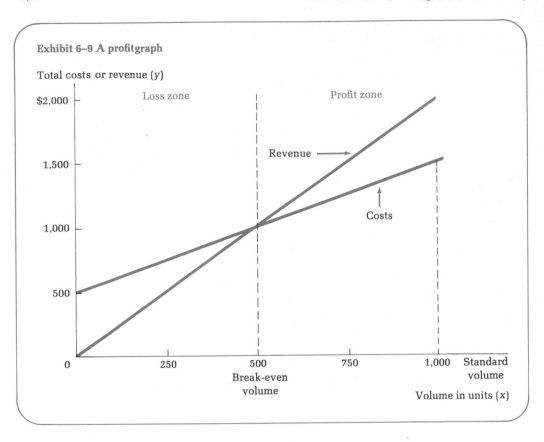

Exhibit 6–9 A profitgraph

Total costs or revenue (y)

business, standard volume is considerably higher than the break-even volume.

INTERPRETATION OF THE PROFITGRAPH

The profitgraph is a useful device for analyzing the overall profit characteristics of a business. To illustrate such an analysis, assume the following situation, which is the same as that shown in previous diagrams:

Fixed costs........................	$500 per period
Variable costs.....................	$1 per unit
Standard volume...................	1,000 units
Selling price......................	$2 per unit

For simplicity, we shall assume that the company makes only one product. In this situation, total costs at *standard volume* will be $500 (fixed) plus (1,000 × $1) (variable) = $1,500. Assuming that all costs are assigned to the product using an overhead rate that is based on standard volume, then the unit cost of the product will be $1,500 ÷

1,000 units, or $1.50 per unit. At a selling price of $2 per unit, the normal profit will be $0.50 per unit.

Computation of break-even volume. Recall that the break-even volume is the volume at which costs equal revenue.

Since revenue (y) at any volume (x) is $\qquad\qquad px = y$

And costs (y) at any volume (x) is $\qquad\qquad a + bx = y$

And since at the break-even volume,

    costs = revenue:

Therefore the break-even volume is the

    volume at which $\qquad\qquad\qquad\qquad px = a + bx$

If we let x equal the break-even volume, then for the above situation, we have

$$\$2x = \$500 + \$1x$$
$$x = 500 \text{ units}$$

At the break-even volume of 500 units, revenue equals 500 units × $2 per unit, which is $1,000, and total costs equal $500 + (500 units × $1 per unit), which is also $1,000.

The equation for the break-even volume, x, can also be stated in the following form:

$$x = \frac{a}{p - b}$$

In words, this equation says that the break-even volume can be found by dividing the fixed costs (a) by the difference between selling price per unit (p) and variable cost per unit (b).

Marginal income. From the relationships of costs and revenue at various volumes, an important conclusion can be drawn: although the profit at standard volume is $0.50 per unit, this unit profit will be earned *only* at the standard volume. At lower volumes the profit will be less than $0.50 per unit, and at higher volumes it will be more than $0.50 per unit. The relationship between costs, revenue, and volume can be summed up by the statement that for each change of one unit in volume, profit will change by $1. This $1 is called the **marginal income** or the **contribution margin.**

Marginal income is the difference between selling price and variable cost per unit.

Starting at the bottom of the relevant range, each additional unit of volume reduces the loss by the amount of marginal income until the break-even volume is reached, and thereafter each additional unit of volume increases profit by the amount of marginal income.

We can use the above notation to express these relationships, adding the symbol i for total income or profit:

$$(p - b)x - a = i$$

In words, total income at any volume is marginal income $(p - b)$ times volume minus fixed cost. In the above example, at standard volume of 1,000 units,

$$(p - b) \quad x \quad - \quad a \quad = \quad i$$
$$(\$2 - \$1) \ 1,000 - \$500 = \$500$$

That is, the marginal income of $1 per unit times 1,000 units minus the fixed cost of $500 gives total income of $500. Stated another way, if the marginal income is $1 per unit and fixed costs are $500, 500 units must be sold before enough revenue will be earned to cover fixed costs. After that, a profit of $1 per unit will be earned.

IMPROVING PROFIT PERFORMANCE

These cost-volume-profit relationships suggest that a useful way of studying the basic profit characteristics of a business is to focus on, not the profit per unit (which is different at every volume), but rather the total fixed costs and the marginal income per unit. In these terms, there are four basic ways in which the profit of a business that makes a single product can be increased:

1. Increase selling prices per unit.
2. Decrease variable costs per unit.
3. Decrease fixed costs.
4. Increase volume.

The separate effects of each of these possibilities are shown in the following calculations and in Exhibit 6–10. Each starts from a situation that is assumed to be "normal": selling price, $2; variable costs, $1 per unit; fixed costs, $500 per period; and volume, 1,000 units. The effect of a 10 percent change in each factor is:

A. A 10 percent increase in selling price would add $200 to revenue and would have no effect on costs; therefore, profit would be increased by $200, or 40 percent.

B. A 10 percent decrease in variable costs would reduce variable costs by $100; profit would therefore increase by $100, or 20 percent.

C. A 10 percent decrease in fixed cost would amount to $50; profit would therefore increase by $50, or 10 percent.

D. A 10 percent increase in volume would increase profit by the marginal income of $1 per unit times an additional 100 units, or $100, which is an increase of 20 percent.

If, instead of varying each factor separately, we look at some of the interrelationships among them, we can calculate, for example, that a 20 percent (i.e., $100) increase in fixed costs could be offset either by a 5 percent increase in selling price, or a 10 percent increase in volume, or a 10 percent decrease in variable costs.

Another calculation made from a profitgraph is the **margin of safety.**

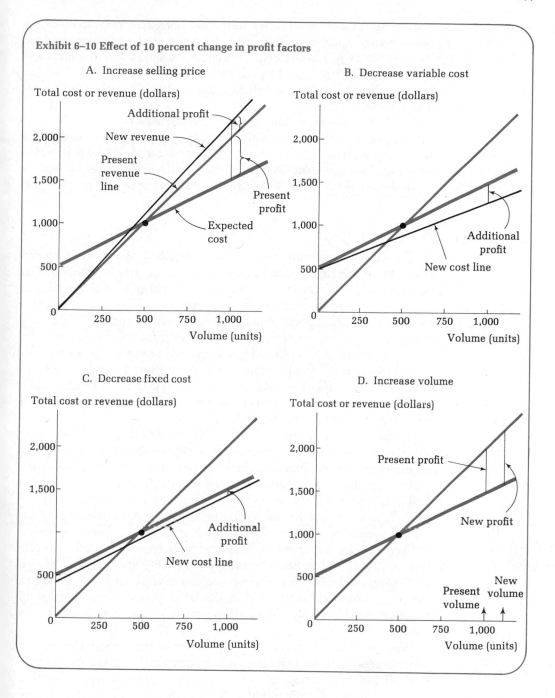

Exhibit 6–10 Effect of 10 percent change in profit factors

A. Increase selling price

Total cost or revenue (dollars)

Additional profit

New revenue

Present revenue line

Present profit

Expected cost

Volume (units)

B. Decrease variable cost

Total cost or revenue (dollars)

Additional profit

New cost line

Volume (units)

C. Decrease fixed cost

Total cost or revenue (dollars)

Additional profit

New cost line

Volume (units)

D. Increase volume

Total cost or revenue (dollars)

Present profit

New profit

New volume

Present volume

Volume (units)

This is the amount or ratio by which the current volume exceeds the break-even volume. Assuming current volume is the same as standard volume, which is 1,000 units, the margin of safety in our illustrative situation is 500 units, or 50 percent, of current volume. Sales volume can decrease by 50 percent before a loss is incurred, other factors remaining equal.

The foregoing calculations assume that each of the factors is independent of the others, a situation that is rarely the case in the real world. An increase in selling price often is accompanied by a decrease in volume, for example. Changes in the factors must therefore usually be studied simultaneously, rather than separately as was done above.

SEVERAL PRODUCTS

The cost-volume-profit relationships described above apply in the situation in which the company makes only a single product. The relationship also holds in the company that makes several products if each product has substantially the same marginal income as a percentage of sales. A profitgraph could be constructed for such a company by using sales revenue, rather than units, as the measure of volume. In such a company each dollar of sales revenue produces the same marginal income as every other dollar of sales revenue. If, as is sometimes the case, the company is able to set selling prices so as to obtain the same marginal income on each of its products, such a profitgraph is a valid representation of its profit characteristics.

If, however, the company makes several products and they have *different* marginal incomes, the depiction of a valid cost-volume-profit relationship is more complicated. If the proportion of the sales of each product to the total remains relatively constant, then a single profitgraph is still valid. It shows the *average* marginal income for all products, rather than the individual marginal incomes of any product.

The proportion of sales of each product in a given period is called the **product mix** in that period. Changes in the product mix affect profits in a way that is not revealed by the type of profitgraph described above. For example, even if sales revenue does not change from one period to the next, profits will increase if in the latter period the proportion of products that have a high marginal income is greater than it was in the first period.

When products have different marginal incomes and when the product mix changes, either of two alternative approaches to cost-volume-profit analysis can be used. One is to treat each product as a separate entity, and to construct a profitgraph for that entity, just as we did for the business as a whole. This method requires that all costs of the business be allocated to individual products. The second approach is to construct a profitgraph that portrays the marginal incomes of the several products separately. The technique for doing this is beyond the scope of this introductory treatment.

Other in-
fluences on
costs

A cost-volume diagram, or a profitgraph, shows only what total costs are expected to be at various *levels* of volume. For example, the diagram shows that the variable cost of 200 units is double the variable cost of 100 units. There are many reasons, other than the level of volume, why the costs in one period are different from those in another period. Some of these are listed below. They will be discussed in more detail in later chapters.

1. *Changes in input prices.* One of the most important causes of changes in a cost-volume diagram is that the prices of input factors change. Inflation is a persistent, and probably permanent, phenomenon. Wage rates go up; salaries go up; material costs go up; costs of services go up. A cost-volume diagram can get seriously out of date, and hence be misleading, if it is not adjusted for the effect of these changes. (Not *all* input prices go up, of course. There have been dramatic reductions in the prices of certain raw materials, for example, reflecting the intro-duction of new production techniques. Such decreases also require that the cost-volume diagram be updated.)

2. The *rate* at which volume changes. Rapid changes in the level of volume are more difficult for factory personnel to adjust to than are moderate changes in volume; therefore, the more rapid the change in volume, the more likely it is that costs will depart from the straight-line, cost-volume pattern.

3. The *direction* of change in volume. When volume is increasing, costs tend to lag behind the straight-line relationship either because the factory is unable to hire the additional workers that are assumed in the cost curve or because supervisors try to "get by" without adding overhead costs. Similarly, when volume is decreasing, there is a re-luctance to lay off workers and to shrink other elements of cost, and this also causes a lag.

4. The *duration* of change in volume. A temporary change of vol-ume, in either direction, tends to affect costs less than a change that lasts a long time, for much the same reasons as were given in the preceding paragraph.

5. *Prior knowledge of the change.* If a production manager has ade-quate advance notice of a change in volume, he can plan for it, and actual costs therefore are more likely to remain close to the cost-volume line than is the case when the change in volume is unexpected.

6. *Productivity.* The cost-volume diagram assumes a certain level of productivity in the use of resources. As the level of productivity changes, the cost changes. As we noted in Chapter 5, overall productivity in the United States tends to increase at a rate of about 3 percent a year, and unit costs are reduced correspondingly.

7. *Experience.* Studies have shown that certain items of costs tend to decrease, per unit, over a period of time as workers and their super-visors become more familiar with the work; as production methods improve; as less work is scrapped and less rework required; as fewer skilled workers need to be used; and so on. These decreasing unit costs

are a function of the learning process, which results in fewer and fewer man-hours being necessary to produce a unit of product as more units of the same product are completed. In some industries, it has been found possible to predict the pattern of such decreases in unit costs, and to express this pattern in what is called a **learning curve** or an **experience curve.**

8. *Management discretion.* Some items of cost change because management has decided that they *should* change. Some companies, for example, have relatively large headquarters staffs, while others have small headquarters staffs. The size of these staffs, and hence the costs associated with their activities, can be varied within fairly wide limits, depending on management's judgment as to what the optimum size is. Such types of cost are called *discretionary costs*. They are discussed in more detail in Part Three.

9. *Measure of volume.* Volume is often measured by sales, either in units or in dollars. Costs are production costs. If the volume of sales does not correspond to the volume of production, the profitgraph may be misleading.

For these reasons, and for others not listed above, it is not possible to predict the total costs of a business in a certain period simply by predicting the volume for that period and then determining the costs at that volume by reading a cost-volume diagram. Nevertheless, the effect of volume on costs and profits is so important that the cost-volume diagram and the profitgraph are extremely useful tools in analysis. In using them, the interpretation of the relationships that they depict must be tempered by the influence of other factors, to the extent that they can be estimated.

Sources of
differential
cost data
Since the items of cost that are differential with respect to a given problem depend on the nature of that specific problem, it is not possible to identify items of differential cost in the accounting system and to collect these costs on a regular basis. Instead, the accounting system is designed so that it can furnish the raw data which is useful in estimating the differential costs for a specific problem. Differential costs are needed for a wide variety of problems, and it is rarely possible that all these needs can be foreseen. In general, the accounting system is designed so that:

a. It identifies items of *variable costs* separately from items of fixed cost, and

b. It identifies the *direct costs* of various cost objectives.

This can be done by the proper classification of accounts. Direct material costs and direct labor costs are variable costs, so no special identification is needed for them. For indirect factory costs and for selling, general, and administrative costs, items of cost that are variable are identified as such in the account structure. Similarly, items of cost that are direct with respect to the principal cost objectives are separately identified in the accounts. This is done, of course, only to the extent that such separate identification is worthwhile.

> *EXAMPLE:* Refer to the laundry and dry cleaning company statement given in Exhibit 6–1. If the company's account structure contained only the account "Salaries and Wages," it would not be possible to identify in the accounts the amount of salaries and wages that were direct to the dry cleaning cost objective and those that were direct to the laundry cost objective. Such identification requires that separate accounts be established for "Wages, Laundry," "Wages, Dry Cleaning," and "Indirect Salaries." In this small business, however, the need for such a separation might not be great enough to warrant making such a separation on a routine basis. If it was decided that separate accounts were not worthwhile, then a special compilation of costs would have to be made in order to do the analysis described in Exhibit 6–1.

DIRECT COSTING

Because of the importance of identifying direct and variable items of cost, some companies use what is called a **direct cost system** (although it would be more logical to call it a **variable cost system). In a direct cost system products are charged only with their variable production costs.** These consist of direct labor costs, direct material costs, and those items of factory indirect costs that are variable. All fixed costs are charged as expenses of the current period. This practice is *not* in accordance with generally accepted accounting principles, because these principles require that an appropriate share of *all* factory costs be assigned to products; nevertheless, some companies use it for internal purposes. The conventional cost accounting system, as described in Chapters 2 and 3, is also called an **absorption cost system,** to indicate that fixed costs are absorbed as a part of product costs.

In direct costing, fixed production costs are viewed as being essentially costs that are associated with being in a state of readiness to produce rather than costs associated with the actual production of specific units of product. Fixed costs are said to be "time" costs, whereas variable costs are said to be "activity" costs. Proponents of direct costing assert that management can be misled if these fixed costs are intermingled with variable costs in the measurement of inventory and costs of goods sold. Appendix B discusses this point in more detail. Direct costing is the extreme case of differences of opinion about which items of costs are **product costs** and which are expenses of the current period, that is, **period costs.**

As pointed out above, variable costs are collected and separately identified in an absorption cost system. The difference is that in an absorption cost system, fixed costs are allocated to products whereas in a direct cost system no such allocations are made.

The relationships between cost, volume, and profit depicted in the form of diagrams and equations in the latter part of this chapter are similar to those depicted in the contribution analysis that was described in the early part of the chapter. For the purpose of solidifying your grasp of these relationships and also to show the correspondence between contribution analysis and the diagrams and equations, you are asked to recast the data on the four separate ways of changing profits (increase selling price, decrease variable costs, decrease fixed costs, and increase volume) in the form of a contribution analysis and to compare each of these to the "normal" situation, which is given below:

Normal situation:

Revenue ($2 × 1,000 units)........................	$2,000
Less variable costs ($1 × 1,000 units)...............	1,000
Contribution margin.............................	$1,000
Less fixed costs................................	500
Profit.......................................	$ 500

Before examining the solutions given below, make the same calculations for each of the four situations described. The analyses are:

10 percent increase in selling price:

Revenue ($2.20 × 1,000 units).....................	$2,200
Less variable costs..............................	1,000
Contribution margin.............................	$1,200
Less fixed costs................................	500
Profit.......................................	$ 700

Increase in profit: ($700 − $500) ÷ 500 = 40%

10 percent decrease in variable costs:

Revenue.......................................	$2,000
Less variable costs ($0.90 × 1,000 units)............	900
Contribution margin.............................	$1,100
Less fixed costs................................	500
Profit.......................................	$ 600

Increase in profit: ($600 − $500) ÷ 500 = 20%

10 percent decrease in fixed costs:

Revenue.......................................	$2,000
Less variable costs..............................	1,000
Contribution margin.............................	$1,000
Less fixed costs ($500 × 90%).....................	450
Profit.......................................	$ 550

Increase in profit: ($550 − $500) ÷ 500 = 10%

10 percent increase in volume:

Revenue ($2 × 1,100 units)........................	$2,200
Less variable costs ($1 × 1,100 units)...............	1,100
Contribution margin.............................	$1,100
Less fixed costs................................	500
Profit.......................................	$ 600

Increase in profit: ($600 − $500) ÷ 500 = 20%

Summary   Differential costs (or revenues) are those that are different under one set of conditions than they would be under another set of conditions. Differential costs are always constructed for a specified set of conditions. Variable costs are an important category of differential costs in situations in which changes in volume are involved, because total variable costs are different at each level of volume, in contrast with fixed costs which are unaffected by changes in volume.

The technique called *contribution analysis* finds the contribution margin, which is the difference between revenue and variable costs. Analysis of the relationships revealed by a contribution analysis is useful in making decisions on problems in which a proposed course of action affects the contribution margin of the business as a whole or of some segment thereof.

The level of volume has an important effect on costs. The effect can be depicted in a cost-volume diagram, or, if the relationship is approximately linear, by the equation $a + bx = y$. The diagram, and the equation, state that the total costs (y) at any volume are the sum of the fixed costs (a) plus the unit variable costs (b) times the number of units (x). These relationships hold only within a certain range of volume, the relevant range.

When a revenue line is added to a cost-volume diagram, it becomes a *profitgraph*. The profitgraph shows the relationship between revenue and costs (and hence the profit or loss) at any volume within the relevant range. It can be used to analyze the probable consequences of various proposals to change the basic relationships depicted therein. Since profit is affected by factors other than volume, however, the profitgraph does not tell the whole story.

Appendix A   THE LEAST-SQUARES METHOD

If the variable measured on the vertical axis is designated y and that on the horizontal axis x, then *any* straight line is described by the equation, $y = a + bx$. In order to describe a *specific* straight line, we must assign specific numerical values to the two constants (or "parameters"), a and b.

> *EXAMPLE:* Exhibit 6–11 shows the line $y = 2 + \frac{1}{2}x$. Notice that the line cuts the y axis at a value of 2, and that for each unit increase in x, y increase one-half unit.

The technique of fitting a straight line by the method of least squares makes use of this equation for a straight line. It fits a straight line through a series of observations of x, values such that the **squares of the distances of each observation from the line is at a minimum** (hence "least squares"). Distances from the points representing individual observations to the line of best fit are measured *vertically,* that is, parallel to the y axis.

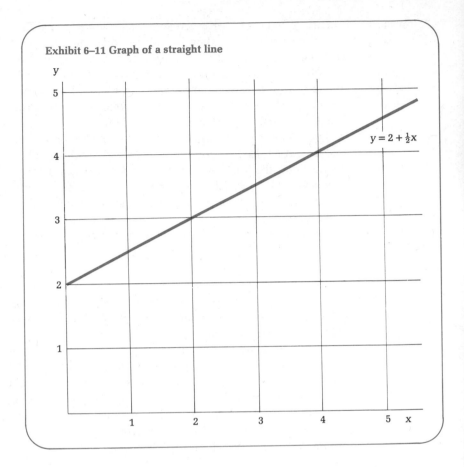

Exhibit 6–11 Graph of a straight line

$y = 2 + \frac{1}{2}x$

To compute the parameters for the least-squares line, we write down in two adjacent columns every value of x and beside each value of x the corresponding value of y. In a third column we put the square of each value of x and in the fourth column, we put the product of each x times the corresponding y (i.e., xy). We then total each column and use the symbol Σx^2 to denote the sum of the squares of the x values, and Σxy to denote the sum of the products of x times the corresponding y. (Notice that Σx^2 does *not* denote the square of the sum of the x's, nor does Σxy denote the total of the x's times the total of y's; each pair of values is treated separately.) We then determine the parameters a and b in the equation for a straight line by solving the two simultaneous "normal equations":

$$Na + b(\Sigma x) = \Sigma y$$
$$a(\Sigma x) + b(\Sigma x^2) = \Sigma xy$$

N is the number of items, that is, the number of x, y pairs.

Suppose we have the following observations of costs and volume in four periods:

	Volume (Units)	Costs
	0	$10
	1	12
	2	13
	3	15

We write the figures:

(1) x	(2) y	(3) x^2	(4) xy
0	10	0	0
1	12	1	12
2	13	4	26
3	15	9	45
$\Sigma x = 6$	$\Sigma y = 50$	$\Sigma x^2 = 14$	$\Sigma xy = 83$

Therefore,

$$\Sigma x = 6,\ \Sigma y = 50,\ \Sigma x^2 = 14,\ \Sigma xy = 83,\ N = 4;$$

and the normal equations given above become

$$50 = 4a + 6b$$
$$83 = 6a + 14b$$

To solve for a and b, multiply the first equation by 3 and the second equation by 2 and get—

$$150 = 12a + 18b$$
$$166 = 12a + 28b$$

Subtract the first equation from the second and get—

$$16 = 10b$$
$$b = 1.6$$

Therefore, $50 = 4a + 9.6$ (from the first normal equation with 9.6 written in place of $6b$):

$$4a = 40.4$$
$$a = 10.1$$

Therefore, the equation of the least-squares line is:

$$y = 10.1 + 1.6x$$

In terms of cost analysis

$$a = \text{Fixed cost per period} = \$10.1$$
$$b = \text{Variable cost per}$$
$$\text{unit of volume} = 1.6$$

Most computers and some minicalculators have programs that will calculate a least-squares line directly after the x, y values are entered.

Appendix B   EFFECT OF DIRECT COSTING ON INCOME

When the number of units of product *sold* in a given period is different from the number of units *manufactured* in that period, a direct cost
system gives a quite different net income figure for the period than does
an absorption cost system. The difference is demonstrated in Exhibit 6–12. The assumed situation is as follows:

Selling price..............................	$100 per unit
Costs:	
Variable manufacturing.....................	25 per unit
Fixed manufacturing.......................	140 per period
Selling and administrative.................	30 per period

Assuming that four units are manufactured each period, the product
costs per unit will be as follows:

	Product Costs per Unit	
	Absorption Costing	*Direct Costing*
Variable costs............................	$25	$25
Fixed manufacturing cost..................	35	0
Product cost per unit.................	$60	$25

In Period No. 1 four units are manufactured, but only two units are
sold. The other two units are in finished goods inventory as of the end
of the period. The income reported under absorption costing is higher
than that reported under direct costing. This is because in absorption
costing $70 of fixed manufacturing cost has become part of the cost of
the two units that are in finished goods inventory and hence do not
affect income for the period, whereas in direct costing the entire $140
of fixed manufacturing cost affects income for the period.

Exhibit 6–12

Comparison of absorption costing and direct costing

PERIOD 1. PRODUCTION EXCEEDS SALES

Units manufactured = 4
Units sold   = 2

Income Statements

	Absorption Costing		*Direct Costing*
Sales revenue.....................................	$200		$200
Cost of goods sold...............................	120		50
Gross margin.....................................	$ 80		$150
Fixed manufacturing costs........................		$140	
Selling and administrative.......................	30	30	170
Income (or loss)..................................	$ 50		$(20)
Ending inventory (2 units).......................	120		50

Exhibit 6–12 (continued)

PERIOD 2. SALES EXCEEDS PRODUCTION

Units manufactured = 4
Units sold   = 6

Income Statements

	Absorption Costing		Direct Costing
Sales revenue (6 units)........................	$600		$600
Cost of goods sold............................	360		150
Gross margin................................	$240		$450
Fixed manufacturing costs......................		$140	
Selling and administrative.....................	30	30	170
Income or (loss).............................	$210		$280
Ending inventory............................	0		0

In Period 2, four units are manufactured but six units are sold (i.e., the four units manufactured in Period 2 plus the two units that were in finished goods inventory). In this period, the income reported under absorption costing is lower than that reported under direct costing. This is because the cost of goods sold under absorption costing includes the $70 of fixed manufacturing cost that had become attached to the two units that were in finished goods inventory, whereas in direct costing this $70 was part of the expense of Period 1.

Important terms	Differential cost	Input measures
	Variable cost	Output measures
	Fixed cost	Profitgraph
	Semivariable cost	Break-even volume
	Contribution margin	Marginal income
	Relevant range	Learning curve
	High-low method	Direct cost system
	Scatter diagram	Absorption cost system
	Drift	

Questions for discussion

1. The accounts contain an item, "Wages earned, $1,000." Describe, so as to distinguish between them, situations in which this $1,000 would be (a) a product cost, (b) a direct cost, (c) a variable cost, (d) a differential cost, (e) an indirect cost, and (f) a fixed cost.

2. "All items of cost can change, but only certain items are variable." Explain and illustrate each half of this sentence.

3. "My records show that gasoline costs me 5 cents a mile, regardless of how many miles I drive my car, whereas my insurance cost obviously varies with the number of miles I drive. Therefore, gasoline is a fixed cost and insurance is a variable cost." Comment.

4. Refer to Exhibit 6–1. If the business was considering buying a building rather than renting it, what items of cost would be differential?

Include both items of cost listed on Exhibit 6–1 and items *not* listed thereon.

5. Explain in your own words the differences between full costs and differential costs.

6. In all the examples given in the text, unit cost decreases as volume increases. Can you think of circumstances in which unit cost would *increase* with an increase in volume?

7. The cost-volume diagram, Exhibit 6–5, does not identify semivariable costs. Why?

8. "The cost-volume diagram shows the relationship between costs and volume under the conditions prevailing at a certain time." How would Exhibit 6–5 be affected if (a) there was an increase in wage and salary rates? (b) if the company added a safety engineer? (c) if direct material costs per unit decreased? (d) if the company purchased an automatic machine to perform certain operations that currently are done manually?

9. How would the unit cost diagram in Exhibit 6–6 be affected by each of the changes listed in Question 8?

10. In Exhibit 6–5, the top of the relevant range is a volume of 1,200 units. What conditions could cause a difference in cost behavior at a volume higher than 1,200 units?

11. Describe methods for estimating the fixed cost per period and the variable cost per unit of volume.

12. Identify the numbered components on the profitgraph in Exhibit 6–13.

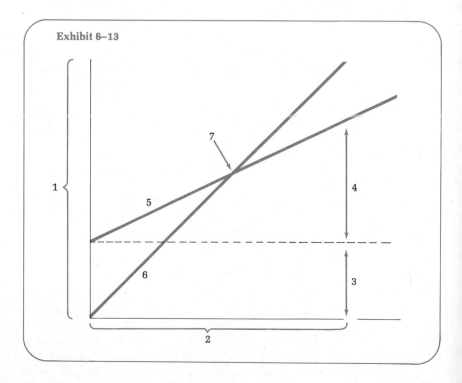

Exhibit 6–13

13.   Under what circumstances could machine-hours appropriately be used as a measure of volume on a profitgraph?

14.   Under what circumstances can a profitgraph such as that shown in Exhibit 6–9 be used if a company makes several products? Why is it invalid under other circumstances?

15.   Why are differential costs not labeled as such in an accounting system?

Problems   6–1.   The graphs in Exhibit 6–14 relate to the actions of certain costs involved with the operation of a summer basketball camp for boys:

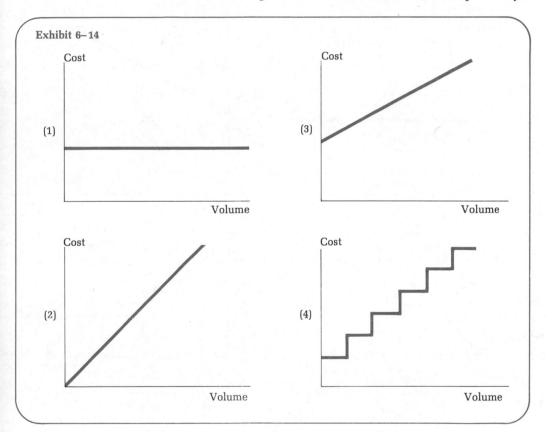

Exhibit 6–14

Required:

1.   Title each graph to show the type of cost it describes (fixed, variable, semivariable, etc.).

2.   From the list of costs described below select those which each graph describes:

Costs
(a) Cost of food served campers.
(b) Counsellors' salaries. An additional counsellor is hired for every 20 campers enrolled over the first 100.
(c) Repairs and maintenance. The maintenance foreman is on salary. Other repairs and labor depend on funds available as campers increase.
(d) Depreciation of camp real estate and equipment.

6-2. The graphs in Exhibit 6–15 relate to the behavior of certain costs involved in the operation of a mechanical arts course offered by a local corporation in a program of adult education:

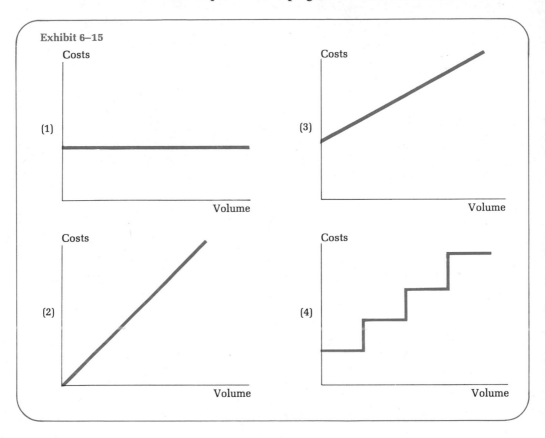

Exhibit 6–15

Required:
1. Title each graph to show the type of cost it describes (fixed, variable, semivariable, etc.).
2. From the list of costs described below select those which each graph describes:

Costs
(a) Cost of raw materials used by students.
(b) Depreciation of machinery and equipment used.

(c) Cost of blueprints and manuals. Extra copies must be acquired for every 6 students who enroll over the minimum
number of 24.

(d) Utilities and maintenance. Utilities remain constant each
month, but maintenance tends to vary with the usage of
machinery and equipment.

6–3. Bolter Company sells two products, A and B. In 1974 it sold 2,000
units of A at $100 per unit. It had purchased these 2,000 units at a
cost of $60 per unit, and had repackaged them at an additional
cost of $10 per unit. It sold 2,000 units of Product B at $50 per
unit. The purchase cost of these units was $35 per unit, and there
were no repackaging costs. All other costs of Bolter Company were
fixed. In 1974 they amounted to $60,000, and were allocated to
Products A and B in proportion to sales revenue.

Required:

1. Prepare an income statement for 1974 in which all costs are
assigned to each product.
2. Prepare an income statement for 1974 that shows the contribution of each product and for the company as a whole. Discuss the differences between this income statement and the income statement prepared in Part 1.
3. In 1975, it is expected that the sales price of Product B must
be decreased to $40 per unit in order to meet competition, other
conditions remaining as in 1974. Prepare an estimated income
statement for 1975.
4. Under the circumstances given in (3), should Product B be
discontinued?

6–4. Austin Company sells two products, A and B. In 1974 it sold 3,000
units of Product A and 1,000 units of Product B. For Product A,
the unit selling price was $100, and the unit purchase cost was $60.
For Product B, the unit selling price was $100, and the unit pur-
chase cost was $70. A sales commission of 10 percent of the selling
price was paid for each product. All other costs were fixed. They
totalled $80,000, and $40,000 was allocated to each product.

Required:

1. Prepare an income statement for 1974 in which all costs are
assigned to each product.
2. Prepare an income statement for 1974 that shows the contribution of each product and for the company as a whole. Discuss
the differences between this income statement and the income
statement prepared in Part 1.
3. Should Product B be discontinued?
4. In 1975, it is expected that the sales volume of each product
will be 2,000 units, other conditions remaining as in 1974.
Prepare an estimated income statement for 1975.

5. What accounts for the difference in net income of 1975 as compared with that of 1974?

6–5. Two competing food vendors were located side by side at a state fair. Both occupied buildings of the same size, paid the same rent, $1,250, and charged similar prices for their food. Vendor A employed three times as many employees as B and had twice as much income as B even though B had more than half the sales of A. Other data:

	Vendor A	Vendor B
Sales	$8,000	$4,500
Cost of goods sold	50% sales	50% sales
Wages	$2,250	$ 750

Required:

1. Present the data given in the form of a marginal income analysis statement.
2. Explain why Vendor A is twice as profitable as Vendor B.
3. By how much would Vendor B's sales have to increase in order to justify the doubling of the number of employees at the same rate of pay if his desired net income is $350?

6–6. The Downtown Department Store is concerned about the profitability of Departments A and B. A condensed income statement for Department A for 1974 follows:

Sales		$100,000
Cost of goods sold		50,000
Gross margin		$ 50,000
Wages	$24,000	
Fixed expense	20,000	44,000
Income		$ 6,000

Employees worked full time. The percentage gross margin for both departments A and B was the same at 50 percent, but Department B had only $36,000 sales and a fourth of the wages of A. Fixed expenses allocated to Department B were $20,000.

Required:

1. Which department is the more profitable? Why?
2. Present the data given in the form of a marginal income analysis statement.
3. By how much would the sales of Department A have to increase in order to justify the addition of a $2,000 display case estimated to last ten years, if the same income is desired from Department A as it currently has?

6–7. Production costs in Department A for the preceding six months were as follows:

	Month					
	Jan.	*Feb.*	*Mar.*	*Apr.*	*May*	*June*
Units of production...........	200	280	260	300	240	260
Total cost........	$8,000	$9,600	$9,300	$9,900	$8,700	$9,500

Required:

1. Estimate fixed and variable costs by the high-low method.
2. Estimate fixed and variable costs by drawing a scatter diagram.
3. If production in a certain month is estimated to be 250 units, what is your estimate of total cost?

6–8. Production costs in Department B for the preceding six months were as follows:

Month	*July*	*Aug.*	*Sept.*	*Oct.*	*Nov.*	*Dec.*
Units of production...........	1,000	1,200	1,400	1,100	900	800
Total cost........	$3,100	$3,500	$3,600	$3,100	$2,900	$2,600

Required:

1. Estimate fixed and variable costs by the high-low method.
2. Estimate fixed and variable costs by drawing a scatter diagram.
3. If production in a certain month is estimated to be 1,200 units, what is your estimate of total cost?

6–9. Using the formula $y = a + bx$ for the cost at any volume, and the formula $px = a + bx$ for the break-even volume, answer the questions below, using the data following:

Fixed costs per period..........................	$45,500
Variable costs per unit..........................	$ 25
Standard sales volume per period (units)...........	30,000
Selling price per unit..........................	$ 60

Required:

1. Calculate the total cost at standard volume.
2. Calculate the break-even point in units.
3. Calculate the profit or loss at standard volume.
4. What is the marginal income?
5. Compute the income which would result at the standard volume if both the variable cost per unit and the selling price per unit increased by 20 percent.

6–10. Using the formula $y = a + bx$ for the cost at any volume, and the formula $px = a + bx$ for the break-even volume, answer the questions below, using the data following:

```
Fixed costs..........................  $60,000
Variable costs at standard volume........  $12,000
Standard volume......................   6,000 units
Selling price per unit.................  $    20
```

Required:

1. Calculate the total cost at standard volume.
2. Calculate the break-even point in units.
3. Calculate the profit or loss at standard volume.
4. How much loss will be incurred with the sale of two units less than the break-even units?
5. Compute the income which would result at standard volume if the fixed costs and total sales both decreased by $5,000.

6–11. The 1975 budget for Collegiate Gift Shoppe contains the following data:

```
Total assets.......................  $180,000
Revenues...........................   200,000
Total expenses.....................   160,000
Fixed expenses.....................    40,000
```

Required:

1. What is the *formula* for estimating the income at various volumes under these circumstances?
2. What is the expected break-even point for 1975?
3. If the maximum capacity of this firm is $300,000 sales without further investment, what is the maximum potential rate of return on assets?
4. If $10,000 of fixed expenses could be transferred to variable costs of sales, what is the dollar effect on—
    (a) Income, and
    (b) Break-even point?

6–12. The 1975 budget for the College Soda Shop contains the following data:

```
Liabilities........................  $ 40,000
Capital stock......................    42,500
Retained earnings..................     7,500
Sales..............................   100,000
Fixed expenses.....................    20,000
Variable expenses..................    60,000
```

Required:

1. What is the *formula* for estimating the income at various volumes under these circumstances?
2. What is the break-even volume in 1975?

3. If the maximum capacity of this firm is $150,000 of sales utilizing the current level of assets, what is the maximum potential rate of return on these assets?

4. If the cost of goods sold can be reduced by $5,000 by changing suppliers, what is the dollar effect on—
   (a) Net income, and
   (b) Break-even point?

6–13. Mr. Blaine, manager of the Radio Hut, a retail store specializing in radio, stereo, and tape equipment, is trying to decide whether there is a predictable relationship between store wages and sales volume. Employees of the store include general office help and two full-time clerks, whose costs were the same each week. In periods of peak activity part-time clerks are hired. Average weekly amounts for selected accounts for the last year are as follows:

Sales...................... $12,500
Wages..................... 1,155 (total)
Wages..................... 625 (part-time clerks)

Required:

1. Use the formula $y = a + bx$ to predict the future amount of wages for a week when estimated sales will be $15,000.

2. If sales increased enough to warrant the addition of another full-time clerk adding $150 a week to wages, predict (a) the wages expected to be paid part-time clerks in a week when sales were $20,000, and (b) the total wages which will be paid.

3. What sales volume would warrant the expenditure of $800 a week for part-time help, assuming fixed wages remained the same as in (1) above?

4. Does there seem to be a predictable relationship between wages and sales volume that can aid Mr. Blaine in future planning? Explain.

6–14. The manager of Motor-Magic Shop, a repair business specializing in the maintenance and repair of small engines and motors, is studying costs in relation to service revenue. He is currently concerned with the relationship of wages paid mechanics to sales revenue. The shop employs two full-time mechanics who are paid $150 each per week, and uses part-time help who are students from a local vocational training program when volume is more than these two mechanics can handle. They are paid on an hourly basis. Last year, part-time wages averaged $72 per week, and sales averaged $800 per week.

Required:

1. Use the formula $y = a + bx$ to predict the future amount of wages for a week in which sales are expected to be $900.

2. What weekly revenue would warrant wages of $180 per week for part-time workers?
3. A bookkeeper was hired at the wage rate of $120 per week. Predict the total wages which would be paid in a week which had total sales of $950.
4. Does there seem to be a predictable relationship between wages and sales volume? Explain.

6–15. The condensed income statement for a line of antique bottles manufactured by Reproductions, Inc., for the past year follows:

Sales...............................	$60,000
Cost of goods sold.......................	50,000
Gross margin............................	$10,000
Selling and administrative expense........	18,000
Net Loss...............................	$(8,000)

The costs include certain costs which would be incurred whether the bottles were made or not. Fixed product costs included in cost of goods sold amount to $26,000, and other fixed costs amount to $14,-000.

Required:

1. Restate the results of operations for the antique bottle line in a form which management would find more useful in making a decision as to whether to continue to make antique bottles.
2. Which is more profitable, to continue or discontinue the bottle line?
3. What factors would become relevant to management's decision if there is an offer to buy the bottle operations?

6–16. Following are simplified data for costs and volume in four months:

Month	*Volume (units)*	*Cost*
September.....................	4	$6
October......................	3	5
November.....................	5	7
December....................	2	4

Required:

Compute fixed and variable cost by the method of least squares.

6–17. The controller of LaMay, Inc., wants to compare the operating results of direct costing and absorption costing using data taken from company records for the first three years of operations. Unit production costs are computed each year, using Fifo to assign inventory costs to revenue. There are no ending inventories of goods in process in any year. The following data are available:

Units	Year 1	Year 2	Year 3
Beginning inventory of finished goods....	0	4,000	2,000
Production...........................	5,000	2,000	4,000
Sales................................	1,000	4,000	4,000

Costs and Revenues	Year 1	Year 2	Year 3
Sales................................	$50,000	$200,000	$200,000
Raw material used....................	75,000	30,000	60,000
Direct labor.........................	50,000	20,000	40,000
Fixed factory overhead...............	60,000	60,000	60,000
Selling and administrative costs........	6,500	14,000	14,000

Required:

1. Prepare an income statement for each of the three years using direct costing.
2. Prepare the net income for each of the three years using absorption costing.
3. What accounts for the discrepancy between the income computed under the different method?

7 Alternative choice decisions

Purpose of
the chapter

In Chapter 6 we introduced the concept of differential costs and differential revenues, and we described techniques for identifying these types of costs and revenues and for using them in the analysis of problems that involved changes in volume. In Chapter 7, our purpose is to describe the use of differential costs in analyzing several other types of problems. These problems can be designated *alternative choice* problems, for in each case the manager seeks to choose the best one of several alternative courses of action.

Nature of
alternative
choice
problems

In an alternative choice problem two or more alternative courses of action are specified and the manager chooses the one that he believes to be the best.[1]

In many alternative choice problems, the choice is made on a strictly judgmental basis; that is, there is no systematic attempt to define, measure, and assess the advantages and disadvantages of each alternative. A person who makes a judgmental decision may do so simply because he is not aware of any other way of making up his mind, or he may do so, and with good reason, because the problem is one in which a systematic attempt to assess alternatives is too difficult, too expensive, or simply not possible. No mathematical formula will help solve a problem in which the attitudes or emotions of the individuals involved are dominant factors, nor is there any point in trying to make calcula-

---

[1] In a broad sense, *all* business problems involve a choice among alternatives. The problems discussed here are those in which the alternatives are clearly specified.

196

tions if the available information is so sketchy or so inaccurate that the results would be completely unreliable.

In many other situations, however, it is useful to reduce at least some of the potential consequences of each alternative to a quantitative basis and to weigh these consequences in a systematic manner. In this and the next two chapters, we discuss techniques for making such an analysis.

BUSINESS OBJECTIVES

In an alternative choice problem, the manager seeks the *best* alternative. "Best" refers to that alternative which is most likely to accomplish the objectives of his organization. Although it is safe to say that the dominant objective of a business is to earn a profit, such a statement is not specific enough for our present purpose.

When investors furnish funds to a business, they do so in the expectation of earning a return, that is, a profit, on these investments. Presumably the more profit that is earned on a given investment, the greater the satisfaction of the investors. This idea leads to the economists' statement that the objective of a business is to *maximize the return on its investment*. The maximization idea, however, is too difficult to apply in most practical situations. The businessman does not know, out of all the very large number of alternative courses of action available to him, which one will produce the absolute maximum return on investment. Furthermore, return on investment is not the *only* objective of a business. Many actions which could increase return on investment are ethically unacceptable. Setting selling prices that charge all the traffic will bear is one example. For these reasons, the idea that an important objective of a business is to earn a *satisfactory* return on its investment is more realistic and more ethically sound than the idea that the sole objective is to maximize return on investment.

Satisfactory return on investment is an important objective, but it is by no means the only objective of a business. In many practical problems, personal satisfaction, friendship, patriotism, self-esteem, or other considerations may be much more important than return on investment. The company may have other measurable objectives, such as maintenance of its market position, stabilization of employment, avoidance of undue risk, or increasing its net income as reported on its income statement.[2] When these considerations are important or dominant, the solution to the problem cannot be reached by the techniques discussed here. The most these techniques can do is show the effect on return on investment of seeking some other objective. The problem then becomes

---

[2] For reasons to be described in Chapter 8, net income as measured by generally accepted accounting principles does not necessarily reflect the "well-offness" of a business.

one of deciding whether the attainment of the other objective is worth the cost.

Steps in
analysis

The analysis of most alternative choice problems involves the following steps:

1. Define the problem.
2. Select the most likely alternative solutions.
3. Measure and weigh those consequences of each selected alternative that can be expressed in quantitative terms.
4. Evaluate those consequences that cannot be expressed in quantitative terms and weigh them against each other and against the measured consequences.
5. Reach a decision.

In this book, we focus primarily on information that can be expressed in quantitative terms. Thus, we are here interested primarily in Step 3 of the above list. Brief mention will be made of the other steps.

STEPS 1 AND 2. DEFINITION OF THE PROBLEM AND OF ALTERNATIVE SOLUTIONS

Unless the problem is clearly and precisely defined, quantitative amounts that are relevant to its solution cannot be determined. In many situations, the definition of the problem, or even the recognition that a problem exists, may be the most difficult part of the whole process. Moreover, even after the problem has been identified, the possible alternative solutions to it often are by no means clear at the outset.

> *EXAMPLE:* A factory manager is considering a machinery salesman's proposal that a certain machine should be used to produce automatically a part that is now being produced by manual methods. At first glance, there may appear to be two alternatives: (*a*) continue to make the part by manual methods or (*b*) buy the new machine. Actually, however, several additional alternatives should perhaps be considered, such as these: (*c*) buy a machine other than the one recommended by the salesman, (*d*) improve the present method of making the part, or even (*e*) eliminate the manufacturing operation altogether and buy the part from an outside source. Some thought should be given to these other possibilities before attention is focused too closely on the original proposal.

On the other hand, the more alternatives that are considered, the more complex the analysis becomes. For this reason, having identified all the possible alternatives, the analyst should eliminate on a judgmental basis those that are clearly unattractive, leaving only a few for detailed analysis.

In most problems, one of the alternatives is to continue what is now being done, that is, to reject a proposed change. This alternative is referred to as the **base case.**[3] It is used as a benchmark against which other alternatives are compared. Note that there must always be at least two alternatives. If only one course of action is open, the company literally has "no choice"; therefore, it has no decision and no need for analysis.

STEP 3. WEIGHING AND MEASURING THE QUANTITATIVE FACTORS

Usually, a number of advantages and a number of disadvantages are associated with each of the alternatives. The task of the decision maker is to evaluate each of the relevant factors and to decide, on balance, which alternative has the largest net advantage. If the factors, or variables, are expressed solely in words, such an evaluation is an exceedingly difficult task.

> *EXAMPLE:* Consider the statement: "A proposed manufacturing process will save labor, but it will result in increased power consumption and require additional insurance protection." Such a statement provides no way of weighing the relative importance of the saving in labor against the increased power and insurance costs. If, by contrast, the statement is "The proposed process will save $1,000 in labor, but power costs will increase by $200 and insurance costs will increase by $100," the net effect of these three factors can easily be determined; that is, $1,000 − ($200 + $100) indicates a net advantage of $700 for the proposed process.

The reason why we try to express as many factors as possible in quantitative terms is demonstrated in the above illustration: once we have done this, it becomes easy to find the net effect of these factors by the simple arithmetic operations of addition and subtraction.

STEP 4. EVALUATING THE UNMEASURED FACTORS

For most problems, there are important factors that are not measurable; yet the final decision must take into account all differences between the alternatives being considered, both those that are measured and those not measured. The process of weighing the relative importance of these unmeasured factors, both as compared with one another and as compared with the net advantage or disadvantage of the measured factors, is a judgmental process.

It is easy to underestimate the importance of these unmeasured factors. The numerical calculations for the measured factors often

---

[3] For convenience, the base case may be identified as Case 1, and the other alternatives as Case 2, Case 3, etc.

require hard work, and they result in a figure that has the appearance of being definite and precise; yet all the factors that influence the final number may be collectively less important than a single factor that cannot be measured. For example, many persons could meet their transportation needs less expensively by using public conveyances rather than by operating an automobile, but they nevertheless own an automobile for reasons of prestige, convenience, or other factors that cannot be measured quantitatively.

To the extent that calculations can be made, these make it possible to express as a single number the net effect of many factors that bear on the decision. They therefore reduce the number of factors that must be considered separately in the final judgment process that leads to the decision; that is, they narrow the area within which judgment must be exercised. Rarely, if ever, do they eliminate the necessity for this crucial judgment process.

STEP 5. REACHING A DECISION

After his first attempt to identify, evaluate, and weigh the factors, the decision maker has two choices: (1) he can seek additional information or (2) he can make a decision and act on it. Many decisions could be improved by obtaining additional information, and it is usually possible to obtain such information. However, obtaining the additional information always involves effort (which means cost), and what is more important, it involves time. There comes a point, therefore, when the businessman concludes that he is better off to act than to defer a decision until more data have been collected.

Differential costs

In Chapter 6 we introduced the type of cost construction called differential costs. Since differential costs are normally used in analyzing alternative choice problems, we now discuss them in more depth.

If some alternative to the base case (i.e., the present method of operation or "status quo") is proposed, differential costs are those that will be different under the proposed alternative than they are in the base case. Items of cost that will be unaffected by the proposal are not differential. The term **out-of-pocket costs** is used generally to mean the same thing as differential cost. There is no general category of costs that can be labeled "differential." Direct labor costs are differential in many problems; but if in a specific situation people are going to be employed regardless of which alternative is adopted, labor costs are not differential. For example, it can be demonstrated that a given quantity of manuscript pages or letters can be typed in less time with an electric typewriter than with a nonelectric typewriter, but an actual saving in labor costs will result from the purchase of an electric typewriter only if the time thus freed is used productively for some other purpose.

EXAMPLE: A company is considering the possibility of buying Part No. 101 from an outside supplier instead of manufacturing the part as it is now doing. In this case the base case is to continue manufacturing Part No. 101, and the alternative (or Case 2) is to purchase Part No. 101 from the outside supplier. All revenue items, all selling and administrative expenses, and all production costs other than those directly associated with the manufacture of Part No. 101 will probably be unaffected by the decision. If so, there is no need to consider them. Items of differential cost could be as follows:

	If Part No. 101 Is Manufactured (Base Case)	If Part No. 101 Is Purchased (Case 2)	Difference −	Difference +
Direct material........	$ 570	0	$ 570	
Purchased parts.......		$1,700		$1,700
Direct labor..........	600	0	600	
Power...............	70	0	70	
Other costs...........	150	0	150	
Total..........	$1,390	$1,700	$1,390	$1,700
				−1,390
Net differential cost...				$ 310

Since costs would be increased by $310 if Part No. 101 were purchased, the indication is the proposal to purchase Part No. 101 should be rejected.

MECHANICS OF THE CALCULATION

There is no prescribed format for making a comparison of the differential costs of the several alternatives. The arrangement should be that which is most convenient and which most clearly sets forth the facts to the decision maker.

EXAMPLE: For the problem described in the preceding example, the same result can be obtained, with somewhat less effort, if the total differential costs of each alternative are calculated instead of finding the difference for each item of cost, viz:

	If Part No. 101 Is Manufactured	If Part No. 101 Is Purchased
Direct material.....................	$ 570	$ 0
Purchased parts....................	0	1,700
Direct labor......................	600	0
Power...........................	70	0
Other costs.......................	150	0
Total.....................	$1,390	$1,700
		−1,390
Difference (disadvantage of purchasing).....................		$ 310

Or, exactly the same result can be obtained by figuring the net differences between the alternatives, viz:

		Costs if *Part No. 101* *Is Purchased*
Purchase price of Part No. 101..........		$1,700
Costs saved by not manufacturing		
Part No. 101:		
Direct material.....................	$570	
Direct labor.......................	600	
Power...........................	70	
Other costs......................	150	
Total costs saved................		−1,390
Net disadvantage in purchasing........		$ 310

COSTS THAT ARE UNAFFECTED

Although items of cost that are unaffected by the decision are not differential and may be disregarded, a listing of some or all of these unaffected costs nevertheless may be useful so as to insure that all cost items have been considered. If this is done, it is essential that the unaffected costs be treated in exactly the same way under each of the alternatives. The net difference between the costs of the two alternatives, which is the result we seek, is not changed by adding equal amounts to the cost of each alternative.

> *EXAMPLE:* Part No. 101 is one component of Product A. It may be convenient to list each of the items of cost, and perhaps even the revenue, for each of the alternatives, as in Exhibit 7–1. The difference in profit is the same $310 that was arrived at in the earlier examples. This is because the proposal to purchase Part No. 101 had no effect on the revenue of Product A, nor on the costs of Product A, other than those already listed.

Exhibit 7–1

Calculation of differential profit

	Profit on Product A			
		Base Case		*Purchase of* *Part No. 101*
Revenue.........................		$10,000		$10,000
Costs:				
Direct material..................	$1,570		$1,000	
Purchased parts.................	0		1,700	
Direct labor....................	3,000		2,400	
Power..........................	200		130	
Other costs.....................	450		300	
Occupancy costs.................	800		800	
General and administrative.........	3,000		3,000	
Total costs...................		9,020		9,330
Profit..........................		$ 980		$ 670
		670 ←		
Differential in profit................		$ 310		

The calculation in Exhibit 7–1 requires somewhat more effort than those in the preceding examples, but it may be easier to understand, and the practice of listing each item of cost and revenue helps to insure that no differential costs are overlooked.

DANGER OF USING FULL COST

The full costs that are measured in a full cost accounting system may be misleading in alternative choice problems. In particular, when estimating differential costs, items of cost that are allocated to products should be viewed with skepticism. Full costs usually do not reflect, and are not intended to reflect, the differential costs for most alternative choice problems. A company may allocate overhead costs to products as 100 percent of direct labor; but this does not mean that if direct labor costs are decreased by $600 by purchasing Part No. 101, there will be a corresponding decrease of $600 in overhead costs. Overhead costs may not decrease at all; they may decrease, but by an amount less than $600; or they may even increase, as a result of an increased procurement and inspection work load resulting from the purchase of Part No. 101. In order to estimate what will actually happen to overhead costs, we must go behind the overhead rate and analyze what will happen to the various elements of overhead.

> *EXAMPLE:* The full costs of Product A, as shown on Exhibit 7–1, included an item of $800 for occupancy costs and an item of $3,000 for general and administrative costs. Occupancy cost is the cost of the building in which Product A is manufactured, and the $800 represents the share of total occupancy cost that is allocated to Product A. If Part No. 101, one part in Product A, is purchased, the floor space in which Part No. 101 is now manufactured no longer would be required. It does not necessarily follow, however, that occupancy costs would thereby be reduced. The costs of rent, heat, light, and other items comprising occupancy costs might not be changed at all by the decision to purchase Part No. 101. Unless the actual amount of occupancy cost were changed, this item of cost is not differential.
>
> Similarly, general and administrative costs of the whole company probably would be unaffected by a decision to purchase Part No. 101; unless these costs would be affected, they are not differential.

FRINGE BENEFITS

Labor costs are one of the important items of cost in many business decisions. The real cost of labor is significantly higher than the actual amount of wages earned. It includes such items as the employers' taxes for old-age and unemployment compensation; insurance, medical, and pension plans; vacation and holiday pay; and other fringe benefits. For business in general, these benefits average about 25 percent of wages earned, although there is a wide variation among different companies.

In estimating differential labor costs, fringe benefits usually should be taken into account.

OPPORTUNITY COSTS

Opportunity cost measures the opportunity which is lost or sacrificed when the choice of one course of action requires that an alternative course of action be given up. Opportunity costs are not measured in accounting records, and they are not relevant in many alternative choice problems, but they are significant in certain situations. In general, if accepting an alternative requires that facilities or other resources must be devoted to that alternative that otherwise could be used for some other purpose, there is an opportunity cost, and it is measured by the profit that would have been earned had the resources been devoted to the other purpose.

> *EXAMPLE:* If the floor space required to make Part No. 101 can be used for some other revenue-producing purpose, then the sacrifice involved in using it for Part No. 101 is an opportunity cost of making that part. This cost is measured by the income that would be sacrificed if the floor space is used for Part No. 101; this is not necessarily the same as the allocated occupancy cost per square foot of floor space as developed in the cost accounting system.
>
> If the floor space used for Part No. 101 could be used to manufacture another item that could be sold for a profit of $400, the $400 then becomes a cost of continuing to manufacture Part No. 101. The inclusion of this item would change the numbers as calculated in previous examples as follows:

	If Part No. 101 Is Manufactured (Base Case)	If Part No. 101 Is Purchased	Difference
Differential costs, as above........	$1,390	$1,700	+$310
Opportunity cost of floor space.....	400	0	− 400
Net differential cost (in favor of purchasing).....................			$ 90

The inclusion of this item of opportunity cost therefore changes the results of the calculation; the alternative of purchasing Part No. 101 now has a lower cost.

Opportunity costs are by their very nature "iffy." In most situations, it is extremely difficult to estimate what, if any, additional profit could be earned if the resources in question were devoted to some other use.

VARIABLE COSTS

The term "differential costs" does not have quite the same meaning as the term "variable costs." Variable costs are those that vary directly with changes in the volume of output. By contrast, differential costs are always related to specific alternatives that are being analyzed. If, in a specific problem, one of the alternatives involves a change in volume, then differential costs may well be the same as variable costs. Depending on the problem, however, the differential costs may include nonvariable items. A proposal to change the number of plant watchmen and their duties, for example, involves no elements of variable cost.

Marginal costs and **incremental costs** are terms used in economics for what accountants call variable costs. The marginal or incremental cost of a product is the cost of producing one additional unit of the product. Thus, marginal or incremental costs may be the same as differential costs in those problems in which an alternative under consideration involves changing the volume of output.

ESTIMATES OF FUTURE COSTS

Differential costs are estimates of what costs will be in the future. Nevertheless, in many instances our best information about future costs is derived from an analysis of historical costs. One can easily lose sight of the fact that historical costs, per se, are irrelevant. Historical costs may be a useful guide as to what costs are likely to be in the future, but using them as a guide is basically different from using them as if they were factual statements of what the future costs are going to be.

Except where future costs are determined by long-term contractual arrangements, differential costs are necessarily estimates, and they usually cannot be close estimates. An estimated labor saving of $1,000 a year for five years, for example, implies assumptions as to future wage rates, future fringe benefits, future labor efficiency, future production volume, and other factors that cannot be known with certainty at the time the estimate is prepared. Consequently, there is ordinarily no point in carrying computations of cost estimates to several decimal places; in fact, there is a considerable danger of being misled by the illusion of precision that such meticulous calculations give.

Book value of fixed assets. An element of historical cost that seems to cause considerable difficulty is the book value of fixed assets and the related depreciation expense. The book value of fixed assets is a **sunk cost.** A sunk cost exists because of actions taken in the past, not because of a decision made currently; therefore, a sunk cost is *not* a differential cost. No decision made by man can change what has already happened. The past is history; decisions made now can affect only what *will* happen in the future.

It is sometimes suggested that when a proposed alternative results in the disposition of an existing machine, the depreciation on that machine will no longer be a cost, and that the saving in depreciation expense should therefore be taken into account as an advantage of the proposed alternative. This is not so. This argument overlooks the fact that the book value of the machine will, sooner or later, be recorded as a cost, regardless of whether the proposed alternative is adopted. If the alternative is not adopted (i.e., the base case), depreciation on the machine will continue, whereas if the alternative *is* adopted, the remaining book value will be written off when the machine is disposed of. In either case, the total amount of cost is the same, so the book value is not a differential cost.

> *EXAMPLE:* A new production process is proposed as a substitute for operations now performed on a certain machine. The machine was purchased six years previously for $10,000, and depreciation on it has been recorded at $1,000 a year, a total of $6,000 to date. The machine therefore has a book value of $4,000. The machine has zero market value, that is, the cost of removing it just equals its value as scrap metal. The new process is estimated to require $1,100 of additional direct labor costs annually, but operating costs of the machine, which are $500 a year, will be saved. The cost analysis of differential costs is shown in Part A of Exhibit 7–2. The analysis indicates that the new process will have additional costs of $600 a year, and that it therefore should not be adopted.
>
> It is sometimes argued, however, that this calculation neglects the $1,000 annual saving in depreciation costs that will occur if the machine is disposed of, and that the new process will therefore save $400 a year (= $1,000 − $600), rather than incurring additional costs of $600 a year. This is a fallacious argument. The fact is that if the new process is accepted, the book value of the machine must be written off; and this amount exactly equals the total depreciation charge over the remaining life of the machine. Thus, there is no differential cost associated with the book value of the existing machine. If the new process is adopted, $4,000 of book value will be written off; whereas if the new process is not adopted, the same $4,000 will be recorded as depreciation expense over the next four years.
>
> The irrelevance of sunk costs can be demonstrated by comparison of two income statements for the complete time periods of the remaining life of the machine, one showing the results of operations if the new process is adopted and the machine is scrapped, and the other showing the results if the process is continued on the present machine. Such a comparison is made in Section C of Exhibit 7–2. This illustration demonstrates that there would be a loss of $2,400 over a four-year period, or $600 a year, if the new process were adopted.

The cost of an asset is supposed to be written off over its useful life. In the above example, we know by hindsight that this was not done, for if it had been done, the book value of the machine would be zero at the time it was disposed of. This was an error, but it was an error made in the past, and no current decision can change it.

If the machine had a market value, this fact *would* be a relevant consideration, since its disposal would then bring in additional cash. If the income tax effect of writing off the loss on disposal were different from the tax effect of writing off depreciation over the four-year period, the

Exhibit 7–2

Irrelevance of sunk costs

A. *Differential costs, one year*

	Base Case	If New Process Is Adopted
Additional direct labor costs....	$ 0	$1,100
Machine operating costs.......	500	0
Total.................	$500	$1,100
		−500
Net differential costs..........		$ 600

(Depreciation is not a differential cost)

B. Net differential costs, four years
   ($600 × 4)............... $2,400

C. *Proof: Income statements for four-year period*

		Base Case		If New Process Is Adopted
Sales revenue................		$1,000,000		$1,000,000
Costs:				
Costs unaffected by the decision................	$700,000		$700,000	
Process direct labor costs....	0		4,400	
Machine operating costs.....	2,000		0	
Depreciation on machine....	4,000		0	
Loss on disposal of machine..	0		4,000	
Total costs............		706,000		708,400
Profit..		$ 294,000		$ 291,600
		−291,600		
Decrease in profit if new process is adopted........		$ 2,400		

effect of taxes is relevant. (The method of allowing for this tax effect will be discussed in Chapter 9.) The book value of the machine itself is not relevant. Ultimately, the book value is going to be charged against income, but whether this is done through the annual depreciation charge or through a lump-sum write-off makes no ultimate difference.

IMPORTANCE OF THE TIME SPAN

The question of what costs are relevant depends to a considerable extent on the time span of the problem. If the proposal is to make only one unit of Part No. 101, only the direct material costs may be relevant; the work could conceivably be done without any differential labor costs if workers were paid on a daily basis and had some idle time. At the other extreme, if the proposal involves a commitment to manufacture Part No. 101 over the foreseeable future, practically all items of manufacturing costs would be differential.

In general, the longer the time span of the proposal, the more items
of cost are differential. In the very long run, all costs are differential.
Thus, in very long-run problems, differential costs include the same
elements as full costs, for in the long run one must consider even the
replacement of buildings and equipment, which are sunk costs in the
short run. (Although the items are the same, the amounts are different,
since alternative choice problems involve future costs, not historical
costs.) In many short-run problems, relatively few cost items are subject
to change by a management decision.

**Types of
alternative
choice
problems**

As noted earlier, a dominant objective of a business is to earn a
satisfactory return on investment. The return on investment percentage
is profit divided by investment. Profit is the difference between revenue
and costs. Thus, three basic elements are involved in a company's return
on investment: (1) costs, (2) revenue, and (3) investment, or

$$\frac{\text{Revenue} - \text{Costs}}{\text{Investment}}$$

Although the general approach to all alternative choice problems is
similar, it is useful to discuss three subcategories separately. First, there
are problems that involve only the cost element. In these problems,
since revenue and investment elements are unaffected, the best alternative
is normally the one with the lowest cost. Problems of this type are discussed in the next section. Second, there are problems in which both the
revenue and costs elements are involved. Problems of this type are discussed in the latter part of this chapter. Third, there are problems that
involve investment as well as revenue and costs. These are discussed in
Chapters 8 and 9.

**Problems
involving
costs**

Illustrative of problems involving costs are the following questions:
Will a proposed new method of doing something cost less than the
present method? Which of several proposed methods is the best? Should
we manufacture a certain part or buy it from an outside vendor? Shall
we produce on one shift or two shifts? Shall we shut down the plant
temporarily? Problems of this type are often called **tradeoff problems:**
we wish to find out whether the differential costs of a proposed alternative are such that the alternative is a worthwhile tradeoff for the base
case.

We shall discuss the following types of problems in this category:

1. Methods changes.
2. Make or buy.
3. Economic order quantity.

METHODS CHANGES

In a problem involving a methods change, the base case is to maintain the *status quo,* and the alternative being proposed is the adoption of some new method. The method may be associated with manufacturing products or with any other activity that is part of the operation of the business. The cost analysis for many problems in this class is quite simple. The costs of continuing the present method are estimated and compared with the estimated costs under the proposed method. If the differential costs of the proposed method are significantly lower, the method should be adopted (unless nonquantitative considerations are present). Thus, if a new method of routing the product through the several machines in a department is found to save two hours of labor per unit, at a cost of $8 per hour, the differential savings is $16 per unit; the analysis therefore indicates that the proposed method should be adopted.

A practical difficulty in such problems is in deciding whether certain items of costs are in fact differential. If, for example, the computed labor time in the base case is 20 hours, and under the proposed method, labor time is estimated to be 18 hours, the calculated saving is two hours. This calculated savings may not be a real saving, however. If the number of employees is indeed reduced by 10 percent, or if the employees use the additional two hours to do other productive work, then the amount of the savings is genuine. If no change in the size of the work force or in its use occurs, then the labor cost is not differential, and the proposed method will not in fact add to profits.

MAKE OR BUY

Make-or-buy problems are among the most common type of alternative choice problems. At any given time, a business performs certain activities with its own employees, and it pays outside firms to perform certain other activities. It constantly seeks to improve the balance between these two types of activities by asking: Should we contract with some outside party to perform some function that we are now performing ourselves? Or, should we ourselves perform some activity that we now pay someone else to do? The possibilities are practically endless. They include such questions as whether to manufacture or to buy a given part which was illustrated in a preceding section, contracting for computer services, contracting for all or part of maintenance work, or hiring an outside legal firm rather than having lawyers on the company payroll. Make-or-buy problems even include such fundamental alternatives as whether to turn the entire selling function over to brokers or commission agents, or whether to discontinue manufacturing operations and become solely a marketing organization.

As the example given above for Part No. 101 shows, the cost of the outside service (the "buy" alternative) usually is easy to estimate; the problem is to find the differential costs of the "make" alternative. Perhaps the greatest difficulty in analyzing such problems is in deciding on the appropriate time span to be covered by the analysis. The Part No. 101 example pinpoints this problem. The analysis given above indicated that the cost of purchasing Part No. 101 was $1,700 and the estimated differential cost of manufacturing was $1,390, so there was an estimated saving from "making" of $310. But this saving might be earned only in the very short run. As noted above, in the longer run, overhead costs might in fact become differential. Thus, for an item that is currently being made, as a general rule, the "make" alternative is often attractive in short-run situations, especially when idle facilities exist, but the "buy" alternative may be attractive when a longer time span is considered.

Another problem in evaluating make-or-buy alternatives is that of controlling quality. There are many services which an outside specialist may perform more satisfactorily than company personnel, especially if the amount of services required is a relatively insignificant part of the company's activities. Most companies buy letterheads and forms from an outside source, for example. On the other hand, if the company performs the service itself, it may have better control over its quality than if it relies on an outside source. These are highly judgmental matters.

ECONOMIC ORDER QUANTITY

When the manufacture of a product involves setup costs that are incurred only once for each lot manufactured, the question arises of how many units should be made in one lot. If the demand is predictable and if sales are reasonably steady throughout the year, **the optimum quantity to manufacture at one time,** called the economic lot size or **economic order quantity,** is arrived at by considering two offsetting influences—setup costs and inventory carrying costs. Exhibit 7–3 shows how two alternative policies for an item with annual sales of 1,200 units, occurring at an even rate of 100 per month, affect inventory levels and the number of setups. Part A shows that if the whole 1,200 units were manufactured in one lot, only one setup a year would be necessary, but inventory carrying costs would be high, since the inventory would start with 1,200 units and would average 600 units over the year.[4] By contrast, as shown in Part B, the manufacture of four lots of 300 units each (i.e., one lot each quarter) would involve four times as much setup cost but a relatively low inventory carrying cost since there would be an average of only 150 units in inventory at any one time.

---

[4] Inventory is 1,200 units immediately after the lot has been manufactured and declines to zero a year later. Assuming that the decline is at a roughly even rate throughout the year, the average inventory for the year is one half the sum of the beginning plus ending inventories; thus: $\frac{1}{2}$ $(1,200 + 0) = 600$.

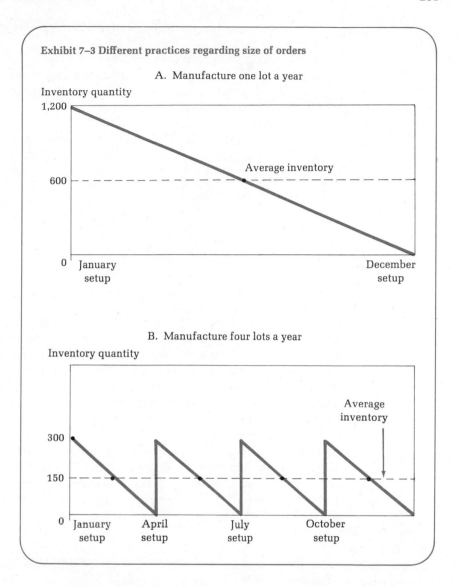

Exhibit 7–3 Different practices regarding size of orders

A. Manufacture one lot a year

Inventory quantity

1,200

600 — — — — — — — — — — — — — — — — Average inventory

0 January
   setup

December
setup

B. Manufacture four lots a year

Inventory quantity

Average
inventory

300

150 — — — — — — — — — — — — — — — — — — —

0 January   April   July   October
   setup   setup   setup   setup

Total cost will be at a minimum when the increase in inventory carry-ing cost resulting from adding one more unit to a lot is equal to the corresponding decrease in setup costs per unit. A model has been developed that determines the optimum balance between setup costs on the one hand and inventory carrying costs on the other hand. The amount is called the economic order quantity. The equation is:

$$Q = \sqrt{\frac{2SR}{CK}}$$

In this equation:

Q = Economic order quantity (number of units in one lot).
S = Setup costs for one setup.
R = Annual requirements in units.
K = Inventory carrying charge, expressed as a percentage of average inventory value.
C = Factory cost per unit.

EXAMPLE: Estimates for a certain item are:

S (setup cost)............................	$300
R (annual requirements)..................	1,200 units
K (carrying charge)......................	20%
C (factory cost).........................	$10 per unit

$$\text{Economic order quantity} = \sqrt{\frac{2 \times \$300 \times 1,200}{\$10 \times 0.2}}$$
$$= \sqrt{360,000}$$
$$= 600 \text{ units}$$

Since 1,200 units are required per year, there must be $1,200 \div 600 = 2$ lots manufactured per year.

The costs used in this equation are differential costs. The differential setup costs include the extra labor costs involved in making the setup, plus fringe benefits on this labor, plus any differential overhead costs associated with making a setup. The differential inventory carrying charge includes an estimate of interest costs, and of the costs associated with the occupancy of warehouse space.

The above example had to do with manufacturing an item. The same approach can be used to determine the economic order quantity for *purchasing* an item from an outside vendor. Instead of "setup costs," the differential purchasing costs are incorporated in the formula. These include the costs of placing the order, receiving the goods, and paying the invoice.

Problems involving both revenue and costs   In the second class of alternative choice problems, both costs and revenues are affected by the proposal being studied. Insofar as the quantitative factors are concerned, the best alternative is the one with the largest difference between differential revenue and differential cost, that is, the alternative with the most **differential income.**

The following types of problems will be discussed:

1. Contribution pricing.
2. Discontinuing a product.
3. Sale versus further processing.
4. Other marketing tactics.
5. Cost/benefit analysis.

CONTRIBUTION PRICING

In Chapter 5, techniques for using cost to arrive at the "normal" or "target" price for a product were described. Briefly, the approach is to add up the full costs of the product, add a profit margin that produces a satisfactory return on investment, and use the result as a first approximation to the price which is then adjusted to take account of competitive conditions. This is the approach that is used for the great majority of pricing decisions in American business.

Although full cost is the normal basis for pricing, and although a company must recover its full cost or eventually go out of business, there are some pricing situations where differential costs and revenues are appropriately used. In normal times, a company may refuse to take orders at prices that will not yield a satisfactory profit; but if times are bad, such orders may be accepted if the differential revenue obtained from them exceeds the differential costs involved. Differential costs are the costs that will be incurred if the order is accepted and that will not be incurred if it is not accepted. Differential revenue is the revenue that will be earned if the order is accepted and that will not be earned if it is not accepted. The company is better off to receive some revenue above its differential costs than to receive nothing at all. Such orders make some contribution to profit,[5] and such a selling price is therefore called a **contribution price,** to distinguish it from a normal price.

Dumping, which is the practice of selling surplus quantities of a product in a selected marketing area at a price that is below full costs, is another version of the contribution idea. However, dumping may violate the Robinson-Patman Amendment in domestic markets, and is in general prohibited by trade agreements in foreign markets.

It is difficult to generalize on the circumstances that determine whether full costs or differential costs are appropriate. Even in normal times, an opportunity may be accepted to make some contribution to profit by using temporarily idle facilities. Conversely, even when current sales volume is low, the contribution concept may be rejected on the grounds that the low price may "spoil the market," or that orders can in fact be obtained at normal margins if the sales organization works hard enough.

EXAMPLE: The estimated differential unit costs of Product X, in the relevant range of volume, are:

	Cost per Unit
Direct material costs	$ 1.20
Direct labor costs	5.60
Variable overhead costs	1.40
Variable marketing costs	3.00
Total differential costs	$11.20

---

[5] Some persons refer to this as a contribution to fixed costs and profit.

Any selling price above $11.20 will produce differential income. For example, if the item can be sold for $14 per unit, the differential income is $2.80 per unit. The company would be $2.80 better off to sell a unit than not to sell it, even though its full costs are more than $14 per unit.

DISCONTINUING A PRODUCT

If the selling price of a product is below its full cost, then conventional accounting reports will indicate that the product is being sold at a loss, and this fact may lead some people to recommend that the product be discontinued. Actually, such an action may make the company worse off rather than better off. It is better to have a product that makes some contribution to overhead and profit than not to have the product at all. An analysis of differential revenues and differential costs is the proper approach to problems of this type. The contribution analysis described in Chapter 6 illustrates such an approach.

> *EXAMPLE:* Hanson Manufacturing Company makes three products, A, B, and C. Exhibit 7–4 shows the profit or loss on each product as reported on the full cost basis. Note that Product B has sales revenue of $2,594,000, full costs of $2,911,000, and hence a loss of $317,000. Should Product B be discontinued because it is being sold at a loss?
>
> The costs that are relevant for this analysis are differential costs; the full costs shown on Exhibit 7–4 are not appropriate. If we ask

Exhibit 7–4

Hansen Manufacturing Company product costs, 1974 (in thousands)

	Product A	Product B	Product C	Total	Direct	Allocated	Basis of Allocation
Rent.............	$ 587	$ 457	$ 388	$ 1,432		x	Sq. ft.
Property taxes.....	62	50	40	152		x	Sq. ft.
Property insurance.	52	40	53	145		x	Val. of equip.
Direct labor.......	1,445	995	768	3,208	x		
Indirect labor.....	398	273	212	883		x	Direct labor
Power...........	22	25	30	77		x	Machine-hours
Light and heat....	15	13	10	38		x	Sq. ft.
Building service....	10	8	7	25		x	Sq. ft.
Materials.........	909	232	251	1,392	x		
Supplies.........	52	48	35	135	x		
Repairs..........	18	15	10	43	x		
Total.........	$3,570	$2,156	$1,804	$ 7,530			
Selling expense....	910	458	470	1,838		x	$ Val. of sales
General and administrative...	345	130	178	653		x	$ Val. of sales
Depreciation......	165	127	165	457		x	Val. of equip.
Interest..........	52	40	53	145		x	Val. of equip.
Total cost.....	$5,042	$2,911	$2,670	$10,623			
Sales (net)........	5,257	2,594	2,862	10,713			
Profit or (loss).....	$ 215	$ (317)	$ 192	$ 90			

what costs are differential if Product B should be discontinued, then it is clear that the costs related to the building, to equipment, and to general administration, are not likely to be affected. These costs would continue (except in the unlikely event that part of the building could be sold); therefore, they are not differential costs. The differential costs are principally the direct labor and direct material costs, and certain other items that are labeled as direct.

If Product B were dropped, the revenue earned from it would of course be lost. Exhibit 7–5 shows the differential costs and revenues

Exhibit 7–5

Effect of discontinuing Product B (differential costs and revenues) (in thousands)

Decrease in revenue..........................		$2,594
Decrease in costs:		
Direct labor...............................	$995	
Materials..................................	232	
Supplies..................................	48	
Repairs...................................	15	1,290
Decrease in profits if Product B		
discontinued..............................		$1,304

in this situation. It shows that if Product B had not been sold in 1974, costs would have been reduced by $1,290,000 but that revenues would have been reduced by $2,594,000, so the company would have been worse off by $1,304,000. Under these circumstances, Product B should not be dropped.[6]

Before a final decision is reached, other alternatives need to be considered. For example, if a new product with a higher profit margin could be found to use the facilities now used to make Product B, then it might indeed be desirable to drop Product B and to add the new product.

SALE VERSUS FURTHER PROCESSING

Many companies, particularly those that manufacture a variety of finished products from basic raw materials, must address the problem of whether to sell a product that has reached a certain stage in the production process or whether to do additional work on it. Meat-packers, for example, can sell an entire carcass of beef, or they can continue to process the carcass into hamburger and various cuts, or they can go even farther and make frozen dinners out of the hamburger. The de-

---

[6] This conclusion is based on the analysis of the available data. In a practical situation, further study would be warranted to determine if other items of cost are differential.

cision requires an analysis of the differential revenues and differential costs.

Let us designate the alternative of selling the product at a certain stage as the base case and that of processing it further as Case 2. For the base case, the relevant numbers are the sales revenue less any differential costs that are required to market the product at that stage. For Case 2, the numbers are the (presumably higher) sales revenue for the processed product, less the differential costs of the additional processing. If the differential income (i.e., revenue minus costs) of further processing exceeds that of the base case, then Case 2 is preferred. The important point to note about this analysis is that all costs incurred up to the point in the production process where this decision takes place may be disregarded. These costs are incurred whether or not additional processing takes place, and they are therefore not differential.

> *EXAMPLE:* A meat-packer is considering whether to sell unprocessed meat (base case) or to process it into frozen dinners (Case 2). Estimates of differential revenues and costs per pound are:

	Base Case (Sell Unprocessed)	Case 2 (Process)	Difference
Revenue......................		$0.70	$1.30	$0.60
Differential marketing costs.....	$0.03	$0.20	
Differential material cost.......	...	0.10	
Other differential costs.........	...	0.18	
Total differential costs....	−0.03	−0.48	$0.45
Differential income...........	$0.67	$0.82	$0.15

Since the differential income for Case 2 is $0.15 higher than that for the base case, the alternative of making frozen dinners appears to be attractive. Neither the cost of the steer nor the cost of slaughtering and dressing it is relevant since these costs are incurred under both alternatives.

OTHER MARKETING TACTICS

The same analytical approach can be used for a number of other marketing problems, such as deciding which customers are worth soliciting by sales personnel and how often the salesperson should call on each customer; deciding whether to open additional warehouses or, conversely, whether to consolidate existing warehouses; deciding whether to improve the durability of a product in order to reduce the number of maintenance calls; and deciding on the minimum size of order that will be accepted.

COST/BENEFIT ANALYSIS

Revenue is a measure of the output of a profit-oriented organization. Nonprofit organizations also have outputs, but many of them cannot measure these outputs in monetary terms. Similarly, the outputs of many responsibility centers within an organization cannot be expressed as revenue. In these situations a comparison of differential costs and differential revenues is not possible. Nevertheless, it is sometimes possible to use a similar approach by comparing differential costs, not with differential revenues but with some measure of the benefits that are expected as a consequence of incurring the additional costs. This approach is called a **cost/benefit analysis.**

Cost/benefit analysis is widely used in nonprofit organizations. It is also used in profit-oriented companies for analyzing such proposals as spending more money to improve safety conditions, or to reduce pollution, or to improve the company's reputation with the public, or to provide better information to management.

In a cost/benefit analysis, the cost calculations are usually straightforward; the difficult part of the analysis is the estimate of the value of the benefits. In many situations, no reliable estimate of the quantitative amount of benefits can be made. In such situations, the anticipated benefits are carefully described in words, and then the decision maker must answer the question: Are the perceived benefits worth *at least* the estimated cost? For example, "If we add $25,000 to the costs of the market research department, will the increased output of the department be worth at least $25,000?" The answer to this question is necessarily judgmental, but the judgment can be aided by a careful estimate of the differential costs and a careful assessment of the probable benefits.

ESTIMATING SALES

In problems in which both revenues and costs are differential, the most difficult part of the analysis usually is the estimate of the sales volumes for the alternatives being considered. No one knows *for sure* what will happen to sales volume if the product is priced on a contribution basis, or if a product is sold after further processing rather than being sold in a less finished state, or if additional sales personnel are hired, or if additional warehouses are operated. Nevertheless, the analysis requires that estimates of sales volume be made. Some companies employ sizable market research staffs which prepare such estimates. They may test a proposed marketing tactic in a few cities to find out what happens to sales volume before making the decision to extend the tactic nationwide. Notwithstanding these efforts, the fact remains that in a free market economy the customer is king, his decision determines how many sales are made, and it is most difficult to estimate in advance what his decision will be.

USE OF PROBABILITIES

All the numbers used in alternative choice problems are estimates of what will happen in the future. In the foregoing examples, we used **single value** estimates; that is, each estimate was a single number representing someone's best estimate as to what differential costs or revenues would be. Some companies are experimenting with estimates made in the form of probability distributions rather than as single numbers. Instead of stating, "I think sales of Item X will be $100,000 if the proposed alternative is adopted," the estimator develops a range of possibilities, together with his estimate of the probability that each will occur. These separate possibilities are weighted by the probability that each will occur. The sum of these weighted amounts is called the **expected value** of the probability distribution. It is computed as in the following example:

Possibilities Sales Volume	Estimated Probability	Weighted Amount
(a)	(b)	(a × b)
$ 60,000	0.1	$ 6,000
80,000	0.1	8,000
100,000	0.4	40,000
120,000	0.2	24,000
140,000	0.2	28,000
	1.0 Expected value.............	$106,000

The probability 0.1 opposite $60,000 means that there is 1 chance in 10 that sales will be $60,000. The sum of the probabilities must always add to 1.0.

The expected value of $106,000 would be used as the best estimate of differential revenue. If a single value estimate rather than an expected value were used, it would be $100,000 because this is the number with the highest probability. The $106,000 expected value is a better estimate of sales because it incorporates the whole probability distribution.

Businessmen do not find it easy to develop estimates in the form of probability distributions; but if they can do so, the validity of the estimates can be greatly increased.

Demonstration case

As a device for demonstrating your understanding of the fact that the cost elements that are relevant in an alternative choice problem vary with the nature of the problem, consider the costs that are relevant for various decisions that may be made about owning and operating an automobile. A study made by Runzheimer and Company and published by the American Automobile Association gives the national average cost in early 1973 of operating a 1973 eight-cylinder Chevrolet Impala four-door hardtop (equipped with standard accessories—radio, automatic transmission, and power steering) as follows:

	Average per Mile
Variable costs:	
Gasoline and oil............................	3.35 cents
Maintenance.............................	0.78
Tires......................................	0.62
Total variable costs....................	4.75 cents

	Amount per Year
Fixed costs:	
Fire and theft insurance......................	$ 45
Other insurance.............................	322
License and registration......................	28
Depreciation................................	777
Total fixed costs........................	$1,172

The automobile is driven 10,000 miles a year. Assume that these costs are valid estimates of future costs (which actually is not the case because of inflation). You are asked to state the differential costs that are relevant in answering these questions:

1. You own an automobile like that described above and have it registered. You are thinking about making a trip of 1,000 miles. What is the differential cost?

2. You own an automobile but have not registered it. You are considering whether to register it for next year or to use alternative forms of transportation that you estimate will cost $1,000 for the 10,000 miles you expect to drive. Should you register it? (Disregard convenience and other nonquantitative factors.)

3. You do not own an automobile but are considering the purchase of the automobile described above. If your estimate is that you will drive 10,000 miles per year for five years and that alternative transportation will cost $1,000 per year, should you do so?

The answers to these questions are:

1. When a person owns an automobile, already has it registered, and is deciding whether it is worthwhile to make a proposed trip, the relevant costs are 4.75 cents a mile times the estimated mileage of the trip; a trip of 1,000 miles therefore has a differential cost of $47.50. The fixed costs are not relevant since they will continue whether or not the trip is made.

2. When a person owns an automobile and is deciding whether to (*a*) register it for a year or (*b*) leave it idle and use some other form of transportation, the relevant costs are the insurance and fees of $395 plus 4.75 cents a mile times the 10,000 miles he expects to travel by automobile, a total of $870. The $395 has become a cost because it is affected by the decision as to registration. If alternative transportation costs $1,000 a year, he is well advised to register the automobile.

3. When a person is deciding whether to (*a*) buy an automobile or (*b*) use some other means of transportation, the relevant costs are $1,172 a year plus 4.75 cents a mile times the 10,000 miles he expects

to travel per year, or $1,172 + $475 = $1,647. If alternative transportation costs $1,000 a year, he is well advised to use alternative transportation.

Each of the above answers is, of course, an oversimplification because it omits nonquantitative factors and relies on averages. In an actual problem, the person would have data that more closely approximated the costs of his own automobile.

Summary   When an alternative choice problem involves changes in costs but not changes in revenue or investment, the best solution is the one with the lowest differential costs, insofar as cost information bears on the solution. Although historical costs may provide a useful guide to what costs will be in the future, we are always interested in future costs, and never in historical costs for their own sake. In particular, sunk costs are irrelevant. The longer the time span involved, the more costs are differential. Among the problems involving changes in cost are: proposed changes in methods, make-or-buy problems, and economic order quantity problems.

When the problem involves both cost and revenue considerations, differential revenues, as well as differential costs, must be estimated. Among the problems in this area are: contribution pricing (i.e., selling below normal price temporarily in order to obtain some differential income); discontinuing a product; sale versus further processing; other marketing tactics; and cost/benefit analysis. When revenue cannot be estimated, cost/benefit analysis is helpful in certain types of problems.

Differential cost and revenue rarely provide the answer to any business problem, but they facilitate comparisons and narrow the area within which judgment must be applied in order to reach a sound decision.

Important terms

Alternative choice problem	**Make or buy**
Base case	**Economic order quantity**
Out-of-pocket costs	**Differential income**
Opportunity cost	**Contribution price**
Marginal cost	**Expected value**
Incremental cost	**Cost/benefit analysis**
Sunk cost	

Questions for discussion

1.   A company has heard that a new machine has been developed that might be better than a machine it now uses for a certain production operation. List the steps it should go through in investigating this matter.

2. In connection with the new machine referred to in Question 1, give examples of quantitative and nonquantitative factors that should be considered, and distinguish between these two types of factors.

3. What is the advantage of using numbers to express the importance of factors in an alternative choice problem?

4. Explain in your own words the story told by Exhibit 7–1. In particular, how do you reconcile the direct material costs given there with the direct material cost of $570 for the same item given in earlier examples?

5. "Overhead costs are allocated to products at 200 percent of direct labor costs. This means that if direct labor costs increase, overhead costs also increase. Therefore, if direct labor costs are differential, so are overhead costs." Do you agree?

6. Opportunity costs, as such, are not recorded in accounting records. Why?

7. Historical costs are irrelevant in alternative choice problems, but the numbers used in many such problems are in fact historical costs. Explain this apparent paradox.

8. The book value of a machine on the balance sheet is genuinely an asset, but in alternative choice problems this asset amount is disregarded. Why?

9. In Exhibit 7–2, the $4,000 book value of an existing machine was disregarded in Part A but included in two places on Part C. Explain why the treatment in the two parts is equivalent (i.e., consistent).

10. Suppose the machine referred to in Exhibit 7–2 could be sold for $1,000. Should this $1,000 enter into the calculation? If so, what happens to the $3,000 difference between the market value of $1,000 and the book value of $4,000?

11. An accounting principle is "cost or market, whichever is lower." How can a machine be carried on the balance sheet as an asset at $4,000 if its market value is only $1,000?

12. The book value of a machine is a sunk cost. However, if the same machine is rented rather than owned, the rental payments are *not* a sunk cost. Explain this apparent paradox.

13. "In the very long run, all costs are differential." Explain what this means.

14. In a certain company, return on investment is calculated as follows:

$$\frac{\text{Revenue } \$100 - \text{Costs } \$80}{\text{Investment } \$200} = 10 \text{ percent}$$

Give *four* ways in which the return on investment could be increased to approximately 11 percent.

15. Under some circumstances, a reduction of two hours of labor time required to make a product reduces differential costs and in other circumstances it does not. Distinguish between these circumstances, with examples.

16. Holvelt Company manufactures and sells power lawnmowers. It owns

its factory and a separate office building. List some of the make-or-buy alternatives that the company might consider.

17. If allocated costs can give misleading impressions, as on Exhibit 7–4, then why should cost allocations be made?

18. "A company must recover its full costs or eventually go out of business." Do you agree? Why?

19. An analyst estimated that a proposed new advertising campaign would increase sales of a certain product by 10 percent. Since sales currently were $1,487,462, he estimated the differential revenue at $148,746.20. What wrong impression could this number give? What number should he have used?

20. Airlines have special low rates for families who fly on certain days. Explain why they do this, using concepts described in this chapter. Under what circumstances should airlines have low rates for students?

Problems

7–1. Vapner Construction Company wants to establish a decision rule on when to rent a house trailer for an on-site construction office, and when to build an on-site office. Trailers of the kind which Vapner uses can be rented for $100 per month, with a minimum rental of eight months. Construction of an on-site office generally costs Vapner $900 for materials, 20 percent of which are salvagable upon dismantling, and $1,200 in labor. Other costs would be unaffected.

Required:

In terms of length of construction project, when should Vapner rent a trailer and when should it construct its own on-site office?

7–2. DBA Chemical Company is considering changing the material content of chemical compound 12XC2, which it produces in batches, on order, for one customer in the plastics industry. DBA salesmen have been informed by the customer that if the order lead time for 12XC2 could be reduced to 10 days from the present 17 days, orders for the compound would double. 12XC2 cannot be carried in inventory due to rapid deterioration after completion.

12XC2 is produced in batches of 10,000 pounds, using special equipment. The compound is made up of various petroleum by-products and other chemicals. The company's chief chemist has informed sales management that substitution of Chemical B for Chemical A in the mix would not change the quality of the product and would cut the processing time in half. Processing time is presently 14 days.

The sales department, in conjunction with company cost accountants, prepared a summary of the cost data for 12XC2 under the present processing method and has also summarized the changes which would result if Chemical B were substituted for Chemical A, as follows:

Costs for Compound 12 × C2	*Per Pound*
Materials (except for Chemical A).................	$0.20
Chemical A.....................................	0.05
Labor (3 men @ $3/hour × 24 hours × 14 days	
÷ 10,000 pounds).............................	0.3024
Overhead (@ 65% of direct material dollars, 85%	
fixed).......................................	0.1625
Full cost.................................	$0.7149

Summary of Changes as a Result of Substituting Chemical B for Chemical A

1. Labor time and costs per pound cut in half.
2. $0.18 material cost component per pound of 12XC2 for Chemical B.
3. Sales volume will double from 180,000 pounds annually to 360,000 pounds annually.

Required:

If DBA can sell 12XC2 at $0.62 per pound, would you recommend acceptance of the proposed change in the manufacturing method?

7–3. A manufacturer of motorcycles has been operating at 80 percent of plant capacity. In order to utilize more capacity the plant manager is considering making a headlight which had previously been purchased for $6.10 per unit. The plant has the equipment and labor force necessary to manufacture this light, which the design engineer estimates would cost $1.40 for raw materials and $3 for direct labor. The plant overhead rate is $2 per direct labor dollar of which $1.20 is variable cost.

Required:

Should the company make the light or continue to buy it from an outside supplier? Support your answer with appropriate computations and reasons.

7–4. Seavy Equipment Company produces a line of wrought-iron lawn ornaments. Current sales average 70 percent of the 100,000 unit plant capacity, and a large contractor has offered the company an order for 10,000 ornaments at $7 each. The usual selling price is $10 per unit. Company cost accountants have computed the cost per ornament as follows:

Variable costs of materials and labor...................	$5
Fixed costs.......................................	3
	$8

Acceptance of the 10,000-unit order is not expected to change the total fixed costs.

Required:

Should Seavy accept the order for 10,000 units at $7 each? Support your answer with appropriate computations.

7–5. Hooker Rubber Company has been offered a contract to supply 500,000 automobile tires to a large car manufacturer at a price of $7.50 per tire. Hooker's full cost of producing the tire is $8. The normal sales price for the tire is $10 to both distributors and some selected retailers. Variable costs per tire amount to $7; however, in order to meet the needs of the auto manufacturer, Hooker will have to cut its sales to regular customers by 100,000 tires annually. The auto maker has clearly indicated that it will enter into the agreement only if Hooker will agree to supply all 500,000 of the tires requested.

Required:
Should Hooker accept the offer?

7–6. Dairy Pure Stores, a small supermarket chain, is considering opening all its stores on Sundays. Salary expense for a Sunday would amount to $8,000, and other additional costs would be approximately $1,300. If the gross margins on sales at Dairy Pure average 15 percent, what volume of sales must the chain generate on a Sunday to make opening worthwhile?

7–7. Delta Venus Swimsuit Company is considering dropping its line of ladies' beach robes. A 1974 product statement for the robe line follows:

Revenue...............................	$417,000
Cost of goods sold....................	378,000
Gross margin..........................	$ 39,000
Selling and administrative expenses....	60,000
Net Loss..............................	$(21,000)

Factory overhead accounts for 26 percent of the cost of the goods sold and is one-third fixed. These data are believed to reflect conditions in the immediate future.

Required:
Should Delta Venus drop the beach robe line?

7–8. Franklin Speedway owns an automobile drag strip with a seating capacity of 4,000. The price per ticket has been $1.75, with an average attendance of 3,600 at the weekly races which are run 50 times a year. Direct costs are $0.25 per person. and other costs are $80,000 per year. The company can increase seating capacity to 8,000 seats for an annual rental fee of $14,000. Direct costs per person remain the same.

Required:
How much would average attendance have to increase in order to make such a move worthwhile?

7–9. Johnson's Health Club sponsors boxing matches twice a week for 25 weeks during fall and winter. The charge per ticket has been

$3.50 with an average attendance of 900 spectators at each match. In an effort to increase attendance, the club manager is considering decreasing the ticket price. There are 1,000 seats available now, but for an added $15,000 per year, capacity can be tripled. Yearly fixed costs are now $90,000 and variable costs are $0.25 per spectator. Expected ticket sales and attendance follow:

Price per Ticket	Estimated Attendance
$3.50	900
3.00	1,250
2.50	1,750
2.00	2,000

Required:

1. Prepare an analysis showing which of the four ticket prices should be adopted.
2. Calculate the difference in income which would result if the price were changed to the amount calculated in (1) above.

7–10. Tracy Enterprises can produce 10,000 snow blowers a month at capacity operations. Average normal production and sales have been 8,000 per month, but an economic slump in the area has caused the sales manager to believe he can only sell 4,000 units through usual outlets during the coming month. Tracy has received an offer from a large mail-order concern requesting a total of 5,000 units of production. Tracy would receive $150 per unit. The blowers could be sold through regular channels for $160 each, the amount which the company feels allows for a satisfactory return on investment. Monthly fixed costs are $400,000; and the variable costs of production, distribution, and administration are $60 per unit.

Required:

1. Compute the cost of a snow blower which would need to be recovered if a profit of $45 per unit was desired on the mail-order contract.
2. How much does it cost Tracy to produce and sell a snow blower? Why do you feel this is the most reasonable cost?
3. What should Tracy do: use regular channels or sell to the mail-order firm?

7–11. Scoville Manufacturing Company has just received an order for 2,500 garden tillers for which the buyer, a large agricultural cooperative, would pay $108 each. Average tiller production and sales have been 4,000 per month, but an economic recession in the area has caused management to believe that only 2,000 tillers could be sold through usual channels. Scoville has the capacity to produce 5,000 units per month with a fixed monthly cost of $200,000 and variable production, distribution, and administrative costs of $30 per unit, which management feels has provided a satisfactory return on investment. The regular selling price is $115 per unit.

Required:

1. Compute the cost of a tiller which would need to be recovered if a total profit of $87,000 was desired from the cooperative order.
2. Calculate what you feel is the full cost to Scoville of one tiller. Why do you feel this is reasonable?
3. What should Scoville do: take the cooperative offer or manufacture to sell through regular channels? Why?

7–12. The Novelty Manufacturing Company makes a line of glassware and is reviewing the profitability of its line of glass ashtrays. A condensed income statement for ashtray operations for last year follows:

Sales....................................	$30,000
Cost of sales...........................	25,000
Gross margin...........................	$ 5,000
Distribution costs:	
Direct.............................	$ 6,500
Indirect and allocated..............	2,500
Net Loss..............................	$(4,000)

The cost of sales includes $3,000, and the distribution costs include $2,000 which would be incurred whether ashtrays were made or not. Allocated costs include $1,000 for delivery expenses which is allocated by weight and other factors pertinent to the cost of deliveries.

Required:

1. Restate the operating results shown in a form which management would find more useful in making its decision as to the profitability of the ashtray line.
2. If the period costs are unavoidable, should the company continue the ashtray line?
3. What factors would become relevant to management's decision if there is an offer to sell the ashtray portion of the business?

7–13. Duke Electronics is considering entering into the field of television manufacturing. Management has located a plant which it can rent for $120,000 annually. With an investment of 1.4 million dollars in equipment and machinery, the plant's physical capacity of an estimated 50,000 T.V.'s annually could be obtained. Variable manufacturing costs are estimated to be $120 per T.V. set, and Duke has a guaranteed market for all its output with a national retailing chain at a price of $155 per set. The plant equipment under consideration has an estimated life of 20 years with a 10 percent salvage value. Other fixed expenses are estimated to be $1.2 million annually for the venture.

Required:

Can Duke Electronics break even on this venture?

7–14. Canterbury, Inc., makes several different products. Each product may be produced several different times a year. As part of an effort to control costs, the controller wants to determine the economic lot size of a production run of Product M. The factory cost per unit is $10.30, setup costs are $300, the inventory carrying charge is 23 percent, and there are expected to be 15,000 units of M produced annually.

Required:

What is the most economical number of units of Product M to produce in one production run?

7–15. Silby Company needs to acquire 50,000 units of Material A to fill production orders for the year. It costs $50 to place an order, and $3 per unit to carry the inventory of Material A per year.

Required:

What is the most economical number of units to order at any one time?

7–16. Ace Fastener Company, a manufacturer of nails, has received a request from Sunshine Builders for Ace to supply Sunshine with 10 100-pound kegs of nails per week for a one-year period, at a price of $5.15 per keg. Ace is presently working at 100 percent capacity for one eight-hour shift and would have to incur overtime expense in order to meet Sunshine's request. Ace's normal sales price for nails is $5.65 per 100-pound keg.

The steel used for manufacture of nails is purchased by Ace at a cost of $80 per ton. Ace experiences a 5 percent material waste factor in production. Labor costs per 100 pounds of output are $0.50; however, overtime production would increase labor costs by 50 percent. Overhead, which is currently 18 percent variable and 82 percent fixed, is allocated on a 100 percent-of-direct-labor-dollars basis.

Required:

Should Ace Fastener Company accept Sunshine's order at the $5.15 per keg price?

7–17. In mid-1970, in reaction to the sharply declining demand for can openers which resulted from the introduction of the "tab top" can, Al Keen, manager of the Kitchen Implements Division (K.I.D.) of Household Products, Inc., has gathered cost data on the division's "Party Time" can opener, in the hope that some action can be taken to reverse the upward spiral of cost per unit.

The data accumulated by Mr. Keen shows, among other things, that it may be more profitable to purchase the plastic handles which are attached to the "Party Time" can opener then to continue to produce them. K.I.D. has frequently been approached by J. E. Plastics Company salesmen who have offered (1) to produce the handles for K.I.D. and sell them to K.I.D. for 4¢ each, and (2) to purchase

K.I.D.'s plastic-handle producing machinery for $27,000 if a sufficiently large contract for handles can be agreed upon.

The data shows that in 1967, handles could be produced for $0.0291125 each with volume at 1.2 million handles annually, as follows:

		1967	
		Annual	*Per Unit*
Factory overhead:			
Depreciation...........	$2,500		
Supervision...........	7,000		
Supplies..............	1,000		
Utilities..............	2,000		
Maintenance..........	500	$13,000	1.08333¢
Labor................		13,200	1.10000
Materials.............		8,735	.72792
		$34,935	2.91125¢

Demand for handles has dropped to a level of 300,000 units annually, and Mr. Keen, recognizing the fixed nature of most of the overhead items, knows that per-unit cost at this reduced level of volume may well exceed the 4¢ per-unit cost of purchase.

Additional data:

1. Variable costs per unit have remained unchanged between 1967 and 1970.

2. Estimated annual factory overhead for 1970 is as follows:

Depreciation......................	$ 2,500
Supervision......................	5,000
Supplies.........................	800
Utilities.........................	1,500
Maintenance.....................	550
	$10,350

3. The net book value of the plastic-handle producing machinery was $32,500 at January 1, 1970.

Required:

Should Mr. Keen accept the offer of J. E. Plastics Company?

7–18. ABC Electronics was contemplating the manufacturing of a component part of an electronic testing device which the company sold. Parts were presently being purchased for $6.17 each. Terms of the arrangement were 2/10, net 30, f.o.b. seller's factory. Shipping charges amounted to $0.08 per unit.

Company cost accountants estimated that after an initial training period of one week, the five men need to assemble the parts would average 66 completed parts, for a normal seven-hour workday. Net material costs per unit would amount to $4.30 if the part were to be produced. The plant manager estimated that one foreman would have to devote about 25 percent of his time to supervision of the men, and that demand for the component part would remain relatively constant at 16,500 units annually. Labor rates were as follows:

Assembly labor	$2.80 per hour
Supervision	4.25 per hour

Required:

1. Should ABC Electronics make the component part or continue to buy it?
2. Will either increases or decreases in demand for the component part change your answer to (1) above?
3. Establish a make-or-buy decision rule for this component part to include rules for:
   a. When to utilize overtime hours (assume overtime pay to be 150 percent of regular pay)
   b. When to hire addition workers.

7–19. Fine Foods, Inc., a regional supermarket chain, orders 400,000 cans of frozen orange juice per year from a California distributor. A 24-can case of frozen juice delivered to the Fine Foods central warehouse costs $4.80, including freight charges. Fine Foods borrows funds at a 10 percent interest rate to finance its inventories.

The Fine Foods purchasing agent has calculated that it costs $200 to place an order for frozen juice, and that the annual storage expenses for one can of juice (electricity, insurance, handling) amounts to $0.05 per can.

Required:

1. How many cans of frozen juice should Fine Foods request in each order?
2. If the California distributor offers Fine Foods a 10 percent discount off the delivery price for minimum orders of 80,000 cans, what should Fine Foods do?

7–20.

CASE
Liquid
Chemical
Company*

The Liquid Chemical Company manufactured and sold a range of high-grade products throughout Great Britain. Many of these products required careful packing, and the company had always made a feature of the special properties of the containers used. They had a special patented lining, made from a material known as GHL, and the firm operated a department especially to maintain its containers in good condition and to make new ones to replace those that were past repair.

Mr. Walsh, the general manager, had for some time suspected that the firm might save money, and get equally good service, by buying its containers from an outside source. After careful inquiries, he approached a firm specializing in container production, Packages, Ltd., and asked for a quotation from it. At the same time he asked Mr. Dyer, his chief accountant, to let him have an up-to-date statement of the cost of operating the container department.

Within a few days, the quotation from Packages, Ltd., came in. The firm was prepared to supply all the new containers required—at that time running at the rate of 3,000 a year—for $125,000 a year, the contract to run for a guaranteed term of five years and thereafter to be renewable from year to year. If the required num-

---

* Copyright David Solomons, University of Pennsylvania.

ber of containers increased, the contract price would be increased proportionally. Additionally, and irrespective of whether the above contract was concluded or not, Packages, Ltd., undertook to carry out purely maintenance work on containers, short of replacement, for a sum of $37,500 a year, on the same contract terms.

Mr. Walsh compared these figures with the cost figures prepared by Mr. Dyer, covering a year's operations of the container department of the Liquid Chemical Company, which were as follows:

Materials...		$70,000
Labor..		50,000
Department overheads:		
Manager's salary...............................	$ 8,000	
Rent...	4,500	
Depreciation of machinery.......................	15,000	
Maintenance of machinery.......................	3,600	
Other expenses.................................	15,750	
		46,850
		$166,850
Proportion of general administrative overheads.......		22,500
Total Cost of Department for Year.................		$189,350

Walsh's conclusion was that no time should be lost in closing the department and in entering into the contracts offered by Packages, Ltd. However, he felt bound to give the manager of the department, Mr. Duffy, an opportunity to question this conclusion before he acted on it. He therefore called him in and put the facts before him, at the same time making it clear that Duffy's own position was not in jeopardy; for even if his department were closed, there was another managerial position shortly becoming vacant to which he could be moved without loss of pay or prospects.

Mr. Duffy looked thoughtful and asked for time to think the matter over. The next morning, he asked to speak to Mr. Walsh again, and said he thought there were a number of considerations that ought to be borne in mind before his department was closed. "For instance," he said, "what will you do with the machinery? It cost $120,000 four years ago, but you'd be lucky if you got $20,000 for it now, even though it's good for another four years at least. And then there's the stock of GHL (a special chemical) we bought a year ago. That cost us $100,000, and at the rate we're using it now, it'll last us another four years or so. We used up about one fifth of it last year. Dyer's figure of $70,000 for materials probably includes about $20,000 for GHL. But it'll be tricky stuff to handle if we don't use it up. We bought it for $500 a ton, and you couldn't buy it today for less than $600. But you wouldn't have more than $400 a ton left if you sold it, after you'd covered all the handling expenses."

Walsh thought that Dyer ought to be present during this discussion. He called him in and put Duffy's points to him. "I don't much like all this conjecture," Dyer said. "I think my figures are pretty conclusive. Besides, if we are going to have all this talk about 'what will happen if,' don't forget the problem of space we're faced with. We're paying $8,500 a year in rent for a warehouse a couple of miles away. If we closed Duffy's department, we'd have all the warehouse space we need without renting."

"That's a good point," said Walsh. "Though I must say, I'm a bit worried about the men if we close the department. I don't think we can find room for any of them elsewhere in the firm. I could see whether Packages can take any of them. But some of them are getting on. There's Walters and Hines, for example. They've been with us since they left school 40 years ago. I'd feel bound to give them a severance allowance—$1,500 a year each, say."

Duffy showed some relief at this. "But I still don't like Dyer's figures," he said. "What about this $22,500 for general administrative overheads. You surely don't expect to sack anyone in the general office if I'm closed, do you?" "Probably not," said Dyer, "but someone has to pay for these costs. We can't ignore them when we look at an individual department, because if we do that with each department in turn, we shall finish up by convincing ourselves that directors, accountants, typists, stationery, and the like don't have to be paid for. And they do, believe me."

"Well, I think we've thrashed this out pretty fully," said Walsh, "but I've been turning over in my mind the possibility of perhaps keeping on the maintenance work ourselves. What are your views on that, Duffy?"

"I don't know," said Duffy, "but it's worth looking into. We shouldn't need any machinery for that, and I could hand the supervision over to a foreman. You'd save $3,000 a year there, say. You'd only need about one fifth of the men, but you could keep on the oldest. You wouldn't save any space, so I suppose the rent would be the same. I shouldn't think the other expenses would be more than $6,500 a year." "What about materials?" asked Walsh. "We use about 10 percent of the total on maintenance," Duffy replied.

"Well, I've told Packages, Ltd., that I'd let them know my decision within a week," said Walsh. "I'll let you know what I decide to do before I write to them."

Required:

1. Assuming no additional information can be readily obtained, what action should be taken?
2. What, if any, additional information do you think is necessary for a sound decision?

8 Capital investment decisions

Purpose of
the chapter
In Chapter 7 we discussed those types of alternative choice problems which involved the use of differential *costs,* and differential *revenues.* In Chapters 8 and 9 we extend the discussion to problems that involve differential *investments.* These are problems in which the proposal is to invest funds, that is, capital, at the present time in the expectation of earning a return on this money over some future period. Such problems are called *capital investment problems.* They are also called *capital budgeting problems* because a company's capital budget is a list of the investment projects which it has decided to carry out. In these problems, the only new element is the consideration of the differential investment; costs and/or revenues are treated in the same manner as already discussed in Chapter 7.

The analysis of capital investment problems is complicated. It is important that these problems be solved correctly because they often involve large sums of money and because they may commit or "lock in" the business to a certain course of action over a considerable period in the future. The basic approach is described in Chapter 8, and some variations on this approach and some additional considerations are discussed in Chapter 9.

The concept
of present
value
WHAT IS PRESENT VALUE?

The analysis in this chapter is built around a concept called *present value,* which we shall define shortly. Many people have great difficulty in understanding this concept, and we shall therefore discuss it care-
232

fully.[1] The reason for this difficulty may stem from a failure to appreciate that there is a fundamental difference between the operation of a business and the conduct of one's personal affairs.

Children are taught that it is a good thing to put money into a piggybank; their parents congratulate them when the bank is finally opened and the accumulated coins are counted out. But a businessman's heart is not gladdened when he takes out of his "piggybank" only the same amount that he put into it. He expects that his money will earn more money.

By their emphasis on piggybanks, parents encourage children to believe that it is better to have money in the future than to spend it today. Stated more formally, parents teach that the value of money today is *less than* its value at some future time. The businessman thinks differently. He expects that money that he invests today will increase in amount as time passes because he expects to earn a profit on that investment. It follows that an amount of money that is available for investment today is more valuable to the businessman than an equal amount of money that will not be available until some time in the future. This is because the money available today can be invested to earn still more money, whereas money that has not yet been received obviously cannot be invested today. If a businessman is asked, "Would you prefer to have a dollar today or a promise of receiving a dollar a year from now?" He answers, "Of course, I prefer a dollar today because I can put that dollar to work and end up a year from now with more than a dollar." To the businessman, therefore, the value of money today is *more than* its value at some future time.

The value of money today is called its *present value*. The present value of $1 that is available today is, obviously, $1. The present value of $1 that is not available today, but that will be available at some future time, is less than $1. How much less, is a matter to be discussed in a following section.

To make this idea more concrete, consider the Able Company. Its management expects that the company can earn a return of 10 percent per year on funds that are invested in the company's assets. (Incidentally, the rate of return is invariably expressed on a *per annum* basis; that is, the statement "return of 10 percent" is invariably taken to mean "10 percent per year.") If Able Company invested $100 today for a year, at an anticipated return of 10 percent, it would expect to have $110 at the end of the year. Thus $100 invested today is expected to have a *future value* of $110 a year from today. Conversely, it can be said that the expectation of having $110 a year from today has a *present value* of $100 if funds are expected to earn 10 percent; that is, the value

---

[1] This concept is introduced in *Fundamentals of Financial Accounting,* Chapter 10, in relation to certain financial accounting matters. If you have difficulty with the discussion that follows, we suggest that you read that chapter.

of $110 to be received a year from today is equal to the value of $100 today.

Suppose Able Company expects to receive $100 a year from now. What is the present value of that amount? In a following section, the technique for answering this question is described, but for now, the answer simply is stated: the present value of $100 to be received a year from now is $90.91 if the business expects to earn 10 percent on its investments. That this *is* the correct answer can easily be demonstrated. If $90.91 is invested today for a year at 10 percent, it will earn 10 percent of $90.91, or $9.09, which added to the $90.91 makes $100. This exercise leads to a definition of present value:

> **The present value of an amount that is expected to be received at a certain time in the future is the amount which if invested today at a designated rate of return would cumulate to the specified amount.**

FINDING PRESENT VALUES

It is easy to demonstrate, as was done above, that the present value of $100 to be received one year from now at a rate of return of 10 percent is $90.91. For periods that are longer than a year, the arithmetic is more complicated because of the force of compound interest. Thus, we can demonstrate that at a 10 percent rate of return, $100 expected to be received two years from today has a present value of $82.64 because in the first year 10 percent of this amount, or $8.26, will be earned, bringing the total to $90.90, and in the second year 10 percent of $90.90, or $9.09, will be earned, bringing the total to $100. (The amount does not come exactly to $100 because the calculations were not carried to enough decimal places.)

In Chapter 10 of *Fundamentals of Financial Accounting* the formula is given for calculating the present value of a payment of $1 to be received n years hence at an interest rate i. It is:

$$\frac{1}{(1 + i)^n}$$

The same formula is applicable to the investment problems discussed here. The term i, which stood for "interest rate" in *Fundamentals of Financial Accounting*, refers to "rate of return," as used above. Indeed, economists refer to the rate used in investment problems as an interest rate, but businessmen customarily use "earnings rate" or "rate of return" for the same notion. We shall not use the formula directly, however, because it is more convenient to use a table of present values computed from it.[2] Such a table, for the present value of $1, is Table A, which

---

[2] Also, as will be explained in Chapter 16, computer programs and mini-calculators are available that handle the calculations automatically.

appears on page 553. Table A is the same as the table given in *Funda-mentals of Financial Accounting,* except that here the numbers have been rounded to three decimal places rather than four places. Three decimal places provide adequate precision for business problems of the type we shall be discussing. The present value amounts used in the above examples were taken from Table A. The number opposite Year 1 in the 10 percent column is $0.909. Since this is the present value of $1, to be received a year from now, the present value of $100 is 100 times this, or $90.90.

Inspection of Table A will reveal two fundamental points about present value:

1. **Present value decreases as the number of years in the future in which the payment is to be received increases.**

> *EXAMPLE:* For a rate of return of 10 percent, some present values of $1 are:

Time	$ Present Value
1 year hence	0.909
5 years hence	0.621
10 years hence	0.386
20 years hence	0.149

2. **Present value decreases as the rate of return increases.**

> *EXAMPLE:* For an amount to be received five years hence, some present values of $1 are:

At a Rate of Return of—	$ Present Value
6%	0.747
10	0.621
15	0.497
20	0.402

APPLICATION TO INVESTMENT DECISIONS

When a company purchases a machine, it makes an **investment;** that is, it commits funds today in the expectation of earning a return on those funds over some future period. Such an investment is similar to that made by a bank when it loans money. The essential character-istic of both types of transactions is that funds are committed today in the expectation of earning a return in the future. In the case of the bank loan, the future return is in the form of interest plus repayment of the principal. In the case of the machine, the future return is in the form of earnings generated by profitable operation of the machine. We shall designate such earnings as the **cash inflow.**

When a company is considering whether or not to purchase a new machine, the essential question that it seeks to answer is **whether the future cash inflow is likely to be large enough to warrant making the**

investment. The problems discussed in this chapter all involve this general question: It is proposed that a certain amount be invested at a specific date (which for convenience we shall label "today") in the expectation that a return will be earned on the investment in future years following the investment date. The question is whether the amount of anticipated future earnings, or cash inflow, is large enough to justify investing these funds in the proposal. Illustrative of these problems are the following:

1. *Replacement.* Shall we replace existing equipment with more efficient equipment? The future expected cash inflow on this investment is the cost savings resulting from lower operating costs, or the profit from additional volume produced by the new equipment, or both.
2. *Expansion.* Shall we build or otherwise acquire a new plant? The future expected cash inflow on this investment is the profits from the products produced in the new plant.
3. *Cost reduction.* Shall we buy equipment to perform an operation now done manually, that is, shall we spend money in order to save money? The expected future cash inflow on this investment is the savings resulting from lower operating costs.
4. *Choice of equipment.* Which of several proposed items of equipment shall we purchase for a given purpose? The choice often turns on which item is expected to give the largest return on the investment made in it.
5. *Buy or lease.* Having decided that we need a building or a piece of equipment, should we lease it or should we buy it? The choice turns on whether or not the investment required to purchase the asset will earn an adequate return because of the savings that will result from avoiding the lease payments.
6. *New product.* Should a new product be added to the line? The choice turns on whether the expected cash inflow from the sale of the new product is large enough to warrant the investment in equipment, working capital, and the costs required to make and introduce the product.

Note that all these problems involve two quite dissimilar kinds of amounts. First, there is the investment, which is usually made in a lump sum at the beginning of the project. Although not literally made "today," it is made at a specific point in time which for analytical purposes is called "today," or **"Time Zero."** Second, there is a stream of cash inflows, which it is anticipated will result from this investment, usually over a period of years.

These two types of amounts cannot be compared directly with one another because they occur at different points in time. As we have seen, the present value of $1 today is $1, but the present value of $1 that is to be received at some time in the future is less than $1. Thus, in order to make a valid comparison, we must bring the amounts involved to equivalent values at the same point in time. This could be done in any of a number of ways. We could, for example, convert all the amounts to future values, that is, their equivalent values at the termination of the project. It is more convenient, however, to convert them to *present values,* that is, to the values at Time Zero. In order to do this, we need not adjust the amount of the investment since it is already stated at its Time Zero or present value. We need only to convert the stream of future cash inflows to their present value equivalents, and we can then compare them directly with the amount of the investment. To do this, we multiply the cash inflow for each year by the present value of $1 for that year at the appropriate rate of return. This process is called **discounting** the cash inflows. The rate at which the cash inflows are discounted is called the **required rate of return.**

The difference between the present value of the cash inflows and the amount of investment is called the net present value. If the net present value is zero or a positive number, the proposal is acceptable.

> *EXAMPLE:* A proposed investment of $1,000 is expected to produce a cash inflow of $600 per year for each of the next two years. The assumed rate of return is 10 percent. The present value of the cash inflows can be compared with the present value of the investment as follows:

	Year	Amount	Present Value of $1 @ 10%	Total Present Value
Investment..............	0	$1,000	1.000	$1,000
Cash inflow.............	1	600	0.909	$ 545
	2	600	0.826	496
		Present value of cash inflows		$1,041
		Net present value		$ 41

The proposed investment is acceptable.

After the amounts of cash inflow has been made comparable with the amount of investment, the basic decision rule is:

> **A proposed investment is acceptable if the present value of its future expected net cash inflows equals or exceeds the amount of investment.**

This is a general rule, and some qualifications to it will be discussed in a later section. To apply it, the approach is as follows:

1. Estimate the amount of investment.
2. Estimate the amount of cash inflow in each future year.
3. Find the present value of these cash inflows. This is done by discounting the cash inflow amounts at the required rate of return.
4. Subtract the amount of investment from the total present value.

We shall recapitulate by listing and defining the terms used in the above process:

Investment means the amount of funds committed to a project at time zero.

Cash inflow means the amounts expected to flow into the company as a consequence of making the investment. Usually cash inflows are expected for several years in the future.

Discounting means finding the present value of future cash inflows.

Required rate of return means the rate at which future cash inflows are discounted in order to find their present value. It is also called the **required earnings rate** or the **discount rate.**

Net present value means the amount by which the total present value of cash inflows exceeds the investment.

RETURN ON INVESTMENT

So far, we have shown how the present value of amounts to be received in the future can be calculated if cash inflows and the rate of return are given. It is useful to look at the situation from another viewpoint: How can the rate of return be calculated when the investment and the cash inflows are given?

Consider the familiar situation of a bank loan. When a bank lends $1,000 and receives interest payments of $80 at the end of each year for five years, with the $1,000 loan being repaid at the end of the fifth year, the bank correctly is said to earn a return of 8 percent on its investment of $1,000. Note that the return percentage is always expressed on an annual basis and that it is found by dividing the annual return by the amount of the investment outstanding during the year. In this case, the amount of loan outstanding each year was $1,000 and the return was $80 in each year, so the rate of return was $80 ÷ $1,000, or 8 percent.

If, however, a bank lends $1,000 and is repaid $250 at the end of each year for five years, the problem of finding the return becomes more complicated. In this situation, only part of the $250 annual cash inflow represents the return, and the remainder is a repayment of the principal. It turns out that this loan also has a return of 8 percent, in the same sense as the loan described in the preceding paragraph: namely, the $250 annual payments will repay the loan itself and in addition will provide a return of 8 percent of the *amount of principal still outstanding each year*. The fact that the return is 8 percent is demonstrated in Exhibit 8–1. Of the $250 repaid in the first year, $80, or 8 percent of the $1,000 then outstanding, is the return, and the remainder, or $170, reduces the investment, or principal, making it $830. In the second year, $66 is a return of 8 percent on the $830 of investment then outstanding, and the remainder, $184, reduces the investment to $646. And so on. (The residual of $3, rather than $0, at the end of the fifth

Exhibit 8–1

Demonstration of meaning of return on investment

Year	Cash Inflow (a)	Return at 8% of Investment Outstanding (b)	Balance, to Apply against Investment c = (a − b)	Investment Outstanding End of Year (d)
0....................	$...	$...	$...	$1,000
1....................	250	80	170	830
2....................	250	66	184	646
3....................	250	52	198	448
4....................	250	36	214	234
5....................	250	19	231	3*

* Arises from rounding.

year arises strictly from rounding; the true return is slightly less than 8.000 percent.)

It can be seen from the above examples that when an investment involves annual interest payments with the full amount of the investment being repaid at its termination date, the computation of the return is simple and direct; but when the annual payments combine both principal and interest, the computation is more complicated. Some business problems are of the simple type. For example, if a business buys land for $1,000, rents it for $80 a year for five years, and then sells it for $1,000 at the end of five years, the return is 8 percent. Many business investment decisions, on the other hand, relate to depreciable assets, whose characteristic is that they have no, or very little, resale value at the end of their useful life. The cash inflow from these investments must therefore be large enough for the investor both to recoup the investment itself during its life and also to permit him to earn a satisfactory return on the amount not yet recouped, just as in the situation shown in Exhibit 8–1.

The concept of present value and the concept of return on investment are intimately related. To demonstrate this point, the following example applies the present value calculation to the one-year investment that was described above, for which we already know the rate of return.

> EXAMPLE: Should a proposed investment of $1,000 with expected cash inflow of $1,080 one year from now be accepted if the required rate of return is 8 percent? In Table A, we find that the present value of $1 to be received one year hence at 8 percent is $0.926. The present value of $1,080 is therefore $1,080 × $0.926 = $1,000. In summary,

> | | |
> |---|---|
> | Investment..................................... | $1,000 |
> | Present value of cash inflow @ 8%.............. | 1,000 |
> | Net present value............................. | 0 |

> The proposal is acceptable.[3]

---

[3] In order to illustrate certain points, the numbers given in this and certain other examples have been structured so that the amount of investment is almost

STREAM OF CASH INFLOWS

The cash inflows on most business investments are not a single amount, as in the preceding example, but rather a series of amounts received over several future years as in Exhibit 8–1. The present value of the stream of cash inflows can be found by discounting each year's cash inflow by the appropriate factor from Table A.

EXAMPLE: Is a proposed investment of $1,000 with expected cash inflow of $250 a year for five years acceptable if the required rate of return is 8 percent? The present value of the cash inflows can be computed as follows:

Year	Cash Inflow (a)	Present Value of $1 at 8% (from Table A) (b)	Present Value (a × b)
First.	$250	0.926	$231
Second.	250	0.857	214
Third.	250	0.794	198
Fourth.	250	0.735	184
Fifth.	250	0.681	170
Total Present Value.			$997

The total present value of the cash inflows is slightly less than $1,000, which means that the rate of return on the proposed investment would be slightly less than 8 percent; therefore, the proposal is not acceptable.

The above computation using Table A was laborious. Table B (page 554) has, for many problems, a more convenient set of present value amounts than those in Table A. It shows the present value of $1 to be received annually for *each* of the next *n* years in the future. Each number on Table B was obtained simply by cumulating, that is, adding together, the amounts for the corresponding year and all preceding years in the same column on Table A.[4] Table B can be used directly to find the present value of a stream of *equal* cash inflows received annually for any given number of years; therefore it reduces considerably the arithmetic required in problems of the type illustrated in the preceding

the same as the present value of cash inflows. Since the numbers are estimates, with an inevitable margin of error, the decision in a real-world problem would not be as clear-cut as the examples indicate. This point is discussed in a subsequent section.

[4] Table B is technically known as a table of "Present Value of an Annuity of $1." It also appears in *Fundamentals of Financial Accounting*, Chapter 10.

example. Note that in order to use Table B, the amount of cash inflows must be the same for each year.

> *EXAMPLE:* Assume the same facts and question as in preceding example. Table B shows that present value of $1 *for each year* for five years at 8 percent to be $3.993; therefore, the present value of $250 a year for five years is 250 × $3.993 = $997, which is the same result as that computed in the preceding example.

Although the values in Table B are cumulative from year 1, they can be used also to find the present value of a stream of cash inflows between any points in time. The procedure is to subtract the value for the year *preceding* the first year of the cash inflow from the value for the last year of the cash inflow.

> *EXAMPLE:* What is the present value of $1,000 a year to be received in years 6 through 10 if the required rate of return is 8 percent? *Solution:*

Time Period	Present Value of $1 per Year at 8%
For 10 years	$6.710
For years 1–5	3.993
Difference (=years 6–10)	$2.717
For $1,000 a year: $1,000 × 2.717 = $2,717	

OTHER PRESENT VALUE TABLES

Tables A and B are constructed on the assumption that cash inflows are received once a year and on the last day of the year. For many problems this is not a realistic assumption because cash in the form of increased revenues or lower costs is likely to flow in throughout the year. Nevertheless, annual tables are customarily used in business investment problems, on the grounds that they are easier to understand than tables constructed on other assumptions, such as monthly or continuous compounding, and that they are good enough considering the inevitable margin of error in the basic estimates.

The calculations in this book will therefore use annual tables: Table A, the present value for a single amount to be received *n* years from now; and Table B, the present value of a stream of equal amounts to be received for each of the next *n* years. The two tables are often used in combination, as illustrated in the next example, which also relates the computation discussed here to the concept of return on investment discussed at the beginning of this section.

> *EXAMPLE:* Is a proposed investment of $1,000 with annual cash inflows of $80 a year for the next five years with the $1,000 to be repaid at the end of five years acceptable if the required rate of return is 8 percent? *Solution:* As shown by the following calculation, the cash inflows have a present value of $1,000, so the proposal is acceptable:

Year	Payment	8% Discount Factor	Present Value
1–5...............	$80/year	3.993 (Table B)	$ 319
End of 5..........	$1,000	0.681 (Table A)	681
Total present value........			$1,000

Estimating the variables

This completes the description of the concept and mechanics of calculations involving a proposed investment. In general, the analysis can be presented in the following format (in this case for a proposed $1,000 investment, with earnings of $400 a year for five years, and a required rate of return of 10 percent):

Investment.. $1,000
Present value of cash inflows $400 × 3.791
    (= PV at 10% for 5 years)........................ 1,516
                Net present value........................... $ 516

We now turn to a discussion of how to estimate each of the four elements involved in such calculations. These are:

1.   The required rate of return;
2.   The amount of cash inflow in each year;
3.   The economic life, which is the number of years for which cash inflows are anticipated; and
4.   The amount of investment.

REQUIRED RATE OF RETURN

When a bank loans money at an interest rate of, say, 7 percent, it does so with the expectation that it *almost certainly* will receive $70 per year interest for every $1,000 it loans. When a company makes an investment in machinery, plant or similar income-producing assets, the return is much less certain. The return depends on the cash inflows that actually will be generated by the investment, and, as will be explained in the next section, these cash inflows usually cannot be estimated accurately in advance. Because of this greater uncertainty, the businessman ordinarily requires a greater return on investments in tangible assets than a banker requires on a loan. The selection of an appropriate required rate of return is a crucial top-management decision.

Two alternative ways of arriving at the required rate of return will be described: (1) trial and error, and (2) cost of capital.

Trial and error. Recall that the higher the required rate of return, the lower the present value of the cash inflows. It follows that the higher the required rate of return, the fewer investment proposals will have cash inflows whose present value exceeds the amount of the investment. Thus, if a given rate results in the rejection of many proposed investments that management intuitively feels are acceptable, there is an indication that this rate is too high, and a lower rate is selected. Conversely, if a given rate results in the acceptance of a flood of projects, there is an indication that it is too low. As a starting point in this trial-and-error process, companies often select a rate of return that other companies in the same industry use.

Cost of capital. In economic theory, the required rate of return should be equal to the company's **cost of capital,** which is the cost of debt capital plus the cost of equity capital, weighted by the relative amount of each in the company's capital structure.

> *EXAMPLE:* Assume a company in which the cost of debt capital (e.g., bonds) is 4 percent and the cost of equity capital (e.g., common stock) is 15 percent, and in which 40 percent of the total capital is debt and 60 percent is equity.[5] The cost of capital is calculated as follows:

Type	Capital Cost	Weight	Weighted
Debt (bonds)...............	4%	0.4	1.6%
Equity (stock)..............	15	0.6	9.0
Total.................		1.0	10.6%

Thus, the cost of capital is 10.6 percent or, rounded, 11 percent. In the above example, the 4 percent used as the cost of debt capital may appear to be low. It is low because it has been adjusted for the income tax effect of debt financing. The reason for making such an adjustment is discussed in Chapter 9.

The difficulty with the cost-of-capital approach is that, although the cost of debt capital is usually known within narrow limits, the cost of equity capital is difficult to estimate realistically.[6] Presumably, the rate of return that investors expect, which is the cost of equity capital, is reflected in the market price of the company's stock, but the market price is also influenced by such other factors as general conditions of the economy, investors' estimate of the company's future earnings, and dividend policy. Techniques for isolating the cost of equity capital from these other factors are complicated; moreover, they do not usually give reliable results. For this reason, the cost-of-capital approach is not widely used in practice.

---

[5] For a more complete description of debt capital and equity capital, see *Fundamentals of Financial Accounting,* Chapters 11 and 12.

[6] For methods of deriving such estimates, see Hunt, Williams, and Donaldson, *Basic Business Finance: Text and Cases* (4th ed.; Homewood, Ill.: Richard D. Irwin, Inc., 1970).

Selection of a rate. Most companies use a judgmental approach in establishing the required rate of return. Either they experiment with various rates, by the trial-and-error method described above, or they judgmentally settle upon a rate of 10 percent, 15 percent, or 20 percent because they feel that elaborate calculations are likely to be fruitless. In the examples in this book, a required rate of return of 10 percent is usually used. This seems to be a widely used rate in industrial companies, and it is the rate prescribed by the federal government for use in the analysis of proposed government investments. Few industrial companies would use a lower rate than 10 percent. Higher rates are used in certain industries in which profit opportunities are unusually good.

Allowance for risk. The required rate of return is higher than the general level of interest rates, that is, the rates at which banks and other financial institutions are willing to loan money.[7] The reason is that capital investments made by a business have a higher degree of risk and uncertainty than do bank loans. When a bank loans money, it has a high expectation of receiving a series of cash inflows that will equal the principal plus the stated amount of interest. The return from most business capital investment projects is much less certain; both the economic life of the project and the cash inflow in each year of its life can be, at best, only roughly estimated.

The required rate of return that is selected by the techniques described above applies to investment proposals of *average* risk. For essentially the same reason that the required rate of return for capital investment projects in general is higher than interest rates on bank loans, the return expected on an individual investment project of greater-than-average risk and uncertainty should be higher than the average rate of return on all projects. Conceptually, it would be possible to use a higher-than-average required rate of return in the calculation of the net present value of projects of higher-than-average risk and uncertainty, but in practice many companies do not do this. Instead, they either introduce an element of conservatism into the calculations by deliberately shortening the estimate of economic life or lowering the estimate of cash inflows, or they take the risk characteristics into account as a judgmental matter when the final decision on the project is made. A few companies use mathematical techniques that are designed to incorporate an allowance for uncertainty; these techniques are described in advanced texts.

CASH INFLOW

The earnings from an investment are essentially the additional *cash* that the company estimates will flow in as a consequence of making the investment as compared with what the company's cash inflow would be if it did not make the investment. The *differential* concept emphasized

---

[7] Under unusual economic conditions, bank interest rates do exceed the required rate of return, but such situations are temporary.

in Chapters 6 and 7 is therefore equally applicable here, and the discussion in Chapters 6 and 7 should carefully be kept in mind in estimating cash inflows for the type of problem now being considered. In particular, recall that the focus is on cash inflows; accounting numbers derived from the accrual concept or from the allocation of overhead costs are not necessarily relevant.

Consider, for example, a proposal to replace an existing machine with a better machine. What are the cash inflows associated with this proposed investment? We note first that the existing machine must still be usable, for if it can no longer perform its function, there is no alternative and hence no analytical problem; it *must* be replaced. The comparison, therefore, is between (A) continuing to use the existing machine (the base case) and (B) operating the proposed machine (Case 2). The existing machine has certain labor, material, power, repair, maintenance, and other costs associated with its future operation. If the alternative machine is proposed as a means of reducing costs, there will be different, lower costs associated with its use. The difference between these two amounts of cost is the cash inflow anticipated if the new machine is acquired. These cash inflows usually are estimated on an annual basis.

Note that the cash inflows are arrived at by comparing the estimated costs associated with the proposed machine with the estimated costs associated with continuing to operate the existing machine. The relevant costs are therefore differential costs, the costs that are different in the proposed investment from those in the base case.

If the proposed machine increases the company's productive capacity, and if the increased output can be sold, the differential income on this increased volume is a cash inflow anticipated from the use of the proposed machine. This differential income is the difference between the added sales revenue and the incremental costs required to produce that sales revenue; these costs usually include direct material, direct labor, direct selling costs, and any other costs that would not be incurred if the increased volume were not manufactured and sold.

Depreciation. **Depreciation on the proposed equipment is not an item of differential cost.** Depreciation is omitted from the calculation of net present value because the procedure itself allows for the recovery of the investment, and to count depreciation as a cost would be taking it into account twice. When we say (as in a preceding example) that an investment of $1,000 which produced a cash inflow of $400 a year for five years has a net present value of $516 at a required earnings rate of 10 percent, we mean that the cash inflow is large enough to (1) recover the investment of $1,000, (2) earn 10 percent on the amount of investment outstanding, and (3) earn $516 in addition. The recovery of investment is equivalent to the sum of the annual depreciation charges that are made in the accounting records; therefore it would be incorrect to include a separate item for depreciation in calculating cash inflow.

Depreciation on the existing equipment is likewise not relevant because the book value of existing equipment represents a sunk cost. For the reason explained in Chapter 7, sunk costs should be disregarded.

Make-or-buy proposals. In Chapter 7 we discussed the type of problem in which the company is considering buying from an outside vender a product which it is now making. Ordinarily, such a proposal does not involve an investment. The converse of this problem, in which the company is considering making an item that it is now buying, *does* involve an investment and therefore belongs in this chapter. The cash inflow on such a proposal is the *difference* between the price paid to the outside vendor and the cash costs that will be incurred if the product is manufactured.

> EXAMPLE: Part No. 102 is currently purchased from an outside vendor at a price of $10 per unit. It is proposed that the part be manufactured. The cash costs of making the part, including direct labor, direct material, and other direct costs are estimated to be $6 per unit. Annual consumption is 1,000 units. The cash inflow is:
>
> | | |
> |---|---:|
> | Purchase cost of Part No. 102 (1,000 × $10)............. | $10,000 |
> | Cost of making Part No. 102 (1,000 × $6)............... | −6,000 |
> | Cash inflow.................................... | $ 4,000 |

Buy-or-lease proposals. The proposal under consideration may be whether to buy an asset or to lease it. (Usually, such a problem is analyzed *after* the basic decision to acquire the asset has been made.) If the asset is bought, the purchase price represents an investment. If the asset is leased, no investment is required but a series of lease payments must be made instead. By buying the asset, the necessity for making these lease payments is avoided, and the avoidance of these payments therefore constitutes the cash inflows on the investment. If the lessor agrees to perform certain services, such as maintenance or insurance, then these should be subtracted from the lease payments because such services would also be required if the asset were purchased, and they therefore are not differential.

> EXAMPLE: A company has decided to acquire a computer. It can be purchased for $100,000, or it can be leased for $22,000 a year. The lease payment includes maintenance, which the company estimates is worth $2,000 a year. The estimated economic life of the computer is eight years. The calculation is as follows:
>
> | | | |
> |---|---:|---:|
> | Investment............................... | | $100,000 |
> | Cash inflow: | | |
> | Saving in lease payments.................. | $22,000 | |
> | Less maintenance included in payments..... | 2,000 | |
> | Annual cash inflow................... | $20,000 | |
> | Present value of cash inflows: | | |
> | $20,000 × 5.335 (8 yrs, 10% Table B).... | | 106,700 |
> | Net present value................. | | $ 6,700 |

Conclusion: The machine should be purchased.

Uncertainties. Since investments in machinery and other operational assets are usually expected to produce cash inflows for a number of years, the earnings estimates may well extend a considerable distance into the future. The farther ahead one attempts to make estimates, the more uncertain they become. Estimates of the relatively distant future must be treated accordingly; that is, as rough approximations rather than as numbers that have a high degree of precision.

Inflation. A particularly troublesome aspect of estimating cash inflows is what assumption to make about future changes in price levels. If the analyst believes, as many people do, that labor rates and material prices will generally tend to move upward indefinitely, it may be desirable to incorporate in the estimate of cash inflows an explicit adjustment for the effect of inflation. For example, if there is an estimated annual savings of direct labor of 1,000 hours per year, and if the current direct labor cost is $5 per hour, the annual savings will be $5,000 currently, but it will be some other amount if the hourly cost changes in the future. If annual wage increases of 5 percent are foreseen, then the saving will be $5,250 in the second year, $5,512 in the third year, and so on. Despite the likelihood of such increases, many companies do not make an adjustment for inflation. They reason that the rate of inflation is highly uncertain, and that its effect on the total company's operations are so unpredictable that the effort to make the adjustment is not worthwhile, or that cost increases will be offset by equivalent increases in selling prices.

Income taxes. In most investment problems the effect of income taxes must be taken into account. Because the procedure for doing this is fairly complicated, this subject is deferred to Chapter 9.

ECONOMIC LIFE

The economic life of an investment is the number of years over which cash inflows are expected as a consequence of making the investment. Even though cash inflows may be expected for an indefinitely long period, the economic life is usually set at a specified maximum number of years, such as 10, 15, or 20. This maximum is often shorter than the life that is actually anticipated both because of the uncertainty of cash inflow estimates for distant years and because the present value of cash inflows for distant years is so low that the amount of these cash inflows has no significant effect on the calculation. For example, at a discount rate of 10 percent, a $1 cash inflow in Year 21 has a present value of only 15 cents, and the *total* present value of a $1 cash inflow in *each* of the 30 years from Year 21 through Year 50 is only $1.40.

The end of the period selected for the economic life of a proposed investment is called the investment horizon. The word suggests that beyond this time cash inflows are not visible. Economic life can rarely be estimated exactly; nevertheless, it is important that the best possible estimate be made, for the economic life has a significant effect on the calculations.

When a proposed project involves the purchase of equipment, the economic life of the investment corresponds to the estimated useful life of the equipment to the user. There is a tendency, when thinking about the life of a machine, to consider primarily its **physical life;** that is, the number of years the machine will provide service before it wears out. The physical life of an automobile, for example, is about 10 years, and that of a brick building, 50 years or more. Although the physical life is an upper limit, in most cases the economic life of an asset is considerably shorter than its physical life. There are several reasons for this. Technological progress makes machinery obsolete. Improvements will almost certainly be made sometime in all machines now in existence, but the question of *which* machines will be improved and *how soon* the improved machines will be on the market is a most difficult one to answer. Unless special information is available, the answer can be little more than an educated guess. Yet it is a guess that must be made, for the investment in a machine will cease to earn a return when it is replaced by an improved machine.

The economic life also ends when the company ceases to make profitable use of the machine. This can happen because the particular operation performed by the machine is made unnecessary by a change in style or a change in process, or because the market for the product itself has vanished, or because the company decides, for whatever reason, to discontinue the product. A machine for making buggy whips may last physically for 100 years, and there may be no possibility of making technological improvements in it; yet such a machine cannot continue to earn a return on its investment after the buggy whips produced on it are no longer in demand. The uncertainties associated with product demand vary widely with different industries. The equipment used to make a novelty item, such as the hula hoop, may have an economic life of only a few years—perhaps only a single year—whereas the generating and distribution equipment of an electric public utility may reasonably be expected to provide earnings for several decades.

Finally, the economic life of a machine ends if the company goes out of business. Most managements quite properly operate on the premise that the company will be in business for a long time to come. There are instances, however, when management foresees an end to the business, or to a particular part of it, in the relatively near future. In such a case, the economic life of a machine is limited to the period during which management believes the business is going to operate.

The key question is: Over what period of time is the investment likely to generate cash inflows for this company? For whatever reason, when the investment no longer produces cash inflows, its economic life has ended. In view of the uncertainties associated with the operation of a business, most companies are conservative in estimating what the economic life of a proposed investment will be.

INVESTMENT

The investment is the amount of funds that a company risks if it accepts an investment proposal. The relevant investment costs are the differential costs. These are the outlays that will be made if the project is undertaken and that would not be made if it is not undertaken. The cost of the machine itself, its shipping costs, cost of installation, and the cost of training operators are examples of differential investment costs. These outlays are part of the investment, even though some of them may not be capitalized in the accounting records.

Existing equipment. If the purchase of new equipment results in the sale of existing equipment, the net proceeds from the sale reduces the amount of the differential investment. In other words, the differential investment represents the total amount of *additional* funds that must be committed to the investment project. The net proceeds from existing equipment are its selling price less any costs incurred in making the sale and in dismantling and removing the equipment.

> EXAMPLE: Following is the calculation of the investment for the proposed purchase of a Beager shirt-pressing machine for a laundry:

Gross investment:

Cost of new Beager Model 85......................		$18,585
Freight from factory...............................		525
Installation, including new wiring...................		600
Training of operators..............................		300
Gross investment.............................		$20,010
Less: Proceeds from sale of old Beager Model 70:		
Sales price..	$1,000	
Less: packing and crating........................	−100	
Net proceeds..............................		900
Net investment......................................		$19,110

Residual value. A machine may have a **residual value** (i.e., salvage or resale value) at the end of its economic life. In a great many cases, the estimated residual value is so small and occurs so far in the future that it has no significant effect on the decision. Moreover, any salvage or resale value that is realized may be approximately offset by removal and dismantling costs. In situations where the estimated residual value is significant, the net residual value (after removal costs) is viewed as a future cash inflow in the year of disposal and is included with the cash inflows. Other assets, such as repair parts or inventory, may also be released at the end of the project, and these are treated in the same fashion.

> EXAMPLE: The economic life of a proposed riverboat is estimated to be 20 years. Although the boat's physical life is considerably

longer than that, it is believed that technological improvements would warrant the purchase of a new boat at that time. It is estimated that the boat could be sold at the end of 20 years for $50,000. Costs associated with making the sale would be $5,000. The present value of the residual value is computed as follows:

Resale value at end of year 20................................ $50,000
Cost of making the sale....................................... −5,000
　　　Net proceeds.. $45,000
Present value of $45,000 in year 20 at discount of 10% = $45,000 × 0.149 (Table A) = $6,700.

(Note that the present value, which actually works out to $6,705, has been deliberately rounded in view of the uncertainty of the estimate. Even greater rounding, say to $7,000, would be acceptable.)

Sunk costs. In Chapter 7 we emphasized that sunk costs are irrelevant. If $100,000 already has been expended for research on a new product and if the new product will require an additional investment in new facilities of $50,000, the relevant investment figure is $50,000, not $150,000. The $100,000 is a sunk cost. Human nature is such that there is a temptation to try to work sunk costs such as these into the calculation, but this temptation must be resisted. In considering a proposed investment, the analyst must always look forward, never backward. Only future events and their associated costs and revenues are relevant to current decisions.

Investments in working capital. An investment is the commitment, or locking up, of funds in any type of asset. Although up to this point depreciable assets have been used as examples, investments also include commitments of funds to additional inventory and to other current assets. In particular, if new equipment is acquired to produce a new product, additional funds will probably be required for inventories, accounts receivable, and increased cash needs. Part of this increase in current assets may be supplied from increased accounts payable and accrued expenses; the remainder must come from permanent capital. This additional working capital is as much a part of the differential investment as the equipment itself.

Often it is reasonable to assume that the *residual value* of investments in working capital is approximately the same as the amount of the initial investment; that is, that at the end of the project, these items can be liquidated at their cost. Under these circumstances, the amount of working capital is treated as a cash inflow in the last year of the project, and its present value is found by discounting that amount at the required rate of return.

EXAMPLE: A proposed new product is estimated to require an investment of $300,000 in equipment and $100,000 in additional working capital (primarily for accounts receivable and inventory). The economic life of the proposal is estimated to be 10 years. At the end of that time, the equipment is estimated to have a net residual value of zero, but working capital can probably be liquidated at the full amount of $100,000. The calculation of the net investment is as follows:

```
Gross investment:
    Equipment............................. $300,000
    Working capital.......................   100,000
        Gross investment..................... $400,000
Less: Release of $100,000 working capital at end of
      Year 10, discounted at 10%:
    $100,000 × 0.386 (Table A)................   38,600
Net investment............................. $361,400
```

(Note that the format of this example is different than the previous one. Here, the present value of the released working capital is deducted from the investment, whereas in the previous example, it was shown as a cash inflow in the year in which it occurred. Either method is satisfactory; they arrive at the same result.)

Non-
monetary
consider-
ations

We have described the quantitative analysis involved in a capital investment proposal. It should be emphasized that this analysis does not provide the complete solution to the problem because it encompasses only those elements that can be reduced to numbers. A full consideration of the problem involves nonmonetary factors. Many investments are undertaken without a calculation of net present value. They may be necessary for the safety of employees; they may be undertaken for the convenience or comfort of employees (such as a new cafeteria or a new recreation room); they may be undertaken to enhance community relations, or because they are required in order to meet pollution control or other legal requirements, or because they increase plant protection safeguards. For some proposals of this type, no economic analysis is necessary; if an unsafe condition is found, it must be corrected regardless of the cost. For other proposals, these nonmonetary factors must be considered along with the numbers that are included in the economic analysis. For all proposals, the decision maker must take into account the fact that all the numbers are estimates, and that he must apply his own judgment as to the validity of these estimates in arriving at a decision.

Based on a survey of 177 industrial companies, Fremgen reports that only 27 percent believed that the economic analysis was the most critical part of the decision process and only 12 percent believed it was the most difficult.[8] The others said that the proper definition of the proposal, the estimation of cash inflows, and the implementation of a decision after it had been made were more important. Thus, the tech-

---

[8] James M. Fremgen, "Capital Budgeting Practices; A Survey," *Management Accounting*, May 1973, p. 19.

niques described in this chapter are by no means the whole story. They are, however, the only part of the story that can be described as a definite procedure; the remainder must be learned through experience.

THE OVERALL ANALYTICAL PROCESS

The technique described above is often called the **net present value** method. Following is a summary of the steps involved in using this method in analyzing a proposed investment:

1. Select a required rate of return. Presumably, once selected, this rate will be used generally; it need not be considered anew for each proposal.
2. Find the net investment, which includes the additional outlays made at Time Zero, less the proceeds from disposal of existing equipment.
3. Estimate the economic life of the proposed project.
4. Estimate the differential cash inflows for each year or sequence of years during the economic life.
5. Estimate the residual values at the end of the economic life, which consist of the disposal value of equipment plus working capital that is to be released.
6. Find the present value of all the inflows identified in Steps 4 and 5 by discounting them at the required rate of return, using Table A or Table B.
7. Find the net present value by subtracting the net investment from the present value of the inflows. If the net present value is zero or positive, decide that the proposal is acceptable, insofar as the monetary factors are concerned.
8. Taking into account the nonmonetary factors, reach a final decision. (This part of the process is at least as important as all the other parts put together, but there is no way of generalizing about it.)

Demonstra-   As an aid to visualizing the relationships in a proposed investment, it
tion case   is often useful to diagram the flows similar to that illustrated in Exhibit 8–2.

This flow diagram reflects the following investment proposal. A proposed machine will cost $9,000, and $2,000 will be spent to install it. It will replace an existing machine which has a book value of $2,000, but which can be sold for $1,000. It is estimated that the machine will save $2,500 a year in labor costs, that its economic life is five years, and that it can be sold at the end of that time for $2,000, net of removal costs. The company requires a rate of return of 10 percent. Should the proposed machine be purchased?

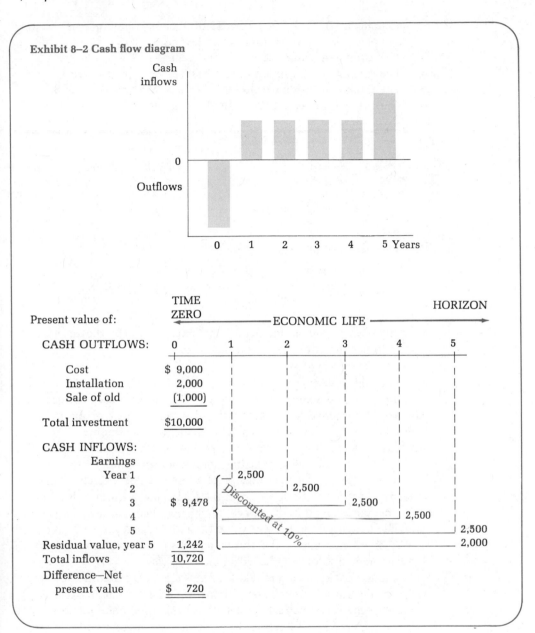

Exhibit 8–2 Cash flow diagram

Present value of:	TIME ZERO		ECONOMIC LIFE			HORIZON
CASH OUTFLOWS:	0	1	2	3	4	5
Cost	$ 9,000					
Installation	2,000					
Sale of old	(1,000)					
Total investment	$10,000					
CASH INFLOWS: Earnings						
Year 1		2,500				
2			2,500			
3	$ 9,478			2,500		
4					2,500	
5						2,500
Residual value, year 5	1,242					2,000
Total inflows	10,720					
Difference—Net present value	$ 720					

Discounted at 10%

Analysis:

(This analysis is arranged in order of the steps given above.)

1. The required rate of return is 10 percent. (The company derived this rate by one of the approaches described above.)

2. The estimated net investment is the $9,000 purchase price, plus the $2,000 installation cost, less the $1,000 resale value of the existing

equipment, or $10,000. The $2,000 book value of the existing equipment is a sunk cost and is irrelevant.

3. The estimated economic life is five years.
4. The estimated cash inflows are $2,500 a year for five years.
5. The estimated residual value is $2,000 at the end of year 5.
6. The present values are computed as follows:

Cash Inflows	Amount	Year	Table	Factor	Present Value
From operations............	$2,500/year	1–5	B	3.791	$ 9,478
Residual..................	2,000	5	A	0.621	1,242
Total present value of inflows...........					$10,720

7. The net present value is

Inflows.............................	$10,720	
Investment.........................	10,000	
Net present value....................	$ 720	

8. Unless there are nonmonetary factors that weight the decision in the other direction, the proposal is acceptable.

Summary   A capital investment problem is essentially one of determining whether the anticipated cash inflows from a proposed project are sufficiently attractive to warrant risking the investment of funds in the project. The investment is typically made at one moment of time, whereas cash inflows occur over a period of time in the future. The analytical technique must take this difference in timing into account. This is done by using the concept of present value, which is that an amount of money to be received in the future has a lower value, today, than the same amount of money that is on hand today. Tables are available that show the present value of amounts that are to be received at any specified time in the future and also amounts that are to be received annually for a specified number of years.

The basic decision rule is that a proposal is acceptable if the present value of the cash inflows expected to be derived from it exceeds the amount of the investment. In order to use this rule, one must estimate: (1) the required rate of return, (2) the amount of cash inflow in each year, (3) the economic life, and (4) the amount of investment.

The required rate of return is the minimum rate that a company expects to earn on its investments. Although usually arrived at judgmentally, it is sometimes possible to arrive at it by computing the company's cost of capital. The cash inflows are discounted at the required rate of return.

Cash inflows are those that are anticipated as a consequence of the investment. They are differential inflows, in the same sense as those discussed in Chapter 7. Depreciation on the proposed assets is disregarded.

Economic life is the number of years that the investment is expected to generate cash inflows. It is never longer than the physical life of the assets acquired, and is usually shorter than the physical life, reflecting the likelihood that technological improvements, the discontinuance of the product line, or other factors will cause a cessation of earnings prior to the expiration of physical life.

The amount of investment is the differential amount of funds that will be committed to the project. It includes not only the invoice cost of the assets themselves but also all costs associated with making the assets ready to begin producing cash inflows. Also, it includes working capital required for the project. The gross amount of investment is reduced by the net proceeds from the sale of assets that are disposed of if the project is undertaken. The present value of the residual value of assets that are sold or released at the end of the economic life may be either subtracted from the investment or added to operating cash inflows.

The foregoing are monetary considerations that can be incorporated in an economic analysis. Nonmonetary considerations are also important in making the actual decision; they are often as important as the monetary considerations and are in some cases so important that no economic analysis is worthwhile.

Important terms		
Present value		**Net present value**
Investment		**Cost of capital**
Cash inflow		**Economic life**
Time Zero		**Investment horizon**
Discounting		**Residual value**
Required rate of return		

Questions for discussion

1. In a "Christmas Club" plan, a person deposits a specified amount weekly in a bank savings account and the total amount accumulated is paid back just before Christmas. No interest, or very little interest, is paid on these deposits. Is a Christmas Club member acting irrationally by depositing money under these conditions? Would a business be acting irrationally if it joined a Christmas Club?

2. A proposal involves an investment of $1,000 and a cash inflow of $200 per year. For how many years must the cash inflows be received if the project is to be acceptable? The required rate of return is 10 percent.

3. Would you prefer cash inflows of $600 a year for four years or cash inflows of $400 a year for six years, assuming your required rate of return is 10 percent? Explain. Is there any required rate of return that would change your answer?

4. The procedure described in the chapter assumes that investment outlays are made at one moment of time, Time Zero. Actually, the construction of a building may require outlays over a period of a year or more. How may the procedure be modified to accommodate this fact?

5. Companies are said to expect higher profits on investments in underdeveloped countries than in Western European countries with stable economic conditions, and this is said to be an example of exploitation of underdeveloped countries. Is there another explanation for this?

6. How does the economic life of a jet aircraft compare with the economic life of the airport runways that the aircraft uses? Why?

7. For each of the following types of investment projects, state how estimates should be made of the investment, the economic life, and the cash inflows:
   (a) Building a new plant.
   (b) Replacing existing equipment with more efficient equipment.
   (c) Buying a machine to perform an operation now done manually.
   (d) Adding a new product.

8. Table B is used to find the present value of a stream of equal annual cash inflows. Suppose that payments were $250 a year in each of years 2, 3, 4, and 5, and $300 in year 1. Without making calculations, explain how Table B could be used in such a situation.

9. If the required rate of return is 8 percent and the investment is $1,000, is the proposal described in Question 8 acceptable? Answer without making calculations. (Hint: Compare these facts with those in the example on page 240.)

10. Why is the cost-of-capital method not widely used in practice?

11. Is a stream of cash inflows that is relatively certain preferable to a stream of cash inflows of the same annual amount that is relatively uncertain? Why?

12. It is said that investors basically have a choice between eating well and sleeping well. Explain what is meant by this statement, using differences in required rates of return in your explanation.

13. Explain why depreciation on the proposed equipment is omitted from the calculation of net present value.

14. Why is the economic life of a machine usually shorter than its physical life? Is the economic life ever longer than the physical life?

15. A company has invested $100,000 to develop a new item of electronic equipment, but it doesn't operate properly. It then decides to invest $50,000 additional, but the equipment still doesn't work. Under what circumstances would the company be well advised to spend yet another $50,000?

Problems   *Note:* Disregard income taxes in all these problems.

8–1. A bank makes the following offer: If you will deposit $15,000 cash, the bank will immediately give you a brand-new automobile worth $3,800, and it will also return your $15,000 at the end of five years.

Required:
1. What earnings rate is implicit in this offer?
2. If you had $15,000 to invest, would you accept this proposition?

8–2. What is the maximum investment a company would make in an asset expected to produce annual cash inflow of $5,000 a year for 8 years if its required rate of return is 10 percent?

8–3. How much investment per dollar of expected annual cash inflow can a company afford if the investment has an economic life of 7 years and the required rate or return is 15 percent?

8–4. The Bowmar Company is considering three proposed investments, A, B, and C. Each requires an investment of $4,900, and each has an economic life of three years and total cash inflow over that period of $6,000. The pattern of cash inflows for each proposal differs, however, as indicated below:

| | Annual Cash Inflows | | |
Year	A	B	C
1.	$1,000	$2,000	$3,000
2.	2,000	2,000	2,000
3.	3,000	2,000	1,000
	$6,000	$6,000	$6,000

Required:
1. Calculate the net present value of each proposal if the required rate of return is 10 percent.
2. Calculate the net present value of each proposal if the required rate of return is 6 percent.
3. Explain why the results differ.

8–5. Parsons Company is considering the purchase of a new machine to replace an existing machine. The purchase price is $10,000 delivered and installed. The new machine is estimated to produce savings of $2,000 in direct labor and other direct costs annually, as compared with the present equipment. The new machine has an estimated economic life of 10 years and zero residual value. The company requires a rate of return of 20 percent on an investment of this type.

Required (consider each part separately):
1. Assuming the present equipment has zero book value and zero salvage value, should the new machine be purchased?
2. Assuming the present equipment has a book value of $4,800 (cost $8,000, less accumulated depreciation of $3,200) and zero salvage value today, should the new machine be purchased?
3. Assuming the present equipment has a book value of $4,800 and

a salvage value today of $3,000, should the new machine be purchased?

4. Assume that the new machine will save only $1,000 a year, but that its estimated economic life is 20 years. Other conditions are as described in Part 1. Should the new machine be purchased?

5. Assume that estimated savings are $2,500 in each of the first five years and $1,500 in each of the next five years. Other conditions are as described in Part 1. Should the new machine be purchased?

8–6. Parsons Company decided to buy the machine described in Problem 8–5 (hereafter called "Model A" machine). Two years later Model B machine comes on the market. Model B costs $20,000 delivered and installed, and it is estimated to result in annual savings of $5,000 as compared with the cost of operating the Model A machine, and to have an economic life of 10 years. Because the Model B machine is such an improvement, the Model A machine has no resale value.

Required:

1. What action should the company take?
2. If the company purchases the Model B machine, a mistake has been made somewhere because the Model A machine, purchased only two years previously, is being scrapped. How did this mistake come about?

8–7. Shortly before the beginning of 1974 Delbert Company was considering the installation of a new piece of equipment which was designed to automate what had been an operation that required direct labor. Expected results for the first year of operations are as follows:

Cost of equipment.........................	$28,200
Installation cost...........................	1,800
Labor savings, 4,000 hours @ $3..............	12,000
Increased power costs......................	900
Increased insurance and taxes...............	500
Increased maintenance costs.................	1,000

The company did buy the equipment. It actually paid $3,500 for installation costs. In 1974, actual labor hours saved totaled 4,000, but labor rates increased to $3.50 per hour. Other costs were as expected. The expected useful life of the equipment was five years.

Required:

1. Assuming the company has a required earnings rate of 15 percent, should the proposal have been accepted, based on expected results? Show all computations.
2. If costs for the five years remain the same as the actual results of the operations of the first year, what can be said about the management's decision to invest in the equipment?

8–8.   Last year Main Line Company installed a group of machines with the expectation of substantial labor cost savings. The expected results for the first year of operations follow:

Cost of machines, installed......................	$15,000
Useful life.......................................	5 years
Labor savings....................................	$ 6,000
Increased power costs...........................	450
Increased insurance and property taxes...........	550

The company actually paid $15,500 for the machines as installation costs were greater than expected. Actual labor savings were only $5,700. Increased maintenance costs were $600. All other costs were as expected.

Required:

1.   Assuming the company has a required earnings rate of 15 percent, should the proposal have been accepted, based on expected results? Show all computations.
2.   If all other costs remain the same as the actual results of the first year of operations, do you feel this company made a sound investment decision? Comment.

8–9.   A new machine has been developed which will enable Wace Industries to produce its major product at a labor saving of $26,000 per year under current rates. After three years the union contract will be renegotiated and the labor savings are estimated at $30,000 per year for the final two years. Wace is interested in buying this machine, but only has $120,000 budgeted for new equipment. The company can invest these funds at equal risk elsewhere and earn 18 percent.

Required:

Calculate the maximum amount which Wace can afford to invest if the decision is made to purchase this machine under the conditions given.

8–10.   Wyman Company has just developed a new product which should have the following projected cash inflows over the economic life of the product:

Year	Cash Flow
1............................	$35,000
2............................	30,000
3............................	25,000
4............................	20,000

Wyman does not invest in productive assets unless they feel the investment will return at least 20 percent. The equipment necessary to produce the product can be bought or made by Wyman.

Required:

Calculate the maximum amount of capital investment which can be budgeted for if the company undertakes the production of the new product under the conditions shown above.

8–11. "Old faithful" was a plastics extruder, long since fully depreciated, which Tupper Plastics Company had owned since its inception in 1954. It was judged to be able to run indefinitely at its present rate of 75 percent of capacity. It had zero salvage value.

Company engineers informed Mr. Tupper, the president, that a new, more efficient extruder was on the market which could save the company $2,250 per year in reduced labor costs and increased output, 60 percent due to the former and 40 percent due to the latter. The new extruder would cost the company $14,250 delivered and installed. The engineers claimed that its economic life was 20 years. Tupper's required earnings rate was 15 percent.

Required:

1. If the engineers are correct, should the plastic extruder be purchased?
2. Mr. Tupper thought the estimate of economic life was unrealistic. What minimum economic life is necessary in order to justify the investment? (Hint: Use a trial-and-error approach.)

8–12. The Jan Shoe Company was considering the following two investments:

	Investment No. 1	*Investment No. 2*
Initial cash outlay......	$10,000	$10,000
Investment life.........	10 years	10 years
Cash inflows...........	$ 1,500 annually	$17,000 at the end of the 10th year

Required:

Which of the two investments had the higher net present value using a 10 percent discount rate?

8–13. Paul Tenant, a door-to-door vacuum cleaner salesman, normally buys a new car every two years, but is now considering the possibility of leasing an automobile for a two-year period for $74 per month. The auto in question could be purchased by Mr. Tenant for $3,000 and financed by the $1,000 trade-in value of his old car, plus a two-year, $2,000 note at 9 percent interest. If Mr. Tenant purchases the car, he estimates that its value at the end of two years would be $1,450.

The lease agreement calls for the lessee (Mr. Tenant) to provide a $500 deposit to be returned in full at the end of the lease. In addition, the agreement states that the lessee will be responsible for all insurance, maintenance, gasoline, and oil.

Required:

What action would you recommend that Paul Tenant take?

8–14. Bill Coyne is considering opening a self-service laundromat which would require an investment of $54,000 for washers, dryers, and related equipment. Bill estimates that the equipment will have a seven-year life, and seeks a return of 25 percent without regard to tax considerations, which he recognizes will reduce his actual return.

Bill plans to charge $0.50 for the use of a washing machine and $0.25 for the use of a dryer for 25 minutes. He has estimated that he will gross $450 and $225 from the washers and dryers respectively each week. Variable costs would amount to $0.04 per wash for water and electricity and $0.03 per 25-minute dryer cycle for gas and electricity. Bill has estimated that his monthly fixed expenses will consist of rent of $450 and maintenance and cleanup labor of $200.

Required:

Can Bill Coyne obtain the return he desires, given the revenue and expense estimates?

8–15.   Mr. Smith of the Smith-Link Company is considering the purchase of a new machine, to replace older, less efficient machinery with a net book value of $35,000. The new machine carries a $220,000 price tag, which includes delivery and installation. Mr. Smith knows that he will incur a loss of $25,000 on the sale of the old machinery, which bothers him, since he is convinced that the present machinery will probably last as long as the proposed new machinery would. Mr. Smith has estimated the economic life of the new machine to be 30 years. On the other hand, Mr. Smith's cost accountants have told him that the new machinery would save the company $18,650 annually in reduced labor and material costs.

Required:

What would the net present value of the new machinery be if it were to be purchased? Assume a 10 percent discount rate.

Suggestions
for further
reading

Grant, Eugene L., and Ireson, William G. *Principles of Engineering Economy.* 4th ed. New York: Ronald Press Co., 1960.

Hunt, Pearson; Williams, Charles M.; and Donaldson, Gordon. *Basic Business Finance: Text and Cases.* 4th ed. Homewood, Ill.: Richard D. Irwin, Inc., 1970.

Quirin, G. David. *The Capital Expenditure Decision.* Homewood, Ill.: Richard D. Irwin, Inc., 1967.

Solomon, Ezra (ed.). *The Management of Corporate Capital.* Glencoe, Ill.: Free Press, 1959.

Terborgh, George. *Business Investment Policy.* Washington, D.C.: Machinery and Allied Products Institute, 1958.

Weston, J. Fred, and Woods, Donald H. *Basic Financial Management: Selected Readings.* Belmont, Calif.: Wadsworth Publishing Co., 1967.

9 Additional aspects of investment decisions

Purpose of the chapter This chapter completes the discussion of the analysis of capital investment decisions. First, it describes how the effect of income taxes is to be taken into account in such analyses. The effect of income taxes on other types of business decisions is also discussed. Next, we describe other techniques for making analyses of investment problems that supplement, or are used in place of, the net present value technique described in Chapter 8. These techniques are the discounted cash flow method, the payback method, and the unadjusted rate of return method. Finally, we describe the application of the present value concept to a class of problems called "preference problems."

Income taxes NATURE OF INCOME TAX IMPACT

In Chapters 7 and 8, we intentionally disregarded the impact of income taxes on the calculation of costs and earnings of proposed alternative courses of action. Obviously, income taxes do affect a company's profitability. If a proposed price increase is estimated to increase a company's profit by $100,000, disregarding income taxes, and if the government takes 50 percent of profit in the form of income tax, then the price increase will add only half of the $100,000, or $50,000, to net income. In general, any course of action that increases profits also increases the amount of income tax that the company must pay.

With a few important differences (some of which are discussed below), the amount of income subject to an income tax (i.e., taxable income) is calculated in the same way that a company calculates net income for financial accounting purposes. Thus, as a general rule, if

262

the income tax rate is 50 percent, the government takes 50 cents out of every dollar that the company adds to its income before income taxes.

The actual tax rate varies among companies. The federal rate is 22 percent on the first $25,000 of corporate income, and 48 percent on all income above that amount. Since the problems we are analyzing involve proposed *increases* in income, the 22 percent rate is not relevant except in small corporations. Neither is its average tax rate relevant.

> *EXAMPLE:* Company X has taxable income of $100,000. It therefore pays income tax as follows:

	Taxable Income	Rate	Tax
	$ 25,000	22%	$ 5,500
	75,000	48	36,000
Total......................	$100,000	41.5%	$41,500

> Its *average* tax rate is 41.5 percent. If, however, Company X increased its taxable income by $10,000, its income taxes would be increased by 48 percent of the $10,000, or $4,800. Since the *differential* income is taxed at the 48 percent rate, both the 22 percent rate and the average rate can be disregarded. As emphasized repeatedly in Chapters 7 and 8, the income that is relevant in the analysis of alternative choice problems is the differential income.

In addition to the federal tax, most states impose income taxes of a few percent, and so do some cities. In the problems and examples in this chapter, we shall assume an income tax rate of 51 percent.[1] The term "net income," without a qualifying term, is always supposed to refer to income after income taxes have been deducted. Nevertheless, in order to avoid any possibility of confusion, the term **aftertax income** is often used for net income, and the term **pretax income** is used for income before the deduction of income taxes. Similarly, we shall refer to the **pretax cash inflow,** which is the same as the cash inflow discussed in Chapter 8, and to the **aftertax cash inflow,** which is the cash inflow after income taxes have been taken into account.

For many alternative choice problems, assuming a tax rate of 51 percent, aftertax income is 49 percent of pretax income. Thus, if a proposed cost reduction method is estimated to save $10,000 a year

---

[1] Although the general principles for calculating income taxes are unlikely to change, rates and some other details change from year to year. This discussion is based on the situation that existed in 1973. Although the rule of thumb that income taxes take half of taxable income is usually satisfactory, for illustrative purposes, we prefer not to use a 50 percent rate. If such a rate were used, we would have difficulty in communicating which of the numbers in the calculations referred to the income tax and which referred to the net income after tax, since the two numbers would be identical.

pretax, it will save $4,900 a year aftertax. Although $4,900 is obviously not as welcome to the shareholders as $10,000 would be, the proposed cost reduction method would increase income, and, in the absence of arguments to the contrary, the decision should be made to adopt it. This is the case with *all* the alternative choice problems discussed in Chapter 7. Income taxes reduce the differential income by the amount of the tax bite; however, a proposal that shows additional income on a pretax basis will also show additional income on an aftertax basis. For this reason, calculations for problems of the type discussed in Chapter 7 (e.g., contribution pricing, new methods, make or buy) are customarily made on a pretax basis, in the interests of simplicity.

When depreciable assets are involved in a proposal, however, the situation is quite different. In proposals of this type, **there is no simple relationship between pretax cash inflow and aftertax cash inflow** primarily because depreciation is disregarded in estimating the operating cash inflow of such proposals, whereas depreciation is an expense that is taken into account in calculating taxable income. This is the case with the capital investment proposals in Chapter 8. We now describe how income taxes should be taken into account in analyzing such proposals.

TAXES IN CAPITAL INVESTMENT DECISIONS

The basic rule for evaluating a proposed investment, given in Chapter 8, is that the investment is acceptable if the present value of the cash inflows equals or exceeds the amount of the investment.

> *EXAMPLE:* A proposed machine costing $1,000 is expected to produce cash inflows in the form of savings in labor and other costs amounting to $400 a year for five years. At a 10 percent required rate of return, these cash inflows have a present value of $400 × 3.791 (Table B) = $1,516. The proposed investment has a net present value of $1,516 − $1,000 = $516, and it is therefore acceptable if taxes are disregarded.

From the discussion in the preceding section, it might be inferred that if the pretax cash inflows were $400 a year, the aftertax cash inflows would be 49 percent of $400, or $196 per year. If such were the case, the proposal described in the preceding example would not be acceptable because the total aftertax cash inflow would be $196 a year for five years, its present value at 10 percent would be $723 (= $196 × 3.791), and this is less than the investment of $1,000. Actually, the calculation of aftertax cash inflow in this situation is more complicated than simply taking 49 percent of the pretax cash inflow.

As explained in Chapter 8, depreciation is omitted from the calculation of net present value because the procedure itself allows for the recovery of the investment, and to count depreciation as a cost would be taking it into account twice. In calculating the income used as a basis for income taxes (i.e., taxable income), however, depreciation is an expense, just as it is on the usual income statement.

Exhibit 9–1 shows how the $1,000 proposed investment used in the above example would affect the company's income statement and the calculation of its income tax. The relationships shown in that exhibit should be studied carefully. The first pair of columns shows how the company's income statement would appear if it did not purchase the proposed machine, and the next pair of columns shows how the income statement would look if the machine were purchased, other conditions remaining unchanged. Revenue is unaffected. Depreciation expense increases by $200, the annual charge for a $1,000 machine being depreciated over a period of five years on a straight-line basis. Other

Exhibit 9–1

Effect of income taxes on investment calculation

	Annual Income Statements		
	Without Investment (Base Case)	With Investment (Case 2)	Difference
Revenue..............	$1,002,000	$1,002,000	0
Depreciation......... $ 50,000		$ 50,200	+$200
Other expenses....... 851,000		850,600	− 400
Total expense....	901,000	900,800	− 200
Pretax income........	$ 101,000	$ 101,200	+ 200
Income tax (51%)....	51,510	51,612	+ 102
Net Income..........	$ 49,490	$ 49,588	+ 98

expenses decrease $400 a year because of the savings arising from use of the new machine. Pretax income therefore increases by $200, which is the difference between the additional depreciation and the lower amount of other expense. Since income tax is assumed to be 51 percent of taxable income, income tax increases by 51 percent of $200 or $102. Net income therefore increases by $98.

Two important facts should be noted. First, there is no proportionate relationship between the $400 of annual cash inflow and the $102 of additional income tax. In order to calculate the additional income tax, we had to take into account the depreciation expense, as well as the cash inflows. Second, the additional income tax is much less than 51 percent of the $400 cash inflow.

The reason that income taxes are not increased by 51 percent of the additional cash flow is that depreciation offsets part of what would otherwise be additional taxable income. Depreciation is therefore called a **tax shield** in investment calculations. It shields the pretax cash inflow from the full impact of income taxes. Taxable income will not correspond to pretax cash inflows in any problem where depreciation is a significant factor. The increase in taxable income will always be *less than* the increase in pretax cash inflow by the amount of the depreciation expense on the assets acquired.

In order to calculate the aftertax cash inflow, therefore, we must take account of the depreciation tax shield. At the same time, we must be careful not to permit the amount of depreciation itself to enter the calculation of cash inflow because this would lead to the same double counting that was referred to above. We must find the amount of additional income tax, which is indeed a cash outflow, without counting the depreciation expense, which is not a cash outflow. The way to do this is to make a separate calculation of the additional income tax and subtract this from the pretax cash inflow. More specifically, the procedure is as follows:

1. Estimate the pretax cash inflows resulting from the investment, as in Chapter 8.
2. Estimate the additional income tax by, in effect, preparing a regular income statement as in Exhibit 9–1.
3. Subtract the additional income tax from the pretax cash inflows to find the aftertax cash inflows.
4. Discount the aftertax cash inflows at the required rate of return to find the net present value.

> EXAMPLE: Continue with the example of a proposed machine costing $1,000 with estimated pretax cash inflows of $400 a year for five years. The required rate of return is 10 percent.
>
> 1. Pretax cash inflows are, as stated, $400 a year.
> 2. Additional income tax is, as calculated in Exhibit 9–1, $102 a year.
> 3. Therefore, annual aftertax cash inflows are $400 − $102 = $298.
> 4. Cash inflows of $298 a year for five years at 10 percent have a present value of $298 × 3.791 (Table B) = $1,130. The net present value is therefore $1,130 − $1,000 = $130. The proposed investment is acceptable.

Accelerated depreciation. In the preceding example we assumed that depreciation was calculated by the straight-line method. Many companies use one of the accelerated methods of depreciation for tax purposes. (In *Fundamentals of Financial Accounting,* we explain that many companies use a different method of depreciation for tax purposes than they use in their financial accounting.) They use an accelerated method because it increases the present value of the depreciation tax shield; that is, they use an accelerated method because the present value of the depreciation tax shield is relatively high in the early years and correspondingly lower in the later years of the investment. (Recall from Chapter 8 that the present value of an amount to be received in the near future is higher than the present value of the same amount to be received in the more distant future.)

Since under the accelerated methods, the amount of depreciation varies from year to year, calculations of aftertax cash inflows must be made separately for each year; and each must be discounted using present values in Table A; it is not possible to use Table B to find the present value because in order to use Table B the cash inflows must be equal in each year.

EXAMPLE: A proposed machine costing $1,000 is expected to result in additional pretax cash inflows of $320 a year for five years. Assuming a required rate of return of 10 percent and straight-line depreciation, is this a good investment?

The cash inflow of $320 will not be fully taxable; rather, additional taxable income will be $320 *minus* the amount of depreciation expense. If straight-line depreciation is used, additional depreciation expense will be $1,000 ÷ 5 years = $200 per year. The differential income subject to tax will be $320 − $200 = $120. At a tax rate of 51 percent, income taxes will be increased by $120 × 51% = $61, so the aftertax cash inflow will be $320 − $61 = $259. Cash inflows of $259 a year for 5 years at 10 percent have a present value of $259 × 3.791 = $982. Since $982 is less than the $1,000 investment, the proposed investment is not acceptable.

Now, assume the same facts except that depreciation is calculated by the sum-of-years'-digits method, which is one of the accelerated methods that is permitted for tax purposes. The tax deductible depreciation and the aftertax cash inflows for the proposal described above would be as follows:

Year	Pretax Cash Inflow (a)	Depreciation (b)	Inflow Subject to Tax (c = a − b)	Tax at 51% (d)	Aftertax Cash Inflow (e = a − d)
1	$ 320	$ 333	$−13	$−6	$ 326
2	320	267	53	27	293
3	320	200	120	61	259
4	320	133	187	95	225
5	320	67	253	129	191
Total	$1,600	$1,000	$ 600	$306	$1,294

For the first year, depreciation expense would be 5/15 of $1,000, or $333. This amount exceeds the amount of pretax cash inflow by $13, so the tax impact in the first year would be a *reduction* in taxes of 51 percent of $13 = $6. The aftertax cash inflow would be $320 − (−$6) = $326. In the second year, depreciation expense would be 4/15 of $1,000, which is $267. The additional inflow subject to tax would therefore be $320 − $267 = $53. The additional income tax would be $27, making the aftertax cash inflow $293. And so on, for the third, fourth, and fifth year.

The present value of the aftertax cash inflow is found by discounting each of the five aftertax cash inflow amounts in the last column above, as follows:

Year	Aftertax Cash Inflow	Discount at 10% (Table A)	Present Value
1	$ 326	0.909	$ 296
2	293	0.826	242
3	259	0.751	195
4	225	0.683	154
5	191	0.621	119
	$1,294		$1,006

In the above example, note how the use of accelerated depreciation increases the attractiveness of the investment; its present value rises from $982 with straight-line depreciation to $1,006 with accelerated depreciation, and the proposal now meets the criterion that the present value of its net cash inflows exceeds the investment. This result occurs because a larger fraction of the depreciation tax shield occurs in the early years, where present values are relatively high.

INVESTMENT CREDIT

Income tax regulations permit a company under certain specified conditions to take an **investment credit** when it purchases new machinery, equipment, and certain other types of depreciable assets (but not buildings). The investment credit may be as high as 7 percent of the purchase price. It is subtracted directly from the amount of the tax bill. Thus, if a company buys a new machine for $10,000, it can subtract up to 7 percent of that amount, or $700, from its current tax obligation. In terms of the calculation described in Chapter 8, this is a direct reduction of $700 in the net investment. In other words, the cost of the machine can be taken as 93 percent of the invoice amount.[2]

CAPITAL GAINS AND LOSSES

When an existing machine is replaced by a new machine, the net book value of the existing machine is removed from the accounting records. This transaction may give rise either to a gain or to a loss, depending on whether the amount realized from the sale of the existing machine is greater than or less than its net book value (see *Fundamentals of Financial Accounting,* Chapter 9). The income tax treatment of this gain or loss may well differ from the accounting treatment. Depending on the circumstances, (1) it may be included in the calcu-

[2] The investment credit is essentially the same as a cash discount on purchases, as described in Chapter 6, *Fundamentals of Financial Accounting*.

lation of taxable income and thus subject to the regular income tax rate of, say, 51 percent; (2) it may be subject only to a 30 percent tax rate, which is applicable to capital gains; or (3) if the new machine replaces one of "like kind," no gain or loss may be recognized, but, instead, the book value of the replaced machine is added to the cash paid for the new machine. Expert tax advice is needed on problems involving gains and losses on the sale of depreciable assets, for it is difficult to know which of these three alternatives is applicable in a given case. In any event, when existing assets are disposed of, the relevant amount by which the net investment is reduced is the proceeds of the sale, adjusted for taxes.

EFFECT OF INFLATION

Consistent with generally accepted accounting principles, income tax regulations permit the cost of a fixed asset to be written off by means of periodic depreciation charges. Some assets, however, do not decline in market value with the passing of time, and others decline at a rate that is less than the depreciation charge. A well-constructed and well-located office building, for example, is often sold for more than the owner paid for it several years previously. The tax deductions, including depreciation expense, on an investment in such properties may even exceed the rental income, yet the property may nevertheless be an attractive investment because of its "depreciation tax shield" and its ultimate resale value. Such properties frequently are called **tax-sheltered investments**. Calculations of the present value of proposed tax-sheltered investments are made in the same fashion as for any investment. The anticipated resale value is treated as an estimated cash inflow in the year in which sale of the property is planned. Because this resale value is estimated to be relatively high, such investments are relatively more attractive than those in machinery or other assets for which no significant amount of resale value is anticipated.

METHODS OF FINANCING

In accordance with generally accepted accounting principles, interest paid to bondholders for the use of their money is reported as an expense; in contrast, dividends paid to shareholders for the use of their money is not an expense but is a distribution of accumulated earnings. (See *Fundamentals of Financial Accounting*, Chapter 12.) The same principle applies in income taxes; interest is a tax deductible expense, dividends are not. A consequence is that the real cost of debt financing to a company is much less than the stated interest cost. Assuming a tax rate of 51 percent, an 8 percent bond has a real cost of only $8\% \times 0.49 = 3.92$ percent because income taxes are reduced from what they otherwise would be by 51 percent of the amount of interest expense.

> *EXAMPLE:* Assume a company with no debt, taxable income of
> $1,000,000, and a 51 percent income tax rate. Its income tax would
> be $510,000, and its aftertax net income would be $490,000. Assume
> now that the company borrows $2,000,000 at an interest rate of
> 8 percent. It pays $160,000 a year of interest expense. Its taxable
> income, however, is reduced by this $160,000, so its income tax is
> reduced by 51 percent of this or $0.51 \times \$160,000 = \$81,600$. Its
> annual net cash outflow has therefore been increased only by
> $\$160,000 \times 0.49 = \$78,400$ because of the bond issue. This is 3.92
> percent of the amount borrowed ($\$2,000,000 \times 3.92 = \$78,400$).

It would be possible to take this interest deduction into account in
the form of a tax shield, just as was described above for depreciation.
This is done, however, only when the method of financing is an integral
part of the proposed investment. In the more usual situation, as explained in Chapter 8, interest is included as one element in calculating
the required rate of return. When such a calculation is made, it is the
aftertax interest cost that is relevant.

> *EXAMPLE:* In computing a company's cost of capital, what rate
> should be used for bonds that have a pretax interest rate of 8 percent
> if the company expects its income tax rate to be 51 percent?
>   *Answer:* If the income tax rate is 51 percent, the aftertax interest
> cost of the bonds is 1 minus 51 percent = 49 percent of the interest
> rate. The rate to be used for bonds is therefore $0.49 \times 0.08 = 3.9$
> percent.

TAX INCENTIVES

Income tax considerations must be taken into account whenever a
proposal involves the acquisition of depreciable assets. In addition to
this general case, there are a number of special situations in which income tax considerations have a significant effect on the analysis of
alternative choice problems. These involve tax incentives that the
government has provided to encourage what it believes to be socially
desirable actions on the part of business. If the proposal involves the
acquisition of, or the search for, oil, gas, or mineral resources, special
tax regulations relating to depletion need to be taken into account.
The government also provides special income tax treatment for expenses
associated with the hiring and training of members of disadvantaged
minority groups, for expenditures made for pollution abatement, for
business conducted in Puerto Rico, for products that are exported for
sale abroad, and for a number of other special situations. A description
of these special tax treatments is not appropriate for an introductory
text. The point is that businessmen must be familiar with their existence
and must be prepared to call in tax experts whenever a proposal involving these matters is being analyzed so that cash-flow estimates will be
based on correct tax facts.

OTHER TAX CONSIDERATIONS

To round out this discussion of the impact of income taxes on business decisions, we summarize three topics that we discuss in *Fundamentals of Financial Accounting:*

1. It is possible to shift the years in which various revenue and expense elements are recorded in order to obtain the maximum tax advantage. In general, and unless it is anticipated that tax rates will increase, a business should delay recording its revenue for tax purposes as long as is possible and should record its expense as early as is possible. Tax regulations permit a considerable amount of latitude in this respect.

2. In Chapter 12 of *Fundamentals of Financial Accounting,* we describe the three principal forms of business organization: a sole proprietorship, a partnership, and a corporation. Tax matters are an important consideration in deciding which form of organization is best in a given situation.

3. In Chapters 11 and 12 of *Fundamentals of Financial Accounting,* we describe various methods of raising capital for a business. Basically, these boil down to a choice between debt financing and equity financing, that is, a choice between long-term loans or bonds versus various types of stock. Taxes are an important factor in this decision.

Other methods of analysis   So far, we have limited the discussion of techniques for analyzing capital investment proposals to one method, the net present value method. We shall now describe three alternative ways of analyzing a proposed capital investment: (1) the discounted cash-flow method, (2) the payback method, and (3) the unadjusted return on investment method.

DISCOUNTED CASH-FLOW METHOD

When the net present value method is used, the required rate of return must be selected in advance of making the calculations, for this rate is used to discount the cash inflows in each year, so as to find their present value. As already pointed out, the choice of an appropriate rate of return is a difficult matter. The **discounted cash-flow method** avoids this difficulty. **It computes the rate of return which equates the present value of the cash inflows with the amount of the investment;** that is, that rate which makes the net present value equal zero. This rate is called the **internal rate of return,** or the **project rate of return.**

If the management is satisfied with this rate of return, then the project is acceptable; if the internal rate of return is not high enough, then the project is unacceptable. In deciding what rate of return is "high enough," the same considerations as those involved in selecting a required rate of return apply (see Chapter 8).

The term "discounted cash flow" is not a descriptive name for this method, for the net present value method also involves the discounting of cash flows. The name is widely used, however. This method is also called the **time-adjusted-return method** or the **investor's method.**

Level inflows. If the cash inflows are level—that is, the same amount each year—the computation is simple. It will be illustrated by a proposed investment of $1,000 with estimated cash inflow of $250 a year for five years. The procedure is as follows:

1. Divide the investment, $1,000, by the annual inflow, $250. The result, 4.0, is called the *investment/inflow ratio.*

2. Look across the five-year row of Table B. The column in which the figure closest to 4.0 appears shows the rate of return. Since the closest figure is 3.993 in the 8 percent column, the return is slightly less than 8 percent (just as it was in Exhibit 8–1).

3. If management is satisfied with a return of slightly less than 8 percent, then it should accept this project (aside from nonquantitative considerations). If it requires a higher return, then it should reject the project.

The number 4.0 in the above example is simply the ratio of the investment to the annual cash inflows. Each number in Table B shows the ratio of the present value of a stream of cash inflows to an investment of $1 made today, for various combinations of rates of return and numbers of years. The number 4.0 opposite any combination of year and rate of return means that the present value of a stream of inflows of $1 a year for that number of years discounted at that rate is $4. The present value of a stream of inflows of $250 a year is in the same ratio; therefore it is $250 times 4, or $1,000. If the number is less than 4.0, as is the case with 3.993 in the example above, then the return is correspondingly less than 8 percent.

In using Table B, in this method, it is usually necessary to interpolate, that is, to estimate the location of a number that lies between two numbers appearing in the table. There is no need to be precise about these interpolations because the final result can be no better than the basic data, and the basic data are ordinarily only rough estimates. A quick interpolation, made visually, is usually as good as the accuracy of the data warrants. Computation of a fraction of a percent is rarely warranted.

Computing several returns. Since the most uncertain estimate of all is often the number of years during which there will be cash inflows (i.e., the economic life), it is often useful to locate several combinations of years and rates that have the specified investment inflow ratio. For example, an investment of $20,000 and annual cash inflow of

$4,000 give a ratio of 5. Some of the combinations found on Table B for a ratio of 5 are as follows:

If the Life Is:	Then the Rate of Return Is About:		If the Required Rate of Return Is:	Then the Life Must Be at Least:
6 years............	6%	*Or*	6%...........	6 + years
8 years............	12%	*figured*	10%...........	7 + years
10 years............	15%	*another*	15%...........	10 years
12 years............	17%	*way:*	18%...........	14 years

If the proposed investment is expected to have a longer life, *and* if the required rate of return is lower than any one of the combinations selected, the investment is acceptable; otherwise, it is not acceptable.

Uneven inflows. If cash inflows are not the same in each year, the internal rate of return must be found by trial and error. The cash inflows for each year are listed, and various discount rates are applied to these amounts until a rate is found that makes their total present value equal to the amount of the investment. This rate is the internal rate of return. This trial-and-error process can be quite tedious if the computations are made manually; however, computer programs are available that perform the calculations automatically.

PAYBACK METHOD

The number referred to above as the investment/inflow ratio is called the **payback** because **it is the number of years over which the investment outlay will be recovered or paid back from the cash inflow** *if* the estimates turn out to be correct; that is, the project will "pay for itself" in this number of years. If a machine costs $1,000 and generates cash inflow of $250 a year, it has a payback of four years.

Payback is often used as a quick, but crude, method for appraising proposed investments. If the payback period is equal to or only slightly less than the economic life of the project, then the proposal is clearly unacceptable. If the payback period is considerably less than the economic life, then the project begins to look attractive.

If several investment proposals have the same general characteristics, then the payback period can be used as a valid way of screening out the acceptable proposals. For example, if a company finds that production equipment ordinarily has a life of 10 years and if it requires a return of at least 15 percent, then the company may specify that new equipment will be considered for purchase only if it has a payback period of 5 years or less; for Table B shows that a payback period of 5 years is equivalent to a return of approximately 15 percent if the life is 10 years. Stating the criterion in this fashion avoids the necessity of explaining the present value concept to supervisors in the operating organizations.

The danger of using payback as a criterion is that it gives no consideration to differences in the length of the estimated economic lives of various projects. There may be a tendency to conclude that the shorter the payback period, the better the project; whereas a project with a long payback may actually be better than a project with a short payback if it will produce cash inflows for a much longer period of time.[3]

UNADJUSTED RETURN ON INVESTMENT METHOD

The *unadjusted return* method computes the net income expected to be earned from the project each year, in accordance with the principles of accounting, including a provision for depreciation expense. The **unadjusted return on investment is found by dividing the annual net income by either the amount of the investment or by one half the amount of investment.** (The use of one half the investment is on the premise that over the whole life of the project, an average of one half the initial investment is outstanding because the investment is at its full amount in Time Zero and shrinks gradually to nothing, or substantially nothing, by its terminal year.)

Since normal depreciation accounting provides, in a sense, for the recovery of the cost of a depreciable asset, one might suppose that the return on an investment could be found by relating the investment to its income after depreciation, but such is *not* the case. We described earlier the calculations for an investment of $1,000, with cash inflow of $250 a year for five years. These calculations showed that the present value of the cash inflows equaled $1,000 when discounted at a required rate of return of 8 percent. In other words, such an investment has a return of 8 percent. In the unadjusted return method, the calculation would be as follows:

Gross earnings	$250
Less depreciation ($\frac{1}{5}$ of $1,000)	200
Net Income	$ 50

Dividing net income by the investment ($50 ÷ $1,000) gives an indicated return of 5 percent. But we know that this result is incorrect; the true return is 8 percent. If we divide the $50 net income by one half the investment, that is, $500, the result is 10 percent, which is also incorrect.

This method is called the unadjusted return method because it makes

---

[3] The simple payback method takes no account of present value; that is, it does not recognize that cash inflows in early years have a higher present value than cash inflows in later years. In order to overcome this weakness, the *discounted payback* method has been developed. The simple payback period is the number of years required to make cash inflows equal the amount of investment. The discounted payback period, by contrast, is the number of years of cash inflows that are required to (*a*) recover the amount of the investment, *and also* (*b*) earn the required rate of return on the investment during that period. Since the method is relatively new and not yet widely used, it is not described in detail here. The computations can be quite complicated if done manually, but are a simple task for a computer.

no adjustment for the differences in present values of the inflows of the various years; that is, it treats each year's inflows as if they were as valuable as those of every other year, whereas actually the prospect of an inflow of $250 next year is more attractive than the prospect of an inflow of $250 two years from now, and that $250 is more attractive than the prospect of an inflow of $250 three years from now, and so on.

The unadjusted return method, based on the gross amount of the investment, will always *understate* the true return. The shorter the time period involved, the more serious is the understatement. For investments involving very long time periods, the understatement is insignificant. If the return is computed by using one half the investment, the result is always an *overstatement* of the true return. No method which does not consider the time value of money can produce an accurate result.

Until fairly recently, the unadjusted return method was widely used, and it is still used in companies whose managers are unaware of the importance of the present value concept. Despite its conceptual weakness, the unadjusted return method does have a place in capital investment analysis, for it shows the effect of a proposal on the company's income statement. This effect, which is not shown in present value computations, may be significant in certain situations because of the importance that investors attach to the amount of net income reported on the income statement.

Preference problems

There are two classes of investment problems, called, respectively, *screening* problems and *preference* problems. **In a screening problem the question is whether or not to accept a proposed investment.** The discussion so far has been limited to this class of problem. A great number of individual proposals come to management's attention, and by the techniques described above, those that are worthwhile can be screened out from the others.

In **preference problems** (also called **ranking** or **rationing** problems), a more difficult question is asked: **Of a number of proposals, each of which has an adequate return, how do they rank in terms of preference?** If not all the proposals can be accepted, which ones do we prefer? The decision may merely involve a choice between two competing proposals, or it may require that a series of proposals be ranked in order of their attractiveness. Such a ranking of projects is necessary when there are more worthwhile proposals than there are funds available to finance them, which is often the case.

CRITERIA FOR PREFERENCE PROBLEMS

Both the discounted cash-flow and the net present value methods are used for preference problems.

If the discounted cash-flow method is used, **the preference rule is as follows: the higher the internal rate of return, the better the project.** A project with a return of 20 percent is said to be preferable to a project with a return of 19 percent.

If the *net present value method* is used, the present value of the cash inflows of one project cannot be compared directly with the present value of the cash inflows of another unless the investments are of the same size. Most people would agree that a $1,000 investment that produces cash inflows with a present value of $2,000 is better than a $1,000,000 investment that produces cash inflows with a present value of $1,001,000, even though they each have a net present value of $1,000. In order to compare two proposals under the net present value method, therefore, we must relate the size of the discounted cash inflows to the amount of money that is risked. This is done simply by dividing the present value of the cash inflows by the amount of investment, to give a ratio that is generally called the *profitability index*. **The preference rule then is as follows: the higher the profitability index, the better the project.**

COMPARISON OF PREFERENCE RULES

Conceptually, the profitability index is superior to the internal rate of return as a device for deciding on preference. This is because the discounted cash-flow method will not always give the correct preference as between two projects with different lives or with different patterns of earnings.

> *EXAMPLE:* Proposal A involves an investment of $1,000 and cash inflow of $1,200 received at the end of one year; its internal rate of return is 20 percent. Proposal B involves an investment of $1,000 and cash inflows of $300 a year for five years; its internal rate of return is only 15 percent. But Proposal A is *not* necessarily preferable to Proposal B. It is preferable only if the company can expect to earn a high return during the following four years on some other project in which the funds released at the end of the first year are reinvested. Otherwise, Proposal B, which earns 15 percent over the whole five-year period, is preferable.[4]

The incorrect signal illustrated in the above example is not present in the profitability index method. Assuming a required rate of return of 10 percent, the two proposals described above would be analyzed as follows:

---

[4] Note that this problem arises when a choice must be made between two competing proposals, only one of which can be adopted. If the proposals are non-competing and the required rate of return is less than 15 percent, then both of them are acceptable.

Proposal (a)	Cash Inflow (b)	Discount Factor (c)	Present Value (d = b × c)	Investment (e)	Index (f = d ÷ e)
A........	$1,200 − 1 yr.	0.909	$1,091	$1,000	1.09
B........	$ 300 − 5 yr.	3.791	1,137	1,000	1.14

The profitability index signals that Proposal B is better than Proposal A, which is in fact the case if the company can expect to reinvest the money released from Proposal A so as to earn only 10 percent on it.

Although the profitability index method is conceptually superior to the discounted cash-flow method, and although the former is also easier to calculate since there is no trial-and-error computation, the discounted cash-flow method is widely used in practice. There seem to be two reasons for this. First, the profitability index method requires that the required rate of return be established before the calculations are made, whereas many analysts prefer to work from the other direction; that is, to find the internal rate of return and then see how it compares with their idea of the rate of return that is appropriate in view of the risks involved. Second, the profitability index, like any index, is an abstract number that is difficult to explain; whereas the internal rate of return is similar to interest rates and earnings rates with which every business-man is familiar.

Comparison of methods

As a means of summarizing and comparing all the analytical methods described in Chapters 8 and 9, we shall now apply these methods to a simple fact situation, as follows: Two capital investment proposals are under consideration. Case 1 involves an investment of $1,000 with estimated pretax cash inflows of $400 a year for five years. Case 2 involves an investment of $10,000 and pretax cash inflows of $3,000 a

Exhibit 9–2

Methods of evaluating investment proposals

	Case 1	Case 2
Assumed facts and estimates:		
Investment...	$1,000	$10,000
Life, years.......................................	5	10
Annual pretax cash inflow............................	$ 400	$ 3,000
Annual aftertax cash inflow..........................	$ 298	$ 1,980
Analytical results:		
Net present value.................................	$ 130	$ 2,167
Profitability index................................	1.13	1.22
Internal rate of return.............................	15%	15%
Payback, years...................................	3.4	5
Unadjusted return, initial investment..................	10%	10%
Unadjusted return, average investment.................	20%	20%

year for 10 years. The income tax rate is estimated to be 51 percent, straight-line depreciation is used for tax purposes, and the required rate of return is 10 percent. These facts, together with computations made under various methods, are summarized in Exhibit 9–2.

First, we must calculate the annual aftertax cash inflow. The calculation has already been made for Case 1 in a previous example. For Case 2, the aftertax inflow is calculated as follows:

Annual cash inflow will be increased by...........................	$3,000
These inflows will be shielded from income taxes by the amount of	
depreciation, which is $10,000 ÷ 10 =........................	1,000
So the amount of additional taxable income is...................	$2,000
Additional tax is 51% of $2,000, or............................	$1,020
Aftertax cash inflow is $3,000 − $1,020, or....................	1,980

We use these numbers in various methods as described below. Calculations are given only for Case 2. (The student might well make the same calculations for Case 1.)

To find the *net present value,* the amount of investment is subtracted from the present value of the stream of aftertax cash inflows:

Present value of aftertax cash inflows = $1,980 × 6.145	
(Table B)..	$12,167
Investment...	10,000
Net present value...................................	$ 2,167

To find the *profitability index,* the present value of the aftertax cash inflow is divided by the investment:

$$\$12,167 \div \$10,000 = 1.22$$

To find the internal rate of return with the *discounted-cash flow method,* the investment/inflow ratio is first calculated. It is $10,000 ÷ $1,980 = 5.05. Then the 10-year row of Table B is examined to find the number closest to this ratio. This is the 5.019 under 15 percent. The internal rate of return is therefore approximately 15 percent.

The *payback period* is the same as the investment/inflow ratio, that is, about five years.

The *unadjusted return* is found by constructing an income statement:

Pretax cash inflows.........................	$3,000
Less depreciation...........................	1,000
Pretax income..............................	$2,000
Income tax (51%)..........................	1,020
Net Income................................	$ 980

The net income, $980, divided by the amount of investment, $10,000, gives a return of about 10 percent. If the average investment of $5,000 (= $10,000 ÷ 2) is used, the return is about 20 percent.

What can we conclude from all these numbers? First, the net present value of both proposals is positive, and the internal rate of return of both projects exceeds the required rate of return of 10 percent. These are valid tests, and they show that both proposals are acceptable.

(These two methods always give the same *screening* signal; that is, if one method says a proposal is acceptable, so will the other.)

From the payback test, we can conclude that the payback period for each proposal is shorter than its life, but we cannot say for sure that this fact, by itself, makes the proposal acceptable because we do not know if it is *enough* shorter to provide an acceptable rate of return.

The unadjusted return understates the true return if it is calculated on the basis of the initial investment, and it overstates the true return if it is calculated on the basis of the average investment. It is not a meaningful figure.

Turning to the more difficult *preference* question, we ask whether Proposal B is more desirable than Proposal A. The profitability index, which is the most valid test, does rank Proposal B higher. The discounted cash-flow method ranks them as equally desirable, each having a rate of return of 15 percent. The payback period does not provide a valid preference measure since there is no way of knowing whether a 5-year project with a payback of three years is preferable to a 10-year project with a payback of five years. The unadjusted return is not a valid measure of preference.

It should be emphasized that the calculation of a variety of measures, as in Exhibit 9–2, was for illustrative purposes only. In the real world, a company would select one principal measure and perhaps supplement it by other measures for special purposes. It would not calculate all these measures routinely.

Concluding comments

ADDITIONAL INTRICACIES

The discussions in this book are introductory. Chapters 8 and 9, however, are even more introductory than most. The concepts and the general approach to solving practical problems are described, but a great many complexities that are encountered in real-life situations are necessarily omitted. For example, we have not described how to handle the situation in which an existing piece of equipment has a shorter useful life than the proposed equipment, or the situation in which some parts of the proposed investment are made prior to Time Zero, or the situation in which investments are made in increments during the life of the project. Such situations are dealt with in the references cited at the end of Chapter 8.

NONQUANTITATIVE FACTORS

Neither have we discussed how to handle the considerations that cannot be reduced to quantitative terms. We repeat the admonition made in Chapter 8: these qualitative factors are usually at least as important as those that are encompassed in the calculations. We omit them simply because there is no way of describing what to do about them other than to say: use good judgment. Indeed, the use of good judgment is the essence of the whole approach. The techniques described in these chapters permit rational analysis of *some* of the important factors. This analysis should be done first. Management should accept the results of this analysis, weigh it together with the qualitative factors, and then make the decision.

NONUSE OF DISCOUNTING

Not every business uses discounting techniques in analyzing investment proposals. In some cases, this is because the manager is not familiar with the techniques. But there is a much better reason in many instances. Some managers, having studied the approach carefully, have concluded that it is like trying "to make a silk purse out of a sow's ear"; that is, in their opinion the underlying estimates of cash flows and economic life are so rough that the refinement of using discounting techniques is more work than it is worth. Therefore they prefer the simple payback method or the unadjusted return.

Those managers who do use one of the discounting methods argue that the extra work involved is small, and that the results, although admittedly rough, are nevertheless better than the results of calculations that do not take into account the time value of money.

Demonstra-   Exhibit 9–3 shows an analysis of an investment proposal made in
tion case   1912, which was a long time prior to the use of present value techniques. The analysis compares the investment and operating costs of three one-horse vans with those of one motor van, which presumably could do the same job. It is an erroneous analysis. Before reading further, it is suggested that the student try his hand at making a valid analysis of this situation, using the data in Exhibit 9–3. The errors are discussed below.

In the first place, note that the calculation includes both the investment cost and the depreciation of this cost (for the van, $2,150 investment and $2,150 depreciation); thus the investment cost is in effect counted twice, which is wrong. Depreciation is the recovery of the investment; it should not be added to the investment itself.[5]

Next, note that an attempt was made to incorporate the notion of present value by including interest as a cost. There are two errors in the method used. First, the rate of interest, 6 percent, is today, as it was then, too low as a measure of the risk of a business investment; it corresponds to a rate for borrowing money. Second, interest was calculated on the initial amount of the investment, which overlooks the fact that

---

[5] Depreciation for the three one-horse vans excluded depreciation on two of the horses, for a reason that is not known. Perhaps it was an attempt to recognize the residual value of the horses.

Exhibit 9–3

Illustration of incorrect investment analysis (from a 1912 advertisement)

DELIVERY VAN

Cost of Operating Three One-Horse Vans for Five Years		Cost of Operating One Schacht Delivery Van for Five Years	
3 Vans at $250 each.	$ 750.00	One Van	$ 2,150.00
7 Horses at $200 each	1,400.00	Gasoline, averaging 60 miles per day,	
3 Sets Harness at $40 per set	120.00	300 days per year, 10 miles per gal	1,440.00
Repairs to harness at $5 per set		Oil at 50¢ gal. 120 miles per gal.	375.00
per year.	75.00	Grease, transmission and cup,	
Repairs to vans, including re-painting	525.00	averaging 15¢ per lb. running 100	
Insurance at $25 per policy	375.00	miles to the lb.	135.00
Wages of three drivers at $15 per week	11,700.00	Battery charging at 50¢ per month	30.00
Wages of stablemen and general help		Tire renewals, averaging 5,000	
(one at $10).	2,600.00	miles per tire	3,300.00
Feed, stabling, Vet. service, shoeing		Oil for lamps	100.00
etc., at $25 per horse per month	4,500.00	Repairs	375.00
Depreciation, 20 percent	1,870.00	Liability and Fire insurance	750.00
Interest on investment at 6 percent	480.00	Driver at $15 per week	3,900.00
	$24,395.00	Incidentals at $25 per year	125.00
		Interest at 6 percent	645.00
		Depreciation at 20 percent	2,150.00
			$15,475.00

Cost of operating three one-horse vans for five years	$24,395.00
Cost of operating one Schacht Delivery Van for five years	15,475.00
Savings in operating van for five years	8,920.00
Net saving, per year, in favor of Schacht Delivery Van	$ 1,785.00

Ask for Diagnosis Blank, fill in and return, and we will analyze your problems for you, and advise you, without prejudice and without incurring any obligation of the feasibility of Motor Trucks or Vans for your delivery service. It will be worth your while.

the funds committed to the investment are gradually released over time. In a rough way, these two errors tend to offset one another, but the extent to which one counterbalances the other is a matter of happenstance. A valid approach would be to use present values rather than simple interest.

Exhibit 9–4 illustrates how the analysis of this investment proposal might be made today. The essential problem is to express the cost of the investment and annual operating costs for each alternative so they can be aggregated correctly. This is done by computing the present value of the stream of future operating costs. We can omit income taxes since they were insignificant in 1912. For the three one-horse vans, the operating costs are given as $3,960 per year. In the absence of other information, a discount rate of 10 percent is assumed. From Table B, we find that a stream of payments of $1 per year for five years, at 10 percent, has a present value of $3.791. Therefore, a stream of $3,960 per year has a present value of $3,960 × 3.791, or $15,010. This, added to the investment, makes the total present value of the costs

Exhibit 9–4

Modern analysis of delivery van proposal

Three one-horse vans:
Investment..................................... $ 2,270
Annual operating costs:
    Repairs..................................... $ 125
    Insurance...................................   75
    Wages......................................   2,860
    Feed, stabling, etc..........................   900
        Total annual operating cost............. $3,960
Present value, 5 years, 10%.....................   15,010
Total present value of costs.................... $17,280

One Schacht delivery van:
Investment..................................... $ 2,150
Annual operating costs:
    Gasoline, oil, grease......................... $ 390
    Tire renewals...............................   650
    Repairs.....................................   75
    Insurance...................................   150
    Wages......................................   780
    Lamp oil, incidentals........................   45
        Total annual operating cost............. $2,090
Present value, 5 years, 10%.....................   7,920
Total present value of costs.................... $10,070
Net Advantage of Schacht Van
   ($17,280 − $10,070)........................ $ 7,210

---

equal to $17,280. The costs of the Schacht delivery van computed in a similar way, comes out to $10,070, so the Schacht delivery van has a net advantage of $7,210.

We might note that the revised calculation uses the same estimates as those used in the original advertisement. For a full-blown analysis, we should also question the assumption that a truck driver will receive the same wages as the driver of a van, that one truck will in fact do as much work as three horse-drawn vans, that gasoline costs 16 cents per gallon, and so on. But we have no way, from the facts given, of addressing such questions.

Summary   The impact of income taxes must be taken into account in analyzing proposed capital investments. This cannot be done by applying the applicable income tax rate to the amount of pretax cash inflows, however, for depreciation shields part of the cash inflows from the effect of income taxes. A separate calculation is made to determine the additional income tax that will result from the proposed investment, and this amount is subtracted from the pretax cash inflows to arrive at the aftertax inflows. The use of accelerated depreciation has the effect of increasing the present value of the depreciation tax shield. In addition to the depreciation shield, the investment credit, capital gains and losses, and the effect of inflation must also be taken into account in analyzing the income tax impact of certain proposed investments.

Income taxes are also an important consideration in deciding on a company's financial structure because the interest expense on bonds is tax deductible, while dividends on stock are not. Incentives provided in the income tax regulations are also important factors in certain situations. Income taxes are also a significant factor in the choice of accounting methods that have the effect of shifting revenue and expense items from one year to another and in deciding on the form of business organization.

In addition to the net present value method of analyzing proposed capital investments discussed in Chapter 8, several other methods are in use. The discounted cash-flow method finds the rate of return that equates the present value of cash inflows to the amount of investment; it is a valid method. The simple payback method finds the number of years of cash inflows that are required to equal the amount of investment. The unadjusted return on investment computes net income according to the principles of accounting and expresses this as a percentage of either the initial investment or the average investment. The simple payback and unadjusted return methods have conceptual weaknesses, but are nevertheless useful if their limitations are understood.

Preference problems are those in which the task is to rank two or more investment proposals in order of their desirability. The profitability index, which is the ratio of the present value of cash inflows to the investment, is the most valid way of making such a ranking. The discounted cash-flow method is also valid in most, but not all, preference problems. Other methods are generally not as useful for ranking purposes.

Important terms	Pretax income	Discounted cash-flow method
	Aftertax income	Internal rate of return
	Pretax cash inflow	Payback method
	Aftertax cash inflow	Unadjusted return on investment method
	Tax shield	Screening problem
	Investment credit	Preference problem
	Tax-sheltered investment	Profitability index

Questions for discussion

1. Is the relevant income tax rate for analyzing investment proposals (a) an average of rates over the past several years, (b) the current rate, or (c) the rate anticipated in the future?

2. Teddall Company expects to pay federal and state income taxes at the following rates:

Nature of Taxable Income	Amount	Rate	Income Tax
First $25,000	$ 25,000	24%	$ 6,000
Puerto Rican income	75,000	0	0
Federal tax only	100,000	48	48,000
Remainder, federal and state tax	800,000	50	400,000
Total	$1,000,000	45.4%	$454,000

What tax rate should it use in analyzing its typical capital investment proposals?

3. Supposing the Congress made the following changes in income taxes, what effect would each probably have on the total amount of capital investments made in the United States? Why?
   (a) Reduction in the income tax rate from 48 percent to 40 percent.
   (b) Elimination of the investment tax credit.
   (c) Permit only straight-line depreciation for tax purposes; forbid the use of accelerated depreciation.
   (d) Permit an investment to be fully depreciated over one half its economic life.

4. For an investment proposal that results in a cost saving, is "cash inflow" as used in the chapter the same as "differential cost" as used in Chapter 7? For an investment proposal that involves additional revenue, is "cash inflow" the same as "differential income"? Explain.

5. In analyzing an investment proposal, why is depreciation excluded from the calculation of pretax cash inflows but included in the calculation of the income tax effect?

6. In your own words, explain how the net difference of $98 in Exhibit 9–1 was derived.

7. Can there be an acceptable proposal to acquire a machine for the purpose of reducing direct labor costs in which the depreciation completely shielded the pretax cash inflow; that is, so that no additional income tax payments would be required? Explain.

8. If the aftertax interest cost of debt financing is so much less than the cost of equity financing, why do companies obtain any capital through equity financing, that is, by selling stock?

9. Explain the difference between the discounted cash-flow method and the net present value method.

10. Under certain circumstances, the reciprocal of the payback period (i.e., annual earnings divided by the investment) is an approximation of the rate of return. Find the internal rate of return for three projects in which the investment is $1,000, annual cash inflows are $300 in each case, and the economic life is respectively (a) 5 years, (b) 8 years, and (c) 10 years. Compare the results with the reciprocal of the payback period (i.e., 30%). Can you generalize from these relationships about the accuracy of the payback reciprocal?

11. Using numbers from the lower portions of the 25 percent, 30 percent, 40 percent, and 50 percent columns of Table B, explain the circumstances under which the reciprocal of the payback period gives the same results as the discounted cash-flow method.

12. In a preference problem, two or more proposals are ranked in order of their desirability. If each of the proposals is acceptable, why does anyone want to know how they rank; that is, why aren't they all accepted?

13. The chapter explains how the numbers for Case 2 in Exhibit 9–2 were derived. Make a similar explanation for Case 1.

14. What are some of the nonquantatitive considerations that are important in a capital investment problem? Can you think of any practical, important problem that does not require the use of judgment?

15. Discuss issues involved in deciding between the following investment opportunities, only one of which can be undertaken. Assume a 10 percent required rate of return.
    Case No. 1. Provides a 17 percent return, with moderate risk, for a 13-year period.
    Case No. 2. Provides a 25 percent return, with moderate risk, for a five-year period.

Problems

Notes: 1. Unless otherwise specified, use the following assumptions in all problems in this chapter:

    Tax rate: 51 percent
    Depreciation method: straight line
    Aftertax required rate of return: 10 percent

    2. Show all computations, labeling each number so that it will be clearly understood.

9–1. A company owned a plot of land that appeared in its fixed assets at its acquisition cost in 1910, which was $10,000. The land was not used. In 1975 the local boys club asked the company to donate the land as the site for a new recreation building. The donation would be a taxable deduction of $110,000, which was the current appraised value. The company's tax rate was 51 percent. Some argued that the company would be better off to donate the land than to keep it or to sell it for $110,000. Assume that, other than the land, the company's taxable income as well as its accounting income before taxes was $10,000,000.

Required:

How would the company's aftertax cash inflow be affected if (a) it donated the land or (b) it sold the land for $110,000? How would its net income be affected?

9–2. The Williams Company is trying to decide whether to continue using an old machine with a remaining useful life of five years, or replace it with a new machine costing $7,000 which is expected to save $1,800 labor costs each year of its five-year life. The old machine is fully depreciated and has no salvage value.

Required:
Should the new machine be acquired?

9–3. The Nelson Corporation has an opportunity to replace an old machine with no book value or salvage value with a new machine costing $10,000 with a 10-year useful life. Expected annual labor savings are $2,000.

Required:
Should the new machine be acquired?

9–4. The Re-Cycle Company is just starting operations with new equipment costing $30,000 and a useful life of four years. At the end of four years the equipment probably can be sold for $6,000. The company is concerned with its cash flow and wants a comparison of straight-line and sum-of-the-years'-digits depreciation to help management decide which depreciation method to use for financial statements and for its income tax return.

Required:
(1)   Calculate the difference in taxable income and cash inflow under each method.
(2)   Which depreciation method is preferable for tax purposes? Why?

9–5. Ecolab, Inc., has acquired new equipment costing $6,000 with an estimated useful life of four years and an estimated salvage value of $1,200. The company wishes to use the depreciation method which gives the better cash flow. Under consideration are the straight-line and the sum-of-the-years'-digits methods.

Required:
(1)   Prepare a schedule which will show the difference in cash flow of the two methods being considered.
(2)   Which depreciation method is preferable for tax purposes?

9–6. Seavy Manufacturing Company owns equipment which it developed and constructed, and which it rents to Timmons Company for $16,000 per year. For this fee the Seavy Company also keeps the equipment repaired and in good working condition. These services cost Seavy $6,000 per year. When built, the equipment cost $60,000. Its useful life when new was estimated at 15 years. In 1974, Seavy has received an offer of $50,000 for the equipment, which is now 10 years old. Any long-term capital gains would be subject to the 30 percent rate.

Required:

(1) Calculate the aftertax income over the next five years (a) if Seavy keeps the equipment and continues to rent it, and (b) if the equipment is sold.

(2) What course of action do you advise the company to follow? Why?

9–7. Thomas Company owns a warehouse which it no longer needs in its own operations. The warehouse was built at a cost of $90,000 10 years ago, at which time its estimated useful life was 15 years. There are two proposals for the use of the warehouse:

(a) Rent it at $24,000 per year, which includes estimated costs of $9,000 per year for maintenance, heat, and utilities.

(b) Sell it outright to a prospective buyer who has offered $75,000. Any capital gain would be taxed at the 30 percent rate.

Required:

(1) Calculate the aftertax income if (a) Thomas Company keeps the warehouse and (b) if Thomas Company sells the warehouse.

(2) Which proposal should the company accept? Why?

9–8. The McGowan Soup Company needs more cold storage space. A building adequate for anticipated needs for the next three years may be leased for $51,000 per year, or the company can build its own storage house on company owned property at a cost of $150,000. At the end of three years the building would have no salvage value. Increased cash inflow is expected to be $60,000 per year before any applicable taxes, straight-line depreciation, or lease payments.

Required:

(1) Calculate the aftertax cash flow for each of the three years if the building is purchased with funds borrowed with interest payable of $7,500, $5,100, and $2,600 for each of the three years, respectively.

(2) Calculate the aftertax cash flow for each year if the building is leased.

(3) Which is more profitable, leasing or buying? Why?

(4) Comment on the decision to acquire the building if the company has a required rate of return of 10 percent after taxes on all such projects.

9–9. The Savory Corporation wants to acquire new equipment with which to make a new product. The equipment may be purchased at a cost of $51,000 or leased for an annual payment of $18,300 per year for three years. The increased cash inflow anticipated is $20,000, per year, before tax considerations and any applicable straight-line depreciation and lease payments. The equipment would have no salvage value at the end of three years.

Required:

(1)   Calculate the aftertax cash flow for each of the three years if the equipment is purchased with $50,000 borrowed funds to be repaid with interest of $2,500, $1,700, and $875 for each of the three years.

9–10.   Arch Williamson, chairman of the computer services committee of Stonewall Company, had originally viewed the question of whether to lease or buy new key-punch equipment as a minor one. He thought back to what he had told Bob Perrotti, the computer services committee's vice chairman. "This key-punch problem is nothing compared to what we went through in 1962 with our initial move to EDP. It's just a question of gathering all the cost, depreciation, and tax data, and massaging the numbers a bit. The answer to the question of lease or buy will become obvious."

Mr. Williamson gathered the following information in discussion with representatives of a large manufacturer of EDP equipment:

(a)   Purchase price of a key-punch unit: $1,500.
(b)   Estimated life of unit: 8 years.
(c)   Salvage value: $100.
(d)   Monthly rental of unit: $20.

Required:

Should the key-punch unit be purchased or leased?

9–11.   (Disregard income taxes in this problem.)
1.   The rate of return for an investment expected to yield an annual cash inflow of $400 is 5 percent. How much is the investment if the investment/inflow ratio is 12.50?
2.   An investment of $9,000 has an investment/inflow ratio of 8.6 and a useful life of 15 years. What is the annual cash inflow? What is the time-adjusted rate of return?
3.   What is the maximum price a company can afford to pay for an asset expected to produce a cash inflow of $6,000 per year for five years if its required rate of return is 8 percent?
4.   How much investment per dollar of expected annual operating savings can a company afford if the investment has an expected life of 10 years and its required rate of return is 12 percent?

9–12.   (Disregard income taxes in this problem.) Compute the following:
1.   An investment of $12,000 has an investment/inflow ratio of 6.2 and a useful life of 12 years. What is the annual cash inflow and the time-adjusted rate of return?
2.   The time-adjusted rate of return for an investment expected to yield an annual cash inflow of $1,500 is 14 percent. How much is the investment if the investment/inflow ratio is 6.14?
3.   What is the maximum investment a company would make in an asset expected to produce annual cash inflow of $5,000 a year for 8 years if its required rate of return is 18 percent?
4.   How much investment per dollar of expected annual operating

savings can a company afford if the investment has an expected life of 7 years and its required rate of return is 15 percent?

9–13. Yale Corporation is considering these two alternative investment proposals, only one of which can be accepted.

	Case 1	Case 2
Added investment....................	$20,000	$20,000
Useful life.........................	5 years	10 years
Expected aftertax inflow.............	$ 5,000	$ 3,000

Required:

Which proposal is the more desirable?

9–14. Jan Shoe Company is considering the following two investment proposals (disregard taxes):

	Case 1	Case 2
Initial cash outlay......	$10,000	$10,000
Investment life.........	10 years	10 years
Cash inflows...........	$ 1,500 annually	$17,000 at the end of the 10th year

Required:

(1) Which of the two investments has the higher net present value using a 10 percent discount rate?
(2) What are the time-adjusted rates of return for each of the two investments?
(3) Which proposal is more desirable? Why?

9–15. Dartmouth Corporation estimates that it will have $50,000 available for capital investments during 1975. Half of this will be reserved for emergency projects and half will be invested in the most desirable projects from the following list. None of the investments has a residual value.

Project Number	Added Investment	Expected Aftertax Cash Inflow	Estimated Life of Project
1	$10,000	$2,500	5 years
2	10,000	3,000	4
3	4,000	500	15
4	2,000	1,000	2
5	5,000	1,250	3

Required:

Rank the projects in order of their desirability.

9–16. The Standard Parts Company has received an offer to bid on some specially machined castings and is trying to decide which of two machines could do the work more profitably. The contract calls for

1,000 units per year for five years for which the company would receive $50 per unit. Below are data related to the use of Machine A and Machine B for the contract, neither of which will be of any use to the company at the end of the contract period, nor will either have a salvage value. Disregard income taxes.

	Machine A		Machine B	
Cost of machine.............	$22,000.00		$40,000.00	
Cost per unit per year:				
Materials and labor.........	29.60		27.65	
Factory overhead (other than depreciation)............	1.40		1.35	
General and administrative expense.................	8.00	$39.00	8.00	$37.00

Required:

Which machine should be used if the contract is won by Standard? Comment on your decision.

9–17. Acme Electronics has received an offer to manufacture components used in submarine sonar equipment at a price of $100,000. With existing equipment Acme could produce the components in one year, the contract limit, or Acme could purchase new equipment which could do the job, and which could be used on other jobs after the contract was completed. The new equipment would be capable of completing the contract in six months. Disregard income taxes.

Below are data related to the existing and proposed equipment:

	Existing	Proposed
Cost of assets employed................	$44,000	$80,000
Cost to produce:		
Materials and labor...................	60,000	53,000
Factory overhead.....................	3,000	6,000
Administrative expenses...............	15,000	15,000
Depreciation per year.................	14,000	24,000

Required:

Should Acme acquire the new equipment or use existing equipment if the contract is received? Comment.

9–18. Samuel Jones is considering the purchase of 62 acres of land, presently owned by Talcott and leased from Talcott by Weeden. Weeden uses the land as a golf driving range and pays $1,000 per month rental.

The purchase price of the land is $400,000; however, Jones has knowledge of state plans to build a highway which will run adjacent to the property. Jones is convinced that once the highway is built he will be able to sell the land for $650,000. Jones plans to finance the purchase with $100,000 of his own funds, plus a $300,000, five-year, 7.5 percent bank note, with interest payable on a monthly basis.

The plans for the new highway call for its completion in four and a half years, and Jones has been informed by Weeden that a five-year lease on the land at the present rental rate would be agreeable to him. Mr. Jones is aware of some of the risks involved in his plan and as a result wishes to evaluate the proposal, using a 15 percent aftertax required rate of return.

Required:

Assuming the following tax rates

Ordinary income......................... 51%
Capital gains........................... 30%

should Mr. Jones undertake this venture?

part three Responsibility accounting

Part Three introduces the third type of management accounting, which is called responsibility accounting. It is called by that name because the accounting information relates to the activities of responsibility centers. Responsibility accounting collects and reports information that is used in the management control process. Part Three also discusses this process in some detail.

Chapter 10 describes the nature of the management control process and its relationship to other planning and control processes. Although we shall describe in a general way how accounting information is used in the management control process, we shall defer a detailed discussion of these uses to later chapters. In Chapter 11 we discuss budgeting, which is one important phase in the management control process. In Chapters 12–15 we discuss the measurement and evaluation of operating performance, which are other phases in the process.

The fact that the material on responsibility accounting follows Part One on full cost accounting and Part Two on differential accounting is not happenstance. From a pedagogical viewpoint, the concepts discussed in Part Three tend to be less precise, and hence more difficult to grasp, than those in the earlier parts. Moreover, these topics are the least related to the financial accounting information discussed in *Fundamentals of Financial Accounting*. Finally, although our focus is on a new type of information—responsibility costs and revenues—the management control process also uses the management accounting information already discussed in Parts One and Two; an understanding of these other types of management accounting is therefore necessary to a thorough comprehension of the subject matter of Part Three.

For purpose of emphasis, we repeat two points that have been made previously:

1. Each of the three types of management accounting information is used for a different purpose. One must first understand the purpose for which information is to be used in a given situation and then select the information that is appropriate for that purpose.

2. Although the three types of management accounting information are discussed separately, collectively they comprise the overall management accounting system. This system contains raw data that are used to construct full cost information, differential information, or responsibility information. Each of these types of information is then used for the purpose for which it is relevant.

10 The management control process

This chapter gives an overview of the management control process. The management control process takes place in an organization, so the chapter sets the stage by describing organizations and the behavior of people who work in them. Other chapters in Part Three will describe in some detail the use of accounting information in the management control process. The present chapter provides background which is intended to make the detailed discussion in later chapters more meaningful, and it also provides a frame of reference into which the various detailed topics can be fitted.

As pointed out in Chapter 1, an organization—any organization—is a group of persons working together for one or more purposes. It is important to note that an organization consists of human beings. A factory with its machines is not an organization; rather, it is the persons who work in the factory that constitute the organization. It is also important to note that in an organization the human beings work together. A crowd walking down a street is not an organization, nor are the spectators at a football game when they are behaving as individual spectators. But the cheering section at a football game is an organization; its members work together under the direction of the cheerleaders.

MANAGEMENT

An organization has one or more leaders. Except in extremely rare circumstances, a group of persons can work together to accomplish the

295

organization's goals only if they are led. In a business organization, the leaders are called managers, or, collectively, the management. An organization's managers decide what the goals of the organization should be; they communicate these goals to members of the organization; they decide the tasks that are to be performed in order to achieve these goals and on the resources that are to be used in carrying out these tasks; they see to it that the activities of the various parts of the organization are coordinated; they match individuals to tasks for which they are suited; they motivate these individuals to carry out their tasks; they observe how well these individuals are performing their tasks; and they take corrective action when the need arises. The leader of a cheering section performs these functions; so does the president of General Motors Corporation.

ORGANIZATIONAL HIERARCHY

A manager can supervise only a limited number of subordinates. Old Testament writers put this number at 10. Although there can be considerable variation in this number, depending on the nature of the job to be done and on the personality and skill of the manager, clearly there is an upper limit to the number of persons that one manager can supervise directly, and it is a small number. It follows that in a company of any substantial size there must be several layers of managers in the organization structure. If 10 subordinates per manager is taken as a typical number for one organization unit, an organization consisting of a thousand people would have to have at least three layers. Units at the lowest level of the organization would each consist of 10 people. The managers of 10 such units could report to a single superior, and that person therefore would directly supervise these 10 persons and would be responsible for the activities of the entire group of 100. Ten such superiors would be necessary for an organization of a thousand people. Above these superiors there would have to be a top manager to coordinate the work of the 10 units, thus making the three layers. This, of course, is a great oversimplification of the way in which organizations are actually put together, and is intended only to illustrate the point that an organization necessarily consists of a number of units, each headed by a manager, and arranged in several layers. Authority runs from the top unit down through the successive layers. Such an arrangement is called an organization hierarchy.

In Chapter 1, Exhibit 1–1, we showed the organization chart for a relatively small organization. Exhibit 10–1 is a condensed organization chart for a larger organization, one that has several levels in its organization hierarchy. At the top is the board of directors which is responsible to the shareholders for the overall conduct of the company's affairs. Reporting to the board of directors is the president, who is the chief executive officer. In the organization depicted, a number of di-

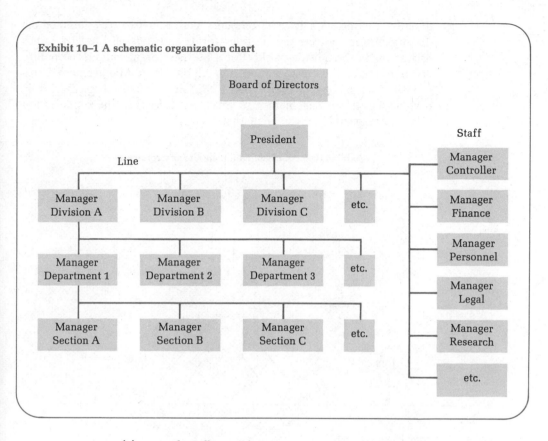

Exhibit 10–1 A schematic organization chart

Board of Directors

President

Staff

Line

Manager Controller

Manager Division A

Manager Division B

Manager Division C

etc.

Manager Finance

Manager Personnel

Manager Department 1

Manager Department 2

Manager Department 3

etc.

Manager Legal

Manager Section A

Manager Section B

Manager Section C

etc.

Manager Research

etc.

visions and staff agencies report to the president. Within each division there are a number of departments, and within each department there are a number of sections. Other names are used for these organization units in different companies, but the names used in Exhibit 10–1 are common.

When the term "organization unit" is used, it can refer to any of the boxes in Exhibit 10–1. Thus, Section A of Department 1 of Division A is an organization unit. Division A itself, including all of its departments and sections, also is an organization unit. Each of these organization units is headed by a manager who is responsible for the work done by the unit. As noted in Chapter 1, these organization units are called responsibility centers. A **responsibility center** is simply an organization unit headed by a responsible manager. The manager is responsible in the sense that he is held accountable for the work done by his organization unit.

ENVIRONMENT

Any organization is a part of a larger society. The world outside the organization itself is called its *environment*. The organization is continually reacting with its environment. This is a two-way interaction: the organization affects the outside world, and it is affected by forces originating in the outside world. For a business organization, the nature of these interactions is suggested by Exhibit 10–2. Management is responsible for managing the organization, but since the organization is part of society, management also must see to it that the organization acts as a respectable member of that society.

Exhibit 10–2 An organization and its environment

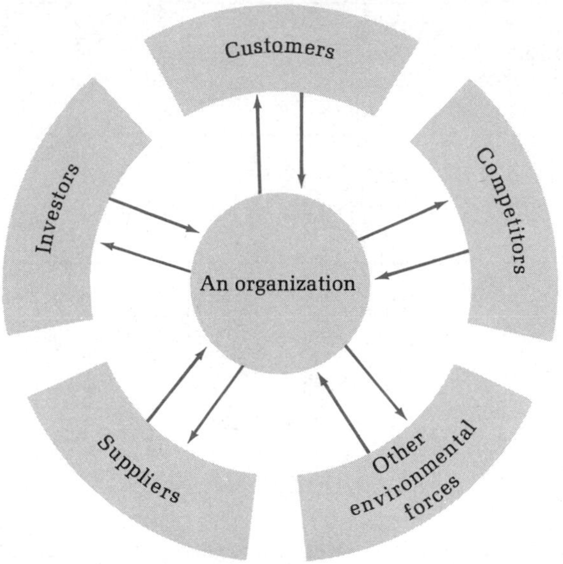

* This illustration was developed by Professor Charles Christenson.

Planning and control processes

Two of the important activities in which managers engage involve the use of accounting information. These are (1) planning and (2) control. *Planning* is deciding what should be done and how it should be done. It is an activity that goes on at all levels in an organization. When a salesman decides what customers he will call on tomorrow, he is engaged in planning. When the president decides to carry out a five-year expansion program, he also is engaged in planning. *Control* is assuring that desired[1] results are attained. It is also an activity that is carried on throughout the organization. When the foreman observes how diligently the employees are working, he is engaged in control, and so is the president when he discusses the latest report on performance with one of his vice presidents.

---

[1] "Desired" results are not necessarily the same as "planned" results. Changes in circumstances that occur after a plan has been prepared may make it desirable to depart from the plan.

Although planning concepts could be discussed separately from control concepts, such a discussion would imply a sharper separation of these management activities than actually occurs. Thus, instead of describing planning first and control second, we shall organize the description of planning and control around three main processes: (1) strategic planning, (2) management control, and (3) operational control. Although either the words "planning" or "control" occurs in the name of each of these processes, it should be understood that all three processes involve *both* planning activities and control activities; the names merely suggest the relative emphasis on planning as compared with the emphasis on control. Our interest in this book is primarily in the management control process, but in order to see how this process relates to the other aspects of the management task, we shall discuss the other processes briefly.

STRATEGIC PLANNING

As noted in Chapter 1, an organization chooses certain strategies in order to achieve its goals, and these determine the nature of its operations. The organizers of a company do not decide simply that, for example, they are "going into the shoe business." They must be more specific than this. Should they manufacture shoes or buy them from another company? Should the shoes be men's shoes, women's, or children's? What should be the quality level and the corresponding price range? How large should the factory be? What manufacturing process should be used? Should a factory be built or should rented facilities be used? Should the shoes be sold to distributors, to retail stores, or directly to consumers? How much of the funds required to start the business should come from shareholders and how much should be borrowed? What is the best source of borrowed funds? Answers to questions like these determined the initial character of the business.

A business entity and its environment are dynamic, not static. As time goes on, the situation changes, and questions similar to those listed above need to be addressed again and again. The process of raising these basic questions and deciding what to do about them is what is meant by strategic planning. Specifically,

> **strategic planning is the process of deciding on the goals of the organization, on changes in these goals, on the resources used to attain these goals, and on the policies that are to govern the acquisition, use, and disposition of these resources.**

MANAGEMENT CONTROL

Once the strategies of an organization have been decided upon, it is management's responsibility to see that they are carried out. In a small business, this may involve primarily the development of an informal implementation plan by the manager, his explanation to other members of the organization of what he wants done, and his subsequent observations to ascertain how well the members carry out the tasks assigned to them. This face-to-face control is feasible only in the tiniest of organizations, however. In a company with many separate organization units, each with its own specialized job to do, the strategies must be communicated to the managers of all these units, a formal implementation plan must be developed, and the efforts of each manager must be brought into harmony with one another. This is the management control process. Its definition is:

> **Management control is the process by which managers assure that resources are obtained and used effectively and efficiently in the accomplishment of the organization's goals.**

OPERATIONAL CONTROL

The third type of planning and control process is called operational control. It is to be distinguished from management control primarily in that it involves relatively little management judgment and relatively little interaction among managers. Inventory control is a case in point. Management can lay down a rule which says that when the inventory of an item drops to a two months' supply, an order should be placed for x additional units. Records can then be set up which show how rapidly the item is moving out of inventory and what the quantity on hand is. When the quantity reaches the prescribed minimum, a purchase order for x units can be placed without involving a management decision or judgment. Since this process does not involve a management decision or judgment, except in the creation of the initial rules and in handling exceptional situations, it is quite different from the process we have labeled management control. The formal definition is:

> **Operational control is the process of assuring that specific tasks are carried out effectively and efficiently.**

DISTINCTIONS AMONG THE PROCESSES

The purpose of the foregoing brief description of the three planning and control processes is merely to provide an overview that is adequate to place the management control process, in which we are primarily interested, in perspective. As an additional way of explaining the distinction, Exhibit 10–3 shows some of the activities that are classified under each of the three processes.

Although each of the three processes involves both planning activities and control activities, the relative importance of planning and of con-

Exhibit 10–3

Examples of planning and control activities in a business organization

Strategic Planning	Management Control	Operational Control
Choosing company strategies	Formulating budgets	
Planning the organization structure	Planning staff levels	Controlling hiring
Setting personnel policies	Formulating personnel practices	Implementing policies
Setting financial policies	Working capital planning	Controlling credit extension
Setting marketing policies	Formulating advertising programs	Controlling placement of advertisements
Setting research policies	Deciding on research projects	
Choosing new product lines	Choosing product improvements	Deciding on work flows
Acquiring a new division	Deciding on plant rearrangement	Scheduling production
Deciding on nonroutine capital expenditures	Deciding on routine expenditures	Controlling construction of new assets
	Formulating decision rules for operational control	Controlling inventory
	Measuring, appraising and improving management performance	Measuring, appraising, and improving workers' efficiency

trol differs for the different processes, as indicated roughly in Exhibit 10–4. At one extreme, the strategic planning process involves primarily planning, but a certain amount of control is necessary to insure that the information and analyses that are necessary as a basis for strategic decisions are assembled and made available to the decision maker at the proper time, and to insure that strategic problems, once identified, are resolved rather than allowed to fall between the cracks. At the other extreme, operational control involves primarily control activities; most of the effort is devoted to insuring that prescribed rules and procedures are being carried out. Some planning is involved in operational control, however. Preparing detailed work schedules, deciding how various work stations are involved, and deciding how to handle special situations that are not covered by the prescribed rules, are examples of planning activities.

The management control process, which is between these two extremes, involves approximately equal amounts of planning activities and control activities. Each activity is as important as the other, and managers spend roughly the same amount of time on each. Moreover, in management control, planning activities are closely related to control activities. We shall, for example, discuss the use of the budget as a planning tool in Chapter 11, and in Chapter 14 we shall describe how information in the same budget is used for control purposes.

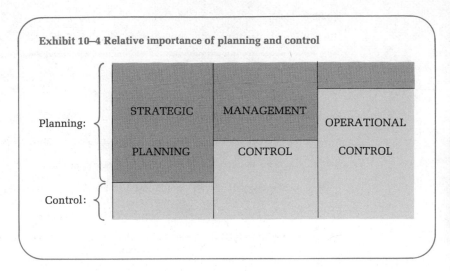

Exhibit 10–4 Relative importance of planning and control

Steps in the management control process

Much of the management control process involves informal communication and interactions. Informal communication occurs by means of memoranda, meetings, conversations, and even by such signals as facial expressions. Although these informal activities are of great importance, they are not amenable to a systematic description. In addition to these informal activities, most companies also have a *formal* management control system. It consists of some or all of the following phases, each of which is described briefly below and in more detail in succeeding chapters:

1. Programming.
2. Budgeting.
3. Operating and accounting.
4. Reporting and analysis.

As indicated in Exhibit 10–5, each of these activities leads to the next. They recur in a regular cycle, and together they constitute a "closed loop."

PROGRAMMING

Programming is the process of deciding on the programs that the company will undertake and the approximate amount of resources that are to be allocated to each program. Programs are the principal activities that the organization has decided to undertake in order to implement the strategies that it has decided upon. In a profit-oriented company, each principal product or product line is a program. If several product lines are manufactured in the same plant, the plant itself and additions or modifications to it may be identified as a program. There are also various research and development programs, some aimed at

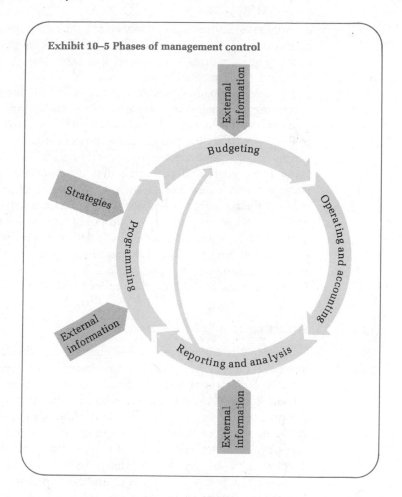

Exhibit 10–5 Phases of management control

improving existing products or processes, others searching for marketable new products. Program decisions are made within the context of the goals and strategies that have previously been decided upon. Decisions as to what the goals and strategies should be are part of the strategic planning process rather than the management control process.

There are two separate aspects of the programming phase. One aspect is analyzing and deciding on specific proposed programs. The nature of such proposals and the techniques that are used to analyze them have already been described in Chapters 7–9. In particular, such proposals usually involve capital investment decisions of the type discussed in Chapters 8 and 9.

The other aspect of the programming phase involves fitting together the separate program proposals into an overall plan for the company, which is called a **long-range plan.** Such a plan shows programs for a number of years ahead—usually 5 years, but possibly as few as 3 or (in the case of certain public utilities) as many as 20. Many companies do not have a formal long-range plan; they rely instead on reports or understandings as to specific, important facets of their programs, particularly the amounts to be invested in capital assets and the means of financing these assets.

In those companies that do develop a formal long-range plan, programming is usually kept separate from budgeting, an activity to be described in the next section. Assuming that the company's fiscal year begins January 1, the programming process would begin the preceding spring. At that time top management discusses and decides on changes in its basic goals and strategies, and disseminates these to divisional managers and other line executives. Managers of individual divisions prepare their programs, following the guidelines set forth by top management. These programs cover proposed actions for a number of years in the future. In the summer or early fall, these proposed programs are discussed at length with top management, and out of these discussions emerges a program for the whole company. This approved program forms the basis of the budgeting process, which begins in the fall.

BUDGETING

A budget is a plan expressed in quantitative, usually monetary, terms that covers a specified period of time, usually one year. In the budgeting process each program is translated into terms that correspond to the responsibility of those managers who have been charged with executing the program or some part of it. Thus, although the plans are originally made in terms of individual programs, in the budgeting process the plans are translated into terms of responsibility centers. The process of developing a budget is essentially one of negotiation between the manager of a responsibility center and his superior. The end product of these negotiations is an approved statement of the revenues that are expected during the budget year, and the resources that are to be used in achieving the company's goals for each responsibility center and for the company as a whole. The budgeting process will be described in more detail in Chapter 11.

OPERATING AND ACCOUNTING

During the period of actual operations, records are kept of resources actually consumed (i.e., costs) and the revenues actually earned. These records are structured so that costs and revenue data are classified both by programs and by responsibility centers. Data classified according to programs are used as a basis for future programming, and data classified by responsibility centers are used to measure the performance of responsibility center managers. For the latter purpose, data on actual results are reported in such a way that they can be readily compared with the plan as set forth in the budget.

REPORTING AND ANALYSIS

The management control system serves as a communication device. The information that is communicated consists of both accounting and nonaccounting data, and of both data generated within the organization and data about what is happening in the environment outside the organization. This information keeps managers informed as to what is going on and helps to insure that the work done by the separate responsibility centers is coordinated. This information is conveyed in the form of reports, as discussed in Chapter 15.

Reports are also used as a basis for control. Essentially, such reports are derived from an analysis that compares actual performance with planned performance and attempts to explain the difference. Techniques for making such analyses are described in Chapter 14.

Based on these formal reports, and also on information received through informal communication channels, managers decide what, if any, action should be taken. They may, for example, decide to change the plan as set forth in the budget, and this leads to a new planning process. It is for this reason that the phases shown in Exhibit 10–5 are depicted as a closed loop, with one leading to the next.

Accounting information used in management control The types of management accounting information discussed in Parts One and Two—full cost accounting and differential accounting—are both used in the management control process. Full cost accounting is used to make decisions of the type described in Chapter 5, particularly those relating to pricing products and changes in product specifications. Differential accounting data are the principal type of accounting data used in the programming phase. These data assist managers in deciding what capital investments to make, what the make-or-buy policy should be, and other matters described in Chapters 7–9.

RESPONSIBILITY ACCOUNTING

In addition to the two types already discussed, there is a third type of management accounting information that is specifically designed for the management control process. It is called responsibility accounting. Unlike the construction of differential costs and revenues, which is tailor-made for each problem, responsibility accounting involves a continuous flow of information throughout the organization. This information is intended to be helpful both for planning and for control. A formal definition is:

> **Responsibility accounting is that type of management accounting that collects and reports both planned and actual accounting information in terms of responsibility centers.**

An essential characteristic of responsibility accounting is that it focuses on responsibility centers. This is necessarily the case, for, as we noted above, the management control process is carried on by managers who head responsibility centers, and accounting information useful in this process must therefore relate to their sphere of responsibility. This difference in focus is what distinguishes responsibility accounting from the full cost accounting that was described in Part One. Full cost accounting focuses on products or services rather than on responsibility centers. Although full cost accounting does make use of cost centers, some of which are also responsibility centers, cost centers are used merely as a means to an end. The emphasis is always on the cost of the goods or services, and the cost center is used as a means of assembling items of cost so that they can be assigned to goods and services. (In making this distinction, we do not mean to imply that full cost accounting and responsibility accounting are two separate accounting systems. As noted in Chapter 2, they are closely related and are more accurately described as two parts of the management accounting system.)

> EXAMPLE: Company X makes two products, No. 1 and No. 2. It has two production departments, A and B, each of which is a production cost center. It also has two general and administrative departments, C and D. The full costs of its products for a month are assembled and reported as shown in Part A of Exhibit 10–6.

Exhibit 10–6

Contrast between full costs and responsibility costs

A. Full Costs

	Product No. 1		Product No. 2	
	Total	*Per Unit*	*Total*	*Per Unit*
Volume (units)...................	2,000		1,000	
Cost item:				
Direct material.................	$14,000	$ 7.00	$ 6,000	$ 6.00
Direct labor....................	8,000	4.00	5,000	5.00
Factory indirect................	3,000	1.50	2,000	2.00
General and administrative........	6,000	3.00	3,000	3.00
Total costs...............	$31,000	$15.50	$16,000	$16.00

B. Responsibility Costs

	Departments (Responsibility Centers)			
	A	*B*	*C*	*D*
Cost item:				
Direct material....................	$18,000	$ 2,000		
Direct labor.......................	4,000	9,000		
Supervision.......................	700	900	$ 800	$1,400
Other labor costs..................	600	800	2,100	3,100
Supplies..........................	500	400	100	200
Other costs.......................	300	800	500	800
Total costs.................	$24,100	$13,900	$3,500	$5,500

Note that from this information, it is impossible to identify what costs the manager of any department was responsible for. In particular, the costs of the two general and administrative departments are lumped together and are allocated first to production cost centers and then to products by means of an overhead rate. The full cost data show the total costs of Departments C and D to be $6,000 + $3,000 = $9,000, but they do not indicate how much of the $9,000 is the responsibility of the manager of Department C and how much is the responsibility of the manager of Department D.

By contrast, responsibility accounting does identify the amount of costs that each of the four departmental managers is responsible for, as shown in Part B of the exhibit.

Note that Part B, however, does not show the costs of the two products. Both types of information are needed. Note also that the totals on the two parts are the same. The two parts are different arrangements of the same underlying data.

Another important characteristic of responsibility accounting is implicit in the description of organizations given earlier in this chapter. Since the management control process influences the behavior of managers, in considering what type of accounting information is useful we must consider how accounting information affects human behavior. In Part Two, by contrast, our description of the use of differential accounting information was strictly impersonal; we made no mention of the behavior of the human beings who used this information in analyzing alternative choice problems. There was no need to bring these behavioral characteristics into the discussion because the process was essentially an economic analysis, and economics does not deal, except peripherally, with the behavior of individuals. By contrast, in our discussion of responsibility accounting, we shall have much to say about human behavior and how managers are influenced by the nature of the accounting information they receive.

Management control system characteristics

Responsibility accounting is the principal type of accounting that is used in the management control process. Following is a list of the principal characteristics of the management control system:

1. As already noted, a management control system focuses on *responsibility centers.*

2. The information in a management control system is of two general types: (1) *planned data,* that is, programs, budgets, and standards; and (2) *actual data,* that is, information on what is actually happening, both inside the organization and in the environment.

3. Ordinarily, a management control system is a *total* system in the sense that it embraces all aspects of a company's operation. It needs to be a total system because an important management function is to assure that all parts of the operation are in balance with one another;

and in order to examine balance, management needs information about each of the parts.

4. With rare exceptions, the management control system is *built around a financial structure;* that is, resources and revenues are expressed in monetary units. Money is the only common denominator which can be used to combine and compare the heterogeneous elements of resources (e.g., hours of labor, type of labor, quantity and quality of material, amount and kind of products produced). Although the financial structure is usually the central focus, nonmonetary measures such as minutes per operation, number of persons, and reject and spoilage rates are also important parts of the system.

5. The management control process tends to be *rhythmic;* it follows a definite pattern and timetable, month after month and year after year. In budget preparation, which is an important activity in the management control process, certain steps are taken in a prescribed sequence and at certain dates each year: dissemination of guidelines, preparation of original estimates, transmission of these estimates up through the several echelons in the organization, review of these estimates, final approval by top management, and dissemination back through the organization. The procedure to be followed at each step in this process, the dates when the steps are to be completed, and even the forms to be used can be, and often are, set forth in a policies and procedures manual.

6. A management control system is, or should be, a *coordinated, integrated system;* that is, although data collected for one purpose may differ from those collected for another purpose, these data should be reconcilable with one another. In particular, it is essential that data on actual performance be structured in the same way—that is, have the same definitions and the same account content as—data on planned performance. If this is not done, valid comparisons of actual and planned performance cannot be made. In a sense, the management control system is a *single* system, but it is perhaps more accurate to think of it as a set of interlocking subsystems, one for programming, another for budgeting, another for accounting, and another for reporting and analysis.

Behavioral aspects of management control

The management control process involves human beings, from those in the lowest responsibility center of the organizational hierarchy up to and including each member of top management. The management control process in part consists of inducing these human beings to take those actions that will help attain the company's goals and to refrain from taking actions that are inconsistent with these goals. Although for some purposes an accumulation of the costs of manufacturing a product is useful, management cannot literally "control" a product, or the costs of making a product. What management does—or at least what it attempts to do—is **control the actions of the people who are responsible for incurring these costs.** The discipline that studies the behavior of people in organizations is called **social psychology.** It is this discipline, rather than economics, that provides the underlying principles that are relevant in the control process. We shall note briefly some aspects of behavior that are essential to an understanding of the management control process.

BEHAVIOR OF PARTICIPANTS

Each person in an organization is called a **participant.** A person becomes a participant—that is, he[2] joins an organization—because he believes that by doing so he can achieve his *personal* goals. His decision to contribute to the productive work of the organization once he has become a member of it is also based on his perception that this will help achieve his personal goals.

An individual's personal goals can be expressed as **needs.** Some of these needs are **material** and can be satisfied by the money that he earns on the job; that is, he needs enough money to provide for himself and for his family. Other needs are **psychological.** People need to have their abilities and achievements recognized; they need social acceptance as members of a group; they need to feel a sense of personal worth; they need to feel secure; they need the freedom to exercise discretion; they may need a feeling of power and achievement.

The relative importance of these needs varies with different persons, and their importance also varies with the same person at different times. For some people, earning a great deal of money is a dominant need; for others, monetary considerations are much less important. Only a relatively few people attach much importance to the need to exercise discretion or the need for achievement,[3] but these few persons tend to be the leaders of the organization. The relative importance that persons attach to their own needs is heavily influenced by the attitude of their colleagues and of their superiors.

MOTIVATION

Individuals are influenced both by the expectation of reward and by the fear of punishment. **Reward is the satisfaction of a need, and pun-**

---

[2] Although the male pronoun is used in place of the awkward "he or she," it should be understood that these observations apply equally to both men and women.

[3] McClelland argues that there is a relationship between the strength of the achievement motivation of the leaders of an organization and the success of that organization and that a similar relationship helps explain why certain countries have a rapid economic growth at certain times while others do not. See David McClelland, *The Achieving Society* (1971); and David C. McClelland and David G. Winter, *Motivating Economic Achievement* (New York: The Free Press), 1969).

ishment is the deprivation of satisfaction. Individuals tend to be more strongly motivated by reward than by punishment.

Monetary compensation is an important means of satisfying certain needs, but beyond the subsistence level the amount of compensation is not necessarily as important as nonmonetary rewards. Nevertheless, the amount of a person's earnings is often important indirectly as an indication of how his achievement and ability are regarded. (A person earning $50,000 a year may be disgruntled if a colleague of perceived equal ability receives $51,000 a year.)

The effectiveness of reward or punishment diminishes rapidly as the time elapses between an action and the reward or punishment administered for it. This is why it is important that reports on performance be made available and acted on quickly. Management control cannot wait for the annual financial statements that appear three months or so after the year has ended.

Needs may be unconscious, or they may be expressed as aspirations or goals. Motivation is weakest when the person perceives a goal as being either unattainable or too easily attainable. Motivation is strong when the goal can be attained with some effort and when the individual regards its attainment as important in relation to his needs.

A person tends to accept reports of his performance more willingly and to use them more constructively when they are presented to him in a manner that he regards as objective; that is, without personal bias.

Persons are receptive to learning better ways of doing things only when they personally recognize the inadequacies of their present behavior. Beyond a certain point, pressure for improved performance accomplishes nothing. This optimum point is far below the maximum amount of pressure that conceivably could be exerted. (When the coach says, "Don't press; don't try too hard," he is applying this principle.)

GOAL CONGRUENCE

Since an organization does not have a mind of its own, the organization itself literally cannot have goals. The "organizational goals" that we have referred to are actually the goals of top management. Top management wants these organizational goals to be attained, but other participants have their own personal goals that *they* want to achieve. These personal goals are the satisfaction of their needs. In other words, participants act in their own self-interest.

The difference between organizational goals and personal goals suggests the central purpose of a management control system: **the system should be designed so that actions that it leads people to take in accordance with their perceived self-interest are actions that are also in the best interests of the company.** In the language of social psychology, the management control system should encourage **goal congruence;** that is, it should be structured so that the goals of participants so far as feasible are consistent with the goals of the organization as a whole.

Perfect congruence between individual goals and organizational goals does not exist, but as a minimum the system should not encourage the individual to act *against* the best interests of the company. For example, if the management control system signals that the emphasis should be only on reducing costs, and if a manager responds by reducing costs at the expense of adequate quality or if he responds by reducing costs in his own responsibility center by measures that cause a more than offsetting increase in costs in some other responsibility center, he has been motivated, but in the wrong direction. It is therefore important to ask two separate questions about any practice used in a management control system:

1. What action does it motivate people to take in their own perceived self-interest, and
2. Is this action in the best interests of the company?

AN EXAMPLE: MAINTENANCE COSTS

As an illustration of how management control practices affect the behavior of individual managers, let us consider the problem of the control of maintenance costs. The maintenance function is that of insuring that buildings and equipment are in good condition. This function is in part the responsibility of the maintenance department, which incurs costs when it makes repairs or does other maintenance work; and it is in part the responsibility of managers of the operating departments who can influence the amount of required maintenance work by how well they take care of their building and equipment on a day-to-day basis. In addition, some maintenance work, such as outside painting, is required simply because of the uncontrollable forces of nature. Each manager understands that top management expects him to keep his costs at an optimum level in order to attain the organizational goal of earning a satisfactory profit. There are at least a dozen ways in which the costs of the maintenance department can be assigned to the several operating departments, and each gives a different "message" to the department managers as to how they should view their responsibility for maintenance. Here are a few of the possibilities and the implications that each is likely to convey:

> Method No. 1: Do not assign any maintenance costs to the operating departments.

Message: The operating manager has no responsibility for maintenance costs. He requests the maintenance department to do the maintenance work that needs to be done, and the maintenance department has the responsibility for complying with these requests. This system does not motivate the operating manager to curb unnecessary requests for maintenance work, nor does it cause him to be concerned about the way in which his equipment is treated in the course of departmental operations, nor does it cause him to facilitate the work of maintenance crews.

> Method No. 2: Allocate total maintenance costs to the operating departments on the basis of the volume of activity in these departments.

Message: Maintenance costs in total are expected to vary proportionately with the level of plant activity. However, the manager of each operating department has no direct responsibility for maintenance work; and the maintenance department, as in the first method, has full responsibility. The manager receives such a message because the amount of maintenance costs allocated to his department is influenced by the method of allocation rather than by actions that he personally takes, so the method does not motivate him to be strongly concerned about the amount of maintenance costs. The operating manager is told what his "fair share" of total maintenance costs is, which possibly may make him interested in the magnitude of such costs in the factory as a whole.

> Method No. 3: Charge departments for individual maintenance jobs at a prescribed cost for each type of job.

Message: The operating foreman is responsible for situations that create the need for maintenance work, such as machine breakdowns; and the maintenance department is responsible for the cost of doing a given maintenance job. The operating manager therefore need not be concerned with the efficiency with which maintenance men work because once he has requested that the job be done, he will be charged a prescribed amount no matter how much is actually spent in doing the job.

> Method No. 4: Charge each department for maintenance work at a prescribed hourly rate for each hour that a maintenance man works in the department.

Message: The operating manager is responsible both for situations that create the need for maintenance work and for the time taken by the maintenance people to do the work. He therefore is motivated to see to it that the maintenance men work efficiently. (This may create a conflict between the operating manager and the maintenance department manager because the latter is also concerned with how efficiently his men work.)

Each of these methods motivates the operating manager differently. The best method is the one that motivates the manager to act as top management wants him to act. If top management decides that maintenance work should be the complete responsibility of the maintenance experts and that the operating managers should not be burdened with any concern about maintenance, the first method is appropriate. If, although placing most of the responsibility on the maintenance department, top management wants operating managers to have some concern about the magnitude of maintenance costs, the second method is appropriate. The third method conveys top management's intention that the operating manager should have a considerable responsibility for the control of maintenance costs, and the fourth method conveys this intention even more strongly. Depending on what top management wishes to accomplish, any one of these methods, or other methods not listed, or some combination of them, may be best for a given company.

The above example indicates the considerations that are important in structuring responsibility accounting information. These considerations are basically different from those involved in full cost accounting, where the purpose is to measure the amount of resources used for products or services, or from those involved in differential accounting, where the purpose is to estimate the amounts that are differential for a proposed course of action. Neither full cost accounting nor differential accounting is influenced by behavioral considerations; in responsibility accounting, behavioral considerations are dominant.

COOPERATION AND CONFLICT

From the description given earlier in this chapter, it easily could be inferred that the way in which organizational goals are attained is that the top manager makes a decision, he communicates that decision down through the organizational hierarchy, and managers at lower levels of the organization proceed to implement it. It should now be apparent that this is *not* the way in which an organization actually functions. Because individuals have their own goals, and because they react in different ways, this view of what happens in an organization is unrealistic.

What actually happens is that each subordinate reacts to the instructions of top management in accordance with how those instructions affect the subordinate's personal needs. Since usually more than one responsibility center is involved in carrying out a given plan, the interactions between their managers also affects what actually happens. For example, although the manager of the maintenance department is supposed to see to it that the maintenance needs of the operating departments are satisfied, if there is friction between the maintenance manager and an operating manager, the needs of that operating manager's department may, in fact, be slighted. For these and many other reasons, **conflict** exists within organizations.

At the same time, the work of the organization will not get done unless its participants work together with a certain amount of harmony. Thus, there is also **cooperation** in organizations. Participants realize that unless there is a reasonable amount of cooperation, the organization will dissolve, and the participants will then be unable to satisfy *any* of the needs which motivated them to join the organization in the first place.

An organization attempts to maintain an appropriate balance between the forces that create conflict and those that create cooperation.

Some conflict is not only inevitable, it is desirable. Conflict results in part from the competition among participants for promotion or other forms of need satisfaction; and such competition is, within limits, healthy. A certain amount of cooperation is also obviously essential, but if undue emphasis is placed on engendering cooperative attitudes, the most able participants will be denied the opportunity of demonstrating their full potentialities.

Implications for management control
The principles of social psychology suggest some ideas that are directly relevant to the management control process. Some of these are listed below.

MANAGEMENT SPONSORSHIP

A management control system will probably be ineffective unless subordinate managers are convinced that top management considers the system to be important. Some systems are installed with no more management backing than the directive, "Let's have a good control system," and with no subsequent interest or action by managements. Such a system, instead of being a part of the management process, becomes a paper shuffling routine whose principal virtue is that it provides employment for a great many clerks.

Action is a sure signal, probably the only effective signal, that management is interested in the control system. Basically, this action involves praise or other reward for good performance, criticism of or removal of the causes for poor performance, or questions leading to these actions. If, in contrast, reports on performance disappear into executive offices and are never heard from again, the organization has reason to assume that management is not paying attention to them. And if management does not pay attention to them, why should anyone else?

PARTICIPATION AND UNDERSTANDING

Control is exercised in part by establishing standards of expected performance and comparing actual performance with these standards. Whatever standard of good performance is adopted, it is likely to be effective as a means of control only if the person being judged agrees that it is an equitable standard. If he does not agree, he is likely to pay no attention to comparisons between his performance and the standard; and he is likely to resent, and if possible reject, an attempt by anyone else to make such a comparison.

The best way to assure this agreement is to ask the person whose performance is to be measured to participate in the process of setting the standard. In order to participate intelligently, the manager needs to understand clearly what the control system is, what he is expected to do, what basis he is going to be judged on, and so on. Such an understanding probably cannot be achieved by written communication. Frequent meetings of supervisors for discussion and explanation are required.

The process of educating the individuals involved in the system is necessarily a continuous one. Not uncommonly, a system is introduced with a loud fanfare, works well for a time, and then gradually withers away in effectiveness as the initial stimulus disappears.

REWARDS

Many management control systems rely for the strength of their motivation on the attitude and actions that top management takes in response to reported performance. In some situations a quite simple signal can be effective.

> EXAMPLE: In the New York City government there was a project to sort out and discard files on those Medicaid cases that had been closed. These files occupied 1,200 file cabinets. When the job started, each clerk was examining an average of 150 files a day, which was unsatisfactory. The supervisor then made the following change: instead of discarding files in a common container, each clerk was asked to pile them in front of his or her work station. As the piles mounted, it became apparent to everyone how much work each clerk was doing. Production immediately increased to 300 files a day.[4]

At the other extreme, the reward can be that the manager's compensation is related to his performance, that is, managers are paid a performance bonus. In view of the importance which many people attach to monetary compensation, this is a strong motivation indeed. In some cases it is too strong, for unless the standards are very carefully worked out, incessant arguments will go on about the justice and equity of the reported results. If the system is being used only for praise or blame, inequities in the figures can be allowed for when interpreting the results, but this is not possible when a bonus is computed mechanically on the basis of reported performance. Thus, a bonus plan is most successful when there is general agreement that the basis of measurement is fair.

FOCUS ON LINE MANAGERS

Since subordinates are responsible to their superiors, they should receive praise, criticism, and other forms of reward and punishment from their superiors. Staff people should not be directly involved in these motivation activities (except with respect to control of the staff organizations themselves). Line managers are the focal points in man-

---

[4] From *Management Accounting*, December 1972, p. 63.

agement control. They are the persons whose judgments are incorporated in the approved plans, and they are the persons who must influence others and whose performance is measured. Staff people collect, summarize, and present information that is useful in the process, and they make calculations that translate management judgments into the format of the system. There may be many such staff people; indeed, the control department is often the largest staff department in a company. However, the significant decisions and control actions are the responsibility of the line managers, not of the staff.

NEED FOR INTERNAL CONSISTENCY

The control system gives "signals" as to the nature of performance that is expected. It is important that these signals be consistent with one another. Inconsistencies between the performance actually desired by top management and the standard as perceived by operating managers can arise when different aspects of performance are being measured in separate parts of a control system. If a supervisor's performance as to quality is being measured in one subsystem, his performance as to cost control in another, and his performance as to volume in a third, he may be uncertain as to the relative weights that he should attach to these three aspects of performance. He will tend to regard one of these aspects as more important than the others, but his choice may be different from what management actually intends.

INDIVIDUAL DIFFERENCES

As pointed out above, individuals differ in their needs and in their reactions to rewards and punishments of various types. An important function of the manager at each level is to adapt his application of the system to the personalities and attitudes of the individuals whom he supervises. Thus an impersonal system can never be a substitute for interpersonal actions; rather, the system is a framework that should be adapted by the manager to fit individual situations.

Summary   There are three planning and control processes in an organization. (1) *Strategic planning* deals with decisions on goals and the strategies for achieving these goals. (2) *Management control,* the process on which we focus, assists managers in assuring that goals are accomplished efficiently and effectively. (3) *Operational* control is the process of assuring that specific tasks are carried out effectively and efficiently.

The management control process consists of a recurring cycle of interrelated phases: programming, which involves making decisions as to what programs should be undertaken; budgeting, which is the development of a plan for the forthcoming year; operating and accounting, which includes the collection of information on what actually occurred; and reporting and analysis, which involves the use of this information as a basis for corrective action and for making new plans.

The management control process involves human beings. The principles of social psychology are therefore relevant. Of these we have called particular attention to certain principles of motivation. These principles, rather than those of economics or cost accounting, govern the design of management control systems.

Important terms		
Strategic planning	**Budget**	
Management control	**Responsibility accounting**	
Operational control	**Reward**	
Programming	**Punishment**	
Long-range plan	**Goal congruence**	

Questions for discussion

1. What is the difference between the formal and the informal management control system?

2. Give examples of the types of information that the president of a company that manufactures and sells women's apparel is likely to receive from the several parts of the environment that are depicted in Exhibit 10–2.

3. What are the differences among the planning activities that take place in the strategic planning process, the management control process, and the operational control process, respectively? Give examples.

4. What are the differences among the control activities that take place in the three processes? Give examples.

5. What are the differences between programming and budgeting?

6. Give some examples of programming decisions that might be made in a college or university.

7. What are the differences between full cost accounting and responsibility accounting?

8. Why is a management control system built around a financial structure? Why does it not consist entirely of monetary information?

9. The management control process tends to be rhythmic. Do you suppose this is also the case with the strategic planning process? Why?

10. "The controller presumably knows more about the nature and meaning of responsibility accounting information than anyone else. He therefore should be the principal person who discusses this information with line managers." Comment on this assertion.

11. Why do a participant's personal goals differ from those of the organization of which he is a part? Give some examples.

12. Can all influences on individuals be classified as either rewards or punishments?

13. A school wants its students to (a) work diligently on their studies, and (b) to learn as much as they are capable of learning. What motivational devices might it use for each of these purposes? Might some of these devices conflict with one another?

14. What method of charging maintenance costs to responsibility centers is appropriate under each of the following circumstances:

   a. Top management wants line managers to have complete responsibility for the operation of their responsibility centers.

   b. The responsibility centers are research and development departments. Top management wants them to devote all their energies to research projects.

   c. Top management wants the maintenance department to be responsible for the normal painting and other upkeep work of buildings, but wants the responsibility centers to be responsible for the cost of alterations, such as new partitions.

15. Why are both cooperation and conflict desirable in an organization?

Problems   10–1. Department 12 of the Minow Company manufactures a variety of components for products, one of which is Part No. 106. Data on this part are as follows:

	Monthly Planned Cost, 1974	Actual Cost, June 1974	
Item of Cost	*Per Unit*	*Per Unit*	*Total*
Direct material and direct labor.........	$ 8.00	$ 7.80	$ 7,800
Fixed costs, Department 12.............	2.00	2.20	2,200
Costs allocated to Department 12........	3.00	3.30	3,300
Total........................	$13.00	$13.30	$13,300

Part No. 106 can be purchased from an outside vender for $11.

Required:

What costs are relevant for each of the following purposes:

1. For preparing financial statements for June 1974?
2. For deciding whether to make or buy Part No. 106?
3. For assessing the performance of the manager of Department 12?

10–2. Kentow Company manufactures three products, A, B, and C. It has three marketing managers, one for each product. During the first year of operations, the company allocated its $30,000 of actual advertising expense to products on the basis of the relative net sales of each product. In the second year, the advertising budget was increased to $50,000. Half was spent on general institutional advertising in the belief the company image would be enhanced. The other half was spent $8,000 on Product A, $12,000 on Product B, and $5,000 on Product C. For purposes of income measurement, all advertising expenses continued to be allocated on the basis of sales. Certain data in the second year were as follows:

	Total	Product A	Product B	Product C
Net sales.............	$450,000	$193,500	$126,000	$130,500
Advertising expense.....	50,000	21,500	14,000	14,500
Net income............	55,000	25,500	12,000	17,500

When the marketing manager of Product A received these figures, he complained that his department was charged with an unfair portion of advertising, and that he should be held responsible only for the actual amount spent to advertise Product A.

Required:

1. Comment on the sales manager's complaint.
2. In its responsibility accounting system, how much advertising expense should be charged to the department responsible for marketing Product A?

10–3.   Jersey Company, a distributor of hardware items offers a cash discount of 2 percent for customers paying their accounts within 10 days of sale, but charges 1½ percent per month on all accounts not paid within 30 days of sale. Each department decides which of its customers will be allowed to buy on credit. The net sales of each department are computed by subtracting the cash discount actually taken on department sales. Revenue from finance charges is allocated to the departments on the basis of credit sales made during the current month. A summary of these monthly transactions follows:

	Total	Department 1	Department 2	Department 3
Cash sales............	$ 740,000	$180,000	$260,000	$300,000
Cash discounts........	9,400	3,600	5,200	600
Total sales............	1,340,000	280,000	560,000	500,000
Finance charges collected...........	31,200	5,200	15,600	10,400

Required:

1. Comment on the method of allocating cash discounts and the revenue from finance charges for responsibility accounting purposes.
2. Compute the net revenue due to credit sales, assigning the discounts and finance revenue in a manner which you believe would produce more useful results for management use.

10–4. The Lane Confectionery Company is a wholesaler of candies and tobacco products. At the end of each month the controller prepares statements for each of the three branch managers and the company president. The statement for the current month is as follows:

	Branch 1	Branch 2	Branch 3
Sales.....................	$300,000	$200,000	$400,000
Direct costs:			
Cost of sales...............	$180,000	$124,000	$220,000
Salesmen's salaries...........	34,000	26,000	38,000
Supplies..................	400	300	450
Utilities..................	1,100	900	1,200
Delivery expense.............	5,000	3,800	6,200
Depreciation—branch assets........	20,000	19,200	22,500
Branch contribution............	$ 59,500	$ 25,800	$111,650
Allocated costs:			
Advertising expense...........	12,000	8,000	16,000
Administrative salaries and other			
administrative expense........	32,000	32,000	32,000
Income before Tax.............	$ 15,500	($ 14,200)	$ 63,650

Required:

1. Comment on the strengths and weaknesses of this statement.
2. Comment on the basis of allocation of the overheads.
3. Should Branch 2 be discontinued? Support your answer with appropriate computations.

10–5. Happy Foods, Inc., operates several hundred fast-food drive-in restaurants. As an experiment, the top management selected three nearly identical restaurants and provided a different compensation plan to the manager of each. One manager was paid a flat salary. Another manager was paid 10 percent of net sales. The third manager was paid a salary plus 25 percent of the amount by which he reduced actual operating expenses below the planned amount. Results for the first year were as follows:

	Restaurant		
	A	B	C
Sales......................	$240,000	$200,000	$160,000
Raw food costs................	96,000	80,000	64,000
Gross margin.................	$144,000	$120,000	$ 96,000
Operating expenses			
Wages and salaries.............	$ 90,000	$ 70,000	$ 60,000
Advertising................	30,000	20,000	10,000
Other...................	15,000	15,000	12,000
Total expenses..............	$135,000	$105,000	$ 82,000
Income before Taxes.............	$ 9,000	$ 15,000	$ 14,000

Required:

1. Which compensation plan was probably used in restaurants A, B, and C respectively?
2. As well as you can, explain how the compensation plans affected the performance of the managers.
3. Which of the three plans, or what alternative plan, would you recommend? (Hint: Consider probable long-run as well as short-run effects.)

10–6. Exhibit 10–2 represents the flow of information between an organization and its environments. Taking General Motors Corporation (or any other industrial company if you happen to be more familiar with another one) as an illustrative situation, list a specific example of a piece of information for each of the flows depicted by an arrow on that exhibit. For the box labeled "other environmental forces," think of either the general public or the government, whichever you prefer.

10–7. Rapid Cab Company owns a fleet of 20 taxicabs, each of which has two or three drivers per 24-hour day. Drivers are paid $3 per hour and may keep all tips. Maintenance of cabs is done by the company at its own garage. Profits have been declining, and part of the problem is believed caused by such practices as withholding fares, use of the cabs for personal use, and not trying hard enough to solicit business. In an effort to reduce such activities, the company is considering doing away with the hourly wages and paying each driver 60 percent of the total fares as shown on the meter, less the actual cost of gasoline, oil, tires, and maintenance.

Required:

Discuss the proposed compensation plan.

Suggestions
for further
reading

Atkinson, J. W. *An Introduction to Motivation.* Princeton, N.J.: D. Van Nostrand Co., Inc., 1964.

Caplan, Edwin H. *Management Accounting and Behavioral Science.* Reading, Mass.: Addison-Wesley Publishing Co., Inc., 1971.

Cyert, R. M., and March, J. G., *A Behavioral Theory of the Firm.* Englewood Cliffs, N.J.: Prentice-Hall, Inc., 1963.

Homans, G. C., *Social Behavior: Its Elementary Forms.* New York: Harcourt, Brace & World, Inc., 1961.

Lawrence, P. R., and Lorsch, J. W. *Organization and Environment: Managing Differentiation and Integration.* Boston: Division of Research, Harvard Business School, 1967.

McClelland, D. C. *The Achieving Society.* Princeton, N.J.: D. Van Nostrand Co., Inc., 1961.

11 Budget preparation

Purpose of
the chapter This chapter discusses one of the important activities of the management control process, namely, the preparation of budgets. In order to
understand this activity, one needs to know both what managers and
others do in the course of preparing budgets, which is the *behavioral*
aspect of budgeting, and also how the amounts in the budget are calculated and assembled, which is the *technical* aspect of budgeting. The
text focuses primarily on the behavioral aspect. An Appendix illustrates
the technical aspect by showing the details of budget preparation in a
simple situation. Since the interrelationships among the various parts of
a budget can be understood most clearly if all these parts are grouped
together, the usual practice of having exhibits appear close to the text
material to which they relate has not been followed in this chapter.
Instead, all exhibits appear in the Appendix, where they are arranged
in an order that facilitates the tracing of information from one exhibit
to another.

Uses of the
budget   A budget is a plan that is expressed in quantitative, usually monetary,
terms and that covers a specified period of time, usually one year. The
budget for a business company is frequently referred to as a **profit plan**
since it shows the plan that the company expects to follow in order
to attain its profit goal. The budget is useful for these purposes:

1. For making and coordinating plans,
2. For communicating these plans to those who are responsible for
   carrying them out,
3. In motivating managers at all levels, and

322

4.   As a standard with which actual performance subsequently can be compared.

Planning.   Although basic planning decisions are usually made in the programming process that occurs prior to the beginning of the budget cycle (as described in Chapter 10), the process of formulating the budget leads to a refinement of these plans; and when it discloses imbalances or unsatisfactory overall results, the budgeting process may lead to a change in plans.

Communication.   Management's plans will not be carried out (except by accident) unless the organization understands what the plans are. Adequate understanding includes not only a knowledge of specific plans (e.g., how many units are to be manufactured, what methods and machines are to be used, how much material is to be purchased, what selling prices are to be), but also a knowledge about policies and constraints to which the organization is expected to adhere. Examples of these kinds of information follow: the maximum amounts that may be spent for such items as advertising, maintenance, administrative costs; wage rates and hours of work; and desired quality levels. A most useful device for communicating quantitative information concerning these plans and limitations is the approved budget. Moreover, much vital information is communicated during the process of preparing the budget.

Motivation.   If the atmosphere is right, the budget process can be a powerful force in motivating managers to work toward the goals of the overall organization. Such an atmosphere is created when the manager of each responsibility center understands that top management regards the process as important, and when he participates in the formulation of his own budget in the manner to be described later in this chapter.

Standard for performance measurement.   A carefully prepared budget is the best possible standard against which to compare actual performance, and it is increasingly being used for this purpose. Until fairly recently, the general practice was to compare current results with results for last month or with results for the same period a year ago; this is still the basic means of comparison in many companies. Such a historical standard has the fundamental weakness that it does not take account of either changes in the underlying forces at work or in the planned program for the current year.

> *EXAMPLE:* In a favorable market situation, a certain company increased its volume and its selling prices and hence increased its net income in 1974 by 5 percent over the net income of 1973. If 1974's results are compared with 1973's, there is an apparent cause for rejoicing. However, the company had *planned* to increase profits by 15 percent, and performance when measured against the plan was, therefore, not so good. The company quite properly took steps to find out, and if possible to correct, the factors that caused the difference between actual and budgeted results in 1974.

In general, it is more significant to answer the question, "Why didn't we do what we planned to do?" than the question, "Why are this year's results different from last year's?" Presumably, the principal factors accounting for the difference between this year and last year were taken into consideration in the preparation of the budget. Of course, the budget is a reliable standard only if it has been carefully prepared. If management doubts the realism of the budget, then there is good reason to use last year's performance as a benchmark, for this at least has the merit of being a definite, objective figure.

Types of budgets

Although we have referred to "the" budget, the complete "budget package" in a company includes several items, each of which is also referred to as a budget. We shall therefore refer to the total package as the **master budget,** and shall use appropriate names for each of its components. Exhibit 11–2 (page 344) shows the components used in the company whose budget preparation will be described in detail. The three principal parts of the master budget are:

1. An **operating budget,** showing planned operations for the forthcoming year, including revenues, expenses, and related changes in inventory;
2. A **cash budget,** showing the anticipated sources and uses of cash in that year; and
3. A **capital expenditure budget,** showing planned changes in fixed assets.

We shall first describe the nature of the operating budget and the steps involved in its preparation. We shall then describe the cash budget and the capital expenditure budget. Another document, the *budgeted balance sheet* is derived directly from the other budgets and is therefore not described separately.

The operating budget

PROGRAM BUDGETS AND RESPONSIBILITY BUDGETS

In some companies, the operating budget consists of two parts, a program budget and a responsibility budget. These represent two ways of depicting the overall operating plan for the business, two different methods of slicing the pie; therefore, both arrive at the same final figure for budgeted net income.

The program budget consists of the estimated revenues and costs of the major programs that the company plans to undertake during the year. Such a budget might be arranged, for example, by products lines and show the anticipated revenue and costs associated with each product line. This type of budget is useful to a manager when he is analyzing overall balance among the various programs of the business.

It helps to answer such questions as these: Is the profit margin on each product line satisfactory? Is production capacity in balance with the size and capability of the sales organization? Can we afford to spend so much for research? Are adequate funds available? And so on. A negative answer to any of these questions indicates the necessity for revising the plan. (The Lake Erie Table Company, whose practices are described in the Appendix, does not prepare a program budget.)

The responsibility budget sets forth plans in terms of the persons responsible for carrying them out. It is an excellent control device since it is a statement of the performance that is expected for each manager, against which his actual performance can later be compared. As explained in the Appendix, each manager listed on the organization chart in Exhibit 11–1 is responsible for preparing those parts of the operating budget that correspond to his sphere of responsibility.

In the factory, for example, there should be a responsibility budget for each department, showing the costs that are controllable by the foreman of the department. There may also be a program budget showing planned costs for each product, including both direct costs and allocated costs. The numbers on each set of budgets add up to total factory costs; but if several products were made in a factory in which there are several responsibility centers, the program budget would not be useful for control purposes, since the costs shown on it could not ordinarily be related to the responsibility of specific managers.

In some situations, individual responsibility can be related to specific programs, and in these situations, the program budget does serve as a means of control. The producer of a motion picture or a television "special," for example, has a budget for his particular program, and control is exercised in terms of that budget. This is also the case in the construction of major capital assets: buildings, dams, roads, bridges, ships, weapons systems, and the like.

VARIABLE BUDGETS

If the total costs in a responsibility center are expected to vary with changes in volume, as is the case with most production and sales responsibility centers, the responsibility budget may be in the form of a **variable budget** or **flexible budget.** Such a budget shows the planned behavior of costs at various volume levels. The variable budget is usually expressed in terms of the cost-volume equation described in Chapter 6, that is, a fixed amount for a specified time period plus a variable amount per unit of volume. (Recall from Chapter 6 the basic equation for determining the costs [y] at any volume [x]; it is $y = a + bx$, in which a is the fixed amount and b is the variable amount per unit of volume x.) A variable budget may also be expressed as the costs that are planned at discrete levels of volume; that is, the costs planned at 60 percent of standard volume may be listed in one column,

and costs planned at 70, 80, 90, 100, 110, 120, 130, and 140 percent
of standard volume may be listed in other columns. When discrete
volume levels are shown, a comparison of actual costs with budgeted
costs requires an interpolation whenever the actual volume is between
two of the specified volume levels.

When there is a variable budget, the costs at *one* volume level are
used as part of the master budget. That volume level is the volume at
which the company plans to operate during the budget period.

> *EXAMPLE:* Schedule 6 in the Appendix shows a factory overhead
> budget. The first group of items thereon are for budgeted costs in the
> machining department, as follows:

Account	Variable Budget Formula Fixed	Variable	January Budget ($25,830 DLD)
Supervisory salaries...........	$3,300 + $	0 per DLD*	$ 3,300
Wages......................	500 +	0.13	3,858
Factory supplies.............	0 +	0.11	2,841
Power......................	0 +	0.10	2,583
Depreciation................	1,200 +	0	1,200
Employee benefits...........	400 +	0.15	4,275
Total.................	$5,400 +	$0.49 per DLD	$18,057

* DLD means direct labor dollars, which is the measure of volume used in the illustration.

The columns labeled "variable budget formula" give the variable
budget. The budget for any month is calculated on the basis of the
volume planned for that month. The first three items are examples of
fixed, semivariable, and variable costs, respectively. The supervisory
salaries item is a fixed cost, and the budgeted amount for any month is
the fixed amount, $3,300, regardless of volume. The wages item is a
semivariable cost; the budgeted amount for January is the fixed component, $500, plus the variable component, which is $0.13 times the
$25,830 direct labor dollars budgeted for January, (= $3,358), making a total of $3,858. The factory supplies item is a variable cost; the
budgeted amount for January is $0.11 times the $25,830 direct labor
dollars or $2,841.

In addition to the responsibility budgets for costs, there are also:
• A budget of planned inventory levels of finished products and raw
  materials (Schedule 7);
• A budget of the planned purchases of materials (Schedule 4); and
• A budget for planned manpower levels (Schedule 5).
There may be also a budget for planned personnel promotions, partici-
pation in training programs, and retirements; and budgets for a variety
of other special purposes that are not illustrated in this description.

RELATIONSHIPS AMONG THE BUDGET COMPONENTS

The budget should constitute a coherent whole; therefore, the pieces must be consistent with one another. The costs in the individual production centers in the responsibility budget must add up to the same amount as the total factory product costs in the program budget. The volume level used to calculate budgeted costs from the variable budget must be the volume that is planned for the period. Changes in raw material inventory must be consistent with the planned purchases of raw material and the planned usage of raw material in production. Changes in finished goods inventory must be consistent with production volume and with sales volume. The manpower budget must be consistent with labor costs. All of these relationships are illustrated in the various schedules in the Appendix.

Organization for preparation of budgets
A **budget committee,** consisting of several members of the top management group, usually guides the work of preparing the budget. This committee recommends to the chief executive officer the general guidelines that the organization is to follow, disseminates these guidelines after his approval, coordinates the separate budgets prepared by the various organizational units, resolves differences among them, and submits the final budget to the president and to the board of directors for approval. In a small company, this work is done by the president himself, or by his immediate line subordinate. Instructions go down through the regular chain of command, and the budget comes back up for successive reviews and approvals through the same channels. Decisions about the budget are made by the line organization, and the final approval is given by the chief executive officer, subject to ratification by the board of directors.

BUDGET STAFF

The line organization usually is assisted in its preparation of the budget by a staff unit headed by the **budget director.** As a staff person, the budget director's functions are to disseminate instructions about the mechanics of budget preparation (the forms and how to fill them out), to provide data on past performance that are useful in preparation of the budget, to make computations on the basis of decisions reached by the line organization, to assemble the budget numbers, and to see to it that everyone submits his portion of the budget on time. The budget staff may do a very large fraction of the budget work. It is not the crucial part, however, for the significant decisions are always made by the line organization. Once the members of the line organization have reached an agreement on such matters as labor productivity and wage rates, for example, the budget staff can calculate the detailed amounts for labor costs by products and by responsibility centers; this is a considerable job of computation, but it is entirely based on the decisions of the line supervisors.

The budget staff is like a telephone company. It operates an important communication system; it is responsible for the speed, accuracy, and clarity with which messages flow through the system, but it does not decide on the content of the messages themselves.

Preparing the operating budget

Most companies prepare budgets once a year, and the budget covers a year. Separate budget estimates are usually made for each month or each quarter within the year. In some companies, data are initially estimated by months only for the next three months or the next six months, with the balance of the year being shown by quarters. When this is done a detailed budget by months is prepared shortly before the beginning of each new quarter.

Some companies follow the practice of preparing a new budget every quarter, but for a full year ahead. Every three months the budget amounts for the quarter just completed are dropped, the amounts for the succeeding three quarters are revised if necessary, and budget amounts for the fourth succeeding quarter are added. This is called a **rolling budget.**

The preparation of a budget can be studied both as an accounting process and as also a management process. From an accounting standpoint, one studies the mechanics of the system, the procedures for assembling data, and budget formats. The procedures are similar to those described in *Fundamentals of Financial Accounting* for recording actual transactions, and the end result of the calculation and summarizing operations is a set of financial statements—a balance sheet, income statement, and statement of changes in financial position—identical in format with those resulting from the accounting process that records historical events. The principal difference is that the budget amounts reflect planned future activities rather than data on what has happened in the past.

Since the relationship to financial accounting is so close, we trust that the reader can trace the numbers through the several schedules in the Appendix, using his knowledge of how financial accounting transactions are recorded. We therefore have not provided a detailed description of these schedules. Instead, we shall focus here on the preparation of an operating budget as a *management* process, and we shall now describe the principal steps in that process.

The operating budget consists of several components. In detail, the components vary among companies, but those shown in Exhibit 11–2 are common: a sales budget, an inventory budget, a selling expense budget, a production budget, a materials usage budget, a material purchase budget, a direct labor budget, a factory overhead budget, a cost of goods sold budget, and an administrative expense budget.

Most budget components are affected by decisions or estimates made in constructing other components. Nearly all components are affected by the planned sales volume and decisions as to inventory levels; the purchases budget is affected by planned production volume and decisions as to raw material inventory levels; and so on. Thus, there has to be a carefully worked out timetable specifying the order in which the several parts of the operating budget are developed and the time when each must be completed. In general, the steps covered by this timetable are as follows:

1. Setting planning guidelines.
2. Making the sales budget.
3. Initial preparation of other budget components.
4. Negotiation to evolve final plans for each component.
5. Coordination and review of the components.
6. Final approval.
7. Distribution of the approved budget.

In a company of average complexity, the elapsed time for the whole budget preparation process is approximately three months, with the most hectic part (steps 4, 5, and 6 above) requiring approximately one month. In highly complex organizations, the elapsed time may be somewhat longer. At the other extreme, a small business may go through the whole process in one afternoon.

STEP 1. SETTING PLANNING GUIDELINES

The budget preparation process is *not* the mechanism through which most major policy decisions are made, but rather a means of implementing these decisions. If the company has a formal programming process, most major decisions are made as part of that process. Although some major decisions may be made during the budget preparation process, because the act of preparing the budget may uncover unforeseen problems, these are exceptions to the general rule.

Thus, when budget preparation begins, a great many decisions affecting the budget year already have been made. The maximum level of manufacturing operations has been set by the amount and character of available production facilities. (If an expansion of facilities is to take place during the budget year, the decision would ordinarily have been made a year or more previously because of the time required to build buildings and to acquire and install machinery.) If a new product is to go into volume production, considerable time would have already been spent prior to the budget year on product development, testing, design, and initial promotional work. Thus, the budget is not a *de vovo* creation; it is built within the context of the ongoing business and is governed by programming decisions that have been made previously.

If the company has a formal program or long-range plan (see Chapter 10), this plan provides a starting point in preparing the budget. Alternatively, or in addition, top management establishes policies and guidelines that are to govern budget preparation. These guidelines vary greatly in content in different companies. At one extreme, there may be only a brief general statement, such as, "Assume that industry volume next year will be 5 percent higher than the current year." More commonly, detailed information and guidance are given on such matters as projected general economic conditions, allowance to be made for price increases and wage increases, changes in the product line, changes in the scale of operations, allowable number of personnel promotions, and anticipated productivity gains. In addition, detailed instructions are issued as to what information is required from each responsibility center for the budget, and how this information is to be recorded on the budget documents.

These guidelines would be of great interest to competitors, who would like very much to learn what the company's strategies are, so care is taken to insure that the guidelines are circulated only to those who need to know them. If it is particularly important that a new strategy be concealed, it may be omitted from the guideline statement, with necessary adjustments in the budget being made subsequently at the headquarters level. In the absence of statements to the contrary, the organization customarily assumes that the factors affecting operations in the budget year will be similar to those in the current year.

EXAMPLE: The following guideline statement was developed by the budget committee of a large bank; it is relatively general and brief:

It is customary for the committee to summarize for your general guidance current thinking regarding deposits, loans, and loan rates. The expectations outlined below are for the overall bank. Therefore, it is important that the head of each department analyze the impact of expected general economic trends on the conditions peculiar to his own area of activity in order to project specific goals which he may reasonably expect to attain.

DEPOSITS

There is every indication that money market conditions will be such that demand deposit levels in our area will expand. In our judgment, we anticipate at least a 5 percent growth in demand deposits for all banks. Our overall goal, however, should be set somewhat higher to reflect an improvement in our relative position. Savings deposits will continue to climb moderately. Current rates for time and savings deposits should be used to project interest costs.

LOANS AND LOAN RATES

In all probability, loan demand will slacken seasonally in the early months of next year; in fact, many economists believe that the decline may continue through the second quarter of the year. We firmly believe that sometime between April and July loan demand should strengthen.

For the most part, the recent decline in the prime rate is reflected in the loan rate structure at this time. Accordingly, except where necessary rate adjustments are still anticipated, the existing rate structure should prevail.

EXPENSES

Before preparing the budget, it is imperative that each supervisor closely evaluate controllable expense in his area and consider all means of economizing and reducing costs, particularly in such areas as personnel staffing, overtime, entertainment, stationery, etc. The salary administration policies explained in the Budget Instructions should be strictly followed.

In order to complete the budget for the entire bank by year-end, your full cooperation is necessary in meeting the deadlines which appear in the attached General Instructions.

Budget Committee

STEP 2. MAKING THE SALES BUDGET

The amount of sales and the sales mix (i.e., the proportion represented by each product or product line) govern the level and general character of the company's operations. Thus, a sales plan must be made early in the budget process, for it affects most of the other plans. **The sales budget is different from a sales forecast.** A forecast is merely passive, while a budget should reflect the results of positive actions that management plans to take in order to influence future events. For example, this may be the sales *forecast:* "With the present amount of sales effort, we expect sales to run at about the same level as currently." By contrast, the sales *budget* may show a substantial planned increase in sales, reflecting management's intention to add sales personnel, to increase advertising and sales promotion, or to add or redesign products.

It follows that at the same time the sales budget is prepared, a selling expense budget must also be prepared because the size and nature of the order-getting efforts that are intended to influence sales revenue are given in the selling expense budget. However, in this early stage, it may suffice to show the main elements of selling expense, with such details as the expenses of operating field selling offices left until the next step.

In almost all companies the sales budget is the most difficult plan to make. This is because a company's sales revenue depends on the actions of its customers, which are not subject to the direct control of management. In contrast, the amounts of cost incurred are determined primarily by actions of the company itself (except for the prices of certain cost factors), and therefore can be planned with more confidence.

Basically, there are two ways of making estimates as a basis for the sales budget:

1. Make a **statistical forecast** on the basis of an analysis of general business conditions, market conditions, product growth curves, and the like; or
2. Make an **internal estimate** by collecting the opinions of executives and salespersons. In some companies sales personnel are asked to estimate the sales of each product to each of their customers; in others, regional managers estimate total sales in their regions; in still others, the field organization does not participate in the estimating process.

There are advantages and weaknesses in both the statistical and the internal methods. Both are often used together, but neither can be guaranteed to yield an even reasonably close estimate in view of the inevitable uncertainties of the future. Statistical techniques rest on the assumption that the future is likely to resemble the past. Such an assumption is reasonable in many situations. Thus, if sales have been increasing at the rate of 5 percent a year, and if there is no evidence that new factors will change this rate of increase, it is reasonable to predict that next year's sales will be 5 percent above this year's. This is the simplest type of forecast since it depends only on an extrapolation of past performance. A more complicated, and usually more reliable, procedure is to analyze the several factors that affect sales revenue and then predict the future behavior of each of these factors.

> *EXAMPLE:* Able Pharmacy is the leading drugstore in its town. Its management observes that sales revenue in the past has increased proportionately with (*a*) increase in the local population, and (*b*) increases in the general level of prices, that is, the rate of inflation. If the local population is expected to increase 5 percent next year, and if prices are expected to increase 3 percent, then one could predict a sales revenue increase of about 8 percent. (The arithmetic of combining percentages is more complicated than simple addition, so the mathematically calculated increase is not exactly 8 percent; nevertheless, 8 percent is close enough in view of the margin of error.)

The forecasting technique used in the preceding example is called **correlation,** that is, a change in one number was predicted in terms of the change in another number because there was reason to believe that there was an identifiable association between the movement of the two numbers. Companies are continually searching for factors that correlate with sales revenue as an aid to improving their prediction of this difficult number.

The foregoing description of forecasting techniques omitted the effect on sales revenue of changes in marketing policy. The estimated impact of such changes would be incorporated before the final sales budget was determined.

Schedule 1 in the Appendix shows a completed sales budget.

STEP 3. INITIAL PREPARATION OF OTHER BUDGET COMPONENTS

The budget guidelines prepared by top management, together with the sales plan, are disseminated down through the successive levels in the organization. Managers at each level may add other, more detailed, information for the guidance of their subordinates. When the guidelines arrive at the lowest responsibility centers, the managers of these responsibility centers prepare the budget plans for the items within their sphere of responsibility, working within the constraints specified in the guidelines.

Planning expenses. The manager of a responsibility center makes an estimate of each significant element of expense in his responsibility center. These estimates are made by a combination of analytical techniques and judgment. Techniques for separating the variable and fixed components of cost that were discussed in Chapter 6 are widely used for this purpose. Schedules 3, 5, 6, 9, and 10 in the Appendix reflect such estimates.

Whenever feasible, estimates for physical quantities and for unit prices should be shown separately in order to facilitate the subsequent analysis of performance; that is, material cost is preferably shown as number of pounds times cents per pound, labor costs as number of hours times the hourly wage rate, and so on. The basic reason for such a separation is that different factors, and often different managers, are responsible for changes in the quantity component and the price component, respectively. For example, the purchasing officer is responsible for the cost per pound of raw material purchased, but the factory foreman is responsible for the quantity of raw material used. For similar reasons, the estimates are broken down by product lines, by significant items of cost, and in other ways that will facilitate subsequent analysis of actual performance as compared with the budgeted amounts.

Usually, the most recent data on actual costs is used as a starting point in making the expense estimates. The guidelines may provide specific instructions as to the permitted changes that can be made from current expenses, such as, "Assume a 3 percent price increase for purchased materials and services." In addition to following these instructions, the manager who prepares the budget, that is, the budgetee, expresses his judgment as to the behavior of costs not covered by the instructions.

STEP 4. NEGOTIATION

Now comes the crucial stage in the process from a control standpoint, the negotiation[1] between the budgetee and his superior. The value of the budget as a plan of what is to happen, as a motivating device, and

---

[1] In a perceptive study, Dr. G. Hofstede describes this process as a "game"; see *The Game of Budget Control* (Assen, The Netherlands: Van Gorcum & Co., N.V., 1967). A negotiation is a game, in the formal sense.

as a standard against which actual performance will be measured, depends largely on how skillfully this negotiation is conducted.

Several recent studies have shown that the budget is more effective as a motivating device when it represents a tight, but attainable, goal. If it is too tight, it leads to frustration; if it is too loose, it leads to complacency. The budgetee and his superior therefore seek to arrive at this desirable middle ground.[2]

As did the budgetee, the superior usually must take the current level of expense as his starting point in the negotiations, modifying this according to his perception of how satisfactory the current level is. He simply does not have enough time during the budget review to re-examine each of the elements of expense so as to insure that the budgetee's estimates are optimum. It is a fact, however, that the operation of Parkinson's First Law ("costs tend to increase regardless of the amount of work done") strongly suggests that costs do drift out of line over a period of time, and that the current level of spending may therefore be too high. One way of addressing this problem is to make an arbitrary cut, say 5 percent, in the budget estimates, but this has the weakness of any arbitrary action; it affects the efficient and the inefficient managers alike. Furthermore, if budgetees know that an arbitrary cut is going to be made, they can counter it by padding their original estimates by a corresponding amount.

There are more reasonable tactics for keeping costs in line during the negotiating process. The superior should require a full explanation of any proposed cost increases. He attempts to find reasons why costs may be expected to decrease, such as a decrease in the work load of the responsibility center or an increase in productivity resulting from the installation of new equipment or a new method, recognizing that these prospective decreases may not be voluntarily disclosed by the budgetee. Some managements, knowing that overall productivity in America increases by approximately 3 percent per year, expect similar productivity gains within their companies. As a rough rule of thumb, some companies expect productivity gains to offset inflationary price increases, and consequently expect total costs at a given volume level to show a net change of zero from one year to the next.

For his part, the budgetee defends his estimates. He justifies proposed cost increases by explaining their underlying causes, such as additional work that he is expected to do, the effect of inflation, the need for better quality output, and so on.

---

[2] The policy of some companies is to set the responsibility budget slightly tighter than the performance that reasonably can be expected. When this is done, a "budget reserve" is added to the responsibility budget so as to reduce the total company profit to the amount that reasonably can be expected. Individual managers are, of course, not told what the amount of this reserve is. If no such reserve were provided, the responsibility budget would not match the program budget.

The commitment. The end product of the negotiation process is an agreement which represents an implicit commitment by each party, the budgetee and his superior. By the act of agreeing to the budget estimates, the budgetee says to his superior, in effect: "I can and will operate my responsibility center in accordance with the plan described in this budget." By approving the budget estimates, the superior says to the budgetee, in effect: "If you operate your responsibility center in accordance with this plan, you will do what we consider to be a good job." Both of these statements contain the implicit qualification of "subject to adjustment for unanticipated changes in circumstances" since both parties recognize that actual events, such as changes in price levels and in general business conditions, may not correspond to those assumed when the budget was prepared and that these changes may affect the plans set forth in the budget. In judging whether the commitment is in fact being accomplished as the year progresses, management must take these changes into account.

The nature of the commitment, both as to individual elements of expense and as to the total expense of the responsibility center, may be one of three types: (1) it may represent a ceiling (e.g., "not more than \$X should be spent for books and periodicals"); (2) it may represent a floor (e.g., "at least \$Y should be spent for employee training"); or (3) it may represent a guide (e.g., "approximately \$Z should be spent for overtime"). Often, the individual items are not explicitly identified as to which of these three categories they belong in, but it is obviously important that the two parties have a clear understanding as to which item belongs in which category.

STEP 5. COORDINATION AND REVIEW

The negotiation process is repeated at successively higher levels of responsibility centers in the organizational hierarchy, up to the very top. Negotiations at higher levels may, of course, result in changes in the detailed budgets that have been agreed to at lower level. If these changes are significant, the budget should be recycled back down the organizational hierarchy for revision. If, however, the guidelines are carefully described, and if the budget process is well understood and well conducted by those who participate in it, such recycling ordinarily is not necessary. In the successive stages of negotiation, the person who has the role of superior at one level becomes the budgetee at the next higher level. Since he is well aware of this fact, he is strongly motivated to negotiate budgets with his budgetees that he can then defend successfully with his superiors, for if his superior demonstrates that the proposed budget is too loose, this is a reflection on the budgetee's ability as a manager and as a negotiator.

As the individual budgets move up the organizational hierarchy in the negotiation and review process, they are also examined in relationship to one another, and this examination may reveal aspects of the plan that are out of balance. If so, certain of the underlying budgets may need to be changed. Major unresolved problems are submitted to the budget committee for resolution. The individual responsibility center budgets may also reveal the need to change planned amounts in the program budget, and these changes may in turn disclose that parts of the program appear to be out of balance. Various summary documents, especially the budgeted income statement, the budgeted balance sheet, and the cash-flow budget, are also prepared during this step.

STEPS 6 AND 7. FINAL APPROVAL AND DISTRIBUTION

Just prior to the beginning of the budget year, the proposed budget is submitted to top management for approval. If the guidelines have been properly set and adhered to, the proposed budget should contain no great surprises to top management. This approval is by no means perfunctory, however, for it signifies the official agreement of top management to the proposed plans for the year. The chief executive officer therefore usually spends considerable time discussing the budget with each of the managers who reports to him. After top management approves the budget, it is submitted to the board of directors for final approval.

The approved budget is then transmitted down through the organization. It constitutes authority to carry out the plans specified therein.

VARIATIONS IN PRACTICE

The preceding is a generalized description of the budget process. Not all companies prepare a budget for each responsibility center, and some companies that do develop a comprehensive budget treat the process more casually than is implied in the above description. Some companies formulate their budgets in a process that is essentially the reverse of that described; that is, instead of having budget estimates originate at the lowest responsibility centers, the budget is prepared by a high-level staff, blessed by top management, and then transmitted down to the organization. This **imposed budget** is an unsatisfactory motivating device, and it is therefore not widely used.

REVISIONS

The budget is formulated in accordance with certain assumptions as to conditions that will prevail during the budget year. Actual conditions during the year will never be exactly the same as those assumed, and the differences may be significant. The question then arises as to whether or not the budget should be revised so that it will reflect what is now known about current conditions. There is considerable difference of opinion on this question.

Those who favor revising the budget point out that the budget is supposed to reflect the plan in accordance with which the company is operating, and that when the plan has to be changed because of changing conditions, the budget should reflect these changes. If the budget is not revised, it is no longer a statement of plans, they maintain.

The opponents of revising the budget argue that the process of revision not only is time consuming but also may obscure the goals that the company originally intended to achieve and the reasons for departures from these goals, especially since a revision may reflect the budgetee's skill in negotiating a change, rather than one that reflects an actual change in the underlying assumed conditions. Since revisions for spurious reasons destroy the credibility of the budget, critics refer to such a revised budget as a "rubber standard." Many companies therefore do not revise their budgets during the year, and take account of changes in conditions when they analyze the difference between actual and budgeted performance.

Other companies solve this problem by having two budgets: a **baseline** budget set at the beginning of the year, and a **current budget** reflecting the best current estimate of revenue and expenses. A comparison of actual performance with the baseline performance shows the extent of deviation from the original plan, and a comparison of the current budget with the baseline budget shows how much of this deviation is attributable to changes in current conditions from those originally assumed.

Some managers use current budgets in lieu of reports of actual performance. Such a manager says: "I am not interested in actual costs because I literally can't do anything to control them; they have already happened. What I am interested in is how we now think we are going to come out, compared with how we originally planned to come out, as expressed in the baseline budget. If this comparison is not satisfactory, I can at least investigate what can be done to bring the situation back into line." As someone has said, "We should all be concerned about the future because we will have to spend the rest of our lives there."

The cash budget   The operating budget is usually prepared in terms of revenues and expenses. For financial planning purposes, it must be translated into terms of cash inflows and cash outflows. This translation results in the **cash budget.** The financial manager uses the cash budget to make plans to insure that the company has enough, but not too much, cash on hand during the year ahead.

There are two approaches to the preparation of a cash budget:

1. Start with the budgeted balance sheet and income statements, and adjust the amounts thereon to reflect the planned sources and uses of cash. This procedure is substantially the same as that described for the statement of changes on financial position in Chapter 15 of *Fundamentals of Financial Accounting,* except that the data are estimates of the future rather than historical. Its preparation is therefore not described again here.

2. Analyze those plans having cash-flow implications to estimate each of the sources and uses of cash. This approach as shown in Schedule 11 of the Appendix, and subordinate Schedules 11a and 11b. Some points about this approach are briefly described below.

Collection of accounts receivable is estimated by applying a "lag" factor to estimated sales or shipments. This factor may be based simply on the assumption that the cash from this month's sales will be collected next month; or there may be a more elaborate assumption. Schedule 11a is constructed on the assumption that 50 percent of a month's sales are collected in the current month, less a cash discount of 1 percent; that 49.5 percent of the month's receivables are collected in the following month; and that 0.5 percent of the month's receivables are never collected.

The estimated amount and timing of *raw materials purchases* is obtained from the materials purchases budget (Schedule 4). In Schedule 11b the assumption is made that all purchases will be paid for in the month in which they are received; more commonly, a lag factor, similar to that described above, would be applied to the amount of purchases in a given month. This lag factor is the time interval that ordinarily elapses between the receipt of material and the payment of the invoice.

Other operating expenses are often taken directly from the expense budget, since the timing of cash disbursements is likely to correspond closely to the incurrence of the expense. Depreciation and other items of expense not requiring cash disbursements in the current month are excluded. In Schedule 11b, these noncash items include (in addition to depreciation) insurance, taxes, and interest expense because these expenses will be paid for in a different month than that for which the budget illustrated here is prepared. Bad debt expense is also deducted because it does not represent a cash outlay. Capital expenditures are also shown as an outlay, with amounts taken from the capital budget.

Schedule 11 shows how cash plans are made. The company desires a minimum cash balance of $50,000 as a cushion against unforeseen needs. From the budgeted cash receipts and cash disbursements, a calculation is made of whether the budgeted cash balance exceeds or falls below this minimum. In January and February the budgeted cash balance exceeds the minimum. In this company no action is planned, but in other situations, the company might well decide to invest the extra cash in marketable securities. In March, the budget indicates a cash deficiency of $87,916; consequently, plans are made to borrow $90,000 to offset this deficiency. The lower portion of the cash budget therefore shows the company's financing plans.

The capital
expenditure
budget

The **capital expenditure budget** is essentially a list of what management believes to be worthwhile projects for the acquisition of new plant and equipment together with the estimated cost of each such capital investment project, and the timing of capital expenditures. Proposals for capital expenditure projects may originate anywhere in the organization. The capital expenditure budget is usually prepared separately from the operating budget, and in many companies it is prepared at a different time and cleared through a capital appropriations committee that is separate from the budget committee. Since capital acquisitions often require several years to complete and since the important ones usually are associated with new programs, the capital expenditure budget can just as well be classified as part of the programming process rather than as part of the annual budgeting process.

In the capital expenditure budget, individual projects are often classified by purposes such as the following:

1. Cost reduction and replacement.
2. Expansion and improvement of existing product lines.
3. New products.
4. Health and safety.
5. Other.

Proposals in the first two categories usually are susceptible to an economic analysis in which the net present value can be estimated. Some proposals for the addition of new products can also be substantiated by an economic analysis, although in a great many situations the estimate of sales of the new product is pretty much a guess. Proposals in the other categories usually cannot be sufficiently quantified so that an economic analysis is feasible.

Each proposed capital investment, except those for minor amounts, is accompanied by a justification. For some projects, the net present value or other measure of desirability can be estimated by methods described in Chapters 8 and 9. Other projects, such as the construction of a new office building or remodeling of employee recreation rooms, are justified on the basis of improved morale, safety, appearance, convenience, or other subjective grounds. A lump sum usually is included in the capital budget to provide for capital expenditure projects that are not large enough to warrant individual consideration by top management.

As proposals for capital expenditures come up through the organization, they are screened at various levels, and only the sufficiently attractive ones flow up to the top and appear in the final capital expenditure budget. On this document, they are often arranged in what is believed to be the order of desirability. Estimated expenditures are shown by years, or by quarters, so that the cash required in each time period can be determined. At the final review meeting, which is usually at the board-of-director level, not only are the individual projects discussed but also the total amount requested on the budget is compared with estimated funds available. Many apparently worthwhile projects may not be approved, simply because the funds are not available.

Approval of the capital budget usually means approval of the projects *in principle,* but does not constitute final authority to proceed with them. For this authority, a specific authorization request is prepared for the project, spelling out the proposal in more detail, perhaps with firm bids or price quotations on the new assets. These **authorization requests** are approved at various levels in the organization, depending on their size and character. For example, each foreman may be authorized to buy production tools or similar items costing not more than $100 each, provided his total for the year does not exceed $1,000; and at the other extreme, all projects costing more than $500,000 and all projects for new products, whatever their cost, may require approval of the board of directors. In between, there is a scale of amounts that various echelons in the organization may authorize without the approval of their superiors.

An increasing number of companies use procedures to follow up on capital expenditures. These include both checks on the spending itself and also an appraisal, perhaps a year or more after the project is completed, as to how well the estimates of cost and revenue actually turned out.

Summary

Budgets are used as a device for making and coordinating plans, for communicating these plans to those who are responsible for carrying them out, for motivating managers at all levels, and as a standard with which actual performance subsequently can be compared. In a comprehensive budget system, there is a package of interrelated budgets, including the operating budget, the variable budget, the cash budget, the capital expenditure budget, and perhaps others.

The operating budget is prepared within the context of basic policies and plans that have already been decided upon in the programming process. The principal steps are as follows: (1) dissemination of guidelines stating the overall plans and policies and other assumptions and constraints that are to be observed in the preparation of budget estimates; (2) preparation of the sales plan; (3) preparation of other estimates by the managers of responsibility centers, assisted by, but not dominated by, the budget staff; (4) negotiation of an agreed budget between the budgetee and his superior, which gives rise to a bilateral commitment by these parties; (5) coordination and review as these initial plans move up the organizational chain of command; (6) approval by top management and the board of directors; and (7) dissemination of the approved budget back down through the organization.

The *cash budget* translates revenues and expenses into cash receipts (inflows) and disbursements (outflows) and thus facilitates financial planning.

The *capital expenditure budget* is a price list of presumably worthwhile projects for the acquisition of new capital assets. Often it is prepared separately from the operating budget. Approval of the capital expenditure budget constitutes only approval in principle, for a subsequent authorization is usually required before work on the project can begin.

Appendix   THE MECHANICS OF BUDGET PREPARATION*

Following is a detailed description of the mechanics involved in preparing a budget. It is presented primarily to illustrate the relationships among the various parts. It should be emphasized that this example deals with mechanics only. It does not describe the judgmental process that led to the assumptions on which the budget was based, nor the process of negotiation that led to approval of the estimates. In order to save space, only the data for three months are shown. In actuality, the budget was prepared for the first three months and for each of the other three quarters of the year. The company involved is the Lake Erie Table Company, Inc.

The Lake Erie Table Company (LET) employs 128 people (21 in sales, 24 in administration, and 83 in production). Exhibit 11–1 is the company's organization chart. The LET Company manufactures and sells directly to retailers (department stores, discount houses, furniture stores) along the eastern seaboard, two folding card tables, the Royal and Superior models. The Royal and Superior card tables have suggested retail prices of $24.95 and $18.95, respectively, and are sold to the retailers at $15.00 and $11.40, respectively, which is approximately 40 percent off of the retail price. Both tables have tubular steel frames with a baked enamel finish. Both tops are made of plywood covered with vinyl. Both tables come in forest green, desert tan, or fruitwood color. Each table requires the same amount of direct labor and factory overhead to manufacture. Although the Royal has only slightly more material in it, the company can sell the Royal to retailers for $3.60 more than the Superior.

Exhibit 11–2 shows the relationships among the various schedules that constitute the budget. The responsibility for the preparation of the various schedules parallels the responsibility structure of the organization as defined in the organization chart.

---

* Based on material developed by Professor Thomas E. Lynch, Columbia University. Used by permission.

Exhibits 11–3 through 11–7 contain basic data and calculations that are part of the budget preparation.

The master budget is made up of the following schedules:

Schedule 1:   The *sales budget* is the responsibility of the sales vice president. The sales budget is the foundation of all other budgets since they are related partially or completely to the budgeted sales volume. The sales budget is influenced by the planned unit sales price and the planned advertising and selling expenses. The planned unit sales prices are decided by top management.

Schedule 2:   The *production budget* and all of the budgets supporting it (Schedules 3 through 6) are the responsibility of the production vice president. The production budget is prepared after the sales budget and inventory budget (Schedule 7).

Schedule 3:   The *materials usage budget* is prepared by the supervisors of the machining and assembly departments. The machining department supervisor prepares the estimates for materials A and B, and the assembly department supervisor prepares the estimates for materials C and D.

Schedule 4:   The *materials purchase budget* is the responsibility of the purchasing manager who in this case is also the production vice president. It is his responsibility to provide the planned unit purchase price for raw materials.

Schedule 5:   The *direct labor budget* is the responsibility of the managers of the machining and assembly departments. They prepare estimates of their departments' total direct labor hours. The budgeted rate per hour is prepared by the industrial relations department.

Schedule 6:   The *factory overhead budget* is also the responsibility of the production department managers. The production and direct labor budgets provide the basis for projecting the planned volume of work for the machining and assembly departments, which in turn is used in planning the volume of work in the maintenance and general factory overhead departments.

Schedule 7:   The *inventory budget* reflects the planned inventory policy of top management and is prepared by the budget director. The company uses first-in, first-out cost flow for all inventories.

Schedule 8:   The budget director uses all of the preceding budgets to prepare the *cost of goods sold budget.*

Schedule 9:   Each district sales manager prepares his own *selling expense budget* concurrently with his sales budget. The sales vice president prepares the general sales overhead budget and approves the district sales managers' budgets.

Schedule 10:   The controller and industrial relations manager prepare their departmental budgets and the administrative vice president

prepares the general *administrative budget* and approves the accounting and industrial relations budgets.

Schedule 11, 11a, and 11b: The chief financial officer, in this case the
controller, is responsible for preparing the *cash budget.* Note that
some expenses such as insurance, taxes, and interest do not require
an immediate cash outlay and some expenses such as depreciation
and bad debts expense never require a cash outlay.

Schedules 12 and 13:   The budgeted *income statement* and *balance
sheet* are prepared by the budget director.

Capital budget.   The capital budget is not illustrated. Note, however,
that the company's planned capital expenditures have been included in
the cash budget, Schedule 11. This $300,000 outlay represents that
portion of the long-range capital spending budget that will materialize
in March.

The completed budget is discussed with the company president; after
he approves it, he presents it to the board of directors for their
approval.

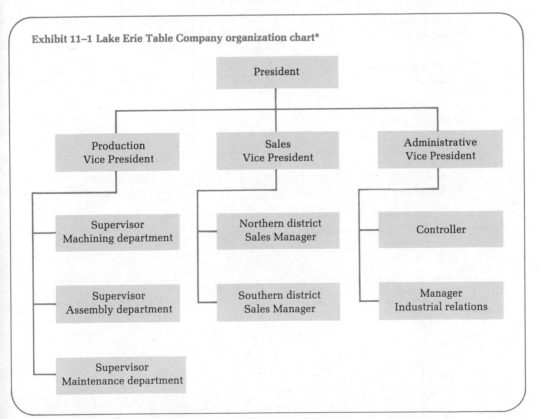

Exhibit 11–1 Lake Erie Table Company organization chart*

* *Note:* Each box represents one of the 11 responsibility centers of the company.

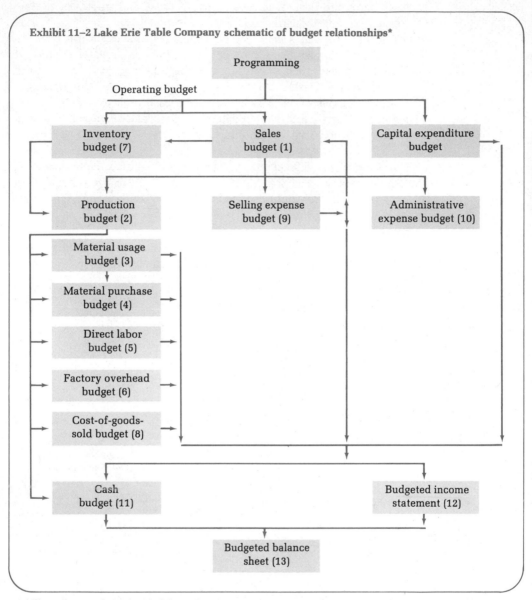

Exhibit 11–2 Lake Erie Table Company schematic of budget relationships*

* Figures in parentheses are schedule numbers.
Note: This exhibit should be examined carefully and then Schedules 1 through 13 should be examined also and integrated into this framework.

Exhibit 11–3

LAKE ERIE TABLE COMPANY
Bill of Material
Royal and Superior Folding Card Tables*

Part Identifi-cation	Description	Raw Material Required Royal	Superior
A	Tubular steel legs: 1 in. diameter × 30 in. length...	10 ft.	
	1 in. diameter × 27 in. length...		9 ft.
B	Plywood top: ½ in. × 41 in. diameter............	12 sq. ft.	
	½ in. × 3 sq. ft...................		9 sq. ft.
C	Vinyl top: 41 in. diameter......................	12 sq. ft.	
	3 sq. ft............................		9 sq. ft.
D	Assembly kit (1 in. flat steel edging, bolts, hinges, cardboard packing)..........................	1	1

* The *Royal* folding card table is a *round* table with a 41 in. diameter and is 30 in. high. The *Superior* folding card table is a 36 in. *square* table and is 27 in. high. Both tables use the same materials, but the Royal uses slightly more material. Both tables require the same amount of direct labor to manufacture.

Exhibit 11–4

LAKE ERIE TABLE COMPANY
Cost Sheet

			Estimated Cost per Table	
			Royal	Superior
Machining Department				
	Quantity	Price		
Materials:				
A—Steel legs..................	10 ft.	$0.12	$1.20	
	9 ft.	0.12		$1.08
B—Plywood top..............	12 sq. ft.	0.10	1.20	
	9 sq. ft.	0.10		0.90
	Time	Rate		
Direct labor:				
Each table..................	9 min.	$6.00	0.90	0.90
	DLD	Budgeted Rate		
Budgeted factory overhead (see Exhibit 11–5):				
Variable rate per DLD*.......	0.90	0.51	0.46	0.46
Fixed rate per DLD..........	0.90	0.46	0.414	0.414
Machining cost per unit...			$4.194	$3.754
Assembly Department				
	Quantity	Price		
Materials:				
C—Vinyl top................	12 sq. ft.	$0.02	$0.24	
Vinyl top................	9 sq. ft.	0.02		$0.18
D—Assembly kit............	1	1.00	1.00	1.00
Direct labor:				
Each table..................	12 min.	$5.00	1.00	1.00
	DLD	Budgeted Rate		
Budgeted factory overhead (see Exhibit 11–6):				
Variable rate per DLD........	1.00	0.561	0.561	0.561
Fixed rate per DLD..........	1.00	0.472	0.472	0.472
Assembly cost per unit....			$3.273	$3.213
Total cost per unit to manufacture.....................			$7.447	$6.967

* Direct labor dollar.

Exhibit 11–5

LAKE ERIE TABLE COMPANY
Machining Department Cost Budget
For the Quarter Ending March 31, 1975

Volume: $77,670 direct labor dollars (DLD); 12,945 direct labor hours (DLH)
          (Schedule 5)

	Royal	*Superior*
Material and labor estimates (Exhibit 11–4):		
Material...	$2.40	$1.98
Labor time..	9 min.	9 min.
Labor rate per hour............................	$6.00	$6.00

	Fixed per Quarter	*Variable per DLD*
Variable budget for overhead costs (Schedule 6):		
Supervision......................................	$ 9,900	. . .
Wages...	1,500	$0.13
Factory supplies................................	. . .	0.11
Power..	. . .	0.10
Depreciation.....................................	3,600	. . .
Insurance and taxes on employees...................	1,200	0.15
Maintenance (F = 240 hrs. × $6.442; V = 258 hrs. × $6.442 = $1,662 ÷ $77,670 SDLD = $0.02) (see Exhibit 11–7)........................	1,546	0.02
General factory overhead, allocated (see Exhibit 11–7)................................	17,934	. . .
	$35,680	
($35,680 ÷ $77,670 DLD = $0.46 per DLD).........	$0.46	$0.51
Overhead rate per DLD (= $0.46 + $0.51)............		$0.97

Exhibit 11–6

LAKE ERIE TABLE COMPANY
Assembly Department Cost Budget
For the Quarter Ending March 31, 1975

Volume: $86,300 direct labor dollars (DLD); 17,260 direct labor hours (DLH) (Schedule 5)

	Royal	*Superior*
Material and labor estimates (Exhibit 11–4):		
Material...	$1.24	$1.18
Labor time......................................	12 min.	12 min.
Labor rate per hour.............................	$5.00	$5.00

	Fixed per Quarter	*Variable per DLD*
Variable budget for overhead costs (Schedule 6):		
Supervision.....................................	$14,400	. . .
Wages..	2,100	$0.17
Factory supplies................................	. . .	0.10
Power..	. . .	0.12
Depreciation....................................	3,000	. . .
Insurance and taxes on employees.................	1,800	0.15
Maintenance (F = 240 hrs. × $6.442; V = 286 × $6.442 = $1,842 ÷ $86,300 SDLD = $0.021) (see Exhibit 11–7)......................	1,546	0.021
General factory overhead, allocated (see Exhibit 11–7).................................	17,934	. . .
	$40,780	
($40,780 ÷ $86,300 DLD = $0.472 per DLD)........	$ 0.472	$0.561
Overhead rate per DLD (= $0.472 + $0.561).........		$1.033

Exhibit 11–7

LAKE ERIE TABLE COMPANY
Computation of Budget Factory Overhead Rate
For the Quarter Ending March 31, 1975

	Total	*Service Departments*		*Producing Departments*	
		Gen. Fact. Over-head	*Mainte-nance*	*Ma-chining*	*As-sembly*
Total factory overhead.......	$164,625	$36,600	$5,865	$54,258	$67,902
Allocations*:					
1. General factory over-head.................		36,600	732	17,934	17,934
2. Maintenance.........			$6,597	3,207	3,390
Total..............	$164,625			$75,399	$89,226
Direct labor dollars (DLD) from Schedule 5........				$77,670	$86,300
Budgeted factory overhead rate per DLD...........				$0.9708	$ 1.034
Variable and fixed portions of factory overhead rate:					
Variable.................				$ 0.51	$ 0.561
Fixed....................				0.46	0.472
Total................				$ .97	$ 1.033

* Allocation bases:
1. Relative floor space: 2 percent for maintenance and 49 percent each for machining and assembly.
2. Planned direct repair hours:
   Machining: 80 hours per month (fixed) plus one hour for every 50 direct labor hours (from Schedule 5) equals 258 variable hours for a total of 498 repair hours.
   Assembly: 80 hours per month (fixed) plus one hour for every 50 direct labor hours (from Schedule 5) equals 286 variable hours for a total of 526 repair hours.

$$\frac{\$6,597}{1,024 \text{ hrs.}} = \$6.442 \text{ per planned repair hour.}$$

Schedule 1

LAKE ERIE TABLE COMPANY
Sales Budget
For the Quarter Ending March 31, 1975

District and Product	Unit Price	January Units	January Amount	February Units	February Amount	March Units	March Amount	Quarter Total Units	Quarter Total Amount
Northern:									
Royal.........	$15.00	6,000	$ 90,000	6,000	$ 90,000	6,100	$ 91,500	18,100	$ 271,500
Sup..........	$11.40	10,000	114,000	10,000	114,000	10,300	117,420	30,300	345,420
Total			$204,000		$204,000		$208,920		$ 616,920
Southern:									
Royal.........	$15.00	4,000	$ 60,000	4,000	$ 60,000	4,000	$ 60,000	12,000	$ 180,000
Sup..........	$11.40	8,000	91,200	8,000	91,200	8,200	93,480	24,200	275,880
Total			$151,200		$151,200		$153,480		$ 455,880
Totals:									
Royal.........	$15.00	10,000	$150,000	10,000	$150,000	10,100	$151,500	30,100	$ 451,500
Sup..........	$11.40	18,000	205,200	18,000	205,200	18,500	210,900	54,500	621,300
		28,000	$355,200	28,000	$355,200	28,600	$362,400	84,600	$1,072.800

Estimated sales for April, which are necessary for the production budget, are:

	April Sales in Units	
	Royal	*Superior*
Northern district.........................	6,200	10,400
Southern district.........................	4,200	8,200
	10,400	18,600

Schedule 2

LAKE ERIE TABLE COMPANY
Production Budget (Units)
For the Quarter Ending March 31, 1975

Product	January	February	March	Quarter Total	April
Royal:					
Units to be sold*...............	10,000	10,000	10,100	30,100	10,400
Add: Planned ending inventory†...	10,000	10,100	10,400	30,500	10,400
Total.....................	20,000	20,100	20,500	60,600	20,800
Less: Planned beginning inventory‡.........................	9,800	10,000	10,100	29,900	10,400
Units to be produced............	10,200	10,100	10,400	30,700	10,400
Superior:					
Units to be sold*...............	18,000	18,000	18,500	54,500	18,600
Add: Planned ending inventory† ..	18,000	18,500	18,600	55,100	18,600
Total.....................	36,000	36,500	37,100	109,600	37,200
Less: Planned beginning inventory‡.........................	17,500	18,000	18,500	54,000	18,600
Units to be produced...........	18,500	18,500	18,600	55,600	18,600
Quarter total.....................	28,700	28,600	29,000	86,300	29,000

* From Schedule 1.
† At the end of any month the company wishes to maintain a basic inventory of the next month's sales.
‡ From Schedule 7.

Schedule 3

<hr>

LAKE ERIE TABLE COMPANY
Materials Usage Budget (Units)
For the Quarter Ending March 31, 1975

	Royal			*Superior*			*Total*		
Material and Month	*Pro- duction Planned**	*Units Re- quired†*	*Units Needed for Pro- duction*	*Pro- duction Planned**	*Units Re- quired†*	*Units Needed for Pro- duction*	*Units Needed for Pro- duction*	*Unit Cost†*	*Total Material Cost*
A									
January......	10,200	10	102,000	18,500	9	166,500	268,500	$0.12	$32,220
February.....	10,100	10	101,000	18,500	9	166,500	267,500	0.12	32,100
March.......	10,400	10	104,000	18,600	9	167,400	271,400	0.12	32,568
Total........	30,700		307,000	55,600		500,400	807,400		$96,888
B									
January......	10,200	12	122,400	18,500	9	166,500	288,900	0.10	$28,890
February.....	10,100	12	121,200	18,500	9	166,500	287,700	0.10	28,770
March.......	10,400	12	124,800	18,600	9	167,400	292,200	0.10	29,220
Total........	30,700		368,400	55,600		500,400	868,800		$86,880
C									
January......	10,200	12	122,400	18,500	9	166,500	288,900	0.02	$ 5,778
February.....	10,100	12	121,200	18,500	9	166,500	287,700	0.02	5,754
March........	10,400	12	124,800	18,600	9	167,400	292,200	0.02	5,844
Total........	30,700		368,400	55,600		500,400	868,800		$17,376
D									
January......	10,200	1	10,200	18,500	1	18,500	28,700	1.00	$28,700
February.....	10,100	1	10,100	18,500	1	18,500	28,600	1.00	28,600
March........	10,400	1	10,400	18,600	1	18,600	29,000	1.00	29,000
Total........	30,700		30,700	55,600		55,600	86,300		$86,300

Quarter Totals	*A*	*B*	*C*	*D*	*Total*
January......	$32,220	$28,890	$ 5,778	$28,700	$ 95,588
February.....	32,100	28,770	5,754	28,600	95,224
March.......	32,568	29,220	5,844	29,000	96,632
Total........	$96,888	$86,880	$17,376	$86,300	$287,444

* From Schedule 2.
† From Exhibit 11–3.

Schedule 4

LAKE ERIE TABLE COMPANY
Materials Purchases Budget (Units)
For the Quarter Ending March 31, 1975

Material and Month	Units Needed for Production*	Add Ending Inventory†	Total Units Required	Less Beginning Inventory	Purchases Units	Unit Cost	Total Cost
A							
January	268,500	267,500	536,000	268,500	267,500	$0.12	$32,100
February	267,500	271,400	538,900	267,500	271,400	0.12	32,568
March	271,400	271,400	542,800	271,400	271,400	0.12	32,568
Total	807,400	810,300	1,617,700	807,400	810,300		$97,236
B							
January	288,900	287,700	576,600	288,900	287,700	0.10	$28,770
February	287,700	292,200	579,900	287,700	292,200	0.10	29,220
March	292,200	292,200	584,400	292,200	292,200	0.10	29,220
Total	868,800	872,100	1,740,900	868,800	872,100		$87,210
C							
January	288,900	287,700	576,600	288,900	287,700	0.02	$ 5,754
February	287,700	292,200	579,900	287,700	292,200	0.02	5,844
March	292,200	292,200	584,400	292,200	292,200	0.02	5,844
Total	868,800	872,100	1,740,900	868,800	872,100		$17,442
D							
January	28,700	28,600	57,300	28,000	29,300	1.00	$29,300
February	28,600	29,000	57,600	28,600	29,000	1.00	29,000
March	29,000	29,000	58,000	29,000	29,000	1.00	29,000
Total	86,300	86,600	172,900	85,600	87,300		$87,300

Quarter Totals	A	B	C	D	Total
January	$32,100	$28,770	$ 5,754	$29,300	$ 95,924
February	32,568	29,220	5,844	29,000	96,632
March	32,568	29,220	5,844	29,000	96,632
	$97,236	$87,210	$17,442	$87,300	$289,188

* From Schedule 3.
† At the end of any month the company wishes to maintain a basic inventory of the next month's units needed for production.

Schedule 5

LAKE ERIE TABLE COMPANY
Direct Labor Budget
For the Quarter Ending March 31, 1975

Month and Dept.	*Royal* Units to Be Produced	Hours per Unit	Total Hours	*Superior* Units to Be Produced	Hours per Unit	Total Hours	*Total* Dept. Hours	Rate per Hour	Labor Cost
Jan.									
Machining.......	10,200	0.15	1,530	18,500	0.15	2,775	4,305	$6.00	$ 25,830
Assembly........	10,200	0.20	2,040	18,500	0.20	3,700	5,740	5.00	28,700
			3,570			6,475	10,045		$ 54,530
Feb.									
Machining.......	10,100	0.15	1,515	18,500	0.15	2,775	4,290	6.00	$ 25,740
Assembly........	10,100	0.20	2,020	18,500	0.20	3,700	5,720	5.00	28,600
			3,535			6,475	10,010		$ 54,340
Mar.									
Machining.......	10,400	0.15	1,560	18,600	0.15	2,790	4,350	6.00	$ 26,100
Assembly........	10,400	0.20	2,080	18,600	0.20	3,720	5,800	5.00	29,000
			3,640			6,510	10,150		$ 55,100
Quarter Totals									
Machining.......	30,700	0.15	4,605	55,600	0.15	8,340	12,945	6.00	$ 77,670
Assembly........	30,700	0.20	6,140	55,600	0.20	11,120	17,260	5.00	86,300
			10,745			19,460	30,205		$163,970

Schedule 6

LAKE ERIE TABLE COMPANY
Factory Overhead Budget
For the Quarter Ending March 31, 1975

Department and Account	Variable Budget Formula	January (DLD, $25,830)*	February (DLD, $25,740)	March (DLD, $26,100)	Total (DLD, $77,670)
Machining:					
Supervisory salaries	$3,300 + $ 0 per DLD	$ 3,300	$ 3,300	$ 3,300	$ 9,900
Indirect labor	500 + 0.13	3,858	3,846	3,893	11,597
Factory supplies	0 + 0.11	2,841	2,831	2,871	8,543
Power	0 + 0.10	2,583	2,574	2,610	7,767
Depreciation	1,200 + 0	1,200	1,200	1,200	3,600
Employee benefits	400 + 0.15	4,275	4,261	4,315	12,851
Total	$5,400 + $0.49 per DLD	$18,057	$18,012	$18,189	$ 54,258
Assembly:		(DLD, $28,700)	(DLD, $28,600)	(DLD, $29,000)	(DLD, $86,300)
Supervisory salaries	$4,800 + $ 0 per DLD	$ 4,800	$ 4,800	$ 4,800	$ 14,400
Indirect labor	700 + 0.17	5,579	5,562	5,630	16,771
Factory supplies	0 + 0.10	2,870	2,860	2,900	8,630
Power	0 + 0.12	3,444	3,432	3,480	10,356
Depreciation	1,000 + 0	1,000	1,000	1,000	3,000
Employee benefits	600 + 0.15	4,905	4,890	4,950	14,745
Total	$7,100 + $0.54 per DLD	$22,598	$22,544	$22,760	$67,902
Maintenance:		(DRH, 341)†	(DRH, 340)	(DRH, 343)	(DRH, 1,024)
Supervisory salaries	$1,100 + $ 0 per DRH	$ 1,100	$ 1,100	$ 1,100	$ 3,300
Indirect labor	400 + 0	400	400	400	1,200
Factory supplies	0 + 0.60	205	204	206	615
Depreciation	100 + 0	100	100	100	300
Employee benefits	150 + 0	150	150	150	450
Total	$1,750 + $0.60 per DRH	$ 1,955	$ 1,954	$ 1,956	$ 5,865
General factory overhead (all fixed):					
Salaries and wages		$ 6,000	$ 6,000	$ 6,000	$ 18,000
Employee benefits		600	600	600	1,800
Factory supplies		100	100	100	300
Power, water, fuel, and phone		550	550	550	1,650
Insurance and taxes		950	950	950	2,850
Depreciation		4,000	4,000	4,000	12,000
Total		$12,200	$12,200	$12,200	$ 36,600
Total factory overhead		$54,810	$54,710	$55,105	$164,625

* Direct labor dollars.
† Direct repair hours.

Schedule 7

LAKE ERIE TABLE COMPANY
Inventory Budget
For the Quarter Ending March 31, 1975

	January 1, 1975 Beginning Inventory*			*March 31, 1975* Ending Inventory†		
Inventory	*Units*	*Unit Cost*	*Total Amount*	*Units*	*Unit Cost*	*Total Amount*
Raw materials:						
Material A............	268,500	$0.12	$ 32,220	271,400	$0.12	$ 32,568
Material B............	288,900	0.10	28,890	292,200	0.10	29,220
Material C............	288,900	0.02	5,778	292,200	0.02	5,844
Material D............	28,000	1.00	28,000	29,000	1.00	29,000
Total...............			$ 94,888			$ 96,632
Finished goods:						
Royal................	9,800	7.447	$ 72,981	10,400	7.447	$ 77,449
Standard.............	17,500	6.967	121,923	18,600	6.967	129,586
Total..............			$194,904			$207,035
Total inventory..........			$289,792			$303,667

* Estimated amount.
† From Schedules 2 and 4.

Schedule 8

LAKE ERIE TABLE COMPANY
Cost of Goods Sold Budget*
For the Quarter Ending March 31, 1975

Schedule Reference

	Raw materials used:		
7	Inventory, January 1, 1975...................	$ 94,888	
4	Purchases of raw materials...................	289,188	
	Total..................................	$384,076	
7	Less inventory, March 31, 1975................	96,632	
3	Cost of raw materials used......................		$287,444
5	Direct labor................................		163,970
6	Factory expenses.............................		164,625
	Total manufacturing cost..................		$616,039
7	Add beginning finished goods inventory.........		194,904
	Total cost of goods available for sale.........		$810,943
7	Less ending finished goods inventory............		207,035
	Total cost of goods sold...................		$603,908†

* The company does not have any goods in process inventory at the beginning or end of any month. If the company did have goods in process inventories, the beginning goods in process would be added to the total manufacturing costs and the ending goods in process would be deducted from the total manufacturing costs.

† As a check,

	Royal	*Superior*
Total sales for the quarter are...................................	30,100	54,500
Cost to manufacture, from Exhibit 11–5.........................	$7.447	$6.967
Total cost of goods sold is $603,857.............................	$224,155	$379,702

The slight difference of $51 ($603,908–$603,857) is due to rounding.

LAKE ERIE TABLE COMPANY
Selling Expense Budget
For the Quarter Ending March 31, 1975

Department and Account	Variable Budget Formula	January (Sales, $204,000)	February (Sales, $204,000)	March (Sales, $208,920)	Total (Sales, $616,920)
Northern district:					
Salaries and wages	$ 3,300 F + $ 0 per $100 sales	$ 3,300	$ 3,300	$ 3,300	$ 9,900
Sales commissions	0 F + $5.00	10,200	10,200	10,446	30,846
Employee benefits	330 F + 0.50	1,350	1,350	1,375	4,075
Telephone	400 F + 0	400	400	400	1,200
Travel and entertainment	6,375 F + 0	6,375	6,375	6,375	19,125
Office rent and supplies	1,475 F + 0	1,475	1,475	1,475	4,425
Freight-out	120 F + 0.50	1,140	1,140	1,165	3,445
Total	$12,000 F + $6.00 per $100 sales	$24,240	$24,240	$24,536	$ 73,016
Southern district:		(Sales, $151,200)	(Sales, $151,200)	(Sales, $153,480)	(Sales, $455,880)
Salaries and wages	$ 3,100 F + $ 0 per $100 sales	$ 3,100	$ 3,100	$ 3,100	$ 9,300
Sales commissions	0 F + $5.00	7,560	7,560	7,674	22,794
Employee benefits	310 F + 0.50	1,066	1,066	1,077	3,209
Telephone	340 F + 0	340	340	340	1,020
Travel and entertainment	4,875 F + 0	4,875	4,875	4,875	14,625
Office rent and supplies	1,275 F + 0	1,275	1,275	1,275	3,825
Freight-out	100 F + 0.50	856	856	867	2,579
Total	$10,000 F + $6.00 per $100 sales	$19,072	$19,072	$19,208	$ 57,352
General sales overhead (all fixed):					
Salaries and wages		$ 4,600	$ 4,600	$ 4,600	$ 13,800
Employee benefits		460	460	460	1,380
Depreciation—office equipment		140	140	140	420
Advertising		6,000	6,000	6,000	18,000
Telephone		220	220	220	660
Travel and entertainment		400	400	400	1,200
Office supplies		180	180	180	540
Total		$12,000	$12,000	$12,000	$ 36,000
Total selling expenses		$55,312	$55,312	$55,744	$166,368

Schedule 10

LAKE ERIE TABLE COMPANY
Administrative Expense Budget
For the Quarter Ending March 31, 1975

Department and Account	January	February	March	Total
Controller:				
Salaries and wages..............................	$ 9,500	$ 9,500	$ 9,500	$ 28,500
Insurance and taxes on employees..................	950	950	950	2,850
Office supplies.....................................	330	330	330	990
Depreciation—office equipment.....................	220	220	220	660
Loss on bad debts ($0.50 per $100 sales*)...........	1,776	1,776	1,812	5,364
Total.......................................	$12,776	$12,776	$12,812	$ 38,364
Industrial relations:				
Salaries and wages..............................	$ 4,500	$ 4,500	$ 4,500	$ 13,500
Insurance and taxes on employees..................	450	450	450	1,350
Travel and entertainment..........................	200	200	200	200
Office supplies.....................................	50	50	50	150
Depreciation—office equipment.....................	100	100	100	300
Total.......................................	$ 5,300	$ 5,300	$ 5,300	$ 15,900
General administration:				
Salaries and wages..............................	$10,400	$10,400	$10,400	$ 31,200
Insurance and taxes on employees..................	1,040	1,040	1,040	3,120
Office supplies.....................................	200	200	200	600
Depreciation—office equipment and building.........	2,060	2,060	2,060	6,280
Insurance and taxes—real estate and property........	500	500	500	500
Power, fuel, water, and telephone..................	700	700	700	2,100
Interest expense................................	500	500	500	1,500
	$15,400	$15,400	$15,400	$ 46,200
Total administrative expenses..................	$33,476	$33,476	$33,512	$100,464

* This is the only expense that varies with sales, hence, no variable budget is needed for these three responsibility centers.

Schedule 11

LAKE ERIE TABLE COMPANY
Cash Budget
For the Quarter Ending March 31, 1975

Schedule Reference	*Item*	*January*	*February*	*March*
Given	Beginning cash balance.....................	$ 50,000	$118,527	$189,317
11a	Budgeted cash receipts.....................	349,074	351,648	355,212
	Total cash available.......................	$399,074	$470,175	$544,529
	Budgeted cash disbursements:			
11b	Operations............................	$280,547	$280,858	$282,445
	Capital expenditures*...................	0	0	300,000
	Total cash disbursements....................	$280,547	$280,858	$582,445
Given	Minimum cash balance desired...............	50,000	50,000	50,000
	Total cash needed..........................	$330,547	$330,858	$632,445
	Excess (or deficiency)†.....................	$ 68,527	$139,317	$(87,916)
	Financing:			
Given	Bank loan.............................	0	0	90,000
	Bank repayments........................	0	0	0
	Ending cash balance.......................	$118,527	$189,317	$ 52,084

* Estimated cost of new equipment to be purchased in March.
† Minimum cash balance desired plus any excess or less any deficiency and plus any loans less any repayments.

Schedule 11a

LAKE ERIE TABLE COMPANY
Schedule of Cash Receipts and Ending Balances in Accounts Receivable*
For the Quarter Ending March 31, 1975

Item		January	February	March
December, 1974 sales†	$350,000			
Collected in January	49½%	$173,250		
January, 1975 sales	355,200			
Collected in January: 50%	177,600			
Less 1% cash discount	1,776	175,824		
Collected in February	49½%		$175,824	
February, 1975 sales	$355,200			
Collected in February: 50%	177,600			
Less 1% cash discount	1,776		175,824	
Collected in March	49½%			$175,824
March, 1975 sales	$362,400			
Collected in March: 50%	181,200			
Less 1% cash discount	1,812			179,388
Total collections		$349,074	$351,648	$355,212
Add cash discounts		1,776	1,776	1,812
Total reduction of receivables		$350,850	$353,424	$357,024
Accounts receivable beginning balances (½ of previous month's sales)		$175,000	$177,600	$177,600
Add sales during the month		355,200	355,200	362,400
		$530,200	$532,800	$540,000
Less reductions from above		350,850	353,424	357,024
Accounts receivable ending balance		$179,350	$179,376	$182,976

* Collection schedule:
   1.   50 percent of month's sales are collected during the month and a 1 percent cash discount is taken.
   2.   49½ percent of month's receivables are collected the following month.
   3.   One-half percent of month's receivables are never collected and are written off at the year-end.
  † This is a given amount.

Schedule 11b

<hr>

LAKE ERIE TABLE COMPANY
Schedule of Cash Disbursements
For the Quarter Ending March 31, 1975

Schedule Reference	Item	January		February		March	
4	Materials*..................	$95,924		$96,632		$96,632	
	Less 1%, discount........	959	$ 94,965	966	$ 95,566	966	$ 95,566
5	Direct labor†................		54,530		54,340		55,100
6	Factory overhead‡..........	$54,810		$54,710		$55,105	
	Less:						
	Depreciation...........	6,300		6,300		6,300	
	Insurance and taxes.....	950	47,560	950	47,460	950	47,855
9	Selling expenses............	$55,312		$55,312		$55,744	
	Less: Depreciation........	140	55,172	140	55,172	140	55,604
10	Administrative expenses.....	$33,476		$33,476		$33,512	
	Less:						
	Depreciation...........	2,380		2,380		2,380	
	Insurance and taxes.....	500		500		500	
	Interest expense..........	500		500		500	
	Bad debts expense........	1,776	28,320	1,776	28,320	1,812	28,320
	Total disbursements........		$280,547		$280,858		$282,445

* All material expenditures are in the same month the purchase is made and a 1 percent cash discount is taken.
† Disbursements for labor assumed to be in the same month as incurred.
‡ Overhead disbursements are in the same month the expenditure is incurred except: (1) depreciation and bad debts expense do not require cash outlays; (2) insurance and taxes on real estate and personal property are paid in July of each year; (3) interest is paid on April 1 and October 1.

Schedule 12

LAKE ERIE TABLE COMPANY
Budgeted Income Statement
For the Quarter Ending March 31, 1975

Schedule Reference			
1	Sales.....................................		$1,072,800
8	Cost of goods sold........................		603,908
	Gross margin..........................		$ 468,892
	Less:		
9	Selling expenses.......................	$166,368	
10	Administrative expenses................	100,464	266,832
	Net income before taxes..................		$ 202,060
Given	Less federal income taxes (48%)...........		96,989
	Net Income.............................		$ 105,071

Schedule 13

LAKE ERIE TABLE COMPANY
Budgeted Balance Sheet
As of March 31, 1975

Assets

Current Assets:			
Cash (Schedule 11).....................................		$ 52,084	
Accounts receivable (Schedule 11a).......................	$ 182,976		
Less: Allowance for uncollectible (Schedule 10)*..........	5,364	177,612	
Inventories (Schedule 7)................................		303,667	$ 533,363
Fixed Assets:			
Land (given)..		$ 50,000	
Buildings (given)....................................	$1,000,000		
Less: Accumulated depreciation (given).................	100,000	900,000	
Equipment (given)....................................	1,000,000		
Less: Accumulated depreciation (given).................	425,000	575,000	1,025,000
Total Assets....................................			$1,558,363

Liabilities

Current Liabilities:			
Accrued interest payable (Schedule 11b).................		$ 1,500	
Accrued insurance and taxes on real estate personal property (Schedule 11b)............................		4,350	$ 5,850
Long-Term Liabilities:			
Notes payable—$100,000 due January 1, 1980; 6% interest payable on April 1 and October 1 (see Schedule 10).......			100,000

Shareholders' Equity

Common stock, $1 par value, 200,000 shares authorized; 100,000 shares outstanding (given).........................			100,000
Paid-in capital in excess of par (given)......................			400,000
Retained earnings:			
Beginning balance (given)...............................		$847,442	
Plus estimated earnings (Schedule 12)....................		105,071	952,513
Total Liability and Shareholders' Equity.............			$1,558,363

* The debit to bad debt expense each month is offset by a credit to allowance for uncollectible accounts which had a zero balance at January 1, 1975.

Important | Profit plan | Commitment
terms | Master budget | Imposed budget
| Operating budget | Baseline budget
| Program budget | Current budget
| Responsibility budget | Cash budget
| Variable (or flexible) budget | Capital expenditure budget
| Rolling budget | Authorization request

Questions
for
discussion

1. Distinguish between the technical and the behavioral aspects of budget preparation.

2. Explain the purposes for which a budget would be used in a large automobile dealership, such as the Morgan Ford Company described in Chapter 1.

3. Explain the relationship between a program budget and the program that results from the programming process.

4. The example on page 326 shows a variable budget formula for a machining department. What would the factory overhead budget for this department be in a month when planned production volume is $30,000 direct labor dollars?

5. Distinguish between the role of the line organization and the role of the staff in budget preparation. Does the budget director function in a line capacity when he prepares the budget for his own office?

6. What is the difference between a sales budget and a sales forecast?

7. The management team of a small printing shop consists of the president, the production manager, the sales manager, and the controller. They meet one afternoon, and at the end of the afternoon have prepared a budget for the coming year. Describe briefly, step by step, what probably happened that afternoon, identifying the part that each person played.

8. Budget amounts may represent (a) a ceiling, (b) a floor, or (c) a guide. Which is appropriate for each of the items listed on Schedules 9 and 10 of the Appendix? Why?

9. Why is an imposed budget an unsatisfactory motivating device?

10. A frequently revised budget is sometimes called a "rubber standard." Where do you suppose this term originated? What derogatory implication does this term have?

11. Suppose that a current budget is prepared as carefully as is humanly possible. Can management use such a budget in lieu of actual reports on performance?

12. On a capital expenditure budget, individual projects often are listed in order of their desirability. Is "desirability" the same as net present value?

13. Trace through each schedule of the Appendix so that you can describe what is being done on each and their interrelationship. One good way

of doing this is to start with the budgeted income statement and balance sheet (Schedules 12 and 13), and work backwards to find the source of each number on these statements.

Problems   11–1.   Exotic Gifts, Ltd., is preparing a budget for the second quarter of the current calendar year. The March ending inventory of merchandise was $106,000, which was higher than expected. The company prefers to carry ending inventory amounting to the expected sales of the next two months. Purchases of merchandise are paid for by the end of the next month, and the balance due on accounts payable at the end of March was $24,000. Budgeted sales follow:

April.........	$40,000	July............	$72,000
May..........	48,000	August..........	56,000
June..........	60,000	September.......	60,000

Required:

Assuming a 25 percent gross profit margin is budgeted, prepare a budget showing the following amounts for the months of April, May, and June:
1. Cost of goods sold.
2. Purchases required.
3. Cash payments for merchandise purchases.

11–2.   Homecraft, Inc., has just received a franchise to distribute humidifiers on the eastern seaboard. The company commenced business on January 1, 1974 with these assets:

Cash.............	$45,000	Delivery equipment..	$640,000
Inventory.........	94,000	Office equipment.....	160,000

(All equipment has useful life of 20 years and no residual value.) First-quarter sales are expected to be $360,000, and should be doubled in the second quarter. Third-quarter sales are expected to be $1,080,000. One percent of sales are considered to be uncollectible. The gross profit margin should be 30 percent. Variable selling expenses except bad debts are budgeted at 12 percent of sales, and fixed selling expenses at $48,000 per quarter, exclusive of depreciation. Variable administrative expenses are expected to run 3 percent of sales, and fixed administrative expenses should total $34,200 per quarter.

Required:

Prepare an operating budget for the first quarter of 1974 and another for the second quarter of 1974.

11–3.   Home Equipment Center has been organized to sell a line of lawn and garden equipment. The company began operations on January 1, 1974 with the following assets:

Cash..................... $ 11,250
Inventory...............   23,500
Land....................   25,000
Buildings and equipment... 200,000 (useful life 20 years, and no residual value), of which $160,000 relates to selling and $40,000 to general and administrative activities.

Sales for January, February, and March are expected to be $90,-000; they are expected to be $180,000 for the next three months, and $270,000 for the three months after that. Certain expenses are expected to vary with sales as follows:

	Percent of Sales Dollars
Cost of sales.............................	70
Bad debts................................	1
Variable selling..........................	12
Variable administrative...................	3

Expenses not expected to vary with sales:

Selling.........................	$12,000 per quarter
Administrative..................	8,550 per quarter
Depreciation...................	2,500 per quarter

Required:

Prepare an operating budget for the first and second quarters of operations for Home Equipment Center.

11–4. Wallace Box Company manufactures cardboard cartons which are used by other manufacturers to package a wide variety of consumer products. The sales vice president has gathered various items of information as a basis for top management's decision as to the sales budget for 1975, as follows:

Sales revenue in 1974 is estimated to be $8,000,000, based on actual sales for the first 10 months. This is an estimated 5 percent of all cardboard cartons sold in Wallace's marketing territory. A trade association forecasts that industry sales, in units, will increase 4 percent in 1975 as compared with 1974.

The sales staff estimates that selling prices will be at least 5 percent higher in 1975, and may well be 8 percent higher.

Sales estimates for each territory, obtained from the salesmen responsible for that territory, add up to $9,500,000 for 1975. In the past such estimates have tended to be somewhat optimistic. Included in the $9,500,000 is a sizable increase in one territory that reflects an estimated $300,000 of sales to the Marvel Company, a possible new customer. Discussions with Marvel have been underway for several months, and the salesman is "practically certain" that Marvel will give its carton business to Wallace in 1975.

The financial vice president, who keeps well informed on general business conditions, believes that the trade association forecast is too high. His own estimate is that industry sales in units will not increase at all in 1975.

The sales vice president, on the other hand, not only believes that the trade association forecast is reliable but he also believes that Wallace's market share (i.e., percentage of industry sales) will be 5.4 percent of industry sales in units.

Required:
1. Set boundaries on the sales budget for 1975; that is, state the lowest amount and the highest amount of sales revenue that you believe top management should reasonably consider.
2. Within this range, what number would you use as the sales budget for 1975?

11–5. The Mitchell Company is compiling a cash forecast for 1975, its second year of operations. Total sales and unpaid customer balances have been estimated for the first four months of 1975 as follows:

	Sales	Unpaid Customer Balances
January	$67,000	$13,000
February	57,000	12,500
March	37,500	10,500
April	37,500	14,000

During 1974 cash and credit sales have been approximately equal. Customers on the average pay their bills on the following schedule:

90 percent of accounts receivable at the beginning of the month are collected in that month.

60 percent of credit sales during the month are collected that month.

2 percent of credit sales become bad debts and are written off.

Required:
Prepare a budget of cash sales and collections on credit sales expected for the first four months of 1975.

11–6. Smith, Inc., estimates sales and collections of accounts receivables quarterly. The sales budget for 1975 follows:

	Total Sales	Beginning Receivables Balance
First quarter	$33,500	$6,500
Second quarter	28,500	6,250
Third quarter	18,750	5,250
Fourth quarter	18,750	7,000

Cash and credit sales have been approximately equal each month in the past. Of the amounts carried as a balance at the beginning of each quarter, 2 percent are considered uncollectible and 90 percent will be collected in that quarter. Before the quarter ends, 70 percent of the credit sales for the quarter will be collected.

Required:

Prepare a schedule giving the cash budget for sales and receivables collections for next year.

11–7.   Imports, Inc., is preparing a budget for the first quarter of next year. Sales are budgeted at $20,000 for January, $25,000 for February, $32,000 for March, $38,000 for April, and $30,000 for May. When merchandise is purchased it is paid for within 30 days, and the company intends to keep an inventory of at least two months' expected sales on hand. The December 31 inventory of the current year was $55,000 because of an unexpected slump in sales, and accounts payable were $10,000. The gross profit margin is budgeted at 25 percent.

Required:

Prepare a budget of the following amounts for the months of January, February, and March:
1.   Cost of goods sold.
2.   Purchases required.
3.   Cash payments for merchandise purchases.

11–8.   At the end of the first quarter of 1973, Soloman, Inc., had a cash balance of $12,600, accounts receivable of $80,000, and accounts payable of $53,400. All liabilities are paid in one month after they have been incurred. Customers pay for 80 percent of credit sales by the end of the next month, 15 percent by the end of the second month, and 3 percent by the end of the third month. Budgeted amounts for the second quarter of 1973 follow:

	April	May	June
Cash sales	$24,000	$18,000	$32,000
Sales on account	65,000	42,000	60,000
Purchases on account	48,000	43,000	38,000
Cash payments:			
Salaries and wages	7,000	7,000	7,800
Delivery truck		18,000	
Dividends			8,000
Interest	2,400	2,400	2,400
Miscellaneous	3,600	4,600	4,200

Required:

Prepare a cash budget which will show for each month:
1.   The beginning cash balance.
2.   Cash receipts.
3.   Cash disbursements.
4.   The cash balance at the end of the month.

11–9.   On December 31, 1973, Davidson Sales had a cash balance of $7,000, an accounts receivable balance of $40,000, and an accounts payable balance of $27,000. Budgeted amounts for January, February, and March of 1974 follows.

	January	February	March
Cash sales................................	$12,000	$10,000	$15,000
Credit sales..............................	27,000	20,000	29,000
Purchases on account....................	25,000	20,500	18,000
Cash payments to be made:			
Salaries and wages....................	3,500	3,600	4,000
Rent..................................	1,000	1,000	1,000
Miscellaneous........................	1,500	2,200	2,000
Fixed asset purchases.................	0	8,000	0
Dividend payments....................	0	0	3,500

80 percent of credit sales are collected in the next month, 15 percent the second month, and 3 percent the third month, the remainder being uncollectible. Purchases are routinely paid for within a month.

Required:

Prepare a cash budget which will show for each month:
1. The beginning cash balance.
2. Cash receipts.
3. Cash disbursements.
4. The cash balance at the end of the month.

11–10. Homecraft, Inc., whose operations are described in Problem 11–2, also is preparing a cash budget for the first two quarters of 1974. In addition to the data given in Problem 11–2, the following estimates are available:

Other franchise holders collect 75 percent of receivables in the quarter in which a sale is made and 24 percent in the following quarter. Sixty percent of merchandise purchases and two thirds of operating expenses will be paid for in the quarter in which the purchase is made, and the balance in the following quarter. Ending inventory of each quarter should be equal to a third of the cost of sales of the coming quarter. An additional $90,000 investment will have to be made at the end of June to handle the expected increase in sales volume in the third quarter.

Required:

1. Prepared a cash budget for the first and second quarters of 1974.
2. Assuming that a minimum cash balance of $20,000 is desired at all times, what steps would you advise Homecraft to take at the end of each of the first two quarters?

11–11. Home Equipment Center, referred to in Problem 11–3, is also preparing a cash budget for the first two quarters of 1974. In addition to the data given in Problem 11–3, the following estimates are available:

Three fourths of the receivables will be paid in the quarter in which the sale is made and 24 percent in the following quarter. Sixty percent of merchandise purchased and two thirds of operating expenses will be paid for in the quarter in which the purchase is made, and the balance in the following quarter. The ending inventory of each quarter should be equal to one third of the amount of estimated cost of sales for the coming quarter. An additional $22,500 investment will have to be made at the end of the second quarter to handle the increased sales volume expected in the third quarter.

Required:

1. Prepare a cash budget for the first and second quarters of 1974.
2. Assuming that a minimum cash balance of $5,000 is desired at all times, what steps would you advise Home Equipment Center to take at the end of each of the first two quarters?

11–12. Charles McVea, president of the McVea Company, a wholesaling establishment, asks your assistance in preparing a budget of cash receipts and disbursements for the next two months, October and November. The company borrowed $90,000 on August 5, to help meet the peak seasonal cash needs, the note becoming due on November 30. There is some question in the president's mind about whether the cash position of the company will be strong enough to pay off the note on time.

The September 30, trial balance of the company shows, among other things, the following account balances:

Cash...	$ 14,200
Accounts receivable........................	227,000
Allowance for bad debts...................	9,100
Inventory......................................	193,800
Accounts payable..........................	86,000
Notes payable...............................	124,000

The McVea Company sells one product only. Sales price of the product is $100 and terms are uniform to all customers: 2 percent discount if paid within the first 10 days of the month subsequent to purchase, otherwise due by the end of the month subsequent to purchase. Historically the company has experienced a 60 percent collection within the discount period, an 85 percent collection within the month subsequent to purchase, and a 98 percent collection within the second month subsequent to purchase. Uncollectables average 2 percent of sales.

The company has projected annual sales for the current year ending December 31 of $1.5 million. Sales for recent months and estimates of sales for the remainder of the year follows:

August.....................................	$180,000
September................................	200,000
October (estimate).....................	220,000
November (estimate)..................	280,000
December (estimate)..................	150,000

All purchases of merchandise are payable within 10 days. Accordingly, month-end balances in accounts payable represent approximately 33 percent of the purchases of merchandise made in the month then ended. The unit purchase price is $68. Target ending inventory is set at 80 percent of next month's estimated sales in units.

Selling and administrative expenses for the year are estimated to total $400,000, of which 40 percent is fixed (including depreciation of $32,000). Variable selling and administrative expenses vary directly with sales, and all selling and administrative expenses are paid as incurred.

Required:

1. Prepare a cash budget for the McVea Company for the months of October and November.
2. Will the company be able to meet the $90,000 note due at the end of November?

11–13.   Below is the December 31, 1972 balance sheet of Bonus Bakers:

BONUS BAKERS
Balance Sheet
As of December 31, 1972

Assets

Current Assets:

Cash	$ 3,750
Accounts receivable	4,125
Prepaid rent	1,500
Prepaid insurance	450
Total Current Assets	$ 9,825

Fixed Assets:

Improvements to leased building	$12,775
Baking equipment	13,300
Baking utensils	1,310
	$27,385
Less: Accumulated depreciation	8,308
Total Fixed Assets	$19,077
Total Assets	$28,902

Liabilities

Current Liabilities:

Accounts payable	$ 4,219
Accrued expenses	182
Short-term notes payable	3,000
Total Current Liabilities	$ 7,401
Long-term notes payable	$ 7,000
Total Liabilities	$14,401

Shareholders' Equity

Common stock (par $10)	$ 6,000
Retained earnings	8,501
Total Shareholders' Equity	$14,501
Total Liabilities and Shareholders' Equity	$28,902

Estimates and additional information are as follows:

a) Estimated 1973 sales, net of discounts and allowances: $105,-000. Sales typically follow an even month-to-month pace, with no noticeable seasonal trends.

b) The company moved into its present building on July 1, 1972. Rent of $3,000 for one year in advance was paid on July 1, 1972. Beginning in July 1973 rent of $250 per month will be paid in cash for the current month.

c) Accounts receivable are expected to continue to experience a one-half month turnover cycle. All sales are on account.

d) Flour, yeast, and all other baking materials are purchased and consumed so quickly that no inventory accounts for these items is maintained. They are expensed upon purchase. The December 31, 1972, balance of accounts payable consists solely of this type of purchase and represents 12½ percent of total 1972 purchases of baking materials.

e) It is estimated that 1973 cost of goods sold will be as follows:

Raw materials..............................	$35,200
Direct labor...............................	25,650
Fixed factory overhead (cash)*................	4,160
Variable factory overhead....................	7,895
	$72,905

* Excludes depreciation and includes only $1,500 of rent payments.

f) The company holds an insurance policy for $1,000,000 of liability coverage. The policy runs from year to year from April 1 to March 30. The annual premium of $1,800 is due in April, and its cost is considered an administrative expense.

g) When the company moved to its new building, two bank notes totaling $10,000 were signed, the first being due in June 1973 for $3,000, and the second being due in January 1977 for $7,000. Both notes bear interest at 8 percent, payable on June 30 and December 31.

h) Data on fixed assets are as follows:

Asset	Purchase Date	Life	Cost	Depreciation Method
Improvements...........	7–1–72	10 yrs.	$12,775	SL
Baking equipment.......	1–1–68	15	12,000	SYD
Baking equipment.......	7–1–72	5	1,300	SYD
Baking utensils.........	1–1–68	10	1,310	SYD

All fixed assets are considered to have a zero salvage value.

i) Selling and administrative expenses other than the insurance and interest are estimated to total $24,600 in 1973, or $2,050 per month.

j) It is expected that accrued expenses balance, which is for raw materials, will remain essentially unchanged for an indefinite period.

k) Management does not anticipate the payment of any dividends during the coming year.

Required:

1. Prepare a budgeted income statement for Bonus Bakers for 1973 and a balance sheet as of December 31, 1973 (ignore tax considerations).
2. Prepare a cash budget on a monthly basis for Bonus Bakers for the year 1973.

11–14. Paul Barton and Robert Doyle formed a partnership to provide professional accounting services to a consortium of businessmen in a medium sized mid-western town. The partnership hired seven employees, rented an office, purchased supplies, and contracted to purchase company automobiles for the two partners. Barton & Doyle recognized that their initial investments in the business of $4,000 each would probably not be enough to get them over the initial cash squeeze which most new businesses encounter during their first months of operation and are accordingly faced with the problem of determining their exact month-to-month cash needs so that a loan agreement can be reached with a local bank.

Monthly salary expense for the seven employees amounted to $6,200 of which Barton & Doyle estimate 55 percent, 65 percent, and 70 percent will be billable to clients at the rate of 250 percent of base pay over the first three months respectively. The partners estimated that billable hours as a percentage of total hours will level off at 75 percent by the fourth month of operations. Mr. Barton and Mr. Doyle expect to bill approximately 50 percent of their time to clients at the rate of 300 percent of their monthly draw, which they have agreed will be $1,000 each per month.

Rent on the office space amounted to $720 per month. The invoice for office supplies amounting to $1,200 will become due during the first month of operation, while the payment for the two automobiles amounting to $6,400 need not be made until the second month of operation.

Required:

Assuming that collection of monthly billings to clients takes place in the succeeding month, and that Barton & Doyle wish to keep a minimum cash balance on hand of $2,000, what loan requirements will the partnership have during each of the first four months of operation?

11–15. In early January, McCartney Sales, a medium size retailing establishment, was considering a change in its credit policy, whereby customers previously refused charge accounts would be granted accounts with relatively low ($100–$200) credit limits. McCartney's president, Leonard P. Harrison, estimated that the present monthly sales volume of $400,000 would increase by 50 percent with the change in policy, which can be put into effect by the end of the month.

Management of McCartney Sales recognized that as the new policy takes effect, not only would sales volume and the level of accounts receivable rise, but in addition, inventories and salaries would also unavoidably increase. Salaries, which currently were $60,000 per month were expected to increase by 25 percent. Inventories, costing an average of 70 percent of selling price, were expected to increase in proportion to sales. Sales on account presently made up 75 percent of total sales and averaged a 45-day turnover rate. It was estimated that the additional sales obtained through the change in policy would be 90 percent on account and average a 60-day lag for collection.

McCARTNEY SALES
Pro forma Balance Sheet as of January 31
(in thousands of dollars)

Cash	$ 200	Liabilities	$ 700
Accounts receivable	450	Owners' equity	510
Inventory	560	Total Liabilities	
Total Assets	$1,210	and Owners' Equity	$1,210

Required:

Assuming the following, prepare pro forma balance sheets and income statements for McCartney Sales for the months of February, March, April, and May.

1. The new credit policy is put into effect at the end of January.
2. Expenses other than cost of goods sold and salaries are fixed at $50,000 per month.
3. A minimum cash balance of $100,000 must be maintained.
4. Expansion of accounts receivable and inventory levels are to be financed with surplus cash and debt.

Suggestions for further reading

Chamberlain, Neil W. *The Firm: Micro-Economic Planning and Action.* New York: McGraw-Hill Book Co., 1962.

Heiser, Herman C. *Budgeting, Principles and Practices.* New York: The Ronald Press Co., 1959.

Hofstede, G. H. *The Game of Budget Control.* Assen, The Netherlands: Van Gorcum & Co., N.V., 1967.

Steiner, George A. (ed.). *Top Management Planning.* New York: The MacMillan Co., 1969.

Welsch, Glenn A. *Budgeting: Profit Planning and Control.* 3d ed.; Englewood Cliffs, N.J.: Prentice-Hall, Inc., 1972.

12 Standard costs

Purpose of
the chapter
In Chapter 11 we described how estimates of future factory costs were developed as a part of the budgeting process. The present chapter describes a cost accounting system that incorporates such estimates and discusses the usefulness of such a system. This system is called a standard cost system.

Since a standard cost system is one type of cost accounting system, it logically could have been discussed in Part One, along with the description of other cost accounting systems. Discussion has been deferred until now for three reasons. First, although the underlying concept of standard costing is not particularly complicated, there often is difficulty in grasping this concept if it is presented early in a course. A standard cost system *appears* to be a roundabout way of measuring product costs, as contrasted with the straightforward method of collecting actual costs that was described in Part One. We shall see that the opposite is the case; that is, that a standard cost system involves less work than does an actual cost system. Secondly, standard costs are used for several different purposes, and we could not discuss the usefulness of standard costs for some of these purposes early in the book because the purposes themselves had not been described. Standard costs are useful in pricing, the topic discussed in Chapter 5; they are useful in making alternative choice decisions (Chapters 7–9), and they are useful in control (Chapter 10). Third, the development of standard costs has much in common with the formulation of budgets which was discussed in the preceding chapter.

Nature and
uses of stan-
dard costs
NATURE OF STANDARD COSTS

A standard cost is a measure of what an item of cost should be, as contrasted with a record of what it actually was. A standard cost system
374

is a cost accounting system that records standard costs either in addition to, or instead of, actual costs. In an actual cost system,[1] indirect costs are assigned to products by means of a predetermined overhead rate, and this is also the case with a standard cost system. The difference between the two systems is in the way direct costs are measured. An actual cost system collects the *actual amount* of direct costs that are incurred for each product. In a standard cost system, *standard unit costs* are developed for the direct material and direct labor elements of product costs; and it is these amounts, rather than actual costs, that are carried through the system to finished goods inventory.

Because of the similar way in which overhead costs are treated in both a standard cost and an actual cost system, the term *standard cost* applies particularly to direct material cost and direct labor cost. In describing how the system works, however, we shall include overhead costs as well as direct costs, so as to show how total standard factory costs are accumulated.

For direct material, the standard represents the amount of material that should be required to produce a unit of product priced at what the price of this material should be.

> *EXAMPLE:* In a shoe factory, the unit of production may be a case (24 pairs) of shoes, Style 107. In an actual cost system, upper leather, sole leather, heels, and other items of direct material would be requisitioned from raw material inventory for this lot of shoes; the actual cost of this material would be calculated; and this cost would be entered on a cost sheet for this lot of shoes. In a standard cost system, a standard material cost for Style 107 is determined. It is determined perhaps once a year, by methods to be described below. Whenever a lot of Style 107 is manufactured, it is assigned this standard material cost.
>
> If the standard direct material cost is $50 per case, the difference between the two systems is illustrated in the following:

Direct Material Cost, Style 107

Job No.	Quantity (Cases)	Actual Cost System	Standard Cost System
1	1	$ 51.23	$ 50.00
2	1	49.57	50.00
3	5	290.41	250.00
4	2	91.87	100.00

---

[1] As pointed out in Chapter 2, a company could conceivably assign overhead to products by use of actual overhead rates rather than predetermined overhead rates. Purists therefore distinguish between a "normal absorption" system, which uses predetermined overhead rates, and an "actual" system which uses overhead rates determined after the end of the period. In this book we use "actual" to refer to both of these systems because the objective of both is to assign actual costs to products.

The same principle applies to direct labor. Instead of charging each job for the number of hours that each employee actually spends on that job times the actual hourly rate for that employee, the job is charged at a standard direct labor cost for a unit of the product, which is calculated by multiplying the standard number of hours that should be required to manufacture one unit by the standard labor cost per hour.

In an actual cost system, overhead is ordinarily assigned to products by means of a predetermined overhead rate. For example, if the overhead rate is $5 per direct labor hour, and if a job required 100 direct labor hours, then the overhead cost would be calculated as $5 \times 100 = $500. Note that although this calculation is made in what is called an "actual" cost system, the "actual" overhead cost of this job was not necessarily $500. Indeed, there is no way of knowing for sure what the actual overhead cost was, since by definition overhead cannot be traced directly to any given product. In a standard cost system, there would also be a predetermined overhead rate, but the overhead cost of a job would be calculated by multiplying this rate by a *standard* quantity, such as the standard direct labor hours. With this exception, the treatment of overhead costs is the same under the two systems.

Standard costs can be used either with a job order cost system or a process cost system.

In some standard cost systems, standard costs of a job or product are recorded *instead of* actual costs. In other systems, standard costs are recorded *in addition to* actual costs. In a shoe factory, for example, no measurement is made at all of the actual direct material costs of a particular lot of shoes, such as Style 107 referred to in the preceding example. The total cost of all direct material issued to a production cost center for an accounting period, such as a month, is collected, and this total is compared with the total standard direct material cost for all shoes worked on during the period.

As will be explained below, such a comparison is used as a basis for control. The same approach is used for direct labor and overhead cost. This version of a standard cost system is used when the dollar value of individual units of product or jobs is relatively small. When the size of jobs is large, it is worthwhile to record *both* the standard costs and the actual costs of individual jobs.

In summary, the basic objective of an actual cost system is to charge units of products with a fair share of the *actual* costs incurred in making those products, whereas the basic idea of a standard cost system is that **the costs charged to units of products are the costs that should have been incurred on those products rather than the costs that actually were incurred.**

The phrase "standard cost accounting" may appear to be a contradiction of terms. We have learned that accounting is supposed to measure what actually happened; in the case of manufacturing, this is the amount of resources actually used in making a product. A standard cost system, however, does not purport to measure the amount of resources actually used to make a product. As we shall see, there are good reasons for this seeming contradiction.

VARIANCES

The difference between a standard cost and an actual cost is called a **variance.**[2] A standard cost system is arranged so that at appropriate points in the flow of costs, the amount of variance is recorded in one or more variance accounts. A debit balance in a variance account means that actual costs were higher than standard costs; such a variance is called an **unfavorable variance.** A credit balance means that actual costs were lower than standard costs; such a variance is called a **favorable variance.**

USES OF STANDARD COSTS

A standard cost system may be used for any or all of these purposes: (1) it provides a basis for controlling performance, (2) it provides cost information that is useful for certain types of decisions, (3) it may provide a more rational measurement of inventory amounts and of cost of goods sold, and (4) it may reduce the cost of recordkeeping.

Use in control. A good starting point in the control of a manager's performance is to compare what the manager actually did with what he should have done. Standard costs provide a basis for such comparisons.

> *EXAMPLE:* If the standard direct material cost for all the shoes manufactured in a month was $243,107, and if the actual cost of the direct material used on those shoes was $268,539, there is an indication that direct material costs were $25,432 higher than they should have been. Without some standard, there is no starting point for examining the appropriateness of the $268,539 of direct material cost.

As already indicated, differences between actual costs and standard costs are debited or credited to variance accounts. Favorable variances are an indication that performance was better than expected, and unfavorable variances are an indication that performance was worse than expected. These variance accounts are therefore an important aid in analyzing and controlling costs. Their use for this purpose will be discussed in Chapter 14.

Use in decision making. Standard costs are often used as a basis for arriving at normal selling prices, especially when each job is different from other jobs because each is made according to individual customers'

---

[2] The word "variance" has a completely different meaning in statistics; it refers to the amount of dispersion around some measure of central tendency. The two meanings should not be confused.

specifications. This is the "time-and-material" method of pricing described in Chapter 5.

> *EXAMPLE:* A contractor who specializes in painting exteriors of houses estimates that a painter using a brush should be able to paint 60 square feet of surface per hour, and that his earnings (including fringe benefits) should be $6 per hour. He estimates that a crew (consisting of a painter and a helper) using a spray gun should be able to paint 450 square feet of surface per hour, and that the earnings of the two-man crew should be $11 per hour. He estimates his overhead costs to be $2 per direct labor hour, and decides that a satisfactory profit is 10 percent of costs. He calculates hourly rates as follows:

		Brush	*Spray*
1.	Standard direct labor cost per hour...............	$6.00	$11.00
2.	Standard overhead cost per hour ($2 per man)	2.00	4.00
3.	Total standard cost per hour......................	$8.00	$15.00
4.	Standard profit per hour (10%)...................	0.80	1.50
5.	Standard selling price per hour...................	$8.80	$16.50
6.	Standard square feet per hour....................	60	450
7.	Standard price per square foot (5 ÷ 6)............	$0.147	$ 0.037

> To find the price of painting a given house, he estimates the number of square feet of surface that will be painted with a brush and the number of square feet that will be painted with a spray gun, and applies the above standard unit prices, viz:

		Brush	*Spray*
1.	No. of square feet of surface.....................	1,000	10,000
2.	Standard unit price (from above).................	0.147	0.037
3.	Total price (1 × 2).............................	$147	$370

The total standard price of the job (excluding paint) is therefore $147 + $370 = $517.

If he gets the job at that price, he can compare actual cost with the standards used above, and this comparison provides him with a way of detecting the cause of differences between his actual profit and his expected profit.

In alternative choice decisions, of the type discussed in Chapters 7–9, standard costs are often the best available approximation of the differential costs that are relevant in making such decisions.

More rational costs. A third advantage of a standard cost system is that it eliminates what otherwise might be an undesirable quirk in the accounting system. A standard cost system records the same costs for physically identical units of products, whereas, an actual cost system may record different costs for physically identical units of products. In the example of Style 107 shoes given above, the actual direct material cost of each lot was different. The actual direct labor cost of each lot would also be different, depending on such factors as whether the employees who worked on the shoes had a relatively high wage rate because of long seniority. The shoes themselves, however, are physically the same. Realistically, there is no good reason for carrying one pair of

Style 107 in inventory at one cost and another pair of Style 107 at a different amount, or in charging cost of goods sold at different amounts. There is no physical difference in the two pairs of shoes that warrants the conclusion that one pair "cost" more than the other. In a standard cost system, all shoes of the same style would be carried in inventory and charged as cost of goods sold at the same unit cost.

Saving in recordkeeping. Because of the addition of standard costs to the system, it might appear that a standard cost accounting system requires more recordkeeping than an actual cost accounting system. In reality, when standard costs are used instead of actual costs, there may well be a *reduction* in the amount of effort required to operate the system. Consider the example of the shoe factory given above. In an actual cost system, a record must be maintained of the dollar amount of direct material used on each lot of shoes (in the example, each lot of Style 107), that is, requisitions of material from raw materials inventory must identify that the material is to be used for a particular lot of Style 107; the cost of each item of direct material on the requisition must be calculated, and this amount must be entered on the job cost sheet. Similarly, the direct workers must keep track of the time that they spent on each lot of shoes, each of these time records must be priced, and the total direct labor cost must be accumulated and entered on the job cost sheet for each lot.

Much of this work is eliminated in a standard cost system. All the individual material requisitions for a month can be totaled and posted as a single credit to Raw Materials Inventory. Instead of making separate entries for direct material cost on each job cost sheet, one amount, the standard unit material cost, is all that is needed. Neither is there any need for direct workers to keep track of the time they spend on individual lots. One amount, the predetermined standard direct labor cost, is all that is needed.

There is furthermore a considerable reduction in the amount of recordkeeping required for finished goods inventory and cost of goods sold. Since all pairs of Style 107 shoes have the same cost (except when the standard is changed), all of the complications involved in keeping track of costs according to a Lifo, Fifo, or average cost assumption (as described in *Fundamentals of Financial Accounting,* Chapter 7) disappear.

One part of a standard cost system, that of determining the individual standards, does involve additional effort. As will be pointed out in a following section, in many situations the effort required to do this is not great, but there can be no doubt that some effort is involved. The determination of standard unit costs is done only occasionally, however. Once a standard has been determined, it is used for months, or even years, without change.

Generally, there is a saving in recordkeeping costs if the occasional task of determining the standard cost is more than offset by the reduction in detailed recording that occurs each time a job is costed. If the standard cost is not used several times, there is no saving.

> *EXAMPLE:* An automobile company may manufacture several hundred thousand units of a given model in a year. A cost must be attached to each unit, and that cost must be carried through the accounts, from Goods in Process Inventory, through Finished Goods Inventory to Cost of Goods Sold, as the automobile moves from the factory, to the storage lot, and then to the dealer. The job of accumulating the actual direct material and direct labor cost for each of these automobiles would be stupendous. It is a relatively easy matter, however, to have a standard unit cost for the basic model, and for each of the items of optional equipment that may be added to it, and to use this cost in accounting for the automobiles as they move through the inventory accounts to cost of goods sold. A small builder of custom houses, however, would not use a standard cost system (at least not in order to save on recordkeeping). Each house is sufficiently different so that the cost of developing the standard would exceed the saving in recordkeeping. A builder of mass-produced standard houses might or might not use a standard cost system in order to save on recordkeeping costs; the choice would depend on whether a sufficient number of similar houses would be built to warrant the effort of developing standards.

Setting the cost standards   The usefulness of a standard cost system depends in large part on how realistic the individual standards are. To arrive at a good standard does not necessarily require a great deal of extra effort, however. Some companies have shifted to a standard cost system simply by taking the average unit costs obtained from their former actual cost system and using these as standards. This is an easy way to set up a standard cost system, and the resulting standards may be sufficiently reliable if material prices and labor rates are not expected to change significantly and if no substantial opportunities for improving efficiency are foreseen.

More commonly, the standards are built up from an analysis of direct labor, direct material, and overhead requirements. Some comments on this process follow.

SEPARATION OF QUANTITY AND PRICE

Every dollar amount of direct material or direct labor cost in a cost accounting system results from the multiplication of a physical quantity by a price per unit of quantity. For direct material, this is the number of pounds (or other measure) of direct material multiplied by the price per pound, and for direct labor it is the number of minutes or hours of labor times the rate per hour. **In setting a cost standard, it is usually desirable to consider the quantity separately from the unit price, and to maintain their separate identity in the underlying records.** There are two reasons for this. First, and most importantly, a separation of the quantity and price aspects facilitates analysis of the causes of the differences between the actual cost and standard cost, and for assignment of responsibility for these differences. For example, the quantity of direct material used is usually the responsibility of the production department, whereas the price per unit of quantity is the responsibility of the purchasing department. Second, the separation facilitates revision of the standards when the need to do so arises. For example, if the standard unit price of an item of direct material increases, the standard direct material cost can be adjusted simply by multiplying the standard quantity by the new unit price.

TYPES OF STANDARDS

The standard cost of a product can be either an **ideal** standard or a **normal** standard. **An ideal standard represents what the costs would be if production operations were conducted at maximum efficiency;** that is, if waste or spoilage of direct material were at an absolute minimum and if direct workers produced the maximum output they are physically capable of producing and if machines never broke down. **A normal standard (or currently attainable standard) represents the degree of efficiency that reasonably can be expected under prevailing conditions;** that is, direct material costs include an allowance for the probable amount of waste and spoilage, and direct labor costs allow for the fact that workers do not actually work at peak efficiency, and that machines do break down. For a given product, a normal standard cost is of course higher than an ideal standard cost.

In most companies, the cost standards are normal standards since these represent what costs are really expected to be. An ideal standard is a goal toward which managers strive but which they probably cannot attain. Those companies that use an ideal standard argue that inefficiencies should not be built into the standard but rather should be isolated for separate examination and that managers should always strive for the best possible performance. When ideal standards are used, an allowance for inefficiency must be added to the standard cost when it is used for pricing and other decision-making purposes. In the following description, we assume the use of normal standards.

STANDARD DIRECT MATERIAL COST

The standard direct material cost of a product is usually derived from a **bill of materials.** This is simply a list showing the quantity of each item of material that is necessary to manufacture the article. A bill of materials is not prepared solely, or even primarily, for the purposes of the standard cost system. It must be prepared in any event in order to determine how much of what material to purchase, what storage requirements for material are, how much of each item of material should be requisitioned for a given lot, and for other production reasons. Therefore, the amount of additional effort required to develop standard material cost is small. The bill of materials may show only the quantity of material component that is required to make one unit or lot of product, but if there is likelihood that material will be spoiled or wasted during the production process, an allowance for the quantity of material that will probably be lost for these reasons should be included in the calculation of standard material quantity.

The standard direct material cost is obtained by multiplying the standard quantities of material by standard unit prices. The standard unit price of each item of material is ordinarily obtained from the purchasing department. As described in Chapter 3, this is not solely the invoice price; it may also include material-related costs that are involved in bringing the material to the plant and storing it until it is used.

STANDARD DIRECT LABOR COSTS

For direct labor costs, the estimated number of minutes required for each labor operation is often available. Production engineers have various techniques for obtaining such standard times. One is to **time study** each operation, that is, the observer uses a stopwatch to find the time that an efficient worker takes to perform the operation. However, many workers resent such direct observations; some companies are prohibited by union contracts from making them; and they are prohibited by law in many government organizations. An alternative approach is to divide each operation into the **elemental body movements** that are involved in it (e.g., "reaching," "grasping," "turning over"). Standard times for each of these body movements have been developed, and these are added up to find the standard time for the whole operation. Descriptions of these and other methods of arriving at standard time allowances will be found in books on industrial engineering. As was with the case with direct material, these standard labor times are needed not only for the standard cost system but also for other purposes: as a basis for planning labor requirements, for deciding on the best production work flow, for production scheduling, and for measuring worker efficiency.

The standard quantities of direct labor are converted to monetary amounts by multiplying each by a unit price, that is, an hourly labor rate. This rate may include not only wages earned but also an allowance for fringe benefits and other labor-related costs.

STANDARD OVERHEAD COSTS

In Chapter 11 we described the process of preparing budgets for responsibility centers. As a part of this same process, standard overhead

Exhibit 12–1

Example of estimating a semivariable overhead cost material handling versus direct labor hours

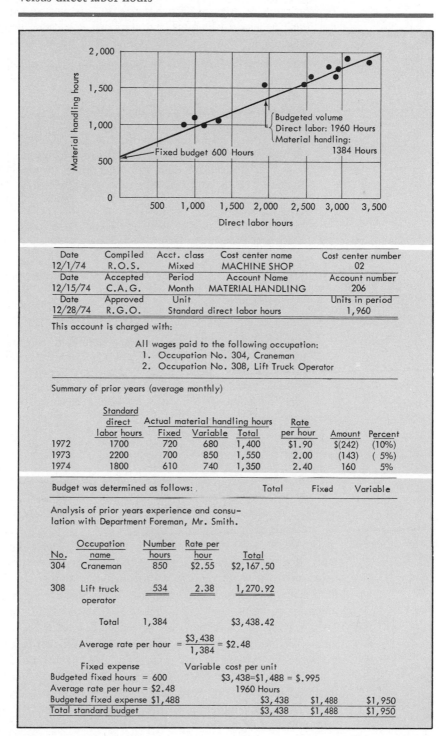

Date 12/1/74	Compiled R.O.S.	Acct. class Mixed	Cost center name MACHINE SHOP	Cost center number 02
Date 12/15/74	Accepted C.A.G.	Period Month	Account Name MATERIAL HANDLING	Account number 206
Date 12/28/74	Approved R.G.O.	Unit Standard direct labor hours		Units in period 1,960

This account is charged with:

    All wages paid to the following occupation:
      1. Occupation No. 304, Craneman
      2. Occupation No. 308, Lift Truck Operator

Summary of prior years (average monthly)

	Standard direct labor hours	Actual material handling hours			Rate per hour	Amount	Percent
		Fixed	Variable	Total			
1972	1700	720	680	1,400	$1.90	$(242)	(10%)
1973	2200	700	850	1,550	2.00	(143)	(5%)
1974	1800	610	740	1,350	2.40	160	5%

Budget was determined as follows:	Total	Fixed	Variable

Analysis of prior years experience and consu-
lation with Department Foreman, Mr. Smith.

No.	Occupation name	Number hours	Rate per hour	Total
304	Craneman	850	$2.55	$2,167.50
308	Lift truck operator	534	2.38	1,270.92
	Total	1,384		$3,438.42

Average rate per hour $= \dfrac{\$3,438}{1,384} = \$2.48$

Fixed expense	Variable cost per unit			
Budgeted fixed hours = 600	$\dfrac{\$3,438 = \$1,488 = \$.995}{1960 \text{ Hours}}$			
Average rate per hour = $2.48				
Budgeted fixed expense $1,488		$3,438	$1,488	$1,950
Total standard budget		$3,438	$1,488	$1,950

rates are determined. We shall therefore not repeat the description here. For the purpose of recalling what the process was and for showing the relationship between budgets and standard costs, one example is given below:

> *EXAMPLE:* Exhibit 12–1 shows the work sheet used in one company to develop both the variable budget and the standard overhead component for material handling labor costs. The top part of the work sheet is a scatter diagram, in which dots show actual material handling hours plotted against direct labor hours (a measure of volume) for each of the preceding 12 months. Summary information for the current and two preceding years is given in a lower block on the chart. Based on this information and after consultation with the departmental foreman as to conditions that are expected in the forthcoming year, the budget analyst arrived at a variable budget for material handling labor, as—

> Fixed expense per month........................ $1,488
> Variable expense per standard direct labor hour.... 0.995

Since normal volume was 1,960 direct labor hours, the *budgeted cost at normal volume* was:

$$\$1,488 + (\$0.995 \times 1.960) = \$3,438$$

Budgeted costs at normal volume would also be used to develop the standard overhead rate. The calculation is not shown on Exhibit 12–1 since it would be made for all overhead items together, rather than for material handling separately. If the only overhead cost were material handling labor, the standard overhead rate would be $3,438 ÷ 1,960 standard direct labor hours = $1.75 per standard direct labor hour.

ADJUSTMENTS IN STANDARDS

Standards usually change over time. Material prices and labor rates are likely to increase, and in many situations the quantity of raw material and labor per unit of product is reduced as better manufacturing methods are discovered. These changes require revisions in standard costs. As a general rule, standard costs are not adjusted more often than once a year unless some highly significant event occurs. Usually, the adjustment does not require a thorough reexamination of all elements in the standard. In some situations, the adjustment involves simply making an across-the-board increase in each standard cost element, say an increase of 3 percent to reflect overall price increases. This method, although only approximate, may be sufficiently accurate for the purposes for which the standards are used. In some companies, the standards are left unadjusted for long periods of time. The variances will then become large, but if the business is not complicated and if management thoroughly understands the underlying forces, the necessary adjustments can be made mentally.

MECHANICS OF THE SYSTEM

Exhibit 12–2 is a flowchart of a standard cost system. The company makes smoking pipes; it is the same situation as that depicted in the flowchart for an actual cost accounting system in Chapter 2, Exhibit 2–2. The circled numbers refer to the transactions described briefly below. It is suggested that the student expand this brief description by describing the nature of each of the debits and credits in the T-accounts; referring back to Chapter 2. This will be useful as a review of the mechanics of a cost accounting system. The following transactions occurred in a certain month:

1. Raw material was received.
2. Direct material was used in the manufacturing process.
3. Direct labor was used in the manufacturing process.
4. Employees were paid the amounts due them.
5. Actual overhead costs were incurred.
6. Overhead costs were debited to Goods in Process Inventory.
7. Pipes were completed and transferred to Finished Goods Inventory.
8. Pipes were shipped to customers.
9. Sales revenue was earned for the same pipes involved in Transaction No. 8.
10. Selling and administrative expenses were incurred.
11. Selling and administrative expenses were closed to Income Summary.
12. Revenue and Cost of Goods Sold accounts were closed to Income Summary.

A comparison of Exhibit 12–2 with Exhibit 2–2 will show that the only difference between the flowchart for an actual cost accounting system and that for a standard cost accounting system is that variance accounts have been introduced in a standard cost system in Transactions No. 1, No. 2, No. 3, and No. 6.

Material price variance. Transaction No. 1 records the receipt of material into Raw Materials Inventory. In an actual cost system, the entry was:

```
Dr.  Raw Materials Inventory.................6,000
     Cr.  Accounts Payable....................      6,000
```

Material was recorded in the Raw Materials Inventory account at the actual price paid, which was $6,000.

In a standard cost system, material is recorded in Raw Materials Inventory at its standard cost, which is here assumed to be $5,900. Since the amount actually owed the vendor was $6,000, the credit to Accounts Payable necessarily is $6,000. The difference of $100 between

Exhibit 12–2
Flow chart of a standard cost system

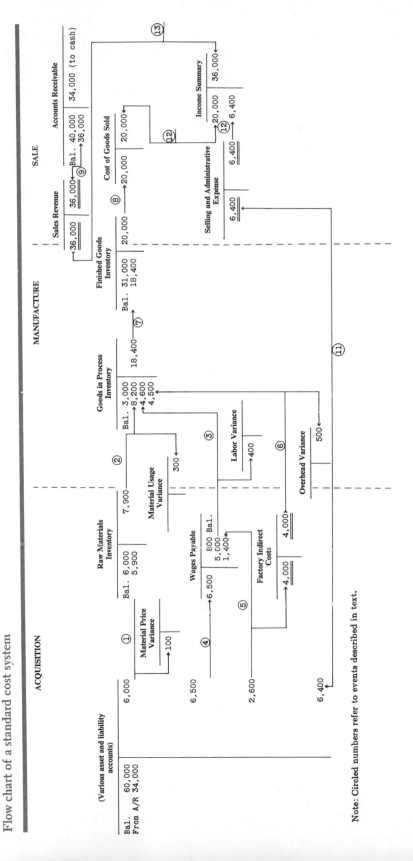

Note: Circled numbers refer to events described in text.

these two amounts is debited to a Material Price Variance account, as in the following:

```
Dr.  Raw Material Inventory...................5,900
     Material Price Variance..................  100
     Cr.  Accounts Payable....................            6,000
```

The **Material Price Variance** account can be explained in either of two ways. *Mechanically,* the account is necessary to satisfy the fundamental requirement that debits must equal credits. *Conceptually,* the account shows the difference between the actual price of the raw material purchased and its standard price. In the above entry, the actual price was higher than the standard price.

> *EXAMPLE:* The standard unit price of the material purchased is $5.90 per pound. If 1,000 pounds are purchased at $6 per pound, the amount owed the vendor is $6,000, but the 1,000 pounds of material is debited to Raw Materials Inventory at its standard price of $5.90 per pound, making the total amount of the debit $5,900. The variance account indicates that $100 more than the standard price was paid.

Material usage variance. Transaction No. 2 records the issuance of raw materials out of inventory and into the manufacturing process. In the actual cost system, the entry was:

```
Dr.  Goods in Process Inventory..............8,000
     Cr.  Raw Materials Inventory............            8,000
```

The actual cost of the materials put into production was $8,000. In the standard cost system, the corresponding entry differs from the above in two respects. First, the credit to Raw Materials Inventory is calculated at the *standard price* of the actual quantity of material withdrawn, rather than the actual price. The standard price is used because, as a consequence of Transaction No. 1, material is carried in Raw Materials Inventory at its standard price rather than its actual price. Secondly, the debit to Goods in Process Inventory is calculated at the *standard cost,* which is the standard quantity required priced at standard unit prices. This debit is here assumed to be $8,200. The difference of $300 between these two amounts is credited to Material Usage Variance. The entry therefore is:

```
Dr.  Goods in Process Inventory..............8,200
     Cr.  Raw Materials Inventory............            7,900
          Material Usage Variance............             300
```

The **Material Usage Variance** does *not* relate to the difference between the actual unit price of the raw material and its standard unit price because both the credit to Raw Materials Inventory and the debit to Goods in Process Inventory were calculated at standard unit prices. The price variance was isolated when the material moved *into* inventory, in Transaction No. 1. The Material Usage Variance arises from either of two causes: (1) the actual *quantity* of material used differed from the standard quantity or (2) the actual raw material used was a different *type* of material, with a different standard unit price, than that specified on the bill of materials.

Direct labor and overhead variances. In Transaction No. 3, relating to direct labor, the procedure is essentially the same. There is a credit to Wages Payable of $5,000 representing the actual direct labor cost of the period, a debit to Goods in Process Inventory of $4,600 representing the standard direct labor cost of the pipes worked on during the period, and a debit to the Labor Variance for the difference of $400. Transaction No. 6 is a corresponding entry for indirect factory cost.

Note that in the above entries, the Material Price Variance and the Labor Variance are debits. These are therefore "unfavorable" variances in the sense that actual costs exceeded standard costs. The Material Usage Variance and the Overhead Variance are credits. They are "favorable" variances in the sense that actual costs were less than standard costs.

In summary, the only mechanical difference between the accounts in a standard cost system and those in an actual cost system is that the former has variance accounts. Variance accounts are necessarily introduced whenever one part of a transaction is at standard cost and the other part is at actual cost.

VARIATIONS IN THE STANDARD COST IDEA

In the system discussed above, standard costs were introduced when raw material entered inventory and when material, labor, and overhead were debited to Goods in Process Inventory. This is common practice, but standards can also be introduced at other points.

Instead of debiting Raw Materials Inventory at standard unit prices, some companies carry raw material at actual cost and make the conversion to standard cost when the raw material is issued for use in the production process. In such a system, there would be no material price variance, and the material variance account would incorporate both the price and the quantity components of the variance.

In another variation of the standard cost idea, the shift from actual to standard is made at a later point in the production process than that shown in Exhibit 12–2. In such a system, elements of cost are charged into Goods in Process Inventory at actual cost, and the shift from

actual to standard is made when the completed products are transferred from Goods in Process Inventory to Finished Goods Inventory.
In this system, there would be only one variance account, and it would
be generated as part of the entry recording this transfer, which is
Transaction No. 7 on Exhibit 12–2.

Some companies do not use a *complete* standard cost system, that is,
a system that treats all elements of cost on a standard basis. They may,
for example, use standard direct labor costs, but actual direct material
costs; or they may do the reverse. The choice depends on the advantages
that are obtainable in the particular situation. Regardless of these
variations, the essential points are: **(1) in a standard cost system, some
or all of the elements of cost are recorded at standard rather than at
actual; and (2) at whatever point a shift from actual to standard is
made, a variance account is generated.**

Demonstra-
tion case
As an illustration of some of the procedural details of a standard
cost system, the system of the Black Meter Company (which is the
disguised name for an actual company) is described below.

DESCRIPTION OF COMPANY

The Black Meter Company manufactures water meters in one
standard design but in a wide range of sizes. The water meters installed
in the basements of most homes are an example of its product. The
meters consist basically of a hard rubber piston that is put in motion
by the flow of water past it, a gear train that reduces this motion and
registers it on a dial, and two heavy bronze castings which are bolted
together around the measuring device.

The company has several production departments. The castings and
many interior parts of meters are cast in the foundry and then are
sent to one of the three machining departments, depending upon their
size. Some of the mechanical parts are sent to a subassembly department where they are assembled into gear trains. Other parts go directly
to the meter assembly department. There are also several departments
that provide service to the production departments.

OVERVIEW OF SYSTEM

Since the company ships meters to customers as soon as they are
completed, it does not have a Finished Goods Inventory account. It
does have Raw Materials Inventory and Goods in Process Inventory
accounts. It uses a standard cost system. Standard costs are established
for each element of direct labor, direct material, and manufacturing
overhead.

During the month, actual costs are accumulated: material is pur-

chased, the earnings of workers are recorded, and manufacturing overhead items, such as water or electricity, are purchased and paid for at
actual cost. Elements of cost are debited into inventory at predetermined
standard costs, however. Since actual costs often are different from
standard costs, variance accounts are necessary. At the end of a month
variances between actual and standard are examined; these variances
assist management control of costs because they focus attention on the
exceptional situations, and avoid the necessity for studying the bulk of
the cost data.

SETTING UP STANDARD COSTS

A standard unit cost is established for every type of material that is
purchased. This is done annually by adjusting the current market price
for any changes that are expected for the following year. For example,
if copper at the end of a year cost 30 cents a pound and no change is
predicted, the standard cost for copper for the next year will be 30 cents
a pound.

Standard rates for direct labor and manufacturing overhead are also
determined annually. These rates are used to assign costs to products
according to the number of standard direct labor hours incurred in the
manufacture of each product. This is done on a departmental basis. For
each production department, the accountants start with data on the
actual direct labor payroll and the number of direct labor hours worked
in each of the past few years. The departmental foreman gives his
opinion as to adjustments that should be made to take account of future
conditions. An amount for total labor cost and an amount for hours
worked under normal conditions of activity is thus arrived at. By divid-

Exhibit 12–3

Department Number	Department name	Labor	Overhead	Total rate
	STANDARD OVERHEAD RATES EFFECTIVE JANUARY 1			
103	Carpenter and pattern shop	$4.06	$3.07	$7.13/hour
104	Toolroom	4.35	3.26	7.61/hour
108	Pattern storage	----	----	8.04/pound
120A	Foundry--molding	4.50	5.78	10.28/hour
120B	Foundry--grinding and snagging	3.50	2.90	6.40/hour
122	Small parts manufacture	3.72	3.38	7.10/hour
123	Interior parts manufacture	3.68	3.73	7.41/hour
124	Case manufacture	3.98	6.02	10.00/hour
125	Plating--rack	----	----	6.50/100 pcs.
130	Train, register, and interior assembly	3.70	3.97	7.67/hour
131	Small meter assembly	3.50	4.01	7.51/hour
132	Large meter assembly	3.90	5.98	9.88/hour
133	Meter testing	4.11	3.56	7.67/hour
134	Meter repair	3.50	3.66	6.16/hour

ing the payroll amount by the normal number of hours, a standard direct labor rate per standard direct labor hour for each department is found.

Overhead costs for a production department include both the overhead costs incurred in that department plus an allocated portion of the costs of service departments. Estimates are made of these amounts for each production department under normal conditions. These estimated total overhead costs are divided by the standard number of direct labor hours for each producing department, the same amount that had been used in calculating the labor rate, to arrive at a manufacturing overhead rate per standard direct labor hour. These rates are given in Exhibit 12–3.

DEVELOPING STANDARD PRODUCT COSTS

The standard hourly rates (which include both direct labor and overhead) are used to develop a standard cost for each type of meter. The form used for this purpose is called a manufacturing order (specifically, foundry order, parts order, or assembly order) because the same form is also used to schedule actual production. Examples of these calculations are given in Exhibits 12–4, 12–5, 12–6, and 12–7.

Exhibit 12–4

		FOUNDRY ORDER								Order No.		
Drawing No.			Part 5/8" HF Chamber Rings			Material Cost						
Material	Gov't Bronze 100 Pcs. 91.0# at 0.3265/#						$29.712					
Weight			Plating		Econ. Lot	Pattern Cost		0.04		$3.64		
Rate No.	Std. Man-Hrs. per 100 Pcs.	Std. Basic Rate	Prod. Center	Oper. No.	Operations and Tools	Machine	Man No.	Std. Rate /Hr.	Man No.	Total Cost	Total	
	1.76		120 A	1	Mold	Match Plate		10.28		18.093		
	0.45		120 B	2	Grind	Wheel		6.40		2.88		
	0.68		120 B	3	Snag	Bench		6.40		4.35		
										58.675		

Exhibit 12–5

RR–7						PARTS ORDER					
Drawing No. X-2408			Part 5/8" HF Chamber Rings					Material Cost		Order No.	
Plating H.T. & E.T.			Material Gov't Bronze 100 pieces 89#					$58.675			
Econ. Lot 2,000										Quantity Ordered	
Rate Number	Hours per 100 Pcs.		Setup St'd.	Prod. Center	Oper. No.	Operations and Tools	Machine	Man No.	Std. Rate /Hr.	Total
	St'd.	Allw'd.								
	0.75			122	1	Broach out let #734	P.P.		7.10	5.325
	0.55			123	2	Finish tap plate bore and face	Heald		7.41	4.076
	0.93			123		Drill 6 holes	Drill		7.41	6.891
	0.47			123	3	C-sink-3 holes tap plate side	Drill		7.41	3.483
	0.17			123		Tap 3 holes tap plate side	Heskins		7.41	1.260
	5.00			123	4	Rough & Finish inside & outside	Heald		7.41	37.050
	0.20			123		C-sink 3 holes on bottom	Drill		7.41	1.482
	0.30			123	5	Tap 3 holes on bottom	Drill		7.41	2.223
	0.47			123		Spline inside	Spliner		7.41	3.483
	0.50			123	6	Spline outside	Miller		7.41	3.705
	5.80			123		Dress	Bench		7.41	42.978
					7					170.631

The examples show the development of the standard cost of a ⅝-inch HF Meter.

Exhibit 12–4 shows the calculation for a ⅝-inch Chamber Ring which is manufactured in the foundry, and which is one component of the ⅝-inch HF Meter. As in the case with most parts, costs are calculated for a lot of 100 units. The standard material cost is figured in the second line of the foundry order, Exhibit 12–4. These parts are cast from bronze that has a standard cost of $0.3265 a pound. Since the standard weight of 100 pieces is 91 pounds, the standard material cost is $0.3265 × 91 = $29.712, as shown in the "Material Cost" box. The $0.04 figure in the pattern cost box is a standard pattern cost per pound; this is multiplied by the 91 pounds to give the $3.64 standard pattern charge.

In order to apply the standard direct labor and manufacturing overhead rates to any part, it is necessary to have the standard direct labor hours for the operations involved in making that part. These are obtained from time studies and are entered in the first column of the foundry order. The standard time to mold 100 chamber rings is 1.76 direct labor hours; to grind them, 0.45 hours, and to snag them, 0.68 hours.

Exhibit 12–6

ASSEMBLY ORDER												
Drawing No. 2400		Assembly 5/8" Disc Interior						Sheet No. of				
Used on Assemblies of 5/8" HF & HD Meters								Order No.				
Parts of Assembly		Cost		Part of Assembly		Cost		Quantity Ordered				
K-2408 Chamber Ring		170.631										
K-2414 Chamber Top Plate		73.550						Date Ordered				
K-2418 Chamber Bot. Plate		70.120										
K-2465 Disc Piston Assem.		149.010						Date Wanted				
K-2422 Disc. Chbr. Diaphragm		7.660										
				K-4521 Chamber Screws (6)		7.000						
Rate No.	Std. Man–Hrs. Per 100 Pcs.	Std. Basic Rate	Prod. Center	Oper. No.	Operations and Tools	Machine	Man No.	Std. Rate /Hr.	Man No.	Total Cost	Total
	2.6		130	1	Assemble Top Plate to Ring	Bench		7.67		19.942	
	0.9		130	2	Fit Abutment for Interior	Bench		7.67		6.903	
	1.1		130	3	Mill & Scrape Diaphragm for Interior	Bench		7.67		8.437	
	2.9		130	4	File Diaphragm Slots in Piston	Bench		7.67		22.243	
										528.496	

In the first column of numbers of the right-hand side of the foundry order, the combined standard direct labor and manufacturing overhead rate per standard direct labor hour for the operation is recorded. For example, Exhibit 12–3 shows the labor and overhead rate for molding in Department 120A as $10.28 per standard direct labor hour, and this amount appears on the foundry order for the molding operation. It is multiplied by the standard direct labor time of 1.76 hours to give a standard cost of labor and overhead of $18.093. The same procedure is followed for the other two foundry operations. The total standard foundry cost of 100 chamber rings is $58.675.

Exhibit 12–5 accumulates additional standard costs for these 100 chamber rings as they pass through the parts manufacture department. They enter the parts department at the standard cost of $58.675, the same cost at which they left the foundry. After the operations listed on Exhibit 12–5 have been performed on them, they become finished chamber rings. These operations have increased the standard cost to $170.631. As shown in Exhibits 12–5 and 12–6 these parts are assembled into 5/8-inch HF disc interiors, and finally into 5/8-inch meters. In each of these assembly operations standard costs are added; the total standard cost of 100 meters is $1,760.596.

Exhibit 12–7

ASSEMBLY ORDER							
Drawing No. 2735	Assembly 5/8" HF ET FB				Sheet No.	of	
Used on Assemblies of					Order No.		
Parts of Assembly	**Cost**	**Parts of Assembly**		**Cost**			
2761 Top Case	270.60	K-5030 5/8" HF Dur. Bolt	(6)	62.880	Quantity Ordered		
K-2776 Casting Gasket	13.25	K-4630 5/8" HF ac Nut	(6)	35.440			
X-2770 Bottom Case	100.14	K-5068 5/8" HF Washers	(6)	20.140			
2779 Casting Strainer	16.95	2782 Chamber Pin		3.966	Date Ordered		
3209 5/8" Closed Train	600.01	6172 Misc. Train Conn.		17.120			
2400 5/8" HF Int. Assem.	528.496						
2412 5/8" HF Sand Plate	15.00				Date Wanted		

Rate No.	Std. Man-Hrs. per 100 Pcs.	Std. Basic Rate	Prod. Prod. Center	Oper. No.	Operations and Tools	Machine	Man No.	Std. Rate /Hr.	Man No.	Total Cost	Total
	4.6		131	1	Assem. Train and Strainer to Case	Bench		7.51		34.546	
	5.6		131	2	Assem. Int. & Bottom to Meter	Bench		7.51		42.058	
										1760.596	

In the same manner, standard costs are calculated for all the meter sizes that the Black Meter Company manufactured. These standards are revised annually to recognize any significant changes in the costs of labor, materials, or overhead.

ACCOUNTING ENTRIES

All direct material, direct labor, and manufacturing overhead costs are debited to Goods in Process Inventory at standard costs. Actual costs are collected in total for the period, but no actual costs are collected for individual meters.

Material. As soon as any material is purchased, the standard cost of that material is penciled on the vendor's invoice. Each purchase is journalized in an invoice and check register. This register contains columns in which to credit the actual cost of the material to Accounts Payable, to debit an inventory account for the standard cost, and to debit or credit the difference to a purchase price variance account. When material is issued for use in production, the quantity is the standard amount (e.g., 91 pounds in the example shown in Exhibit 12–4), and the entry crediting Raw Materials Inventory and debiting

Goods in Process Inventory is made at the standard cost (e.g., $29.712 in the example shown in Exhibit 12–4).

Labor.   The basic document for recording direct labor costs is the job timecard. Each productive employee fills out such a card for each order on which he or she works during a week. The timecard reproduced as Exhibit 12–8 shows that Mr. Harris worked all week on one order. On the timecard he records the quantity finished, the actual hours he worked, and the allowed, or standard, hours. A payroll clerk enters each employee's daywork rate, the standard direct labor rate for that department, and extends the actual and standard direct labor cost of the work completed.

Exhibit 12–8

Mach. No.	Prod. Center	Quantity Ordered	Order Number	
	130	3,000	2I-86572	Clock No. 337
	Part Name			
	5/8" Cl. Trains			
Prev. Quan. Fin.	Oper. No.	Operation Name		
O	9	Finish Assem.		
Quan. Finished	Std. Hours Per 100	Std. Hours	Std. Rate	Standard Labor
2,300	1.75	40.25	3.70	148.92
Quan. Finished			TIME CARD	
2,300				Name B. HARRIS
	Stop	Actual Hours	D.W. Rate	Earnings
Sept. 20	40.0	40.0	3.65	146.00
	Start			Gain or Loss
Sept. 16	00.0	Foreman		2.92

By totaling all the job timecards, the payroll clerk obtains the actual wages earned by each employee in each department, and also the total standard labor cost of the work done in each department. These amounts are the basis for an entry which credits accrued wages for the actual amount and debits Goods in Process Inventory account for the standard amount of direct labor. The variance is recorded in a direct labor variance account.

Manufacturing overhead.   For each department, a cost clerk multiplies the standard direct labor hours worked by the manufacturing overhead rate for that department (as obtained from Exhibit 12–3); this gives the amount of standard manufacturing overhead cost for the department for that month. This amount is debited to Goods in Process Inventory. During the month actual manufacturing overhead expenses have been accumulated in the invoice and check register and in various adjusting entries. The difference between the sum of the actual overhead costs and the standard manufacturing overhead cost is the manu-

Exhibit 12–9

Carbon copy of sales invoice

Village of Vernon,
Attn: Village Clerk,
Vernon, N.Y.

Village of Vernon, Water Dept.,
Attn: E. J. Blackburn, Mayor
Vernon, N.Y.

STIBBS   Prepaid

10   5/8" x 3/4" Model HF Meters SG SH ET FB & 3/4"

                                                                          248.00

1   Charge Gear #46X -- shipped 8-10-   .88   248.00

                                                Meter   248.00   176.06
                                                Parts   .88   .48

                                Ship gear by P. Post

Exhibit 12–10

Income Statement
June

Net sales...		$1,198,234
Less: Cost of goods sold at standard cost.........	$831,868	
Variances (detailed below)......................	5,357	826,511
Gross manufacturing margin....................		$ 371,723
Selling expense................................	$ 92,107	
General and administrative expense..............	177,362	269,469
Income before income taxes.....................		$ 102,254
Income taxes.................................		49,320
Net Income...................................		$ 52,934

Variances

	Debit	Credit
Favorable variances:		
Material price variance.......................		$ 62,608
Unfavorable variances:		
Material usage.............................	$ 22,457	
Direct labor...............................	16,234	
Overhead..................................	18,560	57,251
Net Variance................................		$ 5,357

Exhibit 12–11
Flowchart

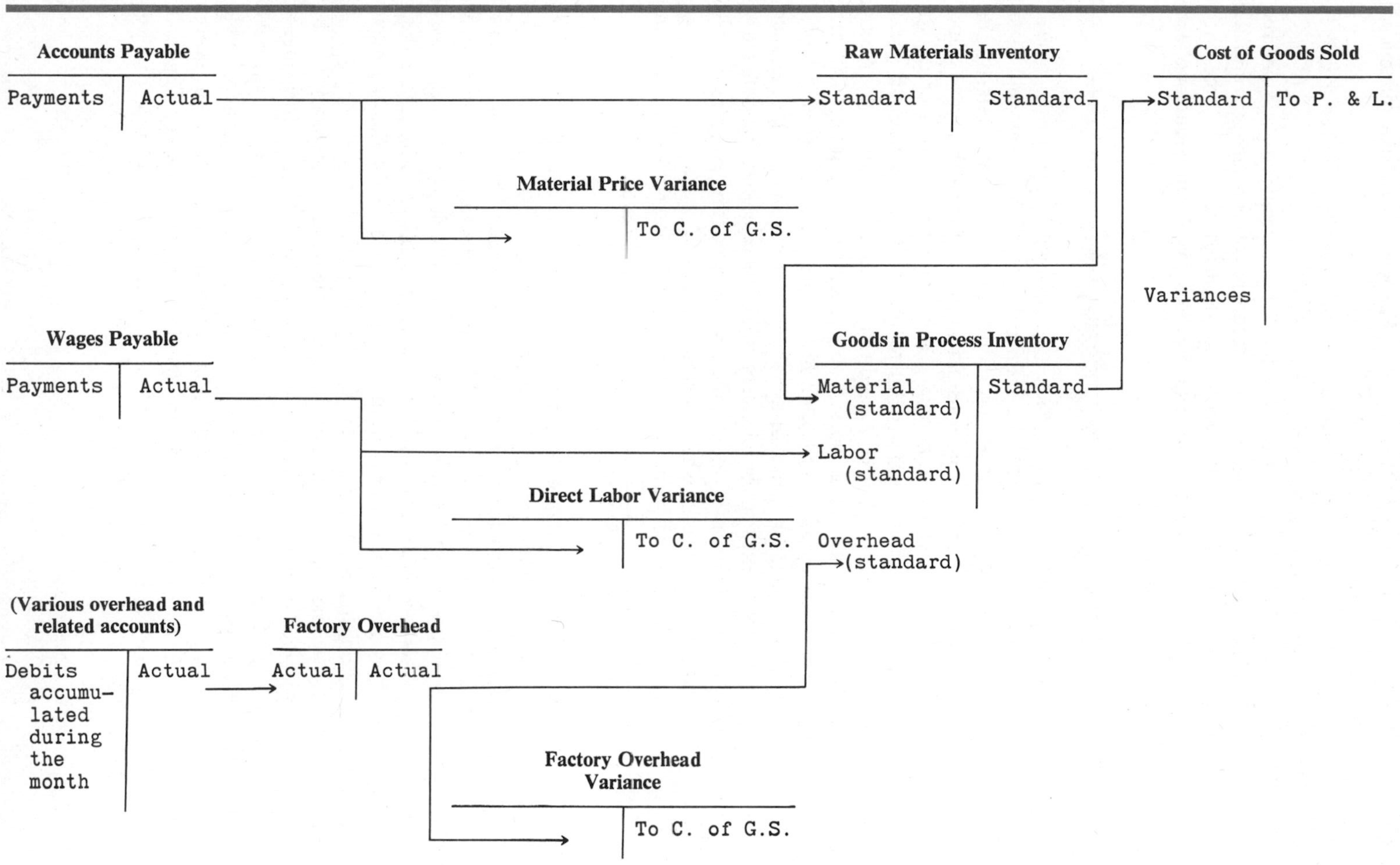

Accounts Payable

Payments	Actual

Material Price Variance

	To C. of G.S.

Raw Materials Inventory

Standard	Standard

Cost of Goods Sold

Standard	To P. & L.

Variances

Goods in Process Inventory

Material (standard)	Standard
Labor (standard)	
Overhead (standard)	

Wages Payable

Payments	Actual

Direct Labor Variance

	To C. of G.S.

Factory Overhead

Actual	Actual

(Various overhead and related accounts)

Debits accumu-lated during the month	Actual

Factory Overhead Variance

	To C. of G.S.

facturing overhead variance, which is debited or credited to the overhead variance accounts.

When these transactions have been recorded, all material, direct labor, and manufacturing overhead have been charged into the Goods in Process Inventory account at standard cost, and three variance accounts have been debited or credited for the difference between actual and standard.

SALES AND COST OF GOODS SOLD

A duplicate copy of each sales invoice is sent to the office where a clerk enters in pencil the standard cost of the items sold (see Exhibit 12–9). At the end of the month the cost clerk totals the figures on these duplicate invoices to get amounts for sales revenue and for the standard cost of those sales. The standard cost is a credit to the Inventory account and a debit to the Cost of Goods Sold account. The total sales amount is a credit to Sales and a debit to Accounts Receivable. When this work is completed, the accounting department is in a position to obtain the monthly income statement (see Exhibit 12–10). Note, incidentally, that although the net amount of the variance on this income statement is relatively small, there are sizable detailed variances that tend to offset one another. Management investigates these variances and takes action when warranted.

A flowchart summarizing the above description appears in Exhibit 12–11.

Summary

The essential idea of a standard cost accounting system is that costs and inventory amounts are recorded at what costs *should* have been rather than what they actually were. At some point in the flow of costs through the system there is a shift from actual costs to standard costs. Wherever this shift occurs, a variance develops. This can be as early in the process as the receipt of raw materials (in which case the variance is a Material Price Variance), or it can be as late as the movement of finished product from the factory to finished goods inventory.

The purposes of a standard cost accounting system are (1) to provide information that can be used in the appraisal of performance, because, as a first approximation, a credit variance indicates good performance and a debit variance indicates poor performance; (2) to provide better information for pricing and other decisions; (3) to overcome the anamoly that results in an actual cost system in which physically identical products have different costs; and (4) to save recordkeeping effort.

Important terms

Standard cost	**Bill of materials**
Variance	**Material price variance**
Unfavorable variance	**Material usage variance**
Favorable variance	

Questions
for
discussion
1. To what extent does an actual cost system, as described in Part One, not measure true actual costs?

2. A credit variance is a favorable variance. In general, do credits to accounts represent "favorable" events?

3. For what purposes are standard cost systems used?

4. A furniture company using an actual job cost accounting system has separate job cost records for each of two dining room tables. The recorded costs of each table are identical except in one respect; namely, the direct labor cost of assembly and finishing was $32 for one table and $36 for the other. This operation required eight hours for each table, but for one table it was performed by an employee who earned $4 per hour, while for the other it was performed by an employee who, because of seniority, earned $4.50 per hour. Did the cost of the two tables differ? Should they be sold at different prices?

5. Explain how a standard cost accounting system can reduce record-keeping costs. Give some examples of companies in which such a system would be *more* expensive than an actual cost system.

6. Describe three ways in which the standard labor cost of an operation can be determined.

7. In your own words describe each numbered transaction in Exhibit 12–2.

8. If raw material is credited out of Raw Materials Inventory at actual cost and debited to Goods in Process Inventory at standard cost, the difference is debited or credited to a materials variance account. What is the difference between such an account and a materials *usage* variance account?

9. In Exhibit 12–1 and related explanations, the standard material handling cost per direct labor hour was stated to be $1.75. How would this number be used in the standard cost system? Explain, step by step, how this number was calculated.

10. Trace through the procedure described for the Black Meter Company. Can you show how the numbers on each exhibit are derived from, or help derive, the numbers on other exhibits? Can you relate each of the forms to the flowchart?

11. Imagine what an actual cost system for Black Meter Company would look like. Would it require less recordkeeping effort? Would it provide useful information to management that the standard cost accounting system does not provide?

12. In what respects, if at all, do the cost flows in the Black Meter Company differ from those depicted in Exhibit 12–2?

13. The forms in Exhibits 12–4, 12–5, and 12–6 are headed "foundry order," "parts order," and "assembly order," respectively. What is probably their principal use? Why are standard cost computations made on these forms rather than on special forms designed for this purpose?

14. Suppose that the direct labor rate for Department No. 120A was in-

creased to $5.50 per hour and that for Department No. 131 was increased to $4.50 per hour. What effect would these changes have on the succeeding exhibits and on the total standard cost of 100 ⅝-inch HF meters?

Problems   **12–1.** Standard unit material and labor costs for the single product manufactured by Farrell Company are as follows:

Standard Unit Costs

Direct material, 10 pounds at $2 per pound.................... $20
Direct labor, 5 hours at $3 per hour........................   15

During June the following transactions occurred:

1. Purchased 1,000 pounds of direct material at $2.10 per pound.
2. Issued 4,100 pounds of material from raw material inventory to manufacture 400 units of product.
3. Incurred direct labor costs of $5,800 in manufacturing these 400 units. (There was neither a beginning nor an ending balance in Goods in Process Inventory.)

Required:
Journalize these transactions.

12–2. Some of the journal entries for Folo Company have been posted to T-accounts as follows:

Accounts Payable		Raw Materials Inventory		Material Price Variance	
	8,000	A	6,000	400	

Wages Payable				Material Usage Variance	
	C				B

Factory Indirect Cost		Goods in Process Inventory		Direct Labor Variance	
10,000	D	6,200			300
		20,000			
		9,900			

				Overhead Variance	
				E	

Required:

What amounts should be entered in place of the letters A, B, C, D, and E?

12–3. A partial income statement for May Pex Company is as follows:

Sales revenue..		$190,000
Standard cost of goods sold:		
Beginning inventory.	$ 18,000	
Cost of goods manufactured.	110,000	
Ending inventory.	−16,000	112,000
Standard gross margin.		$ 78,000

Variances for this accounting period, which were not included in costs of goods manufactured, were:

Favorable direct labor variance of $5,000.
Favorable overhead variance of $3,900.
Unfavorable material usage variance of $3,000.

Required:

Compute the gross margin assuming actual costs were used instead of standard costs.

12–4. An income statement of Mono Company, which used an actual cost system was as follows:

Sales revenue.	$250,000
Cost of goods sold.	158,000
Gross margin.	$ 92,000
Operating expenses.	45,000
Income before Income Taxes.	$ 47,000

Suppose that instead of using an actual cost system the company had used a standard cost system and that in the same period variances were:

Raw materials usage variance.	Dr.	$3,800
Direct labor variance.	Dr.	3,600
Overhead variance.	Cr.	7,500

There were no balances in either Goods in Process Inventory or Finished Goods Inventory. Variance accounts were not closed.

Required:

Calculate what the income before income taxes would have been if a standard cost system had been used.

12–5. Following are standard and actual unit costs of product Z-3 taken from the books of Alkid Company for the month of May:

	Standard Unit Costs	Actual Unit Costs
Raw materials.	10 pounds @ $0.25	11 pounds @ $0.26
Direct labor.	4 hours @ $2.50	5 hours @ $2.55
Factory overhead.	4 hours @ $3.00	4 hours @ $2.95
Units produced.		70,000
Units sold.		68,000

Required:

(1) Compute the total actual and standard costs and the variances for each of the three elements of production cost for the 70,000 units produced.

(2) a. Give an analysis of the elements of cost comprising the finished goods ending inventory at standard cost. There were no beginning inventories, and no ending inventory of goods in process.

    b. Compute the amount of the finished goods ending inventory at actual cost.

12–6. Perry Gadget Company has been manufacturing a product, L 400, for a number of years. Based on past experience the cost of L 400 under normal operating conditions should be as follows:

Standard Cost of One Unit of L 400

Direct materials:	4 pounds @ $2 per pound...........	$ 8
Direct labor:	2 hours @ $3 per hour.............	6
Overhead:	@ 50% of direct labor cost.........	3
	Total......................	$17

The overhead rate is based on the assumption of a normal 20,000 hours of work per month.

Actual results for June production of L 400 were as follows:

Units produced......................	10,000
Material used........................	40,500 pounds
Direct labor hours....................	20,000
Direct material cost, per pound........	$2.10
Direct labor cost, per hour............	$2.80
Actual overhead cost.................	$31,500
Sales, at $25 per unit.................	8,000 units

Required:

(1) Compute the total actual and standard costs and the variances for each of the three elements of production cost for the 10,000 units produced.

(2) a. Give an analysis of the elements of cost comprising the finished goods ending inventory at standard cost. There were no beginning inventories, and no ending inventory of goods in process.

    b. Compute the amount of the finished goods ending inventory at actual cost.

12–7. At the end of the fiscal year of Multi-Products, Inc., the following data appeared in accounts in the general ledger:

	Debits	Credits
Materials inventory.....................	$15,000	$12,000
Finished goods inventory...............	35,000	30,000
Factory indirect costs..................	12,500	12,500
Direct labor cost......................	27,000	27,000
Raw materials variance................	1,400	
Direct labor variance..................		700
Overhead variance.....................	450	

There were no inventories at the beginning of the year. The Raw Materials Inventory, Direct Labor Cost, and Factory Indirect Cost accounts are debited at actual cost.

Required:

(1) Reconstruct the journal entries needed to record the accumulation of standard costs in good in process and the standard cost of goods sold for the year.

(2) Compute the cost of goods sold using actual costs.

12–8. At the end of the first year of operations of the Standard Company, its records reflected the following cost flows:

Accounts Payable		Material Price Variance		Raw Materials Inventory	
XXX	20,000	100		19,900	12,000

Factory Payroll Payable		Direct Labor Variance		Goods in Process Inventory	
XXX	31,000		1,000	12,000 32,000 32,600	65,000

Miscellaneous Accounts				Finished Goods Inventory	
XXX	33,000			65,000	47,000

Factory Overhead		Overhead Variance		Cost of Goods Sold	
33,000	32,600 400	400		47,000	

Required:

(1) Journalize the entries necessary to record the results of operations for the year.

(2) Compute the actual cost of goods sold.

12–9. The standard costs for one unit of product KLM are determined to be as follows:

Direct materials—3 units @ $5................	$15.00
Direct labor—4 hours @ $3.................	12.00
Overhead—$2.50 per hour of direct labor.........	10.00
Standard cost per unit......................	$37.00

Operating results for March:

Purchases of raw materials....................	$88,500
Actual cost of raw materials used............	90,300
Standard cost of raw materials used..........	90,000
Actual direct labor cost.....................	80,970
Actual overhead cost........................	52,300
Units completed in March....................	6,000
Units sold in March.........................	5,000

Inventories: Goods in process, March 1 and
31, zero:
Raw materials, March 1: 4,500 units @ $5
Finished goods, March 1: 800 units @ $37

Required:

Prepare a flowchart which will reflect the accumulation of costs in the inventory accounts for March operations, assuming the uses of a standard cost system in which all differences between actual and standard are removed prior to debits to Goods in Process.

12–10. The standard costs for one unit of product C8J are determined to be as follows:

Direct material, 1.5 pounds @ $2.00....................	$ 3.00
Direct labor, 2.0 hours @ $2.50........................	5.00
Manufacturing overhead, $1 per hour of direct labor.....	2.00
Total standard cost per unit....................	$10.00

Results of operations for January:

Cost of raw materials purchased.......................	$9,500
Actual cost of raw material put into production..........	6,100
Standard cost of raw materials used...................	6,000
Actual direct labor cost..............................	9,900
Actual overhead cost.................................	4,100
Production completed in January in units..............	2,000

There was no unfinished inventory at the end of January
and 900 units were sold.
Inventories, January 1:
Raw materials: 1,500 pounds @ $2
Goods in process: none
Finished goods: 800 units @ $10

Required:

Prepare a flowchart to reflect the results of January operations, assuming the use of a standard cost system in which all differences between actual and standard costs are removed prior to debits to Goods in Process Inventory.

12–11. Total overhead costs expected for the first year of operations of Western Company are estimated to be:

Depreciation of plant and machinery..........	$ 8,000
Taxes.....................................	1,000
Insurance.................................	1,200
Supplies..................................	4,300
Indirect labor.............................	4,500
Power.....................................	2,000
Repairs...................................	2,500
Supervision...............................	6,500
Total.....................................	$30,000

The plant is expected to operate at a normal capacity of five men each working a 40-hour week for 50 weeks. During the first four-week period of operations the following manufacturing transactions took place:

Raw materials with a standard cost of $3,600 were purchased for $3,800, and all were transferred to goods in process. The payroll totaled $2,900 for 800 hours of direct labor. Actual overhead cost for this period amounted to $2,200. The standard cost of direct labor is $3.50 per hour. All work started during the month was completed.

Required:

(1) Construct a flowchart to show the computation of the standard cost of goods manufactured and transferred to finished goods, assuming the use of one manufacturing variance account in which variances are isolated when the goods are transferred to finished goods inventory.

(2) Show what parts of the total manufacturing variance is attributable to differences between actual and standard costs for material, labor, and overheads.

12–12. Debits to the factory overhead account for the Gaylord Company for the month of September resulted from the posting of the following entry:

September 30	Factory Overhead	....	58,000
	Cash.....................		23,000
	Depreciation Expense		30,000
	Prepaid Insurance		1,000
	Property Taxes..............		4,000

Overhead is assigned to product on the basis of $2.50 per direct labor hour. Four hours of work are normal for one unit of product, and 5,000 units were completed during September. Raw materials bought for $115,000 and having a standard cost of $113,-000 were transferred to production. At the beginning of September there was a raw material inventory of $2,200. The payroll for September totaled $57,000 for 19,000 hours at $3 per hour. The planned payroll for the units produced was 20,000 hours at $3. All work started during a month is completed by the end of the month.

Required:

(1) Construct a flowchart to show computation of the standard cost of goods manufactured and transferred to finished goods inventory assuming the use of one manufacturing variance account where variances are isolated when the goods are transferred to finished goods inventory.

(2) Show what parts of the total manufacturing variance is attributable to differences between actual and standard costs for material, labor, and overhead, respectively.

12–13. The following information relates to the operations of the Forrest Woodworking Corporation. For the month of April:

Materials purchased..........................	$ 9,800
Materials used..............................	9,000
Labor......................................	15,000
Heat, light, and power (direct costs)..........	1,128
Supplies used..............................	500
General factory overhead....................	1,200
Machine shop (direct costs).................	800
Inventories, April 1:	
Process I................................	0
Process II...............................	0
Process III..............................	0
Finished goods...........................	1,500

All materials enter Process I at actual cost, and production flows from Process I, to II, to III. All supplies were used by the machine shop. Labor is used by all three processes equally. General factory overhead costs are allocated on the same basis as labor. Utility costs are allocated 20 percent to the machine shop, 60 percent to Process I, and 10 percent each to Processes II and III. The machine shop services only Processes I and II with 75 percent of the work being done for Process I. Six thousand units of product were started and finished during April. There were no units left unfinished at the end of the month, and 5,800 units with a standard cost of $4.50 per unit were sold.

Required:

(1) Complete postings (on a separate sheet of paper) to the following T-accounts to show the accumulation of costs for the standard process cost system described above, and assuming the use of one manufacturing variance account where variances are isolated when goods are transferred to finished goods inventory.

(2) Compute the actual cost per unit manufactured in April.

Selected T-accounts

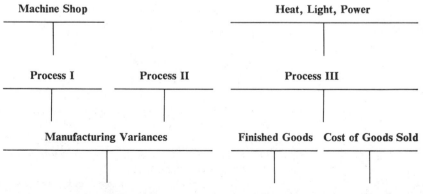

12–14.   Data below was taken from the job cost system of Custom-Craft, Inc., as of August 31:

Job Number	Actual Costs Materials Used	Actual Costs Direct Labor	Direct Labor Hours
501	$2,900	$6,000	2,000
502	3,900	4,000	1,800
503	2,200	3,000	1,300

The heating department incurred direct costs of $830, and the general maintenance department incurred $1,220 direct costs for the month. These costs of the two departments are assigned to jobs on the basis of direct labor hours per job. Actual cost for general factory overhead was $1,200, to be assigned as follows: $80 to each service department, $480 to Job No. 501, $320 to Job No. 502, and $240 to Job No. 503. During August the three jobs were started and finished, with no beginning or ending inventories of unfinished jobs. Job No. 503 was sold and shipped on August 31. The standard cost for labor is $3 per hour. Standard costs for raw materials were $3,000 for Job No. 501, $3,800 for Job No. 502, and $2,200 for Job No. 503. The standard cost for manufacturing overheads was 20 percent of standard direct labor.

Required:

(1) Set up the following T-accounts and make entries to them to reflect the accumulation of costs for the standard job cost system described above, assuming all variances are isolated in one account when jobs are completed: Heating, General Maintenance, General Factory Overhead, Goods in Process, Manufacturing Variances, Finished Goods, and Cost of Goods Sold.

(2) Show for each job the standard costs of material, labor, and overhead.

(3) Show for each job the actual costs of material, labor, and overhead.

12–15. Kodol company prepared its income statements for the current year on three alternative cost accounting systems as follows:

	A	B	C
Sales revenue	$100,000	$100,000	$100,000
Cost of goods sold	33,000	40,000	43,000
	$ 67,000	$ 60,000	$ 57,000
Variances:			
Direct material	...	(2,000)	...
Direct labor	...	(1,000)	...
Factory overhead	...	(5,000)	(5,000)
Gross margin	$ 67,000	$ 52,000	$ 52,000
Other operating expense	55,000	40,000	40,000
Operating Income	$ 12,000	$ 12,000	$ 12,000

Required:

Explain your answers to the following questions:

1. Match the following cost systems with alternatives A, B, and C: (1) standard cost system; (2) actual full cost system; and (3) actual direct cost system.
2. How much, if any, of the factory overhead cost was variable?
3. What was the actual factory overhead cost incurred for the year?
4. What were the nonfactory costs incurred for the year?
5. What percentage was actual factory volume for the year to normal factory volume?
6. Which of the alternative statements was *not* prepared in accordance with generally accepted accounting principles?
7. How did actual direct material cost compare with planned direct material cost?

13 The control structure

Purpose of
the chapter
Chapter 11 described how a company formulates plans for attaining its goals in the year ahead, and Chapter 12 described how the cost aspects of these plans are incorporated in a standard cost system. In Chapters 13, 14, and 15, we shall describe how management uses accounting information to control the company's progress in attaining its goals. Chapter 13 sets the stage for this discussion. It describes organizational arrangements that are intended to facilitate the control process, and it describes concepts that are important in analyzing accounting information that is developed as an aid to control. The application of these concepts will be described in Chapters 14 and 15.

Responsibility centers
Throughout this book we have used the term "responsibility center" to denote any organizational unit that is headed by a responsible manager. As a basis for studying the control process, we now go more deeply into the nature of responsibility centers. Exhibit 13–1 provides a basis for doing this. The top section depicts a machine, which in some important respects is analogous to a responsibility center. A machine, in this case a gasoline engine, (1) uses inputs, (2) to do work, (3) which results in output. In the case of an engine, the input is fuel and air, and the output is mechanical energy.

REALITY VERSUS INFORMATION

Information about the real world gives, at best, an approximation of what the real world actually is like. For example, there is a real-world

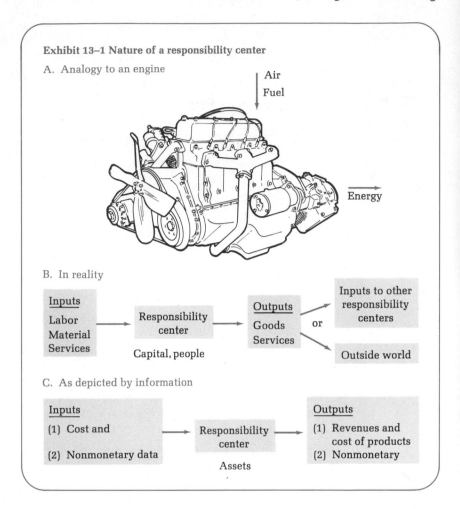

Exhibit 13–1 Nature of a responsibility center

A. Analogy to an engine

Air
Fuel

Energy

B. In reality

Inputs		Outputs		Inputs to other responsibility centers
Labor	Responsibility center	Goods	or	
Material		Services		
Services				Outside world

Capital, people

C. As depicted by information

Inputs		Outputs
(1) Cost and	Responsibility center	(1) Revenues and cost of products
(2) Nonmonetary data		(2) Nonmonetary

Assets

territory called Rhode Island. There are also maps that give information about Rhode Island, and these maps are useful for certain purposes, such as aiding the traveler to find the best route from Providence to Newport. A map does not, however, convey a complete picture of Rhode Island, nor is it intended to do so. Rather, what the cartographer does is to present information that is useful for the purpose for which the map is drawn.

Accounting information is like a map. It is intended to help the user, but it is not, and does not purport to be, a complete picture of reality. Exhibit 13–1 illustrates this difference between reality and information—between the territory and the map. In reality, a responsibility center can be described as in Part B of the exhibit, as follows:

1. It uses resources. These are its **inputs.** They are physical quantities of material, hours of various types of labor, and a variety of services.

2. It *works* with these resources. People are involved in this process. Usually, working capital and fixed assets are also required.
3. As a result of this work, it produces **outputs.** These are classified either as goods, if they are tangible, or as services, if they are intangible. These goods or services go either to other responsibility centers within the company or to a customer in the outside world.

Information about a responsibility center is shown in Part C of the exhibit. This information can be classified as either accounting information or other information. Although we are here interested primarily in accounting information, we must not overlook that fact that much nonaccounting information is relevant in understanding what a responsibility center does.

Accounting measures inputs in terms of cost. Although the resources themselves are physical things such as pounds of material and hours of labor, for the purposes of a management control system it is necessary to measure these physical things with some common denominator so that the physically unlike elements of resources can be combined. That common denominator is money. The monetary measure of the resources used in a responsibility center is *cost.* In addition to cost information, nonaccounting information on such matters as the physical quantity of material used, its quality, the skill level of the work force, and so on, is also useful.

If the outputs of a responsibility center are goods or services sold to an outside customer, accounting measures these outputs in terms of revenue. If, however, products or services are transferred to other responsibility centers within the company, an accounting measure of output is more difficult to obtain. In some situations a revenue measure of output is feasible for such transfers. Alternative measures are the total cost of the goods or services transferred, or a nonaccounting measure, such as the number of units of output.

This general statement of the nature of a responsibility center can be used to help explain three types of responsibility centers which are important in management control systems. These are: (1) expense centers, (2) profit centers, and (3) investment centers.

EXPENSE CENTERS

If the control system measures the expenses (i.e., the costs) incurred by a responsibility center but does not measure the monetary value of its output, the responsibility center is called an expense center. Every responsibility center has outputs; that is, it does something. In many cases, however, it is neither feasible nor necessary to measure these outputs in monetary terms. For example, it would be extremely difficult to measure the monetary value of the accounting department's contribution to the company. Although generally it is relatively easy to measure the monetary value of the outputs of an individual production department, there is no reason for doing so if the responsibility of the department manager is to produce a stated *quantity* of outputs at the lowest feasible cost. For these reasons, most individual production departments, and most staff units are expense centers. For an expense center, the accounting system records the cost incurred, but not the revenues earned.

Expense centers should not be confused with cost centers. An expense center is one type of responsibility center used in the management control process. Recall from Chapter 3 that a *cost center* is a device used in a cost accounting system to collect costs that are subsequently to be charged to cost objectives. In a given company, some expense centers may also be cost centers.

In the interests of completeness, we mention here the **revenue center,** which is a responsibility center in which revenues are recorded. Certain branch sales offices are examples of revenue centers. The following discussion omits further mention of revenue centers as such, since the general concepts applicable to them are a mirror image of those applicable to expense centers.

PROFIT CENTERS

Revenue is a monetary measure of outputs, and expense (or cost) is a monetary measure of inputs, or resources consumed. Profit is the difference between revenue and expense. **If performance in a responsibility center is measured in terms of both (1) the revenue it earns and (2) the expense it incurs, the responsibility center is a profit center.**

Although in financial accounting, revenue is recognized only when it is realized, in management accounting it is necessary to define revenue as a monetary measure of the output of a responsibility center in a given accounting period, *whether or not the company realizes the revenue in that period*. Thus, a factory is a profit center if it "sells" its output to the sales department and records the revenue from such sales. Likewise, a service department, such as the maintenance department, may "sell" its services to the responsibility centers that receive these services. These "sales" generate revenues for the service department, and in these circumstances, the service department is a profit center.

Revenues that arise when one responsibility center "sells" its outputs to other responsibility centers within the company differ from revenues that arise from sales to customers, in that outside sales increase the company's assets (either accounts receivable or cash), while internal sales do not. These internal transfers are therefore called by some people "mere bookkeeping entries." As we shall see, they nevertheless can be important in the management control process.

A given responsibility center is a profit center only if management *decides* to measure its outputs in monetary terms. Revenues for a whole company are automatically generated when the company makes sales to the outside world. By contrast, revenues for an internal organization unit are recognized only if management decides that it is a good idea to do so. No accounting principle *requires* that revenues be measured for individual responsibility centers within a company. With some ingenuity, practically any expense center could be turned into a profit center because some way of putting a selling price on the output of most responsibility centers can be found. The question is whether there are sufficient positive benefits in doing so.

Advantages of profit centers. A profit center resembles a business in miniature. Like a separate company, it has an income statement that shows revenue, expense, and the difference between them, which is profit. Most of the decisions made by the manager of a profit center affect the numbers on this income statement. The income statement for a profit center therefore is a basic management control document. Because his performance is measured by profit, the manager of a profit center is motivated to make decisions about inputs and outputs that will increase the profit that is reported for his profit center. Since he acts somewhat as he would act if he were running his own business, the profit center is a good training ground for general management responsibility. The profit center concept is relatively new. It is becoming increasingly popular, but its possibilities have not yet been fully exploited. The use of the profit center idea is one of the important tools that has made possible the recent tendency of large companies to decentralize.

Criteria for profit centers. Although the profit-center approach has become a powerful force for promoting good management control, it does not work well for all responsibility centers. In deciding on whether to set up a given responsibility center as a profit center, the following points should be kept in mind:

1. Extra recordkeeping is involved if the profit center idea is used. In the profit center itself, there is the extra work of measuring output in monetary terms, and in the responsibility centers that receive its outputs there is the work of recording the cost of goods or services received.

2. When top management *requires* responsibility centers to use a certain service furnished by another responsibility center within the company, the service probably should be furnished at no charge, and the service unit therefore should not be a profit center. For example, if top management requires that internal audits be made, the responsibility centers probably should not be asked to pay for the cost of the internal auditing service, and the internal auditing unit should therefore not be a profit center.

3. If the manager of a responsibility center has little authority to decide on the quantity and quality of its outputs or on the relation of output to costs, then a profit center is usually of little usefulness as a control device. This does not imply that the manager of a profit center must have *complete* control over outputs and inputs, for few, if any, managers have such complete authority.

4. If output is fairly homogeneous (e.g., cement), a nonmonetary measure of output (e.g., hundredweight of cement produced) may be adequate, and there may be no substantial advantage to be gained in converting this output to a monetary measure of revenue.

5. To the extent that a profit center puts a manager in business for himself, it promotes a spirit of competition. Up to a certain point, this is desirable. Beyond that point, however, the device may generate excessive friction between profit centers, to the detriment of the whole company's welfare. Also, it may generate too much interest in short-run profits to the detriment of long-run results. These difficulties are likely to arise when managers have an inadequate understanding of the management job, and they often can be overcome by education. If, however, they cannot be overcome, the profit center technique should not be used.

TRANSFER PRICES

A transfer price is a price used to measure the value of products or services furnished by a profit center to other responsibility centers within a company. It is to be contrasted with a market price, which measures exchanges between a company and the outside world. Internal exchanges that are measured by transfer prices result in *revenue* for the responsibility center furnishing the goods or services and in *cost* for the responsibility center receiving the goods or services. Whenever profit centers are established, transfer prices must also be established. There are two general approaches to the construction of a transfer price: the **market-based price** and the **cost-based price.**

If a market price for the goods or services exists, the market price is usually preferable to a cost-based price. The "buying" responsibility center should ordinarily not be expected to pay more internally than it would have to pay if it purchased from the outside world, nor should the "selling" center ordinarily be entitled to more revenue than it could obtain by selling to the outside world. If the market price is abnormal, as for example when an outside vendor sets a low "distress" price in order to use temporarily idle capacity, then such temporary aberrations are ordinarily disregarded in arriving at transfer prices. The market price may be adjusted for cash discounts and for certain selling costs that are not involved in an internal exchange.

In a great many situations, there is no reliable market price that can be used as a basis for the transfer price, and in these situations, a cost-based transfer price is used. Two general types of cost-based price are discussed in the literature: (1) marginal cost and (2) full cost plus profit. **Marginal cost,** as explained in Chapter 7, has approximately the same meaning as variable cost. The marginal cost approach is consistent with the economic model of the firm that assumes the managers make decisions on the basis of complete knowledge of all factors affecting the firm (see Appendix to Chapter 5), but it is not much used in practice.[1]

If the **full cost approach** is used, the method of computing cost and the amount of profit to be included is set by top management in order to lessen arguments that would otherwise occur between the buying and the selling responsibility centers. If feasible, the cost should be a **standard cost,** for if it is an actual cost, the selling responsibility center can pass along its inefficiencies to the buying responsibility center; these inefficiencies will be included in the transfer price. In some situations, the costs are neither the standard nor the actual costs incurred in the selling responsibility center; they may instead be an estimate of the costs that *would be* incurred by the most efficient producer, if such costs can be estimated. A transfer price based on such estimates of cost may be a better measure of the output of the selling responsibility center than a price based on the manufacturing practices and equipment actually being employed.

Whatever the approach to setting the transfer price, there is usually a mechanism for **negotiating** the price of actual transactions between the buying and the selling responsibility centers. For example, the selling responsibility center may be willing to sell below the normal market price rather than lose the business, which could happen if the buying responsibility center took advantage of a temporarily low outside price. In such circumstances, the two parties negotiate a "deal." Unless both responsibility center managers have complete freedom to act, these negotiations will not always lead to an equitable result because the parties have unequal bargaining powers; that is, the prospective buyer may not have the power of threatening to take its business elsewhere, and the prospective seller may not have the power of refusing to do the work. Thus, there usually needs to be an **arbitration** mechanism to settle disputes concerning transfer prices.

INVESTMENT CENTERS

An investment center is a responsibility center in which the manager is held responsible for the use of assets, as well as for revenues and expenses. It is therefore the ultimate extension of the responsibility idea. In an investment center the manager is expected to earn a satisfactory return on the *capital employed* in his responsibility center.

Measurement of capital employed, or the **investment base,** poses many difficult problems, and the idea of the investment center is so new that there is considerable disagreement as to the best solution of these problems. For example, consider cash. The cash balance of the

---

[1] For the argument for the marginal cost approach, see: Jack Hirshleifer, "On the Economics of Transfer Pricing," *Journal of Business,* July 1956, pp. 172–84; and his "Economics of the Divisionalized Firm," *Journal of Business,* April 1957, pp. 96–108.

company is a safety valve, or shock absorber, protecting the company against short-run fluctuations in funds requirements. Compared with an independent company, an investment center needs relatively little cash, however, because it can obtain funds from its headquarters on short notice. Part of the headquarters cash balance therefore exists for the financial protection of the investment centers, and headquarters cash can therefore logically be allocated to the investment centers as part of their capital employed. There are several ways of allocating this cash to investment centers just as there are several ways of allocating general overhead costs.

Similar problems arise with respect to each type of asset that the investment center uses. A discussion of these problems is outside the scope of this introductory treatment. For our present purpose, we need only state that: many problems exist, there is much disagreement as to the best solution, but despite the difficulties a growing number of companies do find it useful to create investment centers.

Investment centers are normally used only for relatively large units, such as a division that both manufactures and markets a line of products. It has the effect of "putting the manager into business for himself" to an even greater extent than does the profit center. Reports on performance show not only the amount of profit that the investment center manager has earned, which is the case with reports for a profit center, but also the amount of assets that he used in earning that profit. This is obviously a more encompassing report on performance than a report which does not relate profits to assets employed. On the other hand, the possible disadvantages mentioned above for profit centers exist in a magnified form in investment centers. Recordkeeping costs increase, and there is the possibility that the manager will be motivated to act in ways that are not consistent with the long-run best interests of the company as a whole.

Additional control concepts

As background for understanding the control process which will be described in Chapters 14 and 15, we now discuss some of the basic concepts that are relevant in that process. These are:

1. Measurements of effectiveness and efficiency.
2. Controllable costs distinguished from noncontrollable costs.
3. Engineered, discretionary, and committed costs.

Effectiveness and efficiency

The performance of a manager of a responsibility center can be measured in terms of the effectiveness and the efficiency of the work of the responsibility center. **By effectiveness, we mean how well the responsibility center does its job**—that is (to quote the dictionary), "the extent to which it produces the intended or expected results." **Efficiency** is used in its engineering sense—that is, the **amount of output per unit**

of input. An efficient machine is one which produces a given quantity of outputs with a minimum consumption of inputs, or one which produces the largest possible outputs from a given quantity of inputs.

Effectiveness is always related to the organization's objectives. Efficiency, per se, is not related to objectives. An efficient responsibility center is one which does whatever it does with the lowest consumption of resources; but if what it does (i.e., its output) is an inadequate contribution to the accomplishment of the organization's objectives, it is ineffective.

> *EXAMPLE:* If a department that is responsible for processing incoming sales orders does so at a low cost per order processed, it is efficient. If however, the department is sloppy in answering customer queries about the status of orders, and thus antagonizes customers to the point where they take their business elsewhere, the department is ineffective; the loss of a customer is not consistent with the company's goals.

In many responsibility centers, a measure of efficiency can be developed that relates actual costs to some standard—that is, to a number that expresses what costs *should be incurred* for a given amount of output. A budgeted cost or a standard cost is such a standard. Such a measure can be a useful indication of efficiency, but it is never a *perfect* measure for at least two reasons: (1) recorded costs are not a precisely accurate measure of resources consumed, and (2) standards are, at best, only approximate measures of what resource consumption ideally should have been in the circumstances prevailing. Each of these limitations has been discussed in earlier chapters.

In an expense center, effectiveness cannot be measured in monetary terms. This is because effectiveness requires a measurement of outputs, and in an expense center outputs are not measured in monetary terms. In some profit centers, an approximate measure of effectiveness is possible. When a primary goal of the whole organization is to earn profits, then the contribution to this goal by a profit center is a measure of its effectiveness. This is so because in a profit center, both outputs (i.e., revenues) and inputs (i.e., costs) are measured in monetary terms; profit is the difference between them.

Since the amount of profit is influenced both by how effective a manager is and by how efficient he is, the profit in a profit center measures *both* effectiveness and efficiency. When such an overall measure exists, it is unnecessary to determine the relative importance of effectiveness versus efficiency. When such an overall measure does not exist, however, it is feasible and useful to classify performance measures as relating either to effectiveness or to efficiency. In these situations, there is the problem of judging the relative importance of the two types of measurements. For example, how do we compare two maintenance managers, one who incurs higher costs than he should but has an excellent record of keeping equipment in tip-top condition, and the other who incurs lower costs but also has a poor record of equipment break-downs? The former is more effective but less efficient than the latter.

Profit is, at best, only an approximate measure of effectiveness and of efficiency for several reasons: (1) monetary measures do not exactly measure either all aspects of outputs or all inputs, for reasons already given; (2) standards are not accurate; and (3) at best, profit is a measure of what has happened in the short run, whereas we are presumably also interested in the long-run consequences of decisions.

In view of the inadequacies of the profit measure, even under the best of circumstances, and in view of the absence of any profit measure in an expense center, many companies use nonmonetary measures of effectiveness. They may, for example, work out with the managers of responsibility centers a list of the objectives which are to be attained in the year—including such nonmonetary statements as "develop a new organization manual"; "send three persons to management development programs"; "reduce clerical errors by 50 percent"—and they then measure actual performance against these plans. This is called **management by objectives.**

Controllable costs

A second concept that is important in understanding the control process is the distinction between controllable and noncontrollable costs. **An item of cost is controllable if the amount of cost incurred in (or assigned to) a responsibility center is significantly influenced by the actions of the manager of the responsibility center.** Otherwise, it is noncontrollable. There are two important implications of this definition: (1) it refers to a specific responsibility center, and (2) it suggests that controllability results from a *significant* influence rather than from a *complete* influence. Each of these implications is discussed below.

The word "controllable" must be used in the context of a specific responsibility center rather than as an innate characteristic of a given cost item. When the organization is viewed as a complete entity, **all costs are controllable.** For any item of cost, there is someone, some-where in the company, who can take actions that influence it. In the extreme case, costs for any segment of the business can be reduced to zero by closing down that segment; costs incurred in manufacturing a component within the company can be changed by purchasing that component from an outside vendor; and so on. Thus, the important question is not what costs are controllable in general but rather what costs are controllable in a *specific responsibility center,* for it is these costs on which the management control system must focus.

DEGREE OF INFLUENCE

The definition of "controllable" refers to a *significant* influence rather than to *complete* influence because only in rare cases does one individual have complete control over *all* the factors that influence **any** item of cost. The influence that the manager of a manufacturing department has over its direct labor costs may actually be quite limited: wage rates may be established by the personnel department or by union negotiations; the amount of direct labor required for a unit of product may be largely determined by the engineers who designed the product and who specified how it was to be manufactured; and the number of units produced, and hence total direct labor costs, may be influenced by the action of some earlier department in the production process, by the ability of the purchasing department to obtain materials, or by a variety of other factors. Nevertheless, the manager of a manufacturing department usually has a significant influence on the amount of direct labor cost incurred in his department. He has some control over the amount of idle time in his department, the speed and efficiency with which work is done, and other factors which to some extent affect labor costs.

Direct material costs and direct labor costs in a given responsibility center are usually controllable. With respect to the items of overhead cost, some elements are controllable by the responsibility center to which the costs are assigned, but others are not controllable. Indirect labor, supplies, and electricity are usually controllable. So are those charges from service centers that are based on services actually rendered by the service center. **An allocated cost is not controllable by the responsibility center to which the allocation is made.** The amount of cost allocated to a responsibility center depends on the formula used to make the allocation rather than the actions of the responsibility center manager. This is so unless the cost is actually a direct cost that is allocated only for convenience, as in the case of social security taxes on direct labor.

> *EXAMPLE:* The cost of Department A, a production department, for April includes $12,248 of factory overhead which was Department A's allocated share of the $83,422 total factory overhead. The manager of Department A had little, if any, influence on the $83,422 of total factory overhead; that cost was the responsibility of the several factory overhead departments. Neither did the manager of Department A influence what fraction of the $83,422 was assigned to Department A; that amount depended on the particular basis or bases of allocation used. The $12,248 of factory overhead cost was therefore noncontrollable by the manager of the production department.

CONTRAST WITH DIRECT COSTS

The cost of a responsibility center may be classified as either direct or indirect. Indirect costs are allocated to the responsibility center and are therefore not controllable by it, as explained above. All controllable costs are therefore direct costs. Not all direct costs are controllable, however.

EXAMPLE: Depreciation on departmental equipment is a direct cost of the department, but the depreciation charge is often noncontrollable by the departmental supervisor since he may have no authority to acquire or dispose of equipment. The rental charge for rented premises is another example of a direct but noncontrollable cost.

CONTRAST WITH VARIABLE COSTS

Neither are controllable costs necessarily the same as *variable costs,* that is, costs that vary with the volume of output. Some costs, such as indirect labor, heat, light, and magazine subscriptions, may be unaffected by volume, but they are nevertheless controllable. Conversely, although most variable costs are controllable, that is not always the case. In some situations, the cost of raw material and parts, whose consumption varies directly with volume, may be entirely outside the influence of the departmental manager.

EXAMPLE: In an automobile assembly department, one automobile requires an engine, a body, five wheels, and so on, and there is nothing the supervisor can do about it. He is responsible for waste and spoilage of material, but not for the main flow of material itself.

Direct labor, which is usually thought of as the obvious example of a controllable cost item, may be noncontrollable in certain types of responsibility centers. Situations of this type must be examined very carefully, however, in order to insure that the noncontrollability is real. Supervisors tend to argue that more costs are noncontrollable than actually is the case, in order to avoid being held responsible for them.

EXAMPLE: If an assembly line has 20 work stations and cannot be operated unless it is manned by 20 persons of specified skills and hence specified wage rates, direct labor cost on that assembly line may be noncontrollable. Nevertheless, the assumption that such costs are noncontrollable may be open to challenge, for it may be possible to find ways to do the job with 19 persons, or with 20 persons who have a lower average skill classification and hence lower wage rates.

CONVERTING NONCONTROLLABLE COSTS TO CONTROLLABLE COSTS

A noncontrollable element of cost can be converted to a controllable element of cost in either of two related ways: (1) by changing the basis of cost assignment; and/or (2) by changing the locus of responsibility for decisions.

Converting allocated costs to direct costs. As noted above, allocated costs are noncontrollable by the responsibility center to which they are allocated. Many items of cost that are allocated to responsibility centers could be converted to controllable costs simply by assigning the cost in such a way that the amount of costs assigned is influenced by actions taken by the manager of the responsibility center.

> *EXAMPLE:* If all electricity coming into a plant is measured by a single meter, there is no way of measuring the actual electrical consumption of each department in the plant, and the electrical cost is therefore necessarily allocated to each department and is noncontrollable. Electricity cost can be changed to a controllable cost for the several departments in the plant simply by installing electrical meters in each department so that each department's actual consumption is measured.

Services that a responsibility center receives from service units can be converted from allocated to controllable costs by assigning the cost of services to the benefiting responsibility centers on some basis that measures the amount of services actually rendered.

> *EXAMPLE:* As described in Chapter 10, if maintenance department costs are charged to production responsibility centers as a part of an overhead rate, they are noncontrollable; but if responsibility centers are charged on the basis of an hourly rate for each hour that a maintenance man works there and if the head of the responsibility center can influence the requests for maintenance work, then maintenance is a controllable element of the cost of the production responsibility center.

Practically any item of indirect cost could conceivably be converted to a direct and controllable cost, but for some (such as charging the president's salary on the basis of the time he spends on the problems of various parts of the business), the effort involved in doing so clearly is not worthwhile. There are nevertheless a great many unexploited opportunities in many companies to convert noncontrollable costs to controllable costs.

The same principle applies to costs that although actually incurred in a responsibility center are not assigned to the responsibility center at all, even on an allocated basis. Under these circumstances, the material or services are "free" insofar as the head of the responsibility center is concerned, and since he does not have to "pay" for them (as part of the costs for which he is held responsible), he is unlikely to be concerned about careful use of these materials or services.

> *EXAMPLE:* Until relatively recently, the city of New York did not charge residents for the amount of water that they used. When water meters were installed and residents were required to pay for their own use of water, the total quantity of water used in the city decreased by a sizable amount.

Changing responsibility for cost incurrence. The most important decisions affecting costs are made at or near the top of an organization, both because top management presumably has more ability and because it has a broader viewpoint than lower level managers. On the other hand, the farther removed these decisions are from the "firing line," the place where resources are actually used, the less responsive they can be to conditions currently existing at that place. Although there is no way of making a precise distinction, an organization in which a relatively high proportion of decisions are made at the top is said to be *centralized,* and one in which lower level managers make relatively more decisions is said to be *decentralized.*

In the context of our present discussion, a decentralized organization is one in which a relatively large fraction of total costs are controllable in the lower levels of responsibility centers. Many companies have found that if they have a good system for controlling performance, top management can safely delegate responsibility for many decisions, and thus use the knowledge and judgment of the person who is intimately familiar with current conditions at lower levels.

> EXAMPLE: Perhaps the most dramatic example of a shift from centralized to decentralized management is the change that has taken place in Communist countries. Beginning with Yugoslavia in the 1950s, and later extending to the USSR, there has been a recognition that the highly centralized planning and control process envisioned by Lenin simply does not work well in practice. Consequently, individual plant managers have been given much more authority to make decisions affecting the costs of their plants. This shift to decentralization required the installation of a more effective management control system.

REPORTING NONCONTROLLABLE COSTS

In the performance reports for responsibility centers, it is obviously essential that controllable costs be clearly separated from noncontrollable costs. Some people argue that the *separation* of controllable from noncontrollable costs is not enough; they insist that noncontrollable costs should not even be reported. Actually, there may be good reasons for reporting all, or certain types of, the noncontrollable costs assigned to a responsibility center. One reason is that top management may want the manager of the responsibilty center to be concerned about such costs, the expectation being that his concern may indirectly lead to better cost control.

> EXAMPLE: The control report of a production department may list an allocated portion of the cost of the personnel department, even though the foreman of the production department has no direct responsibility for costs of the personnel department. Such a practice can be justified either on the ground that the foreman will refrain from making unnecessary requests of the personnel department if he is made to feel some responsibility for personnel department costs, or on the ground that the foreman may in various ways put pressure on the manager of the personnel department to exercise good cost control in his own department.

Another reason for reporting noncontrollable costs in responsibility centers is that if the manager is made aware of the total amount of costs that are incurred in operating his responsibility center, he may have a better understanding of how much other parts of the company contributes to its operation. Such a practice may boomerang, however, for the manager may conclude that his controllable costs are so small, relative to the costs that he cannot control, that they are not worth worrying about.

EXAMPLE: Exhibit 13–2 shows a control report for a production department. The controllable items of cost are clearly separated from the noncontrollable items, and no variance from budgeted costs is shown for the noncontrollable items in order to avoid any implication that the department manager is responsible for explaining the behavior of these items. The departmental manager is made aware that the total cost of the department is $15,253. Some people would argue, however, that he knows that since $6,248 of this amount is noncontrollable, he may not be adequately concerned about the $9,005 that is controllable and especially about his $488 unfavorable variance, which is only 3 percent of total cost.

Exhibit 13–2

A control report

Department 107		Month: January 1974
Item	Actual Cost	Variance from Budget
Controllable:		
Material spoilage	$ 681	$(107)
Direct labor	5,234	(228)
Indirect labor	1,678	82
Supplies	340	20
Maintenance	822	(235)
Power	450	(20)
Subtotal, controllable	$ 9,005	$(488)
Noncontrollable:		
Rent	$ 763	
Depreciation	1,625	
Allocated costs	3,860	
Subtotal, noncontrollable	$ 6,248	
Total cost	$15,253	

( ) = unfavorable.

Engineered, discretionary, and committed costs

Still another classification of costs is that among (1) engineered, (2) discretionary, and (3) committed costs. Although both engineered and discretionary costs are controllable, the approach to the control of one is quite different from that of the other. Committed costs are not controllable in the short run, but they are controllable in the long run.

ENGINEERED COSTS

Engineered costs are items of cost for which the right or proper amount of costs that should be incurred can be estimated. Direct labor cost is an example. Given the specifications for a product, engineers can determine the necessary production operations and they can estimate, within reasonably close limits, the time that should be spent on each operation. The total amount of direct labor costs that should be incurred can then be estimated by translation of these times into money by means of a standard wage rate, to arrive at a standard labor cost per unit. The standard unit cost multiplied by the number of units of product gives what the total amount of direct labor cost should be. Since production engineering is not an exact science, this amount is not necessarily the exact amount that should be spent, but the estimates can usually be made close enough so that there is relatively little ground for disagreement. In particular, there can be no reasonable ground for denying that there is a direct relationship between volume (i.e., output) and costs; two units require approximately double the amount of direct labor that one unit requires. Similarly, in most situations, direct material costs are engineered costs.

DISCRETIONARY COSTS

Discretionary costs are items of costs whose amount can be varied at the discretion of the manager of the responsibility center. These costs are also called **programmed** or **managed** costs. The amount of a discretionary cost can be whatever management wants it to be, within wide limits. Unlike engineered costs, there is no scientific way of deciding what the "right" amount of cost should be, or at least there is no scientific basis that the management of the particular company is willing to rely on. How much should be spent for research and development? For public relations? For employees' parties and outings? For donations? For the accounting department? No one knows. In most companies, the discretionary cost category includes all general and administrative activities, all order-getting activities, and many items of factory indirect cost.

In the absence of an engineering standard, the amount to be spent for a given item of cost must be a matter of judgment. Usually, this judgment is arrived at by joint agreement between the supervisor concerned and his superior, as part of the budget preparation process. Indeed most of the discussion in the negotiation phase of the budget preparation process (which was described in Chapter 11) occurs with respect to the permitted level of discretionary costs.

Although there is no "right" level for the total amount of a discretionary cost item, there may be usable standards for controlling some of the detail within it.

> *EXAMPLE:* Although no one knows the optimum amount that should be spent for the accounting function as a whole, it is nevertheless possible to measure the performance of individual clerks in the accounting department in terms of number of postings or number of invoices typed per hour. And although we cannot know the "right" amount of total travel expense, we can set standards for the amount that should be spent per day or per mile.

Furthermore, new developments in management accounting result in a gradual shift of items from the discretionary cost category to the engineered cost category. Several companies have recently started to use what they believe to be valid techniques for determining the "right" amount that they should spend on advertising in order to achieve their sales objectives, or the "right" number of sales personnel.

Spurious relationships. The decision as to how much should be spent for a discretionary cost item may take several forms, such as "spend the same amount as we spent last year," or "spend *b* percent of sales," or "spend *a* dollars plus *b* percent of sales." These decision rules result in historical spending patterns which, when plotted against volume, have the same superficial appearance as the patterns of engineered cost. The first type of decision gives a fixed cost line, the second a variable cost line, and the third a semivariable cost line.

These relationships are fundamentally different from those observed for engineered costs, however. For engineered costs, the pattern is inevitable; as volume increases, the amount of cost *must* increase. For discretionary costs, the relationship exists only because of a management decision, and it can be changed simply by making a different management decision.

> *EXAMPLE:* A company may have decided that research and development costs should be 3 percent of sales revenue. There can be no scientific reason for such a decision, for no one knows the optimum amount that should be spent for research and development. In all probability, such a rule exists primarily because management thinks that this is what the company can afford to spend. In this company there will be a linear relationship between sales volume and research and development costs. This is not a cause-and-effect relationship, however; and there is no inherent reason why research and development costs in the future should conform to the historical pattern.

Order-getting costs. As explained in Chapter 4, order-getting costs are those incurred in order to make sales. They include the costs of the selling organization, advertising, sales promotion, and so on. These costs may vary with sales volume, but the relationship is the reverse of that for factory costs: order-getting cost is the independent variable, and sales volume is the dependent variable. Order-getting costs vary not in response to sales volume but rather *in anticipation of* sales volume, according to decisions made by management.[2] They are there-fore discretionary costs.

If management has a policy of spending more for order-getting activities when sales volume is high, then a scatter diagram of the re-lationship between order-getting costs and sales volume will have the same appearance as the diagrams for the relationship between produc-tion costs and production volume (see Exhibit 13–3). The two dia-

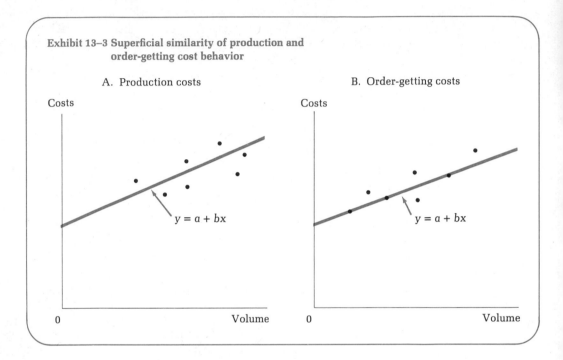

Exhibit 13–3 Superficial similarity of production and
order-getting cost behavior

A. Production costs

B. Order-getting costs

grams should be interpreted quite differently, however. The production cost diagram indicates that production cost *necessarily* increases as volume increases, while the selling cost diagram shows either that selling cost has been *permitted* to increase with increases in volume, or that the higher costs have resulted in the higher volume. Further, subject to some qualifications, it may be said that for total factory indirect costs, the lower they are, the better; whereas low order-getting costs may re-flect inadequate selling effort. The "right" level of order-getting costs is a judgment made by management.

There is not always a direct relationship between order-getting cost and sales volume. Take advertising costs as an example. Management may decide (1) to *increase* advertising expenditures when sales *in-*

---

[2] Exceptions are salesmen's commissions and other payments related to sales revenue. These items of course vary directly with sales revenue.

crease, on the basis that the company can afford to spend more when revenue is high; (2) to spend *the same amount* for advertising, regardless of sales volume; or (3) to *increase* advertising expenditures when sales *decrease,* in the belief that additional effort is necessary to regain lost volume. Each of these policies gives a different line of relationship, and the causal pattern is further obscured by the fact that sales volume is influenced not only by advertising, or indeed order-getting effort in total, but also by general business conditions and other factors outside the company's control.

Zero-base review. In responsibility centers in which the amount of discretionary costs is relatively large, one device for controlling them is occasionally to make an intensive reevaluation of the costs incurred. This is called a **zero-base review.** As the term suggests, a zero-base review examines a certain function or responsibility center "from scratch." The reviewer judges what activities should be undertaken, and then estimates the level of those activities. This approach of starting from a zero base is in sharp contrast with that used in budgeting, in which the starting point usually is the current level of spending.[3]

In making a zero-base review, basic questions are raised about the activity, such as:

1. Should the activity be performed at all?
2. What should the quality level be? Are we doing too much?
3. Should it be performed in this way?
4. How much should it cost?

One way to examine the costs of a function is to make a comparison with the costs of performing similar functions in other parts of the company or in other companies. In some cases information can be obtained from trade associations and similar sources about the average cost of performing certain functions in other companies. Although there are problems of comparability; although, by definition, there is no way of finding a "correct" relationship between cost and output in a discretionary cost situation; although there is a danger in taking an average of other companies' costs as a standard; and although many other criticisms can be raised about such comparisons, they nevertheless can be useful. For example, they often lead to the following interesting question: If other companies can get the job done for $X, why can't we?

A good zero-base review is time consuming, and it is also likely to be a traumatic experience for the managers of responsibility centers. Such a review therefore cannot be made every year; rather reviews are scheduled so that all responsibility centers are covered once every four or five years. Alternatively, a form of zero-base review may be made

---

[3] This practice is sometimes, but erroneously, called *zero-base budgeting.* It is not a part of the annual budgeting process, however, because a zero-base review requires more time than is available in the normal budgeting process.

for the whole company when the need to reduce costs is urgent because of some crisis situation. A zero-base review establishes a new base for the budget, and the annual budget review attempts to keep costs reasonably in line with this base until the next zero-base review is made.

COMMITTED COSTS

Committed costs are those that are the inevitable consequences of commitments previously made. Depreciation is an example; once a company has purchased a building or a piece of equipment, there is an inevitable depreciation charge so long as the building continues to be owned. When the manager of a baseball team has a five-year contract, his salary is a committed cost.

In the short run, committed costs are noncontrollable. They can be changed only by changing the commitment, for example, by disposing of the building or equipment whose depreciation is being recorded, or by buying up the baseball manager's contract.

Summary

In this chapter we have described certain concepts about responsibility centers and about the types of cost incurred in responsibility centers. This description is intended to set the stage for the discussion of the analysis of performance in Chapters 14 and 15.

Responsibility centers can be classified as either expense centers, profit centers, or investment centers. Profit centers and investment centers provide a powerful basis for control in situations in which the manager can make decisions affecting both outputs and inputs, although the device may lead to too much competition between responsibility centers and too much attention to short-term results. When a profit center is used, there usually must be established a transfer price at which outputs of the center are charged to other responsibility centers. If feasible, the transfer price should be based on the market price for the product or service; if there is no market price, the transfer price must be related to cost, usually the full cost of the goods or services.

Two additional cost concepts were introduced. First is the distinction between controllable and noncontrollable costs. Here, the important points are that: (1) "controllable" always refers to a specific responsibility center because all costs are controllable somewhere within the company; and (2) few elements of cost are completely controllable by any one person. Second, is the distinction between engineered, discretionary, and committed costs. Here, it is essential that the nature of discretionary costs be thoroughly understood, and particularly that conclusions be avoided that a given item of discretionary cost necessarily varies with volume or some other factor, just because there has been an apparent statistical relationship between cost and volume.

Important terms	Inputs	Effectiveness
	Outputs	Efficiency
	Expense center	Controllable cost
	Profit center	Engineered cost
	Transfer price	Discretionary cost
	Investment center	Zero-base review
	Investment base	Committed cost

Questions for discussion

1. Distinguish between "reality" and "information," using the terms "territory" and "map" in your explanation.

2. Accounting measures inputs and outputs in terms of costs and revenues, respectively. Give some examples of inputs and outputs that accounting does *not* measure.

3. Distinguish carefully between a "cost center" and an "expense center." Can one department in a company be both?

4. Suggest some inefficiencies or unwise actions that would be revealed on performance reports if a responsibility center were a profit center, that would not be revealed if it were an expense center. Similarly, suggest some inefficiencies or unwise actions that would be revealed if a responsibility center were an investment center, that would not be revealed if it were a profit center.

5. What actions could a profit center manager take that would improve his reported performance but would be against the long-run best interests of the company? (Hint: Consider advertising, training, maintenance.)

6. A certain company has a typing and secretarial pool which various offices may call on for additional assistance when their own staffs are too busy to handle the work load. What factors should be considered in deciding whether or not to make this pool a profit center? If it is made a profit center, how should the transfer price of typing be arrived at? If the typing pool is a profit center, should other departments be permitted to hire temporary outside help to handle their overflow work load?

7. A university operates a bus service partly for the convenience of students who do not have automobiles, partly for student safety, and partly to discourage the use of private automobiles on campus because parking space is limited. Should the university charge a fee to users of the bus service? How does this question relate to the subject matter of this chapter?

8. Under what circumstances should a transfer price be a cost-based price?

9. Departments A and B are profit centers. Department A manufactures stove tops which Department B uses in manufacturing complete stoves. In negotiating a transfer price for the stove tops, under what circumstances would the bargaining power of the two departments be unequal? Is there any way in which the two departments could be given approximately equal bargaining power?

10. What is meant by the term "optimum level of cost"?

11. Why is an allocated item of cost not controllable in the responsibility center to which it is allocated?

12. Review the exhibits given in the Appendix to Chapter 11. Give examples of cost items that probably are engineered, discretionary, and committed, respectively. Give examples of cost items that are controllable and of others that are noncontrollable.

13. Explain the difference between the two diagrams in Exhibit 13–3.

14. Why is a "zero-base budget" rare, or nonexistent?

15. "An item of cost that is committed in the short run is likely to be discretionary in the long run." Explain why. For a given item, what time period is "short run" and what is "long run"?

Problems   13–1. The Box Division of Maple Company manufactures cardboard boxes which are used by other divisions of Maple Company and which are also sold to external customers. The Hardware Division of Maple Company has requested the Box Division to supply a certain box Style K, and the Box Division has computed a proposed transfer price on this box, as follows:

	Per Thousand Boxes
Variable cost................................	$180
Fixed cost...................................	40
Total cost................................	$220
Profit (to provide normal return on assets employed).........................	30
Transfer price.......................	$250

The Hardware Division is unwilling to accept this transfer price because Style K boxes are regularly sold to outside customers for $240 per thousand. The Box Division points out, however, that competition for this box is unusually keen, and that this is why it cannot price the box to external customers so as to earn a normal return. Both divisions are profit centers.

Required:

What should the transfer price be? (Explain your answer.)

13–2. Six months after the Box Division of Maple Company started to supply Style K boxes to the Hardware Division (see Problem 13–1), Eastern Company offered to supply boxes to the Hardware Division for $235 per thousand. The Hardware Division thereupon informed the Box Division that the transfer price should be reduced to $235 because this was now the market price.

Required (explain your answers):

1. Should the transfer price be reduced to $235 per thousand?
2. Under what circumstances should the Box Division refuse to supply boxes to the Hardware Division?

3. If the Box Division refused to supply boxes at $235 per thousand, should the Hardware Division be permitted by top management to buy boxes from the Eastern Company?

4. If outside market prices continued to decrease, and eventually reached $210 per thousand, would this change your answer to any of the preceding questions?

13-3. The Transistor Division of Mador Company manufactures certain components that are used in radio transmitters that the Electronics Division sells to the U.S. Air Force. Data used in the negotiation of a selling price are as follows:

	Cost per Transmitter	
	Transistor Division Components	Complete Transmitter
Components from Transistor Division......	...	$ 220
Other direct material....................	$ 20	480
Direct labor............................	80	100
Indirect costs..........................	100	200
Total cost......................	$200	$1,000
Profit margin..........................	20	100
Price............................	$220	$1,100

The Air Force representative argued that the $1,100 price was too high because profit was double counted.

Required:

1. If Mador Company calculated its profit margin on the basis of assets employed, is the Air Force position correct?
2. If Mador Company calculated its profit on the basis of a markon over cost, is the Air Force position correct?
3. From the data given above, which method of calculating profit did the Mador Company probably use?

13-4. Talbot Corporation has a power generating department that supplies power to other departments. Since this department must be prepared to operate at capacity if the other departments have a heavy need for power, the budget of the power generating department lists the costs that are planned at full capacity operations. In April the department operated at 90 percent of capacity. Its performance report for April was as follows:

	Budget	Actual
Building depreciation..................	$ 24,000	$ 24,000
Building taxes and insurance...........	7,000	8,000
Equipment depreciation................	12,000	12,000
Fuel..................................	90,000	80,000
Direct labor...........................	40,000	35,000
Supplies..............................	10,000	9,000
Miscellaneous........................	4,000	4,000
Total cost.....................	$187,000	$172,000

Required:

Recast this report in a form that would be more useful in assessing the performance of the power generating department. Change any numbers that you believe should be changed, using assumed amounts if you do not know exactly what the amounts should be. Explain the changes that you make.

13–5. Police protection and the operation of a city water works are two common functions of municipal governments. Middletown published a budget for 1974 operations and a report of actual results for 1974 which included the following data:

	Police Department		Water Works	
	Budgeted	Actual	Budgeted	Actual
Revenues.............	$ 0	$ 0	$62,000	$61,000
Expenses.............	60,000	58,000	55,000	57,000

Required:

1. Explain how the efficiency and effectiveness of these two government services could be judged.
2. Discuss the differences between these two services which accounts for the difference in methods of judging efficiency and effectiveness.

13–6. The Bountiful Bread Company delivers bread and pastries daily to retail stores. It has six driver-salesmen assigned to different routes. Each salesman is paid a weekly salary plus a commission based on sales. Route lengths are from 50 to 175 miles, some in densely-settled areas, some in rural areas. All but one route have been operated for several years and are well-established. Each salesman may advertise if he wishes, and the cost is paid by him. Because of complaints from drivers about the mileage differential, and route density differences, the question of developing varying commission rates has arisen.

Required:

Discuss the possibilities of considering each driver-salesman as a profit center for measuring performance.

13–7.

CASE
Bultman
Automobiles,
Inc. (A)

William Bultman, the part owner and manager of an automobile dealership, felt the problems associated with the rapid growth of his business were becoming too great for him to handle alone. (See Exhibit 13–4 for current income statement.) The reputation he had established in the community led him to believe that the recent growth in his business would continue. His long-standing policy of emphasizing new car sales as the principal business of the dealership had paid off, in Mr. Bultman's opinion. This, combined with close attention to customer relations so that a substantial amount of repeat business was available, had increased the company's sales to a new high level. Therefore, he wanted to make organizational changes to cope with the new situation. Mr. Bultman's three "silent partners" agreed to this decision.

Accordingly, Mr. Bultman divided up the business into three departments: a new car sales department, a used car sales department, and the service department. He then appointed three of his most trusted employees as managers of the new departments: John Ward was named manager of new car sales; Marty Ziegel, manager of used car sales; and Charlie Lassen, manager of the service department. All of these men had been with the dealership for several years.

Each of the managers was told to run his department as if it were an independent business. In order to give the new managers an incentive, their remuneration was calculated as a straight percentage of their department's profit.

Soon after taking over as the manager of the new car sales department, John Ward had to settle upon the amount to offer a particular customer who wanted to trade his old car as part of the

Exhibit 13–4

BULTMAN AUTOMOBILES, INC.
Income Statement for the Year Ended December 31, 1964

Sales of new cars....................			$764,375
Cost of new sales....................		$631,281	
Sales remuneration..................		32,474	
			663,755
			$100,620
Allowances on trade*................			23,223
			$ 77,397
Sales of used cars...................		$479,138	
Appraised value of used cars.........	$381,455		
Sales remuneration..................	18,312		
		399,767	
		$ 79,371	
Allowances on trade*................		12,223	
			67,148
			$144,545
Service sales to customers............		$ 69,502	
Cost of work........................		51,397	
		$ 18,105	
Service work on reconditioning:			
Charge............................	$ 47,316		
Cost..............................	48,862	(1,546)	
			16,559
			$161,104
General and administrative expenses...			98,342
Profit before Taxes..................			$ 62,762

* Allowances on trade represents the excess of amounts allowed on cars taken in trade over their appraised value.

purchase price of a new one with a list price of $3,600. Before closing the sale, Mr. Ward had to decide the amount of discount from list he would offer the customer and the trade-in value of the old car. He knew he could deduct 15 percent from the list price of the new car without seriously hurting his profit margin. However, he also wanted to make sure that he did not lose out on the trade-in.

During his conversations with the customer, it had. become apparent that the customer had an inflated view of the worth of his old car, a far from uncommon event. The new car had been in stock for some time, and the model was not selling very well, so Mr. Ward was rather anxious to make the sale if this could be done profitably.

In order to establish the trade-in value of the car, the manager of the used car department, Mr. Ziegel, accompanied Mr. Ward and the customer out to the parking lot to examine the car. In the course of his appraisal, Mr. Ziegel estimated the car would require reconditioning work costing about $200, after which the car would retail for about $1,050. On a wholesale basis, he could either buy or sell such a car, after reconditioning, for about $900. The wholesale price of a car was subject to much greater fluctuation than the retail price, depending on color, trim, model, etc. Fortunately, the car being traded in was a very popular shade. The retail automobile dealers' handbook of used car prices, the "Blue Book," gave a cash buying price range of $775 to $825 for the trade-in model in good condition. This range represented the distribution of cash prices paid by automobile dealers for that model of car in the area in the past week. Mr. Ziegel estimated that he could get about $625 for the car "as is" (that is, without any work being done to it) at next week's auction.

The new car department manager had the right to buy a trade-in at any price he thought appropriate, but then it was his responsibility to dispose of the car. He had the alternative of either trying to persuade the used car manager to take over the car, accepting the used car manager's appraisal price, or he himself could sell the car through wholesale channels. Whatever course Mr. Ward adopted, it was his primary responsibility to make a profit for the dealership on the new cars he sold, without affecting his performance through excessive allowances on trade-ins. This primary goal, Mr. Ward said, had to be "balanced against the need to satisfy the customers and move the new cars out of inventory— and there is only a narrow line between not allowing enough on the used car and allowing too much."

After weighing all these factors, with particular emphasis on the personality of the customer, Mr. Ward decided he would allow $1,200 for the used car, provided the customer agreed to pay the list price for the new car. After a certain amount of haggling, during which the customer came down from a higher figure and Ward came up from a lower one, the $1,200 allowance was agreed upon. The necessary papers were signed, and the customer drove off.

Mr. Ward returned to the office and explained the situation to Ronald Bradley, who had recently joined the dealership as an accountant. After listening with interest to Mr. Ward's explanation of the sale, Mr. Bradley set about recording the sale in the accounting records of the business. As soon as he saw the new car had been purchased from the manufacturer for $2,500, he was uncertain as to the value he should place on the trade-in vehicle. Since the new car's list price was $3,600 and it had cost $2,500, Mr. Bradley reasoned the gross margin on the new car sale was $1,100. Yet Mr. Ward had allowed $1,200 for the old car, which needed $200 repairs and could be sold retail for $1,050 or wholesale for $900. Did this mean that the new car sale involved a loss? Mr. Bradley was not at all sure he knew the answer to this question. Also, he was uncertain about the value he should place on the used car for inventory valuation purposes.

Required:

How should this transaction be recorded so as to motivate properly the managers of the departments involved?

13–8.

CASE
Bultman
Automobiles,
Inc. (B)

Ronald Bradley, the recently appointed accountant of Bultman Automobiles, Inc., was unable to resolve the problem he faced as to the valuation of a trade-in car. The car had been taken in trade at an allowance of $1,200 against the list selling price of the new car of $3,600. The cost of the new car to the company had been $2,500. The old car could be sold wholesale or retail, at prices of about $900 and $1,050 respectively. Bradley decided that he would put down a valuation of $1,200, and then await instructions from his superiors.

When Marty Ziegel, manager of the used car department, found out what Mr. Bradley had done, he went to the office and stated forcefully that he would not accept $1,200 as the valuation of the used car. His comment went as follows:

"My used car department has to get rid of that used car, unless John [new car department manager] agrees to take it over himself. I would certainly never have allowed the customer $1,200 for that old tub. I would never have given any more than $700, which is the wholesale price less the cost of repairs. My department has to make a profit too, you know. My own income is dependent on the gross profit I show on the sale of used cars, and I will not stand for having my income hurt because John is too generous toward his customers."

Mr. Bradley replied that he had not meant to cause trouble, but had simply recorded the car at what seemed to be its cost of acquisition, because he had been taught that this was the best practice. Whatever response Mr. Ziegel was about to make to this comment was cut off by the arrival of William Bultman, the general manager, and Charlie Lassen, the service department manager. Mr. Bultman picked up the phone and called John Ward, the new car sales manager, asking him to come over right away.

"All right, Charlie," said Mr. Bultman, "now that we are all here, would you tell them what you just told me."

Mr. Lassen, who was obviously very worried, said:

"Thanks, Bill; the trouble is with this trade-in. John and Marty were right in thinking that the repairs they thought necessary would cost about $200. Unfortunately, they failed to notice that the rear axle is cracked, which will have to be replaced before we can sell the car. This will use up materials and labor costing about $150.

"Besides this, there is another thing which is bothering me a good deal more. If I did work costing $350 for an outside customer, I would be able to charge him about $475 for the job. The Blue Book[6] gives a range of $460 to $490 for the work this car needs, and I have always aimed for the middle of the Blue Book range. That would give a contribution to my department's gross profit of $125, and my own income is based on that gross profit. Since it looks as if a high proportion of the work of my department is going to be the reconditioning of trade-ins for resale, I figure that I should be able to make the same charge for repairing a trade-in as I would get for an outside repair job. In this case, the charge would be $450."

Messrs. Ziegel and Ward both started to talk at once at this point. Mr. Ziegel, the more forceful of the two, managed to edge Mr. Ward out:

"This axle business is unfortunate, all right, but it is very hard to spot a cracked axle. Charlie is likely to be just as lucky the other way next time. He has to take the rough with the smooth. It is up to him to get the cars ready for me to sell."

Mr. Ward, after agreeing that the failure to spot the axle was unfortunate, added:

"This error is hardly my fault, however. Anyway, it is ridiculous that the service department should make a profit out of jobs it does for the rest of the dealership. The company can't make money when its left hand sells to its right."

William Bultman, the general manager, was getting a little confused about the situation. He thought there was a little truth in everything that had been said, but he was not sure how much. It was evident to him that some action was called for, both to sort out the present problem and to prevent its recurrence. He instructed Mr. Bradley, the accountant, to "work out how much we are really going to make on this whole deal," and then retired to his office to consider how best to get his managers to make a profit for the company.

Required:

How should this transaction be recorded?

13–9.   A week after the events described in Problem 13–8 had occurred,
CASE   William Bultman, part owner and manager of the business, was still
Bultman   far from sure what action to take to motivate his managers to make
Automobiles, a profit for the business. During the week, Charlie Lassen, the
Inc. (C)   service manager, had reported to him that the repairs to the used

---

[6] In addition to the Blue Book for used car prices, there is a Blue Book which gives the range of charges for various classes of repair work. Like the used car book, it is a weekly, and is based on the actual charges made and reported by motor repair shops in the area.

car had cost $387, of which $180 represented the cost of those repairs which had been spotted at the time of purchase, and the remaining $207 was the cost of supplying and fitting a replacement for the cracked axle.

To support his case for a higher allowance on reconditioning jobs, Lassen had looked up the duplicate invoices over the last few months, and had found other examples of the same work that had been done on the trade-in car. The amount of these invoices totaled $453, which the customers had paid without question, and the time and materials that had gone into the jobs had been costed at $335. This included an allocation of departmental overhead, but no charge for general overhead.

In addition, Lassen had obtained from Mr. Bradley, the accountant, the cost analysis shown in Exhibit 13–5. Lassen told Bultman that this was a fairly typical distribution of the service department expense.

Exhibit 13–5

BULTMAN AUTOMOBILES, INC.
Analysis of Service Department Expenses
For the Year Ended December 31, 1964

	Customer Jobs	Recondition- ing Jobs	Total
Number of jobs	183	165	348
Direct labor	$21,386	$19,764	$ 41,150
Supplies	7,412	6,551	13,963
Department overhead (fixed)	6,312	5,213	11,525
	$35,110	$31,528	$ 66,638
Parts	16,287	17,334	33,621
	$51,397	$48,862	$100,259
Charges made for jobs to customers or other departments	69,502	47,316	116,818
Profit (Loss)	$18,105	($ 1,546)	$ 16,559
General overhead proportion			11,416
Departmental profit for the year			$ 5,143

Required:

1. In view of the new information, how should the complete transaction relating to the cars described in Problems 13–7, 13–8, and 13–9 be recorded?

2. Does the system motivate the department managers properly? If not, what changes would you recommend?

14 Analysis of variances

Purpose of
the chapter
In preceding chapters we discussed the preparation of plans for the conduct of future operations and the expression of these plans in the form of budgets and standard costs. In most situations, actual revenues and costs do *not* correspond to the planned revenues and costs. Management wants to know not only *what* the amount of the differences between actual and planned results were but also, and more importantly, *why* these differences occurred. Analytical techniques that are helpful in identifying the causes of the differences between actual results and planned results are discussed in this chapter. Essentially, these techniques decompose the total difference between actual and planned performance into several elements, each of which is called a variance. Having identified how much of the total difference is attributable to each type of variance, management is in a position to fix responsibility and to ask relevant questions. The answers to these questions may suggest the need for corrective action.

Overview of
the analytical
process
We shall refer to the data with which actual performance is being compared as the *budgeted* data because, as emphasized in Chapter 12, a carefully prepared budget is usually the best indication of what performance should be. The same techniques can be used to analyze actual performance in terms of any other basis of comparison, such as performance in some prior period, performance in some other responsibility center, or even the analyst's judgment, based on his own experience as to what constitutes "good" performance. Although our principal focus is in analyzing the performance of responsibility centers

438

in a business company, the same general approach can be used for analyzing any situation in which inputs are used to produce outputs.

In earlier chapters, we have used the term *variance* for the difference between actual costs and standard costs. We shall now broaden the meaning of this word to include the difference between the actual amount and the budgeted amount of *any* revenue or cost item.

An *unfavorable* variance is one whose effect is to make actual net income lower than budgeted net income. **Thus, an unfavorable revenue variance occurs when actual revenue is less than budgeted revenue, but an unfavorable cost variance occurs when actual cost is higher than budgeted cost.** Corresponding statements can of course be made about **favorable** variances.

In looking at the business as a whole, attention ultimately is directed at the "bottom line," that is, at the amount of the net income. If in a certain company budgeted net income in April was $100,000 and actual net income was only $80,000, the $20,000 variance indicates that something went wrong in April. It does not, however, indicates *what* went wrong. In order to take effective action, management needs to know the specific factors that caused the unfavorable variance.

Since the responsibility accounting system collects revenues and costs by responsibility centers, information from this system provides the starting point for such an analysis. Such information helps to pinpoint the responsibility centers in which the variance occurred. The system also provides data that can be used to indicate *why* the variance occurred. As a device for classifying the techniques used for this purpose, we shall use the description of the work of a responsibility center that was given in Chapter 13, which focused on inputs and outputs.

STRUCTURE OF THE ANALYSIS

Net income is the difference between revenues and expenses. Revenues measure outputs, and expenses (or costs) measure inputs. Inputs, it will be recalled, are the resources used by a responsibility center. Thus, we can classify the factors that account for the total variance between actual net income and budgeted net income as related either to revenues or to costs.

Revenues earned from the sale of a product reflect the selling price per unit and the number of units sold, that is, the sales volume. Thus, part of the difference between actual and budgeted revenue for the product is attributable to a variance between actual and budgeted *unit selling prices,* and the remainder is attributable to a variance between actual and budgeted *sales volume.*

Cost variances can be similarly classified. The cost of an item of input is found by multiplying the *quantity* of the resource by its *unit price.* For example, if 1,000 pounds of Material A was actually used in a month, and its actual unit price was $5 per pound, the actual cost of Material A for the month was $5,000. Management often needs to know how much of the cost variance was caused by a difference between actual and budgeted *quantity* and how much by a difference between actual and budgeted *unit price*.

As noted in earlier chapters, unit costs of products also are affected by production volume. If actual volume exceeds budgeted volume, fixed costs are spread over a larger number of units, and the fixed cost per unit is correspondingly reduced. Thus, a difference between actual and budgeted production volume gives rise to a *production volume* variance.

The foregoing is not a complete list of variances. Other types of variances can be identified, but they are not important in most situations. (One other type of variance, the mix variance, is described in the Appendix.) Moreover, not all variances are identified for all elements of cost or revenue. For direct material costs and direct labor costs, the analysis is focused on the quantity and price variances, whereas in the case of overhead costs, variances attributable to the quantity of resources used and to the unit price of these resources are usually not analyzed separately. Instead, these are lumped together into what is called a *spending variance*. Thus, overhead cost variances are classified as either spending variances or production volume variances.

In summary, the total variance between actual and budgeted net income is composed of the following principal elements, each of which is discussed in this chapter:

Revenues:
1. Selling price variance.
2. Sales volume variance.

Direct labor and direct material costs:
3. Quantity variance.
4. Price variance.

Overhead costs:
5. Spending variance.
6. Production volume variance.

Revenue variances

If actual sales revenues in April were $9,900 and budgeted sales revenues were $10,000, there was an unfavorable revenue variance of $100. This $100 is explainable in terms of a variance in unit selling prices and/or a variance in sales volume. The rules for isolating the effect of these two components are as follows:

1. The selling price variance is the difference between the actual unit price and the budgeted unit price, multiplied by the *actual* number of units.
2. The sales volume variance is the difference between the actual sales volume and the budgeted sales volume, priced at the *budgeted* unit price.

The **net variance** (or **total variance**) in revenue is the algebraic sum of the selling price and sales volume variances. It follows that having found either the selling price or the sales volume variance, the other can be found by subtracting this variance from the net variance. The net variance is also, of course, the difference between actual revenues and budgeted sales revenues.

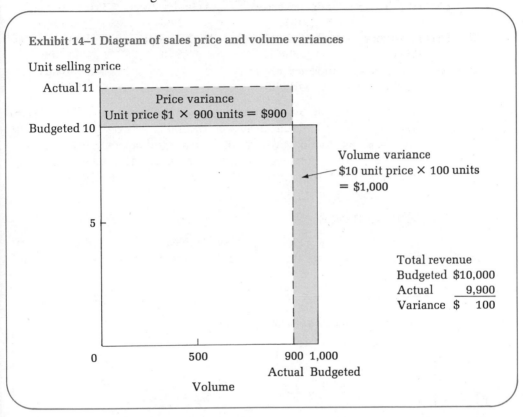

Exhibit 14–1 Diagram of sales price and volume variances

The application of these rules is illustrated in Exhibit 14–1 which is a diagram of this situation:

	Actual	Budgeted
Unit selling price..........................	$ 11	$ 10
Volume, units............................	900	1,000
Revenues (unit price × volume)...........	$9,900	$10,000

In the diagram, the solid rectangle indicates the budgeted revenue (1,000 units × $10 per unit = $10,000), and the dotted rectangle indicates actual revenues (900 units × $11 per unit = $9,900). The variances are the areas where the two rectangles do not coincide. The *selling price* variance is 900 units times $1 per unit, or $900; it is favorable because actual unit price is higher than budgeted unit price. The *sales volume* variance is 100 units times $10 per unit, or $1,000; it is unfavorable because actual volume was less than budgeted volume. The net variance is the algebraic sum of these two variances, or $100 unfavorable; this is also the difference between actual revenues and budgeted revenues.

The calculations are repeated in terms of the rules given above:

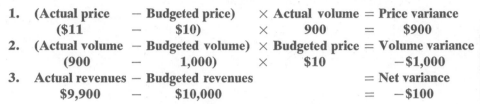

1. **(Actual price   − Budgeted price)   × Actual volume = Price variance**
    ($11   − $10)   ×   900   = $900

2. **(Actual volume − Budgeted volume) × Budgeted price = Volume variance**
    (900   −   1,000)   × $10   −$1,000

3. **Actual revenues − Budgeted revenues   = Net variance**
    $9,900   − $10,000   =   −$100

These equations are set up in such a way that a *plus* (i.e., algebraically positive) result means a favorable variance and a *minus* (i.e., algebraically negative) result means an unfavorable variance, but it is easier to use common sense to determine whether the variance is favorable or unfavorable than it is to remember these relationships.

JOINT VARIANCE

The diagram in Exhibit 14–1 shows clearly the nature of the variances when one of the variances is favorable and the other is un-

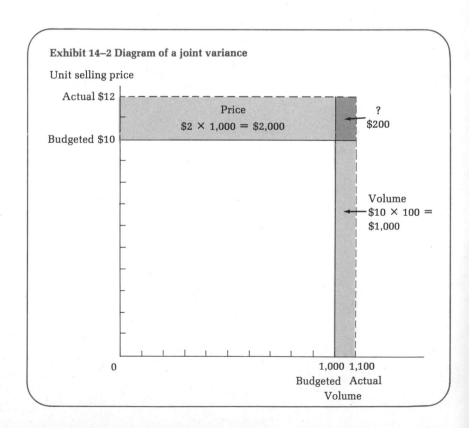

Exhibit 14–2 Diagram of a joint variance

favorable. The situation is less clear, however, when *both* the variances are favorable or when *both* are unfavorable. The nature of the difficulty is illustrated by Exhibit 14–2 which shows the same budgeted performance as in Exhibit 14–1, but actual performance in a month when both the price variance and the volume variance were favorable, as follows:

	Unit Price		*Volume*		*Revenue*
Actual...................	$12	×	1,100	=	$13,200
Budgeted...............	10	×	1,000	=	10,000
Net variance.........					$ 3,200

In this situation, the favorable net variance of $3,200 arises partly because the actual unit price was $2 higher than the budgeted unit price and partly because the actual volume was 100 units more than the budgeted volume. *At least* $2,000 is a selling price variance because the 1,000 budgeted units were sold at the $2 higher price, and *at least* $1,000 is a sales volume variance because the 100 units of additional volume has a budgeted sales price of $10 per unit. There remains $200 of variance to be explained, however. As shown in the upper right-hand corner of Exhibit 14–2, this $200 results from the *combination* of the higher unit price and the larger volume. This **joint variance** is *not* reported separately. The rules stated above have the effect of assigning this $200 as a price variance, as can be seen from this calculation:

1. **(Actual price – Bud. price) × Actual volume = Price variance**

    ($12 – $10) × 1,100 $2,200

2. **Actual volume – Bud. volume × Bud. price = Volume variance**

    (1,100 – 1,000) × $10 = $1,000

Assignment of the joint variance as a selling price variance arises solely because of the way in which the above rules are stated. It would be equally plausible to construct rules such that the joint variance became part of the sales volume variance. It would also be possible to construct rules such that part of the joint variance became a selling price variance and the remainder became a sales volume variance, but these rules are so complicated that few companies think it worthwhile to use them. It is important that whatever rule is selected be used consistently throughout the company.

GROSS MARGIN ANALYSIS

Although many companies analyze output variances in terms of sales revenue, as above, other companies analyze these variances in terms of gross margin. The following data for the month of April will be used to illustrate the difference between these two approaches:

	Budgeted	Actual	Difference
Revenue..........................	$10,000	$10,800	$ 800
Cost of goods sold................	6,000	7,200	(1,200)
Gross margin.....................	$ 4,000	$ 3,600	$ (400)

( ) = unfavorable.

Those companies that make the analysis in terms of revenue focus on the question of why actual *revenue* in April was $800 higher than the budgeted amount, while those companies that make the analysis in terms of gross margin focus on why actual *gross margin* was $400 less than the budgeted amount. In an analysis of gross margin, the portion of the total variance that is attributable to volume is separated from the portion that is attributable to the difference between actual and budgeted unit gross margins.

The **gross margin variance** is the difference between the actual gross margin per unit and the budgeted gross margin per unit multiplied by the actual quantity sold. If the actual gross margin was $3 per unit and if the budgeted gross margin was $4 per unit, there was an unfavorable gross margin variance of $1 per unit. If 1,200 units were actually sold, the gross margin variance was $1,200 (= $1 × 1,200 units).

The **sales volume variance** is the difference between the actual sales volume and the budgeted sales volume (as was the case with revenue), but it is priced at the budgeted gross margin per unit. In the example, if actual sales volume was 1,200 units and budgeted sales volume was 1,000 units, there was a favorable variance of 200 units. In a gross margin analysis, the volume variance would be determined by multiplying 200 units by the budgeted unit gross margin of $4, so the volume variance would be $800.

In the gross margin approach, the difference between actual and budgeted sales volume is valued at the gross margin, which some companies believe is a better measure of the value of a unit of volume than is the selling price. The argument runs that if the company sells one additional unit of product, the transaction increases its net income not by the selling price of that unit but rather by the difference between the selling price and the cost of that unit; that difference is the unit gross margin. The margin approach is particularly relevant when the marketing organization is held responsible for obtaining an appropriate *spread* between cost of goods sold and sales revenue, whatever the cost of goods sold turns out to be. The gross margin approach measures how such a marketing organization has discharged its responsibility.

Some companies do not keep records of budgeted unit selling prices, but they do have a budgeted or standard gross margin percentage; these companies necessarily use the gross margin approach. For example, many department stores do not keep records of the budgeted unit selling prices for the thousands of individual items that they sell. They do, however, have a standard gross margin percentage for each department, and they therefore use the gross margin approach.

On the other hand, in companies whose selling prices cannot be changed in response to short-run changes in product costs, the gross margin is the joint responsibility of the marketing organization and the production organization; the marketing organization is responsible for its revenue component, and the production organization for its cost-of-goods-sold component. In these companies, the use of the gross margin approach would conceal how much of the variance is the responsibility of each organization, and the revenue approach is therefore more appropriate.

Direct labor and direct material variances

DIRECT LABOR

The standard (i.e., budgeted)[1] direct labor cost of one unit of product is constructed essentially by multiplying the standard time (e.g., standard number of hours) required to produce that unit by a standard rate per unit of time (e.g., standard wage rate per hour). Total standard direct labor cost for *an accounting period,* such as a month, is found by multiplying the standard direct labor cost per unit by the actual number of units of product produced in that period. When employees are paid on an hourly basis, actual direct labor cost for the period is the product of actual hours worked times the actual labor rate per hour. These relationships suggest that it is possible to break the variance between actual and standard direct labor costs into two components:

1. The variance caused by the fact that actual *time* differed from standard time; this is the **labor quantity variance** or **usage variance;** and

2. The variance caused by the fact that actual *labor rates* differed from standard labor rates; this is the **labor price variance** or **rate variance.**

A commonly used pair of rules for isolating the effects of these components follows:

1. The *time variance* is the difference between standard hours and actual hours, priced at the standard rate per hour.

2. The *rate variance* is the difference between the standard rate per hour and the actual rate per hour, multiplied by the actual number of hours.

---

[1] In the discussion of direct labor and direct material we shall use "standard" rather than "budgeted," because the former is more common. In this context, they have the same meaning.

The *net* variance (or *total* variance) in labor costs is the algebraic sum of the time and rate variances. The net variance is also the difference between the actual direct labor cost and the standard direct labor cost.

The standard number of hours is the standard number of hours in the products *actually produced* in the period. It is found by cumulating the standard unit labor hours for each of the units produced. It is *not* the number of hours which may have been planned for the period as shown in the operating budget unless actual production volume is the same as planned volume.

> *EXAMPLE:* A company's operating budget shows that it plans to manufacture 1,000 units of product in May. Each unit has a standard direct labor content of one hour. Actual production in May was only 900 units, however. In applying the above rules, the number to use for standard hours is 900, not 1,000.

As was the case with revenue variances, if both the time and rate variances are unfavorable or if both are favorable, the effect of these rules is to assign the joint portion of the variance to the rate variance.

A sample calculation is described below and diagrammed in Exhibit 14–3. The situation is as follows:

	Actual	*Standard*
Hours required for units produced..........	1,000	900
Wage rate per hour........................	$ 5	$ 4
Direct labor cost.........................	$5,000	$3,600

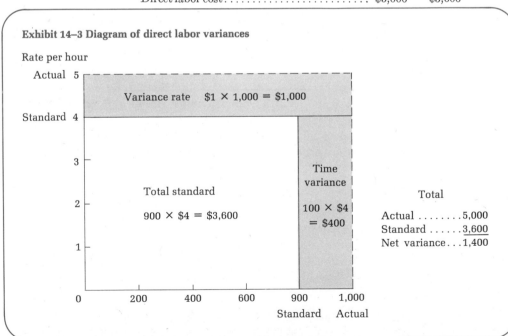

Exhibit 14–3 Diagram of direct labor variances

In this situation, the unfavorable net variance is $5,000 − $3,600 = $1,400. The $1,400 variance is partly the result of the high wage rate and partly the result of the longer time required. The above rules segregate the effect of each factor, as follows:

1. **(Standard hours − Actual hours) × Standard rate = Time variance**
   (900 − 1,000) × $4 = −$400
2. **(Standard rate − Actual rate) × Actual hours = Rate variance**
   ($4 − $5) × 1,000 = −$1,000

Interpretation of the direct labor variance. The reason for attempting to break down the total direct labor variance as described above is that the rate variance is often evaluated differently from the time variance. The rate variance may arise because of a change in wage rates for which the foreman in charge of the responsibility center cannot be held responsible, whereas the foreman may be held entirely responsible for the time variance, because he should control the number of hours that direct workers spent on the production for the period.

This distinction cannot be made in all cases, for there are many situations in which the two factors are interdependent. For example, the foreman may find it possible to complete the work in less than the standard number of hours by using workers who earn a higher than standard rate, and he may be perfectly justified in doing so. Even so, the use of the technique described above may lead to a better understanding of what actually happened.

DIRECT MATERIAL

The variance between actual and standard direct material costs can be broken down into what are commonly called **material usage variance** and **material price variance** by the same technique as that described above for direct labor. The material usage variance is also called the *yield variance*. The diagram in Exhibit 14–3 is made applicable to material costs simply by changing the names:

	Actual	Standard
Quantity (pounds) used in the period	1,000	900
Price per pound	$ 5	$ 4
Material cost	5,000	$3,600

The *usage* or *yield* variance is 100 pounds times $4 a pound, or $400; and the *price* variance is $1 a pound times 1,000 pounds, or $1,000.

In some companies, as described in Chapter 12, the cost accounting system is constructed so that the material price variance is isolated when material is purchased and placed in raw materials inventory. Raw Materials Inventory is debited at standard cost, Accounts Payable (or Cash) is credited at actual cost, and the difference is debited or credited to Material Price Variance. In such a system, the difference between the actual material cost and the standard material cost *is* the usage variance; it need not be calculated separately.[2]

As was the case with direct labor, the separation of direct material into its price and usage components facilitates analysis and control of direct material costs. The price variance is the responsibility of the purchasing department, whereas the usage variance is the responsibility of the department that uses the material.

Spoilage and rework. The material usage variance shows the difference between the actual quantity and the standard quantity of material *put into* the manufacturing process. If the product itself does not pass inspection at the end of the production process or at some intermediate stage, it must either be discarded or sent back to have the defect corrected. If discarded, the labor, material, and overhead costs accumulated on it up to that point constitute **spoilage.** If sent back for correction, the extra **rework** cost is also a cost associated with substandard products. The cost of spoilage and rework is usually classified as an item of factory indirect cost or overhead cost. As such, it is encompassed by the discussion of overhead costs, which is in the next section.

Overhead variances

The net overhead variance, which is the difference between total actual overhead cost incurred in a period and total absorbed overhead cost for that period, can be decomposed into a production volume variance and a spending variance.

PRODUCTION VOLUME VARIANCE

The production volume variance is caused by the presence of fixed costs. Because overhead costs are comprised in part of fixed costs, *unit* overhead costs are greater at low volumes than they are at high volumes.

EXAMPLE: If the variable budget for an overhead item is $500 per period plus $1 per unit of output, overhead costs at various volumes are expected to be as follows:

Volume (In Units)	Budgeted Overhead Cost			Unit Overhead Cost
	Fixed	Variable	Total	
800.............	$500	$ 800	$1,300	$1.62
900.............	500	900	1,400	1.56
1,000.............	500	1,000	1,500	1.50
1,100.............	500	1,100	1,600	1.45
1,200.............	500	1,200	1,700	1.42

---

[2] If actual raw material used is of a different *quality* than that specified in the standard (and hence has a different standard unit price), a sort of price variance is created. Ordinarily, no attempt is made to separate out this variance from the pure usage variance.

Since the unit selling price presumably does not fluctuate with volume, whereas unit overhead costs do change with volume as demonstrated above, unit profit is different at different volumes. Thus, if the actual volume is different from the budgeted volume, a volume variance arises.

In order to measure the production volume variance, the cost-volume relationship described in Chapter 6 must be used.[3] In Exhibit 14–4, the line marked "budgeted" cost shows this direct, but less than proportional, relationship between costs and volume. Costs at any volume are expected to be the fixed amount per period, a, plus the variable rate per unit of volume, b, times the number of units of volume, x.

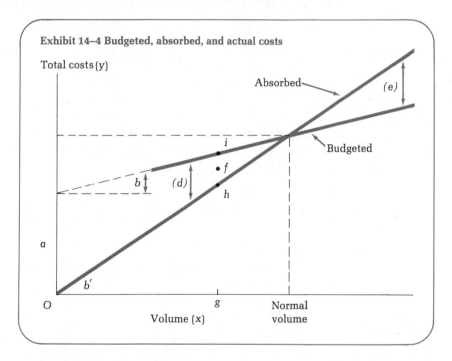

Exhibit 14–4 Budgeted, absorbed, and actual costs

The overhead rate used to allocate overhead costs to products was determined by choosing one level of volume, which was called the *standard volume,* and dividing budgeted total costs at that volume by the number of units of volume. Thus, if the variable budget formula is $500 per period + $1 per unit, and if standard volume is 1,000 units, total budgeted costs for 1,000 units are $1,500, and the overhead rate is $1.50 per unit. Alternatively, the overhead rate can be calculated as follows:

---

[3] The reader may wish to refer back to that chapter to refresh his recollection of this relationship.

	Overhead Rate
Variable costs per unit (at any volume)..............	$1.00
Fixed costs per unit at 1,000 units ($500 ÷ 1,000)......	0.50
Total overhead rate........................	$1.50

At any volume, overhead costs would be *absorbed* or *applied* to product costs at the rate of $1.50 per unit. The line of "absorbed" cost on the diagram shows the total amount of overhead costs that would be absorbed at various volumes. Note that at standard volume, budgeted costs equal absorbed costs, but that at any other volume budgeted costs are different from absorbed costs, as indicated by the spread between the two lines. At lower volumes, costs are expected to be *unabsorbed,* as indicated by the amount *d,* and at higher volumes they are expected to be *overabsorbed,* as indicated by the amount *e.* They are unabsorbed or overabsorbed *because* actual volume differs from standard volume; hence, this amount is the volume variance. The production volume variance results solely from the fact that actual volume in a given period differed from the volume that was used in setting the overhead rate, that is, the standard volume. Also, the production volume variance is attributable solely to the fixed component of the overhead rate; variable overhead costs per unit are, by definition, unaffected by the volume level.

> *EXAMPLE:* Continuing with the numbers used in the preceding example (and shown graphically in Exhibit 14–4), the following table shows the volume variance at various volumes if the overhead rate is $1.50 per unit:

Volume (in Units) (1)	*Absorbed Overhead* 2 = (1) × $1.50	*Budgeted Overhead* (3) (From above)	*Volume Variance* (4) = (2) − (3)
800	$1,200	$1,300	−$100
900	1,350	1,400	− 50
1,000	1,500	1,500	0
1,100	1,650	1,600	50
1,200	1,800	1,700	100

SPENDING VARIANCE

If, whatever the volume level, the actual overhead costs incurred in a period were the same as the budgeted costs for that volume, as shown in the variable budget, the net overhead variance would be entirely attributable to volume. For many reasons, however, actual costs are not likely to be the same as the amount of costs budgeted at the volume level for the period. The difference between actual costs and budgeted costs at the actual level of volume in the period is called the *spending variance.*

The spending variance for overhead costs has the same significance as the *sum* of the quantity and price variances (i.e., the *net variance*) for direct material costs and direct labor cost. Indeed, it would be possible to decompose the spending variance into quantity and price components in the same manner as was described for these direct costs. Most companies do not do this for overhead costs, however, because they do not find this additional breakdown worthwhile.

CALCULATION OF OVERHEAD VARIANCES

The overhead variance, as shown in the accounting records, is the algebraic sum of the volume variance and the spending variance. In order to understand how each variance is calculated, refer again to Exhibit 14–4, which shows these variances graphically. From the relationship indicated there, the procedure for calculating the amount of the variances can be discerned. The situation illustrated in that exhibit is one in which actual costs are at the point marked f, and actual volume is g; that is, actual volume is below standard volume, and actual costs are below the costs budgeted at the actual volume but they are higher than absorbed costs. Absorbed costs at the actual volume are the amount h, and budgeted costs at the actual volume are the amount i. Note that budgeted costs are the amount of costs budgeted for the volume level actually attained in the period. The following relationships will hold:

The **net overhead variance** is the difference between absorbed costs, h, and actual costs, f. In the example, the variance is unfavorable. As is stated above, the net overhead variance is also the algebraic sum of the volume variance and the spending variance.

The **production volume variance** is the difference between absorbed costs, h, and budgeted costs, i. In the example, this variance is unfavorable.

The **spending variance** is the difference between budgeted costs, i, and actual costs, f. In the example, this variance is favorable.

EXAMPLE: Assume that:
- Actual volume in an accounting period is 900 units of product.
- Actual overhead costs are $1,380.
- The variable budget formula is $500 per period plus $1 per unit of product.
- The overhead rate is $1.50 per unit of product.

Then:

Budgeted cost at the actual volume	$= \$500 + \$1(900)$	$= \$1,400$
Absorbed cost at the actual volume	$= \$1.50 \times 900$	$= \$1,350$
Total variance (unfavorable)	$= \$1,350 - \$1,380$	$= -\$30$
Volume variance (unfavorable)	$= \$1,350 - 1,400$	$= -\$50$
Spending variance (favorable)	$= \$1,400 - 1,380$	$= \$20$

INTERPRETATION OF THE VARIANCES

Presumably, the manager is responsible for the spending variance in his responsibility center. Because the variable budget cannot take account of all the noncontrollable factors that affect costs, however, there may be a reasonable explanation for the spending variance. The existence of an unfavorable variance is therefore not, by itself, grounds for criticizing performance. Rather, it is a signal that investigation and explanation are required.

In some situations the manager may also be responsible for the volume variance; that is, his failure to obtain the standard volume of output may result from his inability to keep products moving through his department at the proper speed. The volume variance is more likely to be someone else's responsibility, however. It may result because the sales department was unable to obtain the planned volume of orders, because some earlier department in the manufacturing process failed to deliver materials as they were needed, or because vendors did not deliver raw material when it was needed.

In appraising spending performance, the analyst should look behind the total spending variance and examine the individual overhead items of which it consists. The total budgeted cost is the sum of the budgeted amounts for each of the separate items of cost. A spending variance can and should be developed for each important item; it is the difference between actual cost incurred and the budget allowance for that item. Attention should be focused on significant spending variances for individual elements.

Relation of variances to the accounts

If the company uses a standard cost accounting system, some of the variances described above are identified directly in that system. They are described in Chapter 12, but are repeated here for convenience.

If the system isolates the material price variance when material is purchased, then both the material price and material usage variances appear in the accounts. Otherwise, the accounts show only the net material variance.

The system described in Chapter 12 showed the net direct labor variance. With additional effort, variance accounts could be set up which showed separately the two components of this variance, the labor time variance and the labor rate variance.

The system described in Chapter 12 showed the net factory overhead variance. Again, with additional effort, the volume and spending components of this variance could be shown separately.

Use and limitations of variance analysis

In a given company the techniques used to analyze the differences between actual and budgeted performance depends on management's judgments as to how useful the results are likely to be.

Some companies do not use any formal techniques; others use only a few of those described here; and still others use even more sophisticated techniques. There are no prescribed criteria beyond the general rule that any technique should provide information that is worth more than the costs involved in developing the information.

VALIDITY OF THE STANDARD

Presumably, a particular standard is selected because it is the best available measure of the performance to be expected. Nevertheless, a standard is rarely, if ever, perfect.

Although it is often convenient to refer to "favorable" and "unfavorable" variances, these words imply value judgments that are valid only to the extent that the standard is a valid measure of what performance should have been. Some of the limitations of various types of standards will be discussed in Chapter 15.

Even a standard cost may not be an accurate estimate of what costs "should have been under the circumstances." This situation can arise for either or both of two reasons: (1) the standard was not set properly, or (2) although set properly in the light of conditions existing at the time, those conditions have changed so that the standard has become obsolete.

> *EXAMPLE:* The standard direct labor cost for Product 101 is $6.12 per unit. This may be an inaccurate reflection of the direct labor costs that actually should be incurred for Product 101 because it was derived from an engineering analysis that was wrong, or because it was based on an incorrect wage rate. Or, even though no such errors occurred when the rate was originally set, it may not be an accurate *current* estimate of labor costs for Product 101 because methods changes have occurred that changed the number of minutes required, or because hourly wage rates have changed.

An essential first step in the analysis of a variance, therefore, is an examination of the validity of the standard. Judgments made on the basis of the variance must be tempered by the results of this examination.

It should also be recognized that for the whole category of discretionary costs, the budgeted amount represents not what should have been spent in any cause-and-effect sense, but rather what has been agreed to as the permitted level of spending. For discretionary costs, a variance between budgeted cost and actual cost indicates only that the manager spent more or less than the agreed upon amount. In particular, actual spending that is less than budgeted does not imply "good" performance. Presumably, good performance with respect to a discretionary cost item is spending approximately the amount budgeted, neither more nor less.

Even though the budget is valid, a net variance may not reflect the performance of a responsible supervisor since it may result from a combination of causes, some of which he can control and some of which he cannot control. Analytical techniques make it possible to separate, at least approximately, the controllable portion from the non-controllable portion; however, these techniques are strictly mechanical. At best, they provide a starting point for the tasks of evaluating performance and for discovering the underlying causes of off-budget performance.

NONCOMPARABLE DATA

It is a truism that if data are to be compared, they must be comparable; that is, that the number that is labeled "actual" must refer to the same element—have the same content as—the number that is labeled "budget." One of the annoying problems in real life is that this condition may not always exist. The discrepancy occurs most frequently in "one-shot" analyses, that is, those made for a specific purpose, as contrasted with the recurring analysis of performance that is part of an ongoing control system.

> *EXAMPLE:* In the early 1960s, there was a great deal of public controversy about the decision of the Secretary of Defense to award the contract for the F-111 fighter-bomber plane to General Dynamics Corporation rather than to Boeing Company. Among other things, it was alleged that the General Dynamics price was several hundred million dollars higher than the Boeing price. Actually, the elements of the price calculations of the two companies were not comparable in at least five important respects. When adjustments were made to make them comparable, the General Dynamics price was lower than the Boeing price. (In terms of our analytical framework, Boeing was the "budget" and General Dynamics was the "actual" in this situation.)

Noncomparability can also exist in an ongoing control system. It can exist for some time, without readers of reports being aware of the fact that the content of the "budget" number is not quite the same as the content of the "actual" number. This happens usually because the people who are responsible for preparation of the budget are not the same as the people who are responsible for recording the actual, and unknown to one another, they define terms in slightly different ways.

> *EXAMPLE:* In a certain company, the *standard* direct labor cost included wages earned by direct workers plus all their fringe benefits, including social security taxes, disability insurance, and medical and pension costs. The *actual* direct labor cost included wages earned and most of the fringe benefits, but it did not include pension cost. This discrepancy existed for over a year before being discovered.

SIGNIFICANCE OF VARIANCES

Many detailed calculations must be made in a complete analysis of the difference between budgeted net income and actual net income. As he plows through the detail, the student easily can lose sight of the purpose of the whole exercise, which is to break the total difference into elements such that the *causes* of the difference are revealed. The manager wants to know what portion of the total variance is attributable to each cause so as to decide what, if any, action should be taken. He wants to be able to associate each variance with the person responsible for it. The techniques described in this chapter help the manager to do this. The manager would not personally make the computations, of course; they would be made for him as part of the control process. He needs to know how they are made, however; otherwise, he is likely not to understand their significance.

The calculation of the variances is only the first step in the control process. The existence of variances of significant size raises questions in the manager's mind, and he next takes steps to find out the answers to these questions. The president does not say to the sales manager, "You had an unfavorable sales volume variance; *therefore,* you performed poorly." Rather, he asks: *"Why* did you have an unfavorable sales volume variance?" In other words, the manager does not look upon an unfavorable variance as an automatic basis for criticism, nor on a favorable variance as an automatic basis for praise. Rather, he regards the variances as pointing to situations for which an explanation of underlying causes is required. He seeks to find these causes, and only after he has found them does he act.

In this chapter we have said that the individual variances indicate the *cause* of the difference between actual and budgeted performance. In one sense, they do indicate causes; the material price variance shows how much of the total variance was caused by a difference between actual and standard material prices. The variances do not, however, indicate *why* the difference between actual and standard occurred. Was an unfavorable material price variance the consequence of lack of diligence on the part of the purchasing department in finding the vendor who offered the lowest price, or was it the consequence of an increase in the market price of the material? Variance analysis does not reveal these *underlying causes*. It does reveal the areas in which further investigation is needed in order to determine what the underlying causes were.

Demonstration case   As a way of summarizing the techniques described in this chapter, the complete analysis of a simple situation is shown in Exhibit 14–5. The income statement (Section A) shows a variance between actual and budgeted income of $59. (For simplicity, all amounts except unit costs and revenues are in thousands of dollars; thus $59 means $59,000.) The question is: What accounts for this $59 variance? The answer to this question is given in Section B, which decomposes the

Exhibit 14–5

Computation of variances

A. Income Statements

	Budget	Actual	Variance
Sales..	$540	$551	
Less: Standard cost of goods sold..............	440	418	
Gross margin at standard cost...................	$100	$133	$(33)
Less: Manufacturing variances.................	0	82	(82)
Gross margin..................................	$100	$ 51	$(49)
General and administrative expense..............	40	50	(10)
Income before Taxes..........................	$ 60	$ 1	$(59)

B. Summary of Variances

Unit margin.......................................	$ 38
Sales volume......................................	(5)
Net margin..	33
Material price.....................................	$(16)
Material usage.....................................	4
Labor rate..	(8)
Labor time..	(24)
Overhead volume..................................	(15)
Overhead spending................................	(23)
Net manufacturing.................................	$(82)
General and administrative.........................	(10)
Income Variance...................................	$(59)

( ) = unfavorable.

C. Sales Volume and Margin

	Quantity (Unit)	Unit Margin	Total Margin
Underlying data:			
Budget..........................	200	$0.50	$100
Actual..........................	190	0.70	133
Net margin variance..................			$ 33

Unit margin variance:
(Actual unit margin − Budgeted unit margin) × Actual units = Unit margin variance
    ($0.70   − $0.50)   ×   190   = $38

Sales volume variance:
(Actual volume − Budgeted volume) × Budgeted unit margin = Volume variance
    (190   −   200)   × $0.50   =   ($5)

D. Cost Variances

Underlying Data, Costs

Item	Standard	Actual
Volume	200 units	170 units
Direct material	2 lbs./unit at $0.20/lb.	320 lbs. at $0.25 = $80
Direct labor	0.4 hrs./unit at $2.00/hr.	80 hrs. at $2.10 = $168
Overhead	$100 + $0.50 per unit	$208

Exhibit 14–5 (continued)

Computation of Cost Variances

(1) *Material price variance:*
    Standard price − Actual price × Actual quantity = Material price variance
         $0.20   − $0.25   ×   320   =   ($16)

(2) *Material usage variance:*
    Standard quantity − Actual quantity × Standard price = Material usage
                                                                variance
            340*   −   320   × $0.20   = $4
    * 170 units at 2 lbs. per unit.

(3) *Labor rate variance:*
    Standard rate − Actual rate × Actual hours = Labor rate variance
        $2.00   − $2.10   80   =   ($8)

(4) *Labor time variance:*
    Standard hours − Actual hours × Standard rate = Labor time variance
         68*   −   80 $2.00   =   ($24)
    * 170 units at 0.4 hours per unit.

(5) *Overhead volume variance:*
        Absorbed overhead: 170 units × $1 per unit*...................... $170
        Budgeted overhead: $100 + ($0.50 × 170 units)...................   185
           Volume variance... $ (15)
        * Overhead rate = $100 + ($0.50 × 200 units) ÷ 200 units = $1.00

(6) *Overhead spending variance:*
        Budgeted overhead (as above).................................. $185
        Actual overhead..   208
                                                                     $ (23)

total variance into elements. The remainder of the exhibit shows how each of these elements was found.

REVENUE VARIANCES

The first step in the computation is to analyze the difference between budgeted and actual revenues or margins. We shall here use gross margins rather than revenues. This part of the analysis is shown in Section C. Gross margin is found by subtracting *standard* cost of goods sold (which is $2.20 per unit) from selling prices. Our use of the standard cost of sales figure means that the marketing department is not held accountable for manufacturing cost variances; rather, these are the responsibility of the manufacturing organization.

The unit margin variance is determined by multiplying the actual sales quantities for each product by the difference between actual and budgeted unit margins.

The sales volume variance is the loss or gain in gross margin that results from a difference between actual and budgeted sales volume.

The algebraic sum of the unit margin variance, $38, and the sales volume variance ($5) is the $33 shown as the gross margin variance on the income statement.

Note that revenue or margin variances are favorable when actual is greater than budget, which is of course the opposite situation from cost variances.

> *EXAMPLE:* In Exhibit 14–5, the $33 excess of actual gross margin over standard gross margin is favorable, but the $82 excess of actual manufacturing variances over standard manufacturing variances is unfavorable.

COST VARIANCES

Next we turn to an analysis of the input variances. Note that, as shown in Section D, actual production volume (170 units) is less than actual sales volume (190 units), the difference being made up out of inventory which is carried at standard cost. Carrying the inventory at standard cost means that expense variances are treated as period costs and charged directly to cost of goods sold during the period in which they occur. The labor, material, and manufacturing overhead variances described earlier in the chapter are calculated in Section D. Their algebraic sum equals the $82 unfavorable cost variance noted on the income statement.

An examination of the $10 unfavorable variance in general and administrative expenses completes the analysis of the net profit variance. This is not shown; it would consist of an analysis by class of expense of the amount of and reasons for differences between the budgeted expense and the actual expense.

Summary

Our task is to analyze the difference between actual performance and the performance that was expected under the circumstances. The latter is called "budgeted" performance. The total difference between actual and budgeted net income for the company as a whole can be decomposed into a number of elements. Some or all of these elements also explain the total difference between actual and budgeted performance for a responsibility center within a company.

These elements, or "variances," can be related to outputs and to inputs separately. Those relating to outputs (i.e., revenues) are price or gross margin per unit, and sales volume. Those relating to inputs (i.e., costs) are material price, material quantity, labor rate, labor time, production volume, and overhead spending.

The results of a variance analysis provide a starting point for management action. They suggest questions that need to be asked, although the analysis does not automatically provide the answers to these questions.

Appendix A   MIX VARIANCES

When a process uses several different materials, or several grades of the same material that are supposed to be combined in a standard proportion, a *mix variance* exists if the actual proportion differs from the standard proportion. The mix variance for each item of material is the difference between the actual quantity of material used and the standard proportion (i.e., the quantity that would have been used if the standard proportions were adhered to), priced at the standard price.

To illustrate the calculation of the mix variance, we shall use the situation in Exhibit 14–6. We shall assume that one unit of product uses

Exhibit 14–6

Calculation of mix and price variances

A.   Assumed Situation

	Standard			Actual		
	Quantity (Lbs.)	Unit Price	Total	Quantity (Lbs.)	Unit Price	Total
Material D................	4	$2	$ 8	2	$4	$ 8
Material E................	2	4	8	1	4	4
Material F................	2	8	16	3	6	18
Total................	8	$4	$32	6	$5	$30

B.   Computation of Mix Variance

	Standard* Mix	− Actual Quantity	= Difference	× Standard Price	= Mix Variance
Material D.............	3	2	+1	$2	$ 2
Material E.............	1.5	1	+0.5	4	2
Material F.............	1.5	3	−1.5	8	− 12
Total.............	6	6			−$ 8

* This is the standard proportions 4/8, 2/8, and 2/8 applied to the actual total quantity.

C.   Computation of Price Variance

	Standard Price	− Actual Price	= Difference	× Actual Quantity	= Price Variance
Material D................	$2	$4	−$2	2	−$4
Material E................	4	4	. . .	1	. . .
Material F................	8	6	+ 2	3	+ 6
Price variance.......					$2

Materials D, E, and F in the proportions 4/8, 2/8, and 2/8, respectively. In Section B, the mix variance is calculated by applying these fractions to the *actual* total quantity of material used, 6 pounds; the result is the *standard* mix of the three materials that should be contained in one unit of product, namely, 3 pounds of D, 1.5 pounds of E, and 1.5 pounds of F. The difference between the actual quantity of each material and its standard mix is multiplied by its standard unit price. The algebraic sum of these amounts is the mix variance, which in the example is an unfavorable variance of $8.

The price variance on each material is computed in Section C according to the rule given in the chapter; that is, it is the difference between the standard unit price and the actual unit price, multiplied by the actual quantity.

Computation of the mix variance and price variance in this manner, although complicated, reveals information that might otherwise be concealed. It shows the effect of changes in the price of each material, which is hidden if averages are used. It also shows the effect of varying the mix of materials used to manufacture the product. These two factors may be interrelated; for example, it is quite possible that a higher than standard proportion of one material is used in an attempt to offset the effect of an increased price of another material.

GENERAL USE OF THE MIX CONCEPT

The mix variance came to light when the three items of direct material were examined separately. If direct material is treated as a single item whose quantity is the total quantity and whose price is the *average* unit price of the separate elements of material, as was done in Exhibit 14–5, no mix variance develops. A similar phenomenon exists with respect to direct labor costs. If instead of using the total number of direct labor hours and the *average* hourly wage rate in calculating the labor variances, we had used the number of direct labor hours in each skill category and the hourly wage rate for that skill category, a labor mix variance could be developed. This variance does not have the same meaning as a pure labor rate variance. An unfavorable pure labor rate variance means that a given employee earned more than the standard rate per hour, whereas an unfavorable labor mix variance means that a high proportion of highly paid persons were used during the period. This can happen, for example, when part of the work force is laid off, and those remaining have relatively much seniority, and hence high pay.

Some chemical companies and other companies whose manufacturing process consists primarily of combining several raw materials into finished products compute a mix variance. Most companies do not do so, however. They have decided that the additional information is not worth the cost of calculating it.

The mix concept is perhaps used most commonly in analyzing sales or gross margin variances. It is important to know to which extent the total variance was caused by the "richness" of the sales mix, that is, by the proportion of high price or high margin products.

In general, a mix variance can be developed whenever a cost or revenue item is broken down into components, and the components have different unit prices. When a price variance is computed by use of an average price, we do not know whether the variance is caused by a true difference in prices, or whether it is caused by a change in the proportion of the elements that make up the total, that is, by a change in mix.

Important terms		
Net variance	Material price variance
Selling price variance	Spoilage
Gross margin variance	Rework
Sales volume variance	Net overhead variance
Labor quantity (or usage) variance	Production volume variance
Labor price (or rate) variance	Spending variance
Material usage variance	

Questions for discussion

1. A price variance is usually determined by multiplying a difference in unit prices by a certain measure of volume, and a volume variance is determined by multiplying a difference in volume by a certain measure of unit price. In which case is the "certain measure" the actual, and in which is it the budgeted amount?

2. Describe how Exhibit 14–1 would be drawn if the selling price variance was unfavorable and the sales volume variance was favorable.

3. In Exhibit 14–2, what do the solid rectangle and the dotted rectangle represent, respectively? What area represents the net variance?

4. Describe how Exhibit 14–2 would be drawn if both the variances were unfavorable.

5. As between the sale of new automobiles and the sale of groceries in a supermarket, in which case would the company be more likely to measure a selling price variance and in which a gross margin variance? Why?

6. There is no volume variance for direct material and direct labor, but there is a volume variance for overhead. What accounts for this fact?

7. Changes in unit overhead costs result from the effect of volume on fixed costs. Explain why this is so.

8. On Exhibit 14–4, describe where the point denoting actual cost would be located under each of the following conditions:
   (a) Actual volume exceeds normal volume; actual costs exceed absorbed costs.
   (b) Actual volume exceeds normal volume; there is zero spending variance.
   (c) There is zero net overhead variance.
   (d) There is an unfavorable volume variance and an unfavorable spending variance.

9. Using Exhibit 14–4, and related data, what would the production volume and spending variances be in a month when actual volume was 1,100 units and actual overhead cost was $1,700?

10. In a certain month actual net income was $10,000 less than budgeted net income, and the entire $10,000 was accounted for by an overhead spending variance. In what sense did the variance identify the *cause* of the $10,000 net income variance? In what sense did it *not* identify the cause?

11. In Exhibit 14–5, the production volume variance arose because of the number of units produced and the sales volume variance arose because of the number of units sold. What accounts for the difference between these amounts?

12. Compute the selling price and sales volume variances for the situation described in Exhibit 14–5. What accounts for the difference between budgeted and actual cost of goods sold? (Hint: The standard cost of goods sold was $2.20 per unit.)

Problems   14–1. The diagrams shown in Exhibit 14–7 can represent either sales revenue, direct labor costs, or direct material costs. For each case, identify the letters.

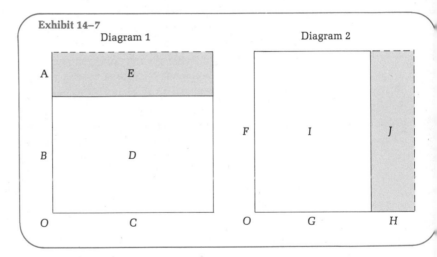

Exhibit 14–7

14–2. Jay and Kay Enterprises have a production overhead budget of $300,000 fixed costs and $200,000 variable costs for a standard monthly volume of 100,000 units of production. Actual overhead costs for the month of February amounted to $485,000, and the company operated at 90 percent of capacity.

Required:
1. Compute the overhead rate.
2. Analyze the net overhead variance.

14–3. Sundry Products, Inc., has the following data for Production Department 20:

Standard hours for production completed.............. 39,800
Unfavorable overhead volume variance................ $ 1,000
Unfavorable overhead spending variance.............. 600
Overhead absorption rate: $8 per standard direct labor hour
Variable costs per standard direct labor hour.......... $ 3

Required:

From these data reconstruct the postings to the factory overhead cost account to show the actual overhead debited and the absorbed overhead credited.

14–4. Brown Company uses a standard cost system in which factory overhead is allocated on the basis of direct labor hours. Results for the month of July appear below:

Actual units of raw materials purchased............. 900
Actual units of raw materials put into process........ 750
Actual direct labor hours used in production......... 425
Standard direct labor hours used in production....... 375
Actual factory overhead costs..................... $3,750
Standard price of one unit of raw material........... $ 6.00
Variances:
  Raw materials price........................... $225.00 Cr.
  Labor time.................................... 175.00 Dr.
  Factory overhead, total....................... 150.00 Cr.
  Materials usage............................... 150.00 Dr.
  Labor rate.................................... 215.50 Dr.

Required:

Use the data above to compute the following:
1. Standard units of material put into process.
2. Standard labor rate per hour.
3. Actual labor rate per hour.
4. Standard factory overhead rate.
5. Factory overhead absorbed into product.
6. Actual cost per unit of materials purchased.

14–5. Given below are the postings to T-accounts of Northeast Company to record manufacturing costs for the month of July. The company uses a standard cost system which removes the material price variance upon purchase, the labor rate variance when labor is charged to Goods in Process, and carries Finished Goods at standard cost.

Accounts Payable		Material Price Variance		Materials Inventory	
xxx	25,000	600		24,400	14,000

Factory Payroll Payable		Material Use Variance		Goods in Process Inventory	
xxx	33,000		400	14,000	55,000
				34,000	
				22,300	

(Various accounts)		Labor Rate Variance		Finished Goods Inventory	
xxx	23,000		1,000	55,200	40,000

Factory Overheads		Labor Time Variance		Cost of Goods Sold	
23,000	22,300	200		40,000	
	700				

Factory Overhead Variance	
700	

Required:
1. Journalize the entries reflected in the postings.
2. Compute the actual Cost of Goods Sold which would appear on the July income statement after closing all variances to Cost of Goods Sold.

14–6. The following data relate to the operations of Smith, Inc., a company using a standard cost system in which factory overhead costs are absorbed on the basis of direct labor hours.

Actual units of raw material put into production.......	300
Actual units of raw material purchased..............	600
Actual direct labor hours used in production..........	170
Standard direct labor hours used in production........	150
Actual factory overhead costs.....................	$1,500
Standard price of one unit of raw material...........	$3
Material price variance..........................	$30 Cr.
Labor time variance.............................	70 Dr.
Factory overhead net variance.....................	60 Cr.
Material usage variance..........................	60 Dr.
Labor rate variance.............................	85 Dr.

Required:
Use the data available above to compute the following:
1. Standard units of raw materials put into production.
2. Standard labor rate per hour.

3. Actual labor rate per hour.
4. Standard factory overhead rate.
5. Factory overhead absorbed into product.
6. Actual raw material cost per unit.

14–7. Below are details of entries to selected T-accounts taken from the records of Midlands Corporation for the month of January. The company uses a standard cost system which removes the raw materials variance due to price upon purchase, the labor rate variance when labor is charged to Goods in Process, and carries Finished Goods at standard cost.

Accounts	Debits	Credits
Accounts Payable	xxx	50,000
Factory Payroll Payable	xxx	66,000
Various Accounts	xxx	46,000
Factory Overheads	46,000	44,600
		1,400
Raw Materials Inventory	48,800	28,000
Goods in Process Inventory	28,000	110,000
	68,000	
	44,600	
Finished Goods Inventory	110,400	80,000
Cost of Goods Sold	80,000	
Material Price Variance	1,200	
Material Use Variance		800
Labor Rate Variance		2,000
Labor Time Variance	400	
Factory Overhead Variance	1,400	

Required:

1. Journalize the entries which resulted in the postings to the accounts above.
2. Compute the actual Cost of Goods Sold which would appear on the January income statement after closing all variances to the Cost of Goods Sold.

14–8. Exhibit 14–8 relates to monthly production for each of four months. The company uses standard costs and monthly budgets for production control. The items illustrated in the chart are overhead costs. Actual overhead costs are shown by the dots initialed to represent the months of September, October, November, and December.

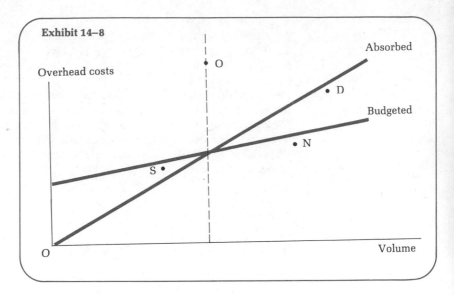

Exhibit 14–8

Required:

Answer the following questions:

1. In what months would the net overhead variance be unfavorable?
2. In what months would a favorable volume variance appear?
3. Based only on the chart, in what two months does the control of overhead seem best?
4. In which of the months was the largest amount added to goods in process inventory?
5. In December was the amount of overhead debited to Goods in Process Inventory more than, less than, or the same as the actual overhead?
6. Which appears to be the larger for this company—the variable or the fixed overheads? How can you tell?

14–9. Exhibit 4–9 reflects the amount of budgeted overhead costs and the amount of absorbed overhead cost at various volumes:

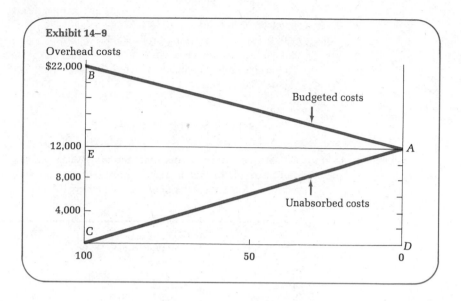

Exhibit 14–9

Required:

Answer the following questions based on the diagram:

1. What are the fixed and variable components of the budgeted costs at standard volume?
2. How much is budgeted for 50 percent of standard volume?
3. Compute the volume variance at 50 percent of standard volume.
4. Compute the spending variance at 50 percent of standard volume if actual overhead costs are $18,000.
5. At what percentage of standard volume will overhead costs begin to be overabsorbed?
6. At what percent of standard volume will the amount of overhead debited to Goods in Process total $8,800, of which $4,800 is fixed?
7. At what percent of standard volume will there be a favorable volume variance?

14–10. The standard cost of Product J is as follows:

Material	3 ft. at $0.50/ft.	$1.50
Direct labor	½ hr. at $2.00/hr.	1.00
Variable overhead	½ hr. at $4.00/hr.	2.00
Fixed overhead	½ hr. at $5.00/hr.	2.50

Standard volume is 200 direct labor hours per month (factory overhead is allocated on the basis of direct labor hours). Selling expenses are $2,000 per month plus $0.50 per unit sold. Administrative expenses $1,000 per month. There were no beginning or ending inventories.

Other information:

1,000 feet of material purchased for $360
240 hours worked at a cost of $504
Actual variable overhead incurred, $984
Actual fixed overhead incurred, $1,250

Required:

Calculate all possible variances.

14–11. As part of its development activity, Vista Land Company had built a road. Its financial vice president was reviewing a report his construction superintendent had sent him:

**Cost Report
Wordsworth Drive**

		Budget		
Description	*Price*	*Quantity*	*Total*	*Actual Cost*
Grading............	$20/hr.	250 hrs.	$ 5,000	$ 5,040
Paving.............	$6/yd.	10,000 yds.	60,000	92,400
Labor..............	$5/hr.	800 hrs.	4,000	3,840
Supervision.........	...	...	2,000	2,000
Overhead...........	...	...	4,000	4,000
			$75,000	$107,280

Notes:

(1) Budget based on a 1,000 yard long road. Actual length was 1,200 yards.

(2) Grading budget based on efficiency factor of 4 yards per hour. Actual performance was 5 yards per hour.

(3) Paving budget based on 10 yards of asphalt per yard of road length. Actually needed 11 yards of asphalt per yard of road length.

(4) Labor based on ⅘ hour per yard of road length. Actual efficiency was same as budget.

The financial vice president wanted to evaluate the performance of the work on Wordsworth Drive. Specifically, he desired to know the reasons why the actual cost of the road exceeded the budget by $32,280.

Required:

Prepare a variance analysis for the Wordsworth Drive project and identify the reasons why cost exceeded budget.

14–12. Howard Machine Works employs two types of labor, skilled and unskilled, in the manufacture of Part No. 66, one of its many products. Standard cost data and actual operating results for the month of January when 100 units of Part No. 66 were manufactured, follow:

	Process	
	Assembly	*Machining*
Type of worker......................	Unskilled	Skilled
Standard hours per unit..............	4	6
Standard labor rate per hour..........	$2.50	$3.50
Actual hours of operation.............	390	600
Actual wages.......................	$836	$2,196
Actual hours for which wages were paid:		
Unskilled........................	380	
Skilled (of which 10 hours were on assembly)....................		610

Required:

Calculate the direct labor time and individual labor rate variances, and the mix variance attributable to the fact that skilled and unskilled labor shifted jobs for 10 hours.

14–13. The Brandon Company has just completed its first year of operations. A condensed income statement follows, showing actual and standard amounts and the variances:

Income Statement

	Standard	*Actual*	*Variance*
Sales................................	$1,400	$1,332	
Cost of goods sold...................	900	800	
Manufacturing variance...............		(10)	
Gross margin.......................	$ 500	$ 522	$22
General and administrative expense....	35	30	5
Income............................	$ 465	$ 492	$27

Other data pertinent to first year operations:

Raw material variances:
Price............................. $15 favorable
Use.............................. $ 4 unfavorable
Direct labor variances:
Rate............................. $10 unfavorable
Time............................. $12 favorable
Overhead variances:
Volume........................... $29 unfavorable
Spending......................... $ 6 favorable

Marketing Data

	Standard Selling Price per Unit	*Expected Sales in Units*	*Actual Units Sold*
Product A..............	$3.20	250	270
Product B..............	3.00	200	180

Required:

The president of Brandon Company has asked you as controller for the following data which you are to supply:

1. How much of the variance in net income was due to the fact that we sold less than expected of Product B and more of Product A?
2. What would have happened to the net income if we had produced the number of units expected?
3. What would have happened to the total net marketing variance if we had sold the number of units of both A and B that we expected to sell, but at the *actual* selling prices per unit?
4. What is the variance due to the fact that actual selling prices were less than expected? Product A sold for $3 per unit.

15 Reports on performance

Previous chapters in Part Three discussed the formulation of budgets and the analysis of variances between budgeted performance and actual performance. The present chapter describes how information regarding performance is communicated to managers and how managers use this information. The vehicle for communicating this information is called a control report. The chapter discusses the general nature of control reports, criteria governing their content, and their uses and limitations. Our focus is primarily on the cost and revenue aspects of performance, but other aspects of performance are discussed briefly.

INFORMATION REPORTS VERSUS CONTROL REPORTS

Reports on what has happened in a business are useful for two general purposes, which may be called information and control, respectively.

Information reports are designed to tell management what is going on. (They are sometimes called "Howgozit" reports to highlight this purpose.) They may or may not lead to action. Each reader studies them to detect whether or not something has happened that requires looking into, and if nothing of significance is noted, which is often the case, the report is put aside without action. If something does strike the reader's attention, an inquiry or an action is initiated. The information on these reports may come from the accounting system, but it may also come from a wide variety of other sources. Information reports derived from accounting records include income statements, balance sheets, statements of changes in financial position, and details on such items as

471

cash balances, the status of accounts receivable, the status of inventories, and lists of accounts payable that are coming due. A list of other possible information reports would be very long indeed. It would include such *internal* information as quantities of material received, sales orders received, production that was not up to quality standards, and absenteeism; and such *external* information as general news summaries, stock market prices, information on the industry from trade associations, and economic information published by the government. An example of an information report is shown in Exhibit 15–1.

Exhibit 15–1

Example of sales information report

SALES AND GROSS PROFIT BY CUSTOMER

BY TERRITORY THROUGH MARCH 1972

CUSTOMER NO.	NAME	TERRITORY NUMBER	SALES DOLLARS MONTH	SALES DOLLARS YEAR-TO-DATE	GROSS PROFIT DOLLARS MONTH	GROSS PROFIT DOLLARS YEAR-TO-DATE	GROSS PROFIT PERCENT OF SALES MONTH	GROSS PROFIT PERCENT OF SALES YEAR-TO-DATE
0007	ABC Company	18	1,000	5,000	200	1,250	20	25
1234	Acme Hardware	18	5,000	10,000	1,100	3,000	22	30
6600	XYZ Company	18	2,500	10,000	1,000	3,500	40	35
	TOTAL Territory 18 — Louisville		8,500*	25,000*	2,300*	7,750*	27*	31*
1300	All Purpose Supply	19	2,000	11,000	900	5,100	45	46
5000	Metro Distributor	19	6,000	42,000	1,800	15,000	30	36
6000	Union Construction	19	23,000	60,000	4,300	17,400	19	29
	TOTAL Territory 19 — Nashville		31,000*	113,000*	7,000*	37,500*	23*	33*
	TOTAL MID–SOUTH REGION		337,900**	1,200,000**	121,000**	400,000*	36**	33**

SALES STATISTICS FOR SPECIFIC CUSTOMER

Customer No. 6600 — XYZ Company

Shipping PLANT	PRODUCT CODE	PRODUCT DESCRIPTION	SALES UNITS MONTH	SALES UNITS Y-T-D	SALES DOLLARS MONTH	SALES DOLLARS Y-T-D	CLAIMS MONTH	CLAIMS Y-T-D	GROSS PROFIT MONTH DOLLARS	GROSS PROFIT MONTH %	GROSS PROFIT Y-T-D DOLLARS	GROSS PROFIT Y-T-D %
1	1111	A–1	200	700	320	1,050	–	–	200	63	630	60
1	1112	A–2	–	50	–	75	–	–	–	–	15	20
1	2222	B–1	–	100	–	125	–	–	–	–	50	40
1	2223	B–2	200	500	200	500	–	–	60	30	150	30
	Total from Plant 1		400	1,350	520	1,750	–	–	260	50	845	48
	Less Freight Absorbed		–	–	–	–	–	–	50	10	150	9
	Gross Profit		–	–	–	–	–	–	210	40	695	39
2	3333	C–1	20	50	50	75	–	–	30	60	25	33
2	3334	C–2	1,000	4,000	1,930	8,175	100	100	860	45	3,740	46
	Total from Plant 2		1,020	4,050	1,980	8,250	100	100	890	45	3,765	46
	Less Freight Absorbed		–	–	–	–	–	–	100	5	960	12
	Gross Profit		–	–	–	–	–	–	790	40	2,805	34
	GRAND TOTALS:											
	Before Freight		–	–	–	–	–	–	1,150	46	4,610	46
	Freight Absorbed		–	–	–	–	–	–	150	6	1,110	11
	After Freight		1,420	5,400	2,500	10,000	100	100	1,000	40	3,500	35

Source: H. V. Stephens, "A Profit-Oriented Marketing Information System," *Management Accounting*, September 1972, p. 40.

Control reports, or **performance reports,** are specifically designed to report on the performance of operating managers, that is, the heads of responsibility centers. The essential purpose of a control report is to compare actual performance in a responsibility center with what performance would have been under the circumstances prevailing, in such a way that reasons for the difference between actual and standard performance are identified and, if feasible, quantified. It follows that three kinds of information are conveyed in such reports: (1) information on what performance *actually was;* (2) information on what *performance should have been;* and (3) reasons for the difference between actual and expected performance.

PURPOSE OF COMPARISONS

The first question to be raised about a comparison between actual and expected performance is: of what use is it? A manager's performance can be measured only *after* he has performed; but at that time the work has already been done, and no subsequent action by anyone can change what has been done. Of what value, therefore, are reports on past performance? There are two valid answers to this question, both of which stem from the behavioral factors that were discussed in Chapter 10.

First, if a person knows in advance that his performance is going to be measured, reported, and judged, he tends to act differently from the way he would have acted had he believed that no one was going to check up on him. (Anyone who has received grades in school should appreciate the importance of this point.)

Second, even though it is literally impossible to alter an event that has already happened, an analysis of how a person has performed in the past may indicate, both to that person and to his superior, ways of obtaining better performance in the future. Corrective action taken by the person himself is important; the system should "help the man help himself." Action by the superior is also necessary. Such action ranges in severity from giving verbal criticism or praise, to suggesting specific means of improving future performance, to the extremes of firing or promoting the person.

INGREDIENTS OF CONTROL REPORTS

For the purpose of considering the information that should be included in a control report, it is useful to recall the description of the responsibility center which was given in Chapter 13. A responsibility center uses resources, which are its *inputs.* These resources can be classified as material, labor, and services; and their consumption is measured in terms of cost. In the operation of the responsibility center, these resources are used to produce *outputs*. These outputs presumably help to achieve the goals of the organization.

Information on outputs can be divided into two categories: (1) *quantity,* that is, how much was done; and (2) *quality,* that is, how well it was done. For a customer invoicing department, for example, the quantity of output may be measured by the number of invoices processed, and the quality of output by the percentage of invoices without errors. Usually, it is easier to measure quantity than to measure quality; for example, it is easier to count the number of invoices processed than to detect and count those that contain errors. Recall also from Chapter 13 that we are interested in two aspects of performance: (1) *effectiveness,* which is how well the responsibility center does its job, and which is therefore related to its outputs; and (2) *efficiency,* which is the ratio of outputs to inputs.

The structure summarized above suggests that actual performance should be compared with expected performance in three dimensions, as indicated by the following questions: **(1) how much was accomplished (i.e., quantity of outputs)? (2) how well was the work done (quality or effectiveness of outputs)? and (3) how much did it cost?**

In some situations, the analysis can be simplified by answering the second question on a "go, no-go" basis; that is, quality was either satisfactory or it was not satisfactory.

> *EXAMPLE:* In a department that fabricates parts, the parts either pass final inspection or they fail to pass inspection and are rejected. There is no need to measure and report the degree of which acceptable parts exceed the quality standards, nor the degree to which rejected parts fall below the quality standards. In this situation, there is therefore no measure of the "amount of quality," that is analogous to measures of the amount of cost.

In these situations, the control reports do not contain information on amount of quality of outputs. When such a simplification is feasible, the reports need answer only the first and third questions, that is, they show information on quantity of outputs and on cost.

In still other situations, the reports can be limited to only the third question. For example, if the manager of a production department has no control over the volume of production and if the quality of work is indicated by the amount of rework costs, his performance may be measured primarily on the basis of cost alone.

In many situations, however, all three questions need to be considered together, and mistakes are made when one facet of performance is given undue emphasis as compared with the others.

> *EXAMPLE:* Until recently the Soviet management control system emphasized the *quantity* of outputs, with substantial bonuses being paid to managers for exceeding volume quotas. Because of this emphasis on quantity, inadequate attention was paid to quality and to

cost. In recent years the Soviet system has been redesigned to provide a more balanced emphasis for all three factors.

CRITERIA FOR CONTROL REPORTS

In the next sections we shall discuss certain criteria that should govern the content of control reports. These are:

1.   Reports should be related to personal responsibility.
2.   Reports should compare actual performance with the best available standard.
3.   Reports should highlight significant information.
4.   Reports should be timely.
5.   Information should be communicated clearly.
6.   Reports should be integrated.
7.   Reports must be worth more than they cost.

As a basis for discussing these criteria, we shall use the set of control reports shown in Exhibit 15–2.

Focus on
personal
responsibility

In this Part Three, we have emphasized *responsibility accounting,* that is, the type of accounting that classifies costs and revenues according to the responsibility centers that are responsible for incurring the costs and generating the revenues. Responsibility accounting therefore provides information that meets the criterion that reports should be related to personal responsibility.

Responsibility accounting also classifies the costs assigned to each responsibility center according to whether they are controllable or noncontrollable. Many control reports show only controllable costs; nevertheless, some of them contain noncontrollable costs for information purposes. In Exhibit 15–2, only controllable costs are reported. Note that these include only direct labor cost and controllable overhead cost. Direct material cost is not included on these reports because in the departments included on these reports neither the quantity nor the price of material used is controllable by the department manager. The manager is responsible, however, for repair and rework costs of material or products that are defective, and this item of controllable cost does appear on the report.

In order to facilitate analysis and corrective action, the total amount of controllable cost is classified by item (also called *object,* or *natural element,* or *function*). Indirect labor, supplies, power, heat, overtime premiums, and spoilage are examples from the long list of cost elements that might be useful in a given situation.

In summary, **responsibility accounting requires that costs be classified: (1) by responsibility centers; (2) within each responsibility center,**

Exhibit 15–2

Package of control reports

A. First (or, lowest) Level Report

Drill Press Department (Foreman)	Actual		(Over) or Under Budget	
	June	Year to Date	June	Year to Date
Output:				
Standard direct labor hours........	1,210	6,060	105	501
Direct labor cost:				
Amount........................	$3,860	$22,140	$ 360	$1,140
Time variance..................			622	1,807
Rate variance..................			(262)	(667)
Controllable overhead:				
Setup costs....................	1,187	7,224	(265)	90
Repair and rework..............	520	2,916	180	91
Overtime premium..............	484	2,748	(75)	(704)
Supplies.......................	215	1,308	(121)	(210)
Small tools....................	260	1,521	160	(82)
Other.........................	644	3,888	91	195
Total.....................	$3,310	$19,605	$ (30)	$ (620)

B. Second Level Report

Production Department Cost Summary (General superintendent)	Amount		(Over) or Under Budget	
	June	Year to Date	June	Year to Date
Controllable overhead:				
General superintendent's office......	$ 1,960	$ 12,300	$ (115)	$ (675)
Drill press.....................	3,310	19,605	(30)	(620)
Screw machine..................	3,115	18,085	90	(135)
Punch press....................	5,740	33,635	(65)	(640)
Plating........................	1,865	9,795	(175)	825
Heat treating..................	3,195	18,015	210	35
Assembly......................	5,340	35,845	(625)	(1,380)
Total.....................	$24,525	$147,280	$ (710)	$(2,590)

	Standard		Variance	
	June	Year to Date	June	Year to Date
Direct labor:				
Drill press.....................	$ 3,860	$ 22,140	$ 360	$1,140
Screw machine..................	5,240	31,760	540	1,560
Punch press....................	3,720	23,850	215	940
Plating........................	1,410	7,370	155	1,410
Heat treating..................	1,630	8,510	180	390
Assembly......................	11,260	68,340	1,570	(310)
Total.....................	$27,120	$161,970	$3,020	$5,130

C. Third Level Report

Factory Cost Summary (Vice president of production)	Amount		(Over) or Under Budget	
	June	Year to Date	June	Year to Date
Controllable overhead:				
Vice president's office..............	$ 2,110	$ 12,030	$ (315)	$ 35
General superintendent's office......	24,525	147,280	(710)	(2,590)
Production control...............	1,235	7,570	(125)	(210)
Purchasing.....................	1,180	7,045	95	75
Maintainance..................	3,590	18,960	(235)	245
Tool room.....................	4,120	25,175	160	(320)
Inspection.....................	2,245	13,680	180	(160)
Receiving, shipping, stores........	3,630	22,965	(70)	(730)
Total.....................	$42,635	$254,705	($1,020)	$(3,655)

	Standard		Variance	
	June	Year to Date	June	Year to Date
Direct labor........................	$27,120	$161,970	$3,020	$5,130

by whether controllable or noncontrollable; and (3) within the controllable classification by cost elements, in sufficient detail to provide a useful basis for analysis.

Selection of a standard

A report that contains information *only* on actual performance is virtually useless for control purposes; it becomes useful only when actual performance is compared with some standard. Standards used in control reports are of three types: (1) predetermined standards or budgets, (2) historical standards, or (3) external standards.

Predetermined standards or budgets, if carefully prepared, are the best formal standards; and they are the basis against which actual performance is compared in many well-managed companies. The validity of such a standard depends largely on how much care went into its development. If the budget numbers were arrived at in a slipshod manner, they obviously will not provide a reliable basis for comparison. Methods for arriving at the best possible budgets and the related standard costs were described in Chapters 11 and 12. This is the type of standard used in Exhibit 15–2.

Historical standards are records of past actual performance. Results for the current month may be compared with results for last month, or with results for the same month a year ago. This type of standard has two serious weaknesses: (1) conditions may have changed between the two periods in a way that invalidates the comparison; and (2) when a manager is measured against his own past record, there may be no way of knowing whether the prior period's performance was acceptable to start with. A foreman whose spoilage cost is $500 a month, month after month, is consistent, but we do not know, without other evidence, whether he is consistently good or consistently poor. Despite these inherent weaknesses, historical standards are used in many companies. There are three principal reasons for their popularity, one of which is unsound.

The unsound reason is tradition. The use of budgets is a comparatively recent development. Some managers who have become accustomed to comparing current performance with past performance feel comfortable with such comparisons and are reluctant to change.

A sound reason for using historical standards is that the budget may not be trusted. Past performance is a firm figure drawn directly from the accounting records; it cannot normally be "fudged." This reason is valid only in companies in which the budgeting process is not well done. A carefully prepared budget is a better standard than past experience because the budget takes account of the effect of changing conditions which tend to make the current situation unlike the past.

The other valid reason for using historical standards is that in a given organization conditions may not in fact change significantly from one year to the next. In the dynamic society in which we live, such organizations are rare, but when this situation does prevail, the work required to prepare a budget may be viewed as being unnecessary.

External standards are standards derived from the performance of responsibility centers other than the one for which the control report is intended. The performance of one branch sales office may be compared with the performance of other branch sales offices, for example. If conditions in these responsibility centers are similar, such a comparison may provide a useful basis for judging performance. The catch is that it is not easy to find two responsibility centers that are sufficiently similar, or whose performance is affected by the same factors, to permit such comparisons on a regular basis. Thus, external standards are more likely to be used in special studies, such as the zero-base review discussed in Chapter 13, than in regular control reports.

Highlighting
significant
information

The problem of designing a good set of control reports has changed drastically since the advent of the computer. When data had to be collected and reported manually, great care had to be taken to limit the quantity of information contained in reports because the cost of preparing them was relatively high. By contrast, the computer can spew out vast quantities of information at a relatively low cost. A computer can print out more figures in a minute than a manager can assimilate in a day. Thus, the current problem is to decide on the *right type* of information that should be given to management. To provide managers with less information than they need is bad, but to deluge them with information that they do not need is almost as bad.

Individual cost and revenue elements therefore should be reported only when they are likely to be significant. Reporting a long list of cost items, many of which have only minor amounts, tends to obscure the few really significant ones. Related minor items should be aggregated into a single item (for example, costs for space heating, electric lighting, and air conditioning can be reported as "utilities"). Other minor items can be lumped together into a catchall classification, "other," as is done in Exhibit 15–2. Because control reports tend to have a standard format, not all the items are likely to be significant in each reporting period; the intent is that the items shown on the report are *likely to be* significant; they are items that the manager *probably* should be concerned about. If, in a given period, an item is not significant, as is the case with several of the items in Exhibit 15–2, the manager simply skips over it.

The significance of an item is not necessarily proportional to its size. Management may be interested in a cost item of relatively small amount if this item is one which is largely discretionary and therefore warrants close attention (such as travel expense, professional dues, or books and periodicals), or if costs incurred for the item may be symptomatic of a larger problem (such as spoilage and rework costs, which may indicate problems of quality control).

ROUNDING

In order to focus on significant information, the numbers in control reports ordinarily are rounded. Some persons report numbers to the last penny, such as

Direct labor............ $127,241.83

In the underlying accounting records, such meticulousness is necessary, but it serves no useful purpose in control reports. The reader doesn't care about the 83 cents; he probably doesn't care about the 241 dollars. He can get an adequate impression about the size of direct labor costs from the $127 thousand. As a rough rule of thumb, three digits of data are usually adequate in control reports (although certain items might have more or less than three digits in order to make a whole column of numbers easy to understand). Thus, the direct labor item above would be reported as $127,000, or the heading of the report would say "000 omitted," or "dollar amounts in thousands."

The amount of rounding depends on the size of the responsibility center. Rounding to thousands of dollars will show three digits of information for items that are between $99,500, and $999,500. For smaller responsibility centers, amounts might be rounded to hundreds of dollars; this is often written as "000 omitted," but with one number to the right of the decimal point, as $127.2. Reports for larger responsibility centers might be rounded to millions of dollars or, as in the case of the Department of Defense, which is the largest organization in the United States, to tenths of billions.

MANAGEMENT BY EXCEPTION

A management control system should operate on the **exception principle.** This principle states that a control report should focus management's attention on the relatively small number of items in which actual performance is significantly different from the standard; when this is done, little or no attention need be given to the relatively large number of situations where performance is satisfactory.

No control system makes a perfect distinction between the situations that warrant management attention and those that do not. For example, although those items for which actual spending significantly *exceeds* the budgeted amount are usually "red flagged" for further investigation, the investigation of these items may reveal that the variance was entirely justified. Conversely, even though actual spending for exactly matches the budget allowance, an unsatisfactory situation may exist.

> *EXAMPLE:* When the general superintendent reads his production de-
> partment cost summary report (Part B of Exhibit 15–2), his attention
> is not called to the performance of the drill press department in June
> because its actual costs were only $30 in excess of standard, an in-
> significant amount. We can observe from the details of drill press per-
> formance in Part A, however, that setup costs, overtime premium, and
> supplies are considerably in excess of standard, and these excesses may
> indicate that problems do exist.

The exception principle is tricky to apply in practice. It is nevertheless a useful starting point for indicating the significance of what would
otherwise be a bewildering mass of data, provided that the need for
some examination of the superficially unexceptional situations is not
overlooked.

The distinction between significant and insignificant results is usually
a matter of judgment. Attempts are currently being made to define
"significant" in statistical terms. Although these statistical approaches
may have applications to business problems in the future, they are not
used to any considerable extent in current control reports.

In order to focus attention on significant matters, control reports
usually omit the arithmetic calculations used to derive the reported
numbers. In Exhibit 15–2, for example, the direct labor time and rate
variances are shown, but not the calculations of these variances, which
were described in Chapter 14.

Note also that Exhibit 15–2 does not show the budgeted amounts, but
only the differences between actual and budget. Some control reports
have three columns: (1) actual, (2) standard (or budget), and (3)
variance. The "standard" column is unnecessary. If a reader should be
interested in what the standard amount is, he can find it by adding
the actual and the variance. It could be argued that the significant information is the variance, and that the actual amount is also unnecessary; however, the actual does provide an indication of the magnitude
of the item, and managers tend to be uncomfortable if a control report
does not contain actual data.

Timing of reports

THE CONTROL PERIOD

**The proper control period, that is, the period of time covered by one
report, is the shortest period of time in which management can usefully
intervene and in which significant changes in performance are likely.**
The period is different for different responsibility centers and for different items of cost and output within responsibility centers. Spoilage
rates in a production operation may be reported hourly, or oftener,
because if a machine starts to function improperly the situation must
be corrected at once. Certain other key cost elements of a production
cost center may be measured daily. Reports on sales orders received or
sales revenue are often made daily or weekly or, as in the case of auto-

mobile manufacturers, every 10 days, because of the variability of this item, its importance, and the necessity for taking prompt action if significant variances occur. Reports on overall performance, particularly those going to top levels of management, usually are on a monthly basis, as in Exhibit 15–2. Top management does not have either the time or the inclination to explore local, temporary problems.

Arguments for a relatively long control period are: (1) performance for a short period of time is influenced by random factors that tend to average out over longer periods; (2) reports that cover short time periods cost more per year and require more time of managers at all levels than reports that cover longer periods; and (3) frequent reports may be associated with unduly restrictive supervision. These considerations in favor of a relatively long control period may be offset, of course, by the necessity for detecting serious trouble quickly: a change in the behavior of a continuous chemical processing operation must be known as soon as it occurs, or there may be an explosion. Also if an out-of-control situation develops, the longer it continues without detection, the more unnecessary costs will be incurred.

REPORT TIMING

The other aspect of report timing is the interval that elapses between the end of the period covered by the report and the issuance of the report itself. Obviously, this interval should be as short as is feasible. For monthly reports, the interval desirably should be less than 10 days. In order to meet this deadline, it may be necessary to make approximations of certain "actual" amounts for which exact information is not available, or to take other shortcuts. Such approximations are worthwhile because an **approximately accurate report provided promptly is far preferable to a precisely accurate report that is furnished so long after the event that no effective action can be taken.** One of the benefits of a computer is that it usually speeds up significantly the process of preparing and issuing reports.

Clarity of communication
Since a control report is a communication device, it obviously is not doing its job unless it communicates the intended message clearly. This is much easier said than done. There is room for much misunderstanding in interpreting the meaning of the numbers on a report. Those who are responsible for designing control reports are therefore well advised to spend much time in choosing terms that convey the intended meaning and in arranging the numbers on the report in a way that emphasizes the intended relationships.

One small, but troublesome, matter is the way of indicating whether variances are favorable or unfavorable. The device used in Exhibit 15–2 is coming to be generally accepted; parentheses are used to indicate

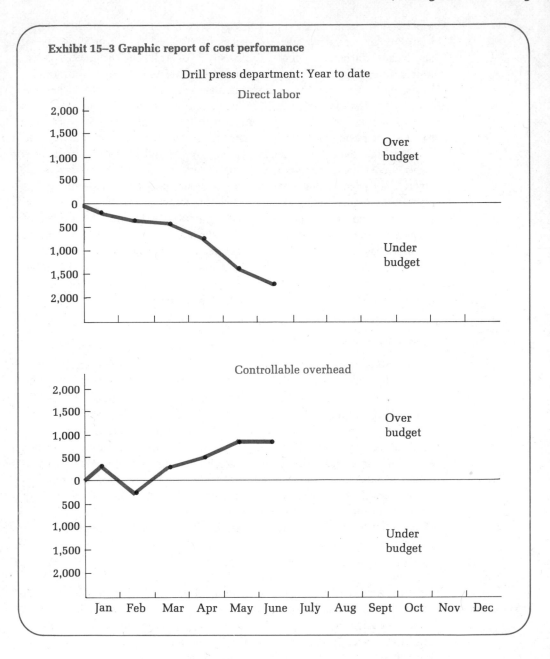

Exhibit 15–3 Graphic report of cost performance

Drill press department: Year to date

unfavorable variances, that is, variances that have the effect of making net income less that the budgeted amount. This means that:

- For **revenue** items, parentheses indicate that actual revenue was **less than** budgeted revenue.
- For **cost and expense** items, parentheses indicate that actual cost and expense was **greater than** budgeted amounts.

Clarity may also be enhanced if the variances are expressed as **percentages** of budget (i.e., variance ÷ budget), as well as in absolute dollars. The percentage gives a quick impression of how important the variance is relative to the budget.

Particularly in reports for profit centers, clarity may be enhanced if **ratios** are used to call attention to important relationships. Such ratios are described in Chapter 16 of *Fundamentals of Financial Accounting*.

Two devices not illustrated in Exhibit 15–2 are often useful in aiding clarity: (1) explanations, and (2) graphs.

Explanatory material may do nothing more than narrate in words the highlights of what the report already says in numbers. For example, a narrative of the report in Part A of Exhibit 15–2 might begin: "Direct labor costs this June were $360 under standard, but this was the net effect of a $622 favorable time variance and a $262 unfavorable rate variance. Controllable overhead was within $30 of budget. . . ." Such a narrative seems to help some managers comprehend the intended message of the report, but it actually does no more than restate what the report itself says. A quite different type of explanation goes farther than this and gives reasons for the most significant items in the report. Such an explanation of Exhibit 15–2 might say, for example: "The unfavorable rate variance was the result of the use of three machine operators in Pay Grade 6, whereas the job called for Pay Grade 5. This has been going on since April because no Pay Grade 5 employees were available. The situation should be corrected before the end of July."

The use of graphs rather than tables of numbers is primarily a matter of personal preference. A graph gives an overall impression of relationships more vividly than does a table, but not as much information can be conveyed by a graph as by a table of comparable size. Some companies use both graphs and tabular reports. Exhibit 15–3 shows a graph that could accompany the report of the drill press department (Exhibit 15–2A). It gives a clear picture of the *trend* of actual costs in relation to budget, but necessarily omits much of the detail that is contained in Exhibit 15–2.

Integrated reports

Monthly control reports should consist of an integrated package; that is, **the reports for lower level responsibility centers should be consistent with and easily relatable to summary reports that are prepared for higher level responsibility centers, and these in turn should be consistent with the summary report for the whole company.**

Parts B and C of Exhibit 15–2 illustrate this process of summarization. Part B is a control report for the next higher level in the organization hierarchy above the individual production departments, the general superintendent. It is a summary report. The drill press department, which is one of several departments for which the general superintendent is responsible, appears as one line on this report. Note that the amounts reported in Part B for the drill press department are the same as the totals on the report for the drill press department, Part A. The superintendent uses this report to identify departments whose total costs appear to be out of line, and he then refers to the detailed reports for these departments. In the situation illustrated, the superintendent probably would be most interested in the punch press and assembly departments because their actual controllable overhead costs were significantly in excess of budget.

Part C is a control report for an even higher level, the total production operation. It includes the general superintendent's departments, as reported in detail on Part B, plus the staff departments that report to the vice president of production, plus the expenses of the vice president's own office. Note that the totals in Part B appear as one line in Part C.

Cost of reporting

It is obvious that a reporting system, like anything else, should not cost more than it is worth. Unfortunately, there are great difficulties in applying this statement to practical situations. Although researchers are attempting in various ways to measure the value of management information, they have not had much if any success. Moreover, it is no simple matter to measure the cost of a given report, partly because most of the preparation costs are joint and partly because the real cost includes not only the preparation cost but also the cost of the man-hours that managers spend reading the report when they might be doing something else.

At least one practical statement can be made: If no one uses a report, it is not worthwhile. Useless reports are not uncommon. They come about because a new problem area created the need for a report at some earlier time and although the problem area disappeared, the report continued. It is therefore worthwhile to review a company's set of reports from time to time and eliminate reports that are no longer needed. A report structure, like a tree, is often better if it is pruned.

It is unfortunately true that **the more relevant a piece of information is, the more difficult it is to measure.** An estimate of future performance is more difficult to make than a record of past performance, but it is more useful. A timely report, that is, one furnished shortly after the events reported on, is more difficult to compile than a report submitted long after the period has ended, but it is more useful. A measurement requiring judgment is more useful than one obtained by reading meters or other objective information, but it is more difficult. Thus, in designing a control report system, a balance must be drawn between what management would like to have and what it is feasible to furnish.

Format of control reports

Exhibits 15–4 and 15–5 are additional examples of well-designed control reports.

Exhibit 15–4 is a control report for a profit center. Note that only a moderate amount of detail is shown, but that there is a breakdown

Exhibit 15–4

Control report for a profit center
($000 omitted)

Month of	June			Division		Seattle Stone	
		This Month				Year to Date	
	Actual	Budget	Better or (Worse)		Actual	Budget	Better or (Worse)
Sales................................	1,665	1,589	76		8,391	7,915	476
Cost of sales:							
Variable cost of sales................	897	963	66		4,930	4,819	(111)
Fixed plant expense..................	232	216	(16)		1,253	1,245	(8)
Production variance..................	27	. . .	(27)		20	. . .	(20)
Total cost of sales................	1,156	1,179	23		6,203	6,064	(139)
Gross margin........................	509	410	99		2,188	1,851	337
Expenses:							
Selling............................	44	40	(4)		238	234	(4)
Administrative......................	64	62	(2)		381	365	(16)
Total expenses....................	108	102	(6)		619	599	(20)
Operating income....................	401	308	93		1,569	1,252	317
Add: other income..................	1	10	(9)		72	18	54
Less: other expense.................	3	2	(1)		20	11	(9)
Pretax Income.......................	399	316	83		1,621	1,259	362

between variable costs and fixed costs. The report compares budget and actual both for the current month and for the year to date, which is common practice.

Exhibit 15–5 shows a relatively sophisticated report for a profit center. Very little detail about elements of revenue or of expense are given. Instead, the emphasis is on the variances, or the nature of the differences between budget and actual.

Exhibit 15–6 shows how *not* to prepare a control report. Some of its deficiencies are:

1. It covers a six months' period, with no indication of performance in the most recent month or quarter. This period is unduly long for effective control.

2. It makes no distinction between controllable and noncontrollable costs. Equipment depreciation and allocated corporate costs, which are noncontrollable, are intermingled with items of controllable cost.

3. It lists items of minor importance, such as part-time salaries, borrowed labor, mimeograph costs, and reproduction costs. Conversely, the "miscellaneous" costs are greater than any single item of controllable cost, except employee cost. The miscellaneous item probably should be reclassified.

4. Readers must make their own comparison of actual and budgeted costs. The variance should have been calculated for them so that they can easily note which variances are large.

Exhibit 15-5

Control report for a profit center

MONTH					YEAR TO DATE		
Income Gain (+) or Loss (−) from		Actual	Ref.	($000 omitted)	Actual	Income Gain (+) or Loss (−) from	
Previous Year	Budget					Budget	Previous Year
220	53	1,307	1	Gross sales to customers			
...	...	52	2	Discounts and allowances			
220	53	1,255	3	Net sales to customers			
17%	4%	%	4	Percent gain (+)/loss (−)	%	%	%
				DOLLAR VOLUME GAIN (+)/LOSS (−) DUE TO:			
100	...		5	Sales price			
120	53		6	Sales volume			
0	0		6a	Trade mix			
−52	−11	433	7	Variable cost of sales			
272	64	822	8	Profit margin			
				PROFIT MARGIN GAIN (+)/LOSS (−) DUE TO:			
104	0		9	Profit volume ratio (P/V)			
168	64		10	Dollar volume			
10%	0%	63 %	11	Profit volume ratio (P/V)	%	%	%
	Income Addition (+)			*Income Addition (+)*			
−40	10	486	12	Total fixed manufacturing cost			
0	0	50	13	Fixed manufacturing cost—transfers			
−182	4	286	14	Plant income (standard)			
−13%	0%	23 %	15	Percent of net sales	%	%	%

January _____ 19
Month

Income Addition (+)
Income Reduction (−)

	−%	−%	101	%
16	Percent performance			
17	Manufacturing efficiency			

Income Addition (+)

				%
18	Methods improvements			30
19	Other revisions of standards			0
20	Material price changes			−16
21	Division special projects			0
22	Company special projects			0
23	New plant expense			0
24	Other plant expenses			−30
25	Income on seconds			0
26				
27				
28	Plant income (actual)			270
29	Percent gain (+)/loss (−)		%	%
30	Percent of net sales		%	22 %
36A				

Increase (+) or Decrease (−)

37	Total employed capital	10,296		
38	Percent return	1%	%	38
39	Turnover rate	4%		1.5

20 _____
Division

Income Addition (+)
Income Reduction (−)

	%	%	%

Income Addition (+)

Increase (+) or Decrease (−)

	%	%	%

EMPLOYED CAPITAL

Exhibit 15–6

Expense center report

NEW JERSEY INSURANCE COMPANY
Budget Report, Corporate Loan Section
First Six Months, 1974

Costs	Budget	Actual
Employee costs:		
Salaries, full time.............................	$109,680	$101,472
Salaries, part time...........................		120
Salaries, overtime............................	1,200	280
Borrowed labor...............................		280
Employee lunches.............................	4,130	3,742
Insurance, retirement, etc....................	13,891	11,845
Social security...............................	3,006	2,742
Total......................	$131,907	$120,201
Direct service costs:		
Photography.................................	$ 655	$ 541
Tracing......................................	292	106
Mimeograph.................................		27
Reproduction................................		14
Total......................	$ 947	$ 688
Other costs:		
Rent...	$ 16,781	$ 16,781
Office supplies...............................	740	1,182
Equipment, depreciation, and maintenance.......	3,096	3,096
Printed forms................................	178	366
Travel.......................................	772	752
Telephone and telegrams......................	910	1,134
Postage......................................	168	156
Allocated corporate costs......................	7,085	6,343
Professional dues.............................	80	80
Miscellaneous................................	1,073	1,165
Total......................	$ 30,883	$ 31,065
Grand total......................	$163,737	$151,944
Number of full-time employees...................	26	24

Use of control reports

FEEDBACK

In electrical engineering, there is a process called *feedback*. It refers to electrical circuits that are arranged so that information about a machine's current performance is fed back in such a way that the future performance of that machine may be changed. A thermostat is a feedback device; if the temperature of a room drops below a prescribed level, the thermostat senses that information and activates the furnace; the furnace then makes heat that increases the room temperature. In an engineering diagram, the circuitry and associated control apparatus is called a *feedback loop*.

Control reports are feedback devices, but they are only one part of the feedback loop. Unlike the thermostat, which acts automatically in response to information about temperature,

itself cause a change in performance. **A change results only when managers take actions that lead to change.** Thus, in management control, the feedback loop requires both the control report *plus* management action. In this section, we describe how that action occurs.

There are three steps in the control process:

1. *Identify* areas that require investigation.
2. *Investigate* these areas to ascertain whether action is warranted.
3. *Act,* when investigation indicates the need for action.

IDENTIFICATION

The control report is useful only in the first step in the process. It suggests areas that seem to need looking into. Although significant variances between actual and budgeted performance are a signal that an investigation may be warranted, they are not an *automatic* signal. The manager interprets the numbers in the light of his own knowledge about conditions in the responsibility center. He may have already learned, from conversations or personal observation, that there is an adequate explanation for the variance, or he may have observed the need for corrective action before the report itself reaches him. Some managers say that an essential characteristic of a good management control system is that **reports should contain no surprises.** By this they mean that managers of responsibility centers should inform their superiors as soon as significant events occur and should institute the necessary action immediately. If this is done, significant information will already have been communicated informally to the superior before he receives the formal report.

The following observations by successful chief executives suggest the importance of these informal channels of communication[1]:

"The main thing is to keep your antenna sensitive, and have an open management. Then the information comes in" (Walter A. Haas, Jr. Levi Strauss & Co.).

"You have to get out yourself and get around, see those flight kitchens, look at that hotel site yourself, get the smell of it and the feel of it, in order to get that extra dimension of understanding" (J. W. Marriott, Jr., Marriott Corporation).

"The identification of what should be tended to by management is itself part of management" (James H. Binger, Honeywell, Inc.).

Difficulties in measuring outputs. In examining the report, the manager attempts to judge both the efficiency and the effectiveness of the responsibility center. In order to do this, he needs information on outputs. Control reports for product departments that manufacture physical products usually contain reliable output information, such as units of products produced, but in many other responsibility centers,

---

[1] "It's no easy trick to be a well-informed executive," *Fortune,* January 1973.

output cannot be expressed in quantitative terms. This is the case with most staff departments of a company, such as the research and development department, the personnel department, the controller department, the treasurer's office, and the general administrative offices. It is also generally the case with nonprofit organizations, such as government bodies of all types, schools, hospitals, foundations, churches, and social welfare organizations. If output is not stated in quantitative terms on the control report, the manager must temper his judgment of the report of cost performance accordingly. Under these circumstances, the report shows, at best, whether the manager of the responsibility center spent the amount that he was supposed to spend. It does not show what he accomplished, that is, his effectiveness, and the reader of the report must therefore form his judgment as to how effective the manager was by other means, usually by conversations with those who are familiar with the work done, or by personal observation.

Engineering and discretionary costs. The reader must also distinguish between items of engineered cost and items of discretionary costs. **With respect to engineered costs, the general rule is "the lower they are, the better."** The objective is to spend as little as possible, consistent with quality and safety standards. The supervisor who reduces his engineered costs below the standard amounts usually should be congratulated. With respect to **discretionary costs,** however, the situation is quite different and much more complicated. **Often, optimum performance consists of spending the amount agreed on,** for spending too little may be as bad as, or worse than, spending too much. A factory manager can easily reduce his current costs by skimping on maintenance or on training; a marketing manager can reduce his advertising or sales promotion expenditures; top management may eliminate a research department. None of these actions may be in the overall best interest of the company, although all of them result in lower costs on the current reports of performance.

In short, **the proper interpretation of a control report involves much more than a look at the size of the variances.** In order to determine what, if any, investigation should be made, the reader brings to bear all his experience regarding the work of the responsibility center, all the information that he has obtained from informal sources, and his intuitive judgment or "feel" for what needs attention.

INVESTIGATION

Usually, an investigation of possible significant areas takes the form of a conversation between the head of a responsibility center and his superior. Such conversations are scheduled shortly after the control reports have been issued. In them, the superior probes to determine whether further action is warranted. More often than not, he learns that special circumstances have arisen that account for the variance between actual performance and the budget. A budget is always prepared under a certain set of assumptions as to the conditions that will prevail. In actual operations, some of these assumptions may not hold. If the changed circumstances are noncontrollable, this, rather than inefficiency of the responsibility center manager, may be the explanation for an unfavorable variance. If such noncontrollable changes exist, the responsibility center manager cannot be justifiably criticized for an unfavorable variance. Corrective action may nevertheless be required, for the unfavorable variance indicates that the company's overall profit is going to be less than planned, and steps to offset this may be feasible in other areas.

Another possible explanation of an unfavorable variance is some unexpected, random occurrence, such as a machine breakdown. The supervisor is unlikely to be as concerned about these random events as he is about tendencies that are likely to continue in the future, unless corrected. Thus, he is particularly interested in variances that persist for several months, especially if they increase in magnitude from one month to the next. He wants to find out what the underlying causes of these trends are, and how they can be corrected.

ACTION

Based on his investigation, the manager decides whether further action is required. Usually, this action takes place at the end of the meeting described above. The superior and the manager should agree on the positive steps that will be taken to remedy unsatisfactory conditions revealed by the investigation. Equally important, if investigation reveals that performance has been good, a "pat on the back" is appropriate.

Of course, in many situations, no action at all is indicated. The superior judges that performance is satisfactory, and that is that. The superior should be particularly careful not to place too much emphasis on short-run performance. **An inherent characteristic of management control systems is that they tend to focus on short-run rather than long-run performance;** that is, they measure current profits rather than the effect of current actions on future profits. Thus, if too much emphasis is placed on results as shown in current control reports, long-run profitability may be hurt. As already noted, it is easy to increase current profits by decreasing research and development maintenance or advertising expenditures, but the long-run effect of such actions may be bad.

Economic appraisal   An analysis of performance in terms of responsibility costs and revenues shows how well the manager of the responsibility center has performed as a manager. A quite separate type of analysis shows how well the responsibility center has performed as an economic entity. Such analyses are made periodically, but not as frequently as monthly, of profit centers and investment centers. Such analyses require the use of full cost accounting rather than responsibility accounting; in fact, the report looks the same as an income statement for a separate business would look.

The control report may show that the profit center manager is doing an excellent job, considering the circumstances, but if the profit center is not producing a satisfactory profit, action may be required regardless of this fact.

> *EXAMPLE:* Current control reports show that a certain downtown branch of a chain of specialty stores is operating at a loss. This loss is explainable by the fact that customers are tending to shop in suburban shopping centers rather than downtown. The store manager is not responsible for this trend. Nevertheless, an economic analysis may reveal no way to put the downtown store on a profitable basis. The decision is therefore made to close this store and open a new store in the suburbs.

There are therefore two essentially different ways in which the performance of a responsibility center is judged. First, there is the control report which focuses on the manager's responsibility for turning in an actual performance that corresponds to the commitment he made during the budget preparation process. **Behavioral** considerations are important in the use of this report. Second, there is the analysis of the responsibility center as an economic entity. In such an analysis, **economic** considerations are dominant.

An economic analysis, such as that illustrated above, may require a revision in plans and budgets. Analysis of the situation revealed in control reports may also require such a revision. Thus, as pointed out in Chapter 10, the management control process is continuous, with analysis of control reports leading to a change in budgets, which in turn become a new standard against which subsequent performance is measured.

Demonstra-   For the purpose of showing how control reports are used, actions
tion case   taken with respect to the reports shown in Exhibit 15–2 are described below. The reader should refer back to this exhibit in order to follow this narrative.

DRILL PRESS DEPARTMENT

The general superintendent studied the report for the drill press department (Part A) since it was one of the departments for which he was responsible. He noted that output on the department in June, as measured by standard direct labor hours, continued to be higher than budget, and he saw no need for investigation in this area. He noted that direct labor cost continued to be below standard, because a favorable time variance more than offset an unfavorable rate variance. He knew from his discussions of earlier reports that the time variance resulted primarily from a methods improvement. He decided that the rate variance was of sufficient importance to investigate.

Looking down the list of controllable overhead costs, he was struck by the unfavorable variance in setup costs for June, especially since there was a favorable variance for the six months to date. He noted that repair and rework costs, which had been out of line in previous months, had a favorable variance in June. The unfavorable variance in supplies seemed to him to be significant, also.

In his regular monthly meeting with the foreman of the drill press department, therefore, the general superintendent raised questions about the direct labor rate variance, setup costs, and supplies. The foreman said that the direct labor rate variance arose because three machine operators were paid a higher rate than the job called for. He had been unable to obtain qualified operators at the standard rates, but he expected to be able to do so during July. The foreman had no concrete explanation for the unfavorable variance in setup costs; it seemed to be an aggregation of unfavorable performance on a number of separate jobs. With respect to supplies, he noted that the unfavorable variance was primarily caused by an unusually large requisition for lubricants, which should suffice for several months.

The superintendent accepted all these explanations except the one about setup costs. He stressed that it was the foreman's responsibility to keep setup costs in line. He balanced this criticism by making complimentary remarks about the favorable variance on repair and rework costs.

PRODUCTION DEPARTMENTS

The vice president of production studied the report for all production departments. He did not raise a question about the drill press department because it had a favorable direct labor variance and an insignificant overhead variance for June. (As already noted, this summary report obscured some offsetting variances that were significant in the report of the drill press department.) He was particularly concerned about the unfavorable overhead variance in the assembly department. He recalled that through April the assembly department had operated close to its budget. He had raised a question about the unfavorable variance on the May report but had been assured that the situation was a temporary one. He was therefore disturbed to note that the unsatisfactory conditions apparently continued in June.

In his regular meetings with departmental foremen, the vice president therefore focused on the assembly department. He did go over the detailed reports of the other departments briefly, because this was his way of demonstrating the importance he attached to the control reports.

He was not satisfied with the explanation given by the assembly department foreman, but neither could he decide on specific corrective action. He did emphasize that he expected costs to be brought back into line promptly. The assembly department foreman seemed to get the message.

THE FACTORY

The president studied the factory cost summary report, preparatory to his meeting with the vice president of production. Of the departments listed thereon, he decided that the general superintendent's departments and the vice president's own office were most in need of discussion, the former because of the relatively large size of the overhead cost variance in June, and the latter because the unfavorable variance, although small in absolute terms, might indicate the beginning of an unsatisfactory trend.

When the president discussed this report with the vice president, the vice president explained that the problem in the general superintendent's departments was primarily focused in the assembly department, and that he would keep close watch on it. The president mentioned the unfavorable variance in the vice president's office only briefly, but with enough emphasis so that the vice president understood the basis for his concern.

Summary

The essential purpose of control reports is to compare actual performance in a responsibility center with what performance should have been under the circumstances prevailing, in such a way that reasons for the difference between actual and expected performance are identified, and, if feasible, quantified. These reports essentially address three questions: (1) how much was accomplished? (2) how well was the work done? and (3) how much did it cost?, although the second question is often answered simply by showing that quality either was or was not satisfactory. The first question relates to effectiveness, and the second to efficiency.

Control reports are governed by the following criteria: they should be related to personal responsibility; they should compare actual performance with the best available standard; they should highlight significant information; they should cover an appropriate time period and should be issued promptly after the end of that period; the information should be communicated clearly by the use not only of dollar amounts but also graphs, percentages, ratios, and narrative explanations; the separate reports should be part of an integrated package; and reports should be worth more than they cost.

A control report identifies areas that require further investigation. The first step of the control process is to study the report to identify such areas. The second step is to investigate each of these areas, usually in a meeting with the manager of the responsibility center involved. The third step is to take action if, after appropriate investigation, action appears to be warranted. This action should include praise, as well as criticism.

| Important terms | **Predetermined standards** **Historical standards** **External standards** **Exception principle** | **Feedback** **Information report** **Control report** |

Questions for discussion

1. What are the differences between an information report and a control report?

2. What use could a sales manager make of Exhibit 15–1? What changes would be necessary to convert this report to a control report? Is it of *any* use for control purposes in its present form?

3. What is meant by the statement that control reports should be related to personal responsibility? Why is this criterion important?

4. What factors can make the budget a less-than-perfect standard against which to judge actual performance?

5. If actual sales revenue is less than budgeted sales revenue, the cause could be *either* that sales effort was unsatisfactory *or* that the amount of budgeted revenue was too high. How can a manager judge which of these possibilities is the more likely?

6. Why do you suppose that some control reports (such as the one in Exhibit 15–5) compare actual performance *both* with budgeted performance and also with performance in the prior year?

7. "Numbers in reports should not be rounded. Rounded numbers indicate a lack of precision, or even sloppiness, and therefore they lessen the credibility of the report." Comment.

8. As a general rule, reports on the quality of output in a highly mechanized department should be prepared more frequently than similar reports in a department that has principally manual operations. Why?

9. A "favorable" cost variance arises when actual costs are less than budgeted costs. Explain, with examples, why a favorable variance sometimes indicates poor performance.

10. In what sense are the three reports shown in Exhibit 15–2 "integrated"?

11. Of the department's listed in Part B of Exhibit 15–2, which one do you judge has the best performance record from the information given? (Caution: You need to consider carefully which of several possible measures is the best.)

12. All the reports used in this chapter omit income tax expense. Why is this omission justified? Under what circumstances would it be desirable to include income tax expense on control reports?

Problems   15–1. The Green Company prepares budgets for each department and for control purposes furnishes each department manager with actual results for comparison. The data relating to Department A for February follow:

	Budget	*Actual*
Sales..................................	$13,000	$17,000
Cost of goods sold....................	7,800	10,600
Gross margin.........................	$ 5,200	$ 6,400
Direct operating expenses*.............	5,000	6,000
Contribution to indirect expenses........	$ 200	$ 400

* Includes fixed expenses of $2,400.

Required:

Rearrange these data and prepare a report for the manager of Department A which will be of more value in analyzing his performance for the month of February. Comment on the results of February operations.

15–2. Brown Enterprises prepares monthly departmental reports in an effort to control costs. Each department has a manager to whom the report is addressed and who is held responsible for the operating results in his department. The report made to Department C for September follows:

	Budgeted	*Actual*
Sales..................................	$39,000	$51,000
Cost of goods sold....................	23,400	31,800
Gross margin.........................	$15,600	$19,200
Direct operating expenses*.............	15,000	18,000
Contribution to indirect expenses........	$ 600	$ 1,200

* Of which $7,200 are costs not varying directly with sales volume at the expected level of sales.

Required:

Prepare a report which will be of more value in analyzing and appraising the performance of the manager of Department C for September. Comment on the operating results.

15–3. Hogate Company pays a bonus to any of its five division managers who increase their percentage of income to sales over that of the year before. The manager of Division A is displeased because of the results of operations of his line for the current year. His division showed a decrease in net income percentage, as can be determined from the following:

	Current Year		Last Year	
Net sales..............		$350,000		$300,000
Cost of goods sold:				
Division fixed costs......	$ 40,000		$ 40,000	
Allocated costs.........	72,000		40,000	
Variable costs..........	100,000	212,000	100,000	180,000
Gross margin............		$138,000		$120,000
Selling and administrative expense:				
Division fixed expenses...	$ 35,000		$ 30,000	
Allocated expenses.......	45,000		36,000	
Variable expenses........	30,000	110,000	27,000	93,000
Income.................		$ 28,000		$ 27,000

The items of allocated costs and expenses represent general costs and expenses of the company which were allocated to the divisions.

Required:

1. Prepare a statement which shows more clearly the performance of Division A.
2. Comment on the method used by the company to calculate bonuses.

15–4. Following are 1974 budget data for the Gateway Corporation:

	Product 1	Product 2	Product 3	Total
Sales.....................	$100,000	$60,000	$40,000	$200,000
Cost of goods sold.........	$ 60,000	$42,000	$32,000	$134,000
Variable operating expenses.	15,000	9,000	6,000	30,000
Product contribution........	$ 25,000	$ 9,000	$ 2,000	$ 36,000
Fixed costs...............				24,000
Net Income before Tax.....				$ 12,000

Actual sales in 1974 were $220,000, but a disappointing loss of $1,000 resulted. The expected pattern of variable expense held, but the pattern of sales did not. Sales revenue of Products 1 and 2 were $40,000 each, sales of Product 3 were $140,000.

Required:

Prepare a report that shows 1974 results in a manner which will clearly explain the unexpected loss of $1,000 to management.

15–5. In order to help department managers to control costs, Pando Company sends each a monthly report comparing actual results with expected results budgeted in advance. An analysis of the effectiveness of the manager's operations for the past month is included. Below are the budgeted and actual results of Department A for November:

	Budgeted	Actual
Sales......................................	$19,500	$25,500
Cost of goods sold......................	11,700	15,900
Gross margin..........................	$ 7,800	$ 9,600
Operating expenses.....................	7,500	9,000
Operating Income......................	$ 300	$ 600

Required:

Prepare a report which analyzes the performance of Department A for November. Department A has allocated to it $3,600 of fixed costs.

15–6.   The foreman of the Machine Shop received the following monthly overhead cost report:

Item	Budget	Actual	Over (under)
Materials handling.................	$ 6,000	$ 6,150	$ 150
Supplies.........................	4,200	4,000	(200)
Depreciation—equipment...........	5,000	7,000	2,000
Training[1].......................	3,500	4,300	800
Building and grounds[2].............	2,700	2,700	0
General plant expense[1].............	1,500	1,600	100
Maintenance[3]....................	4,000	3,800	(200)
Totals....................	$26,900	$29,550	$2,650

Bases of allocation or assignment:
[1] Number of employees.
[2] Dollars of budgeted overhead cost.
[3] Number of hours of maintenance employees' time utilized times a standard rate.

Required:

1.   Discuss the appropriateness of the individual items of the report.
2.   Evaluate the performance of the machine shop foreman.

15–7.   The following data statement of selling expenses was taken from the books of the Manten Company which sells its own line of garden tools:

			(Dollar Amounts in Thousands)					
	1972		1971		1970		1969	
	$	%	$	%	$	%	$	%
Sales revenue............	1,269	100.0	935	100.0	833	100.0	791	100.0
Selling expenses:								
Advertising............	84	6.6	34	3.6	28	3.4	24	3.0
District branch								
expenses*...........	80	6.3	41	4.4	38	4.6	32	4.1
Delivery expense.......								
(own trucks)........	20	1.6	15	1.6	19	2.3	22	2.8
Freight-out...........	21	1.7	9	1.0	11	1.3	8	1.0
Salesmen's salary								
expense............	111	8.7	76	8.1	68	8.2	61	7.7
Salesmen's travel								
expense............	35	2.8	20	2.1	18	2.2	26	3.3
Miscellaneous selling								
expense............	9	0.7	9	1.0	8	1.01	7	0.9
Total............	360	28.4	204	21.8	190	23.01	180	22.8

* Includes such fixed occupancy expenses as rent, advertising, etc.

Required:

What items need further investigation? Why?

15–8. As assistant to the president, prepare a memorandum to the president, summarizing performance and pointing out matters which he should discuss with the manager of the Corporate Loan Section, based on the data in Exhibit 15–6.

15–9. As assistant to the president, prepare a memorandum to the president, summarizing performance and pointing out matters that he should discuss with the manager of the Seattle Stone Division, based on the data in Exhibit 15–4.

15–10. Department A is one of 15 production departments in the Hopewell Company. On December 15, 1974, the following variable budget and planned production schedule were approved:

1975 Variable Budget—Department A

Controllable Costs	Fixed Amount per Month	Variable Rate per Direct Machine-Hour
Salaries.................................	$ 9,000	
Indirect labor...........................	18,000	$0.07
Indirect materials........................		0.09
Other costs..............................	6,000	0.03
	$33,000	$0.19

Production Plan	1975 Total	Jan.	Feb.	Mar.	Balance
Planned output in direct machine-hours.	325,000	22,000	25,000	29,000	249,000

On March 1, 1975, the manager of Department A was informed that his planned output for March had been revised to 34,000 direct machine-hours. He expressed some doubts as to whether this volume could be attained.

At the end of March 1975 the accounting records provided the following actual data for the month for the department:

Actual output in direct machine-hours.........	33,000
Actual controllable costs incurred:	
Salaries...............................	$ 9,300
Indirect labor.........................	20,500
Indirect materials.....................	2,850
Other costs............................	7,510
	$40,160

Required:

1. Prepare a report on performance in March.
2. Suggest what items in this report are especially significant and what possible explanations for these items may be.

15–11.

CASE
Gillette
Safety Razor
Company

On the morning of March 5, Miss Ruth Fillipetti, an employee of the Gillette Safety Razor Company, reported for work in the buffing room of the South Boston plant. At the stock cage she picked up a tray containing handles for one of the current models of the Gillette safety razor. These stamped copper handles had been sent to the buffing department for smoothing and polishing. After being polished, the handles went to the plating department for the final stage in their manufacture.

Miss Fillipetti's job was to smooth and polish the end of the razor handle. In this work she used a power-driven buffer wheel, against which she held the handle. The operation was not a difficult one, but it was not automatic; that is, she was required to place the end of the handle against the buffer wheel manually. For certain models, an automatic machine could be used that required only that the handles be placed on a moving belt of spindles. This belt carried the handles automatically across a buffer wheel. Miss Fillipetti spent the full day of March 5 buffing razor handle ends and by 5 o'clock had completed the smoothing and polishing of 2,100 pieces.

A close check was kept on the amount of work given to Miss Fillipetti and also on the amount of time she spent doing it. Although none of the employees of the Gillette Safety Razor Company was paid on a piece-rate basis, a daily comparison was made of the actual and standard times required to do the work assigned. On the morning of March 6 the timecard for Miss Fillipetti, together with timecards of other employees in the buffing room, was sent upstairs to the accounting department, where work and time requirements were posted and compared with previously established standard times. By 4 o'clock that afternoon—that is, the afternoon of March 6—the complete record of gains and losses with reference to standard times for work done on March 5 was reported back to the foreman in the buffing room. A procedure similar to that used for the buffing department was followed for each of the production departments of the razor division. In some departments the reports were referred to by the foreman when talking privately with operators, but in other departments the reports were posted daily. A portion of the March 5 report for the buffing department is reproduced as Exhibit 15–7.

The time standard set up for the operation of buffing the ends of the razor handles was 375 handles an hour.[5] The normal time to produce 2,100 units at the rate of 375 an hour was 5 hours and 36 minutes. The time records were kept in 5-minute units; and, therefore, the expected time for the work done by Miss Fillipetti on March 5 was listed on the report as $5\frac{7}{12}$ hours. Her day's work actually took $7\frac{11}{12}$ hours, so that a loss of $2\frac{3}{12}$ hours in standard time was indicated. When actual time exceeded standard allowable time, the amount lost was reported on the daily record sheet in red pencil; when actual time was under standard time, the gain was shown in black. A summary for the whole department was shown at the top of each report form.

Once a week the daily summary reports were combined into a weekly report that was furnished each of the foremen and the plant superintendent. From these weekly reports a continuous tabulation was maintained by the plant superintendent. The departmental labor control record for the buffing room shown in Exhibit 15–8 contains data for the three-month period beginning with the week ending December 23, through and including the week ending March 16.

The first column of the departmental labor control record (Exhibit 15–8) gives the normal or standard allowable hours for the volume of work done. Normal hours were the daily average of the "expected" hours shown on the daily report. Columns 2 and 3 of Exhibit 15–8 show the average daily hours lost and gained. Column 4 gives the daily average of actual hours required to do the same work for which the normal operating time is given in column 1. It will be noted that column 1 plus column 2 minus column 3 equals column 4. The entries in column 5, "General Ledger," refer to hours spent on special work ordered by the general office and therefore not part of the normal production flow. Column 6 gives the number of hours' work that was not measured and for which no normal times were available for comparison. Columns 7 and 8 relate to nonproductive time devoted to the work of maintenance and similar work not directly resulting in produced goods. The final columns gives the total number of hours worked in the department.

---

[5] This operation was coded as 195 D 20; the "195" refers to the model, the "D" to the handle of the razor, and the "20" to the operation. A similar code number was given every other operation. The letter "B" was used to refer to the cap of the razor, "C" to the guard, and "A" to the complete razor. The operation on which Miss Fillipetti was engaged, 195 D 20, was known as "cut down and color."

Exhibit 15–7

Daily report of production by operators

GILLETTE SAFETY RAZOR COMPANY
Daily report of production by operators

DATE March 5   490 BUFFING DEPARTMENT

		Operation Number	Ac-count	Production Total Actual	Production Expected per Hour	Hours Expected	Hours Actual	Difference Red-Loss R	Difference Black-Gain B
4126	MOORE, STELLA	195 D 20	502	2800	375	7 [6]	8		6
4126	MOORE, STELLA								
4127	MACCAREY, ELEANOR	1001 DG 25	502	2800			7		
4127	MACCAREY, ELEANOR	195 DG 25	502	400	400	1	1		
4128	MURPHY, ELLEN	1005 R 200	502	200			1	9	
4128	MURPHY, ELLEN	1005 RG 26	502	100				6	
4129	LEIGH, VIRGINIA	139 B 204	502	20000	2250	8	8		11
4129	LEIGH, VIRGINIA								
4130	FILLIPETTI, RUTH	195 D 20	502	2100	375	5	7 [10]	2 [3]	
4130	FILLIPETTI, RUTH								
4131	LURRELLO, HELEN	139 B 24	502	14000	1750	8	8		
4131	LURRELLO, HELEN								

	Operation Number	Ac-count	Production Total Actual	Production Expected per Hour	Hours Expected	Hours Actual	Difference Red-Loss R	Difference Black-Gain B
	195 D 20	502	450	375	1	1		4
	194 H 20	522	600	300	2	3		1 [3]

Total Expected Hours	181 [9]
Total Productive Hours Not Measured	48 [6]
Lost Hours	13 [3]
Gained Hours	5
Nonproductive Hours Charged to This Dept.	50 [4]
Nonproductive Hours Not Charged to This Dept.	2
Loaned Hours	48
Total Actual Hours Worked Included Loaned	343 [10]

No.	Name	Operation Number	Account	Total Actual	Expected per Hour	Expected	Actual	Diff R (Red-Loss)	Diff B (Black-Gain)
4132	CONRAD, HORTENSE	Loaned					8		
4132	CONRAD, HORTENSE								
4133	O'LEARY, KATHARINE	1005 AG 210	502	76			3		
4133	O'LEARY, KATHARINE	195 D 20	502	2275	375	6 [1]	7	18	
4134	WOODROW, ESTHER	139 B 206	502	20000	2250	8 [11]	8		11
4134	WOODROW, ESTHER								
4135	ROVETA, MILDRED	195 C 24	502	12000	1750	6 [10]	8	12	
4135	ROVETA, MILDRED								
4136	CAPRA, JOSEPHINE	1004 A 20	522	500			3 [5]		
4136	CAPRA, JOSEPHINE	195 D 20	502	1600	375	4 [3]	4	4	
4137	CASSIDY, ELINOR	195 D 20	502	2400	375	6 [5]	8	17	
4137	CASSIDY, ELINOR								
4138	LOVITT, MARION	Group							
4138	LOVITT, MARION								
4139	LESLIE, ALTHEA	1004 A 20	522	1100			8		
4139	LESLIE, ALTHEA								
4140	SMITH, MARY	139 B 29	502	14000	1750	8	8		
4140	SMITH, MARY								
4141	GRADY, ANNE	Loaned							
4141	GRADY, ANNE								
4142	LAMB, ELIZABETH	1001 D 211	502	23000	3500	6 [7]	8	15	
4142	LAMB, ELIZABETH								

Exhibit 15–8

Departmental labor control, Department 490—Buffing
(average daily hours)

Week Ending	Normal Hours (1)	Hours Lost (2)	Hours Gained (3)	Actual Measured Hours (4)	General Ledger (5)	Productive Hours Not Measured (6)	Nonproductive Hours (7)	Nonproductive Ratio to Normal Hours (8)	Total Hours (9)
December 9......	212.9	8.0	8.1	212.8	6.4	30.1	50.8	23.86	300.1
16......	183.8	10.5	5.6	188.7	12.7	23.4	51.3	27.91	276.1
23......	192.0	5.5	5.2	192.3	11.9	22.7	51.4	26.77	278.3
January 6......	174.7	9.2	5.0	178.9	2.0	39.8	57.6	32.97	278.3
13......	196.4	24.4	4.9	215.9	1.5	28.2	54.2	27.60	299.8
20......	194.9	14.6	6.1	203.4	4.0	54.5	50.3	25.80	312.2
27......	194.7	11.3	7.5	198.5	8.0	63.0	54.8	28.15	324.3
February 3......	160.8	10.5	4.5	166.8	6.0	106.9	56.7	35.26	336.4
10......	153.8	14.5	3.4	164.9	5.8	86.1	41.7	27.11	298.5
17......	168.4	19.7	5.4	182.7	3.6	72.7	50.9	30.23	309.9
24......	177.1	13.2	3.7	186.6	2.5	72.7	57.5	32.47	319.3
March 2......	192.5	10.6	3.5	199.6	1.8	68.3	54.8	28.47	324.5
9......	201.1	13.2	3.2	211.1	0.4	46.7	54.1	26.90	312.3
16......	169.6	5.4	4.8	170.2	. . .	17.7	56.3	33.20	244.2

A report similar to that shown in Exhibit 15–8 was prepared weekly for each of the departments engaged in manufacturing razors. Exhibit 15–9 shows for the weeks ending March 9 and March 16 the hours lost in each of six departments. The exhibit also shows the total number of hours reported for the departments and the number of measured hours for which losses were computed.

The daily report comparing actual and normal times by operators was prepared for the department foremen. The personnel department did not receive copies of the daily report and, therefore, could not make the operator's performance a formal part of his personnel record. It was estimated that the time of two clerks was required to prepare the daily and weekly reports for the entire razor division.

Required:

1. What is the source, so far as you can judge, of the entries in each of the columns of Exhibit 15–7? If you were handed this report, what would you look for first? Should the plant superintendent request that the daily production report be put on his desk?

2. If Miss Fillipetti's record on operation 195 D 20 continued to be poor, should the department manager refer the matter to the personnel department? Before taking such action, what should the department manager consider?

Exhibit 15–9

Excerpts from production control report, selected departments
(average daily hours)

Department	Hours Lost		Measured Hours		Total Hours	
	Week Ending March 9	Week Ending March 16	Week Ending March 9	Week Ending March 16	Week Ending March 9	Week Ending March 16
Cap and guard..............	0.3	0.7	167.9	208.5	297.2	279.2
Buffing.....................	13.2	5.4	211.1	170.2	312.3	244.2
Handle inspection...........	6.0	2.8	143.2	135.7	157.4	146.2
Wire and plating............	0.1	...	79.3	86.3	18.7	188.1
Handle packing	34.5	50.9	440.2	546.5	535.9	683.4
Auto-strop and probak department................	13.2	7.9	64.4	60.4	186.4	156.1

3. Rank, from best to poorest, the performance of Stella Moore, Ellen Murphy, Ruth Fillipetti, and Esther Woodrow.

4. What purpose could be served by the operating report illustrated in Exhibit 15–7? Is it worth the cost? Should the cost be shared by other reports, perhaps not shown in the case?

5. What is Exhibit 15–8? Why is this type of report called a comparative report? Why are the figures in Exhibit 15–8 in terms of daily averages instead of weekly totals?

6. Look at Exhibit 15–8, *not Exhibit 15–9,* and decide what items you would select to be included in a summary report comparing performance in various departments in the factory.

7. What do Exhibits 15–8 and 15–9 tell other than the number of hours put in by employees? Doesn't management really want to know whether any work was done during those hours?

8. If you were receiving these control reports, what standards would you develop?

15–12.

CASE
Day Company

The president of the Day department store has received the facts tabulated in Exhibit 15–10 from one of the operating executives. He has asked you to comment on the significant points revealed by these data.

Exhibit 15–10

Comparative operating statistics for Department A and similar departments of comparable stores

	1964	*1965*	*1966*	*1967*	*1968*
Department A:					
Sales.....................	$100,000	$104,400	$109,600	$98,800	$100,600
Gross margin.............	$ 25,900	$ 28,814	$ 38,250	$35,469	$ 36,517
Direct expenses...........	$ 8,264	$ 8,601	$ 9,024	$ 8,861	$ 8,980
Indirect expenses..........	20,000	20,880	21,920	24,700	25,150
Total expenses..........	$ 28,264	$ 29,481	$ 30,944	$33,561	$ 34,130
Net Profit (Loss).......	$ (2,364)	$ (667)	$ 7,306	$ 1,908	$ 2,387
Percentages, Department A:					
Sales (1964 = 100).........	100%	104.4%	109.6%	98.8%	100.6%
Gross margin.............	25.9	27.6	34.9	35.9	36.3
Transactions (1966 = 100)...	96	98	100	95	96
Percentages, Similar Departments of Other Stores:					
Sales (1964 = 100).........	100%	106.1%	111.3%	112.7%	114.2%
Gross margin.............	25.1	27.2	29.4	30.1	34.6
Transactions (1966 = 100)...	....	....	100	97	98
Published index of retail prices of products sold in Department A (1966 = 100).......			100	102	103

The data relate to the operating results of Department A, which handles gloves and ladies' hosiery. The president is interested in the results in your analysis because the department adopted a higher markup percentage in pricing goods sold in this department beginning in 1966. The effect of this policy may be noted clearly in the percentage gross margin figures.

Required:

Respond to the president's request.

16 Information processing

Purpose of
the chapter In this book we have focused on the *uses* of accounting information. We have paid relatively little attention to the procedures and mechanics that are employed to collect and summarize this information. Since our viewpoint is that of the manager, such a focus is appropriate. Nevertheless, the manager does need to have some understanding of the mechanics of processing information. Such an understanding helps him appreciate the limitations on the quantity and quality of information that can be made available for his use, the nature of this information, and the speed with which he can reasonably expect to get it. The purpose of this chapter is to give an overall view of systems for processing information.

In *Fundamentals of Financial Accounting* we describe information processing techniques in those chapters in which the transactions themselves were discussed.[1] All of these techniques are relevant in management accounting because management accounting uses the same basic data as are used in financial accounting. In this book we have not described matters relating to information processing as a part of the chapters in which the several types of management accounting data were discussed because each type of data does not have an associated or unique processing technique. Instead, we have deferred such a description until the types of data and their uses have been described, and we now discuss the processing of these data collectively.

---

[1] Specifically, the accounts, the general journal, and the ledger are discussed in Chapter 4; controlling accounts and subsidiary ledgers, in Appendix A to Chapter 6; inventory recordkeeping, in Chapter 7; special journals, in Appendix B to Chapter 8; and payroll accounting in Appendix A to Chapter 10.

Any information processing system has these elements:

1. Recording. There must be some means of recording events at the time they happen. In accounting, such events that are recorded are called transactions. A sales invoice is a record of an individual sales transaction, for example. It is a piece of paper that shows the name and address of the customer, a detailed listing of the name and price of each item that was sold to him, and other pertinent information about the sale.

2. Classifying. The system must be designed in such a way that all the myriad bits of information that are recorded can be arranged in some orderly fashion. In *Fundamentals of Financial Accounting* we state that this is the primary function of the ledger. Data that were originally recorded in chronological order in a journal are rearranged in the ledger in the form of accounts; each account contains all the data that relate to the phenomenon that is defined by the title of the account. Such a rearrangement from chronological order to ledger accounts is necessary if the user is to make any sense out of the flow of data.

3. Summarizing. For some purposes, information must be available in considerable detail. If Mr. Jones, a customer, raises a question about the amount that he owes, records must be available to show exactly what items were sold to Mr. Jones, and the detailed calculation of unit price times quantity for each item. For other purposes, however, only summaries are needed. Management does not have time to assimilate the details of the sales transactions with Mr. Jones and every other customer. Instead, it wants totals of sales by classes of customers, by product groupings, and so on. Thus, the accounts in which information is initially recorded are **building blocks.** They are combined in various ways to produce the summaries that are needed for the several purposes described in this book.

4. Reporting. The information must be made available to those who need it in a form that is understandable to them, preferably one that highlights the important matters that need to be brought to their attention.

CRITERIA FOR INFORMATION PROCESSING

A information processing system should be designed so as to meet the following criteria:

1. Accuracy. The information processed should have an *adquate* degree of accuracy. This does not mean *absolute* accuracy because absolute accuracy often costs too much to attain and because it results in intolerable delays in making the information available. In order to find out exactly how many screws are in an inventory bin, they would have to be counted, which is both time consuming and expensive. An approximation of the number of screws, which can be made just by looking at the size of the pile, is usually sufficiently accurate for management purposes. In arithmetic operations, however, complete accuracy is expected, and this is also the case for certain other important pieces of information, such as the amount of cash in a bank account.

2. Timeliness. Information is used as a basis for decisions. Decisions must be made promptly if they are to influence the course of events. If something is going wrong, management needs to know about it quickly. The need for speed often conflicts with the need for accuracy. A reasonably accurate report on profit for the past month that is available on the fifth working day of the following month is usually much more useful than a precisely accurate report that is not available until several weeks later. However, a report submitted so hastily that it is little more than a guess is not useful either.

3. Clarity. The information must be presented in such a way that the person who receives it understands the message that it is supposed to communicate. If it is vague, or if the reader gets an erroneous impression from it, it cannot serve the purpose for which it is intended.

4. Economy. The information must be recorded, classified, summarized, and reported as efficiently as possible. Overall, the cost of providing the information must be less than the value that users derive from it.

HISTORICAL DEVELOPMENT OF SYSTEMS

The introduction of electronic computers has revolutionized business information processing systems. We shall therefore mention only briefly some important aspects of systems as they existed prior to the time when computers came into general use, and we shall discuss in more detail information processing systems as they exist currently.

MANUAL SYSTEMS

When one thinks of systems, one thinks of *forms*. Although forms are often described as "red tape," they are essential in assuring that the correct data are recorded, and they facilitate the accuracy and clarity with which data are recorded. Once data have been recorded, the processes of classification and summarization require that data be transferred from one form to another. If this copying is done manually, it is expensive, and also copying errors creep in. Thus, the invention of **carbon paper** was a significant development in information processing. A piece of carbon paper permits the same item of information to be recorded in two or more places, without the cost and the possibility of error that is inherent in manual copying.

The process of summarizing also requires **arithmetic.** Most of this arithmetic is simple addition, so the adding machine was an important aid to information processing. More elaborate machines, collectively known as **bookkeeping machines,** essentially combine the functions of carbon paper and of adding machines; that is, they record the information in several places at once, and they simultaneously do the addition that is necessary to provide summaries. Thus, a billing machine may be used simultaneously to (1) prepare the customer's invoice, (2) adjust his ledger account, and (3) provide a summary of sales revenue credits and accounts receivable debits.

PUNCHED CARD MACHINES

From devices that copy and do arithmetic, we next proceed to punched card machines. There is a whole family of such machines. In order for them to operate, a card must be punched for each item of information. Once these cards have been punched, the machines do arithmetic and copy information from one form to another, which are the same operations done by the bookkeeping machines described above. Punched card machines have important advantages over book-keeping machines, however. First, they require much less manpower; once a machine has been properly set up, it will do the arithmetic and recording for an entire batch of invoices or an entire payroll, in contrast with bookkeeping machines, which require that human beings be in-volved in the processing of each invoice or each wage calculation. Second, they operate much more rapidly. Third, if the volume of work is large, they do this work at a much lower cost per unit of information.

In addition, punched card machines perform one type of operation that could not be done by their predecessors; they can **sort** the informa-tion into categories, which greatly facilitates the classifying and sum-marizing operations. For example, punched card machines easily and accurately can sort a set of punched cards containing sales information for each customer into alphabetical order, or by customer size classes, or by geographical region, or in any other way that is useful.

In summary, up until the advent of the computer, machines were developed that facilitated each step of information processing. They increased accuracy, speed, and clarity, and at the same time they re-duced the cost of processing information as compared with manual methods. As we shall see, the computer represents not only further progress in each of these dimensions; it also introduces an entirely new capability that none of its predecessors had.

Automated data processing
:   **Automated data processing** is, as the name suggests, the processing of data without human intervention. It was made possible by the development of **electronic computers.** The first computer for business purposes began operation only in 1951, and growth has been extremely rapid since then. The purpose of this section is to describe what auto-mated data processing is—as background for the following sections in which its use in accounting is assessed. For this purpose a detailed understanding of what goes on inside the computer is not required, any

more than one needs a detailed knowledge of what goes on under the hood in order to understand how to use an automobile.[2]

A general-purpose, digital computer (hereafter, referred to as simply "computer") performs these operations:

1. It stores data.
2. It performs arithmetic operations on data.
3. It compares two pieces of data and determines whether or not they are equal.
4. It sorts, that is, rearranges, data.
5. It prepares reports, displays any desired part of the stored data, or causes some other machine to perform in a prescribed way.

The components of a computer are shown schematically in Exhibit 16–1. They are: input, storage, processing, and output. Each is described below.

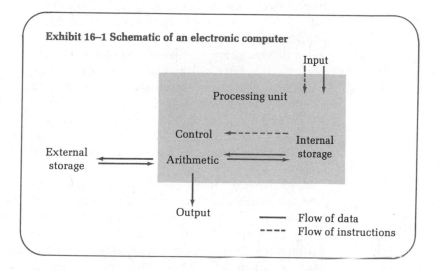

Exhibit 16–1 Schematic of an electronic computer

INPUT

Processing unit

Control

External storage

Arithmetic

Internal storage

Output

—— Flow of data

---- Flow of instructions

INPUT

Computer codes. In the computer each numerical digit, alphabetical letter, or other symbol (e.g., $, %, #, *) is represented by a combination of electrical impulses. Each such combination is called a **computer character.** On the printed page, the character may be represented by code consisting of a combination of black and white dots, as in Exhibit 16–2. Inside the computer, however, the character is not visible or

---

[2] This description is limited to general-purpose, digital computers, thereby omitting (*a*) special-purpose computers and (*b*) analog computers. *Special-purpose* computers are designed to perform a single task (such as calculating the course of an aircraft or missile), or a small number of related tasks. *Analog* computers use approximations rather than cardinal numbers. A slide rule is a manually operated analog computer; it is set at approximately the numbers that are to be computed, and the result of the computation is approximately correct.

Exhibit 16–2 Visual representation of a computer character

Code	Represents
00000000	1
00000000	2
00000000	3
00000000	9
00000000	A
00000000	B
00000000	C

Source: American Standard Code for Information Exchange.

tangible; it is represented by a combination of electrical states, such as the presence or absence of an electrical charge (i.e., the current is either "on" or "off"). These electrical states can be manipulated almost with the speed of electricity (which is the speed of light), and this is the basic reason that the computer operates so rapidly. A computer works on one character at a time, so the usual way of describing the capacity of a computer is in terms of the number of characters that it can store, and the usual way of describing its speed is in terms of the number of characters it can process in one second or other unit of time. As will be explained shortly, the computer user does not need to know what the codes for these characters are because he will never work with them directly.

Input devices. In the input operations, data are fed into the computer, and each character is translated electrically into the code that the computer will use in all subsequent operations. Instructions which tell the computer what to do with these data, called the **program,** are also inputted. In the earliest computers, the input operation involved preparing a punched card for each item of data, and these cards were then fed into the computer. This is still a common input method, but the preparation of punched cards is relatively expensive; in the typical business data processing situation, this step is many times more expensive than all the succeeding operations combined. Punched card input is also relatively slow, the maximum speed being approximately 1,300 characters per second.[3] The usual practice therefore is to convert the original data to computer code in a preliminary operation, often using an inexpensive separate machine, and to hold these data temporarily on magnetic tape. The magnetic tape is used subsequently as input to the main computer. A 2,400-foot reel of magnetic tape can hold 40 million characters, and these can be inputted to the computer at a maximum rate of 300,000 characters per second.

---

[3] All computer characteristics given in this chapter are rough approximations. There is considerable variation among computers, and speed also varies with the nature of the work being done.

Machine-readable input. Not only is the preparation of punched cards expensive and slow, but it also is an operation that is susceptible to errors, since the cards are prepared by human beings. Much work has therefore been done to develop input mechanisms that eliminate most of this manual processing. The first such machine-readable input to come into widespread use was **magnetic ink character recognition** (MICR), which is now used on most bank checks and deposit slips. On such documents, a number identifying the depositor and his bank appears in a form that can be read by humans, viz:

⑆0511⑈0003⑆ 07⑈05141494⑈

The printing ink contains a metallic substance which permits these same characters to be read automatically by the computer. The computer does this by comparing the characteristics of each MICR character with a file of characteristics contained in its memory. When it obtains a match, it creates the corresponding computer code for the character. (This may sound like a cumbersome operation, but recall that it is done at the speed of light.)

Some success has also been achieved with optical devices that will permit the computer to read characters that are printed with ordinary ink. Currently most of these devices work only with characters that conform to a fairly rigid format and that are positioned in a prescribed area of the document. Optical input devices that are able to read ordinary typewritten material are becoming available, and such devices will soon be widely used.

Direct input. Another solution to the input problem is to have input information created automatically by a machine that is located at the point where the transaction originates; this information is either stored on tape or is transmitted by wire directly to the computer.

EXAMPLE NO. 1: In a job shop there may be direct input devices in each department or section. When an employee begins a job, he inserts in the device one card containing his employee number, another card containing the number of the operation he is about to perform, and another with the number of the job. He inserts his employee number card again when the job is completed. The input device notes the beginning and ending time from a clock.

EXAMPLE NO. 2: In a supermarket, a recording device performs all the functions previously performed by the cash register; that is, it adds up the sales price of each item, and classifies the items by departments (e.g., groceries, meat, fresh vegetables). When the price tag on the item is in machine-readable form, as in Exhibit 16–3, the need for handkeying entries into this device is eliminated. An optical scanner performs this operation automatically. The recording device transmits detailed sales information to a central computer. Management can obtain summary information on today's sales for each store in an entire chain of supermarkets a few minutes after the close of business.

Exhibit 16–3

Machine readable retail price tag

Because of the speed and accuracy with which these devices generate input information and also because, if volume is large, the information is generated at a lower cost than previous methods, the use of point-of-sale and other direct input devices is growing rapidly.

STORAGE

The processing unit of the computer works on only one, or a few, characters at one time. A means of storing characters must therefore be provided so that they can be held until the processing unit is ready to work on them. The storage device is also called *memory*. Since the data are represented by combinations of electrical states, the storage medium can be anything in which there are two states and which can be changed from one state to the other electrically. The earliest computers used vacuum tubes which were either "on" or "off." In more recent models the two-state characteristic is obtained by coatings which can be either magnetized or not magnetized, or by cores or metallic film in which the two states are represented by the clockwise or counter-clockwise direction of a magnetic field, or by chemicals which are either energized or not energized.

When a new character is entered into a storage cell, the character that was previously in the cell is automatically erased. Thus, unlike an accounting ledger page, which is also a means of storing information, computer storage can be reused indefinitely.

There are two general categories of storage, internal and external, and several types within each category. They differ essentially because each represents a different tradeoff between cost and access time. **Access time** is the time required to locate a character in storage and transfer it to the place where it will be used.

Internal storage. Internal storage or memory is used in the computing process, to be described next. Since hundreds of thousands of computations are made each second, and since for each computation data must be moved out of memory, worked on, and then returned to memory, it is essential that access time of internal storage be very short. Storage devices with fast access time are much more expensive per character stored than storage devices with slow access time. Because of the high cost, internal storage is relatively small.

External storage. Until shortly before they are needed in a computation, data are stored in external storage devices. Various combinations of these devices may be used in a given computer. At one extreme are fast-access but expensive devices similar to those used for internal storage. At the other extreme are the slow-access but inexpensive magnetic tapes already described. When magnetic tape is used, the tape must be used sequentially which makes the process of searching for a desired piece of information very slow—as long as several minutes, if its general location on the tape is not known. In magnetic disks, the search process is random and much faster than with magnetic tape—from $\frac{1}{20}$ to $\frac{1}{2}$ second (i.e., 50 to 500 milli-seconds) to locate one character. Another large capacity but relatively fast-access storage device is the data cell. A single data cell weighs about 5 pounds and can store 400 million characters. About 200 of these data cells are used in one medium-sized computer system.

PROCESSING

The processing section of the computer consists of a control unit and an arithmetic unit. The **control unit** contains the program and directs the movement of characters out of and back to storage and the manipulation of these characters in the arithmetic unit. The **arithmetic unit** does only two things: (1) it **computes,** that is, performs the arithmetic operations of addition, subtraction, multiplication, and division; and (2) it **compares** two characters and determines whether or not they are equal, and if they are unequal, which one is larger. If a computer only computed, it would be nothing more than a very fast, accurate calculating machine (up to three million additions per second). It is the second operation, that of comparison, that gives the computer its extraordinary power.

> *EXAMPLE:* In February 1968, a fire demolished an Air Force warehouse and destroyed its contents which consisted of 16,000 different items of spare parts for F-4 aircraft. The fire occurred at midnight. By eight o'clock the next morning the computer had located in its records the information on the quantity of each of the 16,000 items stored in that warehouse (out of the several hundred thousand items stored on the whole base; this was a comparison operation); it had deducted these quantities from the inventory record of each item and had computed the quantity to be reordered in accordance with its economic order quantity rules (these were arithmetic operations), and it had prepared 10,000 requisitions (this was a copying operation).

Programming.   **A program is a set of instructions specifying each operation that the computer is to perform.** Data processing procedures consist of a series of operations performed one after the other. The rules for performing each of these operations may vary with the circumstances. For example, a program that processes incoming sales orders that are to be filled from inventory might contain the following steps:

1.   For the first item on the order, compare the quantity ordered with the quantity on hand in inventory. Is the quantity ordered less than the quantity on hand? (Answer "yes" or "no.")

2a.   If *yes,* deduct the quantity ordered from the amount on hand in inventory and prepare a shipping order.

2b.   If *no,* prepare a backorder record (to notify the customer that the quantity ordered is not now available but that it will be shipped when inventory is replenished).

The first instruction above illustrates the comparison feature. It is this feature that permits the computer to handle any conceivable set of circumstances, *providing* that these circumstances have been foreseen and instructions for handling them have been incorporated in the program. This is a large proviso, for it requires the programmer to visualize in advance every contingency that might arise in the procedure that he is programming, and then to provide for that contingency.

As an indication of the possibilities opened up by this comparison feature, a greatly simplified portion of an order processing program is given in Exhibit 16–4. The illustration is in the form of a **block diagram.** A block diagram shows not the detailed instructions but rather the main steps in the program for each of which there will be a detailed set of instructions. Note that at various points the program **branches** into either of two directions, depending on the results of a comparison made at that point.

The comparison, or *logic,* feature also enables the computer to sort records into numerical order, alphabetical order, or any other desired order; to merge two or more sets of records together; to update a set of records, and indeed to manipulate the data in any conceivable way that can be reduced to a written instruction. "Data" as used here means letters as well as numbers. Some computer programs operate on straight textual material; for example, the U.S. Code, the laws of many states, and abstracts of most scientific journal articles are now available on magnetic tape so that a computer can be used to locate references to specific topics.

Computer languages.   In the earliest computers the programmer had to specify each operation in great detail. This is no longer necessary. Instead, the programmer uses a computer language such as BASIC, COBOL, or FORTRAN. He writes his program in the vocabulary and grammar of that language which closely resemble ordinary English and the symbols of algebra. The simplest of these languages, BASIC, can

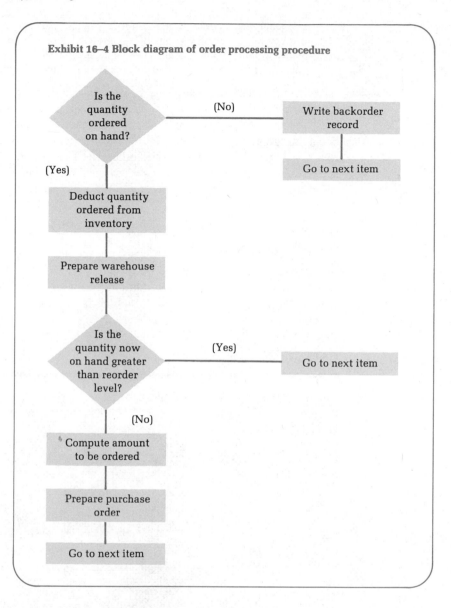

Exhibit 16–4 Block diagram of order processing procedure

be learned by high school students in a few hours. The program is then inputted to the computer and the computer, using a special **compiler program**, translates this program into the detailed instructions that it requires.

> *EXAMPLE:* In Chapter 8, the formula for finding the present value of a future payment of $1 was given as $P = 1 \div (1 + i)^n$. With CAL, which is a widely used computer language, the user would simply input the following instruction:

TYPE 1/ (1 + R) ↑ N FOR R = .1 FOR N = 1 TO 50.

The computer would then compute the 10 percent column of the present value Table A (page 553), the whole operation requiring less than a minute. (Only a fraction of a second of this is computation time; most of the time is required for the input and output operations.)

Users of a computer language also have access to standardized instructions for many procedures such as "sort in alphabetical order," "raise to the nth power," and also whole routines, such as those for linear programming, payroll, and order processing. Some of these routines they can use "as is," while others require modification to fit the needs of a particular company. All these developments simplify and speed up the task of preparing programs for computers.

OUTPUT

The results of the computations appear initially as characters in computer storage. If they are to be printed as *hard copy* on a form or a report, the program instructs the computer how to *format* these reports; that is, the program causes the computer to arrange the data in rows

Exhibit 16–5

Computer input and output

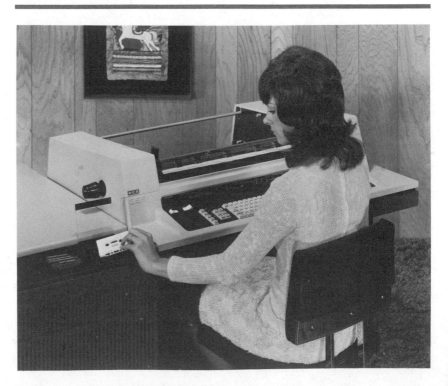

Courtesy of National Cash Register Company.

and columns in whatever format is desired. Some computers will print the results in the form of dots at prescribed locations on the page, thus producing graphs automatically. The output can also be displayed on a cathode-ray tube (a television screen is a cathode-ray tube). The computer can even be connected to a tape file that contains a spoken sound for each number and for certain common words, and this permits its output to be communicated audibly through an ordinary telephone. Exhibit 16–5 shows a terminal which combines input and output devices.

PROCESSING MODES

Computers operate basically in one of two modes, on-line or off-line.

In the **on-line mode,** the computer is kept loaded with a single program and the data required for that program. The user is connected directly to the computer with an input-output device. He inputs his specific problem or question, and the computer solves this problem or answers the question and communicates the output to the user in a few seconds.

> *EXAMPLE:* The first extensive application of on-line processing was for airline seat reservations. The computer storage contains the number of seats currently available on each flight for the next month or so. At each airline reservation counter there is an input-output device. When ticket agents wish to inquire whether space is available on a certain flight, they query the computer via this device. The query is transmitted to the computer over ordinary telephone lines. In a second or so, the computer tells the agent whether the space is available. If the ticket agent then sells the space, the computer is notified via another input, and the computer automatically adjusts its record of space available. In some systems, the computer also calculates the price of the ticket and prints the ticket.

Many banks do deposit accounting with an on-line computer; each teller has an input-output device which is used both to find the current balance in a customer's account and to record deposits and withdrawals at the instant they are made.

In the **off-line** mode, users are not connected directly to the computer. They submit their problems to a computer center which processes these problems and also routine recurring programs. This method of operations is called **batch processing.** The program and data in internal storage are removed from the computer after each job has been completed, and the computer therefore starts fresh with each new job. Thus the payroll computation might be run weekly; order processing work, once a day; financial statements, monthly; and nonroutine jobs, whenever time is available. The off-line mode is much less expensive than the on-line mode, so it is used for those data processing jobs where an immediate response is unnecessary. For example, employees are willing to wait for their pay for a few days after the pay period has ended; therefore payroll programs are usually run off-line.

TIME SHARING

Large computers are constructed so that the processing unit can work on several problems almost simultaneously. Many users can input their problems to the computer, where they are held in storage until time on the processing unit becomes available, usually within a few seconds. The computer then processes the problem and transmits the output back to the user. The airline reservation and bank deposit applications mentioned above are examples of one type of time sharing using the on-line mode. **Time sharing** makes it possible for a small business to have access to a large computer. A computer service company installs an input-output unit in the premises of the small business, and the user pays a monthly fee plus a charge for the minutes (or seconds) of computer time. These computer service companies also have large libraries of programs which they make available to their clients.

MINICALCULATORS

A development that is even more recent than the computer is that of the minicalculator. In the terminology used earlier in this chapter, a

Exhibit 16–6

Minicalculator

Calculation of Rate of Return	
Investment	$1,000
Annual earnings	250
Economic life, years	5

Calculation:		
Enter	5	
Depress		n
Enter	250	
Depress		PMT
Enter	1000	
Depress		PV
		i
Answer:	7.93 percent	

minicalculator is a special-purpose computer since it has a fixed program. The simplest calculators do the four arithmetic operations $(+ - \times \div)$, quietly and at electronic speed. They sell for less than $100.

A more sophisticated calculator will do automatically many of the complicated calculations that occur frequently in a business. Exhibit 16–6 shows such a machine. It is smaller than and weighs less than this book, sells for less than $400, and will do 40 types of calculation.

As an illustration, consider the problem of finding the rate of return on an investment such as the question: What is the rate of return on an investment of $1,000 that earns $250 per year for five years? By the method described in Chapter 9, this involved looking up factors in Table A and making a series of trial-and-error calculations. With the use of the calculator, one simply enters numbers and presses keys as shown in Exhibit 16–6.

| Implications for accounting | With the background of the preceding section, we shall now discuss the effect on accounting that computers are having, and are likely to have in the future. We shall first discuss this impact in general and then in relation to specific types of accounting. |

GENERAL IMPACT

It seems clear that almost all companies will make some use of computers. The individual physician's office, with perhaps one nurse and one secretary, is a very small business, but an increasing number of physicians have their billing and accounts receivable done at computer service centers.

The number of business computers in the United States rose from 1 in 1951 to 1,000 in 1956, to 31,000 in 1966, and to 120,000 in 1973. This growth will undoubtedly continue. Developments in technology are reducing both storage costs and processing costs rapidly. The cost per calculation for computers introduced in the early 1960s was roughly one tenth that of those in use in 1955, and the cost per calculation in the early 1970s is roughly one tenth of that in the early 1960s. Development of better program languages and the increased availability of standard programs will reduce these "software" costs.

As new technological developments lead to still lower processing and storage costs, as programming becomes even simpler, and as more and more standardized programs become available, there will be a corresponding increase in the number of tasks that can be performed less expensively by the computer than by humans. Since the processing of data is very inexpensive once they have been converted to computer code, a business will seek additional ways to use a given item of input data. Consequently, companies will do an increasing amount of their accounting work on computers.

THE INPUT PROBLEM

The least efficient part of computer-oriented information processing is input. As already noted, when input material is prepared by human beings, the process is slow and prone to error. Although the remainder of the processing is extremely fast and virtually 100 percent accurate, the quality of the output can be no better than the quality of the input. (Computer experts refer to this truism as "GIGO"—garbage in, garbage out.) Thus, great efforts are being made to automate the input operation. Devices that will convert ordinary typewritten material into computer language will probably be widely used in the near future, as will machine-readable inputs like the retail price tags described earlier. Most stores, restaurants, and service organizations already use machine-readable credit cards. As inputs become less expensive and more error free, use of computers should expand even more.

Unfortunately, the development of machine-readable input devices has created a new type of input problem, that of fraud. Criminals have found ways to use these devices to steal.

> *EXAMPLE*. Donn B. Parker of Stanford Research Institute described a scheme that was used in a bank in Washington, D.C. The criminal removed all the deposit slips at one writing desk and replaced them with deposits slips on which his own account number was encoded in magnetic ink. For three days every customer who used that writing desk to fill out a deposit slip was actually depositing money into the culprit's account. The thief reappeared, withdrew $100,000 from his account, and walked away. He has not yet been found.[4]

Much time is currently being devoted to plugging such loopholes in data processing systems.

OPERATING DATA

In Chapter 1, we described the main streams of operating data that provide the raw material for financial and management accounting. These streams include data for controlling the production process, for purchasing and materials inventory, for payroll and personnel, for plant and equipment, for sales and accounts receivable, and for cash and other financial transactions. The computer has brought about important changes in these data flows:

1. As noted above, with the computer data are processed more accurately, more rapidly, and at lower cost.
2. The storage capability of the computer permits large quantities of detailed data to be held in a **data bank,** where they are available for use when the need arises.
3. Many routine operations are now performed by the computer rather

---

[4] *Time,* December 25, 1972.

than by human beings. These include certain operations that require that decisions be made. For example, the computer can be programmed to decide when a purchase order should be placed to replenish a routine item carried in inventory, the quantity of that item that should be ordered, and the date when the new stock should arrive; and it can even write the purchase order without human intervention. (Humans are nevertheless necessary to supervise the operation and to make certain that the transaction is actually "routine.") The computer can do this job better than people can do it; "better" in the sense that if its program truly expresses what management intends to be done, the computer will carry out these intentions more accurately and more consistently than the humans normally employed for these routine operations.

FINANCIAL ACCOUNTING

The computer speeds up the process of collecting and summarizing financial accounting information. It permits the use of accounting methods which some companies hitherto were unwilling to use because of the amount of detailed calculations involved, such as more detailed breakdowns of fixed assets in calculating depreciation; more exact methods of accruing pension benefits; and more exact methods of calculating interest, discounts, and premiums on bonds and notes. The computer permits trial runs to be made of the effect of various accounting alternatives on the financial statements.

The computer will calculate all ratios of the type we describe in Chapter 16 of *Fundamentals of Financial Accounting*. Furthermore, a service called COMPUSTAT maintains in its data bank the financial statements and ratios for over 1,500 companies, going back over a period of years, and these are helpful in analyzing the financial statements of the company in question. Another service maintains a computer record of the terminology and accounting principles that companies use on their financial statements, and a company can use this service to find out how widely used various alternative practices are.

The computer has, however, created a new problem. How does one audit a set of accounts when many of the numbers and calculations are invisible, existing only in the form of electrical impulses which are often erased after subsidiary calculations have been completed? The public accounting profession is hard at work on this problem. New tests of computer-produced data are being devised, and safeguards to prevent unauthorized manipulation of the data are being developed.

FULL COST ACCOUNTING

In our discussion of full cost accounting, we pointed out that some practices that were not conceptually sound were justified on the grounds of practicality; the conceptually best method was thought to involve computations that cost more than they were worth. This was particularly the case with procedures for allocating costs. With a computer, it is feasible to use more exact methods of allocating indirect costs to cost centers, cost pools can be narrowly defined and hence more homogeneous, and multiple bases of allocation can be used. Shortcuts in the calculation of direct material and direct labor costs that may have been used on the ground that more exact methods were too expensive, are no longer necessary.

DIFFERENTIAL ACCOUNTING

Many of the problems for which differential costs and revenues are appropriate require extensive calculations. Some companies use approaches that they know to be conceptually unsound simply because they are unwilling to go through the arithmetic required by the better approach. This is one reason given for the use of the payback method in capital investment problems; it is not accurate, but it is simple. With a computer the drudgery of the calculation is eliminated. Computer programs are available that handle make-or-buy problems, buy-or-lease problems, product pricing strategies, capital investment problems, and other problems discussed in Chapters 7, 8, and 9. They make obsolete the argument that a certain procedure should not be used because it is too complicated.

The relevant differential cost and revenue amounts depend on the nature of the particular problem being analyzed. The computer's storage capacity permits large quantities of detailed data to be held in a data bank, and thus makes it practicable to use data that is "tailor-made" to the requirements of a given problem. For example, the wage rate for each job category can be held in the computer and called forth easily when the problem requires it, thus obviating the need to use average wage rates.

Mathematical models. Perhaps most important of all, the computer permits the use of **mathematical models.** Such a model states mathematically the interrelationships among a set of variables that are believed to represent the significant factors in a given situation. The income statement is a model that shows the interrelationships of sales revenues, various elements of expense, and net income, but the relationships on the income statement are expressed in terms of a simple linear equation (revenues − expenses = net income). Much more complicated models are now being used for alternative choice problems. These models are called **simulation models** because they simulate the situation being analyzed, including what the outcome is expected to be if a proposed alternative were adopted.

Models are also available that suggest the optimum alternative out of a wide choice of possible courses of action, with many interacting variables. **Linear programming** is a widely used technique for this purpose.

> *EXAMPLE NO 1:* A company that distributes its products through-out the United States wishes to locate warehouses so as to provide rapid service to its customers at the lowest combination of transporta-tion and warehouse costs. It has a very large number of possible choices as to the location and size of warehouses. Linear programming can be used to suggest the optimum solution.

> *EXAMPLE NO. 2:* A petroleum refinery can make a wide variety of products, and widely varying quantities of each product, from a given quantity of crude oil of a certain chemical composition. The optimum product mix depends on the demand for various products and their relative profitability, and is affected also by limitations of the refinery process with respect to certain products. Linear programming is used by practically all petroleum refineries to find the optimum mix.

The computer makes it feasible to use **multiple correlations** to fore-cast sales revenue. This is a technique that identifies the effect of each of several factors on sales, and is therefore more powerful than the simple correlation technique described in Chapter 11. It is also possible to use a similar technique in preparing variable budgets; that is, in-stead of adjusting costs only for changes in volume, other factors that cause costs to vary can be taken into account.

Some companies are experimenting with an **overall company model** that will predict net income on the basis of an elaborate set of assump-tions as to the behavior of the various factors that affect net income. Because a company is an extremely complicated organism, construction of a realistic model of its complete operations is difficult. If it can be done, however, the company has a powerful tool that can be used to test the consequences of various proposed strategies, and also to assist in budget preparation. In the budget preparation process, for example, managers would be required to make only key decisions and assump-tions, mostly those relating to marketing strategies and discretionary cost items; the model could then be used to produce all the detailed budgets, and it would do so in a way that insured that the budgets for the several parts of the organization were coordinated with one another.

With a computer, standard costs can be revised more frequently. Although standard costs are supposed to be revised whenever there is a significant change in cost factors, this was not feasible in many com-panies. An across-the-board wage increase, for example, in a company that manufactures many different end products, components, and parts, requires recalculation of thousands of separate standard cost cards; many companies did not judge the manual effort required to be worth-while. When standard costs are in a computer's data bank, recalcula-tions are a simple matter.

Fortunately for humans, the computer is limited to operations that can be precisely described. It does not eliminate the need for judgment in defining the problem and in specifying and evaluating the factors that have not been quantified, nor can a computer's calculations produce results that are more accurate than the validity of the data fed into it. Thus, the computer provides great assistance to managers and analysts, but it replaces only the computational part of their work; it does not replace the people themselves.

RESPONSIBILITY ACCOUNTING

The mechanics of programming, budgeting, measuring actual performance, and preparing control reports are facilitated by the use of computers. Computers help to insure that the calculations are accurate. More importantly they shorten the time required to compile and disseminate information and thus make it possible to take corrective action more quickly. Computers also make it feasible to take into account many more variables in analyzing the difference between planned and actual performance, and to use more sophisticated analytical techniques in this process.

The management control process is, however, fundamentally a behavioral process; the computer does not eliminate the manager, nor does its existence alter the basic fact that managers obtain results by working with other human beings.

INTEGRATED DATA PROCESSING

The dream of the system builder is to develop an information processing system in which each relevant bit of raw data is recorded once, and only once. These data are then combined, summarized, and analyzed automatically in a variety of ways so as to produce all the reports and other output documents that the business needs. Such an integrated data processing system can easily be described in general terms, but to develop it in practice is a far more complicated task than any group of mortals has so far been able to accomplish. It now appears that the computer may make feasible such a system, if not for all the data in a business, at least for substantial chunks of them. Such a system will not be developed overnight, but it is a goal that is not now completely fanciful.

Integrated data processing implies a blurring of the distinction that hitherto has existed among different categories of data, and this is a development that is occurring in any event. There is no longer a sharp distinction between financial accounting data and management accounting data, or between input data and output data, or between monetary data and nonmonetary data, or even between numbers and words. The computer processes them all. Thus it may soon be undesirable to discuss management accounting primarily in terms of monetary information; it may be more useful to view it as encompassing all recurring information that is of use to management.

There is a temptation to be too enthusiastic about the future of the computer. At present, computers tend to spew out too much information, and this tends to hinder rather than help managers do their job. But this is almost certainly a temporary condition caused by the haste with which computer programs have been developed and by the necessity for learning how best to use the computer's power. As time goes on, it is reasonable to expect that computer outputs will be better organized and more relevant to management's needs.

Summary   A computer basically does only a few things: it stores data, it makes computations, it makes comparisons, it rearranges data, and it produces reports; however, it does these things a million times faster than a human being can do them, it can perform a long and involved sequence of such operations without human intervention, and it does its work with virtually perfect accuracy. Thus computers are rapidly taking over the routine data processing work of business. It seems likely that they will take over such work in all businesses except the smallest, and those without a number of recurring transactions.

Computers also provide a powerful way of analyzing the data relevant to management problems to all types. They thus improve the quality of such analyses, although the results can be no better than the quality of the raw data, nor can the computer substitute for management judgment.

Important terms

Automated data processing	**On-line mode**
Computer	**Batch processing**
Computer character	**Time sharing**
Computer program	**Data bank**
Computer storage	**Simulation model**
Processing section	

Questions for discussion

1. Information should be "adequately" accurate. A telephone company has considerable cash in the coin boxes of its pay phones. Should it make arrangements to count this cash on December 31 so that the cash item on its balance sheet will be accurate? If not, how should it record this uncounted cash?

2. Consider a sales invoice for a credit sale of $129 to Ralph Jones. Describe the several information processing steps, using what happens to the information on this sales invoice as an example.

3. A manual accounting system classifies a credit sale as a credit to sales and a debit to the customer's account receivable. If a computer were used, what additional information about this transaction might well be recorded in a computer data bank?

4. Explain the advantages that a computer has over punched card machines.

5. If a computer can only determine whether one number is larger than another, how can it sort accounts numbered 14, 12, 13, and 11, so that they end up in numerical order (i.e., 11, 12, 13, 14)?

6. In what sense can a computer handle the placing of purchase orders to replenish inventory better than human beings? In what sense is the computer inferior to human beings in this function?

7. The computer can produce reports faster and more accurately than manual methods. Are such reports always better than manually prepared reports? Why?

8. Assume that a wage increase requires the revision of standard unit direct labor costs. If done manually, the revision of each direct labor unit cost (one for each operation or each product) requires 0.1 hours of clerical time at $4 cost per hour. If done on a computer, the revision effort requires that a program be prepared at a cost of $100, and then a computer operating cost of $0.01 per unit cost. The average product requires 10 direct labor operations. How many products does the company need to have to warrant using the computer for this purpose?

9. Describe in general terms the nature of a computer program that would be used in make-or-buy analysis.

10. A company uses the computer to estimate the net present value of new products it is considering marketing. The computer output for one such proposal reads as follows:

Rate of Return	Net Present Value (000 Omitted)
10%	$1,070
20	501
30	90
32.6	0

The above table was prepared on the assumption that sales volume would be as predicted. Additional tables were prepared on the assumption that sales volume would be 70 percent, 80 percent, 90 percent, and 110 percent, respectively of the predicted amount. If a manual computation of a single net present value required 0.5 hours, how much time, roughly, would be required to calculate this information manually? (The computer time was 11 seconds.)

11. For the information referred to in Question 10, would the computer output be more accurate than the manual calculation? Why?

12. For the information referred to in Question 10, is the computer output more useful than a manual computation showing that the proposal had a net present value of $1,070,000 at a rate of return of 10 percent?

13. If a computer is used for the problem described in Question 10, what aspects of human judgment, if any, are involved in the decision-making process?

Problem   16–1. In 1973 the Wilson Company installed a computer in an office that was readily accessible to members of the controller organization. This terminal was rented from a "computer utility" company and connected to a large computer owned by that company. The terminal was viewed as an experiment. If profitable uses were found, and if sufficient interest developed, it was planned to install similar terminals in other offices.

Mr. Bruce Carroll, controller of the Wilson Company, discussed possible uses of the computer with the salesman of the computer utility. One of these was the equipment replacement problem. The next day, the salesman brought Mr. Carroll a program called PINDX, which he said would aid in solving such problems.

Exhibit 16–7 is a flowchart of this program, and Exhibit 16–8 is a sample of the actual operation of the program as it appeared on the terminal in the Wilson Company office, typed on a continuous roll of paper.

As indicated in Exhibit 16–8 the user activated the program by typing the phrase "RUN PINDX." The computer then asked whether the user wanted instructions printed out. (Presumably, this would be desirable until such time as the user was thoroughly familiar with the program.) Upon receiving a "YES," the computer printed five paragraphs of instructions, and then requested the first piece of information, the "interest rate." On the next line after this request, the computer printed a "?" and the user typed the desired information, in this case 15. The computer continued with its requests, and after "?," the user typed the requested information. The computer then typed the solution.

The problem solved in Exhibit 16–8 is as follows: a proposed machine cost $185,000 and had an economic life of five years. It was estimated to increase certain cash costs by $10,000 per year, and to reduce other costs by $70,000 in year 1, $90,000 in year 2, and $110,000 in each of years 3, 4, and 5. The required rate of return was 15 percent. There was zero residual value. According to the computer, the profitability index was 1.459.

As noted on Exhibit 16–8, the total elapsed time required for running this problem (i.e., from the time Mr. Carroll typed the words PINDX to the printout of the solution) was eight minutes, of which six seconds was actually used in making the computations.

Required:

Did the PINDX program compute the profitability index accurately for the sample problem? (How many minutes did it take you to answer this question?)

Exhibit 16–7 Logical flowchart for profitability index program

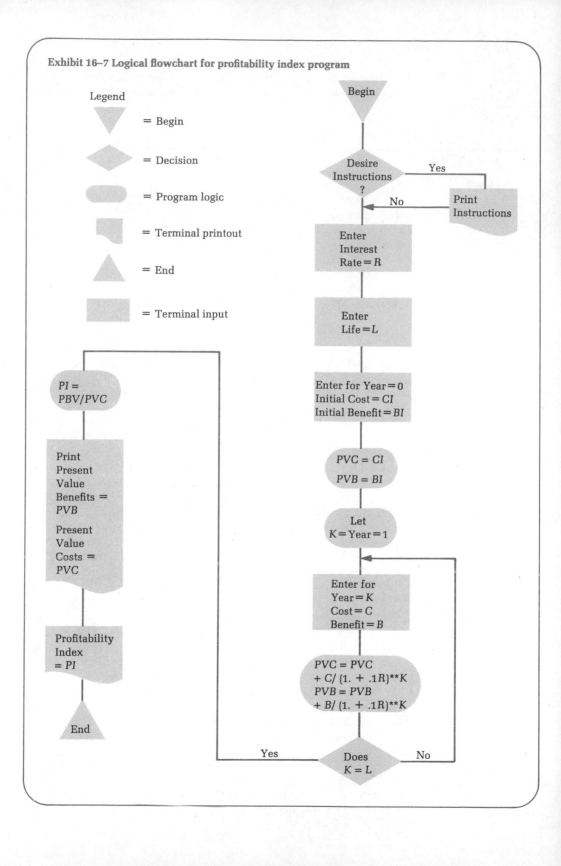

Exhibit 16–8

Computer dialogue

RUN PINDX

PINDX

DO YOU DESIRE USER INSTRUCTIONS (YES OR NO)
? YES

PINDX CALCULATES THE PROFITABILITY INDEX (PV BENEFITS/ PV COSTS) FOR A SET OF CASH FLOWS WHICH THE USER INPUTS.

PINDX WILL FIRST ASK FOR THE INTEREST RATE. (E.G. IF YOU WISH TO USE 10% ENTER 10) NEXT PINDX REQUESTS ECONOMIC LIFE. ENTER THE LIFE OF THE SYSTEM IN YEARS TO THE NEAREST YEAR.

PINDX WILL NOW REQUEST THE COSTS AND BENEFITS FOR TIME = 0 (E.G. CASH FLOWS AT THE BEGINNING OF THE FIRST YEAR.) THE FORMAT FOR THIS INPUT IS THE COST FOLLOWED BY A COMMA FOLLOWED BY THE BENEFIT.

A LOOP IS NOW SET UP TO RUN THE NUMBER OF TIMES YOU HAVE ENTERED AS THE LIFE. IN THIS LOOP PINDX WILL PROMPT THE YEAR NUMBER AND REQUEST THE COST AND BENEFIT FOR THAT YEAR. ALL CASH FLOWS ARE ASSUMED TO OCCUR AT THE YEAR END. THE INPUT FORMAT IS THE SAME AS ABOVE—COST, BENEFIT.

ONCE THE LOOP IS FINISHED, PINDX WILL PRINTOUT THE PRESENT VALUE OF THE COSTS, THE PRESENT VALUE OF THE BENEFITS, AND THE PROFITABILITY INDEX.

NOW GIVE IT A TRY!

ENTER INTEREST RATE
? 15
ENTER LIFE
? 5

ENTER INITIAL COSTS AND BENEFITS FOR TIME = 0
? 185000,0

YEAR = 1
COSTS, BENEFITS
? 10000, 70000

YEAR 2
COSTS, BENEFITS
? 10000, 90000

YEAR = 3
COSTS, BENEFITS
? 10000, 110000

YEAR = 4
COSTS, BENEFITS
? 10000, 110000

YEAR = 5
COSTS, BENEFITS
? 10000, 110000

PRESENT VALUE OF COSTS = 218522
PRESENT VALUE OF BENEFITS = 318830
PROFITABILITY INDEX = 1.459

END PINDX 8 MIN ELAPSED TIME, 6 CPU SECONDS

Suggestions
for further
reading

Blumenthal, Shermann. *Management Information Systems*. Englewood Cliffs, N.J.: Prentice-Hall, Inc., 1969.

Dearden, John; McFarlan, F. Warren; and Zani, William M. *Managing Computer-Based Information Systems*. Homewood, Ill.: Richard D. Irwin, Inc., 1971.

Meier, Robert C.; Newell, W.; and Pozer, H. *Simulation in Business and Economics*. Englewood Cliffs, N.J.: Prentice-Hall, Inc., 1969.

Murdick, Robert G., and Ross, Joel E. *Information Systems for Modern Management*. Englewood Cliffs, N.J.: Prentice-Hall, Inc., 1971.

Sanders, Donald H., *Computers and Management*, New York: McGraw-Hill Book Co., 1969.

17 Summary: The total picture

Purpose of the chapter

When a person studies a photograph or a painting, the eye takes in the total picture and conveys it to the brain; thus, all the parts of the picture and the relationships among the parts can be seen at one time. By contrast, when a person reads a book, instantaneous perception of the whole picture is not possible. The book must be read page by page, and it is only when one has finished the book that the total picture can be perceived. Since the study of a book is spread over a period of time, it is easy for the reader to lose sight of certain individual parts, and particularly how they relate to one another. The purpose of this chapter is to bring together the topics that have been discussed in this book, so as to convey the total picture.

In Chapter 1, a preliminary attempt was made to do the same thing, but the description in that chapter was necessarily general. Without an understanding of the terms and concepts that were discussed throughout the book, the reader could not be expected to have gained a picture of what the subject, management accounting, is.

Overview

In the course of fitting the pieces together, two key points are stressed:

1. **In a given business there is a single accounting system.** It consists of a number of related parts, and the parts are unified within the basic accounting equation: Assets = Liabilities + Owners' Equities.

2. **Different purposes require different accounting constructions.** There is no such thing as "the" cost. Information from the accounting system must be rearranged and modified to meet the needs of these several purposes.

533

COMPLEXITIES OF "COST"

The statement "cost measures the use of resources" is true, but vague. There are few, if any, circumstances in which the word "cost," taken by itself, has an understandable meaning. The word becomes meaningful only when a modifier is coupled with it, and even then the resulting phrase may be subject to a variety of interpretations. Listed below are general categorizations of cost that have been described in this book, and which will be referred to again in this chapter:

- Capital costs and operating costs.
- Product costs and period costs.
- Prime costs.
- Direct costs and indirect costs (or overhead or allocated costs).
- Variable costs and fixed (or nonvariable) costs.
- Full costs.
- Actual costs and standard costs.
- Joint costs and by-product costs.
- Historical costs and estimated costs.
- Differential costs.
- Controllable costs and noncontrollable costs.
- Engineered costs, discretionary costs, and committed costs.
- Responsibility costs.

Much misunderstanding arises in business situations because the parties in a discussion do not communicate clearly what kind of cost they are talking about. In particular, it is important to remember that there is no unambiguous way of stating *"the* cost" of something in any situation in which joint or common costs are involved, and they are involved in most situations.

The appropriate meaning of "cost" depends on the purpose for which the cost information is being used. Consider a factory superintendent's salary. In costing a product for inventory purposes, some fraction of the superintendent's salary is usually included. For overall planning purposes, it is the whole amount of the salary, and not the fractions allocated to individual products, that needs to be studied. As the basis for certain specific decisions (such as whether to buy a new machine), the superintendent's salary is irrelevant and therefore is excluded from the calculations; for other types of decisions (such as whether to shut down the factory), the salary is an important consideration. In measuring the performance of a departmental foreman, the superintendent's salary is not an element of cost, but in measuring the performance of the whole company, it is. In summary, some of these purposes require the full amount of the actual salary, some require a fraction of that amount, some require an estimate of what the amount (full or fractional) will be in the future, and some require that the amount be omitted.

The fact that different purposes require different cost constructions is obvious, but failure to appreciate this fact is perhaps the most important cause both of the misuse of cost figures and of the common but unwarranted criticism that "cost accountants can't be pinned down to a definite statement on what the cost is."

ORGANIZATION OF THE CHAPTER

This book has described a system. Any system can be discussed in terms of (*a*) its structure, that is, what it looks like; and (*b*) its process, that is, how it works. In human biology, for example, anatomy is a study of a structure of the body, and physiology is a study of how the body functions. A similar approach will be used here. We shall start with a description of the accounting structure, and then describe the processes in which accounting information is used.

The accounting structure

OPERATING INFORMATION

In the typical business, vast quantities of data flow through the information system (Chapter 1).[1] When orders are received, records are kept of who has placed the order and exactly what is wanted. The production department is told exactly what to manufacture, how much, and when. The purchasing department places orders for material, and records are maintained of these orders and of the accounts payable that they generate. Inventory records show the quantity and cost of material on hand. Employees are paid the exact amount owed them. Records show the amounts billed to customers, and payments received from customers, and the amounts received from them. These and similar data collectively are called operating information.

Except for a brief description of the use of the computer in processing operating information (Chapter 16), in this book we have not focused on operating information as such; rather we have focused on management accounting information. Most management accounting information is derived from appropriate summaries of operating information. Relatively little information is collected solely for the use of management. It follows that the cost involved in obtaining information for management is only a small fraction of the cost of processing all the information used in a business. Rearrangement and summarization of raw data for management use is a much less expensive job than recording the raw data in the first instance.

MANAGEMENT ACCOUNTING INFORMATION

Exhibit 17–1 gives an overview of the management accounting structure and of the management uses of accounting information.

---

[1] These references indicate the chapter in which an expanded discussion of the topic will be found.

Exhibit 17–1

Cost constructions and their uses

| | | Uses of Cost Information | | | Management Control | |
	Financial Reporting	*Full Cost Measurement*	*Alternative Choice Decisions*	*Planning*	*Control*
Examples	Inventory amounts Cost of goods sold	Target pricing Cost-type contracts	Contribution pricing Make or buy Capital investments	Programming Budget preparation	Performance Measurement
Full cost accounting Direct factory cost	Factory costs only; governed by generally accepted principles	All elements of cost	Note 1	Note 2	Compare actual and standard direct costs
Indirect factory cost Selling and general and administrative			Note 1		
Differential accounting			Tailor-made for each problem, estimates of future	Note 2	
Responsibility accounting			Note 1	Focus on responsibility center	Compare actual and budgeted

Notes:

1. Full cost accounting (except allocated costs) and responsibility accounting may provide raw data that are useful in estimating differential costs
2. In making certain program decisions, both full costs and differential costs are sometimes helpful.

For simplicity, the exhibit has been drawn up in terms of costs, but corresponding statements can be made about revenues. There are three types of cost constructions in management accounting:

1. Full cost accounting.
2. Differential accounting.
3. Responsibility accounting.

Full costs and responsibility costs are collected in the accounts, but differential costs are not. Some individual cost accounts are used both for full costs and for responsibility costs; other accounts are used only for one type of cost construction or the other. Differential costs are constructed in some cases by rearrangement of data obtained from full cost or responsibility cost accounts; in other cases, differential costs are constructed from information that comes from outside the accounting system.

Some companies have an additional set of accounts in order to meet the requirements of regulatory agencies. In general, these accounts are similar to its full-cost accounts.

In addition to this management accounting information, the complete accounting system includes financial accounting information, that is, information used to prepare the financial statements furnished to external parties. Financial accounting is discussed in *Fundamentals of Financial Accounting* and will be referred to here only to the extent necessary to show the relationship between financial accounting and management accounting.

In the following sections, we shall describe the three types of management accounting constructions and we shall then describe the uses of this information by management.

FULL COST ACCOUNTING (CHAPTERS 2, 3, AND 4)

Cost measures in monetary terms the amount of resources used for (or assigned to) a cost objective. A cost objective is anything whose cost is to be measured. In the full cost structure we have used the products that a company manufactures as a case in point. In the absence of more specific information, the term "cost accounting" is usually taken to mean the measurement of costs of manufacturing goods. It could equally well refer to measuring the cost of providing services (such as the various types of telephone calls whose costs are measured by a telephone company), or to measuring the cost of performing a contract. The same principles apply whatever the cost objective may be.

Capital costs and operating costs. Some costs are incurred to build or acquire capital assets. Costs of these capital assets are to be distinguished from operating costs. The following discussion relates only to operating costs.

Factory costs and other costs. The full cost of a product is the sum of its factory cost and its marketing and general and administrative costs; however, the formal accounts usually record only the factory cost of products. This is because only factory costs are used in measuring finished goods inventory amounts on the balance sheet and cost of goods sold on the income statement. It would not be appropriate to include nonmanufacturing costs in finished goods inventory because these costs do not represent resources used in the manufacturing process; in general, these costs are incurred *after* the manufacturing process has been completed.

Factory costs are also, and commonly, called *product costs;* and other costs are called *period costs* because the former enters into the inventory valuation of products, whereas the latter are expenses of the accounting period in which the costs are incurred. It must be understood that the term *product cost* in this context refers only to the factory costs of the product; the full costs of a product include both its factory costs and other costs.

Direct and indirect factory costs (Chapter 3). The factory cost of a product is the sum of (*a*) its direct costs, and (*b*) a fair share of the indirect costs that are incurred for two or more cost objectives, of which the product in question is one.

Direct factory costs. The direct factory costs of a product (usually referred to simply as direct costs) are items of cost that are specifically traced to that product because they are caused by the manufacture of that product. They are usually classified as either (*a*) direct material, -or (*b*) direct labor. They are also called prime costs.

Problems arise in deciding what items of cost should be classified as direct. Conceptually, direct costs should include labor-related costs such as fringe benefits, and material-related costs such as storage and handling costs, but practice varies in this regard. Except for the question of what items to include in the direct cost category, the task of collecting direct costs is straightforward. A large portion of the total paperwork in the accounting system is involved in collecting direct costs, but only a small fraction of the conceptual problems are related to direct costs.

Indirect factory costs. Indirect factory costs are also referred to as *factory overhead costs.* The determination of what share of the total indirect costs of the factory should be assigned to a given product involves difficult conceptual problems; it also involves more complicated procedures than those used for direct costs. Indirect costs are first collected in production cost centers and service cost centers. Total costs of service cost centers are then reassigned to production cost centers, so that all factory costs eventually wind up in some production cost center. The basis of assignment reflects either the relative benefits received by the cost center or the relative amounts of costs caused by the activities of the cost center.

Indirect costs of each production cost center are allocated to products by means of an overhead rate; thus, each product passing through the production cost center is allocated a fair share of its indirect costs. The overhead rate is usually determined in advance of the accounting period. The overhead rate is arrived at by estimating the amount of factory indirect costs in the cost center, estimating the volume or activity level at which the cost center will operate, and then dividing estimated costs by estimated volume; the overhead rate is therefore a cost per unit of volume. Because some costs are fixed, the overhead rate is less for high volumes than it is for low volumes. Because actual volume and actual costs may be different than the amounts that were estimated in advance, it is likely that the amount of indirect costs allocated to products by means of the overhead rate will not exactly equal the actual amount of indirect costs accumulated in the cost center; this results in unabsorbed or overabsorbed overhead.

Job costing and process costing (Chapter 2). Two procedures are used to accumulate the cost of products; the choice between them depends on characteristics of production activity. In a *job cost system,* a record is kept of each product or lot of products going through the factory, and cost items are accumulated on this record. In a *process cost system,* records are maintained by production cost centers only; products are assigned their proportionate share of the costs, both indirect and direct, that are accumulated in the production cost center.

As products move through production costs centers, their costs are accumulated either through job cost or process cost procedures. (It is often said that costs *attach* to products.) Simultaneously, debits to Goods in Process Inventory are made for the total amount of these costs incurred in an accounting period. When products are completed, Goods in Process Inventory is credited and Finished Goods Inventory debited at the accumulated cost. When products are sold, a similar transfer is made from Finished Goods Inventory to Cost of Goods Sold. The costs involved in this process are factory costs, excluding costs that are incurred "beyond the factory exit door."

Joint costs and by-product costs (Chapter 3). Joint costs are costs incurred jointly for two or more products that are produced together at an early stage of the manufacturing process, but which are separated at a stage called the split-off point. They include both direct and indirect factory costs incurred up to the split-off point.

When the intention is to produce as much as possible of one product and as little as possible of another product, the former is called the *main product* and the latter the *by-product*. Special accounting rules apply to the measurement of costs of by-products.

Standard costs (Chapter 12). Instead of, or in addition to, measuring the *actual* costs of a product, a standard cost system records what its costs *should have been*. Standard direct material costs and standard direct labor costs are established. A standard overhead rate is also established, but it is essentially the same as the overhead rate in an actual cost system. As products move through the factory, standard costs are assigned to them; the mechanism is substantially the same as that described above for actual costs, except that at appropriate points variances between actual and standard costs are identified and recorded.

Other costs (Chapter 4). Marketing costs and those general and administrative costs not attributable to the manufacturing process are not assigned to products as part of the process described above; thus such cost elements are not included in inventory or in cost of goods sold. They are period costs. Nevertheless, for certain purposes, it is necessary that full costs, including these other costs, be measured. For these purposes, both direct and indirect nonmanufacturing costs are added to manufacturing costs; this may be done on cost estimating sheets which are not part of the formal accounts. The principles governing the assignment of nonmanufacturing costs to products are the same as those for factory costs. Direct costs are assigned directly, and indirect costs are allocated by means of overhead rates.

DIFFERENTIAL ACCOUNTING (CHAPTERS 6 AND 7)

Differential costs are those items of cost that are expected to be different if a proposed alternative course of action is adopted. The accounts do not record differential costs as such. Such items are always estimates of the future, and the relevant amounts are a function of the specific alternatives being considered. Historical costs obtained from either the full cost structure or the responsibility structure may be useful as a basis for making such estimates.

RESPONSIBILITY ACCOUNTING (CHAPTERS 10 AND 13)

A responsibility center is an organization unit headed by a manager. Since control can be exercised only by human beings who influence other human beings, the focus of control is on the responsibility center. In responsibility accounting, costs are assigned to the responsibility center responsible for incurring them. Many responsibility centers are also cost centers, and in these cases a single set of accounts serves both the purposes of product costing and that of responsibility accounting. Within each responsibility center, the items of costs are classified by object or function (e.g., supervision, supplies, maintenance). Such a classification is not needed for product costing purposes. Conversely, the classification of costs by product is not needed for responsibility accounting purposes. Also, certain cost centers used in product costing are not the responsibility of a single manager (e.g., an "occupancy" cost center in which costs of using physical space are accumulated), and these costs centers are not used in responsibility accounting.

Responsibility accounting includes both *historical* costs and *estimates* of future costs. In most companies, only the historical information is recorded in the formal accounts. Estimates are shown in *programs* or *budgets* that are closely related to, but not a part of, the formal accounts.

Cost categories. Information in the responsibility accounts is classified in ways that are useful to management. The principal categories are listed below.

Variable or fixed (Chapter 6). Variable costs are those that vary with the level of activity or volume; fixed costs do not vary, within a relevant range. Some accounting systems specifically identify items of variable cost. These are called *variable cost systems* (or, but less accurately, *direct cost systems*).

Engineered, discretionary, or committed (Chapter 13). These categories refer to, respectively, costs that are *caused by* the level of activity or volume, costs that change at the *discretion of management,* and costs that are *not subject to change* in the short run. They are usually not identified as such in the accounts, but the distinctions are important in understanding the preparation of budgets and in analyzing reports on performance.

Controllable and noncontrollable (Chapter 13). These categories distinguish those items of cost over which the manager of a responsibility center, respectively, can or cannot exercise a significant amount of control. The distinction is important in analyzing reports on performance.

THE ACCOUNT BUILDING BLOCK

Full cost accounting and responsibility accounting are part of a single system, for which detailed cost information is aggregated in two different ways in different purposes. The lowest common denominator of the system is called the *account building block*. It consists of a single item of cost (e.g., direct material, supplies, overtime) incurred in the *smaller* of either a cost center or a responsibility center. Summaries of cost information are obtained by combining these building blocks in either of two principal ways: (1) by *products* using full cost procedures, or (2) by the hierarchy of *responsibility centers* in the responsibility system.

Uses of accounting information

We turn now to a description of the processes in which the accounting information is used, namely:

1. Financial reporting.
2. Full cost measurement.
3. Alternative choice decision making.
4. Management control.

FINANCIAL REPORTING

Product manufacturing costs are used in measuring goods in process inventory, finished goods inventory, and cost of goods sold in the external financial statements. Expense accounts are also summarized to provide the amounts for expenses on the income statement. The principles and techniques governing the preparation of these financial statements are the subject matter of financial accounting, and are discussed in *Fundamentals of Financial Accounting*.

FULL COST MEASUREMENT (CHAPTER 5)

In conducting its current operations, a business uses full cost information for many purposes.

In a business with several products, and especially in job shops, the most extensive and more frequent use of full cost information is as an aid in arriving at selling prices. In some circumstances, the company may price on the basis of differential costs in order to obtain business that it might otherwise lose. In the great majority of cases, however, companies arrive at the first approximation of the selling price, which is the target price, by following the principle that the price of a product should cover all its direct costs, plus a fair share of its indirect costs, plus a reasonable profit margin. This is the full cost approach to product pricing. In still other situations, the company must sell at prices that exist in the marketplace, and in these situations cost information is useful only in deciding what the company can afford to spend on the product.

Conceptually, selling prices should be based on an estimate of future costs rather than on historical costs as shown in the accounting records. The accounting records nevertheless provide the starting point in the calculation; that is, historical costs are adjusted for estimated changes in cost in order to arrive at the number that is used in deciding on the selling price. If the company has a standard cost system (Chapter 12), the standard unit costs presumably incorporate these adjustments to historical cost, and they are used directly as a basis for pricing. In arriving at the actual selling price, marketing executives adjust the target price according to their judgment of what the best pricing tactic is under the market conditions currently prevailing.

Full costs are also used for many other operating purposes. They are used in situations in which a buyer agrees to pay cost plus a certain profit margin for goods produced or services rendered under a contract. This is the way automobile repair services, TV repairs, job printing, machine shop work, and a great number of other goods and services are priced. Full cost is also the method used for pricing billions of dollars worth of government contracts. Whenever a congressional investigating committee, or any other group asks the question, "What did such-and-such cost?" the answer is usually given in terms of full cost.

ALTERNATIVE CHOICE DECISIONS (CHAPTERS 7, 8, AND 9)

Most business problems require that management make a choice between two or more alternate courses of action; for example, shall we or shall we not buy a proposed new machine? Shall we make a certain part or shall we buy it from an outside vendor?

The best alternative is usually the one that adds the most to profits (or, if additional assets are involved, the alternative that produces the largest return on investment). This test is not always appropriate, however; objectives other than profits usually are relevant in alternative choice problems, and in some situations such objectives are dominant. Accounting information is useful in estimating the costs that are associated with each alternative. These costs are differential costs. If an alternative involves a capital investment, it is the differential investment that is relevant.

In comparing two or more alternatives, the important question to be addressed is how the estimated costs differ; that is, how the costs for one alternative differ from those of the other: this is the concept of differential costs. Costs that are unaffected by either alternative need not be considered at all. In particular, allocated indirect costs can lead to misunderstanding in problems of this type. Since these costs are expressed as overhead rates that are often tied to direct costs, they may give the appearance of varying with whatever measure of activity causes costs to vary; actually the overhead costs may not have such a casual connection with activity.

> EXAMPLE: If the overhead rate is $2 per direct labor dollar, and if one alternative is estimated to require $10,000 of direct labor, it may appear that the alternative will also require $20,000 of overhead; this conclusion is not warranted.

In most alternative choice problems, overhead allocations and the resulting overhead rates should be disregarded; instead, the expected behavior of the various components of overhead should be studied directly.

Neither full cost accounts nor responsibility accounts necessarily contain cost information that is relevant for an alternative choice problem. The task of the analyst is to put together the costs that *are* relevant for the particular problem being examined. In doing this, historical cost accounting information may be used as a starting point—it is adjusted so that it reflects expected future conditions. In making such adjustments, the analyst needs to understand how costs behave, and particularly how costs vary with volume (Chapter 6). Thus, unlike full cost accounting, which is associated with the financial statements, and unlike responsibility accounting, which is associated with the management control process, there is no identifiable part of the accounting structure that is associated with alternative choice decisions. Data from various parts of the structure are massaged and reassembled to fit the requirements of the specific situation being analyzed.

MANAGEMENT CONTROL (CHAPTERS 10, 11, 14, AND 15)

Management control is the process by which managers assure that resources are obtained and used effectively and efficiently in the accomplishment of the organization's goals. The process consists of these steps, in chronological order: programming, budgeting, measuring and appraising performance, and acting on performance. Programming and budgeting are *planning* activities; appraising and acting are *control* activities. In the management control process, behavioral considerations are at least as important as accounting considerations.

Programming (Chapter 10). In the programming activity, management decided on the principal programs that the organization will undertake in the future and on the approximate amount of resources that is to be used for each program. In most companies, the programming activity is relatively unstructured and informal. Differential costs are used in the analysis of proposed programs; but when the proposal covers a long period of time, differential costs are practically equivalent to full costs.

Budget preparation (Chapter 11). In the budgeting activity, an annual profit plan is prepared. The plan is prepared within the context of decisions made during the programming process. It is prepared in terms of responsibility centers, and responsibility costs are relevant.

The planned costs that are decided on in the budgeting activity are used as the basis for calculating overhead rates. If a standard cost system is used, the standard costs are also consistent with the budget.

For those responsibility centers in which overhead costs vary with the level of activity (for either engineering or discretionary reasons), a variable overhead budget is prepared. This budget states a fixed amount per period and a variable amount per unit of output.

Performance measurement, appraisal, and action (Chapters 14 and 15). As performance takes place, actual costs are recorded in the responsibility accounts. These are summarized in reports to management. Among other things, these reports compare actual costs with standard or budgeted costs. Techniques are available for analyzing the variances as a first step in determining their causes (Chapter 14). On the basis of such an analysis of variances, further investigation is conducted and, if warranted, appropriate action is taken.

In making these analyses of variances, distinctions between controllable and noncontrollable costs, between engineered and discretionary costs, and between variable and fixed costs must be understood. These distinctions are not ordinarily reflected in the account classifications. Rather, the identification is made in reports prepared *from* the accounts. In particular, in analyzing the performance of a responsibility center, it is essential that a distinction be made between controllable and noncontrollable costs.

Demonstration case   As a further aid in showing how the elements of an accounting system are related to one another, this section summarizes the accounting system of an actual company (but with a disguised name), the Wallace Box Company.

THE COMPANY AND ITS PRODUCTS

Wallace Box is a well-established manufacturer of paperboard cartons and boxes, primarily as packages for consumer products. The cartons are manufactured in the company's carton factory. The raw material for the carton factory is paperboard which is manufactured in the company's paperboard mill, adjacent to the carton factory. The plant complex also includes a 60,000-square foot warehouse where finished orders are stored pending delivery. The company has approximately 425 employees in 1974. Mr. Edgar Wallace, the president, is also a large stockholder.

The company markets its products within a radius of about 500 miles from its factory. It has seven sales engineers, who are compensated on the basis of a nominal salary, plus commission. Three of them operate from the plant; the other four work out of a sales office in a city that is 200 miles from the plant. The company has an excellent reputation for product quality and customer service. The paperboard and carton industry is characterized by strong competition because of the potential overcapacity that exists in most plants. Because of this overcapacity, competition for large orders is particularly keen, and price cutting is common. Wallace meets this competition by designing special boxes to customer specifications, by actively catering to its customers' wishes, and by strict adherence to promised delivery dates.

The production process requires that the paperboard mill operates continuously on three shifts for maximum efficiency, but the carton factory operates an average of only one and one-half shifts per day.

A partial organization chart is shown as Exhibit 17–2. The paperboard mill and the carton factory are profit centers. In the carton factory are 10 production departments, each consisting of a printing press or a group of similar presses and associated equipment and each headed by a foreman. There are five service departments, which perform functions such as ink manufacture, quality control, and warehouse storage; each is headed by a supervisor. Each of these 15 departments

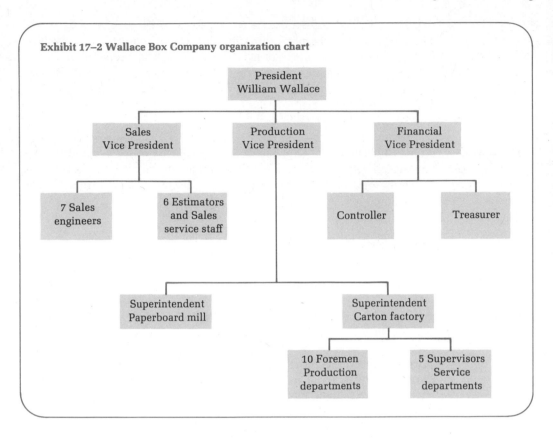

Exhibit 17–2 Wallace Box Company organization chart

is an expense center. The 10 production departments are production cost centers, and the 5 service departments are service cost centers.

PROGRAMMING AND BUDGETING

Wallace Box has no formal mechanism for making program decisions. Mr. Wallace meets informally with his vice presidents and superintendents to discuss changes in strategies. The principal program decisions are those relating to the acquisition of new pieces of equipment. As an aid to making these decisions, a profitability index is calculated for all proposals for equipment acquisitions where the available information is sufficiently reliable to warrant such an analysis. About 85 percent of the proposals in terms of number, but less than 50 percent in terms of dollar magnitude, are in this category.

The controller is responsible for the mechanics of the annual budgeting process. He sees to it that the sales staff prepares sales estimates. These are discussed at length in a meeting attended by Mr. Wallace, the sales vice president, and the controller. After final sales estimates are agreed upon, the controller communicates these estimates to heads of responsibility centers as a basis for their budget preparation.

Some budget items are stated as a fixed amount per month, others are stated as variable amounts per unit of output, and still others are stated as a fixed amount per month plus a variable amount per unit of output. For the production departments, output is measured in terms of machine-hours, and for the service departments it is measured in terms of an appropriate measure of activity, such as pounds of ink manufactured.

Each responsibility center head discusses his proposed budget first with the controller (who has had long experience in the industry and hence can point out discrepancies or soft spots), and, in the case of the carton factory, with the superintendent. Mr. Wallace then discusses the proposed budgets for the board mill and the carton factory with the superintendents of these profit centers. He discusses the marketing budget with the sales vice president. From these discussions, an approved budget emerges. It consists of a master budget showing planned revenues and expenses at the estimated sales volume, a variable budget for each responsibility center showing the fixed amount per month and the variable rate per unit of output for each significant item of expense, a purchasing budget, and a cash-flow budget. The company uses a standard cost system both for control and as a basis for pricing. Standard unit costs and overhead rates are revised if necessary, so that they are consistent with the approved budget.

PRODUCT PRICING

Pricing is a crucial element in the company's marketing tactics. Prices are prepared by the company's estimators for each bid or order, on the basis of sales specifications and the appropriate standard cost elements as shown in tables the company has developed for this purpose. To the calculated amount of total factory costs, there are added allowances for selling and administrative expenses, sales commissions, cash discounts, and a profit margin. These allowances are expressed as percentages, and are based on the budget. A sample price estimate is reproduced as Exhibit 17–3.[2] The price calculated in the estimate is often adjusted, for quotation purposes. It may be lowered to meet competitive conditions, or it may be increased because the design job on the order is judged to be particularly good, or for other reasons. In Exhibit 17–3, the calculated selling price comes to $14.07 per thousand boxes, but the actual quotation was increased to $15.30.

Estimators of several companies meet regularly under the auspices of a trade association to price sample boxes according to their own formulae. Based on these meetings, Mr. Wallace has concluded that

---

[2] Many of the abbreviations and terms in this form are peculiar to the company. The purpose of Exhibit 17–3 is only to illustrate the form used in preparing a price estimate. An understanding of its details is not necessary for this purpose.

Exhibit 17–3

Wallace Box Company

Price Estimate

Item: 1 million boxes, 6 1/16 x 2 3/4 x 1 1/2, printed 2 colors and
varnish, on .024 caliber White Patent Coated, News Backed

PREPARATORY COST	Production Per Hour	Rate	Unit	Material Cost	Mfg. Cost
Original Plates	F. or E.				
Electros 9³/₄ x 9¹/₄		18.94	28	530 32	
Wood				15 99	
Rule				34 09	
Composing					
Die Making	③	4.85	41.8		202 73
Make Ready—Ptg.	2 x	12.80	30.0		384 00
Make Ready—C. & C.	11.55	11.25	15.8		177 75
Total Preparatory Cost				580 40	764 48
QUANTITY COST					
Board 65,005 (3³/₄)	171.00+25			5557 93	
Board (32,5025)				25 00	
Ink		.37	300	111 00	
Ink 30"		.75 / .15	300 / 231	328 95	
Cases Corrugated	700	.30	1429	428 70	
Cellulose Material					
Board, Storage, & Handling		1.87			60 78
Cutting Stock					
Printing		} 22.766			
Cut and Crease					813 09
Stripping	.933-4	.178+ 120			391 60
Cellulose					
Auto Gluing		1.562 .466+11.24			477 24
Hand Gluing					
Wrapping or Packing		6.503			92 93
Inspection					
Total Quantity Cost				6451 58	1835 64
Total Preparatory Cost				580 40	764 48
Total Cost to Make				7031 98	2600 12
Selling & Commercial		45+8 (%+$)			1178 05
Material Forward					2031 98
Shipping 56+		7.25+2	60,287		220 54
Freight and Cartage		.40			241 15
Total Cost					11271 84
Profit		20%			2254 37
Total Selling Price					13526 21
Finished Stock Price					
Commission & Discount		4%			541 05
Total Selling Price					14067 26
Selling Price per M – Calculated					14 07
Selling Price per M – Quoted					15 30

while most of his competitors were shaving prices below formula, Wallace's quoted prices were higher than the calculated estimate about 65 percent of the time, identical about 20 percent of the time, and lower 15 percent of the time. "It all depends on the competition, and on your assessment of the whole situation," he once said.

REPORTS

Each month an income statement is prepared (Exhibit 17–4). It is constructed so as to focus on the performance of the two profit centers.

Exhibit 17–4

WALLACE BOX COMPANY
Income Statement
($000 omitted)

December 1974			*12 Months 1974*	
Actual	*Favorable or (Unfavorable) Variance*	*Board Mill*	*Actual*	*Favorable or (Unfavorable) Variance*
52	12	External sales...............	344	38
168	16	Transfers to carton		
		factory....................	1,970	140
220	28	Total revenues..............	2,314	168
169	(16)	Cost of goods sold...........	1,831	(134)
51	12	Gross margin...............	483	34
	26	Volume variance		48
	(14)	Other variances.............		(14)
		Selling and administrative		
30	(2)	expenses...................	374	(6)
21	10	Board mill profit............	109	28
		Carton Factory		
666	22	Sales.......................	7,968	248
472	(18)	Standard cost of goods sold....	5,664	(130)
194	4	Gross margin................	2,304	118
	8	Price and mix variance........		54
	14	Volume variance.............		64
20	20	Manufacturing variances......	40	40
50	(5)	Selling expenses.............	592	(12)
12	1	Administrative expenses.......	143	7
152	16	Carton factory profit..........	1,609	153
		Company		
173	26	Total factory and mill		
		profits.....................	1,718	181
62	2	Corporate expenses...........	507	18
4	...	Nonoperating income (loss)....	(12)	(2)
107	28	Income before income tax......	1,199	201
53	(13)	Income tax...................	576	(96)
54	15	Net Income..................	623	105

Exhibit 17–5

WALLACE BOX COMPANY
Spending Report
Department 14 (Two Two-Color Meihle Printing Presses)

December 1974			12 Months 1974	
Actual	Spending Variance		Actual	Spending Variance
5,885	(107)	Labor—pressmen..................	81,057	(647)
2,074	(46)	Labor—helpers...................	28,978	(235)
373	120	Press supplies...................	3,279	146
1,472	(604)	Repairs.........................	8,562	120
484	66	Power..........................	6,369	322
242	52	Other controllable overhead........	3,444	461
10,530	(619)	Total controllable costs............	131,689	167
2,426	...	Departmental fixed cost...........	29,112	...
3,352	...	Allocated costs..................	40,224	...
16,308		Total costs......................	201,025	
	(340)	Volume variance..................		1,012
	(959)	Total variance...................		1,179

( ) = unfavorable.

Also, a spending report is prepared for each of the 15 expense centers in the carton factory. An example given is Exhibit 17–5.

In addition, Mr. Wallace receives a variety of other reports on a regular basis. The *internally generated* reports are as follows:

1. Balance sheet, monthly.
2. Selling, general and administrative statement, monthly.
3. Overdue accounts receivable, monthly.
4. Overdue shipments, monthly.
5. Inventory size, monthly.
6. Raw materials shrinkage report, monthly.
7. Cash and securities listing, monthly.
8. Actual sales, weekly, with a monthly comparison of actual and budgeted sales.
9. Carton factory production, monthly. This included operating hours statistics and efficiency percentages.
10. Outstanding orders, weekly.
11. Machine production report, daily.
12. Quality control report, monthly.

Mr. Wallace examines the reports illustrated in Exhibits 17–4 and 17–5 carefully. If there are important departures from plan, he discusses them with the manager responsible. Other reports are prepared primarily for the use of some other executive, and Mr. Wallace receives only an information copy. He may or may not glance at these reports in a given month, but he is certain to do so if he suspects that trouble may be brewing in the area covered by the report.

Mr. Wallace also pays close attention to several *external* reports he receives regularly from the Folding Paper Box Association of America, the industry trade association. They show current economic trends, the probable effects of these trends on different segments of the paperboard carton industry, and sales orders, actual sales, production volume, and other related statistics for all companies in the industry.

Questions
for
discussion

1. Refer to the list of modifiers of the word "cost" that is given on page 534. Which of the modifiers apply to the following numbers in the Wallace Box Company? (Each number has several modifiers.)
   a. On Exhibit 17–3, the total preparatory manufacturing cost of $764.48 (9th line on the exhibit).
   b. On Exhibit 17–3, the board material cost of $5,557.93 (11th line on exhibit).
   c. On Exhibit 17–3, selling and commercial of $1,178.05 (12th line from the bottom).
   d. On Exhibit 17–4, standard cost of goods sold, carton factory, of $472,000 in December.
   e. On Exhibit 17–4, selling expenses, carton factory, of $50,000 in December.
   f. On Exhibit 17–5, labor—pressman in December of $5,885.
   g. On Exhibit 17–5, departmental fixed costs in December of $2,426.
   h. On Exhibit 17–5, allocated costs in December of $3,352.

2. The following questions relate to Exhibit 17–4 and the December 1974 amounts.
   a. A transfer price was used in connection with *two* items. What are these two items?
   b. Assuming that inventory levels did not vary in December, what was the actual cost of goods manufactured in the carton factory?
   c. Why is the assumption in question (b) necessary in order to answer that question?
   d. What is the budgeted amount of corporate expenses?
   e. In December was activity in the board mill above or below the standard volume?

3. The following questions relate to Exhibit 17–5 and the December amounts:
   a. What was the actual cost of labor—pressmen?
   b. What was the budgeted amount of total controllable cost?
   c. What amount of total controllable cost was applied to products?
   d. Why do no amounts appear in the spending variance column for departmental fixed costs and allocated costs?

4. Mr. Wallace is considering the replacement of one of the printing presses in Department 14. Which items of costs appearing on Exhibit 17–5 should be considered in making this decision? In general, what should be done to make these amounts useful as a basis for the decision?

Problems   17–1.   As his assistant, write a memorandum calling Mr. Wallace's atten-
                    tion to matters you think he should be aware of as indicated on Ex-
                    hibit 17–4.

            17–2.   Do the same with Exhibit 17–5.

Table A
Present value of $1

Years Hence	1%	2%	4%	6%	8%	10%	12%	14%	15%	16%	18%	20%	22%	24%	25%	26%	28%	30%	35%	40%	45%	50%
1	0.990	0.980	0.962	0.943	0.926	0.909	0.893	0.877	0.870	0.862	0.847	0.833	0.820	0.806	0.800	0.794	0.781	0.769	0.741	0.714	0.690	0.667
2	0.980	0.961	0.925	0.890	0.857	0.826	0.797	0.769	0.756	0.743	0.718	0.694	0.672	0.650	0.640	0.630	0.610	0.592	0.549	0.510	0.476	0.444
3	0.971	0.942	0.889	0.840	0.794	0.751	0.712	0.675	0.658	0.641	0.609	0.579	0.551	0.524	0.512	0.500	0.477	0.455	0.406	0.364	0.328	0.296
4	0.961	0.924	0.855	0.792	0.735	0.683	0.636	0.592	0.572	0.552	0.516	0.482	0.451	0.423	0.410	0.397	0.373	0.350	0.301	0.260	0.226	0.198
5	0.951	0.906	0.822	0.747	0.681	0.621	0.567	0.519	0.497	0.476	0.437	0.402	0.370	0.341	0.328	0.315	0.291	0.269	0.223	0.186	0.156	0.132
6	0.942	0.888	0.790	0.705	0.630	0.564	0.507	0.456	0.432	0.410	0.370	0.335	0.303	0.275	0.262	0.250	0.227	0.207	0.165	0.133	0.108	0.088
7	0.933	0.871	0.760	0.665	0.583	0.513	0.452	0.400	0.376	0.354	0.314	0.279	0.249	0.222	0.210	0.198	0.178	0.159	0.122	0.095	0.074	0.059
8	0.923	0.853	0.731	0.627	0.540	0.467	0.404	0.351	0.327	0.305	0.266	0.233	0.204	0.179	0.168	0.157	0.139	0.123	0.091	0.068	0.051	0.039
9	0.914	0.837	0.703	0.592	0.500	0.424	0.361	0.308	0.284	0.263	0.225	0.194	0.167	0.144	0.134	0.125	0.108	0.094	0.067	0.048	0.035	0.026
10	0.905	0.820	0.676	0.558	0.463	0.386	0.322	0.270	0.247	0.227	0.191	0.162	0.137	0.116	0.107	0.099	0.085	0.073	0.050	0.035	0.024	0.017
11	0.896	0.804	0.650	0.527	0.429	0.350	0.287	0.237	0.215	0.195	0.162	0.135	0.112	0.094	0.086	0.079	0.066	0.056	0.037	0.025	0.017	0.012
12	0.887	0.788	0.625	0.497	0.397	0.319	0.257	0.208	0.187	0.168	0.137	0.112	0.092	0.076	0.069	0.062	0.052	0.043	0.027	0.018	0.012	0.008
13	0.879	0.773	0.601	0.469	0.368	0.290	0.229	0.182	0.163	0.145	0.116	0.093	0.075	0.061	0.055	0.050	0.040	0.033	0.020	0.013	0.008	0.005
14	0.870	0.758	0.577	0.442	0.340	0.263	0.205	0.160	0.141	0.125	0.099	0.078	0.062	0.049	0.044	0.039	0.032	0.025	0.015	0.009	0.006	0.003
15	0.861	0.743	0.555	0.417	0.315	0.239	0.183	0.140	0.123	0.108	0.084	0.065	0.051	0.040	0.035	0.031	0.025	0.020	0.011	0.006	0.004	0.002
16	0.853	0.728	0.534	0.394	0.292	0.218	0.163	0.123	0.107	0.093	0.071	0.054	0.042	0.032	0.028	0.025	0.019	0.015	0.008	0.005	0.003	0.002
17	0.844	0.714	0.513	0.371	0.270	0.198	0.146	0.108	0.093	0.080	0.060	0.045	0.034	0.026	0.023	0.020	0.015	0.012	0.006	0.003	0.002	0.001
18	0.836	0.700	0.494	0.350	0.250	0.180	0.130	0.095	0.081	0.069	0.051	0.038	0.028	0.021	0.018	0.016	0.012	0.009	0.005	0.002	0.001	0.001
19	0.828	0.686	0.475	0.331	0.232	0.164	0.116	0.083	0.070	0.060	0.043	0.031	0.023	0.017	0.014	0.012	0.009	0.007	0.003	0.002	0.001	
20	0.820	0.673	0.456	0.312	0.215	0.149	0.104	0.073	0.061	0.051	0.037	0.026	0.019	0.014	0.012	0.010	0.007	0.005	0.002	0.001	0.001	
21	0.811	0.660	0.439	0.294	0.199	0.135	0.093	0.064	0.053	0.044	0.031	0.022	0.015	0.011	0.009	0.008	0.006	0.004	0.002	0.001		
22	0.803	0.647	0.422	0.278	0.184	0.123	0.083	0.056	0.046	0.038	0.026	0.018	0.013	0.009	0.007	0.006	0.004	0.003	0.001	0.001		
23	0.795	0.634	0.406	0.262	0.170	0.112	0.074	0.049	0.040	0.033	0.022	0.015	0.010	0.007	0.006	0.005	0.003	0.002	0.001			
24	0.788	0.622	0.390	0.247	0.158	0.102	0.066	0.043	0.035	0.028	0.019	0.013	0.008	0.006	0.005	0.004	0.003	0.002	0.001			
25	0.780	0.610	0.375	0.233	0.146	0.092	0.059	0.038	0.030	0.024	0.016	0.010	0.007	0.005	0.004	0.003	0.002	0.001	0.001			
26	0.772	0.598	0.361	0.220	0.135	0.084	0.053	0.033	0.026	0.021	0.014	0.009	0.006	0.004	0.003	0.002	0.002	0.001				
27	0.764	0.586	0.347	0.207	0.125	0.076	0.047	0.029	0.023	0.018	0.011	0.007	0.005	0.003	0.002	0.002	0.001	0.001				
28	0.757	0.574	0.333	0.196	0.116	0.069	0.042	0.026	0.020	0.016	0.010	0.006	0.004	0.002	0.002	0.001	0.001	0.001				
29	0.749	0.563	0.321	0.185	0.107	0.063	0.037	0.022	0.017	0.014	0.008	0.005	0.003	0.002	0.002	0.001	0.001					
30	0.742	0.552	0.308	0.174	0.099	0.057	0.033	0.020	0.015	0.012	0.007	0.004	0.003	0.002	0.001	0.001	0.001					
40	0.672	0.453	0.208	0.097	0.046	0.022	0.011	0.005	0.004	0.003	0.001	0.001										
50	0.608	0.372	0.141	0.054	0.021	0.009	0.003	0.001	0.001	0.001												

Table B
Present value of $1 received annually for N years

Years (N)	1%	2%	4%	6%	8%	10%	12%	14%	15%	16%	18%	20%	22%	24%	25%	26%	28%	30%	35%	40%	45%	50%
1	0.990	0.980	0.962	0.943	0.926	0.909	0.893	0.877	0.870	0.862	0.847	0.833	0.820	0.806	0.800	0.794	0.781	0.769	0.741	0.714	0.690	0.667
2	1.970	1.942	1.886	1.833	1.783	1.736	1.690	1.647	1.626	1.605	1.566	1.528	1.492	1.457	1.440	1.424	1.392	1.361	1.289	1.224	1.165	1.111
3	2.941	2.884	2.775	2.673	2.577	2.487	2.402	2.322	2.283	2.246	2.174	2.106	2.042	1.981	1.952	1.923	1.868	1.816	1.696	1.589	1.493	1.407
4	3.902	3.808	3.630	3.465	3.312	3.170	3.037	2.914	2.855	2.798	2.690	2.589	2.494	2.404	2.362	2.320	2.241	2.166	1.997	1.849	1.720	1.605
5	4.853	4.713	4.452	4.212	3.993	3.791	3.605	3.433	3.352	3.274	3.127	2.991	2.864	2.745	2.689	2.635	2.532	2.436	2.220	2.035	1.876	1.737
6	5.795	5.601	5.242	4.917	4.623	4.355	4.111	3.889	3.784	3.685	3.498	3.326	3.167	3.020	2.951	2.885	2.759	2.643	2.385	2.168	1.983	1.824
7	6.728	6.472	6.002	5.582	5.206	4.868	4.564	4.288	4.160	4.039	3.812	3.605	3.416	3.242	3.161	3.083	2.937	2.802	2.508	2.263	2.057	1.883
8	7.652	7.325	6.733	6.210	5.747	5.335	4.968	4.639	4.487	4.344	4.078	3.837	3.619	3.421	3.329	3.241	3.076	2.925	2.598	2.331	2.108	1.922
9	8.566	8.162	7.435	6.802	6.247	5.759	5.328	4.946	4.772	4.607	4.303	4.031	3.786	3.566	3.463	3.366	3.184	3.019	2.665	2.379	2.144	1.948
10	9.471	8.983	8.111	7.360	6.710	6.145	5.650	5.216	5.019	4.833	4.494	4.192	3.923	3.682	3.571	3.465	3.269	3.092	2.715	2.414	2.168	1.965
11	10.368	9.787	8.760	7.887	7.139	6.495	5.937	5.453	5.234	5.029	4.656	4.327	4.035	3.776	3.656	3.544	3.335	3.147	2.752	2.438	2.185	1.977
12	11.255	10.575	9.385	8.384	7.536	6.814	6.194	5.660	5.421	5.197	4.793	4.439	4.127	3.851	3.725	3.606	3.387	3.190	2.779	2.456	2.196	1.985
13	12.134	11.343	9.986	8.853	7.904	7.103	6.424	5.842	5.583	5.342	4.910	4.533	4.203	3.912	3.780	3.656	3.427	3.223	2.799	2.468	2.204	1.990
14	13.004	12.106	10.563	9.295	8.244	7.367	6.628	6.002	5.724	5.468	5.008	4.611	4.265	3.962	3.824	3.695	3.459	3.249	2.814	2.477	2.210	1.993
15	13.865	12.849	11.118	9.712	8.559	7.606	6.811	6.142	5.847	5.575	5.092	4.675	4.315	4.001	3.859	3.726	3.483	3.268	2.825	2.484	2.214	1.995
16	14.718	13.578	11.652	10.106	8.851	7.824	6.974	6.265	5.954	5.669	5.162	4.730	4.357	4.033	3.887	3.751	3.503	3.283	2.834	2.489	2.216	1.997
17	15.562	14.292	12.166	10.477	9.122	8.022	7.120	6.373	6.047	5.749	5.222	4.775	4.391	4.059	3.910	3.771	3.518	3.295	2.840	2.492	2.218	1.998
18	16.398	14.992	12.659	10.828	9.372	8.201	7.250	6.467	6.128	5.818	5.273	4.812	4.419	4.080	3.928	3.786	3.529	3.304	2.844	2.494	2.219	1.999
19	17.226	15.678	13.134	11.158	9.604	8.365	7.366	6.550	6.198	5.877	5.316	4.844	4.442	4.097	3.942	3.799	3.539	3.311	2.848	2.496	2.220	1.999
20	18.046	16.351	13.590	11.470	9.818	8.514	7.469	6.623	6.259	5.929	5.353	4.870	4.460	4.110	3.954	3.808	3.546	3.316	2.850	2.497	2.221	1.999
21	18.857	17.011	14.029	11.764	10.017	8.649	7.562	6.687	6.312	5.973	5.384	4.891	4.476	4.121	3.963	3.816	3.551	3.320	2.852	2.498	2.221	2.000
22	19.660	17.658	14.451	12.042	10.201	8.772	7.645	6.743	6.359	6.011	5.410	4.909	4.488	4.130	3.970	3.822	3.556	3.323	2.853	2.498	2.222	2.000
23	20.456	18.292	14.857	12.303	10.371	8.883	7.718	6.792	6.399	6.044	5.432	4.925	4.499	4.137	3.976	3.827	3.559	3.325	2.854	2.499	2.222	2.000
24	21.243	18.914	15.247	12.550	10.529	8.985	7.784	6.835	6.434	6.073	5.451	4.937	4.507	4.143	3.981	3.831	3.562	3.327	2.855	2.499	2.222	2.000
25	22.023	19.523	15.622	12.783	10.675	9.077	7.843	6.873	6.464	6.097	5.467	4.948	4.514	4.147	3.985	3.834	3.564	3.329	2.856	2.499	2.222	2.000
26	22.795	20.121	15.983	13.003	10.810	9.161	7.896	6.906	6.491	6.118	5.480	4.956	4.520	4.151	3.988	3.837	3.566	3.330	2.856	2.500	2.221	2.000
27	23.560	20.707	16.330	13.211	10.935	9.237	7.943	6.935	6.514	6.136	5.492	4.964	4.524	4.154	3.990	3.839	3.567	3.331	2.856	2.500	2.222	2.000
28	24.316	21.281	16.663	13.406	11.051	9.307	7.984	6.961	6.534	6.152	5.502	4.970	4.528	4.157	3.992	3.840	3.568	3.331	2.857	2.500	2.222	2.000
29	25.066	21.844	16.984	13.591	11.158	9.370	8.022	6.983	6.551	6.166	5.510	4.975	4.531	4.159	3.994	3.841	3.569	3.332	2.857	2.500	2.222	2.000
30	25.808	22.396	17.292	13.765	11.258	9.427	8.055	7.003	6.566	6.177	5.517	4.979	4.534	4.160	3.995	3.842	3.569	3.332	2.857	2.500	2.222	2.000
40	32.835	27.355	19.793	15.046	11.925	9.779	8.244	7.105	6.642	6.234	5.548	4.997	4.544	4.166	3.999	3.846	3.571	3.333	2.857	2.500	2.222	2.000
50	39.196	31.424	21.482	15.762	12.234	9.915	8.304	7.133	6.661	6.246	5.554	4.999	4.545	4.167	4.000	3.846	3.571	3.333	2.857	2.500	2.222	2.000

Index

*This book has been set in 10 and 9 point
Times Roman, leaded 2 points. Part numbers
are in 24 point Melior Bold. Part and chapter
titles are in 24 point Melior. Chapter numbers
are in 48 point Melior Bold. The size of the
type page (maximum) is 32 by 48 picas.*